Mathematics
UNLIMITED

HBJ

Harcourt Brace Jovanovich, Inc.

Holt, Rinehart and Winston, Inc.

Orlando · Austin · San Diego · Chicago · Dallas · Toronto

AUTHORS

Francis "Skip" Fennell
Associate Professor of Education
Western Maryland College
Westminster, Maryland

Barbara J. Reys
Assistant Professor of Curriculum
and Instruction
University of Missouri, Columbia, Missouri
Formerly Junior High Mathematics Teacher
Oakland Junior High, Columbia, Missouri

Robert E. Reys
Professor of Mathematics Education
University of Missouri
Columbia, Missouri

Arnold W. Webb
Senior Research Associate
Research for Better Schools
Philadelphia, Pennsylvania
Formerly Asst. Commissioner of Education
New Jersey State Education Department

ILLUSTRATION

Bob Aiese: pp. 32, 33, 44, 78, 79, 221, 358, 359, 420 • Beth Baum: pp. 55, 180, 181, 226, 227 • Steve Cieslawski: pp. 138, 139 • Donald Crews: pp. 162, 163, 206, 292, 294, 295, 388, 415, 416, 418, 419 • Nancy Didion: pp. 14, 15, 140, 141, 216 • Hovik Dilakian: pp. 196, 356 • Betsy Feeney: p. 152 • Mark Giglio: pp. 22, 23, 103, 121, 130, 230, 231, 326, 327 • Deirdre Newman Griffin: pp. 4, 5, 12, 56, 66, 86, 166, 167, 236, 237, 265, 274, 275, 314, 331, 375, 379 • Jim Ludtke: pp. 18, 67, 116, 117, 168, 169, 264, 301, 330, 346, 364 • Linda Miyamoto: pp. 398, 399 • Michael O'Reilly: pp. 16, 106, 120, 260, 261, 286 • David Reinbold: p. 192 • Dixon Scott: pp. 46, 47, 172, 187, 190, 304, 308, 373 • Marti Shohet: pp. 2, 3, 28, 198, 212, 384 • Joel Snyder: pp. 9, 67 • Arthur Thompson: pp. 8, 132, 133, 146-147, 159 • James Torok: pp. 377, 417 • Paul Vaccarello: pp. 92, 93, 240, 241, 308, 309 • Vantage Art Inc.: pp. 16, 341, 345, 365, 372, 381 • Fred Winkowski: pp. 88, 89, 256, 257, 272, 273 • Nina Winters: pp. 6, 20, 37, 182, 183, 210, 211, 248, 249 • Lane Yerkes: pp. 114, 154, 155, 178, 200, 246, 247, 335, 391. B. Colrus: p. H193 • D. Devalle: p. H199 • M. O'Reilly: pp. H108, H187, H192, H194, H200, H206. **Chapter Opener Illustrations:** Jim Owens: pp. 1, 43, 75, 105, 129, 165, 195, 225, 271, 307, 339, 383. **Cover Illustration:** Jeannette Adams.

PHOTOGRAPHY

Alpha/Joe Viesti: p. 283 • Black Star/Dennis Brack: p. 176 • California Historical Society: p. 94 • Stuart Cohen: p. 310 bottom • Bruce Coleman, Inc./Jeff Foott: p. 26 • DPI/Ron Sefton: p. 136; Linda K. Moore: p. 316 • DRK Photo/Tom Bledsoe: p. 84 top; J. Wengle: p. 84 bottom • Duomo/Tony Duffy: p. 62 • Focus on Sports: pp. 51, 64 • Focus West/Dave Black: p. 58 • Michal Heron: pp. 108, 134, 135, 156 • HRW Photo/Elizabeth Hathon: p. 316; Richard Haynes: pp. 52, 54, 55, 77, 110, 111, 228, 229, 250, 251, 318, 319, 321, 323, 392, 393; Ken Karp: p. 282; Photo Researcher: Allen Green, p. 252 • Image Bank/Jay Freis: p. 394; Earl Roberge: p. 118; Grafton M. Smith: p. 80; Merrell Wood: p. 109 • Imagery: p. 296 • International Stock Photo/George Ancona: p. 288 • Lawrence Migdale 1986: p. 337 • Monkmeyer Press/Mimi Forsyth: p. 73 • NASA: pp. 348, 352, 370 • National Center for Atmospheric Research/National Science Foundation: p. 212 • Marvin Newman: pp. 174 top, 175 • Omni-Photo Communications, Inc./Ken Karp: pp. 48-49, 148-149, 204-205, 282, 284, 324-325, 396, 397; John Lei: pp. 10-11, 24-25, 82-83, 144, 242-243, 258-259, 276-277, 278, 280, 290-291, 328 • Photo Researchers, Inc.: pp. 360, 366; Wesley Bocxe: p. 174 bottom; Ron Church: p. 30; Richard Hutchinson: p. 297; Tom McHugh: p. 34; Carleton Ray: p. 19; Earl Roberge: p. 238 bottom • Rainbow/Coco McCoy: p. 112; Linda K. Moore: p. 262 • Carl Roessler: p. 31 • Shostal Associates: p. 208 • Tom Stack & Associates/Don & Pat Valenti: p. 202 • Stock Market/Greg Davis: p. 310 top; Sonja Jacobs: pp. 184, 202, 239; George Juckes: p. 96; Lewis Portnoy: p. 184; Stan Tess: p. 390 • Taurus Photos: p. 311 • Woodfin Camp & Associates/Craig Aurness: pp. 27, 233; Sissie Brimberg: p. 238 top; Dick Durrance: p. 232 top; Robert Frerck: p. 208; David Alan Harvey: p. 26 top; Jeff Lowenthal: p. 312; Robert McElroy: p. 142; Mike Maple: pp. 202, 214; Wally McNamee: pp. 64, 150-151; Chuck Nicklin: p. 12 center; Lentikuva Oy: p. 64; Bill Ross: p. 53; Mike S. Yamashita: p. 12 • Leo de Wys/Ann Chwatsky: p. 127 • Page H187, HBJ Photo/Earl Kogler; H203, Myrleen Ferguson/PhotoEdit; H210.

Printed in the United States of America

ISBN 0-15-351566-X

CONTENTS

4 MULTIPLYING DECIMALS

▶◀

5 DIVIDING WHOLE NUMBERS

▶◀

6 DIVISION: 2-DIGIT DIVISORS

The world's oceans are teeming with life. How many different kinds of creatures can you name? Could you put them in order by length, weight, or speed?

1 PLACE VALUE, ADDITION AND SUBTRACTION
Whole Numbers

Numbers to Hundred Thousands

One hundred twenty-five thousand, four hundred six people have contributed money to help save the whales. Write a number that shows how many people contributed.

125,406 people contributed money.

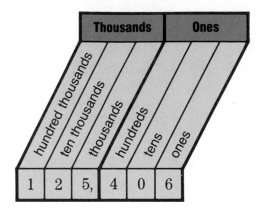

A comma is used to separate large numbers into groups of three digits.

In 125,406:

The value of the digit 1, in the hundred thousands place, is 100,000.
The value of the digit 2, in the ten thousands place, is 20,000.
The value of the digit 5, in the thousands place, is 5,000.
The value of the digit 4, in the hundreds place, is 400.
The value of the digit 0, in the tens place, is 0.
The value of the digit 6, in the ones place, is 6.

Standard form: 125,406
Expanded form: 100,000 + 20,000 + 5,000 + 400 + 6

Checkpoint   Write the letter of the correct answer.

What is the value of the blue digit?

1. 386,846

a. 8
b. 80
c. 800
d. 846

2. 930,834

a. 3
b. 300
c. 3,834
d. 30,000

3. 864,020

a. 0
b. 20
c. 100
d. 200

What is the value of the blue digit?

1. 456,782   **2.** 385,621   **3.** 598,364   **4.** 786,320   **5.** 976,841

6. 304,562   **7.** 343,754   **8.** 600,032   **9.** 750,401   **10.** 806,150

11. 596,321   **12.** 846,329   **13.** 795,423   **14.** 134,769   **15.** 612,439

16. 316,030   **17.** 453,230   **18.** 985,063   **19.** 321,119   **20.** 980,020

21. 409,265   **22.** 763,518   **23.** 547,028   **24.** 993,457   **25.** 821,593

Write in standard form.

26. 80,000 + 7,000 + 900 + 20 + 6

27. 200,000 + 40,000 + 6,000 + 200 + 30 + 1

28. 600,000 + 20,000 + 1,000 + 500 + 90 + 2

29. 50,000 + 3,000 + 500 + 60 + 8

30. 40,000 + 5,000 + 200 + 80 + 5

31. 800,000 + 9,000 + 800 + 7

Write in expanded form.

32. 1,238   **33.** 27,569   **34.** 438,451   **35.** 998,915

36. 342,671   **37.** 357,954   **38.** 529,346   **39.** 82,165

40. 3,972   **41.** 34,602   **42.** 15,045   ★**43.** 707,399

NUMBER SENSE

You can sort a list of numbers by using the number of digits in each number and the value of the front digit of each number as a guide.

134   987

This number is   This number is
close to 100.   close to 1,000.

Sort the list of numbers into two groups:

125; 88; 1,013; 91; 970; 922; 53; 1,321; 988; 879; 85; 1,279; 1,009; 73; 103; 898

1. those close to 100.   **2.** those close to 1,000.

Numbers to Hundred Billions

A. Most of Earth's surface is covered with water. Four oceans—the Pacific, the Atlantic, the Indian, and the Arctic—cover about one hundred twenty-seven million, three hundred forty-eight thousand square miles. Write this number in standard form.

Each group of three digits is called a **period.** Periods simplify the reading and writing of large numbers.

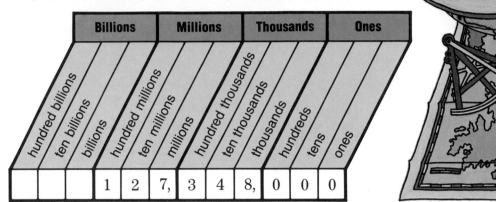

Billions			Millions			Thousands			Ones		
hundred billions	ten billions	billions	hundred millions	ten millions	millions	hundred thousands	ten thousands	thousands	hundreds	tens	ones
		1	2	7,	3	4	8,	0	0	0	

In 127,348,000:

The value of the digit 1, in the hundred millions place, is 100,000,000.
The value of the digit 2, in the ten millions place, is 20,000,000.
The value of the digit 7, in the millions place, is 7,000,000.
The value of the digit 3, in the hundred thousands place, is 300,000.
The value of the digit 4, in the ten thousands place, is 40,000.
The value of the digit 8, in the thousands place, is 8,000.
The value of the digit 0, in the hundreds place, is 0.
The value of the digit 0, in the tens place, is 0.
The value of the digit 0, in the ones place, is 0.

Write in standard form: 127,348,000.

Read: one hundred twenty-seven million, three hundred forty-eight thousand.

B. You can write short word names for large numbers by writing the digits in each period, followed by the name of each period.

127,348,000   27,315,656,423

127 million, 348 thousand   27 billion, 315 million, 656 thousand, 423 ones

What is the value of the blue digit?

1. 228,603,000
2. 755,049,001
3. 100,004,522
4. 591,440,700,000
5. 807,611,882,000
6. 780,049,467,795
7. 492,332,079
8. 561,978,445
9. 893,556,423,009
10. 133,567,238,000
11. 475,506,231,005
★12. 9,000,054,723,976

For 583,247,612,741, write the digits in the

13. billions period.
14. millions period.
15. thousands period.

Write in standard form.

16. 600 million, 29 thousand 500
17. 140 million
18. 845 million, 349 thousand, 1 hundred 1
19. 200 billion, 67 million, 1 thousand, 9 hundred 5

Write the short word name for each.

20. 42,799,928,725
21. 164,989,100,000
22. 608,010,002,700
23. 301,499,500
24. 992,456,204,089
25. 757,322,468,271

CHALLENGE

Ancient Egyptians used *hieroglyphics*, a form of picture writing, to write numbers. They did not use place value.

𐦀 = 1,000	𐦀 = 100
∩ = 10	/ = 1

The Egyptians would write 3,762 like this:

𐦀𐦀𐦀 𝟿𝟿𝟿𝟿𝟿𝟿𝟿 ∩∩∩∩∩∩ //

Write each number.

1. 𝟿𝟿𝟿 ∩∩∩ ////
2. 𐦀 𝟿𝟿𝟿𝟿 ∩∩ ///

Write each number in hieroglyphics.

3. 5,192
4. 4,628
5. 8,325
6. 3,531

Comparing and Ordering

A. A **number line** can be used to compare numbers.

31 32 33 34 35 36 37 38

32 is to the left of 34.
So, 32 *is less than* 34.

Write: 32 < 34.

37 is to the right of 34.
So, 37 *is greater than* 34.

Write: 37 > 34.

You can compare to decide whether two numbers are equal.

34 = 34   34 ≠ 37 | ≠ means not equal to.

B. You can compare without using a number line. Compare the average depths of the Atlantic and the Pacific oceans. Which has a greater average depth?

Atlantic: 3,575 meters   Pacific: 3,940 meters

Compare 3,575 and 3,940.

Line up the digits.	Begin to compare digits at the left.	Continue comparing.
3,575 3,940	3,575 3,940 3 = 3	3,575 3,940 5 < 9

So, 3,575 < 3,940.

The Pacific Ocean has a greater average depth.

C. You can order 4,219; 867; 911; and 298 by comparing.

Line up the digits.	Begin to compare at the left.	Compare the remaining numbers.
4,219 867 911 298	4,219 — Only number with a thousands place; it is the greatest. 867 911 298	911 > 867 867 > 298

From the greatest to the least: 4,219; 911; 867; 298
From the least to the greatest: 298; 867; 911; 4,219

Compare. Use >, <, or = for ●.

1. 47 ● 17

2. 105 ● 204

3. 62 ● 620

4. 80 ● 802

5. 5,468 ● 4,599

6. 11,301 ● 9,098

7. 27,687 ● 21,688

8. 62,546 ● 101,829

9. 878,450 ● 678,405

Order from the least to the greatest.

10. 105; 744; 298; 741

11. 9,056; 821; 1,751; 1,052

12. 301; 6,981; 3,010; 7,059

13. 5,422; 6,001; 542; 512

14. 97; 809; 3,840; 3,048

15. 723; 737; 1,737; 373

Order from the greatest to the least.

16. 588; 198; 258

17. 1,419; 5,712; 2,576

18. 9,082; 482; 9,544

19. 8,222; 3,079; 8,041

20. 22,098; 22,911; 23,004; 21,992

21. 6,776; 6,767; 7,667; 799

22. 54,698; 5,499; 75,001; 57,698

Solve. Use the chart.

23. Which sea is deeper, the Mediterranean Sea or the Caribbean Sea?

24. Scientists have learned that some whales dive to a depth of 3,609 feet. Which seas on the chart have a depth that is greater than the depth to which the whales can dive?

★25. Copy the chart and arrange the seas in order from the shallowest to the deepest.

Sea	Depth
Mediterranean	4,902 feet
Black	3,826 feet
Baltic	282 feet
Caribbean	8,173 feet
North	308 feet

ANOTHER LOOK

Write the number in expanded form.

1. 9,506

2. 89,682

3. 75,897

4. 869,708

5. 456,789,123

6. 3,509,000

PROBLEM SOLVING
A Four-Step Plan

If you have trouble solving a problem, try using the following problem-solving plan. It should help you organize your thinking so that you can find the answer. What is the difference in speed between a sailfish and a swordfish?

FIVE FASTEST FISH

Fish	Speed (mph)
Sailfish	68
Marlin	60
Swordfish	58
Tuna	43
Wahoo	40

Sonia looked at the information in the table. Then she used this four-step plan to solve the problem.

In this step you get ready to solve the problem.

1. QUESTIONS
First, she read the problem carefully to be sure she understood the *question*. She made a note of the important information in the table. Then she stated the problem in her own words.

A sailfish has a speed of 68 mph. A swordfish has a speed of 58 mph. What is the difference between 68 mph and 58 mph?

In this step you plan your solution.

2. TOOLS
Next, Sonia chose the *tools* she would need. Tools are the skills you use to solve problems.

To find the difference between 68 and 58, I'll use subtraction.

In this step you solve the problem.

3. SOLUTIONS
Sonia found the *solution* by applying the tool she had chosen.

$$\begin{array}{r} 68 \\ -58 \\ \hline 10 \end{array}$$

The difference in speed is 10 mph.

In this step you check your answer.

4. CHECKS
Finally, she *checked* her solution to be sure that it answered the question and that it was reasonable.

I can check subtraction by adding.

$$\begin{array}{r} 58 \\ + 10 \\ \hline 68 \end{array}$$

Use the four-step plan to solve each problem.

- State the problem in your own words.
- Tell which tools you will use to solve the problem.
- Solve the problem.
- Check the solution.

For Exercises 1–2, use the table on page 8.

1. What is the difference in speed between the third-fastest fish and the fifth-fastest fish?

2. In an hour, how many more miles does the fastest fish swim than the slowest?

3. Mike found these speeds in his encyclopedia: blue whale, 22 mph; flying fish, 35 mph; salmon, 23 mph; dolphin, 37 mph. Order the speeds from fastest to slowest.

4. A nutrition book gave these calorie amounts for 3-ounce portions of fish: bluefish, 135; sardines, 175; clams, 65; shrimp, 190; salmon, 120. How many calories are there altogether in 3 ounces of shrimp and 3 ounces of salmon?

For Exercises 5–7, use the table.

5. What is the difference in longest life span between a European pike and a giant clam?

LIFE SPANS OF OCEAN CREATURES

Creature	Longest Life Span (yrs)
Giant tortoise	200
Sturgeon	150
Giant clam	100
Killer whale	90
European pike	60

6. Which ocean creature is as much younger than a sturgeon as a giant tortoise is older?

7. Which two ocean creatures, living one after the other, may live to the age of a sturgeon?

8. The weekly catch for one Atlantic coast fishery was: bluefish, 8,254 lb; grouper, 6,909 lb; kingfish, 3,015 lb; redfish, 845 lb; snapper, 8,524 lb. Order the amounts from least to greatest.

9. The weights of five world-record catches are: barracuda, 83 lb; bonefish, 19 lb; black marlin, 1,560 lb; sailfish, 221 lb; tiger shark, 1,780 lb; tarpon, 283 lb. Order the weights from greatest to least.

Properties of Addition

A. Many people are interested in the plant and animal life of a coral reef. John Sparrow takes people out to the reef in his glass-bottom boat. He completes 7 trips Saturday and 8 trips Sunday. How many trips does he complete?

To find how many, you can add.

Addition can be shown in two ways.

$$7 \quad + \quad 8 \quad = \quad 15$$

addend   addend   sum

$$7 \leftarrow \text{addend}$$
$$+\,8 \leftarrow \text{addend}$$
$$\overline{15} \leftarrow \text{sum}$$

John completes 15 trips.

B. Addition has special properties.

Commutative Property If the order of the addends is changed, the sum remains the same.	$3 + 8 = 8 + 3$ $11 = 11$
Zero Property If one of the addends is zero, the sum is equal to the other addend.	$4 + 0 = 4$ $0 + 6 = 6$
Associative Property If the grouping of the addends is changed, the sum remains the same.	$(2 + 4) + 5 = 2 + (4 + 5)$ $6 \quad + 5 = 2 + \quad 9$ $11 = 11$

Complete. Identify the property used.

1. $9 + 3 = 3 + \blacksquare$ **2.** $4 + 7 = \blacksquare + 4$ **3.** $6 + 5 = 5 + \blacksquare$

4. $(2 + 5) + 3 = 2 + (\blacksquare + 3)$ **5.** $6 + (3 + 2) = (\blacksquare + 3) + 2$

6. $4 + (9 + 2) = (\blacksquare + 9) + 2$ **7.** $(3 + 6) + 5 = 3 + (\blacksquare + 5)$

Add.

8. $\begin{array}{r} 4 \\ +7 \end{array}$ 9. $\begin{array}{r} 6 \\ +9 \end{array}$ 10. $\begin{array}{r} 5 \\ +8 \end{array}$ 11. $\begin{array}{r} 9 \\ +8 \end{array}$ 12. $\begin{array}{r} 6 \\ +7 \end{array}$

13. $\begin{array}{r} 8 \\ +9 \end{array}$ 14. $\begin{array}{r} 7 \\ +5 \end{array}$ 15. $\begin{array}{r} 2 \\ +9 \end{array}$ 16. $\begin{array}{r} 8 \\ +4 \end{array}$ 17. $\begin{array}{r} 0 \\ +6 \end{array}$

18. $7 + 8$ 19. $4 + 9$ 20. $5 + 8$ 21. $8 + 7$

22. $8 + 6$ 23. $9 + 6$ 24. $0 + 9$ 25. $6 + 8$

26. $(2 + 2) + 8$ 27. $(3 + 4) + 9$ 28. $(7 + 1) + 3$ 29. $7 + (1 + 3)$

Solve.

★30. $0 + \blacksquare = 9$ ★31. $4 + \blacksquare = 5$ ★32. $7 + \blacksquare = 11$ ★33. $6 + \blacksquare = 15$

★34. $(379 + \blacksquare) + 685 = 379 + (471 + 685)$ ★35. $5,438 + \blacksquare = 3,481 + 5,438$

★36. $562 + (468 + 750) = (562 + \blacksquare) + 750$ ★37. $13,541 + 25,403 = \blacksquare + 13,541$

Solve.

38. On one trip, the passengers spot 7 angelfish. Then they see 6 more angelfish. How many angelfish do the passengers see?

39. Robert and Sarah saw the same number of fish. Robert saw 8 fish in the morning and 9 fish in the afternoon. Sarah saw 9 fish in the morning. How many fish did she see in the afternoon?

40. Look at Ray's chart. How many fish did he spot on each outing? On which outing did he spot more fish?

TROPICAL FISH RAY SAW

Fish	Outing 1	Outing 2
Trunkfish	7	2
Glassfish	4	6

NUMBER SENSE

You can use doubles as an addition shortcut.

Add $6 + 5$.   **Think:** 5 is 1 less than 6.
                        $6 + 6 = 12$ So, $6 + 5 = 11$.

Compute mentally.

1. $7 + 8$ 2. $5 + 4$ 3. $8 + 9$ 4. $8 + 7$ 5. $6 + 7$ 6. $5 + 6$

Related Facts

A. At Buck Island Reef National Monument, snorkelers swim through miles of fragile coral gardens. Nan sees 6 cardinal fish. Then she sees 3 more cardinal fish. How many cardinal fish does Nan see?

To find how many, you can add.

$6 + 3 = 9$ ⟵ sum

Nan sees 9 cardinal fish.
If 3 cardinal fish swim away, how many are left?
To find how many are left, you can subtract.

$9 - 3 = 6$ ⟵ difference

There are 6 cardinal fish left.

B. You can use the numbers 9, 6, and 3 to write a family of facts.

$6 + 3 = 9$	$9 - 3 = 6$
$3 + 6 = 9$	$9 - 6 = 3$

You can use a family of facts to solve a subtraction problem by writing a related addition problem.

$14 - n = 5$ n stands for the missing number.

Think: $9 + 5 = 14$. So, $14 - 9 = 5$.

C. As you subtract, remember:

If 0 is subtracted from a number, the difference is equal to that number.	$7 - 0 = 7$
If a number is subtracted from itself, the difference is 0.	$8 - 8 = 0$
Subtraction is not commutative.	$9 - 4 = 5$ $4 - 9 \neq 5$

Copy and complete.

1. $7 + 8 = 15$
$15 - \blacksquare = 8$

2. $9 + 4 = 13$
$13 - \blacksquare = 9$

3. $6 + 5 = 11$
$11 - \blacksquare = 6$

4. $3 + 9 = 12$
$12 - \blacksquare = 9$

5. $7 + 6 = 13$
$13 - \blacksquare = 7$

6. $8 + 2 = 10$
$10 - \blacksquare = 2$

Subtract.

7. 11
− 8

8. 17
− 8

9. 12
− 4

10. 6
− 5

11. 8
− 4

12. 14
− 7

13. 5
− 1

14. 9
− 2

15. 7
− 2

16. 15
− 15

17. $12 - 12$

18. $10 - 4$

19. $15 - 8$

20. $6 - 4$

21. $8 - 0$

22. $11 - 5$

23. $5 - 2$

24. $4 - 2$

Write a family of facts for each group of numbers.

25. 4, 9, 13

26. 17, 9, 8

27. 13, 6, 7

28. 15, 7, 8

29. 6, 8, 14

30. 5, 3, 2

31. 11, 6, 5

32. 12, 8, 4

Solve for n. Use related facts.

33. $14 - n = 7$

34. $n - 3 = 5$

35. $5 - n = 1$

36. $n - 9 = 9$

Solve for n.

★**37.** $54 + 32 = 86$
$86 - n = 54$

★**38.** $63 + 34 = 97$
$97 - n = 34$

★**39.** $107 + 132 = 239$
$239 - n = 107$

★**40.** $425 + 85 = 510$
$510 - n = 425$

Solve. Use counters or slips of paper to *act out* each story.

41. On her snorkeling trip, Rachel took 17 photographs. She saw that 9 of the photographs were too dark. How many were *not* too dark?

42. Tony took 15 photographs. He gave some of them to his younger sister. He kept 8 for himself. How many did he give to his sister?

43. One day, Luanne saw 6 trunkfish. Ketti saw 2 more trunkfish than Luanne. Altogether, how many trunkfish did the two girls see?

★**44.** Kelly had 2 goldfish. Martha gave her 3 more. Jeff gave her 5 more than Martha gave her. How many goldfish does Kelly have in all?

Front-End Estimation

A. Grouping pairs of numbers to sums of 100 or 1,000 can help you estimate sums.

Group numbers in this box whose sum is about 100.

> **≈ means "is approximately equal to."**

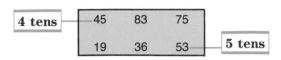

Think: 45 ≈ 4 tens, 53 ≈ 5 tens.
   So, 45 + 53 ≈ 100
   19 + 83 ≈ 100, 75 + 36 ≈ 100.

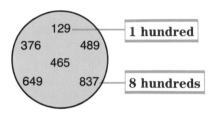

Group numbers in this circle whose sum is about 1,000.
129 + 837 ≈ 1,000
376 + 649 ≈ 1,000   489 + 465 ≈ 1,000

B. Look at the chart of fish tagged by volunteers at the Oceanographic Institute. Their goal was to tag 600 fish daily. Estimate to find whether or not the goal was reached.

Estimate: 115 + 86 + 113 + 175.

You can use front-end estimation.

FISH TAGGED ON TUESDAY

Erica	115
Sean	86
Sally	113
Kevin	175

Add the numbers in the greatest place.

$$
\begin{array}{r}
115 \\
86 \\
113 \\
+175 \\
\hline
3
\end{array}
$$

Adjust by grouping the other amounts.

$$
\left.\begin{array}{r} 115 \\ 86 \end{array}\right\} \text{about } 100
$$

$$
\left.\begin{array}{r} 113 \\ 175 \end{array}\right\} \text{about } 100
$$

Adjustment: 100 + 100 = 200.

Rough estimate: 300.
Adjusted estimate: 300 + 200 = 500.
115 + 86 + 113 + 175 < 600
So, they did not tag enough fish to meet their goal.

Another example:

$$
\left.\begin{array}{r} \$4.67 \\ 3.42 \end{array}\right\} \text{about } \$1
$$
$$
+\ \ 0.85 \quad \text{about } \$1
$$
$$
\$7 + \$1 + \$1 = \$9
$$

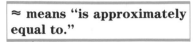

Write the two numbers whose sum is about

1. 100.   85   45   13   35   **2.** 100.   48   75   53   86

3. 50.   17   57   25   35   **4.** 50.   24   49   40   27

5. 1,000.   450   275   560   110   **6.** 1,000.   285   700   100   580

Estimate. Write > or < for ●.

7. 57 + 69 ● 100   **8.** 86 + 97 ● 200   **9.** 46 + 74 ● 100

10. 157 + 294 ● 300   **11.** 219 + 689 ● 1,000   **12.** 895 + 129 ● 900

13. 465 + 789 + 921 ● 2,000   **14.** 389 + 471 + 59 ● 1,000

15. $8.75 + $0.89 ● $10.00   **16.** $5.37 + $1.76 + $1.98 ● $10.00

★**17.** 8,957 + 85 + 125 ● 10,000   ★**18.** 9,875 + 4,327 + 2,756 ● 20,000

Estimate. First write your rough estimate.
Then write your adjusted estimate.

19.	**20.**	**21.**	**22.**	**23.**
54	345	4,276	9,217	$9.57
487	159	345	6,029	8.39
215	95	5,729	5,788	0.95
+ 149	+ 220	+ 3,287	+ 955	+ 9.08

Solve.

24. On a field trip to the Gulf of Mexico, a marine biologist identifies 73 types of coral, 61 types of fish, 22 types of plankton, and 38 types of crustaceans. Did the biologist identify more than 200 types of ocean life?

25. Mary stocks the Oceanographic Institute's exhibit of saltwater fish. She stocks 38 chimera, 69 herring, 117 dogfish, and 478 flounder. About how many saltwater fish is that?

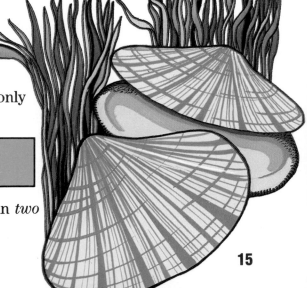

FOCUS: REASONING

Look at the shapes below. Each shape differs in only one way from the shapes next to it.

Rearrange the shapes so that each shape differs in *two* ways from the shapes next to it.

Rounding and Estimating Sums

A. Australia's coral Great Barrier Reef is about 1,250 miles long. To the nearest thousand miles, how long is the reef?

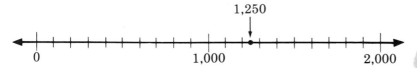

1,250 is between 1,000 and 2,000. It is closer to 1,000. So, to the nearest thousand miles, the reef is 1,000 miles long.

B. Sometimes you have to take a closer look at the digits of a number when rounding. To the nearest hundred miles, how long is the reef?

- Find the place to which you are rounding.
- If the digit to the right is 5 or greater, round up.
- If the digit to the right is less than 5, round down. The digit to the right is 5. Round up.

1,2̲5̲0

1,2̲5̲0

So, to the nearest hundred miles, the reef is 1,300 miles long.

C. Rounding can help you estimate sums.

Estimate 4,857 + 1,426.

The place to which you round depends upon the size of the numbers and how easily you can mentally compute the rounded numbers.

Round each addend to the nearest thousand.	Add the rounded numbers.	Round each addend to the nearest hundred.	Add the rounded numbers.
4,857 → 5,000 + 1,426 → 1,000	5,000 + 1,000 6,000	4,857 → 4,900 + 1,426 → 1,400	4,900 + 1,400 6,300

Both 6,000 and 6,300 are good estimates.

Round each number to the nearest hundred and to the nearest thousand.

1. 5,326   **2.** 4,856   **3.** 7,909   **4.** 1,998   **5.** 6,111   **6.** 2,762

7. 7,283   **8.** 2,931   **9.** 6,270   **10.** 1,635   **11.** 7,469   **12.** 4,983

Round to the nearest ten dollars.

13. $75.75   **14.** $12.13   **15.** $19.99   **16.** $18.90   **17.** $49.99   **18.** $16.75

19. $34.08   **20.** $18.98   **21.** $32.95   **22.** $23.90   **23.** $93.46   **24.** $29.01

Estimate. Write > or < for ● .

25. 723 + 184 ● 1,000   **26.** 8,519 + 2,426 ● 10,000   **27.** 4,326 + 2,148 ● 7,000

28. 423 + 136 + 214 ● 700   **29.** 8,329 + 4,916 + 2,463 ● 17,000

Estimate.

30. 436 + 538   **31.** 568 + 273   **32.** 8,916 + 7,228   **33.** 15,642 + 23,984

34. 426 + 298 + 137   **35.** 5,326 + 4,216 + 5,593   **36.** 14,316 + 12,149 + 27,823

Solve.

37. A scientist in a minisub dives 2,345 feet into the Coral Sea to do some experiments. Then he descends another 1,672 feet. About how deep did the scientist dive?

★38. A commercial diver collected 1,467 pounds of white coral, 1,687 pounds of pink coral, and 2,632 pounds of red coral. About how much coral did the diver collect?

MIDCHAPTER REVIEW

What is the value of the blue digit?

1. 786,213   **2.** 34,077   **3.** 299,493   **4.** 137,244   **5.** 347,214

Order from the least to the greatest.

6. 744; 323; 536   **7.** 2,519; 5,912; 5,291   **8.** 63,246; 63,426; 63,446

Complete.   Round to the nearest hundred.

9. 9 + 3 = ■ + 9   **10.** 0 + ■ = 93   **11.** 16,924   **12.** 901,099

Estimating Differences—Rounding

A. The Aquafest hoped that the exhibition of Biff the Sea Lion would increase daily attendance by about 1,000 people. Last year's daily attendance was 2,516. This year it was 4,326. Estimate whether the goal was reached.

Round to estimate 4,326 − 2,516.
The place to which you round depends upon the size of the numbers and how easily you can compute with the rounded numbers.

Round each number to the nearest thousand.

$$4{,}326 \longrightarrow 4{,}000$$
$$-\ 2{,}516 \longrightarrow 3{,}000$$

Subtract the rounded numbers.

$$\begin{array}{r} 4{,}000 \\ -\ 3{,}000 \\ \hline 1{,}000 \end{array}$$

The goal of about 1,000 was reached.

B. Estimate 2,746 − 593.

Round each number to the nearest hundred.

$$2{,}746 \longrightarrow 2{,}700$$
$$-\ \ \ 593 \longrightarrow \ \ 600$$

Subtract the rounded numbers.

$$\begin{array}{r} 2{,}700 \\ -\ \ \ 600 \\ \hline 2{,}100 \end{array}$$

The difference of 2,746 and 593 is about 2,100.

Estimate by rounding.

1. 8,427 − 3,916	**2.** 5,684 − 3,196	**3.** 7,426 − 783	**4.** 847 − 638	**5.** 3,237 − 759

6. 23,416 − 20,817   **7.** 93,426 − 79,846   **8.** 34,816 − 7,323

Solve.

9. Biff is trained to shoot baskets into a hoop with his nose. In June, Biff made 847 baskets. By July, he had improved enough to make 1,397 baskets. About how many more did he make in July?

PROBLEM SOLVING
Estimation

In some situations, underestimating the answer makes the most sense.

The Oceanographic Museum will give a school lecture series if at least 600 students are interested. The local school boards are asked to estimate the number of students that will attend. Each school made a tally and gave the school board this chart.

STUDENTS INTERESTED IN ATTENDING LECTURES

Faye School 156	Rapp School 236	Gray School 224	Day School 328

To quickly find the number of interested students, the school board estimates. To be sure they have the *minimum* number required, *underestimation* is the best method. Front-end estimation gives an underestimate.

$$\begin{array}{r} 156 \\ 236 \\ 224 \\ + 328 \\ \hline 8 \end{array}$$ Rough estimate: 800

At least 800 students are interested. The museum will sponsor the lecture series.

Estimate to solve.

1. The lectures are held in a 4-section auditorium. At first only the first 112 seats are opened, but the lectures have become so popular that the museum must open the second section of 207 seats, the third section of 234 seats, and then the fourth section of 125 seats. Estimate the minimum number of seats available to the audience.

2. One lecture topic was a project that studied underwater volcanoes. At least 700 samples had to be recorded to make the project a success. The first dive recorded 207 items, the second dive found 218 samples, and the last dive recorded 326 items. Estimate to find whether the project recorded at least the number of samples necessary for success. Was the project a success?

Addition of 2- and 3-Digit Numbers

A. Students from the Webb School visit the Seaquarium as part of their Science Week. They go in two groups. One group has 158 students. The other group has 135 students. How many students visit the Seaquarium? Use place-value blocks to *act out* the story.

Find 158 + 135.

First estimate the sum.

$$
\begin{array}{ccc}
158 & \longrightarrow & 200 \\
+\ 135 & \longrightarrow & +\ 100 \\
\hline
 & & 300
\end{array}
$$

Add the ones. Regroup if necessary.	Add the tens. Regroup if necessary.	Add the hundreds. Regroup if necessary.
$\begin{array}{r} 1 \\ \mathbf{158} \\ +\mathbf{135} \\ \hline 3 \end{array}$	$\begin{array}{r} 1 \\ \mathbf{158} \\ +\mathbf{135} \\ \hline 93 \end{array}$	$\begin{array}{r} \mathbf{158} \\ +\mathbf{135} \\ \hline 293 \end{array}$

293 students visit the Seaquarium.
The answer is reasonably close to the estimate.

B. You add money the same way you add whole numbers. Remember to write the dollar sign and the cents point.

$\begin{array}{r} 1\ 1 \\ \$3.66 \\ +\ \ 2.75 \\ \hline \$6.41 \end{array}$	$\begin{array}{r} 1\ 1 \\ \$2.69 \\ +\ \ 0.83 \\ \hline \$3.52 \end{array}$	$\begin{array}{r} 1\ 1 \\ \$4.67 \\ +\ \ 5.48 \\ \hline \$10.15 \end{array}$

Checkpoint Write the letter of the correct answer.

Add.

1. $\begin{array}{r} 56 \\ +\ 28 \end{array}$	2. $\begin{array}{r} 862 \\ +\ 239 \end{array}$	3. $6.65 + 3.76	4. 647 + 84
a. 28	**a.** 111	**a.** $9.31	**a.** 621
b. 74	**b.** 1,001	**b.** $9.41	**b.** 631
c. 84	**c.** 1,091	**c.** $10.31	**c.** 731
d. 114	**d.** 1,101	**d.** $10.41	**d.** 1,531

Add.

1.	84 + 13	**2.**	31 + 56	**3.**	23 + 53	**4.**	35 + 34	**5.**	$0.66 + 0.43
6.	538 + 145	**7.**	643 + 309	**8.**	866 + 424	**9.**	107 + 773	**10.**	$9.39 + 2.23
11.	27 + 796	**12.**	83 + 129	**13.**	92 + 428	**14.**	285 + 57	**15.**	$1.58 + 0.77
16.	753 + 288	**17.**	47 + 38	**18.**	856 + 939	**19.**	584 + 463	**20.**	$8.06 + 2.29

21. 18 + 17 **22.** 151 + 12 **23.** 77 + 362 **24.** $1.08 + $8.87

25. 739 + 113 **26.** 119 + 78 **27.** 273 + 98 **28.** $1.19 + $0.37

Solve.

29. At one Seaquarium tank, the students see 67 different kinds of fish from Hawaii. In another tank, they see 49 different kinds of fish from Florida. How many kinds of fish do the students see?

30. At the Seaquarium Book Shop, Jo buys two books about the fish she saw. The book about Hawaiian fish costs $2.85. The Florida fish book costs $1.95. How much does Jo spend for the books?

31. The Seaquarium is involved in a special breeding program to help save endangered species. Use the information in the table to write and solve your own addition problems.

NUMBER OF MAMMALS AT THE SEAQUARIUM

Mammal	Total Number (1985)	Number born (1986)
Dolphin	28	5
Manatee	12	3
Whale	7	1

CHALLENGE

Copy and complete each subtraction problem. Use only the digits 3, 7, and 8. Guess. Then check. Then guess again.

1. ▨▨
− ▨▨
—————
5 5

2. ▨▨
− ▨▨
—————
4 9

3. ▨▨
− ▨▨
—————
3 6

4. ▨▨▨
− ▨▨
—————
2 8 6

Addition of Larger Numbers

Every winter, gray whales migrate from their feeding grounds in arctic waters to Baja California. Whale-watchers along the coast first spot the whales 3,295 miles from the feeding grounds. The whales must swim another 1,725 miles before they reach Baja. How far will the whales travel?

Add 3,295 + 1,725.

Add the ones. Regroup if necessary.	Add the tens. Regroup if necessary.	Add the hundreds. Regroup if necessary.	Add the thousands.
1	1 1	1 1 1	1 1 1
3,2 9 5	3,2 9 5	3,2 9 5	3,2 9 5
+ 1,7 2 5	+ 1,7 2 5	+ 1,7 2 5	+ 1,7 2 5
0	2 0	0 2 0	5,0 2 0

The whales will travel 5,020 miles.

Other examples:

```
  1 1 1                1 1 1 1 1
  5 6,8 4 3            $1,6 0 3.8 6
+    5,6 7 2          +    4 9 7.6 4
  6 2,5 1 5            $2,1 0 1.5 0
```

Checkpoint Write the letter of the correct answer.

Add.

1. 8,078
   + 1,546

2. 47,954
   + 31,676

3. $6,725.58 + $298.54

a. 9,514
b. 9,524
c. 9,624
d. 9,651

a. 78,520
b. 78,530
c. 78,630
d. 79,630

a. $6,024.12
b. $6,913.02
c. $7,024.12
d. $70.2412

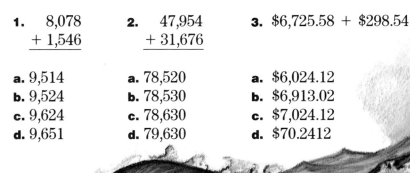

Find the sum.

| **1.** 1,556 + 1,377 | **2.** 3,251 + 5,699 | **3.** 6,847 + 7,068 | **4.** 5,188 + 1,784 | **5.** $43.48 + 5.82 |

| **6.** 69,994 + 22,953 | **7.** 41,923 + 9,884 | **8.** 64,383 + 42,762 | **9.** 26,870 + 16,261 | **10.** $762.47 + 49.72 |

| **11.** 58,659 + 27,343 | **12.** 67,094 + 37,738 | **13.** 40,653 + 37,438 | **14.** 12,009 + 68,994 | **15.** $567.04 + 798.92 |

16. 229,775 + 50,426   **17.** 176,754 + 436,437   **18.** $758.25 + $238.47

19. $2,456.67 + $729.16   **20.** 721,423 + 53,724   **21.** $675.48 + $138.09

22. 3,485 + 7,947   **23.** 8,967 + 36,775   **24.** 96,783 + 4,563

Solve.

25. A whale named Gigi is tagged to track her migration. She swam 1,957 miles during July and 2,443 miles during August. How many miles did Gigi swim during the two months?

26. Whale watchers observe a group of killer whales in Canadian waters. They spend $2,567.85 to rent a ship. They spend $3,853.78 on equipment. How much do they spend in all?

NUMBER SENSE

You can estimate differences by using the front digits of numbers.

	Subtract the front digits.	Write zeros in the other places.
8,369 − 3,629	8 − 3 = 5	8,369 − 3,629 ⟶ 5,000

5,000 is a rough estimate of the difference.

Estimate.

| **1.** 6,243 − 1,427 | **2.** 7,846 − 3,598 | **3.** 4,276 − 3,569 | **4.** 67,416 − 28,497 |

Column Addition

A. Michael uses a minisubmarine to study the plant and animal life of the coral reef. So far, he has noted 132 different types of coral and 47 different types of sea plants. He has also recorded 348 kinds of fish. How many types of coral-reef life has Michael seen?

Add 132 + 47 + 348.

Line up the numbers so that the ones are in a column.

Add the ones. Regroup if necessary.	Add the tens. Regroup if necessary.	Add the hundreds.

$$
\begin{array}{r} 132 \\ 47 \\ +348 \\ \hline 7 \end{array}
\qquad
\begin{array}{r} 132 \\ 47 \\ +348 \\ \hline 27 \end{array}
\qquad
\begin{array}{r} {\scriptstyle 1} \\ 132 \\ 47 \\ +348 \\ \hline 527 \end{array}
$$

Michael has seen 527 types of coral-reef life.

B. You can check your answer by adding up.

$$
\begin{array}{r} {\scriptstyle 1\ 1} \\ 132 \\ 47 \\ +348 \\ \hline 527 \end{array} \Big\uparrow
$$

Checkpoint Write the letter of the correct answer.

Add.

1.
$$\begin{array}{r} 46 \\ 39 \\ +17 \\ \hline \end{array}$$

2.
$$\begin{array}{r} \$12.56 \\ 2.01 \\ +\ 3.15 \\ \hline \end{array}$$

3. 5,329 + 2,438 + 59 + 47,601

1.	2.	3.
a. 82	a. $17.62	a. 44,307
b. 92	b. $17.72	b. 55,407
c. 102	c. $18.72	c. 55,427
d. 822	d. $28.72	d. 184,071

Math Reasoning, page H188

Add. Check by adding up.

1.	2.	3.	4.	5.
29	31	12	44	10
31	11	29	29	22
+ 28	+ 13	+ 69	+ 69	+ 58

6.	7.	8.	9.	10.
$3.15	620	491	$2.81	117
5.21	107	11	1.14	604
+ 1.54	+ 162	+ 274	+ 0.04	+ 229

11.	12.	13.	14.	15.
6,192	2,519	$14.27	6,711	$80.88
1,420	1,228	42.54	2,633	94.16
1,600	3,927	5.17	1,225	56.53
+ 3,837	+ 190	+ 4.30	+ 1,347	+ 71.92

16. 4,246 + 874 + 840   **17.** $1.59 + $29.97   **18.** 353 + 466 + 2,886

19. 327 + 517 + 59 + 73   **20.** 149 + 902 + 65 + 281   **21.** 970 + 784 + 29 + 197

Solve.

22. Patricia made three dives during one day. On her first dive, she spent 37 minutes underwater. Her second dive was 54 minutes long, and her third dive lasted 107 minutes. How much time did Patricia spend underwater that day?

23. Pat bought the following supplies for her diving trip: flippers and a wet suit cost $358.97; goggles and an air tank cost $257.99; an underwater camera cost $287.35. The boat trip and all other expenses amounted to $455.30. What was the cost of Pat's trip?

ANOTHER LOOK

Write >, <, or = for ●.

1. 2,562 ● 2,065

2. 85,689 ● 9,995

3. 6,038 ● 6,039

4. 26,785 ● 2,683

5. 247,850 ● 25,787

6. 478,934 ● 479,734

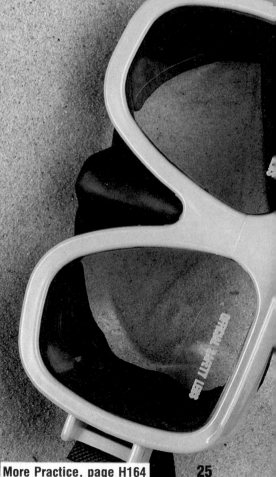

PROBLEM SOLVING
Using Outside Sources Including the Infobank

Sometimes you may have to look in outside resources for the information you need to solve a problem.

Some of the sources in which you can find information are books, magazines, catalogs, and newspapers. You can also obtain information by contacting government agencies, museums, companies, and organizations.

Information from many different sources has been gathered into an Infobank, which you will find on pages 415–420 of this book. You can use this information to solve many problems in this textbook.

Read the following problem.

> Grace needs some equipment for her whale-watching trip. She orders a compass, a canteen, and a flashlight from Explorer's Outfitters, Inc. How much does this order cost?

You need to know the cost of each item that Grace orders. You could find this information by calling Explorer's Outfitters, Inc. You might find an advertisement for this company. Or you could look in the company's catalog.

A part of their catalog appears in the Infobank. Once you find it, you can use the information to solve the problem.

Item	Price
Compass	$11.25
Canteen	3.20
Flashlight	+ 8.75
	$23.20

Grace's order costs $23.20.

Read each problem. Then choose the item in the Infobank that provides the missing information. Write the item.

1. Betsy reads that a man rode on a roller coaster for 258 hours. She wonders if that time is as long as the record-setting ride. Where should she look?

2. The stratosphere starts 10,000 meters above Earth. Where can you look to find how much farther away from Earth the mesosphere starts than the stratosphere?

Use the Infobank to solve.

3. The numbers of blue, humpback, and Bryde's whales differ today from what they were before the whaling boom. Put the current populations of these whales in order from the least to the greatest.

4. The world record for the most words typed in an hour was set by Albert Tangora. To the nearest thousand, how many words did he type?

5. There are box kites, parafoil kites, delta kites, and flat kites. If these four kites without their tails were laid end to end, how many inches long would this row of kites be?

6. Some people are interested in comparing the physical features of United States Presidents. Which President since Herbert Hoover weighed the most?

7. Scientists and oceanographers try to keep track of the whale population. They have discovered that there are more Bryde's whales today than there are blue whales. Estimate how many more Bryde's whales there are than blue whales.

8. Bill reads in the newspaper that the Campabout Store is having a sale on sleeping bags. Each sleeping bag sells for $79.53. Bill finds the same sleeping bag in the Explorer's Outfitters, Inc., catalog. Which store has the better price?

Subtracting 2- and 3-Digit Numbers

A. Scientists begin a two-day trip to follow dolphins along the California coast. The scientists will travel a total of 85 miles. On the first day, they travel 58 miles. How many more miles do they need to travel on the second day?

To find how many miles are needed to complete the trip, you can subtract. Find $85 - 58$.

There are not enough ones.	Regroup. 1 ten 5 ones = 15 ones	Subtract the ones.	Subtract the tens.
$\begin{array}{r} 8\,5 \\ -\,5\,8 \\ \hline \end{array}$	$\begin{array}{r} ^{7}\!\!\not{8}\,^{15}\!\!\not{5} \\ -\,5\,8 \\ \hline \end{array}$	$\begin{array}{r} ^{7}\!\!\not{8}\,^{15}\!\!\not{5} \\ -\,5\,8 \\ \hline 7 \end{array}$	$\begin{array}{r} ^{7}\!\!\not{8}\,^{15}\!\!\not{5} \\ -\,5\,8 \\ \hline 2\,7 \end{array}$

The scientists need to travel 27 miles on the second day.

Add to check your answer.
$$\begin{array}{r} 58 \\ +\,27 \\ \hline 85 \end{array}$$

B. You can subtract money the same way you subtract whole numbers. Remember to write the dollar sign and the cents point and the zero when necessary.

$$\begin{array}{r} ^{15} \\ ^{0}\,^{\not{5}}\,^{10} \\ \$\not{1}.\not{6}\,\not{0} \\ -\;\;0.9\,7 \\ \hline \$0.6\,3 \end{array}$$

You can use addition to check your answer.

$\$0.63 + \$0.97 = \$1.60$

Checkpoint Write the letter of the correct answer.

Subtract.

1.
$$\begin{array}{r} 74 \\ -\,38 \\ \hline \end{array}$$

2.
$$\begin{array}{r} \$8.50 \\ -\;\,1.48 \\ \hline \end{array}$$

3. $350 - 76$

a. 36	**a.** $7.02	**a.** 184
b. 44	**b.** $7.11	**b.** 274
c. 46	**c.** $7.19	**c.** 322
d. 112	**d.** $9.99	**d.** 426

Subtract. Check your answer.

1. 46
   − 13

2. 72
   − 22

3. 84
   − 39

4. 80
   − 65

5. 92
   − 17

6. 295
   − 47

7. 430
   − 125

8. 615
   − 407

9. 848
   − 629

10. $9.81
    − 8.43

11. 371
    − 294

12. 545
    − 367

13. 915
    − 19

14. 250
    − 78

15. $8.82
    − 6.96

16. 345 − 67

17. 298 − 109

18. 814 − 585

19. $9.62 − $0.79

20. 345 − 72

21. 918 − 678

22. 764 − 378

23. $4.57 − $3.88

Find n.

24. $112 − n = 88$

25. $226 − n = 17$

26. $114 − n = 91$

27. $8.72 − n = $1.61

Solve.

28. Marine biologists were studying a group of 117 dolphins. They were able to tag 108 of them. How many dolphins were not tagged?

29. Scientists were studying a group of 93 dolphins. They discovered that 27 of the dolphins were adults. How many of the dolphins were not adults?

30. The Miami Seaquarium is famous for its performing whales and dolphins. The whale show attracted 118 people one day. The next day, 211 people saw the dolphin show. During the two days, how many people watched the shows?

★31. Some scientists teach human words to dolphins. A dolphin named Elvar took 32 weeks to learn five words. Another dolphin, Chee Chee, learned to say the same words in only 23 weeks. How much longer did it take Elvar to learn the words?

CALCULATOR

Use your calculator to solve.

1. 10,101 − 1,010

2. 20,202 − 2,020

3. 30,303 − 3,030

Do you see a pattern? Predict the answer.

4. 90,909 − 9,090

5. 10,010,010 − 100,100

Subtracting Larger Numbers

When he was young, Jack read *20,000 Leagues Under the Sea*, a fantastic story of a submarine voyage. Now, Jack is an underwater explorer. His deepest dive was 4,526 feet in a bathyscaphe. Jack also spent one week in a submarine at a depth of 1,987 feet. How much deeper did Jack go in the bathyscaphe?

You can subtract to compare two numbers.

Find 4,526 − 1,987.

First estimate the difference.

$$
\begin{array}{r}
4{,}526 \longrightarrow 5{,}000 \\
-\,1{,}987 \longrightarrow -\,2{,}000 \\
\hline
3{,}000
\end{array}
$$

Regroup. Subtract the ones.	Regroup. Subtract the tens.	Regroup. Subtract the hundreds.	Subtract the thousands.
1 16	11 4 1 16	14 11 3 4 1 16	14 11 3 4 1 16
4,5 2 6	**4,5 2 6**	**4,5 2 6**	**4,5 2 6**
− 1,9 8 7	**− 1,9 8 7**	**− 1,9 8 7**	**− 1,9 8 7**
9	3 9	5 3 9	2,5 3 9

The bathyscaphe went 2,539 feet deeper than the submarine.

The answer is reasonably close to the estimate.

Other examples:

$$
\begin{array}{r}
8\,13\,15 \\
8{,}9\,4\,5 \\
-\,3{,}2\,6\,7 \\
\hline
5{,}6\,7\,8
\end{array}
\qquad
\begin{array}{r}
12\ 15 \\
4\ 2\ 5\ 10 \\
1\,3\,5{,}3\,6\,0 \\
-\ \ 1\,2{,}4\,7\,5 \\
\hline
1\,2\,2{,}8\,8\,5
\end{array}
\qquad
\begin{array}{r}
11\,13\,12 \\
5\ 7\ 3\ 2\ 12 \\
\$8{,}6\,2\,4.3\,2 \\
-\ \ 4{,}3\,5\,8.6\,7 \\
\hline
\$4{,}2\,6\,5.6\,5
\end{array}
$$

Checkpoint Write the letter of the correct answer.

Subtract.

1. 5,684
    − 3,275

2. 7,518
    − 246

3. $6,557.44 − $2,239.66

a. 1,419	**a.** 7,272	**a.** $4,317.78
b. 2,409	**b.** 7,332	**b.** $4,230.00
c. 2,419	**c.** 7,372	**c.** $4,238.88
d. 23,109	**d.** 7,764	**d.** $4,322.22

Find the difference.

1. 423
   − 264

2. 345
   − 178

3. 743
   − 287

4. 645
   − 283

5. $8.35
   − 5.49

6. 6,832
   − 2,754

7. 3,512
   − 1,674

8. 4,320
   − 2,753

9. 7,543
   − 4,786

10. $36.74
    − 16.98

11. 27,684
    − 16,895

12. 75,374
    − 56,847

13. 32,761
    − 18,775

14. 42,635
    − 24,067

15. $678.41
    − 489.53

16. 689,315
    − 149,878

17. 961,332
    − 710,556

18. 781,121
    − 526,573

19. 864,218
    − 439,629

20. $5,472.31
    − 1,385.85

21. 47,283
    − 6,529

22. 13,529
    − 9,468

23. 129,863
    − 49,127

24. 457,218
    − 70,651

25. $294.63
    − 97.25

26. 3,123 − 373

27. 58,166 − 2,628

28. 516,915 − 376,314

29. 59,656 − 2,468

30. 764 − 598

31. $245.72 − $88.73

Solve.

32. Jack read that in 1952, a submarine made an unsuccessful attempt to sail under the North Pole. That feat was completed in 1958 by the submarine U.S.S. *Nautilus*. How many years after the first attempt were people able to sail under the North Pole?

33. Jack reads a report that during the last ten years, the population of Bryde's whales has decreased by 6,363. Only 33,637 Bryde's whales remain. How many Bryde's whales were there ten years ago?

CHALLENGE

Copy these dots on a sheet of paper. Without lifting your pencil, draw four straight lines that pass through all nine dots.

• • •

• • •

• • •

Subtracting Across Zeros

Scientists keep track of whale populations. The right whale is a protected species. In 1976, scientists counted 3,073 right whales in the world's oceans. Recently, they counted 4,102. By how much did the count increase?

Subtract 4,102 − 3,073.

Regroup tens.
There are no tens
to regroup.
So, regroup hundreds.

$$\begin{array}{r} \overset{0\ 10}{4,1\,\cancel{0}\,2} \\ -\ 3,0\,7\,3 \\ \hline \end{array}$$

Regroup tens.

$$\begin{array}{r} \overset{9}{\underset{}{}}\ \ \ \\ \overset{0\ \cancel{10}12}{4,1\,\cancel{0}\,\cancel{2}} \\ -\ 3,0\,7\,3 \\ \hline \end{array}$$

Subtract.

$$\begin{array}{r} \overset{9}{\underset{}{}}\ \ \ \\ \overset{0\ \cancel{10}12}{4,1\,\cancel{0}\,\cancel{2}} \\ -\ 3,0\,7\,3 \\ \hline 1,0\,2\,9 \end{array}$$

The right whale population has increased by 1,029.

Add to check your answer.

$$\begin{array}{r} 1,029 \\ +\ 3,073 \\ \hline 4,102 \end{array}$$

Other examples:

$$\begin{array}{r} \overset{9}{\underset{}{}}\ \ \\ \overset{2\ \cancel{10}14}{\cancel{3}\,\cancel{0}\,4} \\ -\ \ \ 2\,6 \\ \hline 2\,7\,8 \end{array}$$

$$\begin{array}{r} \overset{9\ 9}{\underset{}{}}\ \ \\ \overset{3\ \cancel{10}\cancel{10}17}{\$\cancel{4}\,\cancel{0}.\cancel{0}\,7} \\ -\ \ \ 2\,8.3\,9 \\ \hline \$1\,1.6\,8 \end{array}$$

$$\begin{array}{r} \overset{13\ 9}{\underset{}{}}\ \ \\ \overset{8\ \cancel{3}\ \cancel{10}10}{5\,\cancel{9}\,\cancel{4},\cancel{0}\,\cancel{0}\,8} \\ -\ 2\,4\,6,2\,2\,7 \\ \hline 3\,4\,7,7\,8\,1 \end{array}$$

Checkpoint Write the letter of the correct answer.

Subtract.

1.
$$\begin{array}{r} 500 \\ -\ 376 \\ \hline \end{array}$$

2.
$$\begin{array}{r} \$70.05 \\ -\ 36.79 \\ \hline \end{array}$$

3.
$$\begin{array}{r} 6,400 \\ -\ 3,725 \\ \hline \end{array}$$

4.
$$\begin{array}{r} 460,052 \\ -\ 235,766 \\ \hline \end{array}$$

1.
a. 124
b. 134
c. 200
d. 224

2.
a. $14.36
b. $33.26
c. $34.26
d. $43.26

3.
a. 2,675
b. 2,685
c. 2,700
d. 3,675

4.
a. 214,286
b. 224,286
c. 234,286
d. 235,714

Find the difference.

1. 700 − 212	**2.** 906 − 527	**3.** 700 − 27	**4.** 800 − 327	**5.** $3.00 − 0.87
6. 4,704 − 2,439	**7.** 51,007 − 7,668	**8.** 27,103 − 17,195	**9.** $150.00 − 147.19	**10.** $400.60 − 384.78
11. 623,400 − 551,982	**12.** 700,000 − 632,757	**13.** $6,012.00 − 2,759.28	**14.** $2,010.01 − 1,754.68	**15.** 260,005 − 199,278

16. 500 − 483   **17.** 5,304 − 418   **18.** 20,055 − 16,739   **19.** 340,781 − 228,627

20. 278,005 − 119,259   **21.** $7,050.70 − $2,193.84   ★**22.** $9,012.21 − $64.79

★**23.** 340,051 − 26,834   ★**24.** $4,010.25 − $38.49   ★**25.** 700,085 − 24,296

Solve. For Problem 27, use the Infobank.

26. Blue whales are the largest creatures on Earth. A blue-whale calf can weigh 2,873 pounds at birth. It weighs 4,000 pounds at the end of one week. How much weight does it gain in one week?

27. Use the information on page 415 to write and solve two of your own word problems.

★**28.** Scientists know that a whale's favorite food is squid. A 60,000-pound whale will often dive 3,000 feet to find squid. If a giant squid weighs 446 pounds, how much heavier is the whale?

CHALLENGE   **Patterns, Relations, and Functions**

What are the next two numbers in the pattern?

1.
5	34	63	■	■

2.
7	33	59	■	■

3.
14	47	80	■	■

4.
320	345	370	■	■

PROBLEM SOLVING
Choosing the Operation

If you read a problem carefully, you may get clues to help you solve the problem. The clues will help you decide whether you should add or subtract.

There were 4 marine biologists in the research group studying the beluga whales. When a new grant was approved, 5 more scientists were hired. How many scientists are there in the research group?

Hints:

If you know	and you want to find	you can
• how many there are in two or more groups	how many there are in all	add.
• how many there are in one group • how many join it	the total number	add.
• how many there are in one group • the number taken away	how many are left	subtract.
• how many there are in each of two groups	how much larger one group is than the other	subtract to compare.
• how many there are in one group • how many there are in part of the group	how many there are in the remaining part of the group	subtract.

Once you have decided, you can solve the problem.

how many are in one group   how many join it   the total number

4   +   5   =   9

There are 9 scientists in the research group.

Write the letter of the operation you would use to solve the problem.

1. A Greek ship had 60 oars. The captain wanted it to go faster. Builders added 34 more oars. How many oars did the ship have then?

a. add   **b.** subtract

2. A British ship arrived in Tahiti with 45 crew members. Some of the crew members liked the island so much that they stayed. The ship left with 28 crew members. How many stayed in Tahiti?

a. add   **b.** subtract

Solve. For problem 8, use the Infobank.

3. A Roman grain ship could haul 800 tons of grain. If workers loaded the ship with 340 tons of grain in one day, how many more tons would they have to load to fill the ship?

4. The *Windjammer* sails into an island bay in the Caribbean. The chain for its anchor is 98 feet long, but the anchor cannot reach the ocean floor. The crew adds 53 more feet of chain to the anchor. How long is the chain?

5. In 1816, passenger ships like the *Blue Star* crossed the Atlantic from Liverpool, England, to New York in 40 days. In 1860, the ship *Andrew Jackson* completed the trip in 15 days. How many more days did it take the *Blue Star* to make the trip?

6. The ancient Egyptians sailed the Nile in boats made of reeds. Some of the boats were 50 feet long. The Vikings sailed the seas in boats as much as 80 feet long. How much longer were the Viking boats than those sailed by the Egyptians?

7. Some Roman galleys were about 150 feet longer than the Viking ships mentioned in problem 6. About how long were they?

8. Use the information on page 419 to solve. How much faster is a hovercraft than an ocean liner?

★9. A ship leaves Calcutta, India, carrying 635 crates of spice. The ship stops to trade in ports in Africa. When it reaches Lagos, Nigeria, it has sold 389 crates of spice. It also takes on 245 more crates of spice. How many crates of spice are on board when the ship sails from Lagos?

★10. A certain kind of boat rides on a cushion of air above the water. It has room for up to 254 passengers and 30 automobiles. If there are 134 passengers and 25 automobiles already on board the boat, how many more autos and passengers can it carry?

CALCULATOR

Study the following example. Write each digit in the correct place in the numeral. Then press the correct calculator keys and read the display upside down. What word do you see?

Example: 7 hundreds, 0 ones, 1 tens   **Numeral:** 710

Calculator Keys: [7] [1] [0]

Display: OIL

Copy and complete the table.

	Numeral	Calculator Keys	Display
1. 5 ones 3 hundreds 7 thousands 4 tens 7 ten thousands	■■,■■■	☐☐☐☐☐	■
2. 3 ten thousands 8 ones 3 millions 9 hundred thousands 3 tens 5 hundreds 1 thousand	■,■■■,■■■	☐☐☐☐☐☐☐	■

You can also use a calculator to find sums and differences that spell out simple sentences. Follow the example then complete the table.

	Calculator Keys	Display
EXAMPLE 518,067 + 12,867 530,934	[5][1][8][0][6][7] [+][1][2][8][6][7][=]	HE GOES
3. 55,145,632 + 2,589,713	☐☐☐☐☐☐☐☐ ☐☐☐☐☐☐☐☐☐☐	■
4. 95,746,215 − 18,594,870	☐☐☐☐☐☐☐☐☐ ☐☐☐☐☐☐☐☐☐☐	■

GROUP PROJECT

"And the Winner is . . ."

The problem: You won the Lucky Travelers Contest. You have a choice of spending a week on a tropical island or in a big city of your choice, with all travel and housing expenses paid. To help you make this decision, draw up for each place a schedule that lists what you would do in one day.

Key Facts

*Things to do
on a tropical island*

- swimming
- sailing
- snorkeling
- collecting seashells
- lying on the beach
- fishing

*Things to do
in a big city*

- sightseeing
- going to museums
- eating at fancy restaurants
- going to sporting events
- seeing plays
- shopping

SCHEDULE

Island Paradise		Dream City	
8:00		8:00	
9:00		9:00	
10:00		10:00	
11:00		11:00	
12:00		12:00	
1:00		1:00	
2:00		2:00	
3:00		3:00	
4:00		4:00	
5:00		5:00	
6:00		6:00	
7:00		7:00	
8:00		8:00	

CHAPTER TEST

Write in expanded form. (page 2)

1. 243,758

Write in standard form. (pages 2 and 4)

2. 50,000 + 2,000 + 900 + 80 + 2

3. 432 million, 348 thousand, 300

Write the short word name. (page 4)

4. 37,453,295,432

Write the value of the blue digit. (pages 2 and 4)

5. 375,060   **6.** 221,039   **7.** 42,304,676,532   **8.** 328,753,021

Compare. Use >, <, or = for ●. (page 6)

9. 323,650 ● 232,567

10. 6,327 ● 7,632

Order from the least to the greatest. (page 6)

11. 3,057; 339; 3,958; 3,032

Order from the greatest to the least. (page 6)

12. 2,473; 22,468; 22,472; 2,508

Estimate. (pages 14, 16, and 18)

13.
$$\begin{array}{r} 34 \\ 793 \\ 157 \\ + 124 \\ \hline \end{array}$$

14.
$$\begin{array}{r} \$6.23 \\ 5.49 \\ 0.75 \\ + 3.04 \\ \hline \end{array}$$

15.
$$\begin{array}{r} 7,615 \\ + 6,523 \\ \hline \end{array}$$

16.
$$\begin{array}{r} 4,623 \\ - 2,157 \\ \hline \end{array}$$

Round to the nearest hundred and thousand. (page 16)

17. 5,639   **18.** 2,898

Round to the nearest ten dollars. (page 16)

19. $65.80   **20.** $83.08

Add. (pages 20, 22, and 24)

21.
$$\begin{array}{r} \$5.62 \\ + 7.39 \\ \hline \end{array}$$

22.
$$\begin{array}{r} 4,382 \\ + 2,634 \\ \hline \end{array}$$

23.
$$\begin{array}{r} 52,757 \\ + 29,039 \\ \hline \end{array}$$

24.
$$\begin{array}{r} 5,778 \\ 3,239 \\ + 87 \\ \hline \end{array}$$

Subtract. (pages 28, 30, and 32)

25.
$$\begin{array}{r} 85 \\ - 73 \\ \hline \end{array}$$

26.
$$\begin{array}{r} 403 \\ - 217 \\ \hline \end{array}$$

27.
$$\begin{array}{r} \$7.43 \\ - 0.65 \\ \hline \end{array}$$

28.
$$\begin{array}{r} 3,200 \\ - 1,576 \\ \hline \end{array}$$

29.
$$\begin{array}{r} 239,865 \\ - 177,598 \\ \hline \end{array}$$

Write the letter of the operation you would use to solve the problem. (pages 34 and 35)

30. Al buys a model of a blue whale for $5.25. Tom buys one for $3.72 more than that. How much does Tom spend?

    a. addition   **b.** subtraction

31. Al works 155 hours at the Aquarium. Tom works there 200 hours. How many more hours does Tom work than Al?

    a. addition   **b.** subtraction

Estimate. (page 19)

32. At the Aquarium, Jake counted 273 blowfish, 157 eels, and 439 angelfish. Estimate the total number of fish that Jake counted.

33. Pablo dives for oysters with his friends. They collect 239 oysters on Monday, 168 on Tuesday, 353 on Wednesday, and 411 on Thursday. About how many oysters do they collect?

BONUS

This place-value chart shows numbers to hundred trillions.

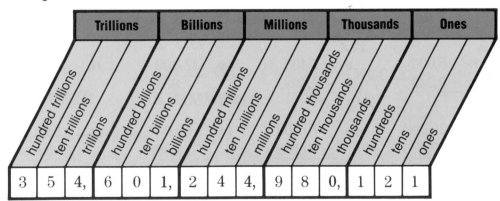

Read: 354 trillion, 601 billion, 244 million, 980 thousand, 121.
Write: 354,601,244,980,121.

Add or subtract. Then compare the answers.
Write >, <, or = for ●.

1.   2,375,987,020,505
    + 4,769,301,512,737

2.   9,301,586,000,121
    + 7,200,392,412,030

3.   357,680,294,027,598
    − 323,455,686,342,000

CUMULATIVE REVIEW

Write the letter of the correct answer.

1. What is the value of the blue digit?
   530,727,654,300

   a. 700
   b. 70,000
   c. 700,000,000
   d. not given

2. Write in standard form:
   500,000,000 + 70,000,000 + 1,000,000 + 70,000 + 1,000 + 80 + 1.

   a. 5,071,981
   b. 50,071,981
   c. 500,071,071,071
   d. not given

3. Compare. Choose >, <, or = for ●.
   549,781 ● 354,892

   a. =
   b. <
   c. >
   d. not given

4. Estimate: 7,469 − 5,188.

   a. 1,000
   b. 2,000
   c. 3,000
   d. 12,000

5. 4,567 + 3,841 + 287

   a. 7,585
   b. 8,695
   c. 8,595
   d. not given

6. Round to the nearest thousand:
   6,539.

   a. 5,000
   b. 6,000
   c. 7,000
   d. not given

7. 4,003 − 2,987

   a. 1,016
   b. 2,984
   c. 2,126
   d. not given

8. Write the word name: 407,300,799.

   a. 407 billion, 300 thousand, 799
   b. 407 million, 300 thousand, 799
   c. 407 billion, 300 million, 799
   d. not given

9. $374.53 + $594.48

   a. $968.01
   b. $968.91
   c. $969.01
   d. not given

10. Order from the greatest to the least:
    62,089; 75,300; 63,411; 57,980.

    a. 75,300; 62,089; 63,411; 57,980
    b. 75,300; 63,411; 62,089; 57,980
    c. 57,980; 62,089; 63,411; 75,300
    d. not given

11. The Halpern Chicken Farm sells 738 cartons of eggs in 6 months. The Whiting Farm sells 287 more cartons than that. How many cartons of eggs does the Whiting Farm sell?

    a. 451
    b. 1,025
    c. 1,225
    d. not given

12. Of 267 acres of farmland, 98 are planted with wheat. Choose the operation to find the number of acres not planted with wheat.

    a. add
    b. subtract
    c. multiply
    d. not given

In sports, athletes continually break world records. What do you think the world record for running 1 mile will be by the year 2000? What about the world record for the 100-meter freestyle in swimming for the same year? Before you begin, find out how the record has changed for each of the two events during the past 30 years.

2 PLACE VALUE, ADDITION AND SUBTRACTION
Decimals

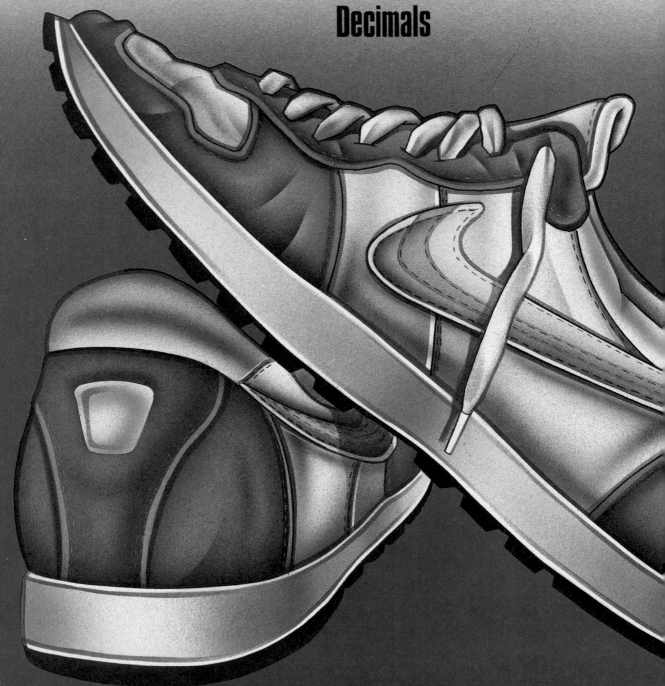

Tenths

A. There are ten rows of seats in one section at one Olympics event. Two of these rows are reserved for reporters and photographers. How can you write a number that describes the portion of rows that are reserved?

You can show the portion of reserved space in a picture. The square is divided into ten equal parts. Each part stands for one tenth. Two parts are shaded.

Ones	Tenths
0	2

Read: two tenths.
Write as a decimal: 0.2.
Write as a fraction: $\frac{2}{10}$.

> Write 0 before the decimal point if there is no digit in the ones place.

Two tenths, or 0.2, of the rows are reserved.

B. You can write a decimal for a number greater than 1.

Ones	Tenths
1	4

Read: one and four tenths.
Write as a decimal: 1.4.
Write as a mixed number: $1\frac{4}{10}$.

Checkpoint Write the letter of the correct answer.

Complete.

1. Seven tenths is written as ■.

a. 0.07
b. 0.7
c. 0.71
d. 7.10

2. Two and five tenths is written as ■.

a. 0.25
b. 2.05
c. 2.5
d. 2 and 0.5

3. 90.1 is read as ■.

a. nine and one tenth
b. ninety and one tenth
c. ninety and one
d. ninety-one

Write as a decimal.

1.   **2.**    **3.**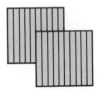

4. one tenth   **5.** one and six tenths   **6.** twelve and nine tenths

7. eight and one tenth   **8.** six tenths   **9.** three and four tenths

Write each decimal on a place-value chart like this.

10. 0.8   **11.** 1.3   **12.** 8.7   **13.** 2.3

14. 2.7   **15.** 4.5   **16.** 67.5   **17.** 15.4

18. 2.3   **19.** 34.7   **20.** 6.7   **21.** 16.8

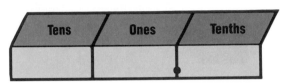

Write the word name for each decimal.

22. 0.3   **23.** 5.5   **24.** 10.3   **25.** 6.9   **26.** 11.1

27. 19.6   **28.** 8.2   **29.** 0.7   **30.** 17.6   **31.** 24.7

Solve.

32. Betty Cuthbert won the gold medal for the 200-meter dash in 1956. Her race time was twenty-three and four-tenths seconds. Write that number as a decimal.

33. In 1948, Mel Patton won the 200-meter dash in 20.1 seconds. If he had been one-tenth second faster, what would his time have been?

NUMBER SENSE

Here is an addition shortcut that can help you add long columns of numbers.

```
  34
  25
+ 16
----
  75
```

Find numbers in the ones column that add up to 10 (4 + 6 = 10). Then finish adding the column: 10 + 5 = 15.

Compute mentally. Look for tens.

1. 35 + 43 + 17   **2.** 28 + 56 + 82   **3.** 43 + 36 + 74   **4.** 15 + 39 + 85

5. 19 + 37 + 63   **6.** 51 + 32 + 98   **7.** 32 + 58 + 12   **8.** 24 + 63 + 23

Hundredths

A. There are 100 members on the Olympic team of one country. There are 48 women on the team. Write the number that describes the portion of women team members.

You can show this in a picture.
The square is divided into one hundred equal parts.
Each part stands for one hundredth.
Forty-eight parts are shaded.

Ones	Tenths	Hundredths
0	4	8

Read: forty-eight hundredths.
Write as a decimal: 0.48.   Write as a fraction: $\frac{48}{100}$.

The number that describes the portion of women team members is forty-eight hundredths, or 0.48.

B. You can write a decimal for a number greater than 1.

Hundreds	Tens	Ones	Tenths	Hundredths
1	2	3	5	8

Read: one hundred twenty-three and fifty-eight hundredths.
Write as a decimal: 123.58. Write as a mixed number: $123\frac{58}{100}$.

Checkpoint Write the letter of the correct answer.

Complete.

1. Twenty-nine hundredths is written as ▓.

a. 0.029
b. 0.209
c. 0.29
d. 29.100

2. 31.15 is read as ▓.

a. thirty-one and fifteen hundredths
b. thirty-one and fifty hundredths
c. thirty-one and fifteen tenths
d. thirty-one and fifteen

46

Write as a decimal.

1. 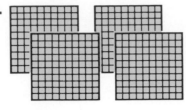 **2.** **3.**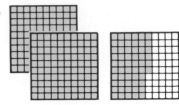

4. seventeen hundredths

5. six and two hundredths

6. forty and fifty-one hundredths

7. three and two hundredths

8. sixty-two hundredths

9. eleven and five hundredths

Copy this place-value chart. Write each decimal
on the place-value chart.

Hundreds	Tens	Ones	Tenths	Hundredths

10. 0.09 **11.** 2.19 **12.** 42.09 **13.** 14.12 **14.** 133.14 **15.** 320.08

16. 740.08 **17.** 69.73 **18.** 1.34 **19.** 87.03 **20.** 292.06 **21.** 100.97

Write the word name for each decimal.

22. 0.01 **23.** 0.38 **24.** 2.95 **25.** 17.63

26. 9.28 **27.** 3.05 **28.** 84.22 **29.** 532.74

Solve.

30. In 1972, Mark Spitz of the United
States set the Olympic record for
the men's 100-meter butterfly with a
time of fifty-four and twenty-seven
hundredths seconds. Write the
record time as a decimal.

31. In 1984, Spitz's Olympic record in
the 100-meter butterfly fell to West
Germany's Michael Gross. The new
record was fifty-three and
eight-hundredths seconds. Write
that as a decimal.

ANOTHER LOOK

Subtract.

1. 30 −17

2. 802 −105

3. 5,020 −2,528

4. 9,006 −2,528

5. $701.10 −565.98

Thousandths

A. A stopwatch can be used to measure the amount of time it takes to run a race. It can measure thousandths of a second. Look at the stopwatch. How would you write the word name for the decimal?

Ones	Tenths	Hundredths	Thousandths
0	7	7	3

Read: seven hundred seventy-three thousandths.
Write as a decimal: 0.773.
Write as a fraction: $\frac{773}{1000}$.

B. You can write a decimal for a number greater than 1.

Thousands	Hundreds	Tens	Ones	Tenths	Hundredths	Thousandths
3	8	2	1	8	7	5

Read: three thousand, eight hundred twenty-one and eight hundred seventy-five thousandths.
Write: 3,821.875.

C. You can write **equivalent** decimals that name the same number.

$$0.8 = 0.80 = 0.800 \qquad 2.6 = 2.60 = 2.600$$

Checkpoint   Write the letter of the correct answer.

Complete.

1. Seven and forty-two thousandths is written as ▧.

a. 0.742
b. 7.0042
c. 7.042
d. 7.420

2. 0.053 is read as ▧.

a. fifty-three thousandths
b. fifty-three hundredths
c. fifty-three tenths
d. five and three thousandths

Write as a decimal.

1. six and thirty-one thousandths
2. twenty-three thousandths
3. six hundred forty-seven thousandths
4. ten and two thousandths
5. fifty-one and two thousandths
6. two hundred and one thousandth

Write the word name for each decimal.

7. 4.513
8. 0.606
9. 0.009
10. 0.112
11. 3.054
12. 0.031
13. 0.500
14. 225.620
15. 6.001
16. 1010.302

Write the value of the blue digit.

17. 0.005
18. 0.068
19. 0.321
20. 1.001
21. 0.809
22. 76.512
23. 100.298
24. 100.298
25. 600.006
26. 50.005

Solve.

27. Al Oerter won gold medals for the discus throw in four Olympics. His best throw was only 18 thousandths of a meter less than the world record. Write this as a decimal.

28. Each runner on a 400-meter relay team had an average time of 9.458 seconds. If each had run 0.002 seconds faster, what would be the average time of each runner?

NUMBER SENSE

You can use what you know about place value to sort lists of decimals less than 1. The most important digit to look at is the digit to the right of the decimal point.

If the digit is 0 or 1, the decimal is close to 0.
If the digit is 4, 5, or 6, the decimal is close to half.
If the digit is 8 or 9, the decimal is close to 1.

The number of digits following this digit does not affect sorting.

Sort the decimals in the box into groups that are

1. close to 0.
2. close to half.
3. close to 1.

0.94	0.436	0.51
	0.004	
0.098	0.11	0.896

PROBLEM SOLVING
Using Broken-Line Graphs and Bar Graphs

A broken-line graph can show how something may have changed over a period of time.

The title states that this graph shows winning times for the men's 100-meter run.

The labels at the left tell you that the times are shown in seconds.

The labels at the bottom of the graph show you selected years of Olympic competition.

Each point on the graph shows the winning time for a selected year of competition.

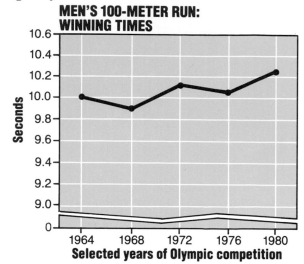

MEN'S 100-METER RUN: WINNING TIMES

A bar graph can help you compare information.

The title states that this graph compares women's 100-meter run times.

The labels at the left tell you that the winning times are shown in seconds. It is important to see that these numbers are not the same as those in the broken-line graph. Be careful when you compare information from different graphs.

The labels at the bottom show selected years of Olympic competition. It is important to see that the years for which information is given in the two graphs are not all the same.

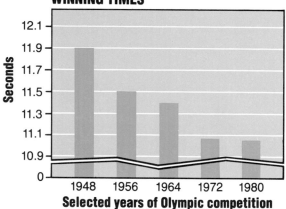

WOMEN'S 100-METER RUN: WINNING TIMES

A break in a graph means that numbers are skipped along the left side of the graph.

You can compare the information on the two graphs. The men's winning time in 1964 was 1.4 seconds faster than the women's winning time for that year.

Can you use the broken-line graph and the bar graph on page 50 to answer each question? Write *yes* or *no*.

1. What were the winning times for the men's and the women's 100-meter runs in 1952?

2. Whose winning time was faster in 1980, the men's or the women's?

Solve.

3. What was the winning woman's time in 1948?

4. What was the winning man's time in 1964?

5. What was the first year in which the men's time was faster than 10.0 seconds?

6. What was the first year in which the women's time was less than 11.5 seconds?

7. Was the time run by the women's winner in 1972 faster than the time run by the men's winner in 1976?

8. Was the time run by the men's winner in 1976 fast enough to have won the race in 1968?

9. Was the time run by the women's winner in 1972 faster than the time run by the men's winner in the same year?

10. If the women's winner in 1964 had been 1 second faster, would her time have been faster than the men's winner in the same year?

11. In general, how have the times for both races changed over the years shown on the two graphs? Have they increased or decreased?

12. What are the differences between the information shown on the men's and the women's graphs?

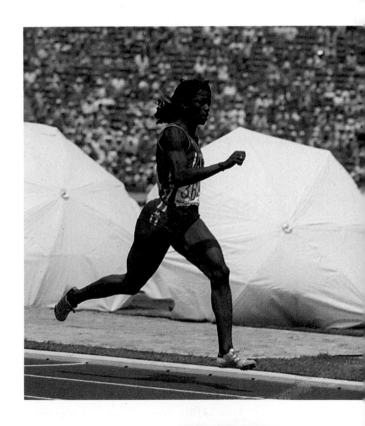

Comparing and Ordering Decimals

A. You can use base-10 blocks to *model* decimals and then compare the decimals.

Step 1: Compare the large block to the flat, the long, and the small cube.

- How many units are there in each kind of shape?

- How do these models compare to one another in size and value?

Step 2: Let the large block stand for one whole.

- What part of the block is the flat? Why?

- What part of the block is the long? Why?

- What part of the block is one small cube? Why?

Step 3: Use the base-10 blocks to show two different decimals.

- Which group of blocks stands for the larger decimal? How can you tell?

- Write the two decimals. How can you use the symbols < and > to show how the two decimals compare?

Use the blocks to compare other decimals. Record each comparison.

Thinking as a Team

1. Do you always need three different shapes of blocks to model a decimal to thousandths? Why or why not?

2. If you had one large block and three small cubes, how would you write the decimal? What does this tell you about when you need to write a zero to the right of the decimal point?

3. Model the decimals 2.4 and 2.40. What do you notice? How do they compare to 2.400?

4. Why is a tenth greater than a thousandth?

B. You can locate decimals on a number line.

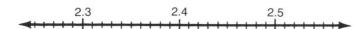

Draw a number line and locate the following points:

2.39   2.5   2.42   2.34

- Which point is farthest to the right? Which decimal is greatest? Why?

Thinking as a Team

1. To compare two decimals, in which place should you first compare digits?

2. How would you list decimals that have an uneven number of digits in order to compare them?

3. Why is it sometimes helpful to use zeros to write one of the decimals being compared as an equivalent decimal?

4. Suppose two decimals have the same digits in all places to the hundredths. What information do you need to find which decimal is greater?

C. You can order a group of decimals by comparing.

Working as a Team

The track team at your school clocked the following times for the 100 meter dash.

Race One		**Race Two**	
Jon:	13.59 seconds	Gene:	13.60 seconds
John:	12.99 seconds	Jim:	12.89 seconds
Jack:	12.59 seconds	Joe:	13.00 seconds
Jose:	13.02 seconds	Julio:	12.54 seconds

List the times in Race One in order from fastest to slowest. List the times in Race Two in order from slowest to fastest.

1. Describe how you ordered the decimals.

2. Who had the fastest time of all? Who had the slowest time?

3. Were there any ties?

Rounding Decimals

A. You can use a number line to explore rounding decimals.

Step 1: Locate these decimals on the number line.

3.1	3.4	3.9	3.2
3.6	3.7	3.8	3.3

- Which of these decimals are closer to 3? Which are closer to 4?

- How would you round 3.5 to the nearest whole number? What do you already know about rounding that would help you?

- Now round 7.8 to the nearest whole number. Draw a number line if it will help you.

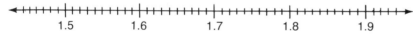

Step 2: Locate 1.84 on the number line.

- The decimals shown on this number line are between which two whole numbers?

- Round 1.84 to the nearest whole number.

- What is 1.84 rounded to the nearest tenth?

Thinking as a Team

1. What rule can you develop about rounding decimals?

2. Write some decimals to the thousandths place. Round each decimal to the nearest hundredth. Then round them to the nearest tenth and to the nearest whole number.

3. What place do you look at first when rounding a decimal to hundredths, to tenths, or to whole numbers?

B. Your mother asks you to go to the grocery store. You have $15 to spend. Here is the list:

1 loaf of bread
1 dozen eggs
1 qt juice
2 melons
1 gal milk
1 lb cheese

When you get to the store, you see this price list on a flyer:

Eggs 1 dozen $0.89	Raisins 1 bag $0.25	Melons each $0.74
Cheese 1 lb $2.29	Milk 1 gal $2.09	Paper Towels 2 rolls $0.79
Juice 1 qt $1.72	Chicken 1 lb $2.59	Bread 1 loaf $1.19

- Quickly check the prices of the items you need to buy to see whether you have enough money. How did you do this?

Thinking as a Team

1. Discuss what other combinations of items you could buy with $15. Make up other lists and trade them with those of your classmates to check.

2. Discuss other times when you might use rounding. Would you round in the same way every time? Why or why not?

Estimating Decimal Sums and Differences

A. As part of her training for the Olympic trials, Jennifer jogs four days each week. She records her distances on a training chart. Use Jennifer's training chart to estimate how many miles she jogged this week.

Day	Distance
Mon.	3.3 mi
Wed.	4.75 mi
Fri.	6.3 mi
Sun.	8.4 mi

Estimate 3.3 + 4.75 + 6.3 + 8.4.

You can estimate by rounding.

Round each number to the nearest whole number.

3.3 + 4.75 + 6.3 + 8.4
↓   ↓   ↓   ↓
3   +   5   +   6   +   8

Add the rounded numbers.

3 + 5 + 6 + 8 = 22

Jennifer jogged about 22 miles this week.

B. When you estimate, round to the place that allows you to mentally compute the rounded numbers.

Estimate $384.48 − $46.64.

Decide to which place value you will round.

To the nearest whole number:

$$\begin{array}{rcl} \$384.48 & \to & \$384 \\ -\ \ \ 46.64 & \to & 47 \\ \hline \end{array}$$

$384 − $47 is difficult to mentally compute; so, round to the nearest ten.

$$\begin{array}{rcl} \$384.48 & \to & \$380 \\ -\ \ \ 46.64 & \to & -\ 50 \\ \hline & & \$330 \end{array}$$

You can see that $380 − $50 is easier to compute. So, the estimated difference of $384.48 − $46.64 is about $330.

Estimate. Write > or < for ●.

1. 6.38 + 1.96 ● 9

2. 15.75 + 4.39 ● 19

3. 2.764 + 1.09 ● 5

4. $15.89 + $1.97 ● $20

5. $39.88 + $7.89 ● $50

6. $13.36 + $5.55 ● $20

7. $8.59 − $2.67 ● $5

8. $20.00 − $14.79 ● $4

9. $34.86 − $26.99 ● $10

10. 11.275 − 1.87 ● 8

11. 26.75 − 15.891 ● 10

12. 1.295 − 1.198 ● 1

13. 8.6 + 4.273 + 9.01 + 3.75 ● 25

14. 19.835 + 5.6 + 4.9 + 27.61 ● 60

Estimate.

15.
```
   4.09
  14.315
+  1.299
```

16.
```
   2.1794
  19.51
+ 36.453
```

17.
```
  93.694
− 23.78
```

18.
```
  19.5
−  8.876
```

Use the catalog of Olympic souvenirs and estimation to help you answer these questions.

19. Is $10 enough to buy B and D?

20. Is $20 enough to buy A, C, and D?

21. Is $10 enough to buy C and D?

22. Is $30 enough to buy C, D, and E?

OLYMPIC-SOUVENIRS CATALOG	
A. Medallion	$4.17
B. Bumper sticker	$5.49
C. Tote bag	$8.95
D. Socks	$4.49
E. Metal trophy	$15.85

Solve.

23. Olympic pole-vault records have risen in the past hundred years. In 1896, the best vault was 10.81 feet. In 1984, the best vault was 18.96 feet. About how many feet higher was the 1984 vault?

24. Sawao Kato scored 115.9 points at the 1968 Olympics in gymnastics. In 1972, he scored 114.65 points. About how many more points did he score in 1968 than in 1972?

MIDCHAPTER REVIEW

Write the place value of the blue digit.

1. 7.012

2. 12.131

3. 6.793

4. 4.29

5. 0.704

Compare. Write >, <, or = for ●.

6. 3.625 ● 3.562

7. 0.6 ● 0.394

Round to the nearest hundredth.

8. 0.125

9. 3.006

10. 2.197

PROBLEM SOLVING
Estimation

Sometimes it is easier to solve a problem by estimating than by finding an exact answer. First you must decide whether to overestimate or underestimate.

> To raise money for a new gym, the Linden School holds a "Sportathon." Tickets cost $2.75 for adults and $1.45 for children. Jean has $12.00. She wants to buy tickets for 1 adult and 1 child. She also wants to have at least $5.45 for lunch. Does she have enough money?

Since Jean wants to be sure she has enough money, she should overestimate her expenses. Round each value up to the next highest dollar.

Adult ticket:	$2.75 $\longrightarrow$	$3.00
Child ticket:	$1.45 $\longrightarrow$	$2.00
Lunch:	$5.45 $\longrightarrow$	+ $6.00
		$11.00 overestimated sum

Since $11 < $12, Jean has enough money.

When the gym committee feels they have earned the $1,750 they need, they will discount all prices. An hour before the Sportathon's end, the committee members will gather information about the amount of money earned. They need to know if they've earned enough so that they can begin to discount the prices.

Since they want to be sure that they've earned the money they need, they should underestimate their earnings. You would not need to calculate an exact sum. Round each value down to the next lowest hundred dollars.

School jackets:	$931.70 $\longrightarrow$	$900
School shirts:	$669.95 $\longrightarrow$	$600
School pennants:	$281.50 $\longrightarrow$	$200
Program ads:	$175.00 $\longrightarrow$	+ $100
		$1,800 underestimated sum

Since $1,800 > $1,750, that is enough to begin to discount.

Explain why you would *underestimate* or *overestimate*.

1. Here is the coach's record for Doris.
   Day 1: 4.8 mi   Day 5: 4.2 mi
   Day 2: 3.6 mi   Day 6: 3.5 mi
   Day 3: 4.4 mi   Day 7: 3.2 mi
   Day 4: 3.9 mi
   Has Doris run at least 24 mi this week?

2. Alan Leibowitz is ordering the following equipment.
Parallel bars:	$119.99
12 mats:	$175.50
1 Vaulting horse:	$151.50

   Mr. Leibowitz has exactly $600. Does he have enough money to pay for his order?

Estimate to solve.

LINDEN SCHOOL—FIRST ROUND GYMNASTICS SCORES

	Floor exercise	Vaulting horse	Balance beam	Uneven bars
Nia:	6.275	7.95	7.9	6.5
Jenny:	6.875	7.25	5.875	6.88
Lisa:	6.75	8.0	5.5	5.5
Lois:	6.95	7.0	6.875	6.0
Karen:	5.75	7.0	6.0	6.0
Alexandra:	7.25	6.875	5.0	5.5

The top three scorers of the first round compete in a second round. The winner is the girl with the highest total for both rounds.

3. Estimate Linden's total for the first round on the vaulting horse.

4. Estimate Linden's total for the first round of the uneven bars.

5. Which event is probably the most difficult? Which is probably the easiest?

6. Lois wanted to score at least 50 points for both rounds. Her second round scores are: 6.55, 7.2, 6.5, and 6.75. Did she reach her goal?

7. The Linden School competes against the Rickert School. Estimate the total for Linden in the first round in all events. (To find the winner, the team members' scores are added together.)

8. The team from the Rickert School scores 45.65 points on the balance beam during the first round. They score 46.85 points during the second round. How many points must the Linden team score during Round 2 to win that event?

Adding Decimals

A. Ingemar Stenmark, a Swedish skier, won a gold medal in the 1980 men's slalom. His first run was clocked at 53.89 seconds. His time for the second run was 50.37 seconds. What was his combined time?

Add 53.89 + 50.37.

Line up the decimal points. Add the hundredths. Regroup if necessary.	Add the tenths. Regroup if necessary.	Add the ones. Regroup if necessary.	Add the tens. Write the decimal point.
$\begin{array}{r} 1 \\ 53.89 \\ +50.37 \\ \hline 6 \end{array}$	$\begin{array}{r} 1\ 1 \\ 53.89 \\ +50.37 \\ \hline 26 \end{array}$	$\begin{array}{r} 1\ 1 \\ 53.89 \\ +50.37 \\ \hline 426 \end{array}$	$\begin{array}{r} 53.89 \\ +50.37 \\ \hline 104.26 \end{array}$

His combined time was 104.26 seconds.

B. You may need to write equivalent decimals before adding.

Add 5.287 + 9.33 + 7.

Line up the decimal points. Add the thousandths.	Add the hundredths.	Add the tenths.	Add the ones. Write the decimal point.
$\begin{array}{r} 5.287 \\ 9.330 \\ +7.000 \\ \hline 7 \end{array}$ $\begin{array}{l} 9.33 = 9.330 \\ 7\ \ \ = 7.000 \end{array}$	$\begin{array}{r} 1 \\ 5.287 \\ 9.330 \\ +7.000 \\ \hline 17 \end{array}$	$\begin{array}{r} 1 \\ 5.287 \\ 9.330 \\ +7.000 \\ \hline 617 \end{array}$	$\begin{array}{r} 5.287 \\ 9.330 \\ +7.000 \\ \hline 21.617 \end{array}$

Checkpoint Write the letter of the correct answer.

Add.

1. 34.8 + 71.23

a. 105.03
b. 105.21
c. 105.31
d. 106.03

2. $56.72 + $13.65

a. $60.37
b. $69.37
c. $70.37
d. $71.37

3. 4.19 + 0.782 + 47.8

a. 0.052772
b. 1.679
c. 52.772
d. 53.772

Add.

1. 10.12
  + 32.26

2. 4.30
  + 0.473

3. 25.231
  + 50.136

4. 21.138
  + 34.451

5. $6.22
  + 2.35

6. 3.19
  + 9.9

7. 2.474
  + 75.84

8. 9.1
  + 4.634

9. 6
  + 8.23

10. $9.74
  + 8.53

11. 3.072
  8.653
  + 9.048

12. 7.651
  1.492
  + 8.648

13. 7.00
  25.67
  + 0.10

14. 0.1
  0.2
  + 9.8

15. $0.08
  2.47
  + 0.52

16. 2.34 + 12.1

17. 15.46 + 8.932

18. 756.9 + 0.78

19. 53.85 + 0.397

20. 1.374 + 85.066

21. $7.07 + $6.42

22. 19.765 + 9.53

23. 2.34 + 0.765 + 3.876

★**24.** (7.4 + 0.920) + 61

★**25.** 0.48 + (58.675 + 9.33)

Solve.

26. In 1980, Eric Heiden won the men's speed-skating event with a time of 38.03 seconds. Karin Enke won the women's event with a time of 41.78 seconds. Estimate to the nearest second how much faster Heiden was.

27. At the 1984 Olympics, Valerie Brisco-Hooks won the women's 200-meter run with a time of 21.81 seconds. She also won the women's 400-meter run in 48.83 seconds. What was her total time for the two events?

28. In a slalom, a skier had a time for her first run of 55.78 seconds and a time for her second run of 56.97 seconds. What was her combined time?

★**29.** In a 100-meter swimming relay, four swimmers had these times: 70.4 seconds, 62.4 seconds, 66.8 seconds, 59.6 seconds. Was their combined time faster or slower than 4 minutes?

NUMBER SENSE

Estimate to check if the answer is reasonable.

1. 2.386 + 0.897 = 2.283

2. 1.043 + 2.98 = 4.023

3. 7.62 + 0.89 = 0.851

4. 3.89 + 4.001 + 7.229 = 15.12

Subtracting Decimals

A. At the 1976 Winter Olympics, Sheila Young of the
United States set an Olympic record in the 500-meter
speed-skating competition. Her time was 42.76 seconds.
In a later competition, she finished the same race in
40.68 seconds. How much faster was her time in the
later competition?

Find the difference: 42.76 − 40.68.

Line up the decimal points. Subtract the hundredths. Regroup if necessary.	Subtract the tenths. Regroup if necessary.	Subtract the ones and the tens. Write the decimal point.
$$\begin{array}{r} 6\ 16 \\ 4\,2.7\,\cancel{6} \\ -\,4\,0.6\,8 \\ \hline 8 \end{array}$$	$$\begin{array}{r} 6\ 16 \\ 4\,2.7\,\cancel{6} \\ -\,4\,0.6\,8 \\ \hline 0\,8 \end{array}$$	$$\begin{array}{r} 6\ 16 \\ 4\,2.7\,\cancel{6} \\ -\,4\,0.6\,8 \\ \hline 2.0\,8 \end{array}$$

Her time was 2.08 seconds faster.

B. You may need to write equivalent decimals before
subtracting.

Find 3.7 − 3.25.

Line up the decimal points.	Subtract the hundredths.	Subtract the tenths.	Subtract the ones. Write the decimal point.
$$\begin{array}{r} 3.7\,0 \\ -\,3.2\,5 \\ \hline \end{array}$$ $3.7 = 3.70$	$$\begin{array}{r} 6\ 10 \\ 3.7\,\cancel{0} \\ -\,3.2\,5 \\ \hline 5 \end{array}$$	$$\begin{array}{r} 6\ 10 \\ 3.7\,\cancel{0} \\ -\,3.2\,5 \\ \hline 4\,5 \end{array}$$	$$\begin{array}{r} 6\ 10 \\ 3.7\,\cancel{0} \\ -\,3.2\,5 \\ \hline 0.4\,5 \end{array}$$ This 0 must be written.

Checkpoint Write the letter of the correct answer.

Subtract.

1. 3.4 − 2.61 **2.** $2.35 − $0.98 **3.** 5.345 − 0.468

a. 0.79	**a.** $1.37	**a.** 2.987
b. 0.81	**b.** $2.47	**b.** 4.877
c. 1.21	**c.** $2.63	**c.** 5.813
d. 6.01	**d.** $3.33	**d.** 5.987

Subtract.

1.   9.78
    − 2.68

2.   7.79
    − 5.14

3.   6.89
    − 5.24

4.   92.34
    − 1.14

5. $29.99
    −   1.92

6.   7.98
    − 5.59

7.   7.34
    − 6.26

8.   67.31
    − 52.17

9. $70.21
    − 36.42

10. $572.92
    − 383.94

11.   25.04
    − 7.16

12.   54.08
    − 5.04

13.   62.42
    − 5.90

14. $36.00
    −   5.65

15. $644.90
    −   4.95

16.   80.6
    − 58.94

17.   60.34
    − 13.8

18.   7.73
    − 5.65

19.   7.31
    − 0.92

20. $766.61
    − 397.84

21. 6 − 0.08

22. 67.9 − 0.39

23. 18.8 − 8.27

24. 58.3 − 0.03

Solve.

25. Thomas Burke of the United States was the winner of the 100-meter dash in the first modern Olympics held in 1896. Burke's time was 12.0 seconds. In 1980, Allen Wells won the same race in 10.15 seconds. Whose time was faster? How much faster?

★**26.** In the 400-meter relay race, four runners race legs of 100 meters each. If the first two runners took a total of 23.36 seconds, the third took 10.33 seconds, and the total time raced was 43.86 seconds, how much time did the last runner take?

FOCUS: REASONING

Some of Sally's friends are John's friends. All of Ron's friends are Sally's friends. From these statements, what can we say about John's friends?

PROBLEM SOLVING
Writing a Number Sentence

When you have trouble deciding how to solve a problem, try writing a number sentence. A number sentence can help you decide how to use the numbers you know to find the number you need.

> In 1980, Ludmila Kondratyeva of the Soviet Union won the women's 100-meter run. Her time was 11.6 seconds. In 1984, Evelyn Ashford, of the United States, won the 100-meter run in 10.97 seconds. How much faster than Kondratyeva did Ashford run the race?

1. List what you know and what you want to find.

Kondratyeva's time was 11.6 seconds. Ashford's time was 10.97 seconds.

How much faster was Ashford's time?

2. Think about how to use this information to solve the problem.

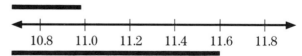

You know how many there are in two groups. You want to find how much larger one group is than another. You can subtract.

3. Write a number sentence. Use n to stand for the number you want to find.

Kondratyeva's − Ashford's = How
time   time   much
                        faster
                        Ashford
                        ran

$$11.6 - 10.97 = n$$

4. Solve. Write the answer. Ashford ran 0.63 seconds faster than Kondratyeva.

$$11.6 - 10.97 = 0.63$$
$$n = 0.63$$

Write the letter of the correct number sentence.
Explain your choice.

1. A diver scored 421.62 points in a platform-diving competition. Another diver scored 8.48 fewer points. What was the second diver's score?

   a. $421.62 + 6.48 = n$
   b. $421.62 - 8.48 = n$
   c. $421.62 + n = 8.48$

2. A skier made 2 slalom runs. His time for the first was 54.67 seconds. His time for the second was 52.48 seconds. What was his combined time?

   a. $54.67 + 52.48 = n$
   b. $54.67 - 52.48 = n$
   c. $52.48 + n = 54.67$

Write a number sentence. Solve.

3. In 1984, Valerie Brisco-Hooks ran the 400-meter race in 21.81 seconds. At the 1980 Olympics, the winning time was 0.22 seconds slower. What was the winning time in 1980?

4. The winning men's high jump in 1984 was 7.71 feet. In 1980, the winning jump was 7.73 feet. In which year was the winning jump higher? How much higher was the winning jump?

5. In 1984, Mary Meagher beat the old 100-meter butterfly swimming record by 1.16 seconds. The old record was 60.42 seconds. What was Mary's time?

6. At the twenty-third Summer Olympics, the United States won 83 gold medals, 61 silver medals, and 30 bronze medals. How many medals did the United States win?

7. One skier scored 225.8 points in ski jumping. Another skier scored 3.6 points higher. What was the second skier's score?

8. One springboard diver scored 503.98 points. A second diver scored 26.09 fewer points. What was the second diver's score?

★9. In running the hurdles, the first runner had a time of 47.79 seconds. The next runner's time was 0.08 seconds slower. The third runner was 1.3 seconds slower than the second runner. What was the third runner's time?

★10. A four-man team entered the 400-meter freestyle relay. The first three swimmers' individual times were 57.31 seconds, 54.83 seconds, and 58.46 seconds. The team's combined score was 222.67 seconds. What was the fourth swimmer's time?

LOGICAL REASONING

Sometimes you can solve a problem by eliminating every possible answer except one.

Mr. and Mrs. Jeffrey had a tennis tournament with their friends, Mr. and Mrs. Kaplan, Mr. and Mrs. Lamson, and Mr. and Mrs. Mossetto. Each player had one partner. Who was Mrs. Jeffrey's partner?

Clues: **a.** Each pair had a man and a woman.
 b. Husbands and wives were not partners.
 c. Mr. Lamson and Mrs. Kaplan were partners.
 d. Mr. Jeffrey's sister is Mrs. Mossetto, but they did not play together.

Copy the table. Write *no* for each pair that is not possible. For each correct pair that you find, write *yes*. Write *no* for the remaining pairs that are no longer possible.

	Mrs. Jeffrey	Mrs. Kaplan	Mrs. Lamson	Mrs. Mossetto
Mr. Jeffrey	no	no		no
Mr. Kaplan		no		
Mr. Lamson	no	yes	no	no
Mr. Mossetto		no		no

1. Who was Mr. Jeffrey's partner?

2. Who was Mrs. Mossetto's partner?

3. Who was Mrs. Jeffrey's partner?

Mr. Andrews, Ms. Baker, Mrs. Carson, Mr. Drew, and Ms. Early each have a different occupation. They work as an electrician, a plumber, a teacher, a pilot, and a doctor. Who is the pilot?

Use the clues and make your own chart to solve.

Clues: **a.** Mr. Drew is on a bowling team with the teacher, the pilot, and Ms. Early.
 b. Mrs. Carson's brother is the plumber.
 c. Ms. Baker is the electrician.
 d. Mr. Andrews is older than the teacher.

GROUP PROJECT

Making a Time Line

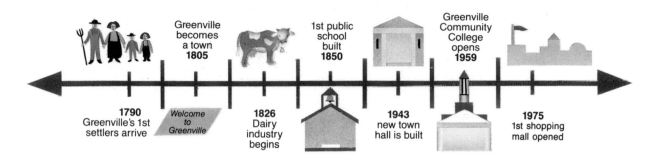

The problem: You and your classmates want to make a time line that shows the history of your town. A time line is a number line that shows dates of important events. Decide which events you want to include. Use the time line on this page as a model to make a time line of your town's history.

You might want to include events such as these:

- the date of the founding of your town
- the dates that famous people lived in your town
- when each public building was constructed
- when industries moved into town
- when your town was named
- when the first settlers moved to your area

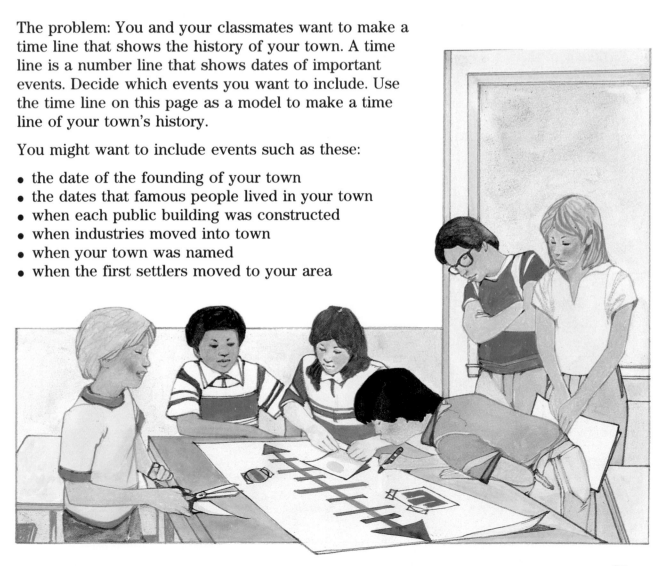

CHAPTER TEST

Write as a decimal. (pages 44, 46, and 48)

1. two and three tenths   **2.** six hundredths   **3.** three thousandths

Write the word name for each decimal. (pages 46 and 48)

4. 0.23   **5.** 6.357

Write the value of the blue digit. (pages 44, 46, and 48)

6. 0.7   **7.** 0.56   **8.** 2.031

Compare. Write >, <, or = for ●. (page 52)

9. 2.35 ● 2.350   **10.** 72.378 ● 72.37

Order from the least to the greatest. (page 52)

11. 25.03; 23.05; 25.35

Round to the nearest whole number, tenth, and hundredth. (page 54)

12. 13.258   **13.** 12.178

Estimate. Write > or < for ●. (page 56)

14. 5.23 + 3.76 ● 8   **15.** 25.323 + 17.282 ● 44

16. 12.65 − 7.87 ● 5   **17.** 35.36 − 5.93 ● 29

Add. (page 60)

18.
$$2.23 + 4.2$$

19.
$$53.6 + 1.539$$

20.
$$2.52 + 0.475$$

21.
$$\$5.25 + 0.83$$

22. 4.35 + 0.4 + 3.7   **23.** 3.251 + 4.73 + 8.9

Subtract. (page 62)

24.
$$2.37 - 1.29$$

25.
$$50.53 - 47.61$$

26.
$$\$73.83 - 59.92$$

27.
$$47.7 - 9.05$$

28. 6 − 0.08   **29.** 18.8 − 8.27

Write a number sentence and solve. (pages 64 and 65)

30. Joe runs the 440-yard dash in 73.56 seconds. Sam's time is 1.72 seconds slower than Joe's time. What is Sam's time?

31. Shirley runs the 220-yard dash in 37.47 seconds. Pat's time is 2.3 seconds faster than Shirley's time. What is Pat's time?

Use the information from the bar graph to solve. (pages 50 and 51)

32. In which year was the 440-yard dash run the fastest?

33. Which years had the closest times in the 440-yard dash?

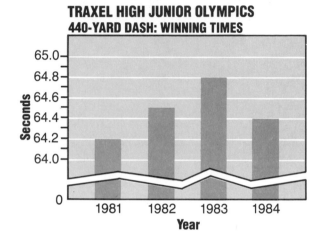

TRAXEL HIGH JUNIOR OLYMPICS
440-YARD DASH: WINNING TIMES

BONUS

This place-value chart shows numbers to ten-thousandths.

Ones	Tenths	Hundredths	Thousandths	Ten-thousandths
1	4	6	9	8

Decimal point

Read: one and 4,698 ten-thousandths.
Write 1.4698.

Add or subtract. Then order the answers from the least to the greatest.

1.	**2.**	**3.**	**4.**	**5.**
3.7126	2.0967	7.2635	6.5938	2.5352
+ 4.2352	+ 5.6384	− 3.8036	− 4.8709	+ 4.8658

RETEACHING

A. Sometimes you may need to write an equivalent decimal before you compare.

Compare 4.92 and 4.9.

Line up the decimal points. Think: 4.9 = 4.90.	Begin by comparing digits at the left.	Continue comparing.	Continue comparing.
4.92 4.90	4.92 4.90 4 = 4	4.92 4.90 9 = 9	4.92 4.90 2 > 0

So, 4.92 > 4.9.

You can see this on a number line.

4.90   4.91   4.92   4.93   4.94   4.95

B. You can order decimals by comparing them.
Compare and order 0.7, 2.08, and 2.069.

Line up the decimal points. Write equivalent decimals.	Begin to compare at the left.	Continue comparing.
0.700 2.080 2.069	0.700 — Think: no ones. 2.080 — So, 0.700 is the 2.069 — smallest number.	8 > 6 2.080 > 2.069

From the least to the greatest, the numbers are 0.7, 2.069, and 2.08.
From the greatest to the least, the numbers are 2.08, 2.069, and 0.7.

Compare. Write >, <, or = for ●.

1. 2.762 ● 2.672   **2.** 53.62 ● 5.362   **3.** 0.372 ● 0.299

4. 9.251 ● 91.25   **5.** 0.040 ● 0.400   **6.** 271.1 ● 72.11

Write in order from the greatest to the least.

7. 2.32, 1.745, 9.33   **8.** 0.07, 0.70, 0.71   **9.** 3.14, 1.579, 4.01

Write in order from the least to the greatest.

10. 7.505, 57.7, 5.07   **11.** 0.002, 0.012, 0.2   **12.** 79.184, 74.189, 79.9

13. 6.112, 6.2, 6.02   **14.** 23.06, 23.07, 23.09   **15.** 4.5, 5.04, 0.54

ENRICHMENT

Checking Accounts

Fred keeps money in a checking account at the bank. He uses a **check register** to record the amounts of his checks and deposits. He sends a check for $21.98 to the Olympic Committee to buy an Olympic coin. Below is a page from Fred's check register.

ITEM NO.	DATE	DESCRIPTION OF TRANSACTION	(−) PAYMENT OR WITHDRAWAL		✓ T	( ) FEE	(+) DEPOSIT OR INTEREST	BALANCE 231	57
096	6/13	U.S. Olympic Comm	21	98				21	98
								209	59
	6/15	Birthday Check					25 00	25	00
								234	59
097	6/21	Ron's Hardware	12	97				12	97
								221	62

The *balance column* shows how much money Fred has in his account after he subtracts the amount of a check or adds the amount of a deposit.

Find the amounts of the missing checks, deposits, or balances.

	(−) PAYMENT OR WITHDRAWAL		✓ T	(−) FEE	(+) DEPOSIT OR INTEREST	BALANCE 313	25
	27	52				27	52
1.						■	■
					13 11	13	11
2.						■	■
					79 58	79	58
3.						■	■

	(−) PAYMENT OR WITHDRAWAL		✓ T	(−) FEE	(+) DEPOSIT OR INTEREST	BALANCE 215	50
					21 35	21	35
4.						■	■
	150	98				150	98
5.						■	■
	37	59				37	59
6.						■	■

On July 1, Fred's balance was $215.27. On July 2, he wrote a check to Harvey's Sock Shop for $13.22. On July 5, he deposited $55.63 in his account. Using this information, copy and complete the register below.

	ITEM NO.	DATE	DESCRIPTION OF TRANSACTION	(−) PAYMENT OR WITHDRAWAL		✓ T	(−) FEE	(+) DEPOSIT OR INTEREST		BALANCE 215	27
7.	031	■	■	■		■				■	■
8.										■	■
9.		■	■					■	■	■	■
10.										■	■

TECHNOLOGY

Here are some LOGO commands.

FD   This moves the turtle forward the number of steps shown.

BK   This moves the turtle backward.

RT   This makes the turtle turn to the right.

LT   This makes the turtle turn to the left.

HOME   This takes the turtle to the center of the screen.

PU   This tells the turtle not to draw a line.

PD   This tells the turtle to begin drawing a line.

PE   This tells the turtle to erase a line.

A LOGO program is called a **procedure.** When you type a procedure's name, the turtle follows all the commands in the procedure. Two or more commands can be on a line. The last command in a procedure must be END.

If you draw a line segment that you wish to erase, use the command PE. Suppose you type FD 100, but meant to type FD 75. Type the command PE BK 25 PD. The turtle will move backward 25 steps and will erase that part of the line segment. Always remember to type PD after using PE. PD tells the turtle to stop erasing and to begin drawing again.

The line segment was drawn by the command FD 105.

1. Write a command to make the line 130 steps long.

2. Write 3 commands to change your new line segment to a length of 85 steps.

3. Write commands for drawing two line segments, each 30 steps long and 15 steps apart.

4. This square was drawn by the following procedure. Rewrite the procedure to turn the square into a rectangle.

```
TO SQUARE
FD 40 RT 90 FD 40 RT 90
FD 40 RT 90 FD 40 RT 90
END
```

★5. This octagon was drawn by the following procedure. Write a procedure that would divide the octagon in half.

```
TO OCTAGON
FD 40 RT 45 FD 40 RT 45 FD 40 RT 45
FD 40 RT 45 FD 40 RT 45 FD 40 RT 45
FD 40 RT 45 FD 40 RT 45
END
```

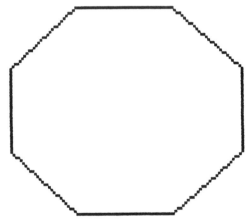

CUMULATIVE REVIEW

Write the letter of the correct answer.

1. Write in standard form:
   500,000 + 60,000 + 4,000 + 300 + 9.

   a. 564,300,009   b. 564,309
   c. 564,390   d. not given

2. Compare. Use >, <, or = for ●.
   597,603 ● 597,630

   a. =   b. <
   c. >   d. not given

3. $597.07 + $789.24

   a. $1,356.21   b. $1,386.31
   c. $1,376.31   d. not given

4. Round to the nearest ten thousand:
   56,000.

   a. 50,000   b. 60,000
   c. 58,000   d. not given

5. Estimate: 4,496 − 2,377.

   a. 1,000   b. 2,000
   c. 4,000   d. 5,000

6. What is the value of the blue digit?
   958,789

   a. 5,000   b. 500
   c. 500,000   d. not given

7. Write in expanded form: 30,579.

   a. 3,000 + 500 + 70 + 9
   b. 30,000 + 500 + 70 + 9
   c. 300,000 + 500 + 70 + 9
   d. not given

8. Write the short word name:
   507,313,896.

   a. 507 billion, 313 million, 896
      thousand
   b. 507 million, 313 thousand, 896
   c. 507 billion, 313 million, 896
   d. not given

9. 7,807 − 6,968

   a. 839   b. 965
   c. 1,949   d. not given

10. 5,798 + 6,055 + 940 + 11

    a. 11,694   b. 12,704
    c. 12,804   d. not given

11. A commercial jet is flying at an
    altitude of 34,059 feet. An air-force
    jet is flying 7,670 feet higher than
    that. How high is the air-force jet
    flying?

    a. 26,389 ft   b. 41,729 ft
    c. 42,629 ft   d. not given

12. An airport runway may be as long
    as 4,783 meters. The clear zone,
    over which the plane flies before
    touching ground, covers 823 meters
    of the total runway. Estimate how
    many meters are not clear zone.

    a. 4,000 m   b. 4,400 m
    c. 5,000 m   d. 5,500 m

74

Plan a white-water rafting trip down the Colorado River through the Grand Canyon. Use a map to decide where your stopping points will be. What kinds of food, supplies, and equipment will you take? How much hiking and rafting will you do? How will you organize your trip?

3 MULTIPLYING WHOLE NUMBERS

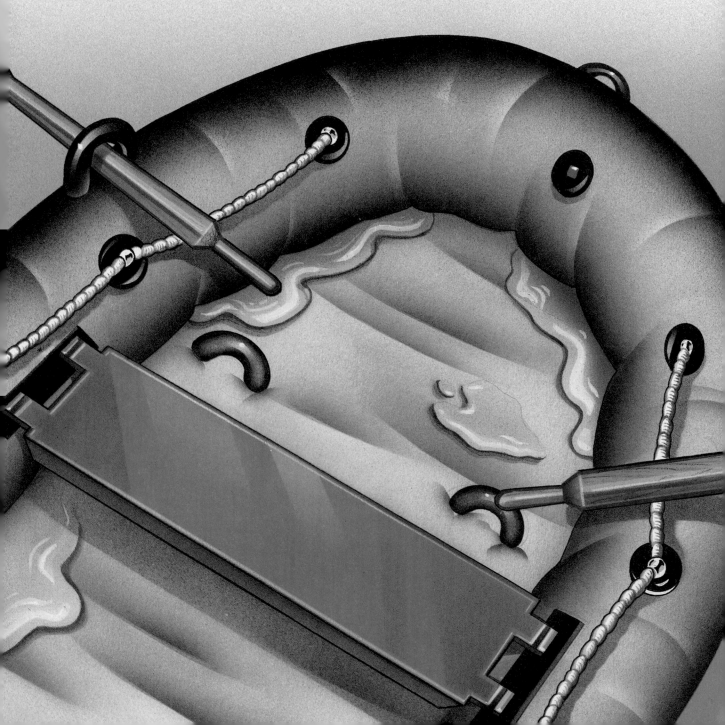

Properties of Multiplication

You can make *models* of rectangles to help you explore properties of multiplication.

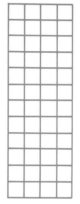

A. Using graph paper, cut out a rectangle that is 4 squares high and 12 squares across.

Cut out another rectangle that is 12 squares high and 4 squares across.

- How many squares are there in each of the rectangles?

- How can you find the number of squares in each rectangle without counting?

- Write number sentences that show how you found the number of squares in each rectangle. What do you notice?

- Draw other pairs of rectangles and repeat what you have done. What do you notice?

Thinking as a Team

You have been exploring the **commutative property** of multiplication. In your own words, describe this property. Compare your description to those of other teams.

B. Using graph paper, cut out a 4 by 10 rectangle. Color it blue. Cut out a 4 by 2 rectangle. Color it red.

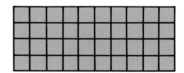

- How many squares are there in the blue rectangle? How many are there in the red rectangle?

  Look at one of the 4 by 12 rectangles. Compare it to the red and blue rectangles.

- What do you notice about the rectangles?

- Write a number sentence that shows a relationship among the three rectangles.

Thinking as a Team

You have been exploring the **distributive property** of multiplication. Describe this property. Compare your description to those of other teams.

C. Work with a partner. Using a calculator, one partner should multiply 23 × (12 × 45). The numbers in the ( ) should be multiplied first. The other partner should multiply (23 × 12) × 45.

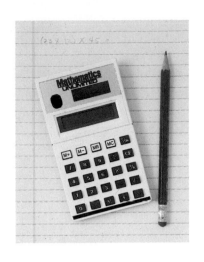

- What do you notice about the way the three factors were grouped when each of you multiplied?
- What do you notice about their products?

Try this using other examples with three factors.

Thinking as a Team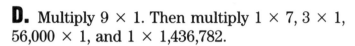

You have been exploring the **associative property** of multiplication. Describe this property. Compare your description to those of other teams.

D. Multiply 9 × 1. Then multiply 1 × 7, 3 × 1, 56,000 × 1, and 1 × 1,436,782.

- What do you notice about each product?

Thinking as a Team

This property is called the **identity property.** Write a rule about this property. Compare your rule to those of other teams.

E. Multiply 7 × 0. Next multiply 8 × 0. Then multiply these numbers:

6,743,879 × 0   0 × 843,559   63 × 434 × 0 × 98,567

- What do you notice about each product?

Thinking as a Team

This property is called the multiplication **property of zero.** Write a rule about this property. Compare your rule to those of other teams.

1. Do all of these properties work with any set of whole numbers? Show some examples.
2. How can you use these properties to help you to multiply mentally?

Multiples of 10

A. Early explorers of the American wilderness marked trails by cutting the bark of trees. This was called *blazing a trail*. If 70 miles of trail are blazed in 1 month, how many miles can be blazed in 10 months?

You can multiply to find how many miles can be blazed in 10 months.

Find 10×70.

Think: $10 \times 70 = (10 \times 10) \times 7 = 100 \times 7$.
So, $10 \times 70 = 700$.

In 10 months, 700 miles of trail can be blazed.

B. Look for a pattern.

$$5 \times 9 = 45 \qquad 50 \times 9 = 450$$
$$5 \times 90 = 450 \qquad 50 \times 90 = 4,500$$
$$5 \times 900 = 4,500 \qquad 50 \times 900 = 45,000$$
$$5 \times 9,000 = 45,000 \qquad 50 \times 9,000 = 450,000$$

Use a calculator to explore other examples, such as:

$$\begin{array}{r} 50 \\ \times\ 60 \\ \hline 3,000 \end{array} \qquad \begin{array}{r} 7,000 \\ \times\ \ 200 \\ \hline 1,400,000 \end{array}$$

Checkpoint Write the letter of the correct answer.

Multiply.

1. $\begin{array}{r} 80 \\ \times\ 10 \\ \hline \end{array}$	2. $\begin{array}{r} 500 \\ \times\ 10 \\ \hline \end{array}$	3. $\begin{array}{r} 700 \\ \times\ 50 \\ \hline \end{array}$	4. $\begin{array}{r} 6,000 \\ \times\ 200 \\ \hline \end{array}$
a. 80	**a.** 50	**a.** 350	**a.** 1,200
b. 800	**b.** 500	**b.** 3,500	**b.** 12,000
c. 8,000	**c.** 5,000	**c.** 35,000	**c.** 120,000
d. 80,000	**d.** 50,000	**d.** 350,000	**d.** 1,200,000

Multiply.

1.	10 $\times\ 4$	2.	20 $\times\ 3$	3.	50 $\times\ 5$	4.	100 $\times\ \ 2$	5.	800 $\times\ \ 7$
6.	200 $\times\ \ 8$	7.	5,000 $\times\ \ \ \ 4$	8.	3,000 $\times\ \ \ \ 3$	9.	70 $\times\ 60$	10.	10 $\times\ 30$
11.	40 $\times\ 30$	12.	300 $\times\ 60$	13.	600 $\times\ 50$	14.	1,000 $\times\ \ \ \ 60$	15.	9,000 $\times\ \ 300$

16. $80 \times 2,000$ **17.** $700 \times 6,000$ **18.** 40×50

19. 200×800 **20.** $3,000 \times 70$ **21.** $4,000 \times 300$

Find n.

★**22.** $6 \times n = 6,000$ ★**23.** $100 \times n = 4,000$ ★**24.** $70 \times n = 56,000$

Solve.

25. Jean-Pierre buys beads to trade during his journey. He buys 30 bags of beads. Each bag contains 600 beads. How many beads does he have to trade?

26. Simple items are good to trade. Jean-Pierre buys 40 cards of sewing needles. Each card holds 60 needles. How many needles does Jean-Pierre buy?

NUMBER SENSE

You can estimate the product of two numbers by multiplying their lead digits and writing in zeros.

Find the lead digit. Multiply.

$$\begin{array}{r} 218 \\ \times\ \ \ 6 \\ \hline 12 \end{array}$$

Count the places after the lead digit.

$$\begin{array}{r} 218 \\ \times\ \ \ 6 \\ \hline 12 \end{array}$$

Two places mean 2 zeros.

Write zeros in the product.

1,200
$6 \times 200 = 1,200$

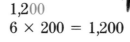

Estimate.

1. 429×3 **2.** 815×6 **3.** 911×2 **4.** 641×5

5. $4,152 \times 3$ **6.** $7,341 \times 5$ **7.** $2,453 \times 4$ **8.** $6,321 \times 9$

PROBLEM SOLVING
Checking for a Reasonable Answer

When you complete a problem, think about your answer. Is it a reasonable answer to the problem? You can often spot an error by thinking about what the value of the answer should be.

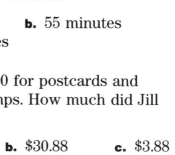

A group of students plan a one-day trip to Denver. They decide they will need to make 2 sandwiches for each person going on the trip. If 9 people go on the trip, how many sandwiches do they need?

a. 11 sandwiches **b.** 18 sandwiches **c.** 180 sandwiches

Without finding the exact answer, you can see that choice **a** is too small and choice **c** is too great. Choice **b** is the most reasonable. You can estimate to check if your choice is a reasonable one. About 5 people could eat 11 sandwiches, and 180 sandwiches would be enough for 90 people. For 9 people, 18 sandwiches would be about right.

Read each problem. Without computing the exact answer, write the letter of the correct answer. Explain your choice.

1. It will cost each student $8 for a bus ticket to Denver. If 9 students go, how much will their total bus fare be?

  a. $810
  b. $17
  c. $72

2. The students decide to spend 90 minutes at Larimer Square, a restored section of Denver. Lynn spends 35 minutes in a crafts shop. How much time does she have to visit the other exhibits?

  a. 3 minutes   **b.** 55 minutes
  c. 125 minutes

3. Julio bought a souvenir gold nugget. He gave the clerk $10. His change was $5.03. How much did he pay for the gold nugget?

  a. $4.97   **b.** $0.03   **c.** $50.30

4. Jill spent $3.00 for postcards and $0.88 for stamps. How much did Jill spend?

  a. $2.12   **b.** $30.88   **c.** $3.88

Read each problem. Without computing the exact answer, write the letter of the correct answer. Explain your choice.

5. John can run 1 mile in 10 minutes. The 16 Street Mall is 1 mile long. How long will it take John to run to the end of the mall and back?

a. 2 hours
b. 2 minutes
c. 20 minutes

6. There are 1,500 animals in the Denver Zoo. On their visit, the students see 357 of these animals. How many of the animals at the Denver Zoo did they not see?

a. 11,430 of the animals
b. 11,857 of the animals
c. 1,143 of the animals

7. The Ballroom in the Children's Museum is filled with thousands of plastic balls. If there are 65 children in the ballroom, and 27 more arrive, how many children are there in the Ballroom?

a. 38 children
b. 92 children
c. 80,092 children

8. The students learn that Denver is called the Mile-High City because its altitude is 5,280 feet. Pikes Peak, also in Colorado, is 14,110 feet high. How much higher than Denver is Pikes Peak?

a. 8,830 feet
b. 18,830 feet
c. 19,650 feet

9. The tour guide explains that the Denver Mint produces about 14 million coins per day. About how many coins are produced there in 10 days?

a. about 14 million coins
b. about 140 million coins
c. about 14 billion coins

10. The mountain road drops in altitude at a rate of 8 meters per minute as it descends into Denver. At that rate, how many meters of altitude would the road drop in 8 minutes?

a. 24 meters
b. 64 meters
c. 180 meters

★11. The bus is caught in a traffic jam 78 miles from home. Traffic moves at only 7 miles per hour. At that rate, how far would the bus be from home after 6 hours?

a. 36 miles
b. 98 miles
c. 143 miles

★12. The group rides on the historic Silverton train. A ticket costs $28 for adults and $14 for children. What is the total fare for 7 children and 2 adults?

a. $1,540
b. $154
c. $252

Estimating Products

A. The Stillmans plan to explore the northwestern part of the United States in their camper. Their trip will last 21 days. They plan to travel 165 miles each day. About how many miles do they plan to travel?

You can estimate a product by rounding each factor to its largest place, and then multiplying.

Estimate 21 × 165.

Round each factor.   **Multiply the rounded factors.**

$$165 \longrightarrow 200$$
$$\times\ \ 21 \longrightarrow\ \ \ \ 20$$

$$\begin{array}{r} 200 \\ \times\ \ \ 20 \\ \hline 4{,}000 \end{array}$$

They plan to travel about 4,000 miles.

B. If one of the factors is a 1-digit number, you can estimate by rounding the other factor and multiplying.

Estimate 5 × 686.

$$\begin{array}{r} 686 \longrightarrow\ \ \ 700 \\ \times\ \ \ 5 \longrightarrow \times\ \ \ 5 \\ \hline 3{,}500 \end{array}$$

C. You can estimate money the same way you estimate whole numbers.

Estimate 9 × $6.89.

9 × $6.89 is about 9 × $7
$$\qquad\qquad 9 \times \$7 = \$63$$

The estimated product of 9 × $6.89 is about $63.00.

Estimate.

1. 43
   × 18

2. 86
   × 24

3. 79
   × 36

4. 16
   × 48

5. 87
   × 59

6. 32
   × 48

7. 324
   × 8

8. 782
   × 6

9. 535
   × 79

10. 424
    × 23

11. 376
    × 34

12. 538
    × 67

13. $3.67
    × 3

14. $2.81
    × 4

15. $6.98
    × 8

16. $8.45
    × 7

17. $8.75
    × 3

18. $7.82
    × 9

19. 17 × 453

20. 23 × 32

21. 34 × 764

22. 16 × 927

23. 88 × 32

24. 76 × 487

★25. 98 × 62

★26. 97 × 99

Solve. For Problem 29, use the Infobank.

27. Larry Stillman takes his camera and 18 rolls of film. Each roll can produce 36 pictures. About how many pictures can Larry take?

28. The family visits Old Faithful, a geyser at Yellowstone Park. The geyser erupts about 22 times a day. If there are 365 days in a year, about how many times will the geyser erupt per year?

29. Before the Stillmans began their trip, they bought camping supplies. Use the information on page 416 to solve. Estimate the total cost of buying one of each item for the 5 members of the family.

★30. The Stillman camper travels 23 miles on 1 gallon of gasoline. If the Stillmans drive 165 miles per day, and gasoline costs $1.13 a gallon, about how much do the Stillmans spend on gasoline each day?

MIDCHAPTER REVIEW

Write the property.

1. $6 \times 0 = 0$

2. $7 \times 5 = 5 \times 7$

3. $6 \times (4 + 3) = (6 \times 4) + (6 \times 3)$

Multiply.

4. 80×20

5. 5×900

6. $400 \times 7,000$

7. 30×600

Estimate.

8. 82×12

9. 72×944

10. 6×543

11. $8 \times \$7.55$

PROBLEM SOLVING
Estimation

Many questions can be answered by using estimated amounts. Sometimes your estimate is too close to the amount you are comparing it to. In this case, you need to find an exact amount.

> The 21 members of the North Fork Bike Club are going to the Mashomack Preserve on Shelter Island, New York. They have to ride a ferryboat to reach the island. The director of the club will pay the ferryboat fare, which is $2.95 per rider. She has $80. Will that be enough?

Although the director can answer this question by finding the exact amount of the fare, she would prefer to round the numbers and estimate.

She rounds. $2.95 ⟶ $3.00   21 members ⟶ 20 members
Then she multiplies. $3.00 × 20 = $60.00 $60.00 < $80.00

She has enough money.

Alfred has $19.06 to spend on souvenirs. He wants 3 maps that cost $3.00 each, a $8.49 Shelter Island sweatshirt, and a bag of shells for $1.76. Does he have enough money?

Alfred estimates.
Maps	(3 × $3.00)	$9.00
Sweatshirt	($8.49)	8.00
Bag of shells	($1.76)	+ 2.00
		$19.00

Since $19.00 is so close to the spending limit—$19.06—Alfred decides to find an exact amount.

Maps	(3 × $3.00)	$9.00
Sweatshirt		8.49
Bag of shells		+ 1.76
		$19.25

Alfred does not have enough money.

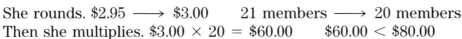

Decide whether you need to find an estimate or an exact answer. Explain your decision.

1. As she enters the preserve, the club director sees a sign that suggests that each visitor contribute $1.85. How much should she put in the contribution box if she pays the suggested amount for each of the 21 members?

2. One member of the club wants to photograph the salt marshes, freshwater ponds, fields, and upland forest that make up the preserve. She has $56.31 with which to buy film. Does she have enough to buy ten $4.99 rolls of film?

Solve. Find an estimate or an exact answer as needed.

3. The operators hope to raise $150.00 per day through visitor contributions to maintain the preserve. The manager counts 101 names in that day's visitor book. If each visitor paid the $1.85 suggested contribution, would they reach their daily goal?

4. The photographer wants to enlarge 3 pictures of otters that were taken at the preserve. To enlarge them, she will have to pay $10 per photo. For how much should she write her check to the photo lab?

5. The operators of the preserve want to find out if they have reached their goal of collecting $450.00 for 3 days.

   The amounts collected are:

   Monday $134
   Tuesday $128
   Wednesday $187

   Did they reach their goal?

6. The whole of Shelter Island is almost 3 times as large as the preserve. The preserve is exactly 2,039 acres. About how large is Shelter Island?

★7. One bike-club member decides to buy a seashell wind chime for $4.95, 3 souvenir plates for $2.00 each, and 4 T-shirts at $6.00 each. He has $34. Does he have enough?

★8. At the restaurant, 10 of the cyclists order the $4.95 broiled-flounder special. Another 5 order the spaghetti dinner at $6.00. The other 6 members order the $9.95 lobster special. These prices do not include tax or tip. The club director says that club dues can pay for $125.00 of the meal's cost. Will the dues cover all of the costs?

Multiplying by 1-Digit Factors

A. New Amsterdam was founded by Dutch traders in 1625. Many ships sailed into its harbor. If 87 ships docked each year, how many ships docked in 9 years?

Multiply 9 × 87.

Multiply the ones. Regroup the 63 ones.

$$\begin{array}{r} 6 \\ 8\ 7 \\ \times\quad 9 \\ \hline 3 \end{array} \qquad \begin{array}{r} 7 \\ \times\ 9 \\ \hline 63 \end{array}$$

Multiply the tens. Then add the 6 tens.

$$\begin{array}{r} 6 \\ 8\ 7 \\ \times\quad 9 \\ \hline 7\ 8\ 3 \end{array} \qquad \begin{array}{r} 8 \\ \times\ 9 \\ \hline 72 \\ +\ 6 \\ \hline 78 \end{array}$$

In 9 years, 783 ships docked.

B. Sometimes you must regroup several times. Find the product of 5 × 219.

Multiply the ones. Regroup the 45 ones.

$$\begin{array}{r} 4 \\ 2\ 1\ 9 \\ \times\quad 5 \\ \hline 5 \end{array} \qquad \begin{array}{r} 9 \\ \times\ 5 \\ \hline 45 \end{array}$$

Multiply the tens. Then add the 4 tens.

$$\begin{array}{r} 4 \\ 2\ 1\ 9 \\ \times\quad 5 \\ \hline 9\ 5 \end{array} \qquad \begin{array}{r} 1 \\ \times\ 5 \\ \hline 5 \\ +\ 4 \\ \hline 9 \end{array}$$

Multiply the hundreds.

$$\begin{array}{r} 4 \\ 2\ 1\ 9 \\ \times\quad 5 \\ \hline 1,0\ 9\ 5 \end{array} \qquad \begin{array}{r} 2 \\ \times\ 5 \\ \hline 10 \end{array}$$

Multiply with money the same way you multiply with whole numbers.

Multiply 4 × $3.65.

$$\begin{array}{r} \$3.65 \\ \times\quad 4 \\ \hline \$14.60 \end{array}$$

Remember to write the dollar sign and the cents point.

Checkpoint Write the letter of the correct answer.

Multiply.

1. $7.26
   × 7

   a. $7.19
   b. $15.82
   c. $50.42
   d. $50.82

2. 23
   × 4

   a. 86
   b. 92
   c. 122
   d. 920

3. 902
   × 6

   a. 5,412
   b. 5,462
   c. 5,472
   d. 54,012

4. 52
   × 9

   a. 468
   b. 477
   c. 4,518
   d. 4,618

Multiply.

1. 42
× 4

2. 61
× 6

3. 73
× 3

4. 84
× 2

5. 50
× 4

6. 67
× 7

7. 86
× 5

8. 54
× 3

9. $0.97
× 4

10. $0.79
× 2

11. 146
× 3

12. 207
× 9

13. 807
× 8

14. $4.37
× 2

15. $9.16
× 4

16. 680
× 9

17. 234
× 4

18. $7.50
× 2

19. $3.54
× 3

20. $1.84
× 7

21. 4 × 31

22. 6 × 16

23. 4 × $3.95

24. 4 × 23

25. 8 × 312

26. 2 × 22

27. 6 × 408

28. 8 × $3.12

Solve.

29. Jonas Bronck came from Denmark with 36 dairy cows. Within a few years, the number of cows increased 6 times. How many cows did Bronck have then?

30. New Yorkers owned 99 ships in 1747. In the next 20 years, the number of ships they owned increased by 5 times. How many ships did New Yorkers own in 1767?

CHALLENGE **Patterns, Relations, and Functions**

Copy the number triangle.

What is the pattern of the numbers in the blue circles?

What is the pattern of the numbers in each row?

Fill in each ○ in the bottom row of the triangle.

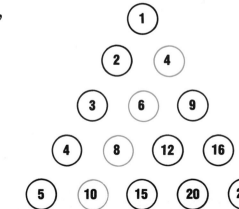

Multiplying Larger Numbers

People from all over the world come to America to explore its wonders. The Giroux family travels from Paris on the Concorde, a supersonic jet plane. It can fly at 1,424 miles per hour. How far can the Concorde fly in 3 hours?

You can multiply as if the same number of miles were flown each hour.

Multiply $3 \times 1,424$.

First estimate the product.

$$
\begin{array}{r}
1,424 \longrightarrow 1,000 \\
\times \quad 3 \longrightarrow \times \quad 3 \\
\hline
3,000
\end{array}
$$

Multiply the ones. Regroup if necessary.	Multiply the tens. Regroup if necessary.	Multiply the hundreds. Regroup if necessary.	Multiply the thousands. Regroup if necessary.

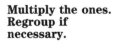

The Concorde can fly 4,272 miles in 3 hours.
The product is reasonably close to the estimate.

Other examples:

$$
\begin{array}{r}
7,941 \\
\times \quad 4 \\
\hline
31,764
\end{array}
\qquad
\begin{array}{r}
63,402 \\
\times \quad 7 \\
\hline
443,814
\end{array}
\qquad
\begin{array}{r}
\$35.27 \\
\times \quad 5 \\
\hline
\$176.35
\end{array}
$$

Checkpoint Write the letter of the correct answer.

Multiply.

1. $\begin{array}{r} 2,436 \\ \times \quad 7 \\ \hline \end{array}$

a. 14,812
b. 15,922
c. 17,052
d. 49,692

2. $\begin{array}{r} \$22.46 \\ \times \quad 4 \\ \hline \end{array}$

a. $22.50
b. $85.34
c. $88.64
d. $89.84

3. $\begin{array}{r} 18,076 \\ \times \quad 7 \\ \hline \end{array}$

a. 76,092
b. 86,702
c. 126,032
d. 126,532

Multiply.

1.	3,440 × 2	**2.**	1,312 × 3	**3.**	2,101 × 4	**4.**	2,315 × 3	**5.**	$34.23 × 2
6.	2,325 × 3	**7.**	3,207 × 3	**8.**	2,016 × 4	**9.**	1,605 × 8	**10.**	$32.15 × 3
11.	12,169 × 4	**12.**	23,064 × 3	**13.**	36,495 × 2	**14.**	33,347 × 3	**15.**	11,248 × 4

16. 3 × 23,055 **17.** 2 × 44,675 **18.** 4 × 2,216 **19.** 8 × $652.43

20. 4 × 12,386 **21.** 2 × 9,909 **22.** 6 × 40,948 **23.** 7 × $732.18

Solve.

24. The Giroux family explores the United States by car. They drive about 1,947 miles per week for 4 weeks. How many miles do they drive?

25. At the Kennedy Space Center in Florida, the Giroux family is amazed to learn that a rocket that travels at 8,426 miles per hour is not fast enough to escape Earth's gravity. The rocket must travel 3 times faster. How fast must the rocket travel?

★**26.** When they wrote the budget for their trip, they had two lists of choices. What is the least cost for 2 people for both hotel and food?

	Cost for 2 persons	Cost for 1 person
Hotel	$75.00 per night	$45.00 per night
Food	$82.00 per day	$37.50 per day

NUMBER SENSE

To help you estimate products, look for factors that are near 10; 100; or 1,000.

Estimate 57 × 98.   **Think:** 98 is close to 100.
$$57 × 100 = 5,700$$

Estimate.

1. 48 × 97 **2.** 73 × 978 **3.** 455 × 103 **4.** 288 × 87

5. 65 × 96 **6.** 387 × 102 **7.** 34 × 989 **8.** 23 × 992

PROBLEM SOLVING
Choosing a Strategy or Method

Write the strategy or method you choose. Then solve.

1. The Santa Fe Trail once linked Independence, Missouri, with Santa Fe, New Mexico. The first stop along the trail was Council Grove. A stage coach traveled 66 miles the first day. It had 54 miles to go before it reached Council Grove. How far from Independence was the first stop?

> Estimation
> Choosing the Operation
> Acting It Out
> Making a Model
> Writing a Number Sentence
> Checking for a Reasonable Answer

2. Suppose a trader bought a knife for $1.72 in Independence and sold it for $8.45 in Santa Fe. How much profit did the trader make?

3. The Council Grove sheriff bought 21 cents' worth of eggs and 16 cents' worth of potatoes. How much money did he spend?

4. A wagon train covered 270 miles of the 800-mile-long Santa Fe Trail. How much farther did it have to go?

5. The Council Grove register showed that 5,819 mules, 478 horses, and 22,738 oxen passed through the town in 1860. Was the number of oxen and horses that passed through Council Grove that year closer to 25,000 or 30,000?

6. The overland mail delivered mail to California in 25 days. The pony express, which replaced the overland mail in 1860, took about 8 days. Was the time saved by pony express on a round trip closer to 20 days or 30 days?

7. In 1803, the Louisiana Purchase increased the size of the United States from about 890,000 square miles to 1,720,000 square miles. Estimate the number of square miles of land gained in the Louisiana Purchase.

★8. Fritz read about the Louisiana Purchase. He read 24 pages on Saturday and twice as many on Sunday. How many pages did Fritz read during the weekend?

PROBLEM SOLVING
Making Change

Sometimes you don't have the exact amount of money to buy an item. You can give the cashier more than the cost of an item, you will receive change.

Carl buys a map of the United States. It costs $7.49. He gives the salesclerk a $10 bill. How much change will he receive? Name the least number of coins and bills he will receive.

You can solve the problem by subtracting the price of the map from the amount given to the salesclerk.

$$\begin{array}{ll} \$10.00 & \longleftarrow \text{amount given to salesclerk} \\ -\quad 7.49 & \longleftarrow \text{price of map} \\ \hline \$2.51 & \longleftarrow \text{Carl's change} \end{array}$$

To find the number of coins and bills, begin with the total cost of the item, and count up to the amount given.

Count from:
$7.49 + 1¢ = $7.50; $7.50 + 0.50 = $8.00; $8.00 + 2.00 = $10.00

| 1 penny | 2 quarters or half-dollar | 2 dollars | amount given |

Solve.

1. Craig buys a coonskin cap. It costs $3.57. He gives the salesclerk a $5 bill. How much change will he receive?

2. Betsy bought moccasins for $12.34. She gave the salesclerk a $20 bill. How much change did she receive?

3. Arthur buys a pioneer powder horn. It costs $8.75. He gives the salesclerk a $10 bill. He receives the smallest number of coins and bills as change. Name them.

4. Jane buys a postcard at the gift shop for $0.20. She gives the salesclerk a $1 bill, and she receives the smallest number of coins or bills as change. Which coins or bills does she receive?

★5. Ted buys 6 commemorative pens at $0.15 each. He gives the salesclerk a $5 bill. How much change will he receive?

★6. Mona buys 4 tickets to the pioneer play at $2.75 each. She gives the salesclerk a $20 bill. She receives the smallest number of coins or bills as change. Name the coins or bills.

Multiplying by 2-Digit Factors

A. The Mason family traveled 129 miles to the start of the Oregon Trail. A guide told them that the trail was 20 times longer than the distance they had already traveled. How long was the Oregon Trail?

To multiply by a multiple of 10, write 0 in the ones place. Then multiply by the tens.

Multiply by ones.	Multiply by tens.
1 2 9	1 2 9
× 2 0	× 2 0
0	2,5 8 0

The Oregon Trail was 2,580 miles long.

B. Find 26 × 99.

Multiply by ones.	Multiply by tens.	Add.
9 9	9 9	9 9
× 2 6	× 2 6	× 2 6
5 9 4	5 9 4	5 9 4
	1 9 8 0	1 9 8 0
		2,5 7 4

Other examples:

79	206	$3.54
× 48	× 71	× 42
632	206	7 08
3 160	14 420	141 60
3,792	14,626	$148.68

Checkpoint Write the letter of the correct answer.

Multiply.

1. 96	**2.** 810	**3.** 95	**4.** 1,673
× 40	× 23	× 41	× 25
a. 384	**a.** 833	**a.** 475	**a.** 37,515
b. 3,640	**b.** 4,050	**b.** 3,695	**b.** 31,725
c. 3,936	**c.** 18,630	**c.** 3,895	**c.** 1,648
d. 3,840	**d.** 19,730	**d.** 3,995	**d.** 41,825

Multiply.

1.	33 × 20	**2.**	42 × 30	**3.**	63 × 50	**4.**	28 × 70	**5.**	121 × 90
6.	56 × 12	**7.**	64 × 16	**8.**	72 × 35	**9.**	82 × 28	**10.**	74 × 23
11.	367 × 70	**12.**	293 × 28	**13.**	105 × 52	**14.**	388 × 26	**15.**	$5.75 × 83
16.	$12.59 × 54	**17.**	$10.45 × 65	**18.**	$31.20 × 27	**19.**	$14.56 × 22	**20.**	$11.43 × 45

21. 68 × 7,847   **22.** 48 × 3,033   **23.** 31 × 9,114   **24.** $48 × 18.77

★**25.** (43 × 5) × 32   ★**26.** (15 × 27) × 52   ★**27.** (54 × 28) × 65

Solve.

28. Most of the wagons left from Independence in the spring. Usually, 187 wagons left each week. How many wagons left in 14 weeks?

29. The wagon train traveled about 13 miles each day along the 2,379-mile trail. If the wagons traveled for 63 days, how much farther did they have to travel?

30. The cooks bought food supplies for the wagon train. They estimated that they would use about 27 pounds of flour each day. If the trip took 165 days, how many pounds of flour did they need?

★**31.** Suppose you are going west with a wagon train. Plan the supplies you would take. Determine the quantities that you would need of tools, nails, food staples, cooking utensils, and fabric.

CALCULATOR

Use your calculator to solve each problem. Look for a pattern in the products.

1. 15,873 × 7   **2.** 15,873 × 14   **3.** 15,873 × 21

4. 15,873 × 28   **5.** 15,873 × 35   **6.** 15,873 × 42

Use the pattern of the products to write the next two problems in this group. What are the products?

Multiplying by 3-Digit Factors

The discovery of gold at Sutter's Mill in California started the famous gold rush of 1849. At one point, 239 gold-seekers, known as "forty-niners," arrived in California each day. How many arrived in that year (365 days)?

First estimate the product.

$$
\begin{array}{r}
365 \longrightarrow 400 \\
\times\,239 \longrightarrow \times\,200 \\
\hline
80{,}000
\end{array}
$$

Multiply by ones.	Multiply by tens.	Multiply by hundreds.	Add.
365	365	365	365
×239	×239	×239	×239
3285	3285	3285	3285
	10950	10950	10950
		73000	73000
			87,235

In that year, 87,235 forty-niners arrived.
The product is reasonably close to the estimate.

Other examples:

$$
\begin{array}{r}
396 \\
\times\,207 \\
\hline
2\,772 \\
0\,000 \\
79\,200 \\
\hline
81{,}972
\end{array}
$$
You can leave out these zeros.

$$
\begin{array}{r}
396 \\
\times\,207 \\
\hline
2\,772 \\
79\,200 \\
\hline
81{,}972
\end{array}
$$

$$
\begin{array}{r}
\$7.89 \\
\times\quad143 \\
\hline
23\,67 \\
315\,60 \\
789\,00 \\
\hline
\$1{,}128.27
\end{array}
$$

Checkpoint Write the letter of the correct answer.

Multiply.

1. 211 × 543

2. 89 × 617

3. $7.39 × 862

a. 2,532	**a.** 10,489	**a.** $118.24
b. 103,573	**b.** 54,813	**b.** $5,074.08
c. 104,573	**c.** 54,913	**c.** $6,085.08
d. 114,573	**d.** 549,130	**d.** $6,370.18

Solve.

1. $\begin{array}{r} 434 \\ \times\, 500 \\ \hline \end{array}$	**2.** $\begin{array}{r} 142 \\ \times\, 300 \\ \hline \end{array}$	**3.** $\begin{array}{r} 322 \\ \times\, 600 \\ \hline \end{array}$	**4.** $\begin{array}{r} 303 \\ \times\, 500 \\ \hline \end{array}$	**5.** $\begin{array}{r} \$3.21 \\ \times\,\ \ 700 \\ \hline \end{array}$
6. $\begin{array}{r} 144 \\ \times\, 827 \\ \hline \end{array}$	**7.** $\begin{array}{r} 293 \\ \times\, 406 \\ \hline \end{array}$	**8.** $\begin{array}{r} 328 \\ \times\, 516 \\ \hline \end{array}$	**9.** $\begin{array}{r} 427 \\ \times\, 404 \\ \hline \end{array}$	**10.** $\begin{array}{r} \$6.02 \\ \times\,\ \ 548 \\ \hline \end{array}$
11. $\begin{array}{r} 701 \\ \times\, 210 \\ \hline \end{array}$	**12.** $\begin{array}{r} 243 \\ \times\, 129 \\ \hline \end{array}$	**13.** $\begin{array}{r} 834 \\ \times\, 201 \\ \hline \end{array}$	**14.** $\begin{array}{r} 429 \\ \times\, 212 \\ \hline \end{array}$	**15.** $\begin{array}{r} \$3.40 \\ \times\,\ \ 192 \\ \hline \end{array}$
16. $\begin{array}{r} 632 \\ \times\, 378 \\ \hline \end{array}$	**17.** $\begin{array}{r} 441 \\ \times\, 146 \\ \hline \end{array}$	**18.** $\begin{array}{r} 701 \\ \times\, 219 \\ \hline \end{array}$	**19.** $\begin{array}{r} 938 \\ \times\, 493 \\ \hline \end{array}$	**20.** $\begin{array}{r} \$4.93 \\ \times\,\ \ 677 \\ \hline \end{array}$

21. 312×104 **22.** 523×928 **23.** 214×310 **24.** $\$1.01 \times 516$

25. 169×805 **26.** 419×301 **27.** 789×938 **28.** $\$4.34 \times 904$

Solve.

29. In 1849, one mining company estimated that it would have to pay each of its miners $295 per year. If the company employed 687 miners, what is its yearly payroll?

30. During 1849, a total of 80,000 miners went to California. Of these, 39,000 took the sea route around Cape Horn. How many miners traveled overland?

31. One rich find was the Calaveras Nugget. It weighed 162 pounds and sold for $269 a pound. How much money was the Calaveras Nugget worth?

★32. A gold miner pays his miners well, for 1849. Each miner must choose whether to be paid $2.17 per day for a 237-day work season or $0.37 per hour for the same number of days. If miners work for 12 hours per day, which rate would the miners probably choose?

CALCULATOR

Find the largest number which, when multiplied by itself, has a product less than or equal to the number given. Guess. Then check. Then guess again.

1. 2,204   **2.** 4,489   **3.** 9,216   **4.** 53,299   **5.** 622,521

PROBLEM SOLVING
Solving Two-Step Problems/Making a Plan

Sometimes you have to use more than one step to solve a problem. Before you can answer the question in the problem, you have to find needed data. Then you use this data to answer the question that was asked. Making a plan can help you solve this kind of problem.

Visitors to California explore its natural wonders and visit its exciting cities. On Monday, a tour company took 148 people on a tour of Hollywood and its movie studios. Each person paid $19. On Tuesday, the tour company received $2,375 from ticket sales. How much more money did the tour company receive on Monday than on Tuesday?

Needed data: How much money was received on Monday?

Plan

Step 1: Find out how much money the tour company received on Monday.
Step 2: Find the difference between Monday's and Tuesday's amounts.

Step 1: Multiply to find out how much the tour company received on Monday.

$$
\begin{array}{r}
148 \\
\times\ \$19 \\
\hline
\$2,812
\end{array}
$$

148 (number of people)
× $19 (amount paid for tour)
$2,812 (total amount received on Monday)

Step 2: Find the difference by subtracting.

$$
\begin{array}{r}
\$2,812 \\
-\ 2,375 \\
\hline
\$\ 437
\end{array}
$$

$2,812 (total received on Monday)
− 2,375 (total received on Tuesday)
$ 437 (more received on Monday than Tuesday)

The tour company received $437 more on Monday than on Tuesday.

Complete the plan by writing the missing step.

1. The Tuolumne River in California's Yosemite National Park is a favorite spot for white-water rafting. One group spent $1,853 for 5 days of rafting. In a second group, each of 7 people paid $280 for 5 days. Which group paid more money?

    Step 1: Find how much money the second group paid.

    Step 2:

2. A group of rafters traveled 168 miles in their first 5 days. In the next 5 days, they traveled 28 miles per day. How many miles did they travel in 10 days?

    Step 1: Find how many miles the group traveled in the next 5 days.

    Step 2:

Make a plan for each problem. Solve.

3. Sara visited Fisherman's Wharf in San Francisco. She had $25.00 in her purse. She paid $8.95 for a lobster lunch. She paid $6.00 for a T-shirt. She bought film for $4.50 and lemonade for $1.25. How much money did Sara have left?

4. The trip from San Francisco to San Diego along the Pacific Coast Highway is 514 miles. Marilyn and her family leave San Francisco. If they drive at 45 miles per hour for 11 hours, how far from San Diego will they be?

5. Marilyn and her family stopped at Carmel. Altogether, they bought 145 shell beads to make necklaces. The beads cost $0.39 each. Marilyn gave the clerk a $100 bill. How much change did she receive?

6. A group of scouts plans to hike 100 miles along the trails of Yosemite National Park. If they hiked 16 miles per day for 6 days, how many miles must they hike the next day?

7. In 1934, 18 farmers set up stands on the outskirts of Los Angeles to start the Farmers Market. Today, 9 times that number of farmers have stands at this popular market. How many more farmers have stands at the market today than did the farmers in 1934?

★8. A souvenir buyer for the San Diego Zoo ordered 175 adult-size T-shirts for $3.50 each. He also ordered 175 child-size T-shirts for $2.95 each. How much more did he spend on the adult-size T-shirts than on the child-size T-shirts?

CALCULATOR

Use your calculator to find the missing digits in the following multiplication problems. Study the example.

Example:

```
    3 6 7
  ×   2 3
  1 ■ 0 1
  7 3 ■
  ■,4 4 1
```

Multiply:

$3 \times 367 = 1{,}1\,0\,1$

$2 \times 367 = 7\,3\,4$

$23 \times 367 = 8{,}4\,4\,1$

The missing digits are 1, 4, and 8.

1.
```
      6 7 8
  ×     4 5
    3 3 ■ 0
  2 ■ 1 2
  3 0,■ 1 0
```

2.
```
      2 2 9
  ×     5 7
    1 ■ ■ 3
  1 ■ 4 5
  1 3,■ 5 3
```

3.
```
      7 8 2
  ×     8 5
    ■ 9 ■ 0
  6 2 ■ 6
  ■ 6,■ 7 0
```

4.
```
      7 0 9
  ×     6 3
    ■ 1 2 7
  ■ 2 ■ 4
  ■ 4,6 ■ 7
```

5.
```
    3,6 2 1
  ×       8 2
      ■ 2 ■ 2
  2 ■ 9 ■ 8
  2 ■ 6,9 2 ■
```

6.
```
    4,7 9 6
  ×       7 6
    2 ■ 7 ■ 6
  3 ■ 5 ■ 2
  ■ 6 ■,4 ■ 6
```

7.
```
      5 8 2
  ×     6 9 1
      5 ■ 2
  5 2 ■ 8
  ■ 4 ■ 2
  ■ 0 ■,1 ■ 2
```

8.
```
    7,9 1 4
  ×       3 8 2
    ■ 5 8 ■ 8
  ■ 3 3 ■ 2
  ■ 3 ■ ■ 2
  ■,0 2 ■,1 ■ 8
```

9.
```
    4,6 8 2
  ×       5 4 ■
    ■ 6 ■ 2
  1 ■ 7 ■ 8
  ■ 3 4 ■ 0
  ■,5 3 ■,9 ■ 2
```

Decide whether you would use mental math, pencil and paper, or a calculator to solve each. Explain your answer, then solve.

10. 16×2

11. 435×8

12. $101{,}101 \times 3$

13. $75{,}357 \times 5$

14. 52×23

15. 20×40

16. 356×206

17. $9{,}376 \times 54$

GROUP PROJECT

Banking on the Alphabet

The problem: Which letter of the alphabet is worth the most? When you write, *a* and *e* are among the most useful letters. You use them often, while you hardly ever use *x* or *z*. Here is a game you can play in which *x* and *z* are among the most valuable letters in the alphabet.

Give each letter a cent value. Begin with *a*, worth $0.01, and go on to *b* ($0.02), *c* ($0.03), and on up to *z*, which is worth $0.26. Use these letter values to answer each question.

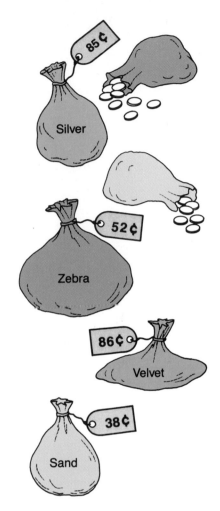

1. Which is more valuable, *gold* or *rust?*

2. How much more is a *diamond* worth than *wood?*

3. Which are worth more, *oysters* or *pearls?*

4. Which is worth the most, a *dime*, a *dollar*, a *penny*, a *nickel*, or a *quarter?* Which is worth exactly $1.00?

5. Find out how much this sentence is worth: *The treasure map is hidden under the floor.*

6. Can you think of a jewel that is worth more than a *ruby?* Don't stop at the ordinary jewels. Try unusual ones from the encyclopedia.

7. Can you come up with any words that are worth more than $1.00? What is the most valuable word you can find? What is the shortest word you can find that is worth more than $1.00?

8. What is the value of your name?

★9. These words are worth exactly $1.00: *chimpanzee, fountain,* and *whistled.* Can you come up with any $1.00 words or names? You might have a contest to see how many $1.00 words you and your classmates can come up with. Then put all your words worth $1.00 or more into a "bank." How much money do you have in the bank?

CHAPTER TEST

Copy and complete. Write the name of the property.
(page 76)

1. $4 \times \blacksquare = 4$

2. $3 \times (7 + 2) = (3 \times 7) + (\blacksquare \times 2)$

3. $(2 \times 6) \times 3 = 2 \times (\blacksquare \times 3)$

4. $9 \times \blacksquare = 8 \times 9$

Multiply. (page 76)

5. $(4 \times 2) \times 6$

6. $(5 \times 8) \times 0$

Multiply. (pages 76, 78)

7.
$$\begin{array}{r} 4 \\ \times 9 \\ \hline \end{array}$$

8.
$$\begin{array}{r} 10 \\ \times 3 \\ \hline \end{array}$$

9.
$$\begin{array}{r} 400 \\ \times 2 \\ \hline \end{array}$$

10.
$$\begin{array}{r} 600 \\ \times 50 \\ \hline \end{array}$$

11. 300×700

12. $2{,}000 \times 60$

13. $7{,}000 \times 400$

Estimate. (page 82)

14.
$$\begin{array}{r} 94 \\ \times 61 \\ \hline \end{array}$$

15.
$$\begin{array}{r} \$3.79 \\ \times 8 \\ \hline \end{array}$$

16.
$$\begin{array}{r} 342 \\ \times 53 \\ \hline \end{array}$$

17.
$$\begin{array}{r} \$4.65 \\ \times 8 \\ \hline \end{array}$$

Multiply. (pages 76, 86, 88, 92, and 94)

18.
$$\begin{array}{r} 53 \\ \times 2 \\ \hline \end{array}$$

19.
$$\begin{array}{r} \$5.89 \\ \times 3 \\ \hline \end{array}$$

20.
$$\begin{array}{r} \$23.95 \\ \times 5 \\ \hline \end{array}$$

21.
$$\begin{array}{r} 38{,}244 \\ \times 7 \\ \hline \end{array}$$

22. 36×42

23. 73×19

24. 368×37

25. $\$4.57 \times 62$

26. $2{,}305 \times 84$

27. $\$15.82 \times 51$

28. 422×505

29. $\$7.39 \times 134$

Solve. (pages 80–81, 84–85, and 96–97)

30. Each year, the North Shore Hiking Club makes plans to hike through one of America's many national parks. As a souvenir for the members of the club who participate in the hike, park officials design T-shirts and caps with the park's name and the date of the hike. This year, the club budgets $200.00 for the purchase of the shirt/cap sets. If 9 members buy the sets for $15.25 each, how much is left of the $200.00 budget?

31. The club chooses to hike the Assateague National Seashore off the coast of Maryland and Virginia. The members plan the distance they want to cover well in advance. This way, if there is extra time left after the planned hike, they can do some exploring. They planned to hike 21 miles per day for 7 days. If they hike an extra 7 miles on the fifth day, how many miles will they have hiked after 5 days?

32. The North Shore Hiking Club has a total of 32 members. Each member pays $15.00 dues each year. The club has budgeted $400.00 for hikes and other activities. Estimate to find whether the membership dues will be enough to cover the budgeted items.

33. One club outing included a group lunch for the 12 members who went on the hike. If each hiker was expected to eat a sandwich, an apple, and juice, how many items needed to be packed? Write the letter of the reasonable answer.

    a. 12   **b.** 36   **c.** 72

BONUS

Solve.

1. $3,267 \times 1,043$	**2.** $6,500 \times 2,368$	**3.** $8,492 \times 5,321$	**4.** $7,378 \times 8,765$	**5.** $5,480 \times 4,325$
6. $4,073 \times 2,120$	**7.** $8,245 \times 1,004$	**8.** $1,239 \times 1,183$	**9.** $7,132 \times 1,946$	**10.** $3,747 \times 2,139$

RETEACHING

When you multiply by more than 1 digit, be careful to line up your products in the correct place. You can use zeros to help you.

Multiply 329 × 487.

Multiply by ones.	Multiply by tens.	Multiply by hundreds.	Add.
487	487	487	487
× 329	× 329	× 329	× 329
4383	4383	4383	4 383
	9740	9740	9 740
		146100	146 100
			160,223

Use zeros to line up the products correctly.

Multiply.

1. 753
× 480

2. 420
× 141

3. 530
× 274

4. 603
× 578

5. 810
× 780

6. 825
× 104

7. 750
× 410

8. 885
× 480

9. 927
× 210

10. 390
× 168

11. 810
× 178

12. 630
× 265

13. 447
× 177

14. 396
× 279

15. 384
× 263

16. 565
× 454

17. 609
× 548

18. 761
× 648

19. 976
× 794

20. 650
× 190

21. 664 × 647

22. 465 × 118

23. 944 × 710

24. 329 × 138

25. 320 × 268

26. 811 × 440

27. 250 × 623

28. 638 × 684

29. 902 × 129

30. 312 × 390

31. 308 × 121

32. 917 × 375

ENRICHMENT

Exponents

Steve has an album of stamps that commemorate the exploration of America. Each page of his album has 10 rows of stamps, with space for 10 stamps in each row. How many stamps are on each page?

You can multiply 10×10. When you multiply a number by itself, you can write the factors in **exponent form.**

10×10 can be written as 10^2.

The 2 is an exponent. It shows how many times that 10 is used as a factor.

$10^2 = 10 \times 10 = 100$

There will be 100 stamps on each page.

Other examples:

$7^1 = 7$
$2^3 = 2 \times 2 \times 2 = 8$
$3^4 = 3 \times 3 \times 3 \times 3 = 81$

Write the number and the exponent.

1. $4 \times 4 \times 4$

2. $6 \times 6 \times 6 \times 6 \times 6$

3. $8 \times 8 \times 8 \times 8$

4. $10 \times 10 \times 10 \times 10 \times 10 \times 10$

5. $7 \times 7 \times 7$

6. $2 \times 2 \times 2 \times 2 \times 2 \times 2 \times 2 \times 2$

7. 5×5

8. $3 \times 3 \times 3$

Write the product. You may use a calculator to help you.

9. 2^5 **10.** 4^4 **11.** 7^2 **12.** 10^4 **13.** 3^5

14. 8^1 **15.** 9^3 **16.** 5^2 **17.** 5^4 **18.** 8^2

19. 10^3 **20.** 3^2 **21.** 6^4 **22.** 9^2 **23.** 4^5

24. 5^5 **25.** 2^4 **26.** 10^1 **27.** 3^3 **28.** 1^7

CUMULATIVE REVIEW

Write the letter of the correct answer.

1. $17.91 - 9.17$

   a. 8.74   **b.** 8.84
   c. 8.86   **d.** not given

2. $83.97 + 17.48$

   a. 101.35   **b.** 101.45
   c. 101.55   **d.** not given

3. $59.73 - 0.07$

   a. 59.66   **b.** 59.76
   c. 59.80   **d.** not given

4. $6.39 + 14.8 + 0.013$

   a. 20.6   **b.** 21.203
   c. 21.23   **d.** not given

5. Order from the least to the greatest:
4.851, 0.485, 48.7, 4.80.

   a. 4.80, 4.851, 0.485, 48.7
   b. 48.7, 4.80, 4.851, 0.485
   c. 0.485, 4.80, 4.851, 48.7
   d. not given

6. Write as a decimal: six hundred
thirty-eight thousandths.

   a. 0.638   **b.** 6.380
   c. 600.38   **d.** not given

7. $497,603 - 19,937$

   a. 366,777   **b.** 387,666
   c. 377,666   **d.** not given

8. $759 + 623 + 1,114$

   a. 1,496   **b.** 2,486
   c. 2,496   **d.** not given

9. $615,101 - 317,011$

   a. 298,090   **b.** 302,111
   c. 308,191   **d.** not given

10. Compare. Use $>$, $<$, or $=$ for ●.
340,597 ● 340,579

   a. $>$ **b.** $<$
   c. $=$ **d.** not given

11. $\$623.00 + \$319.00$

   a. $932.00   **b.** 942
   c. $942.00   **d.** not given

12. Estimate: $425.2 + 289.7$

   a. 600   **b.** 700
   c. 800   **d.** 7,000

13. Simon's time in the 100-yard dash is
11.53 seconds. After practicing, he
improves his time to 11.29 seconds.
Let $n =$ the amount of
improvement in his time. Choose
the correct number sentence to
solve the problem.

   a. $11.53 + 11.29 = n$
   b. $11.53 - 11.29 = n$
   c. $11.53 \times 11.29 = n$
   d. not given

14. Deborah swims the 100-meter
freestyle in 58.67 seconds. This is
5.32 seconds faster than her time
last year. Choose the operation to
find Deborah's time last year.

   a. add   **b.** subtract
   c. multiply   **d.** not given

Flick a switch. A light goes on. Push a button. The dryer starts. Does the electricity used in your home and school seem to come from nowhere? How far away is the source of electricity in your community? How is electricity usage measured in your community? How does the electric company decide how much to charge?

4 MULTIPLYING DECIMALS

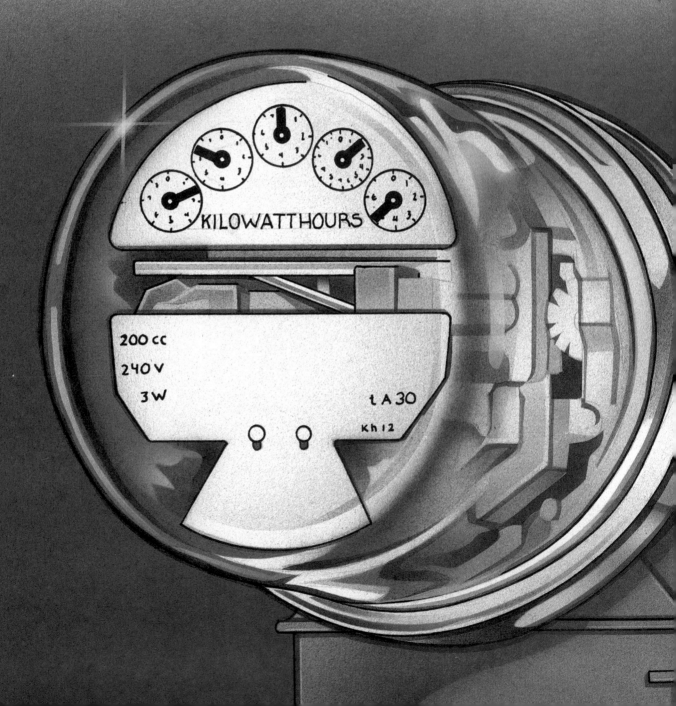

Estimating Decimal Products

A. Wally burns coal in his fireplace for heat. He burns 1.75 kg of coal each hour. If he uses the fireplace for 4.5 hours, about how much coal does he use?

Estimate 4.5 × 1.75.

You can estimate decimal products the same way you estimate whole-number products.

Round both factors to their greatest place.

$$1.75 \rightarrow 2$$
$$\times \quad 4.5 \rightarrow 5$$

Multiply the factors.

$$2$$
$$\times 5$$
$$\overline{10}$$

Wally burns about 10 kg of coal in 4.5 hours.

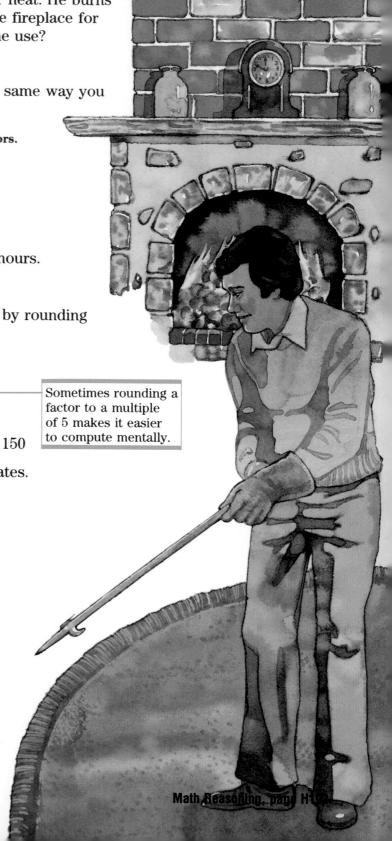

B. You can estimate decimal products by rounding several different ways.

Estimate 6.2 × 26.483.

$$6.2 \times 26.483$$
$$\downarrow \qquad \downarrow$$
$$6 \times \quad 30 = 180$$

$$6.2 \times 26.483$$
$$\downarrow \qquad \downarrow$$
$$6 \times \quad 25 = 150$$

> Sometimes rounding a factor to a multiple of 5 makes it easier to compute mentally.

Both 180 and 150 are reasonable estimates.

Other examples:

$$24.6 \rightarrow \quad 20 \qquad 25$$
$$\times \quad 4.7 \rightarrow \times \ 5 \ \text{or} \times \ 5$$
$$\overline{\qquad \quad 100 \qquad 125}$$

$$76.2 \rightarrow \quad 80 \qquad 75$$
$$\times 3.75 \rightarrow \times \ 4 \ \text{or} \times \ 4$$
$$\overline{\qquad \quad 320 \qquad 300}$$

$$\$46.75 \rightarrow \quad \$50 \qquad \$45$$
$$\times \quad 2.03 \rightarrow \times \quad 2 \ \text{or} \quad \times \ 2$$
$$\overline{\qquad \quad \$100 \qquad \$90}$$

106

Estimate. Write > or < for ●.

1. 2.7×8.3 ● 15 **2.** 3.4×7.4 ● 32 **3.** 3.7×5.1 ● 23

4. 5.4×23.7 ● 130 **5.** 3.2×61.2 ● 171 **6.** 6.3×47.7 ● 312

7. 2.1×8.64 ● 19 **8.** 3.72×8.5 ● 38 **9.** 4.4×32.43 ● 102

10. $2.1 \times \$4.68$ ● $\$9$ **11.** $3.5 \times \$15.76$ ● $\$75$ **12.** $5.4 \times \$36.25$ ● $\$149$

13. 2.46×9.15 ● 27 **14.** 6.8×87.49 ● 573 **15.** 6.34×75.9 ● 485

16. 7.6×26.3 ● 250 **17.** $7.92 \times \$7.58$ ● $\$64$ **18.** 3.89×56.47 ● 242

Estimate.

19. $\begin{array}{r} 9.8 \\ \times\ 4.2 \\ \hline \end{array}$
 20. $\begin{array}{r} 15.8 \\ \times\ 8.23 \\ \hline \end{array}$
 21. $\begin{array}{r} 22.19 \\ \times\ 3.27 \\ \hline \end{array}$
 22. $\begin{array}{r} \$9.39 \\ \times\ 6.8 \\ \hline \end{array}$
 23. $\begin{array}{r} \$7.52 \\ \times\ 4.4 \\ \hline \end{array}$

Solve.

24. The hydroelectric plant where Sam works produces 38,300 kilowatts of electricity. After new generators are installed, the power capacity of the plant will rise 1.5 times. About how many kilowatts of electricity will the plant produce?

★25. A steam-turbine plant produced 11.67 million kilowatts of electricity. New turbines were added to raise the plant's energy capacity 2.3 times, but it only rose 1.8 times. About how many kilowatts does the plant produce? About how much more is this than the plant's previous capacity?

CALCULATOR

Use your calculator to solve these multiplication exercises. Look for a pattern.

$0.1089 \times 9 = $ ▓
$0.10989 \times 9 = $ ▓
$0.109989 \times 9 = $ ▓

Use the pattern to compute these exercises mentally.

1. 0.10999989×9 **2.** 0.1099989×9 **3.** 0.109999989×9

PROBLEM SOLVING
Working Backward

Sometimes you need to work backward to solve a problem. You start with what you know at the end and work back to the beginning.

Rosa used pipe cleaners, paper clips, and toothpicks to build a model of a power plant. She used three times as many toothpicks as pipe cleaners and 10 more paper clips than toothpicks. She used 76 paper clips. How many pipe cleaners did she use?

She knows that:

1. she used 76 paper clips
2. she used 10 more paper clips than toothpicks
3. she used three times as many toothpicks as pipe cleaners.

She needs to use a flowchart to find the number of pipe cleaners she used.

Step 1 Show the steps of the problem.

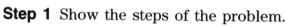

Step 2 Use opposite operations to work backward.

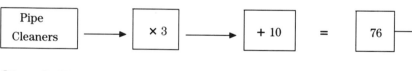

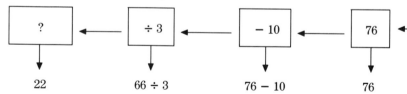

She used 22 pipe cleaners to build her model.

How can you check your answer? Use the answer to work forward to find the number of paper clips.

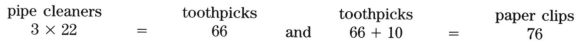

pipe cleaners   toothpicks   toothpicks   paper clips
    3 × 22   =   66   and   66 + 10   =   76

Solve. Work backward if you need to. Work forward to check your answers.

1. Doug uses nails, screws, and wooden dowels to build a model. He uses four times as many screws as wooden dowels, and 14 fewer nails than screws. He uses 82 nails. How many wooden dowels does he use?

2. Kathy gives 10 light bulbs to Lauren for her project on energy. This is twice as many as she gives to Erik. She keeps 8 light bulbs for her project. How many light bulbs did Kathy start with?

3. Alex cuts a piece of aluminum into 3 sections that are the same length. After he cuts off 3 inches from one of the sections, he is left with a section that is 7 inches long. What was the length of the piece of aluminum he started with?

4. Julie bought light bulbs for her energy project. She broke 3 of them on the way home. Within the next day, she broke 4 more. By the time she finished working on her project, she had broken 1 more but had 4 left. How many light bulbs did Julie have at the beginning of her project?

5. Write a problem that can be solved by working backward. Ask others to solve it.

CALCULATOR

Use your calculator to solve.

1. Marsha bought some apples. First, she gave 2 to Erica. Next, she gave 3 to Todd. Finally, Marsha gave 4 apples to Judy. She then had 8 apples left. How many apples did Marsha buy?

2. Arthur, Brett, Carl, and Dave were having a contest to see who could bowl the highest score. Arthur scored 10 more points than Dave, and Dave scored 7 more points than Carl. Carl scored 9 points less than Brett. Brett scored 75. What were the scores of the others?

Multiplying Decimals and Whole Numbers

A. Computing with decimals and whole numbers is alike in some ways and different in some ways.

Shade 15 squares on a 10 by 10 grid to show 15 hundredths or 0.15. Cut out the 15 hundredths. Team up with two other people. Tape each of your 0.15 models next to each other on another hundred square.

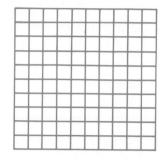

Thinking as a Team

1. Are the combined shaded squares more than one half of the hundred square? Tell why.

2. Look at these problems:

$$\begin{array}{r} 15 \\ \times\ 3 \\ \hline 45 \end{array} \qquad \begin{array}{r} 0.15 \\ \times\ \ 3 \\ \hline 0.45 \end{array}$$

   - How are they alike?
   - How are they different?
   - Which product is more? Why?
   - Which is shown by your model?

3. Use your calculator to find 0.15 + 0.15 + 0.15 and 3 × 0.15. Are the answers the same?

B. Use another hundred square. Shade 25 squares to show 25 hundredths or 0.25. Cut out the 25 hundredths. Team up with three other people. Tape your 0.25 models next to one another on another hundred square.

Thinking as a Team

1. Are the combined shaded squares less than a whole, equal to a whole, or more than a whole?

2. Look at these problems:

$$\begin{array}{r} 25 \\ \times\ 4 \\ \hline 100 \end{array} \qquad \begin{array}{r} 0.25 \\ \times\ \ 4 \\ \hline 1.00 \end{array}$$

   - How are they alike?
   - How are they different?
   - Which product is more? Why?
   - Which is shown by your model?

3. Use your calculator to find 0.25 + 0.25 + 0.25 + 0.25 and 4 × 0.25. Are the answers the same? Does the calculator display decimals differently from the way in which we write them? Can you think of a reason why?

C. Use another hundred square. Shade 80 squares to show 80 hundredths or 0.80. Fold the square in half.

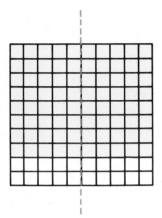

Thinking as a Team

1. Is the number of shaded squares in each half more or less than 50? Tell why.

2. What is half of 0.80?

3. Look at these problems:

$$\begin{array}{r} 80 \\ \times\ 5 \\ \hline 400 \end{array} \qquad \begin{array}{r} 0.80 \\ \times\ 0.5 \\ \hline 0.400 \end{array}$$

   - How are they alike?
   - How are they different?
   - Which product is more? Why?
   - Which is shown by your model?
   - Is one half of 0.80 the same as 0.5 × 0.80?
   - Use your calculator to find 5.0 × 8.0 and then 0.5 × 8.0. What does the display show for each? Look at the decimal point in each product. What do you notice?

4. Apply what you have learned. Do the computation for the first problem. Then use it to help you find the answers to the other problems.

$$\begin{array}{cccccc} 24 & 24 & 2.4 & 24 & 2.4 & 0.24 \\ \times\ 51 & \times\ 5.1 & \times\ 5.1 & \times\ 0.51 & \times\ 0.51 & \times\ 0.51 \end{array}$$

How do you know where to place the decimal point? Discuss your answers with the class.

PROBLEM SOLVING
Making an Organized List

Sometimes you can solve a problem by organizing the given information in the form of a list.

The Wayne School is planning a "Sources of Energy" fair. Students will make exhibits that will be displayed on tables set up in the schoolyard. Each table can hold 2 exhibits.

> Allen, Beth, Carl, Dina, Elliot, and Fay will each enter exhibits. How many possible pairs can be formed from these 6 exhibits?

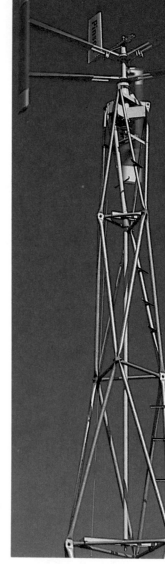

Make a list to show all the possible pairs, or combinations. Let the first letters of the students' names stand for the 6 exhibits.

Allen's exhibit can be displayed alongside any of the 5 other exhibits.

A and B
A and C
A and D
A and E
A and F

Beth's exhibit can be displayed alongside 4 other exhibits. You don't need to include B and A, because that is the same as A and B.

B and C
B and D
B and E
B and F

Carl's exhibit can be paired with 3 other exhibits.

C and D
C and E
C and F

Dina's exhibit can be displayed alongside 2 other exhibits.

D and E
D and F

Elliot's exhibit can be paired with the 1 remaining exhibit.

E and F

Count the number of combinations.

$5 + 4 + 3 + 2 + 1 = 15$

So, 15 combinations can be formed from the 6 exhibits.

Solve. Make a list if needed.

1. George decides to add 1 more energy exhibit. Now there are 7 energy exhibits. How many different pairs of energy exhibits are possible?

2. Allen, Joan, Kim, and Larry want to prepare exhibits about nuclear power. Their teacher asks them to work together in pairs. How many possible pairs are there?

3. Working in pairs, 4 boys and 4 girls design exhibits about coal. Each pair is made up of 1 boy and 1 girl. How many possible pairs are there?

4. Ronnie, Dale, and Gerry are the finalists in the "Best Exhibit" contest. Prizes will be given for first, second, and third place. In how many different orders could the 3 finalists finish?

5. There will be 4 "Wind Power" exhibits on display at the fair. Dean, Emma, and Frank will take turns demonstrating the exhibits. Each of the 3 students will demonstrate each exhibit twice. How many demonstrations on wind power will there be?

6. Dean has 4 coins in his pocket: a quarter, a dime, a nickel, and a penny. If Dean uses only 2 coins, how many possible combinations that amount to more than 25 cents can he make?

7. Emma has 5 coins in her pocket: a half-dollar, a quarter, a dime, a nickel, and a penny. How many combinations of 4 coins can she make?

8. Jim has 21 pennies, 4 nickels, and 2 dimes in his pocket. In how many ways can he make 21 cents?

9. Nora's demonstration about the use of energy is a prizewinner. After each demonstration, Nora and her 4 assistants each distribute 8 pamphlets about solar energy. Nora gave 6 demonstrations. How many pamphlets did Nora and her team distribute?

10. If each of the books on a display rack covers 2 of the following power-source topics—electricity, natural gas, coal, oil, and nuclear power—how many books are there on the display rack? If each book covered 3 of the topics, would there be more or fewer books on the rack?

Multiplying Decimals

A. The average home in the United States uses about 8.4 kilowatt-hours of electricity every day. How much electricity would such a home use in 2.5 days?

Multiply 2.5 × 8.4.

Multiply as you would with whole numbers.

$$\begin{array}{r} 8.4 \\ \times\ \ 2.5 \\ \hline 4\,2\,0 \\ 1\,6\,8\,0 \\ \hline 2\,1\,0\,0 \end{array}$$

Place the decimal point so that the product has as many places as the sum of the decimal places in the factors.

$$\begin{array}{rl} 8.4 & 1 \text{ place} \\ \times\ \ 2.5 & +\,1 \text{ place} \\ \hline 4\,2\,0 & \\ 1\,6\,8\,0 & \\ \hline 2\,1.0\,0 & 2 \text{ places} \end{array}$$

The average home would use 21 kilowatt-hours of electricity in 2.5 days.

Other examples:

$$\begin{array}{r} 0.25 \\ \times\ \ 0.6 \\ \hline 0.150 \end{array}$$

Write this 0.

$$\begin{array}{r} 0.78 \\ \times\ \ 3.9 \\ \hline 702 \\ 2\,340 \\ \hline 3.042 \end{array}$$

B. When multiplying money, round your answer to the nearest whole cent.

$$\begin{array}{rl} \$2.59 & 2 \text{ places} \\ \times\ \ 1.3 & +\,1 \text{ place} \\ \hline 777 & \\ 2\,590 & \\ \hline 3.367 & 3 \text{ places} \end{array}$$

$3.367 rounds to $3.37.

114

Multiply.

1. 0.35
× 0.3

2. 0.57
× 0.5

3. 0.9
× 0.25

4. 0.52
× 0.7

5. 0.65
× 0.3

6. 0.54
× 0.7

7. 0.92
× 1.4

8. 0.24
× 4.5

9. 0.62
× 1.4

10. 0.94
× 3.8

11. 25.87
× 0.3

12. 14.01
× 39

13. 0.66
× 7.4

14. 0.4
× 0.3

15. 13.67
× 0.4

16. 0.6 × 78

17. 0.52 × 13.4

18. 0.91 × 5.8

19. 0.42 × 6.3

20. 0.2 × 27.48

21. 0.8 × 4.84

22. 0.11 × 16

23. 0.6 × 3.27

Multiply. Round the product to the nearest cent.

24. $0.31
× 0.6

25. $26.85
× 0.5

26. $7.37
× 0.4

27. $1.38
× 0.9

28. $2.75
× 0.7

29. $0.50 × 0.37

30. $0.30 × 28.38

31. $3.67 × 5.98

32. $0.50 × 22.09

Solve.

33. The Wu family uses an average of 391.4 kilowatt-hours of electricity each month. They pay $0.18 per kilowatt-hour. What is their average monthly bill?

34. The Wu family installs storm windows. They cost $212.49, but there is a rebate of 0.2 of the price. How much do they receive as their rebate?

35. To save on their electric bill, the Wu family stopped using a space heater. The heater had cost $0.43 per hour and had been used 3.5 hours daily. How much money was saved per day?

36. It costs $0.03 per hour to use a 100-watt lightbulb and $0.02 per hour for a 75-watt bulb. If you replace the 100-watt bulbs in your house with 75-watt bulbs, how much would you save in 5 hours?

MIDCHAPTER REVIEW

Estimate.

1. 6.2 × 7.8

2. 4.29 × 25.18

3. 18.8 × 7.32

4. 6.92 × $6.49

Multiply.

5. 0.9 × 8

6. 56 × 3.14

7. 0.16 × 17

8. 49 × 8.707

9. 23 × 7.28

10. 19 × 0.657

11. 29 × 65.33

12. 84 × 18.9

More Multiplying Decimals

Some solar-energy cells supply only 0.005 kilowatts of energy per minute. Tom Pearson's small electric generator supplies 3.5 times this amount of energy. How much energy does the generator supply?

Multiply 3.5 × 0.005.

Sometimes you need to write zeros in the product to place the decimal point correctly.

Multiply as you would with whole numbers.

$$\begin{array}{r} 3.5 \\ \times\,0.0\,0\,5 \\ \hline 1\,7\,5 \end{array}$$

Add zeros to show the correct number of decimal places. Place the decimal point in the product.

$$\begin{array}{rl} 3.5 & \text{1 place} \\ \times\,0.0\,0\,5 & +\text{3 places} \\ \hline 0.0\,1\,7\,5 & \text{4 places} \end{array}$$

The generator supplies 0.0175 kilowatts per minute.

Other examples:

$$\begin{array}{rl} 0.1 & \text{1 place} \\ \times\,0.08 & +\text{2 places} \\ \hline 0.008 & \text{3 places} \end{array}$$

$$\begin{array}{rl} 1.3 & \text{1 place} \\ \times\,0.002 & +\text{3 places} \\ \hline 0.0026 & \text{4 places} \end{array}$$

$$\begin{array}{rl} \$1.01 & \text{2 places} \\ \times\,0.05 & +\text{2 places} \\ \hline \$0.0505 & \text{4 places} \end{array}$$

$0.0505 rounded to the nearest cent is $0.05.

Checkpoint   Write the letter of the correct answer.

Multiply.

1. 0.08 × 1.2

2. $\begin{array}{r} 0.3 \\ \times\,0.12 \end{array}$

3. 0.04 × 0.05

a. 0.86
b. 0.096
c. 0.96
d. 0.960

a. 0.036
b. 0.36
c. .360
d. 360

a. 0.0002
b. 0.002
c. 0.0200
d. 0.2000

116

Multiply.

1. 0.07 × 0.3	**2.** 0.31 × 0.3	**3.** 0.16 × 0.4	**4.** 0.25 × 0.3	**5.** 0.08 × 0.3
6. 0.03 × 1.6	**7.** 0.02 × 2.5	**8.** 0.04 × 1.7	**9.** 0.03 × 2.2	**10.** 0.02 × 2.4
11. 0.27 × 0.3	**12.** 0.02 × 1.9	**13.** 0.42 × 0.2	**14.** 0.04 × 1.4	**15.** 0.51 × 0.1

16. 1.1 × 0.07   **17.** 0.08 × 0.8   **18.** 3.6 × 0.02   **19.** 0.03 × 0.5

20. 0.06 × 0.5   **21.** 3.1 × 0.03   **22.** 4.3 × 0.02   **23.** 0.05 × 0.9

Multiply. Round the product to the nearest cent.

24. $4.17 × 0.02	**25.** $3.92 × 0.02	**26.** $3.17 × 0.03	**27.** $1.03 × 0.07	**28.** $2.43 × 0.04

Solve. For Problem 30, use the Infobank.

29. A power plant produces 0.048 kilowatt-hours of electricity per person. A second plant produces twice as much. How much electricity is produced by the second plant?

30. Use the information on page 416 to find the cost of using 8 hours of electricity in New York, El Paso, and Chicago. Then write and solve your own word problem.

CALCULATOR

Try to multiply 0.00004 × 0.00007 . Most calculators cannot display the answer because there are not enough spaces to show the complete product. To find the correct answer, multiply 4 × 7 . Then place the decimal point in the correct place. Your product should be 0.0000000028.

Use this technique with your calculator to find the product.

1. 0.00026 × 0.00003   **2.** 0.00038 × 0.00047   **3.** 0.000065 × 0.00103

4. 0.000394 × 0.000072   **5.** 0.00269 × 0.00589   **6.** 0.01256 × 0.000021

PROBLEM SOLVING
Identifying Needed Information

Some problems do not contain all the information needed to solve them. Sometimes you can find this information. Sometimes you cannot. Use the checklist to help you solve the problem.

> If you burned a 100-watt light bulb day and night for a whole year, you would use about 880 kilowatt-hours of electricity. How much would this cost?

Use the checklist to solve the problem.

What information is needed? the price of a kilowatt hour of electricity

Checklist	Yes	No
Do I already know the information?		✓
Can I find the information		
in a magazine article?		✓
in a reference book?		✓
from another person/the electric company?	✓	
Am I really stuck?		✓

You can contact your local electric company to find the cost per kilowatt-hour in your area. You can then multiply that amount by 880 to find the total cost.

Choose the information you would need to solve each problem. Write the letter of the correct answer.

1. The Lees spend $67.40 yearly to run their air conditioner. How much money could they save by using a large fan instead?

   a. the number of summer months
   b. the cost of running a large fan
   c. the size of the fan

2. The price of heating oil tripled between 1978 and 1983. How much did the price go up?

   a. the price of oil in 1978
   b. the amount of oil produced in 1983
   c. the amount of oil used in 1978

Solve. If there is not enough information, write what information you would need.

3. From a 42-gallon barrel of crude oil, 19.5 gallons of gasoline can be made. How many gallons of gasoline can be made from 50 barrels of crude oil?

4. In 1984, Hawaiians paid 11.29¢ per kilowatt hour for electricity. To the nearest cent, how much did 8 kilowatt-hours cost in Hawaii in 1984?

5. The Grand Coulee Dam and the John Day Plant are the first- and the second-largest hydroelectric plants in this country. The Grand Coulee can produce 6,494,000 kilowatts of power. How much less power does the John Day produce?

6. The Steger family's color TV used 320 kilowatt-hours of electricity last year. The cost per kilowatt-hour was 7.52¢. To the nearest cent, how much did it cost the Stegers to use their TV for one year?

7. In 1984, the normal yearly cost of operating a clothes dryer was $74.67. How much higher was the cost in 1984 than in 1983?

8. If the price of gasoline was $1.36 per gallon, how much would it cost to drive a car a distance of 5,000 miles?

9. In 1983, coal produced 0.25 of our electric power, gas produced 0.1, and nuclear power produced 0.125. What part of our electrical power was not produced by coal, gas, nuclear power, or hydroelectric power?

10. About 5.7 barrels of crude oil provide the same amount of energy as 2,000 pounds of coal. How many barrels of oil would provide the same amount of energy as 4,000 pounds of coal?

MATH COMMUNICATION

Read this poem.

The moon shining in the water
Looks like a silver coin
Dropped at my feet.

What is the second word you read? What is the sixth word? What are the last four words?

How do you read a poem? Your eyes follow a specific path.

- You start with the first word at the left in the top line.

- You read across the line, from left to right to the end.

- Then you return to the left and move down a line.

- Then you read from left to right again.

You don't read across, from left to right, in math. How would you solve this problem? What number would you write first? second? third?

$$\begin{array}{r} 48 \\ \times\ 7 \\ \hline \end{array} \qquad \begin{array}{r} 48 \\ \times\ 7 \\ \hline 6 \end{array} \qquad \begin{array}{r} \overset{5}{4}8 \\ \times\ 7 \\ \hline 6 \end{array} \qquad \begin{array}{r} \overset{5}{4}8 \\ \times\ 7 \\ \hline 336 \end{array}$$

When you multiply those numbers, you work from bottom to top and move from right to left.

Read each problem below. Write down the order in which you read and write numbers.

1. $\begin{array}{r} 59 \\ +\ 43 \\ \hline \end{array}$ **2.** $\begin{array}{r} 625 \\ -\ 86 \\ \hline \end{array}$ **3.** $\begin{array}{r} 63 \\ \times\ 9 \\ \hline \end{array}$

GROUP PROJECT

Fuel Costs—A Burning Question

The problem: Your family wants to cut down its heating bill. They are considering buying a fireplace or a wood stove to replace the oil burner. Read the facts below. Decide whether or not your family should replace the oil burner with a fireplace or a wood stove. Discuss the reasons with your classmates.

Key Facts

- There will be a cost to convert from oil to wood-burning methods of heating.
- It would cost about $220.00 per month to heat your home with oil during the winter.
- It would cost about $130.00 per month during the winter to heat your home with a fireplace or a wood stove.
- A fireplace will not be affected by a power shortage.
- A fireplace needs to be cleaned daily.
- Oil is delivered to your house.
- You must cut and transport wood yourself.
- You must obey any regulations about fireplaces and wood stoves.

CHAPTER TEST

Estimate. Write > or < for ●. (page 106)

1. 1.3×5.9 ● 10   **2.** 2.6×8.4 ● 16   **3.** 7.2×4.1 ● 30

4. $3.7 \times \$54.19$ ● $170   **5.** $5.4 \times \$91.20$ ● $500

Estimate. (page 106)

6. $\begin{array}{r} 6.2 \\ \times\ 7.4 \\ \hline \end{array}$ **7.** $\begin{array}{r} \$12.75 \\ \times\ \ \ \ 5.2 \\ \hline \end{array}$ **8.** $\begin{array}{r} 9.4 \\ \times\ 3.8 \\ \hline \end{array}$ **9.** $\begin{array}{r} \$25.39 \\ \times\ \ \ \ 6.3 \\ \hline \end{array}$

Multiply. (pages 110, 114, and 116)

10. $\begin{array}{r} 27 \\ \times\ 0.4 \\ \hline \end{array}$ **11.** $\begin{array}{r} 69 \\ \times\ 0.3 \\ \hline \end{array}$ **12.** $\begin{array}{r} 31 \\ \times\ 0.9 \\ \hline \end{array}$ **13.** $\begin{array}{r} 47 \\ \times\ 0.2 \\ \hline \end{array}$

14. $\begin{array}{r} 55 \\ \times\ 4.1 \\ \hline \end{array}$ **15.** $\begin{array}{r} 88 \\ \times\ 6.4 \\ \hline \end{array}$ **16.** $\begin{array}{r} 11 \\ \times\ 8.7 \\ \hline \end{array}$ **17.** $\begin{array}{r} 36 \\ \times\ 9.2 \\ \hline \end{array}$

18. $\begin{array}{r} \$27.11 \\ \times\ \ \ \ 0.5 \\ \hline \end{array}$ **19.** $\begin{array}{r} 32.56 \\ \times\ \ \ \ 0.4 \\ \hline \end{array}$ **20.** $\begin{array}{r} 0.73 \\ \times\ 8.2 \\ \hline \end{array}$ **21.** $\begin{array}{r} \$0.94 \\ \times\ \ \ \ 3.3 \\ \hline \end{array}$

22. 0.04×0.2 **23.** 0.004×3.1 **24.** $0.03 \times \$2.03$

25. 0.008×4.2 **26.** 0.3×41.84 **27.** 0.19×50.6

28. $4.2 \times \$12.37$ **29.** $0.06 \times \$31.94$

Solve. If there is not enough information, write what information is needed to solve. (pages 118 and 119)

30. Pat helps his family conserve gasoline by riding his bike to school. Pat figures out that his average speed while bicycling to school is 4.5 miles per hour. Pat's older brother, Phil, can ride 3 times as fast as that. What is the speed of Pat's younger brother?

31. Sally and her family are conserving energy by riding bicycles and walking whenever possible. One day, Sally rode her bicycle 27.53 miles. Her sister, Jane, rode her bicycle 4 times that distance. How many miles did Jane ride?

Solve. (pages 112 and 113)

32. The fifth grade class at Palston Elementary prepares a report on energy. The students are given a choice of 4 topics from which they must choose 2. The topics are solar energy, windmills, nuclear power, and water power. How many different combinations are there to choose from?

33. To go with the energy reports, 6 students will make drawings of 3 of the 4 topics. How many different combinations of topics can there be?

BONUS

Solve.

1. $(2.35 \times 4.76) + (3.03 \times 4.1)$

2. $(7.21 \times 4.36) - (0.74 \times 5.63)$

3. $(0.98 \times 4.31) + (6.2 \times 4.07)$

4. $(5.32 \times 0.63) - (0.06 \times 0.14)$

5. $(3.75 \times 4.09) - (0.11 \times 0.23)$

6. $(0.57 \times 0.35) + (7.59 \times 3.16)$

7. $(0.12 \times 4.97) + (5.07 \times 3.1)$

8. $(4 \times 2.5986) - (0.1 \times 3.54)$

RETEACHING

You need to count the decimal places in the factors in order to place the decimal point correctly in the product.

Multiply 3.7 × 4.052.

Multiply as you would with whole numbers.

$$\begin{array}{r} 4.052 \\ \times \quad 3.7 \\ \hline 28364 \\ 121560 \\ \hline 149924 \end{array}$$

Place the decimal point so that the product has as many places as the sum of the decimal places in the factors.

$$\begin{array}{rl} 4.052 \rightarrow & 3 \text{ places} \\ \times \quad 3.7 \rightarrow & + 1 \text{ place} \\ \hline 2\ 8364 & \\ 12\ 1560 & \\ \hline 14.9924 & \quad 4 \text{ places} \end{array}$$

Other examples:

$$\begin{array}{rl} 1.34 \rightarrow & 2 \text{ places} \\ \times \quad 0.2 \rightarrow & + 1 \text{ place} \\ \hline 0.268 \rightarrow & 3 \text{ places} \end{array}$$

$$\begin{array}{rl} 1.23 \rightarrow & 2 \text{ places} \\ \times \quad 3 \rightarrow & + 0 \text{ places} \\ \hline 3.69 \rightarrow & 2 \text{ places} \end{array}$$

$$\begin{array}{rl} 0.09 \rightarrow & 2 \text{ places} \\ \times \quad 7.5 \rightarrow & + 1 \text{ place} \\ \hline 0.675 \rightarrow & 3 \text{ places} \end{array}$$

Multiply.

1. $\begin{array}{r}0.445\\ \times\ \ 0.6\\ \hline\end{array}$	**2.** $\begin{array}{r}3.35\\ \times\ 0.1\\ \hline\end{array}$	**3.** $\begin{array}{r}0.769\\ \times\ \ 0.8\\ \hline\end{array}$	**4.** $\begin{array}{r}0.448\\ \times\ 16.9\\ \hline\end{array}$	**5.** $\begin{array}{r}41.2\\ \times 0.06\\ \hline\end{array}$
6. $\begin{array}{r}0.012\\ \times\ 10.6\\ \hline\end{array}$	**7.** $\begin{array}{r}7.12\\ \times 0.04\\ \hline\end{array}$	**8.** $\begin{array}{r}3.42\\ \times\ 6.9\\ \hline\end{array}$	**9.** $\begin{array}{r}9.8\\ \times 7.4\\ \hline\end{array}$	**10.** $\begin{array}{r}0.06\\ \times\ 8.9\\ \hline\end{array}$
11. $\begin{array}{r}21.02\\ \times\ 0.03\\ \hline\end{array}$	**12.** $\begin{array}{r}0.073\\ \times\ \ 3.8\\ \hline\end{array}$	**13.** $\begin{array}{r}6.108\\ \times\ \ 0.6\\ \hline\end{array}$	**14.** $\begin{array}{r}3.81\\ \times\ 0.3\\ \hline\end{array}$	**15.** $\begin{array}{r}8.12\\ \times\ 0.6\\ \hline\end{array}$
16. $\begin{array}{r}7.644\\ \times\ \ 0.7\\ \hline\end{array}$	**17.** $\begin{array}{r}0.699\\ \times\ \ 6.5\\ \hline\end{array}$	**18.** $\begin{array}{r}2.397\\ \times\ \ 0.7\\ \hline\end{array}$	**19.** $\begin{array}{r}3.981\\ \times\ \ 0.9\\ \hline\end{array}$	**20.** $\begin{array}{r}1.07\\ \times 0.33\\ \hline\end{array}$

21. 2.7×0.35 **22.** 0.89×3.06 **23.** 0.37×0.64 **24.** 3.4×1.067

25. 0.4×2.39 **26.** 1.44×0.23 **27.** 0.374×6.3 **28.** 6.07×2.4

ENRICHMENT

Scientific Notation

The speed of light is about 300,000 kilometers per second. Large numbers like this are often written in **scientific notation.**

Scientific notation is based on powers of 10.

$$10 = 10^1 \qquad 100 = 10^2 \qquad 1,000 = 10^3 \qquad 10,000 = 10^4$$

Notice that the exponent equals the number of zeros in the standard numeral.

Scientific notation has two factors. One factor is a number between 1 and 9. The other factor is a power of 10.

Write 300,000 in scientific notation.

Move the decimal point to the right of the first digit.

$$3 . 0\ 0\ 0\ 0\ 0$$

Count the number of places you moved the decimal point to find the power of 10.

$$3 . 0\ 0\ 0\ 0\ 0 \qquad \boxed{\text{5 decimal places}}$$

$$300,000 = 3 \times 100,000 = 3 \times 10^5$$

Written in scientific notation, 300,000 is 3×10^5.

The speed of light is also expressed as 186,000 miles per second. Write 186,000 in scientific notation.

Move the decimal to the right of the first digit.

$$1 . 8\ 6\ 0\ 0\ 0$$

Count the number of places you moved the decimal point to find the power of 10.

$$186,000 = 1.86 \times 100,000 = 1.86 \times 10^5$$

Written in scientific notation, 186,000 is 1.86×10^5.

Write each number in scientific notation.

1. 80,000
2. 500,000
3. 2,000,000
4. 36,000
5. 783,000
6. 18,000,000

Write the number.

7. 4×10^4
8. 5.5×10^4
9. 9×10^5
10. 2.1×10^4
11. 3.04×10^5
12. 1.3×10^7

125

TECHNOLOGY

This procedure in LOGO draws the square that is shown in the picture.

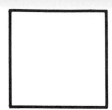

TO SQUARE
FD 40 RT 90 FD 40 RT 90 FD 40 RT 90 FD 40 RT 90
END

Here is a shorter way to write the same procedure.

TO SQUARE
REPEAT 4 [FD 40 RT 90]
END

The REPEAT 4 command means that the two other commands are repeated 4 times.

Suppose you wanted to change the lengths of the square's sides. An easy way to do this is to use a **variable.**

A LOGO variable is part of a procedure that changes. When a procedure uses a variable, you must give the variable a value. This example draws a square.

TO SQUARE :SIDE
REPEAT 4 [FD :SIDE RT 90]
END

The variable is :SIDE. Always use the colon (:) in a variable. When you type the procedure name, you also type a number that tells the turtle the value to give the variable. So, to draw a square that has sides equal to the ones above, type this.

SQUARE 40

To change the lengths of the square's sides, substitute a different number for 40.

1. Identify the variable in this procedure name.

   TO DASHEDLINE :DASH

   REPEAT 3 [FD :DASH PU FD :DASH PD]

   END

2. How long is each dash if you type this command?

   DASHEDLINE 15

3. Write a command to tell the turtle to draw SQUARE with sides that are 75 steps long.

4. Identify the variable in the procedure below. Then copy the figure, and follow the procedure to finish the drawing. (The sides are 50 steps long in this drawing.)

   TO GUESS :SIZE
   REPEAT 5 [FD :SIZE RT 72]
   END

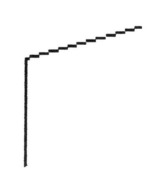

5. What is the figure?

6. Write a command to tell the turtle to use sides of 100 steps for this figure.

127

CUMULATIVE REVIEW

Write the letter of the correct answer.

1. 6 × 13,459

   a. 60,754   **b.** 68,404
   c. 80,754   **d.** not given

2. Estimate: 728 × 3.

   a. 2,000   **b.** 2,010
   c. 2,100   **d.** 21,000

3. 32 × 47

   a. 1,404   **b.** 1,504
   c. 2,305   **d.** not given

4. (6 × 0) × 9

   a. 0   **b.** 54
   c. 540   **d.** not given

5. 609 × $7.58

   a. $4,615.22   **b.** $4,617.32
   c. $4,719.00   **d.** not given

6. 40 × 70,000

   a. 280,000   **b.** 2,800,000
   c. 28,000,000   **d.** not given

7. Compare. Choose >, <, or = for ●.
0.117 ● 0.12

   a. <   **b.** >
   c. =   **d.** not given

8. Write the standard form:
3 million, 62 thousand, thirty.

   a. 3,062,030   **b.** 3,620,030
   c. 3,620,300   **d.** not given

9. 53,906 − 29,749

   a. 23,657   **b.** 24,007
   c. 24,157   **d.** not given

10. 0.11 + 7.971 + 6.5

   a. 13.581   **b.** 14.581
   c. 145.81   **d.** not given

11. Write as a decimal:
sixty-eight thousandths.

   a. 0.68   **b.** 6.8
   c. 0.068   **d.** not given

Interpret the bar graph.

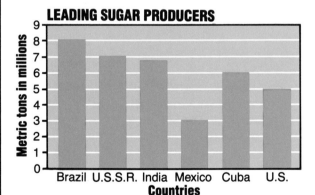

LEADING SUGAR PRODUCERS

12. What country produces the most sugar?

   a. India   **b.** Brazil
   c. U.S.S.R.   **d.** not given

13. How much sugar is produced by both Cuba and the U.S.S.R.?

   a. 11,000,000 tons
   b. 12,000,000 tons
   c. 13,000,000 tons
   d. not given

Help your class organize a Sports Festival Day. Plan ten different games. Each person must play a minimum of 3 games. Most of the games should be group games, but you may include one or two individual games.

5 DIVIDING WHOLE NUMBERS

Division Facts

A. Jim's baseball team calls itself the Doubledays in honor of Abner Doubleday, the founder of the game. The team buys 36 uniform shirts with the team name on them. The shirts are packed 9 to a box. How many boxes do they buy?

You can subtract to find how many groups of 9 there are in 36.

$36 - 9 = 27$; $27 - 9 = 18$; $18 - 9 = 9$; $9 - 9 = 0$
There are four 9's in 36.

It is easier to divide to find the number of groups.

Find $36 \div 9$.

Think: ■ $\times$ **9 = 36.**
$4 \times 9 = 36$ **So, $36 \div 9 = 4$.**

The team buys 4 boxes of shirts.

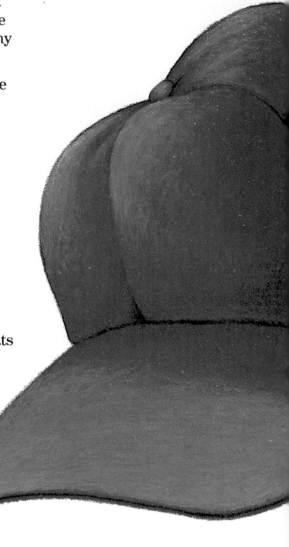

B. The team also purchases 48 new baseball caps. They are packed equally into 6 boxes. How many hats are packed into each box?

You can divide to find the number in each group.

Divide $6\overline{)48}$.

Think: ■ $\times$ **6 = 48.**
$8 \times 6 = 48$ **So, $6\overline{)48}^{\,8}$.**

There are 8 hats packed into each box.

C. Division can be shown in three ways.

$$9\overline{)63}^{\,7} \longleftarrow \text{quotient}$$
$9\overline{)63} \longleftarrow$ dividend
$\uparrow$
divisor

$$63 \div 9 = 7$$
    $\uparrow$ $\uparrow$ $\uparrow$
dividend divisor quotient

dividend $\longrightarrow \dfrac{63}{9} = 7$
divisor $\longrightarrow$
           $\uparrow$
      quotient

Math Reasoning, page H195

Divide.

1. $6\overline{)48}$ 2. $8\overline{)32}$ 3. $7\overline{)56}$ 4. $4\overline{)28}$ 5. $3\overline{)27}$

6. $9\overline{)72}$ 7. $8\overline{)64}$ 8. $5\overline{)30}$ 9. $3\overline{)21}$ 10. $6\overline{)54}$

11. $5\overline{)15}$ 12. $9\overline{)18}$ 13. $4\overline{)36}$ 14. $6\overline{)36}$ 15. $7\overline{)35}$

16. $6\overline{)42}$ 17. $9\overline{)81}$ 18. $7\overline{)28}$ 19. $3\overline{)12}$ 20. $4\overline{)36}$

21. $5\overline{)45}$ 22. $8\overline{)72}$ 23. $3\overline{)18}$ 24. $7\overline{)42}$ 25. $9\overline{)27}$

26. $54 \div 6$ 27. $20 \div 4$ 28. $24 \div 3$ 29. $28 \div 4$ 30. $63 \div 9$

31. $14 \div 2$ 32. $49 \div 7$ 33. $63 \div 7$ 34. $40 \div 5$ 35. $18 \div 6$

36. $56 \div 8$ 37. $42 \div 6$ 38. $27 \div 9$ 39. $32 \div 4$ 40. $20 \div 5$

41. $63 \div 7$ 42. $30 \div 6$ 43. $45 \div 5$ 44. $81 \div 9$ 45. $24 \div 8$

46. $\frac{42}{7}$ 47. $\frac{25}{5}$ 48. $\frac{16}{4}$ 49. $\frac{35}{7}$ 50. $\frac{28}{4}$

Solve.

51. The team runs 3 laps around the field before every game. At the end of the 8-game season, how many laps has the team run?

52. The Doubledays' bleachers can seat 81 people. If there are 9 rows and each row has an equal number of seats, how many seats are there in each row?

53. When the Doubleday team won the championship, the coach divided a box of 18 brand-new baseballs equally among his 9 players. How many baseballs did each player receive?

★54. At the end of the season, 77 people were invited to the team's party. Of the people invited, 5 did not go. The rest of the guests were seated at 8 tables, with an equal number at each table. How many guests were there at each table?

CHALLENGE

1. The divisor is 6 and the dividend is 54. What is the quotient?

2. The quotient is 7 and the dividend is 49. What is the divisor?

3. The divisor is 9 and the quotient is 8. What is the dividend?

4. The dividend is 32 and the divisor is 4. What is the quotient?

Related Facts

A. The Explorer Club is planning a canoe trip to retrace French explorer Louis Joliet's 1673 journey up the Mississippi River. They plan to paddle 63 miles in all, traveling the same number of miles each day for 7 days. How many miles will they travel each day?

Find $7\overline{)63}$.

Think: $\blacksquare \times 7 = 63$.

$9 \times 7 = 63$ So, $63 \div 7 = 9$.

They will travel 9 miles each day.

B. You can write four number sentences using 7, 9, and 63. The number sentences make up a family of facts.

$9 \times 7 = 63$ $63 \div 9 = 7$
$7 \times 9 = 63$ $63 \div 7 = 9$

Use these facts to help you find missing factors.

Complete the number sentence $9 \times \blacksquare = 63$.

Think: $63 \div 9 = 7$.   So, $\blacksquare = 7$.

C. These rules will help you divide.

Any number divided by 1 is that number.	$8 \div 1 = 8$
0 divided by another number, except 0, is 0.	$0 \div 6 = 0$
Any number, except 0, divided by itself is 1.	$5 \div 5 = 1$
A number can never be divided by 0. Think: $\blacksquare \times 0 = 7$. There is no solution.	$7 \div 0 = \blacksquare$

Divide.

1. $5\overline{)35}$ 2. $9\overline{)9}$ 3. $4\overline{)32}$ 4. $6\overline{)36}$ 5. $7\overline{)49}$

6. $3\overline{)24}$ 7. $9\overline{)45}$ 8. $5\overline{)40}$ 9. $7\overline{)63}$ 10. $9\overline{)27}$

11. $7\overline{)0}$ 12. $5\overline{)20}$ 13. $6\overline{)54}$ 14. $3\overline{)18}$ 15. $8\overline{)64}$

16. $4\overline{)24}$ 17. $3\overline{)21}$ 18. $6\overline{)48}$ 19. $5\overline{)45}$ 20. $8\overline{)32}$

21. $36 \div 4$ 22. $16 \div 4$ 23. $48 \div 8$ 24. $54 \div 9$ 25. $9 \div 1$

26. $64 \div 8$ 27. $14 \div 2$ 28. $\frac{42}{6}$ 29. $\frac{18}{2}$ 30. $\frac{72}{9}$

Write a family of facts for each set of numbers.

31. 3, 4, 12 32. 30, 5, 6 33. 21, 7, 3 34. 7, 56, 8 35. 9, 7, 63

Complete each number sentence.

36. $6 \times \blacksquare = 48$ 37. $9 \times \blacksquare = 36$ ★38. $20 \div \blacksquare = 4$ ★39. $45 \div \blacksquare = 5$

Solve.

40. The club plans a picnic at Stony Meadows Park for members and their families. They expect 72 people. The park's picnic tables can seat 8 people each. How many picnic tables will the club need?

★41. The club sponsors a day of sailboat races. In one race, 4 boats compete. Each boat has 7 people aboard. In a second race, twice the number of people take part, and they race 7 sailboats. If there is an equal number of people per boat, how many are aboard each boat in the second race?

NUMBER SENSE

You can use division rules and related facts to mentally compute these exercises.

1. $2,350 \div \blacksquare = 1$
2. $\blacksquare \div 84,650 = 0$
3. $3,450 \div \blacksquare = 3,450$
4. $5 \times 145 = 725$
   $\blacksquare \div 5 = 145$
5. $38 \times 3,552 = 134,976$
   $\blacksquare \div 38 = 3,552$
6. $27 \times 6,854 = 185,058$
   $185,058 \div 6,854 = \blacksquare$

Quotients and Remainders

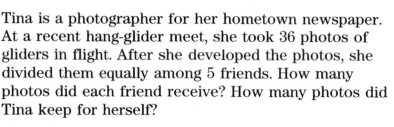

Tina is a photographer for her hometown newspaper. At a recent hang-glider meet, she took 36 photos of gliders in flight. After she developed the photos, she divided them equally among 5 friends. How many photos did each friend receive? How many photos did Tina keep for herself?

Find $36 \div 5$.

Think: ■ × 5 is close to 36.

$$6 \times 5 = 30$$
$$7 \times 5 = 35$$
$$8 \times 5 = 40 \qquad \text{Too great.} \qquad \text{So, use 7.}$$

$$
\begin{array}{r}
7 \text{ R1} \\
5)\overline{3\ 6} \\
3\ 5 \\
\hline
1
\end{array}
$$

Multiply: $7 \times 5 = 35$.
Subtract: $36 - 35 = 1$.
Compare: $1 < 5$.
Write the remainder.

The remainder tells you how many Tina kept for herself.

Each of Tina's friends received 7 photographs. She kept 1 for herself.

You can check division by multiplying and adding the remainder.

$$
\begin{array}{rl}
7 & \longleftarrow \text{quotient} \\
\times\ 5 & \longleftarrow \text{divisor} \\
\hline
35 & \\
+\ 1 & \longleftarrow \text{remainder} \\
\hline
36 & \longleftarrow \text{dividend}
\end{array}
$$

The answer should be the same as the dividend.

Checkpoint   Write the letter of the correct answer.

Divide and check.

1. $55 \div 6$

a. 8 R7
b. 9
c. 9 R1
d. 10

2. $6)\overline{41}$

a. 5 R11
b. 6 R5
c. 7
d. 7 R1

3. $74 \div 9$

a. 7 R11
b. 8
c. 8 R2
d. 9

Divide.

1. $4\overline{)34}$ 2. $3\overline{)26}$ 3. $5\overline{)32}$ 4. $7\overline{)45}$ 5. $5\overline{)21}$

6. $3\overline{)20}$ 7. $6\overline{)37}$ 8. $6\overline{)41}$ 9. $7\overline{)50}$ 10. $8\overline{)44}$

11. $5\overline{)28}$ 12. $9\overline{)74}$ 13. $7\overline{)60}$ 14. $8\overline{)52}$ 15. $5\overline{)41}$

16. $6\overline{)39}$ 17. $8\overline{)31}$ 18. $9\overline{)84}$ 19. $5\overline{)26}$ 20. $4\overline{)13}$

21. $9\overline{)88}$ 22. $5\overline{)43}$ 23. $2\overline{)21}$ 24. $9\overline{)47}$ 25. $3\overline{)23}$

26. $40 \div 6$ 27. $32 \div 4$ 28. $80 \div 9$ 29. $65 \div 8$ 30. $25 \div 5$

31. $53 \div 7$ 32. $62 \div 9$ 33. $73 \div 8$ 34. $38 \div 9$ 35. $48 \div 9$

36. $31 \div 9$ 37. $43 \div 5$ 38. $19 \div 2$ 39. $75 \div 7$ 40. $60 \div 8$

41. $89 \div 9$ 42. $44 \div 6$ 43. $30 \div 4$ 44. $46 \div 5$ 45. $21 \div 2$

46. $\frac{62}{8}$ 47. $\frac{50}{6}$ 48. $\frac{28}{3}$ 49. $\frac{75}{8}$ 50. $\frac{58}{7}$

Solve.

51. Tina takes photos of each of the 8 teams. She promised each team an equal number of prints. If she has only 79 sheets of printing paper, how many prints can she make for each team?

★52. Tina's photographs of the hang gliding are so good that many people want to buy copies. Tina makes 18 prints and sells them in sets of 3. She sells another 45 prints in sets of 5. How many sets of prints does Tina sell?

CALCULATOR

Divide, using your calculator. What does it display?

1. $4\overline{)13}^{\,3\,R1}$ 2. $4\overline{)14}^{\,3\,R2}$ 3. $4\overline{)15}^{\,3\,R3}$

4. $4\overline{)81}^{\,20\,R1}$ 5. $4\overline{)214}^{\,53\,R2}$ 6. $4\overline{)339}^{\,84\,R3}$

PROBLEM SOLVING
Choosing the Operation

You can use the hints in a problem to help you decide whether you should multiply or divide the numbers in the problem to find the answer.

Jan wears a weight belt when she goes scuba diving. She puts 6 weights on her belt. Each weight has a mass of 0.25 kg. What is the total mass of the weights on Jan's belt?

Hints:

If you know	and you want to find	you can
• how many groups there are • that the number in each group is the same • how many there are in each group	how many there are in all	multiply.
• how many there are in all • that the number in each group is the same • how many there are in each group	how many groups	divide.
• that the number in each group is the same • how many there are in all • how many groups there are	how many in each group	divide.

Once you have decided, you can solve the problem.

how many in each group   how many groups   how many in all
        0.25   ×   6   =   1.5

The weights have a total mass of 1.5 kg.

Write the letter of the operation you should use to solve the problem.

1. A group of 24 students wants to rent rowboats. Each boat will hold 4 students. How many boats should be rented?

   a. multiplication
   b. division

2. During an exciting softball game, 3 runs were scored each inning. To break a tie, 10 innings were played. How many runs were scored during the game?

   a. multiplication
   b. division

Solve.

3. When the Dixieland Debs played at the bandshell, 156 students went to hear them. Before the concert ended, 17 of the students left to go to swimming practice. How many students remained at the concert?

4. Forty students visit the City Museum while they are at the park. The teachers separate them into 8 groups of equal size. How many students are there in each group?

5. Each student is given an apple or an orange for lunch. One teacher hands out 26 apples and twice that number of oranges. How many oranges does the teacher hand out?

6. After lunch, the students organize a volleyball tournament. There are 36 students who want to play, and each team has 9 players. How many teams are there in the tournament?

7. Four students rent horses. They each pay $20. How much do they pay altogether?

8. There were 12 students who wanted to have a relay race. If each team has 4 students in it, how many teams can there be?

★9. It costs $25 to rent a tennis court for an hour. Each court holds 4 players. Some students want to play, but they do not want to spend more than $5.50 each. If they split the cost of renting a court equally among 4 players, would each pay more or less than $5.50?

★10. Before leaving, 19 of the students bought Central Park T-shirts. The shirts were $3 each. The sale price was $7 for 3 shirts. If each student received a shirt and the total spent was $45, how many sets of 3 did they buy? How many shirts were bought individually?

Divisibility

A. Often, groups of counters can be used to *model* numbers and operations with numbers. This activity will help you discover some rules about division of whole numbers.

Step 1: Separate 15 counters into groups of 2.

	Number of Counters				
	15	14	13	12	11
Size of Groups 2					
3					
5					

- Were you able to form groups of equal size, with no counters remaining? Copy the chart. Write yes or no in the first blank space below 15.

Step 2: Separate 15 counters into groups of 3. Then separate the 15 counters into groups of 5.

- Were you able to form groups of equal size, with no counters remaining in each case? Write yes or no on the chart.
- You can say that the number 15 is **divisible** by those numbers. For example, 15 is divisible by 3 because you can separate 15 counters into groups of 3 with no counters remaining.

Step 3: Take 14 counters. Separate them into groups of 2. Record your results on the chart. Do the same for groups of 3 and groups of 5. Record your results. Repeat this with 13 counters, 12 counters, and so on to 3 counters. Record your results.

Working as a Team

1. All of the numbers that are divisible by 2 are **even** numbers. Numbers that are not divisible by 2 are **odd** numbers. Write a rule for finding even and odd numbers.

2. Make lists of ten other numbers divisible by 3 and ten other numbers divisible by 5. Write rules for finding the numbers in each of these lists.

3. Add the digits of each number divisible by 3. Divide each of the sums by 3. What do you notice? Write a new rule for finding numbers divisible by 3.

B. Use your rules to decide which of the following numbers are divisible by 2 and which are divisible by 5. Test your answers with a calculator.

425	6,337	13,796	1,585	26,420
12,474	48,240	405	33,100	589

- How can you tell whether there is a remainder when you use a calculator?

- Did your rules work?

- Which of these numbers are divisible by 10?

Thinking as a Team

1. Look at the numbers that are divisible by 10. Write a rule for finding numbers that are divisible by 10.

2. Using your rule, make a list of five other numbers that are divisible by 10.

3. Try to find a rule about numbers that are divisible by 6.

4. How can rules like these help you tell whether a quotient is reasonable?

5. Is every number divisible by 1? Why?

6. Is every number except 0 divisible by itself? Why?

7. Is every number divisible by 0? Why?

8. Describe how you would use a model to show whether 89 is divisible by 9.

9. Is 89 divisible by 9? Draw a model to show whether 89 is divisible by 9.

10. Is 89 divisible by any number from 2 to 10? Use models for help.

Estimating Quotients

A. In preparation for the Craft and Hobby Fair, 7 friends plan to make a patchwork quilt. They will need 1,974 squares of fabric. If each one brings an equal number of squares, about how many squares will each person bring?

Estimate $1,974 \div 7$.

Decide on the number of digits in the quotient.

Divide the thousands: Think: $7\overline{)1}$. Not enough thousands.
Divide the hundreds: Think: $7\overline{)19}$.

So, the quotient begins in the hundreds place.

It will have 3 digits.
$$7\overline{)1,974}$$

Think: $2 \times 7 = 14$.
$$\overset{2}{7\overline{)1,974}}$$
$3 \times 7 = 21$ Too great. So, use 2.

Write zeros for the other digits. $7\overline{)1,974} \longrightarrow 200$
You can say that each person will bring about 200 squares.

B. The next step is to decide how accurate your estimate is.

Think: 1,974 squares will be needed. If each person brings 200 squares, will that be enough?
$7 \times 200 = 1,400$; $1,400 < 1,974$.
So, 200 squares will not be enough.
It is an underestimate.

Each person will bring more than 200 squares.

Write how many digits the quotient will contain.

1. $6\overline{)358}$ 2. $8\overline{)927}$ 3. $5\overline{)236}$ 4. $4\overline{)647}$ 5. $9\overline{)493}$

6. $8\overline{)6,531}$ 7. $7\overline{)4,346}$ 8. $2\overline{)2,659}$ 9. $5\overline{)5,893}$ 10. $9\overline{)8,453}$

11. $3\overline{)24,876}$ 12. $9\overline{)82,543}$ 13. $4\overline{)45,208}$ 14. $6\overline{)72,349}$ 15. $7\overline{)49,876}$

Estimate. Write the letter of the correct answer.

16. $4\overline{)347}$ **a.** 8   **b.** 80   **c.** 800

17. $7\overline{)784}$ **a.** 1   **b.** 10   **c.** 100

18. $9\overline{)6,453}$ **a.** 7   **b.** 70   **c.** 700

19. $3\overline{)3,642}$ **a.** 10   **b.** 100   **c.** 1,000

20. $4\overline{)14,386}$ **a.** 30   **b.** 300   **c.** 3,000

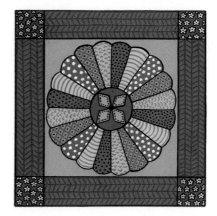

Estimate.

21. $5\overline{)359}$ 22. $6\overline{)285}$ 23. $4\overline{)138}$ 24. $2\overline{)359}$ 25. $9\overline{)897}$

26. $4\overline{)6,398}$ 27. $3\overline{)2,497}$ 28. $6\overline{)3,621}$ 29. $5\overline{)4,672}$ 30. $8\overline{)5,789}$

31. $3\overline{)26,786}$ 32. $8\overline{)13,463}$ 33. $7\overline{)45,671}$ 34. $6\overline{)92,526}$ 35. $4\overline{)15,628}$

Solve.

36. Marge sews pillows at the crafts fair. She uses 2 yards of fabric for every pillow. If Marge used 386 yards of fabric, could she sew 200 pillows?

37. Jim makes ceramic coffee mugs for the crafts fair. He uses 3 pounds of clay for each mug. If Jim has 230 pounds of clay, about how many coffee mugs can he make?

MIDCHAPTER REVIEW

Divide.

1. $64 \div 8$ 2. $81 \div 9$ 3. $28 \div 4$ 4. $\dfrac{63}{7}$ 5. $\dfrac{45}{9}$

6. $7\overline{)59}$ 7. $9\overline{)34}$ 8. $6\overline{)41}$ 9. $\dfrac{70}{8}$ 10. $\dfrac{69}{9}$

Is the number divisible by 2? Write *yes* or *no*.

11. 37   12. 48   13. 56   14. 85   15. 74

PROBLEM SOLVING
Writing a Number Sentence

You can write a number sentence to help solve a word problem. Number sentences help you find the number you need by using the numbers you know.

> Tara belongs to the Roamers Bicycle Club. The club cycled 72 miles through the Napa Valley during an 8-day trip. They cycled the same number of miles each day. How many miles did the Roamers ride each day?

1. List what you know and what you want to find.

In 8 days, the club biked 72 miles. They biked the same distance each day. How many miles did they bike each day?

2. Think about how to use this information to solve the problem.

You know the number in each group is the same. You can divide to find how many in each group.

3. Write a number sentence. Use n to stand for the number you want to find.

miles biked in all	÷	hours biked	=	miles biked each day
72	÷	8	=	n

4. Solve. Write the answer.
$n = 9$
The club biked 9 miles each day.

Math Reasoning, page H196

Read the problem. Write the letter of the correct number sentence. Explain your choice.

1. One Saturday, Jamie rode his 10-speed bicycle 81 miles. That is 9 times the number of miles his little brother, Pete, rode that day. How many miles did Pete ride?

   a. $9 \div 81 = n$
   b. $81 \times 9 = n$
   c. $81 \div 9 = n$

2. Lynn will ride in a bike-a-thon to raise money for a community park. Lynn's pledges amount to $10.97 for every mile she rides. If Lynn rides 25 miles, how much will she raise for the park?

   a. $\$10.97 \div 25 = n$
   b. $1 \times \$10.97 = n$
   c. $25 \times \$10.97 = n$

Write a number sentence. Solve.

3. On one outing, the Hudson Valley Bike Club rode 45 miles from Newburgh to West Point. The bikers made the trip in 5 hours. How many miles did they travel each hour?

4. The Walla Walla Bike Club plans a three-week bike trip to San Diego. The club needs $1,550.00 for the hotel and food. There is $344.83 in the club's treasury. How much more money is needed?

5. There are 3 bikers who ride in a 15-mile relay race. If each biker rides an equal number of miles, how many miles does each biker ride?

6. The 8 members of a bike club decide to split equally the cost of bicycling caps. The total cost is $32. How much must each club member pay?

7. The bikers decide to ride 83 miles per day until they reach the beaches of northern California. If they stop after 15 days, how many miles have they ridden?

8. The fastest recorded speed ever ridden on a bicycle is 78 miles in one hour. At that speed, how many miles would be traveled in 7 hours of biking?

★9. Renee takes $85.00 on a bike trip. She spends $7.95 for a sweatshirt and $6.95 for film. If she spends $15.25 for a concert ticket, how much money will she have left?

★10. Tom and Sandy rode on a bicycle built for two. They biked 6 miles in 36 minutes. At that rate, how far would Tom and Sandy travel in 54 minutes?

2-Digit Quotients

The *Tour d'Avalon* bicycle race attracts 283 riders. Before the race, all the cyclists ride by the reviewing stand in rows of 9. How many full rows of riders are there? How many riders are there in the last row?

Divide to find how many rows: $9\overline{)283}$.

Divide the hundreds. Think: $9\overline{)2}$. Not enough hundreds.

Divide the tens.

Think: $9\overline{)28}$.
Write 3.

$$\begin{array}{r} 3 \\ 9\overline{)283} \\ 27 \\ \hline 1 \end{array}$$
Multiply.
Subtract.
Compare.

Divide the ones.
Bring down the 3.
Think: $9\overline{)13}$.
Write 1.

$$\begin{array}{r} 3\,1 \text{ R4} \\ 9\overline{)283} \\ 27\downarrow \\ \hline 13 \\ 9 \\ \hline 4 \end{array}$$
Multiply.
Subtract.
Compare.
Write the remainder.

Check.

$$\begin{array}{r} 31 \\ \times\ 9 \\ \hline 279 \\ +\ 4 \\ \hline 283 \end{array}$$

There are 31 full rows of riders.
There are 4 riders in the last row.

Other examples:

$$\begin{array}{r} 15 \text{ R3} \\ 6\overline{)93} \\ 6 \\ \hline 33 \\ 30 \\ \hline 3 \end{array}$$

$$\begin{array}{r} 97 \\ 5\overline{)485} \\ 45 \\ \hline 35 \\ 35 \\ \hline 0 \end{array}$$

$$\begin{array}{r} 41 \text{ R3} \\ 4\overline{)167} \\ 16 \\ \hline 7 \\ 4 \\ \hline 3 \end{array}$$

Checkpoint Write the letter of the correct answer.

Divide.

1. $7\overline{)84}$

2. $163 \div 6$

3. $5\overline{)127}$

a. 10 R4
b. 11 R3
c. 11 R7
d. 12

a. 20 R3
b. 27
c. 27 R1
d. 216

a. 21 R2
b. 25
c. 25 R2
d. 26

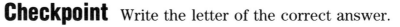

Divide.

1. $2\overline{)64}$ **2.** $3\overline{)72}$ **3.** $2\overline{)94}$ **4.** $4\overline{)76}$ **5.** $6\overline{)90}$

6. $2\overline{)49}$ **7.** $4\overline{)78}$ **8.** $3\overline{)85}$ **9.** $4\overline{)97}$ **10.** $2\overline{)55}$

11. $2\overline{)164}$ **12.** $9\overline{)162}$ **13.** $7\overline{)182}$ **14.** $8\overline{)392}$ **15.** $9\overline{)315}$

16. $7\overline{)573}$ **17.** $3\overline{)229}$ **18.** $3\overline{)131}$ **19.** $9\overline{)650}$ **20.** $6\overline{)486}$

21. $6\overline{)427}$ **22.** $8\overline{)310}$ **23.** $7\overline{)217}$ **24.** $4\overline{)386}$ **25.** $9\overline{)709}$

26. $124 \div 8$ **27.** $212 \div 5$ **28.** $321 \div 3$ **29.** $654 \div 9$ **30.** $336 \div 8$

31. $417 \div 5$ **32.** $556 \div 8$ **33.** $301 \div 4$ **34.** $628 \div 8$ **35.** $374 \div 9$

36. $\frac{616}{7}$ **37.** $\frac{525}{5}$ **38.** $\frac{488}{6}$ **39.** $\frac{268}{4}$ **40.** $\frac{715}{8}$

Solve.

41. The race will last for 8 days and will cover a total of 528 miles. If the riders travel the same number of miles each day, how many miles do they cover the first day?

42. The Woodside Team practiced for a total of 144 hours in 8 weeks. They practiced for the same number of hours each week. For how many hours did they practice each week?

43. A bicycle team from Claremont will donate $0.25 to a local charity for each mile they race. They race a total of 528 miles. How much money will the charity receive?

★44. After the race, each of the 287 riders and 64 staff members received 2 free T-shirts. The shirts were packed 9 to a box. How many boxes of shirts were needed?

ANOTHER LOOK

Subtract.

1.
$$\begin{array}{r} 32,465 \\ -\ 3,523 \\ \hline \end{array}$$

2.
$$\begin{array}{r} 654 \\ -\ 571 \\ \hline \end{array}$$

3.
$$\begin{array}{r} 1,786 \\ -\ 787 \\ \hline \end{array}$$

4.
$$\begin{array}{r} 23,777 \\ -\ 19,499 \\ \hline \end{array}$$

5.
$$\begin{array}{r} 65,434 \\ -\ 65,404 \\ \hline \end{array}$$

6.
$$\begin{array}{r} 5,748 \\ -\ 4,999 \\ \hline \end{array}$$

7.
$$\begin{array}{r} 22,222 \\ -\ 21,311 \\ \hline \end{array}$$

8.
$$\begin{array}{r} 98,000 \\ -\ 27,564 \\ \hline \end{array}$$

9. $76,298 - 54,323$ **10.** $6,040 - 3,506$ **11.** $60,763 - 28,975$

3-Digit Quotients

Each year, volunteers help to clean Central Park. If 3,548 volunteers are separated into 4 groups of the same size, how many are in each group?

You can divide to find the number in each group. $4\overline{)3{,}548}$

First estimate by finding the first number and writing zeros in the other places.

$$4\overline{)3{,}548} \longrightarrow 800$$
with 8 above.

Divide the hundreds.
Think: $4\overline{)35}$.

$$
\begin{array}{r}
8 \\
4\overline{)3{,}548} \\
\underline{32} \\
3
\end{array}
$$

Divide the tens.
Think: $4\overline{)34}$.

$$
\begin{array}{r}
88 \\
4\overline{)3{,}548} \\
\underline{32} \\
34 \\
\underline{32} \\
2
\end{array}
$$

Divide the ones.
Think: $4\overline{)28}$.

$$
\begin{array}{r}
887 \\
4\overline{)3{,}548} \\
\underline{32} \\
34 \\
\underline{32} \\
28 \\
\underline{28} \\
0
\end{array}
$$

There are 887 volunteers in each group.
The answer is reasonably close to the estimate.

Other examples:

$$
\begin{array}{r}
767\ \text{R2} \\
6\overline{)4{,}604} \\
\underline{42} \\
40 \\
\underline{36} \\
44 \\
\underline{42} \\
2
\end{array}
\qquad
\begin{array}{r}
212\ \text{R1} \\
4\overline{)849} \\
\underline{8} \\
4 \\
\underline{4} \\
9 \\
\underline{8} \\
1
\end{array}
$$

Checkpoint   Write the letter of the correct answer.

Divide.

1. $4\overline{)1{,}172}$ **a.** 29 R3   **b.** 213   **c.** 290 R2   **d.** 293

2. $4{,}382 \div 7$ **a.** 620 R2   **b.** 625 R7   **c.** 626   **d.** 711 R5

3. $3{,}431 \div 5$ **a.** 610 R1   **b.** 680 R1   **c.** 686 R1   **d.** 687

Divide.

1. $2\overline{)430}$ 2. $3\overline{)981}$ 3. $2\overline{)650}$ 4. $3\overline{)684}$ 5. $4\overline{)864}$

6. $6\overline{)679}$ 7. $6\overline{)710}$ 8. $3\overline{)449}$ 9. $8\overline{)973}$ 10. $5\overline{)682}$

11. $5\overline{)4,560}$ 12. $9\overline{)7,128}$ 13. $8\overline{)4,472}$ 14. $3\overline{)2,847}$ 15. $6\overline{)2,813}$

16. $9\overline{)5,717}$ 17. $2\overline{)1,463}$ 18. $6\overline{)1,900}$ 19. $7\overline{)2,487}$ 20. $5\overline{)4,056}$

21. $423 \div 2$ 22. $3,159 \div 4$ 23. $1,984 \div 7$ 24. $788 \div 4$ 25. $840 \div 7$

26. $4,308 \div 6$ 27. $5,672 \div 9$ 28. $5,323 \div 6$ 29. $1,629 \div 3$ 30. $6,204 \div 7$

31. $\frac{832}{7}$ 32. $\frac{2,067}{4}$ 33. $\frac{4,405}{5}$ 34. $\frac{729}{6}$ 35. $\frac{5,887}{9}$

Solve.

36. A running club is holding a race in the park. There are 1,967 runners entered, and they are divided equally into 7 heats. How many runners are there in each heat?

37. Tickets for the park merry-go-round cost $1.25. One afternoon, 252 people buy tickets. How much money do they spend for merry-go-round tickets?

38. The 5 soccer leagues that play in the park were looking for new players. There were many more applicants than expected. Each league has at least 165 players. Refer to the chart to decide if there are enough players to have 6 leagues play each day.

SOCCER LEAGUES

Day	Number of applicants
Monday	1,040
Wednesday	935
Friday	1,105

CHALLENGE

If the sum of the digits of a number is 9, then the number is divisible by 9.

342     $3 + 4 + 2 = 9$ $9 \div 9 = 1$
342 is divisible by 9.

Is the number divisible by 9? Write *yes* or *no*.

1. 1,234   2. 3,105   3. 4,203   4. 7,104   5. 226   6. 4,112

Dividing Larger Numbers

Stamp collecting has been called the "king of hobbies and the hobby of kings." Michael has been collecting stamps since he was very young. He has divided his collection of 13,418 stamps equally among 7 albums. How many stamps are there in each album? How many additional stamps does he have?

Find 13,418 ÷ 7.

To place the first digit of the quotient

Think: 7)$\overline{1}$.　　Not enough ten thousands.

Think: 7)$\overline{13}$.　　Place the first digit of the quotient in the thousands place.

```
      1,9 1 6  R6              Check.
 7)1 3,4 1 8                      1,916
   7 ↓                          ×     7
   ───                          ───────
   6 4                          13,412
   6 3 ↓                      +       6
   ───                        ─────────
     1 1                        13,418
       7 ↓
     ─────
       4 8
       4 2
       ───
         6
```

There are 1,916 stamps in each album.
He has 6 additional stamps.

Other examples:

```
    5,484 R3        14,571 R3        2,283 R1         24,234
 8)43,875         5)72,858        3)6,850         4)96,936
   40               5               6               8
   ──               ──              ──              ──
   3 8              22              8               16
   3 2              20              6               16
   ──               ──              ──              ──
     67             2 8             25               9
     64             2 5             24               8
     ──             ──              ──              ──
       35            35             10              13
       32            35              9              12
       ──            ──             ──              ──
         3            8              1              16
                      5                             16
                      ──                            ──
                      3                              0
```

Divide. Multiply to check your answer.

1. 4)4,484   2. 7)9,485   3. 6)7,686   4. 3)9,399

5. 3)8,553   6. 8)9,068   7. 4)5,133   8. 2)6,785

9. 3)28,143   10. 6)35,076   11. 7)22,225   12. 5)47,358

13. 7)57,154   14. 9)38,267   15. 8)74,684   16. 4)65,823

17. 6)36,726   18. 7)63,798   19. 8)63,456   20. 4)35,105

21. 7)4,347   22. 9)13,212   23. 4)22,796   24. 8)45,056

25. 5,143 ÷ 4   26. 7,389 ÷ 6   27. 35,169 ÷ 3   28. 83,330 ÷ 2

29. 89,185 ÷ 3   30. 6,375 ÷ 5   31. 15,724 ÷ 8   32. 77,777 ÷ 6

33. 6,408 ÷ 9   34. 1,244 ÷ 4   35. 9,786 ÷ 3   36. 3,084 ÷ 6

37. 4,984 ÷ 7   38. 9,858 ÷ 3   39. 36,732 ÷ 6   40. 23,120 ÷ 5

Solve.

41. Michael finds a box of old stamp albums in his attic. He takes a few stamps for his own collection and divides the remaining 35,682 into 6 equal groups to sell as starter kits. How many stamps are there in each starter kit?

★42. Michael files stamps of different countries in envelopes with 5 stamps in each. He has 750 Israeli stamps, 506 Spanish stamps, and 231 German stamps. How many full envelopes will Michael have?

FOCUS: REASONING

There are 16 students in a fourth-grade class. The diagram shows how many students belong to school clubs.

There are 2 students who only belong to the computer club.

There are 3 students who belong to both the chorus club and the art club only.

1. How many are in all three clubs?

2. How many students are in the computer club?

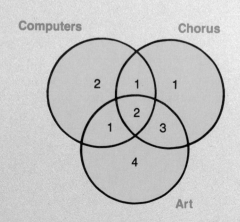

PROBLEM SOLVING
Choosing/Writing a Sensible Question

Asking the right questions can help you organize information and make appropriate decisions.

The Calamity Falls Jug Band wants to go to the Bluegrass Festival at the state fair to compete in the band contest. The members decide to give a concert to raise money to cover their expenses. The band members meet to discuss their plans.

First, the band members have to decide how much money they need to raise. Answering which of these questions will help them determine what their expenses will be?

- What is the cost of transportation? The cost of transportation is important information. It will cost the band more to travel farther.
- How many people are there in the band? The number of people in the band is important information. Each person's expenses will have to be covered.
- Which of the band members plays the banjo? It is not important to know which of the band members plays the banjo. This information will not affect the band's expenses.
- How long will the band stay at the fair? The length of time that the band will spend at the fair is important information. The cost of meals and hotel rooms will be an important part of the band's expenses.

In order to determine the band's expenses, it is important to know the cost of transportation, the number of people in the band, and the length of time that the band will stay at the fair. It will not help to know which of the band members plays the banjo.

Read each statement. Then write the letter of the question that the band does *not* need to answer before making a decision.

1. The band wants to know what its chances are of winning the contest.

   a. How long has the band played together?
   b. Has the band entered a contest before?
   c. Has the band ever played under another name?
   d. What other bands have entered the contest?

2. The band members have to decide whether they want to stay overnight at the fair.

   a. How much money does the band have?
   b. Who has organized the contest?
   c. Where do they need to be the next day and at what time?
   d. At what time will the band play during the contest?

Read each statement. Then formulate two questions that the band should answer before making a decision.

3. The band has to decide where to hold the fund-raising concert.

4. A date has to be set for the concert.

5. The band has to decide which songs to play at the contest.

6. The band has to decide how many songs to play at the contest.

7. The band has to decide how much to charge for tickets to the fund-raising concert.

8. The band has to decide when to arrive at the state fair.

9. The band has to decide where to eat at the state fair.

10. The band members have to decide what to do with extra money they have left after their trip.

Zeros in the Quotient

Kite flying is a national pastime in China, Korea, Japan, and Malaysia. Some of the kites are so big that it takes 3 people to fly them. If 624 people were flying these large kites in a contest, how many kites were in the air? Divide 3)624.

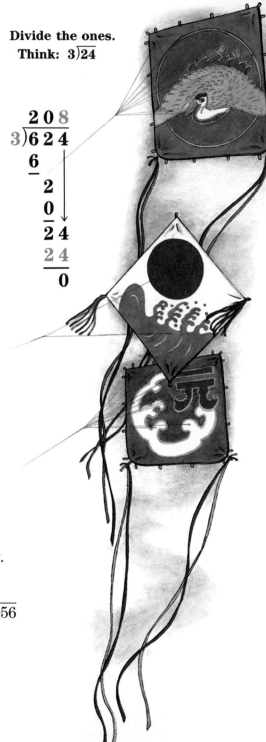

Divide the hundreds.

Think: 3)6

$$
\begin{array}{r}
2 \\
3\overline{)6\,2\,4} \\
\underline{6}
\end{array}
$$

Divide the tens.

Think: 3)2

Not enough tens.

Write 0.

$$
\begin{array}{r}
2\,0 \\
3\overline{)6\,2\,4} \\
\underline{6} \\
2 \\
\underline{0} \\
2
\end{array}
$$

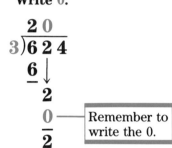 Remember to write the 0.

Divide the ones.

Think: 3)24

$$
\begin{array}{r}
2\,0\,8 \\
3\overline{)6\,2\,4} \\
\underline{6} \\
2 \\
\underline{0} \\
2\,4 \\
\underline{2\,4} \\
0
\end{array}
$$

There were 208 large kites in the air.

Other examples:

$$
\begin{array}{r}
10\text{ R3} \\
5\overline{)53} \\
\underline{5} \\
3 \\
\underline{0} \\
3
\end{array}
\qquad
\begin{array}{r}
2,006 \\
3\overline{)6,018} \\
\underline{6} \\
0 \\
\underline{0} \\
1 \\
\underline{0} \\
18 \\
\underline{18} \\
0
\end{array}
$$

Checkpoint Write the letter of the correct answer.

Divide.

1. 4)8,052

   a. 213
   b. 2,010 R2
   c. 2,013
   d. 2,130

2. 18,540 ÷ 6

   a. 309
   b. 3,009
   c. 3,090
   d. 3,900

3. 7)14,056

   a. 208
   b. 2,008
   c. 2,080
   d. 2,800

Divide.

1. $3\overline{)612}$ **2.** $9\overline{)945}$ **3.** $4\overline{)832}$ **4.** $3\overline{)903}$ **5.** $6\overline{)648}$

6. $4\overline{)83}$ **7.** $7\overline{)72}$ **8.** $3\overline{)62}$ **9.** $2\overline{)611}$ **10.** $4\overline{)810}$

11. $5\overline{)751}$ **12.** $8\overline{)967}$ **13.** $6\overline{)845}$ **14.** $5\overline{)604}$ **15.** $7\overline{)769}$

16. $3\overline{)1,521}$ **17.** $5\overline{)3,540}$ **18.** $3\overline{)1,590}$ **19.** $6\overline{)5,760}$ **20.** $4\overline{)2,428}$

21. $6\overline{)16,234}$ **22.** $8\overline{)48,363}$ **23.** $7\overline{)35,526}$ **24.** $6\overline{)12,430}$ **25.** $9\overline{)36,430}$

26. $5\overline{)27,753}$ **27.** $3\overline{)62}$ **28.** $3\overline{)27,029}$ **29.** $6\overline{)3,644}$ **30.** $2\overline{)34,001}$

31. $30,060 \div 6$ **32.** $749 \div 7$ **33.** $13,206 \div 8$ **34.** $74 \div 9$

35. $54,200 \div 2$ **36.** $67,451 \div 5$ **37.** $6,328 \div 7$ **38.** $66,003 \div 5$

39. $2,418 \div 3$ **40.** $36,160 \div 6$ **41.** $1,452 \div 7$ **42.** $3,417 \div 2$

43. $45,445 \div 5$ **44.** $12,031 \div 4$ **45.** $18,907 \div 9$ **46.** $42,498 \div 6$

Solve. For Problem 49, use the Infobank.

47. The box kite was invented in Australia in the 1890's by Lawrence Hargrave. He used 8 sticks for each kite. How many kites could he have built with 13,616 sticks?

48. The United States Weather Bureau flew long trains of box kites to collect weather data. A total of 408 kites in 4 separate trains were flown. How many kites were there in each train if each train had the same number of kites?

49. Use the information on page 417 to solve. Which kite requires the most sticks to build? Which kites need a tail longer than 3 feet?

★50. Japanese families celebrate Children's Day by flying 1 fish kite for each son. If 6 families have 2 sons each and 3 families have 3 sons each, how many kites do these families fly in all?

NUMBER SENSE

Compute mentally.

1. $(63 \div 9) \times 3$ **2.** $(48 \div 6) \times 8$ **3.** $(35 \div 7) \times 4$ **4.** $(72 \div 8) \times 5$

5. $(14 \div 2) \times 6$ **6.** $(24 \div 3) \times 4$ **7.** $(27 \div 9) \times 6$ **8.** $(32 \div 8) \times 6$

Dividing with Money

The Silver Star Amusement Park has a special weekday price for tickets: $14.25 for 3 tickets. Tim, Patty, and Carrie buy tickets together. What is the cost of each of their tickets at the weekday rate?

Find: $14.25 ÷ 3.

To divide amounts of <u>money</u>, think of the amounts as whole numbers. For 3)$14.25, think: 3)1,425.

```
      $4.7 5
3)$1 4.2 5
   1 2 ↓
     2 2
     2 1 ↓
       1 5
       1 5
         0
```

Remember to write the dollar sign and the cents point.

Check.

```
    $4.75
  ×     3
  $14.25
```

The cost of each ticket is $4.75.

Other examples:

```
    $0.73
8)$5.84
  5 6
  24
  24
   0
```

```
    $0.05
6)$0.30
   30
    0
```

Checkpoint Write the letter of the correct answer.

Divide.

1. $75.42 ÷ 6

a. $12.07
b. $12.57
c. $14.23 R4
d. $125.70

2. 8)$876.48

a. $19.56
b. $109 R4
c. $109.06
d. $109.56

3. $185.80 ÷ 4

a. $41.45
b. $46.20
c. $46.45
d. $46.00 R1

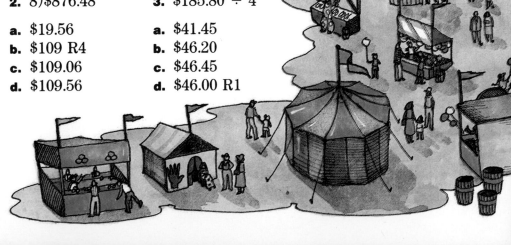

Divide. Check by multiplying.

1. $6\overline{)\$0.54}$ 2. $3\overline{)\$0.81}$ 3. $7\overline{)\$0.84}$ 4. $5\overline{)\$0.65}$

5. $4\overline{)\$2.36}$ 6. $5\overline{)\$1.55}$ 7. $3\overline{)\$4.86}$ 8. $7\overline{)\$6.51}$

9. $8\overline{)\$70.56}$ 10. $5\overline{)\$14.85}$ 11. $4\overline{)\$22.52}$ 12. $3\overline{)\$65.73}$

13. $5\overline{)\$800.55}$ 14. $6\overline{)\$651.24}$ 15. $8\overline{)\$209.20}$ 16. $2\overline{)\$140.56}$

17. $\$19.80 \div 6$ 18. $\$29.37 \div 3$ 19. $\$69.65 \div 7$ 20. $\$305.84 \div 2$

21. $\$475.15 \div 5$ 22. $\$10.84 \div 4$ 23. $\$229.36 \div 2$ 24. $\$706.23 \div 9$

25. $\$26.88 \div 4$ 26. $\$318.51 \div 9$ 27. $\$728.49 \div 7$ 28. $\$521.04 \div 6$

29. $\$972.54 \div 3$ 30. $\$612.18 \div 6$ 31. $\$408.80 \div 2$ 32. $\$23.45 \div 7$

Solve.

33. The Upside-Down-Inside-Out is Tim's favorite ride. He spends $4.55 to ride it 7 times. How much does each ride cost?

34. Carrie likes the Looper-Dooper ride. She rides it 12 times. She spends $1.35 on each ride. How much money does she spend on the Looper-Dooper?

35. Tim, Carrie, and Patty eat lunch at the park. They each have a hamburger and a glass of milk. Patty buys an apple, Tim buys a bag of peanuts, and Carrie buys an orange. They decide to split the bill evenly. Look at the menu. How much does each pay?

SILVER STAR PARK MENU

Hamburger $1.35
Apple $0.50
Orange $0.40
Peanuts $0.60
Milk $0.75

ANOTHER LOOK

Multiply.

1. 727×11 2. $8{,}207 \times 10$ 3. $23{,}654 \times 21$ 4. $98{,}001 \times 30$

5. 111×30 6. $4{,}004 \times 17$ 7. $39{,}100 \times 41$ 8. $75{,}320 \times 50$

PROBLEM SOLVING
Interpreting the Quotient and the Remainder

Sometimes when you divide to solve a problem, the quotient is not a whole number. If the answer is a quotient that has a remainder, read the question again. Be sure that the answer you write really answers the question. You may need to:

1. drop the remainder
2. round the quotient to the next-greater whole number, or
3. use only the remainder.

The Lenox family is planning a gathering at Lake Tiorati State Park. They want to reserve cabins for 27 family members. No more than 4 people are allowed to sleep in a cabin.

Divide:

$$\begin{array}{r} 6 \text{ R}3 \\ 4\overline{)27} \\ 24 \\ \hline 3 \end{array}$$

Read each question. Think about how the answers differ for each question.

Question	Action	Answer
1. How many cabins can be completely filled?	Drop the remainder.	6 cabins can be completely filled.
2. How many cabins are needed to house all the people?	Round the quotient to the next-greater whole number.	7 cabins are needed. (There will be 3 people left after the 6 cabins are filled.)
3. How many people will be in the cabin that is not completely full?	Use only the remainder.	The cabin that is not completely full will house 3 people.

Write the letter of the correct answer.

1. There are 17 members of the Lenox family who plan to drive to the lake together. If they can fit 5 people into each car, how many cars will they need for the trip?

$$5\overline{)17} \quad \begin{array}{c} 3 \text{ R2} \end{array}$$

   a. 2
   b. 3
   c. 4

2. The Lenox children want to rent a rowboat. It costs $9 per hour to rent a boat. The children have $22. For how many hours can they rent a rowboat?

$$9\overline{)22} \quad \begin{array}{c} 2 \text{ R4} \end{array}$$
$$\underline{18}$$
$$4$$

   a. 2 hours
   b. 3 hours
   c. 4 hours

Solve.

3. Joseph Lenox's family decides to camp in tents. There are 5 people in the family. If each tent holds 2 people, how many tents will they need?

4. Anna Lenox estimates that they will need at least 54 hot dogs for the cookout. If hot dogs are sold 8 to a package, how many packages must she buy?

5. Lou Lenox baked enough bran muffins so that each of the 27 family members could have one muffin. He packed the muffins 6 to a box. He brought only full boxes. How many boxes did he bring?

6. Maria Lenox makes 2 quarts (64 ounces) of lemonade. How many 6-ounce glasses of lemonade can she fill completely with the lemonade she has made?

7. The Lenox children decide to organize volleyball games on the beach. There are 17 family members who want to play. Each team will have 8 players. Extra players will be substitutes. How many substitutes will there be?

8. Some boys and girls at the lake want to form separate teams for relay races. There are 9 boys and 10 girls. Each relay team can have 4 members. Any extra people will be judges. How many teams are there?
How many judges will be girls?

How many judges will be boys?

CALCULATOR

You can use a calculator to practice estimating and finding quotients.

Use the numbers given in the boxes to complete each exercise.

Divisors
2   3   4
5   6   7
8   9

Dividends	
567	1,842
585	2,265
816	2,344
1,408	3,440
1,456	6,510
952	1,530
	2,608

Quotients	
107	247
176	293
189	453
208	652
238	

1. ■)1,4 8 2   ▢▢▢

2. ■)■,■■■   9 3 0

3. 3)■■■   ▢▢▢

4. 5)■,■■■   ▢▢▢

5. ■)9 6 3   ▢▢▢

6. 4)■■■   ▢▢▢

7. ■)■■■   2 0 4

8. 8)2,■■■   ▢▢▢

9. ■)■,■■■   9 2 1

10. ■)■■■   1 9 5

11. 8)■,■■ 8   ▢▢▢

12. 4)■,■■■   ▢▢▢

13. ■)■,■■■   3 0 6

14. 7)■,■■■   ▢▢▢

15. ■)■,■■■   4 3 0

Decide whether you would use mental math, pencil and paper, or a calculator to solve each. Explain your answer, then solve.

16. 203
        + 415

17. 1,045
        − 976

18. 311
        ×   5

19. 6)3,660

20. 5,986
        + 6,157

21. 12,986
        − 6,986

22. 425
        × 25

23. 9)888

GROUP PROJECT

Car Wash or Raffle

The problem: Your class needs to raise $500 in two months for a trip to the state fair. They're considering sponsoring a car wash or holding a raffle. Discuss these two ideas with your classmates. Choose one based on the information below.

Key Facts

Car Wash

- You can wash cars in the school parking lot.
- The school will provide soap and water, but you need to provide the buckets, rags, and brushes.

Raffle

- You think students will be willing to pay $0.50 for a raffle ticket.
- Local businesses or parents can contribute prizes to the raffle.
- The sixth-grade class held a successful raffle last month.

Key Questions

- How many cars do you need to wash?
- How many students will help?
- How would you advertise?
- What price will you charge?
- Do you need to hold more than one car wash?

- Where will you hold the raffle?
- How many items should you raffle?
- How many tickets do you need to sell?
- How would you advertise?

CHAPTER TEST

Divide. (pages 130, 132, 134, 144, 146, 148, 152, and 154)

1. $5\overline{)45}$

2. $6\overline{)6}$

3. $\frac{0}{9}$

4. $\frac{30}{7}$

5. $9\overline{)166}$

6. $8\overline{)384}$

7. $\frac{474}{6}$

8. $\frac{623}{7}$

9. $3\overline{)635}$

10. $5\overline{)426}$

11. $\frac{727}{7}$

12. $\frac{27,755}{5}$

13. $\frac{2,421}{3}$

14. $\frac{12,424}{6}$

15. $9\overline{)36,439}$

16. $8\overline{)489,216}$

17. $5\overline{)\$765.45}$

18. $4\overline{)\$24.52}$

19. $17,521 \div 7$

20. $2,613 \div 4$

21. $\$6.58 \div 7$

22. $\$0.93 \div 3$

Copy the chart. Write a check in the box if the dividend
is divisible by the divisor. (page 138)

		Dividend		
		23.	**24.**	**25.**
		695	1,258	26,780
Divisor	2			
	5			
	10			

Estimate. (page 140)

26. $6\overline{)435}$

27. $3\overline{)714}$

28. $8\overline{)4,729}$

29. $6\overline{)55,289}$

Solve. (pages 136–137, 142–143, 150–151, and 156–157)

30. There were 777 people entered in the Rocktown Easter-egg hunt last year. The entrants were divided into groups of 7 people each. How many groups took part in the hunt? Write the letter of the operation you would use to solve the problem.

a. multiplication
b. division

31. The Rocktown Racquet Rompers held a tennis tournament. Each day, all the tickets were sold out, for a total of 1,928 tickets for the 4-day event. How many tickets were sold each day? Write a number sentence and solve.

32. There were 358 people at the Racquet Rompers Club dinner. If 4 people could sit at each table, how many tables were needed? How many people were seated at the last table?

33. The Racquet Rompers want to send 3 members to the New York State championship. Write the letter of the question that the team does *not* need to answer before deciding who should go.

a. Who is the best player?
b. Which tennis racquets should they buy?
c. How much will the trip cost?

BONUS

An input-output chart is a table that lists a series of operations to be performed on a number. The number you start with is the input. The number you end up with is the output. What happens if you input the number 11 to the chart at the right?

The output is 66.

Use the input-output chart to find the outputs of these numbers

1. 7   **2.** 10   **3.** 12   **4.** 9

5. 4   **6.** 5   **7.** 2   **8.** 3

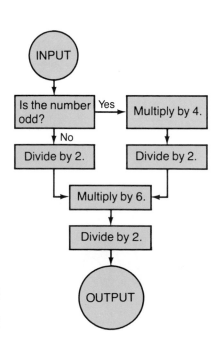

RETEACHING

Sometimes when you divide whole numbers, you need to write zeros in the quotient. Remember to multiply the divisor by the zero and write the product.

Divide $4\overline{)8,375}$.

Divide the thousands. Think: $4\overline{)8}$.	Divide the hundreds. Think: $4\overline{)3}$. Not enough hundreds. Write 0.	Divide the tens. Think: $4\overline{)37}$.	Divide the ones. Think: $4\overline{)15}$.

$$\begin{array}{r} 2 \\ 4\overline{)8,375} \\ \underline{8} \end{array}$$

$$\begin{array}{r} 2\,0 \\ 4\overline{)8,375} \\ \underline{8}\downarrow \\ 3 \\ \underline{0} \\ 3 \end{array}$$
← Write 0 in the quotient.
← Remember to write the 0.

$$\begin{array}{r} 2\,0\,9 \\ 4\overline{)8,375} \\ \underline{8} \\ 3 \\ \underline{0}\downarrow \\ 37 \\ \underline{36} \\ 15 \end{array}$$

$$\begin{array}{r} 2,093\ \text{R3} \\ 4\overline{)8,375} \\ \underline{8} \\ 3 \\ \underline{0} \\ 37 \\ \underline{36}\downarrow \\ 15 \\ \underline{12} \\ 3 \end{array}$$

Divide.

1. $6\overline{)1,254}$ 2. $7\overline{)1,456}$ 3. $5\overline{)535}$ 4. $6\overline{)5,418}$ 5. $4\overline{)3,216}$

6. $8\overline{)5,684}$ 7. $3\overline{)992}$ 8. $6\overline{)2,462}$ 9. $9\overline{)2,797}$ 10. $5\overline{)2,554}$

11. $7\overline{)35,342}$ 12. $3\overline{)91,911}$ 13. $8\overline{)56,723}$ 14. $8\overline{)56,640}$ 15. $4\overline{)28,152}$

16. $4,824 \div 6$ 17. $2,748 \div 9$ 18. $28,270 \div 7$ 19. $61,612 \div 4$

20. $81,814 \div 8$ 21. $4,593 \div 9$ 22. $18,161 \div 6$ 23. $30,632 \div 3$

162

ENRICHMENT

Short Division

You can use short division when you have a 1-digit divisor. Multiply and subtract mentally.

Find the quotient: $4\overline{)2{,}696}$

Divide the thousands. $4\overline{)2}$ Not enough thousands.

Divide the hundreds.

$4\overline{)26}$

Write the remainder next to the tens.

$$\begin{array}{r} 6 \\ 4\overline{)2{,}6\,^296} \end{array}$$

Divide the tens.

$4\overline{)29}$

Write the remainder next to the ones.

$$\begin{array}{r} 6\ 7 \\ 4\overline{)2{,}6\,^29\,^16} \end{array}$$

Divide the ones.

$4\overline{)16}$

Write the remainder if necessary.

$$\begin{array}{r} 6\ 7\ 4 \\ 4\overline{)2{,}6\,^29\,^16} \end{array}$$

The Spoke-n-Four Bicycle Company tests its new 15-speed models with four long-distance relays. The cyclists pass through mountains, deserts, and unpaved sections of road. Within each relay, each cyclist rides an equal number of miles.

Below is a mileage chart that lists the four relays. Copy the chart, and use short division to find the number of miles ridden by each cyclist.

	Relay 1	Relay 2	Relay 3	Relay 4
Total number of miles	1,107	1,024	788	935
Number of cyclists	9	8	4	5
Number of miles ridden by each cyclist	▪	▪	▪	▪

163

CUMULATIVE REVIEW

Write the letter of the correct answer.

1. 0.079×53

    a. 4.177   **b.** 4.187
    c. 41.87   **d.** not given

2. 0.05×0.08

    a. 0.004   **b.** 0.040
    c. 0.40   **d.** not given

3. 72×36.519

    a. 2,529.368   **b.** 2,629.358
    c. 2,629.378   **d.** not given

4. 0.07×3.9

    a. 0.0273   **b.** 0.273
    c. 2.73   **d.** not given

5. $\$4.50 \times 7.3$

    a. $29.75   **b.** $32.75
    c. $32.85   **d.** not given

6. Estimate: 7.12×14.7.

    a. 78   **b.** 105
    c. 200   **d.** 7,000

7. 197×373

    a. 66,981   **b.** 72,481
    c. 73,481   **d.** not given

8. $4.081 + 9.764 + 10.159$

    a. 20.004   **b.** 21.040
    c. 24.004   **d.** not given

9. Compare. Write $>$, $<$, or $=$ for ●.
0.9 ● 0.899

    a. $<$ **b.** $>$
    c. $=$ **d.** not given

10. $938,620 - 419,598$

    a. 419,021   **b.** 519,022
    c. 521,178   **d.** not given

11. $370,004 - 298,557$

    a. 71,447   **b.** 72,557
    c. 82,557   **d.** not given

12. What is the value of the blue digit?
658,932,541

    a. 500   **b.** 5,000
    c. 50,000   **d.** not given

13. Jerry and Bob saw two baseball games last month. Tickets for the first game cost $4.50 each. Tickets for the second game cost $5.75 each. How much did Jerry and Bob spend on their tickets?

    a. $18.40   **b.** $19.50
    c. $20.50   **d.** not given

14. Attendance at Game 1 of the baseball season was 4,327 people. Total attendance for the season was about 8 times that amount. About how many people attended the games for the season?

    a. 3,500   **b.** 35,000
    c. 350,000   **d.** 500,000

People do amazing things to have their names entered into record books. Think of an activity that a group of friends could do. You might try to make the world's biggest sandwich or play the world's longest game of baseball. How many people and how much time would you need to break the record?

6 DIVISION: 2-DIGIT DIVISORS

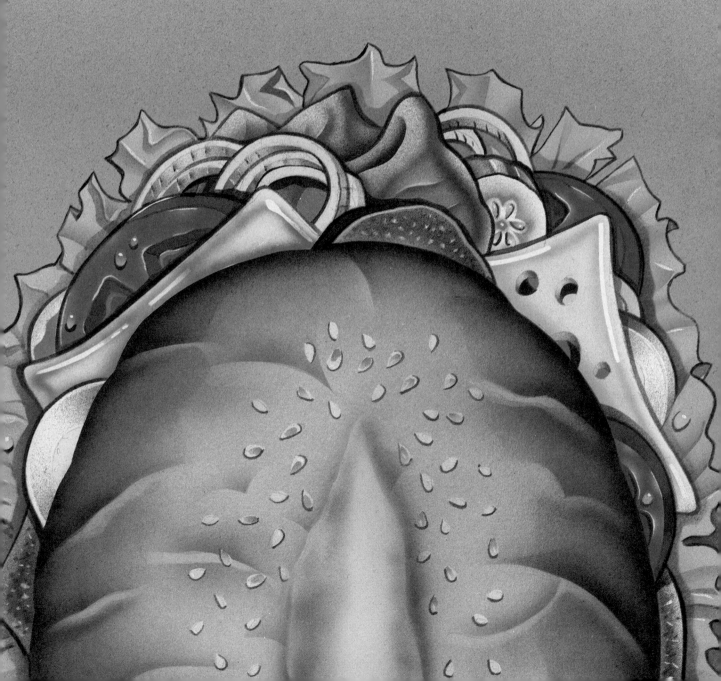

Dividing by Multiples of 10

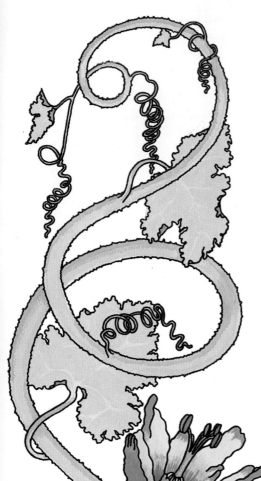

People try to become listed in record books in many ways. One way is to grow giant fruits and vegetables.

A. Marcy grows a 560-pound pumpkin. If she weighs 70 pounds, how many times as heavy as Marcy is her pumpkin?

Divide $560 \div 70$.

You can use division facts to help you divide greater numbers.

Think: $56 \div 7 = 8$.
$\qquad$ $560 \div 70 = 8$.

The pumpkin is 8 times as heavy as Marcy.

Other examples:

$45 \div 9 = 5$ $\qquad$ $30 \div 5 = 6$ $\qquad$ $63 \div 7 = 9$
$450 \div 90 = 5$ $\qquad$ $300 \div 50 = 6$ $\qquad$ $630 \div 70 = 9$

B. Patterns can help you divide by multiples of 10.

$56 \div 8 \ = 7$ $\qquad$ $36 \div 6 \ = 6$
$560 \div 80 = 7$ $\qquad$ $360 \div 60 = 6$
$5{,}600 \div 80 = 70$ $\qquad$ $3{,}600 \div 60 = 60$

Divide.

1. $10\overline{)80}$ 2. $30\overline{)60}$ 3. $20\overline{)80}$ 4. $30\overline{)90}$ 5. $20\overline{)40}$

6. $60\overline{)60}$ 7. $30\overline{)60}$ 8. $40\overline{)80}$ 9. $10\overline{)80}$ 10. $10\overline{)50}$

11. $60\overline{)180}$ 12. $90\overline{)540}$ 13. $20\overline{)180}$ 14. $30\overline{)210}$ 15. $20\overline{)120}$

16. $30\overline{)180}$ 17. $20\overline{)100}$ 18. $40\overline{)360}$ 19. $40\overline{)320}$ 20. $30\overline{)210}$

21. $40\overline{)80}$ 22. $20\overline{)60}$ 23. $30\overline{)30}$ 24. $10\overline{)40}$ 25. $40\overline{)280}$

26. $20\overline{)180}$ 27. $30\overline{)180}$ 28. $40\overline{)80}$ 29. $10\overline{)10}$ 30. $50\overline{)50}$

31. $90 \div 30$ 32. $60 \div 20$ 33. $80 \div 20$ 34. $80 \div 40$ 35. $90 \div 90$

36. $\frac{70}{70}$ 37. $\frac{90}{10}$ 38. $\frac{360}{40}$ 39. $\frac{490}{70}$ 40. $\frac{450}{50}$

Solve.

41. Marcy reads in the *Guinness Book of World Records* that the world's heaviest orange weighed 90 ounces. If this orange had been sectioned into 10 equal slices, how much would each slice have weighed?

42. A farmer whom Marcy knows grows a giant 240-pound watermelon. The average watermelon weighs about 30 pounds. How many average watermelons would equal the weight of this giant watermelon?

CHALLENGE

Multiply or divide to find ▦.

1.

×	7	▦	▦	▦
▦	28	24	▦	20
▦	21	18	12	15
8	▦	▦	▦	▦
▦	35	30	20	25

2.

×	▦	▦	60	▦	70
5	200	50	▦	150	▦
▦	▦	70	▦	210	490
3	120	▦	▦	90	▦
▦	240	60	360	180	420

Estimating Quotients

A. Macy's in New York is one of the largest department stores in the world. In one year, it uses almost 6,000 miles of twine and ribbon to wrap packages, 4,000 miles of tape, and about 7,000,000 folding boxes!

The department store in Black Hills is small, but it still uses many supplies. In 22 days, the store uses 6,975 folding boxes. On the average, how many boxes did it use every day?

Since the store probably did not use the same number of boxes each day, this is a good situation in which to estimate the quotient.

Decide on the number of digits in the quotient.

Divide the hundreds. Think: $22\overline{)69}$.
The quotient begins in the hundreds place.

It will have 3 digits.

$$22\overline{)6{,}975}$$

Think: $3 \times 22 = 66$. Write 3.

$$\begin{array}{r} 3 \\ 22\overline{)6{,}975} \end{array}$$

Write zeros for the other digits.

$$22\overline{)6{,}975} \rightarrow 300$$

You can say that the store uses about 300 boxes every day.

B. The next step is to decide how accurate your estimate is.

Think: 300 boxes are used every day. If the store uses 300 boxes each day, will it use 6,975 in 22 days?

$300 \times 22 = 6{,}600; 6{,}600 < 6{,}975$.
So, more than 300 boxes are used.
300 is an underestimate.

The store uses more than 300 folding boxes every day.

Other examples:

$21\overline{)646} \longrightarrow 30$ $21\overline{)987} \longrightarrow 40$ $32\overline{)978} \longrightarrow 30$

$22\overline{)8{,}956} \longrightarrow 400$ $75\overline{)9{,}825} \longrightarrow 100$ $37\overline{)7{,}955} \longrightarrow 200$

Write how many digits the quotient will contain.

1. $69\overline{)828}$ **2.** $13\overline{)702}$ **3.** $57\overline{)855}$ **4.** $16\overline{)848}$ **5.** $42\overline{)630}$

6. $12\overline{)1,428}$ **7.** $79\overline{)4,898}$ **8.** $17\overline{)1,751}$ **9.** $62\overline{)4,526}$ **10.** $19\overline{)2,698}$

11. $36\overline{)4,356}$ **12.** $43\overline{)688}$ **13.** $77\overline{)9,702}$ **14.** $14\overline{)686}$ **15.** $81\overline{)8,667}$

Estimate. Write the letter of the correct answer.

16. $11\overline{)297}$ **a.** 2   **b.** 20   **c.** 200

17. $29\overline{)319}$ **a.** 1   **b.** 10   **c.** 100

18. $45\overline{)3,290}$ **a.** 80   **b.** 800   **c.** 8,000

19. $71\overline{)1,988}$ **a.** 20   **b.** 200   **c.** 2,000

20. $96\overline{)8,514}$ **a.** 9   **b.** 90   **c.** 900

Estimate.

21. $22\overline{)286}$ **22.** $24\overline{)744}$ **23.** $32\overline{)982}$ **24.** $22\overline{)857}$ **25.** $91\overline{)876}$

26. $81\overline{)7,452}$ **27.** $72\overline{)1,686}$ **28.** $64\overline{)3,508}$ **29.** $42\overline{)3,159}$ **30.** $22\overline{)1,848}$

31. $23\overline{)7,383}$ **32.** $93\overline{)5,247}$ **33.** $11\overline{)2,453}$ **34.** $61\overline{)1,037}$ **35.** $82\overline{)7,532}$

Solve.

36. Janice's hardware store sells 800 boxes of nails every year. About how many boxes of nails does the store sell each month?

37. The True-Built Lumber Store sold 9,750 board feet of lumber last summer. About how much lumber was sold each day? (HINT: the store was open 78 days during the summer.)

NUMBER SENSE

It is easy to divide a number mentally by 5.
Since $10 = 5 \times 2$, you can divide the number by 10.
Then multiply by 2.

Divide. $5\overline{)600}$ Think: $600 \div 10 = 60$ $60 \times 2 = 120$.

Compute mentally.

1. $5\overline{)700}$ **2.** $5\overline{)900}$ **3.** $5\overline{)1,300}$ **4.** $5\overline{)2,300}$

PROBLEM SOLVING
Choosing a Strategy or Method

Write the strategy or method you choose. Then solve.

Checking for a Reasonable Answer
Estimation
Acting It Out
Choosing the Operation
Using a Graph
Writing a Number Sentence
Guessing and Checking
Solving Two-Step Problems/Making a Plan
Identifying Needed Information

1. Bamboo is one of the fastest-growing plants. Some kinds grow 3 feet per day. At that rate, how long would it take the bamboo to reach a height of 50 feet?

2. A human being is about 15 times bigger than a cat. Yet a cat has 14 more bones in its body than a human has. A cat has 230 bones. How many bones does a human being have?

3. It is estimated that by the age of 18, the average child in the United States has watched 17,000 hours of television. About how many years is that?

4. *Moving at a snail's pace* means a top speed of only 0.0313 mile per hour. At that rate, how many miles can a snail go in 3 hours?

5. Some snails move slowly even for snails. One kind of snail can't move faster than 0.00036 mile per hour. At that speed, how far would that kind of snail travel in 24 hours?

6. Lulu visits Mount Waialeale in Hawaii. It is the rainiest place on Earth. Rain falls about 350 days per year. Lulu wants to send some postcards of the mountain. What must she know before she can figure the cost of the postage?

7. Jeff is buying paint to protect the playground equipment. At Store A, 3 gallons of paint cost $32.97. At Store B, 5 gallons of paint cost $49.95. Which store sells paint at a lower cost? How much money per gallon will he save at the cheaper store?

Write the strategy or method you choose. Then solve.

8. What was the first year in which the winning time for the women's 200-meter run was less than 23 seconds?

9. What is the trend in running times for the women's 200-meter run?

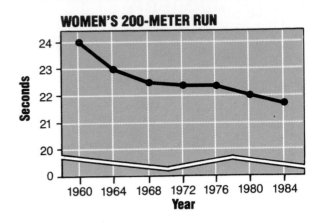

WOMEN'S 200-METER RUN

10. In 1980, an English pilot flew around the world in slightly more than 44 hours. The trip covered 23,068 miles. About how many miles per hour did the pilot travel?

11. How fast can you write? The English novelist John Creasey wrote 564 books in 42 years. About how many books did he write per year?

12. Two of the best-selling videocassettes of all time are *Raiders of the Lost Ark* and *Star Wars*. *Raiders* is the leader. More than 600,000 cassettes have been sold. That's 4 times the number of *Star Wars* cassettes. About how many Star Wars cassettes have been sold?

13. The greatest recorded snowfall took place in Silver Lake, Colorado, in 1921. During a 24-hour period, an average of 3.17 inches of snow fell per hour. About how much snow fell in 24 hours?

14. The average price of gasoline in the United States shot up from about $0.65 per gallon in 1978 to $1.35 in 1981. How much more would it have cost Ms. Stroad to fill her tank in 1981 than in 1978?

15. In 1983, cars traveled an average of 16.33 miles per gallon. A car that had a 12-gallon tank was driven 500 miles. How many times did the driver have to fill the tank to complete the trip?

16. Peter bought a poster for $5.28 including tax. He paid with a $10 bill and received the smallest possible number of coins and bills as change. Which coins and bills did he receive?

17. Look back at your answers to the problems you have solved. Are the answers reasonable? Have you answered the questions that were asked in the problems?

1-Digit Quotients

Deltiology, or collecting postcards, is the third most-popular hobby in the world. It probably began in 1869 when the first postcards were issued.

Jimmy decides to become an ace deltiologist. During the month of August, he collects 217 postcards. He collected about the same number of cards each day. On the average, how many postcards does he collect daily?

There are 31 days in August. Divide $217 \div 31$.

Divide the hundreds. Think: $31\overline{)2}$. Not enough hundreds. Divide the tens. Think: $31\overline{)21}$. Not enough tens.

Divide the ones.
Think: $31\overline{)217}$, or $3\overline{)21}$.
Estimate 7.

$$
\begin{array}{r}
7 \\
31\overline{)217} \\
217 \\
\hline
0
\end{array}
$$
Multiply.
Subtract and compare.

Check.
$$
\begin{array}{r}
31 \\
\times\ 7 \\
\hline
217
\end{array}
$$

Jimmy collects an average of 7 postcards daily.

Other examples:

$$
\begin{array}{r}
4\ \text{R1} \\
42\overline{)169} \\
168 \\
\hline
1
\end{array}
\qquad
\begin{array}{r}
3\ \text{R4} \\
21\overline{)67} \\
63 \\
\hline
4
\end{array}
\qquad
\begin{array}{r}
9\ \text{R18} \\
40\overline{)378} \\
360 \\
\hline
18
\end{array}
$$

Checkpoint Write the letter of the correct answer.

Divide.

1. $53\overline{)424}$

a. 7 R3
b. 7 R73
c. 8
d. 8 R20

2. $365 \div 88$

a. 3 R61
b. 3 R101
c. 4
d. 4 R13

3. $\frac{196}{32}$

a. 5 R36
b. 6
c. 6 R4
d. 6 R14

Math Reasoning, page H197

Divide.

1. $23\overline{)69}$ 2. $36\overline{)72}$ 3. $12\overline{)48}$ 4. $33\overline{)99}$ 5. $20\overline{)80}$

6. $31\overline{)97}$ 7. $42\overline{)94}$ 8. $56\overline{)78}$ 9. $40\overline{)85}$ 10. $24\overline{)77}$

11. $34\overline{)238}$ 12. $56\overline{)224}$ 13. $21\overline{)168}$ 14. $91\overline{)728}$ 15. $30\overline{)270}$

16. $73\overline{)528}$ 17. $68\overline{)359}$ 18. $40\overline{)198}$ 19. $84\overline{)428}$ 20. $93\overline{)567}$

21. $32\overline{)99}$ 22. $86\overline{)602}$ 23. $54\overline{)436}$ 24. $30\overline{)90}$ 25. $72\overline{)393}$

26. $67\overline{)409}$ 27. $90\overline{)368}$ 28. $43\overline{)387}$ 29. $54\overline{)498}$ 30. $91\overline{)637}$

31. $341 \div 74$ 32. $69 \div 11$ 33. $326 \div 81$ 34. $83 \div 41$ 35. $277 \div 70$

36. $93 \div 31$ 37. $139 \div 23$ 38. $254 \div 63$ 39. $560 \div 80$ 40. $39 \div 13$

41. $\frac{320}{53}$ 42. $\frac{264}{44}$ 43. $\frac{76}{35}$ 44. $\frac{49}{22}$ 45. $\frac{495}{70}$

Solve.

46. At first, Jimmy keeps his postcards in a shoe box. When his collection grows to 500 cards, he decides to buy albums. How many albums does he need if he can fit 80 postcards in each one?

47. Jimmy buys postcards at flea markets and antique shops. He counts 105 listings for antique shops in the telephone book. How long will it take him to contact every shop if he calls 35 shops each day?

48. Jimmy buys several postcard collections. He sorts through them and finds 132 duplicate European travel cards. A friend offers him 3 United States cards in exchange for each one. How many United States cards can Jimmy get?

★49. Jimmy organizes a postcard exhibit at the local historical society. One afternoon he sorts through the museum's 182 golden-age postcards. He discards 42 cards and arranges the remaining cards in groups of 35. How many groups of cards are there?

ANOTHER LOOK

Multiply.

1. 254×27 2. 723×59 3. 174×92 4. 632×12 5. 774×41

2-Digit Quotients

The same number of calories is used in 8 hours of sleep as in running for 52 minutes.

A. Pete trained to run in the New York City Marathon. He ran for a total of 1,092 hours during a year's time. If he ran the same number of hours each week, how many hours did he run each week?

There are 52 weeks in a year. Divide $52\overline{)1{,}092}$.

Divide the thousands. Think: $52\overline{)1}$. Not enough thousands.
Divide the hundreds. Think: $52\overline{)10}$. Not enough hundreds.

Divide the tens.
  Think: $52\overline{)109}$, or $5\overline{)10}$.
  Estimate 2.

$$\begin{array}{r} 2 \\ 52\overline{)1{,}092} \\ \underline{104} \\ 5 \end{array}$$

Multiply.
Subtract and compare.

Divide the ones.
  Think: $52\overline{)52}$, or $5\overline{)5}$.
  Estimate 1.

$$\begin{array}{r} 21 \\ 52\overline{)1{,}092} \\ \underline{104}\downarrow \\ 52 \\ \underline{52} \\ 0 \end{array}$$

Multiply.
Subtract and compare.

Pete ran 21 hours each week.

B. To divide amounts of money, think of the amounts as whole numbers. Remember to write the dollar sign and the cents point in the quotient.

$$\begin{array}{r} \$0.11 \\ 43\overline{)\$4.73} \\ \underline{43}\downarrow \\ 43 \\ \underline{43} \\ 0 \end{array}$$ Think: $43\overline{)473}$.

Checkpoint Write the letter of the correct answer.

1. $41\overline{)897}$

a. 21 R36
b. 21 R6
c. 21
d. 22

2. $62\overline{)5{,}273}$

a. 13 R25
b. 75 R23
c. 85 R3
d. 85

3. $71\overline{)6{,}668}$

a. 93
b. 93 R65
c. 98
d. 98 R61

Divide.

1. $39\overline{)819}$ 2. $55\overline{)605}$ 3. $22\overline{)880}$ 4. $67\overline{)\$9.38}$ 5. $56\overline{)\$8.40}$

6. $34\overline{)767}$ 7. $28\overline{)294}$ 8. $54\overline{)774}$ 9. $21\overline{)526}$ 10. $72\overline{)962}$

11. $83\overline{)6,806}$ 12. $79\overline{)4,819}$ 13. $21\overline{)1,701}$ 14. $62\overline{)\$35.96}$ 15. $71\overline{)\$60.35}$

16. $52\overline{)4,273}$ 17. $61\overline{)5,595}$ 18. $88\overline{)3,612}$ 19. $83\overline{)5,588}$ 20. $42\overline{)2,794}$

21. $36\overline{)468}$ 22. $61\overline{)5,663}$ 23. $80\overline{)5,079}$ 24. $52\overline{)1,924}$ 25. $74\overline{)969}$

26. $4,588 \div 62$ 27. $2,065 \div 64$ 28. $\$9.66 \div 23$ 29. $489 \div 34$ 30. $6,338 \div 80$

31. $\frac{2,785}{75}$ 32. $\frac{1,786}{21}$ 33. $\frac{\$32.68}{76}$ 34. $\frac{846}{35}$ 35. $\frac{332}{22}$

Solve.

36. As a warm-up for the New York City Marathon, Pete enters the Parker City Minimarathon. There are 1,035 runners that enter the race. They line up in 45 rows with an equal number of runners in each row. How many runners are there in each row?

37. The New York City Marathon begins in Staten Island. Some of the runners are brought to the starting line from Manhattan by bus. If 5,345 runners sign up for bus transportation, and each bus holds 65 people, how many buses will be needed?

★38. Greta sells marathon buttons along the route. The buttons come packed 7 dozen to a box. Each box costs $12.60. She sells the buttons for $0.75 each. What is her profit on each button?

MIDCHAPTER REVIEW

Divide.

1. $20\overline{)40}$ 2. $30\overline{)96}$ 3. $60\overline{)554}$ 4. $\frac{675}{50}$ 5. $70\overline{)772}$

6. $54\overline{)441}$ 7. $33\overline{)104}$ 8. $\frac{179}{26}$ 9. $\$6.44 \div 28$ 10. $23\overline{)184}$

11. $83\overline{)1,117}$ 12. $333 \div 17$ 13. $21\overline{)\$8.82}$ 14. $37\overline{)445}$ 15. $6,447 \div 70$

PROBLEM SOLVING
Estimation

Sometimes when you make plans, you have to provide estimated amounts.

> Penny wrote a report about the Pentagon for her class. She explained that the Pentagon is located in Washington, D.C., and is the world's largest office building. It covers 29 acres of land. It also has the world's largest private phone system. Penny's class decides to visit the Pentagon on their class trip to Washington. The bus trip will be 240 miles long. The class wants to arrive at 2:00 P.M. What is the best time to leave?

To solve this problem, you need to provide an average speed of travel. There is no way to know the exact speed of the bus, but the class can provide an estimated figure. They base their estimate on past experiences.

- The speed limit is 55 mph on highways and 35 mph on side streets. Most of the trip is made on highways.
- There may be tie-ups due to construction or traffic.
- There may be delays due to bus problems.

The class looks at several possible averages they could use: 35 mph, 40 mph, 55 mph, and 60 mph.

They decide to use 40 mph as the most reasonable estimate of how quickly they will travel.

240 mi ÷ 40 mph = 6 h
The class decides to allow 6 hours for the bus ride. They agree to leave at 8:00 A.M.—6 hours before they want to reach the Pentagon.

Some of the students have decided to go to Washington by plane instead of by bus. The students have to decide the time to board the plane and the amount of money to allow for transportation. Decide whether each question needs to be answered. If it does, decide whether an exact answer needs to be found, or whether an estimate is enough. Write *need not answer, need exact answer,* or *estimate.*

1. How much is plane fare?

2. At what time is the plane scheduled to take off and land?

3. How long is the cab ride to and from the airport?

4. How much time will it take to register at the hotel and take a bus to the Pentagon?

5. How many pounds of luggage can be taken on board?

6. How much are souvenirs at the airport?

7. How much is cab fare to and from the airport? (Cabs in both cities use a set rate, not a meter.)

8. What is the cost of a hotel room?

Use the information to answer the questions.

9. The hotel bill and 2 lunches at the Pentagon will be paid for with funds raised by the class's yard sale. About how much money will they spend on 2 lunches and 6 hotel rooms for 2 nights? Will this year's yard-sale earnings cover the expenses?

- There are 12 students in the group.
- A luncheonette near school charges $2.75 for a tuna sandwich, $3.50 for a hamburger, and $0.70 for a glass of milk.
- Hotel rooms with double occupancy—2 people to a room— range from $45 to $65 per night.
- The last four-years' yard sales earned:
  Year 1—$892.46   Year 2—$936.12
  Year 3—$1,045.10   Year 4—$902.26

PROBLEM SOLVING
Checking That the Solution Answers the Question

Pay special attention to the question that is asked in a problem. Be sure that you answer it.

Read each problem carefully.

1. In 1973, two teenagers were the first to pedal across the United States on a bicycle built for two. Their trip covered 4,837 miles. It began on February 4 and ended on June 5. About how many months did their trip take?

2. In 1973, two teenagers were the first to pedal across the United States on a bicycle built for two. Their trip covered 4,837 miles. It began on February 4 and ended on June 5. To the nearest hundred miles, about how many miles did they travel each month?

Both of these problems give you the same information, but each problem asks a different question. The answer to each question will be different also. The first problem asks a question about time; the answer is about 4 months. The second problem asks a question about distance; the answer is about 1,200 miles.

Which sentence answers the question? Write the letter of the correct answer.

1. One of the most popular songs of all time is "Yesterday" by Paul McCartney and John Lennon. During an 8-year period, 1,186 versions of the song were recorded. If the same number of versions were recorded each year, about how many versions were recorded each year?

   a. about 148 versions
   b. about 9,488 versions
   c. about 8 versions

2. Cats have an amazing homing instinct. Once, a cat left behind in California found its way back home to Oklahoma. The trip took 14 months and covered about 1,400 miles. If the cat left in September, in which month did it return to its home?

   a. 100 miles
   b. 1,200 miles
   c. November

Solve.

3. The world's largest ball of string weighs about 20,000 pounds and is almost 13 feet wide. It took the owner 28 years to gather the string. Estimate the average number of pounds of string that he collected each year.

4. Karen Stevenson won a contest by using a toothpick to eat the most baked beans in the shortest amount of time. Karen ate 2,780 beans in 30 minutes. If she could keep eating at that rate, how many beans would she eat in 1 hour?

5. The fastest-selling record in history was *John Fitzgerald Kennedy—A Memorial Album*. After it went on sale for $0.99, the record sold 4,000,000 copies in 6 days. Estimate how much money the record earned in that time.

6. The largest marching band ever assembled had 2,560 members. They marched on August 31, 1982, in a state parade in Malaysia. If there were about 30 marchers in each row, estimate how many rows there were.

7. Fifteen-year-old Patty Wilson set a world record in women's distance running in 1978. She ran 1,310 miles in 42 days. If she ran the same number of miles each day, estimate the number of miles she ran each day.

8. Otto E. Funk walked 4,165 miles from New York City to San Francisco while playing a violin. His walk began on December 14, 1928, and ended 183 days later, on June 16, 1929. For how many months did he walk?

LOGICAL REASONING

In the stamp club, 12 of the members collect U.S. stamps. 9 members collect foreign stamps. 5 of these members collect both U.S. and foreign stamps. How many members does the club have?

This Venn diagram can be used to solve the problem. There are

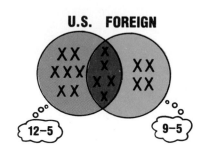

U.S.   FOREIGN

12−5   9−5

7 members who collect *only* U.S. stamps.

5 members who collect both U.S. and foreign stamps.

4 members who collect *only* foreign stamps.

So, there are 7 + 5 + 4 = 16 members in the club.

Draw Venn diagrams and complete.

1. For the track and field team,
16 members enter track events.
11 members enter field events.
6 of these enter both track and field events.

The team has ▨ members.

2. For the coin-collecting club,
13 members collect U.S. coins.
14 members collect foreign coins.
10 of these members collect both U.S. and foreign coins.

The club has ▨ members.

3. For language classes,
16 students take Spanish.
19 students take French.
4 of these students take both Spanish and French.

▨ students take Spanish and/or French.

4. At the class picnic,
19 students played soccer.
12 students played volleyball.
11 of these students played both soccer and volleyball.

▨ students played soccer and/or volleyball.

★5. For the baseball club, 14 students collect cards from the National League.
3 students collect only National League cards.
18 students belong to the club.

▨ students collect only American League cards.

★6. At the swim meet,
16 members swam in relays.
5 members swam in relays and individual events.
25 members swam in the meet.

▨ members swam only in individual events.

GROUP PROJECT

Fabulous Facts

The problem: Fabulous facts can be found in ordinary daily events. There might be a fabulous fact to be found in your home. Think about how many hours of TV you watch each day. How much TV do your classmates watch? How many hours do you and your classmates spend watching TV in a year? Use the chart to discover a fabulous fact in your classroom.

Key Questions

- If there were 30 students in your class, and you all watched the same TV program, you'd chart this as 30 hours of TV watching for that program alone—and that's for only one week. What if you watch different programs?
- How many hours of regular programming do you watch in a week? How many hours do your classmates spend?
- How much time do you spend watching sports events and spectacles in a week? your classmates?
- How many hours of movies do you and your classmates watch in a week?

	Mon.	Tues.	Wed.	Thurs.	Fri.	Sat.	Sun.
Me							
Classmates							

Find your weekly total.

Add your classmates' totals for the week to your total. Find the total hours of TV watched for the year. Is this a fabulous fact?

CHAPTER TEST

Divide. (pages 166, 172, 174, 180, and 182)

1. $20\overline{)80}$

2. $30\overline{)60}$

3. $\frac{92}{32}$

4. $\frac{277}{91}$

5. $86\overline{)586}$

6. $29\overline{)68}$

7. $27\overline{)1,134}$

8. $83\overline{)5,624}$

9. $54\overline{)2,259}$

10. $\frac{488}{13}$

11. $\frac{3,116}{19}$

12. $\frac{9,659}{87}$

13. $7,584 \div 75$

14. $3,791 \div 54$

15. $1,078 \div 37$

16. $36\overline{)7,596}$

17. $62\overline{)8,194}$

18. $\frac{29,782}{73}$

19. $\frac{26,952}{33}$

20. $46\overline{)44,436}$

21. $55\overline{)3,610}$

22. $62\overline{)43,555}$

23. $28\overline{)\$0.84}$

24. $\$95.00 \div 19$

25. $\$5.04 \div 84$

Estimate. Write the letter of the correct answer.
(page 168)

26. $12\overline{)373}$ **a.** 1   **b.** 20   **c.** 30

27. $34\overline{)1,726}$ **a.** 5   **b.** 40   **c.** 50

28. $3,816 \div 42$ **a.** 80   **b.** 90   **c.** 900

29. $\frac{8,956}{73}$ **a.** 80   **b.** 12   **c.** 100

Solve. Use the information to answer the question.
(pages 176 and 177)

30.

The ancient Indian city of Mohenjo-Daro had giant public pools. The same pools still exist today. Scientists are interested in how fast the pools could be filled by using only the waters from the river. Which questions would help the scientists find this information? For each question, is an exact answer needed, or will an estimate be enough? Write *need not answer*, *need exact answer*, or *estimate*.

a. How much water will fill the pools?

b. How old are the pools?

c. How fast does the river flow?

d. Who built each pool?

31. The American Museum of Natural History in New York City is the largest museum in the world. Fran's class holds 2 bake sales to raise money for a trip to the museum. They must pay for admission, lunch, and transportation. Estimate whether they will have enough money to pay for the trip.

- There are 18 students.
- Lunch will cost $3.75 for a full meal, or $2.50 for a hamburger.
- Admission is a suggested donation of $0.75.
- Bus fare is $0.90 one way or $1.50 round trip.
- The first bake sale earned $37.45, and the second earned $78.27.

Write the letter of the correct answer. (pages 184 and 185)

32. Each of the blocks used to build Stonehenge weighed about 50.2 tons. If 60 stones were used, how much did the entire monument weigh?

a. 1 block

b. 200.8 years

c. 3,012 tons

33. The blocks used to build the Cheops pyramid weighed 2.8 T each. Cheops is 480 ft 11 in. high. How much would the top 10 blocks weigh together?

a. 10 T

b. 28 T

c. 2.8 T

BONUS

1. $221\overline{)15,691}$

2. $349\overline{)28,765}$

3. $415\overline{)63,755}$

4. $621\overline{)21,221}$

5. $376\overline{)36,096}$

6. $31\overline{)32,348}$

RETEACHING

Sometimes you need to correct your estimate when you divide.

Divide $97\overline{)7{,}234}$.

Divide the thousands. Think: $97\overline{)7}$. Not enough thousands.
Divide the hundreds. Think: $97\overline{)72}$. Not enough hundreds.

Divide the tens.
Think: $97\overline{)723}$, or $9\overline{)72}$.
Estimate 8.

$$\begin{array}{r} 8 \\ 97\overline{)7{,}234} \\ \underline{7\,76} \end{array}$$

Multiply. Too great.
You need to correct the estimate.

Try 7.

$$\begin{array}{r} 7 \\ 97\overline{)7{,}234} \\ \underline{6\,79} \\ 44 \end{array}$$

Multiply.
Subtract and compare.

Divide the ones.
Think: $97\overline{)44}$, or $9\overline{)44}$.
Estimate 4.

$$\begin{array}{r} 74 \text{ R56} \\ 97\overline{)7{,}234} \\ \underline{6\,79} \\ 444 \\ \underline{388} \\ 56 \end{array}$$

Multiply.
Subtract and compare.
Write the remainder.

Divide.

1. $45\overline{)2{,}482}$ **2.** $33\overline{)2{,}636}$ **3.** $63\overline{)5{,}459}$ **4.** $54\overline{)1{,}511}$

5. $68\overline{)2{,}922}$ **6.** $45\overline{)1{,}484}$ **7.** $23\overline{)964}$ **8.** $33\overline{)493}$

9. $14{,}936 \div 37$ **10.** $4{,}493 \div 65$ **11.** $29{,}988 \div 73$ **12.** $2{,}035 \div 52$

13. $52{,}242 \div 83$ **14.** $5{,}432 \div 61$ **15.** $3{,}693 \div 44$ **16.** $15{,}836 \div 22$

17. $\$7.44 \div 12$ **18.** $\$10.08 \div 18$ **19.** $\$25.52 \div 29$ **20.** $\$22.56 \div 48$

$$97\overline{)723} \qquad 45\overline{)2{,}482} \qquad 97\overline{)44}$$
$$97\overline{)7{,}234} \qquad\qquad 9\overline{)72}$$

ENRICHMENT

Integers

Integers can be used to represent such things as distances above and below sea level.

A mountain is 2 km above sea level.
The height is written as $^+2$ km.
An ocean trench is 2 km below sea level.
The depth is written as $^-2$ km.
Sea level is written as 0.

Write an integer for each.

1. 4 km above sea level

2. 6° above zero

3. a 7-yard gain

4. a loss of $7.00

5. a 4-point penalty

6. a 6-foot fall

Integers can also be used to represent opposites.

EXAMPLES: 4° above zero → $^+4$ 4° below zero → $^-4$
a savings of $6.00 → $^+6$ a loss of $6.00 → $^-6$

You can show integers on a number line.

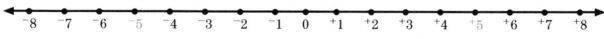

Negative integers   Positive integers

You read $^-5$ as "negative 5."   You read $^+5$ as "positive 5."
$^-5$ is 5 units to the left of 0. $^+5$ is 5 units to the right of 0.

Zero is neither a positive integer nor a negative integer.

Write an integer and its opposite for each.

7. a loss of $5.00

8. 9 feet below sea level

9. 7° above zero

10. a 5-point loss

11. 8 meters below sea level

12. a 4-foot climb

Solve.

13. A child digs a hole 5 feet deep in the sand. If 0 represents the surface, what integer would you use to represent the depth of the hole?

TECHNOLOGY

A PRINT statement is a BASIC instruction that tells the computer to print on the screen. If you are computing with the computer, you can use parentheses to tell the computer which operations to do first. The computer uses * for multiplication and / for division.

1. Write what the computer prints when you type this instruction and then press RETURN or ENTER.

   PRINT 48 / (2 * 4)

2. Write what the computer prints when you RUN this program.

   10   PRINT (6 + 6) / 6
   20   PRINT (2 + 2) / (2 − 1)
   30   PRINT 12 − (2 * 3)
   40   PRINT (5 − 3) * 4
   50   PRINT "WHO DO WE APPRECIATE"

A computer can also store the value of a number.

10   LET X = 17
20   PRINT X

When this program is RUN, the LET statement stores 17 in a **variable** called X. A variable is a location that the computer uses to store a number. If you want to see the value of a variable, you must tell the computer to print it.

3. Write what is printed when this program is RUN.

   10   LET A = 5 * 5
   20   LET B = 30 / 6
   30   PRINT B
   40   PRINT A
   50   END

You have just seen two programs that use variables X, A, and B to store numbers. You can make up your own variable names. Here are some rules for naming variables.

The name of a variable can be a single letter.
B   W   K   I
The name of a variable can be any two letters.
AP   RL   WT
The name of a variable can be one letter and one number.
V2   K9   T3
But the name of a variable cannot start with a number.
6F   14   8W

4. Write the variables that you can use to store numbers.

A	TR	P4	DD	HI
67	G5	14	H	MA
R2	D2	LF	W	P

5. Finish this program. It should find and print the difference between 15 and 9.

```
10   ▨
20   PRINT DF
```

6. Write a program that stores the product of 5 and 6 in a variable and prints it out.

Here is a program that prints the average of three numbers.

```
10   LET A = 15
20   LET B = 9
30   LET C = 6
40   LET AV = (A + B + C) / 3
50   PRINT AV
```

In line 40, the program first adds the values of A, B, and C to find 30. Then it divides 30 by 3 to find 10, and stores 10 in AV.

7. What is printed when this program is RUN?

8. Rewrite this program so that it prints the average of 22 and 8. Copy the whole program.

CUMULATIVE REVIEW

Write the letter of the correct answer.

1. $228.06 ÷ 7

   a. $31.48　　　　　b. $32.00
   c. $32.58　　　　　d. not given

2. 239 ÷ 7

   a. 34　　　　　　　b. 34 R1
   c. 35　　　　　　　d. not given

3. 53,687 ÷ 7

   a. 7,659 R4　　　　b. 7,669 R4
   c. 7,770 R1　　　　d. not given

4. 25 ÷ ■ = 1

   a. 0　　　　　　　b. 25
   c. 1　　　　　　　d. not given

5. Estimate: 18,593 ÷ 6.

   a. 1,500　　　　　b. 2,000
   c. 3,000　　　　　d. 4,000

6. Which number is divisible by 5?

   a. 45,306　　　　　b. 51,355
   c. 56,987　　　　　d. not given

7. 479 × 326

   a. 156,154　　　　b. 158,152
   c. 166,254　　　　d. not given

8. Write in standard form:
   seven and three hundred
   eighty-seven thousandths.

   a. 7.387　　　　　b. 70.387
   c. 7,387　　　　　d. not given

9. 78.42 − 63.28

   a. 14.44　　　　　b. 15.14
   c. 17.04　　　　　d. not given

10. $5,013.00 − $3,698.79

    a. $1,314.21　　　b. $1,324.51
    c. $2,111.45　　　d. not given

11. 3.7 × 0.04

    a. 1.48　　　　　b. 14.8
    c. 148　　　　　　d. not given

12. 3,619 + 4,578 + 1,255 + 543

    a. 9,755　　　　　b. 9,995
    c. 10,215　　　　　d. not given

13. A convoy of trucks must carry 150
    new cars to the showroom. If each
    truck can carry 8 cars, how many
    trucks are needed?

    a. 18　　　　　　b. 19
    c. 20　　　　　　d. not given

14. There are 279 people in the
    woodworking classes, and 31
    people in each class. Let n = the
    number of classes. Choose the
    correct number sentence to solve
    the problem.

    a. 279 × 31 = n　　b. 279 − n = 31
    c. 279 ÷ 31 = n　　d. not given

Often when you see a streak of lightning, it is followed by thunder. Have you ever noticed that you do not hear the thunder immediately? That is because sound moves more slowly than light. How could you find the distance between you and a storm?

7 DIVIDING WITH DECIMALS
Metric Measurement

Multiplying and Dividing Decimals by 10; 100; and 1,000

A. Generally, 10 centimeters of snow contain as much moisture as 1 centimeter of rain. How much snow would there have to be to equal the moisture in 1.37 centimeters of rain?

Find 10×1.37.

$1 \times 1.37 = 1.37$	To multiply by
$10 \times 1.37 = 13.7$	10, move the decimal point one place to the right.
$100 \times 1.37 = 137.$	100, move the decimal point two places to the right.
$1,000 \times 1.37 = 1,370.$	1,000, move the decimal point three places to the right.

Write zeros in the product, as needed, in order to place the decimal point correctly.

There would have to be 13.7 centimeters of snow to equal the moisture in 1.37 centimeters of rain.

B. Find $52.6 \div 10$.

$52.6 \div 1 = 52.6$	To divide by
$52.6 \div 10 = 5.26$	10, move the decimal point one place to the left.
$52.6 \div 100 = 0.526$	100, move the decimal point two places to the left.
$52.6 \div 1,000 = 0.0526$	1,000, move the decimal point three places to the left.

Write zeros in the quotient, as needed, in order to place the decimal point correctly.

Checkpoint Write the letter of the correct answer.

Multiply or divide.

1. $269.3 \div 10$ **a.** 0.2693 **b.** 2.693 **c.** 26.93 **d.** 2,693

2. $1,000 \times 0.999$ **a.** 0.00099 **b.** 99.9 **c.** 999 **d.** 990

Multiply or divide.

1. $38 \div 10$ **3.8**   **2.** $72.48 \div 100$ **3.** $251.74 \div 100$ **4.** $9{,}612.5 \div 1{,}000$

5. 10×456.2 **6.** 100×392 **7.** 100×84.87 **8.** $1{,}000 \times 7.169$

9. $5{,}348 \div 1{,}000$ **10.** $1{,}000 \times 68.412$ ★**11.** $2{,}815.4 \div 10{,}000$ ★**12.** $0.0564 \times 10{,}000$

Copy and complete each chart.

	×	10	100	1,000
13.	45.62	▓	▓	▓
14.	1.386	▓	▓	▓
15.	▓	371.5	▓	▓
16.	▓	▓	▓	9,351
17.	▓	▓	748.2	▓

	÷	10	100	1,000
18.	348.6	▓	▓	▓
19.	73.915	▓	▓	▓
20.	0.4157	▓	▓	▓
21.	▓	23.48	▓	▓
22.	▓	▓	▓	0.005682

Solve.

23. Scientists at the Mount Jackson Weather Station found that a total of 53.5 centimeters of snow had fallen at their station during a 10-week period. What was the average weekly snowfall?

24. Snowstorms in Howe usually leave 3.4 centimeters of snow on the ground. Recently 10 times the usual amount of snow fell on Howe. How much snow is that?

25. The average height of the waves at the beach in Palmville is 1.5 feet. After a recent hurricane, the waves were 10 times the average height. How high were the waves after the hurricane?

★**26.** A hurricane is 650 miles south of Miami, Florida. It is moving toward Florida at a speed of 10 miles per hour. How far will it be from Florida in 10 hours? How long will it take to reach Florida?

ANOTHER LOOK

Find the product.

1.
$$\begin{array}{r} 0.07 \\ \times\, 31.7 \\ \hline \end{array}$$

2.
$$\begin{array}{r} 0.08 \\ \times\ \ 13 \\ \hline \end{array}$$

3.
$$\begin{array}{r} 41.2 \\ \times\, 0.06 \\ \hline \end{array}$$

4.
$$\begin{array}{r} 9.8 \\ \times\, 7.4 \\ \hline \end{array}$$

5.
$$\begin{array}{r} 0.03 \\ \times\ \ 0.5 \\ \hline \end{array}$$

6. 0.42×46.6 **7.** 0.05×3.1 **8.** 0.6×8.12 **9.** 0.04×0.3

PROBLEM SOLVING
Guessing and Checking

Sometimes the best way to solve a problem is to make a guess. Read the problem to find clues. Make a guess. Check to see whether it answers the question. If not, try again.

> In a single day in 1979, a record number of inches of rain fell on Alvin, Texas. The record was a 2-digit number. The sum of its digits is 7. It is not evenly divisible by 2 or 5, and it is less than 60. What is the number?

The first two clues in the problem tell you that the missing number has two digits whose sum is 7. List each 2-digit number whose two digits add up to 7.

16   25   34   43   52   61   70

The next clue in the problem tells you that the number is not divisible by 2 or 5. So, you can eliminate 16, 25, 34, 52, and 70 because they *are* divisible by either 2 or 5. That leaves 43 and 61.

The last clue in the problem tells you that the number is less than 60.
So, your answer is 43.

Now check your answer:
- Is it a 2-digit number? yes
- Is the sum of the digits 7? yes
- Is the number *not* evenly divisible by 2 or 5? yes
- Is the number less than 60? yes

So, in a single day, a record 43 inches of rain fell on Alvin, Texas.

Solve. If you use the guess-and-check method, show your guesses and checks.

1. A snowstorm is considered a blizzard when its winds reach a certain number of miles per hour. This is a 2-digit number. The sum of the digits is 8. The difference between the digits is 2. The number is evenly divisible by 5. At how many miles per hour is a snowstorm considered a blizzard?

2. In 1982, a 2-day blizzard blanketed Denver, Colorado. The number of inches of snow that fell is a 2-digit number that is evenly divisible by 2 and 3. The sum of its digits is 6. If you multiply the number by 3, the product has a 2 in the ones place. How many inches of snow fell during the blizzard?

3. The average low temperature in Dublin, Ireland, is 1°C lower than the average low temperature in London, England. The product of the two temperatures is 72. What are the two temperatures?

4. The average high temperature in Hamburg, West Germany, is 1°F higher than the average high temperature in Copenhagen, Denmark. The sum of the two temperatures is 183. What are the two temperatures?

5. Marcia bought a thermometer for $1.79. She paid for it with 14 coins. What were they?

6. Nicholas spent $4.96 for a book about weather. He paid with 4 dollar bills and 6 coins. What were the coins?

7. In a single month in 1942, a record number of inches of rain fell on Puu Kukui, Maui, Hawaii. This is a 3-digit number. The sum of the digits is 8. The digit in the tens place is 0. The number is *not* evenly divisible by 2, 4, or 5. If you multiply the number by 3, the product is less than 1,000. What is the record number?

8. Santiago, Chile, averages 6 times more rain in October than in January. Both the number of inches of rain that fell in October and the number that fell in January were less than 1. The numbers are decimals, in tenths. The difference between them is 0.5. Their sum is less than 0.9. How much rain fell in October and in January?

9. There are 18 animals in a barnyard. Some of them are rabbits and the rest are chickens. There are 58 animal feet in the barnyard. How many chickens are there?

10. There are 24 vehicles in a parking lot. Some are cars and the rest are motorcycles. The vehicles have 60 wheels altogether. How many cars are there?

Centimeters and Millimeters

A. As many as 100 tiny ice crystals can cling together to form a snowflake. Some snowflakes can measure as long as 2 centimeters.

A **centimeter (cm)** is a metric unit of length used to measure small objects or distances. Find 2 cm on this metric ruler.

B. Each centimeter is divided into ten units called **millimeters (mm).**

> 1 centimeter (cm) = 10 millimeters (mm)

A millimeter is used to measure the length of very small objects. The thickness of a dime is about a millimeter. Measure the length of this icicle to the nearest centimeter and to the nearest millimeter.

1 mm

The icicle measures 6 centimeters to the nearest centimeter.

The icicle measures 58 millimeters to the nearest millimeter.

This measurement can also be expressed as 58 mm, or 5.8 cm.

C. You can find the distance around an object by measuring its sides and then finding the sum of the measures. Find the distance around this shape.

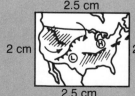

2.5 cm

2 cm   2 cm $2 + 2.5 + 2 + 2.5 = 9$

2.5 cm

The distance around the shape is 9 cm.

Measure the length of the piece of string to the nearest

1. ▪ cm   **2.** ▪ mm   **3.** ▪ cm ▪ mm

Draw a line that measures

4. 3 cm   **5.** 10 cm   **6.** 17 cm   **7.** 24 mm   **8.** 6 mm

9. 12 mm   **10.** 8.2 cm   **11.** 0.7 cm   **12.** 31.2 cm   **13.** 14.8 cm

Measure to find the distance around each shape.

14. 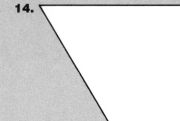   **15.**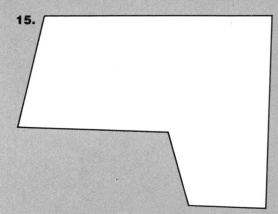

NUMBER SENSE

How long is each item? Copy and complete the table. First estimate each length to the nearest centimeter. Then measure.

Object	Estimate	Measure
A book	▪	▪
An eraser	▪	▪
Your index finger	▪	▪
A piece of chalk	▪	▪

Meters and Kilometers

A. **Meters (m)** and **kilometers (km)** are metric units of length.

1 centimeter (cm) = 10 millimeters (mm)
1 meter (m) = 100 centimeters (cm)
1 kilometer (km) = 1,000 meters (m)

The length of a baseball bat is about 1 meter.

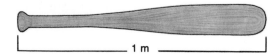

1 m

The distance a person can walk in 15 minutes is about 1 kilometer.

B. To rename larger units with smaller units, you can multiply.

2 cm = ■ mm   5 m = ■ cm   9 km = ■ m
2 × 10 = 20   5 × 100 = 500   9 × 1,000 = 9,000
2 cm = 20 mm   5 m = 500 cm   9 km = 9,000 m

C. To rename smaller units with larger units, you can divide.

7 mm = ■ cm   4 cm = ■ m   8 m = ■ km
7 ÷ 10 = 0.7   4 ÷ 100 = 0.04   8 ÷ 1,000 = 0.008
7 mm = 0.7 cm   4 cm = 0.04 m   8 m = 0.008 km

Checkpoint   Write the letter of the correct answer.

Complete.

1. 16 cm = ■ mm   **a.** 0.16   **b.** 1.6   **c.** 160   **d.** 1,600
2. 756 mm = ■ m   **a.** 0.0756   **b.** 0.756   **c.** 75.6   **d.** 756,000
3. 53 km = ■ m   **a.** 0.053   **b.** 0.53   **c.** 530   **d.** 53,000

Which unit would you use to measure?
Write *millimeter, centimeter, meter,* or *kilometer.*

1. the length of a soccer field

2. the distance to the sun

3. the length of a pen

4. the length of a thumbnail

5. the height of a tree

6. a day's car ride

7. the length of a straw

8. the length of an ant

Choose the appropriate unit. Write *millimeter,
centimeter, meter,* or *kilometer.*

9. A car travels at 55 ▧ an hour.

10. A man is 2 ▧ tall.

11. A house is 10 ▧ high.

12. A plane flies 500 ▧ in a day.

13. A paper clip is 4 ▧ long.

14. A pair of scissors is 5 ▧ long.

Complete.

15. 48 km = ▧ m

16. 0.01 m = ▧ cm

17. 27 km = ▧ m

18. 11 m = ▧ km

19. 93 cm = ▧ m

20. 38.2 m = ▧ km

21. 3 km = ▧ m

22. 47.2 m = ▧ cm

23. 209.5 km = ▧ m

24. 4,967 m = ▧ km

25. 6,035 mm = ▧ cm

26. 0.386 cm = ▧ mm

27. 0.32 m = ▧ cm

28. 7,004 m = ▧ km

29. 835.7 cm = ▧ mm

Solve. For Problem 31, use the Infobank.

30. Weather satellites orbit Earth at an altitude of 1,400,000 meters. What is this altitude in kilometers?

31. Use the information on page 418 to solve. Calculate the widths, in kilometers, of each of the three lowest bands of Earth's atmosphere.

NUMBER SENSE

Estimate to check if the quotient is reasonable.

1. $13\overline{)33.54}$ quotient 1.58

2. $6\overline{)23.34}$ quotient 3.89

3. $2\overline{)24.16}$ quotient 2.03

4. $78\overline{)79.56}$ quotient 1.02

5. $8\overline{)0.688}$ quotient 0.86

6. $34\overline{)9.01}$ quotient 0.265

PROBLEM SOLVING
Identifying Extra Information

One year, 108.3 cm of rain fell in Rio de Janeiro, Brazil. That was 28.9 centimeters less rain than fell in Brasília, Brazil's capital city. Rio de Janeiro's rainfall was 3 times as great as that of Santiago, Chile. What was the rainfall in that year in Santiago, Chile?

A problem may contain more information than you need to answer the question that is asked. If the problem you are reading seems to contain extra information, follow these steps.

1. Study the question.
   What was the rainfall in Santiago?

2. List the information in the problem.
   a. Rio de Janeiro's rainfall was 108.3 cm.
   b. Rio de Janeiro's rainfall was 28.9 cm less than that of Brasília.
   c. Rio de Janeiro's rainfall was 3 times as great as that of Santiago, Chile.

3. Cross out the information that will not help you answer the question. (Cross out *b*.)

4. Use the information that is left to solve the problem.

Solve: $108.3 \div 3 = 36.1$.

There were 36.1 centimeters of rainfall that year in Santiago, Chile.

Write the letter of the information that is not needed.

1. Bridgeport, Connecticut, lies 87 km northeast of New York City. In 1976, Hurricane Belle traveled from New York to Bridgeport in about 3 hours. In Bridgeport, its winds were recorded at 124 km per hour. At what speed did Hurricane Belle travel from New York to Bridgeport?

   a. Bridgeport is 87 km from New York City.
   b. Belle's winds were recorded at 124 km per hour.
   c. Belle took about 3 hours to reach Bridgeport from New York.

2. At 1:00 P.M., a typhoon was reported heading toward Manila at 23.3 km per hour. It hit Manila 4 hours later. At 6:00 P.M., it struck Cavite, 16 km away. How far from Manila was the typhoon at the time of the first report?

   a. The typhoon was first reported at 1:00 P.M.
   b. It was moving at 23.3 km per hour.
   c. Cavite, 16 km from Manila, was hit at 6:00 P.M.

Solve.

3. Canton, China, had 161.5 cm of rain in one year. Shanghai had 53 cm of rain in the same year. Tientsin had only 29.2 cm of rain. That year, about how many times as great as Shanghai's rainfall was Canton's?

4. The greatest amount of rain in a 30-day period fell 125 years ago in a town in India. The town was drenched with 929.99 cm of rain. To the nearest tenth of a centimeter, what was the average daily rainfall?

5. In 1982, 54.6 cm of snow fell on Springfield, Missouri. Almost 9.4 cm more than that fell on Kansas City. Marquette, Michigan, had 8 times as much snow as Springfield. How much snow fell on Marquette?

6. The greatest snowfall in one year measured 31.1 meters. It fell on Mount Rainier, Washington. Mount Rainier is 4,393 meters high. To the nearest tenth of a meter, what was the average monthly snowfall?

7. In Honolulu, Hawaii, the average wind speed is 18.8 km per hour. That is almost twice the average for Chattanooga, Tennessee. On Mount Washington, in New Hampshire, the average wind speed is 3 times as great as that in Honolulu. What is the wind speed on Mount Washington?

8. Probably the heaviest recorded rainfall fell on the island of Guadeloupe, in 1970. In one minute, 3.84 cm of rain fell. At that rate, 230.4 cm of rain would fall in one hour. How many centimeters of rain fell per second?

Liters and Milliliters

A. Maria collects rainwater in a 1-liter jug for her school science project. One rainy day, she collects 364 milliliters of water.

Milliliters (mL) and **liters (L)** are metric units of capacity.

1 liter (L) = 1,000 milliliters (mL)

A carton of milk holds about 1 liter.

An eyedropper holds about 1 milliliter.

B. To rename larger units with smaller units, you can multiply.

4 L = ▨ mL
4 × 1,000 = 4,000
4 L = 4,000 mL

C. To rename smaller units with larger units, you can divide.

8 mL = ▨ L
8 ÷ 1,000 = 0.008
8 mL = 0.008 L

Checkpoint Write the letter of the correct answer.

Complete.

1. 78 L = ▨ mL
a. 0.078
b. 780
c. 7,800
d. 78,000

2. 863 mL = ▨ L
a. 0.0863
b. 0.863
c. 8.63
d. 863,000

3. 119 L = ▨ mL
a. 0.119
b. 1.19
c. 11,900
d. 119,000

4. 47 mL = ▨ L
a. 0.0047
b. 0.047
c. 0.47
d. 47,000

Which unit would you use to measure the capacity?
Write *milliliter* or *liter*.

1. a thermos
2. a teaspoon
3. a canteen
4. a bucket
5. a thimble
6. a carton of juice
7. an aquarium
8. a test tube
9. a raindrop
10. a water-storage tank
11. a gas tank in a car
12. an oil drum
13. a water glass
14. a water trough
15. an ink bottle

Complete.

16. 6 L = ▨ mL
17. 12 L = ▨ mL
18. 0.91 L = ▨ mL
19. 3.3 L = ▨ mL
20. 27 mL = ▨ L
21. 789 mL = ▨ L
22. 15 mL = ▨ L
23. 357 mL = ▨ L
24. 0.4 L = ▨ mL
25. 269 L = ▨ mL
26. 128 mL = ▨ L
27. 4.087 L = ▨ mL
28. 1 mL = ▨ L
29. 10 L = ▨ mL
30. 3,974 mL = ▨ L
31. 23.087 L = ▨ mL
32. 578 mL = ▨ L
33. 0.56 L = ▨ mL
34. 141 L = ▨ mL
35. 0.099 L = ▨ mL
36. 2 mL = ▨ L
37. 79.002 mL = ▨ L
38. 8.091 L = ▨ mL
39. 2,965 mL = ▨ L

Solve.

40. Scientists find 6 milliliters of pollutants in a 30-liter tank of rainwater. How many milliliters of pollutants are there in each liter of rainwater?

41. After a six-month cleanup, scientists found only 2 milliliters of pollutants in a 30-liter tank of rainwater. How many milliliters of pollutants were there now in each liter? How many fewer milliliters is this than the earlier measurement?

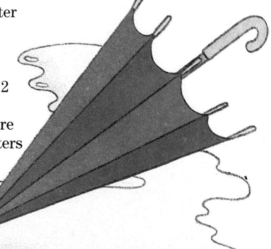

FOCUS: REASONING

Jim has a large vat full of water. He wants to measure out 1 liter of the water, but he does not have a 1-liter container. He does have a 4-liter container and a 7-liter container. How can he measure exactly 1 liter of the water?

4 L   7 L

Kilograms, Grams, and Milligrams

A. Although hailstones can be as large as softballs, most of them are the size of peas. A hailstone that had a mass of 800 grams fell on Coffeyville, Kansas, in 1970.

Kilograms (kg), **grams (g)**, and **milligrams (mg)** are metric units of mass.

> 1 gram (g) = 1,000 milligrams (mg)
> 1 kilogram (kg) = 1,000 grams (g)

A feather has a mass of about 1 gram.

An iron has a mass of about 1 kilogram.

A grain of sand has a mass of about 1 milligram.

B. To rename larger units with smaller units, you can multiply.

4 g = ▦ mg	2kg = ▦ mg	6 kg = ▦ g
4 × 1,000 = 4,000	2 × 1,000,000 = 2,000,000	6 × 1,000 = 6,000
4 g = 4,000 mg	2 kg = 2,000,000 mg	6 kg = 6,000 g

C. To rename smaller units with larger units, you can divide.

7 mg = ▦ g	9 mg = ▦ kg	8 g = ▦ kg
7 ÷ 1,000 = 0.007	9 ÷ 1,000,000 = 0.000009	8 ÷ 1,000 = 0.008
7 mg = 0.007 g	9 mg = 0.000009	8 g = 0.008 kg

Checkpoint Write the letter of the correct answer.

Complete.

1. 38 g = ▦ kg
- **a.** 0.0038
- **b.** 0.038
- **c.** 3.8
- **d.** 3,800

2. 938 mg = ▦ g
- **a.** 0.938
- **b.** 9.38
- **c.** 93,800
- **d.** 938,000

3. 78 g = ▦ mg
- **a.** 0.078
- **b.** 7.8
- **c.** 7,800
- **d.** 78,000

4. 49 kg = ▦ g
- **a.** 0.049
- **b.** 490
- **c.** 4,900
- **d.** 49,000

Which unit would you use to measure the mass? Write *milligram*, *gram*, or *kilogram*.

1. A car
2. A snowflake
3. An adult
4. A pencil
5. A flashcube
6. A book
7. An airplane
8. A bicycle
9. An apple
10. A needle
11. A chair
12. A house
13. A bee
14. A desk
15. An elephant
16. A telephone
17. An ice cube
18. A tractor

Complete.

19. 19 kg = ■ g
20. 1.2 kg = ■ g
21. 47 g = ■ mg
22. 25 kg = ■ g
23. 64 g = ■ kg
24. 35 mg = ■ g
25. 345 mg = ■ kg
26. 29.4 g = ■ kg
27. 0.01 g = ■ mg
28. 498 g = ■ kg
29. 3,732 mg = ■ kg
30. 34.3 g = ■ mg
31. 0.045 kg = ■ g
32. 1,095 mg = ■ g
33. 278 kg = ■ mg
34. 56.4 g = ■ kg
35. 89.9 kg = ■ g
36. 576 g = ■ mg
37. 780 mg = ■ kg
38. 52.9 kg = ■ g
39. 7,897 mg = ■ g
40. 8.9 kg = ■ mg
41. 0.11 g = ■ mg
42. 9 kg = ■ mg

Solve.

43. The mass of a hailstone is about 1 gram. After one hailstorm, 9.8 kg of hailstones were scraped off the roof of a building. About how many hailstones fell on the roof?

44. A scientist is flying in an airplane that, including its cargo, has a total mass of 3,500 kg. The plane releases 1,200 kg of rain-making chemicals into the clouds. How much does the plane now weigh?

CHALLENGE Patterns, Relations, and Functions

Lou uses a balance scale to find the mass of a sea gull that has been injured. He balances the scale by placing the bird in one tray, and placing known masses in the other tray. The bird's mass is 1.5 kg. Look at the table. Find at least four combinations of masses that Lou can use to find 1.5 kg.

KNOWN MASSES

Mass	Number available
1 kg	1
0.75 kg	1
0.5 kg	2
0.25 kg	4
0.01 kg or 10 g	10

PROBLEM SOLVING
Solving Multistep Problems/Making a Plan

Making a plan can help you solve complicated problems. Write down the steps you need to take to solve the problem.

> The year after the drought, Bayville had a total of 37.58 cm of rain. That is 2 times the amount of rain that fell during the drought year of 1983. In 1982, Bayville had 1.5 times the amount of rain that fell in 1983. What is the total amount of rainfall for the years 1982, 1983, and 1984?

Needed data: How much rain fell in 1983?
How much rain fell in 1982?

Plan
Step 1: Find the amount of rainfall in 1983.
Step 2: Find the amount of rainfall in 1982.
Step 3: Find the total amount of rainfall for the years 1982, 1983, and 1984.

Step 1:

amount of rainfall in 1984	÷	2	=	amount of rainfall in 1983
37.58 cm	÷	2	=	18.79 cm

Step 2:

amount of rainfall in 1983	×	1.5	=	amount of rainfall in 1982
18.79 cm	×	1.5	=	28.185 cm

Step 3:

amount of rainfall in 1982	+	amount of rainfall in 1983	+	amount of rainfall in 1984	=	total amount of rainfall
28.185 cm	+	18.79 cm	+	37.58 cm	=	84.555 cm

The total amount of rainfall was 84.555 cm.

Write the missing step or steps in the plan.

1. Bayville has a seawall 11.7 m high. Water at the seawall is usually 8.2 m deep. Before a storm, a stack of sandbags 1 m high is placed on the seawall. The water rises 4 m. Will the water go over the sandbags on the seawall?

   Step 1: Find the height of the seawall and the sandbags.
   Step 2: Find the height of the water during the storm.
   Step 3:

2. Ed and Jo leave Crewe on Friday night. There are 28 cm of snow on the ground. The average daily snowfall is 3 cm. The day Ed and Jo arrived, there were 13 cm of snow on the ground. On which day of the week did Ed and Jo arrive at Crewe?

   Step 1: Find out how much snow fell while they were there.
   Step 2:

   Step 3:

Make a plan for each problem. Solve.

3. Taking a shower instead of a bath saves 40 liters of water. Using the dishwasher instead of washing dishes by hand saves 36 liters. Each of the 5 people in a family takes 1 shower each day, and the dishwasher is run 2 times daily. How many liters of water are saved each day?

4. A weather balloon measures 5 m wide. As it rises, it expands. At a height of 27,000 m, it bursts. The balloon's width expands 0.5 m for every 1,000 m it rises. What was the width of the weather balloon just before it burst at 27,000 m?

5. A blizzard dumped 16.8 cm of snow on Bayville in 7 days. The snow fell at the same rate during the 7 days. How many centimeters of snow fell in the first 5 hours of the storm?

6. When the ice freezes to a thickness of 10 cm, officials let 50 people skate on Bayview Pond at one time. How many cm thick would the ice have to be if only 5 people wanted to skate?

★7. The water at the Bayville seawall is 8.3 m deep before a storm. The water level rises 1.4 m every hour. People add 0.8 m of sandbags to the 11.7 m wall each hour. The storm lasts 4 hours. What is the difference in height between the water level and the seawall after 4 hours?

★8. John measures how much rain has fallen during each hour of a rainstorm. In the first hour, 1.5 cm fell. In the second hour, 1.25 cm fell, and 1.0 cm fell in the third hour. If the rainfall continues to decrease at the same rate, how much rain will have fallen after 5 hours of the rainstorm?

MATH COMMUNICATION

Read this paragraph.

name of a person jerry went to the librarian and asked beginning of exact words where can i find the card catalog pause please question end of exact words

A few symbols would make these sentences easier to read and understand.

Jerry went to the librarian and asked, "Where can I find the card catalog, please?"

Symbols such as commas, capital letters, and question marks make sentences easier to read. They also save space. Math has symbols, too. You already know the symbols $>$, $+$, $\neq$, $<$, $\times$, $\div$.

1. Tell what they mean.

2. Write three other symbols, and tell what they mean.

Use these symbols to rewrite each of the following problems: $>$, $<$, $=$, $°$, $+$, $-$, $\times$, $\div$, $\$$, $\neq$.

3. 0.07 ▦ 70

4. 32 ▦ F = freezing

5. 637 ▦ 729

6. 140 ▦ 35 = 4

7.
$$\begin{array}{r} 372 \\ \underline{\blacksquare\ 6} \\ 2{,}232 \end{array}$$

8.
$$\begin{array}{r} 49 \\ \underline{\blacksquare\ 4} \\ 196 \end{array}$$

9.
$$\begin{array}{r} \$7.12 \\ \underline{+\ 3.81} \\ \blacksquare 10.93 \end{array}$$

10.
$$\begin{array}{r} 792 \\ \underline{\blacksquare 312} \\ 480 \end{array}$$

Use symbols to write a number sentence that will solve each word problem. Then solve each problem.

11. The earliest English colony in North America, Roanoke, was started 22 years before the founding of Jamestown. Jamestown was founded in 1607. When was Roanoke founded?

12. John Adams became our second President in 1797. His son John Quincy Adams became President in 1825. How many years after his father became the President did John Quincy Adams begin his presidency?

GROUP PROJECT

Planning for the Summer

The problem: This summer you want to earn enough money to buy and to do certain things. You have plenty of time, so start now! To make the most of your vacation, plan a budget for the summer. Make a chart like the one below to help you.

Key Questions

- How do you plan to earn money?
- How will you budget your money?
- What expenses will you have?
- How much money do you plan to spend on clothes?
- What kind of activities are you planning?
- How much will they cost?

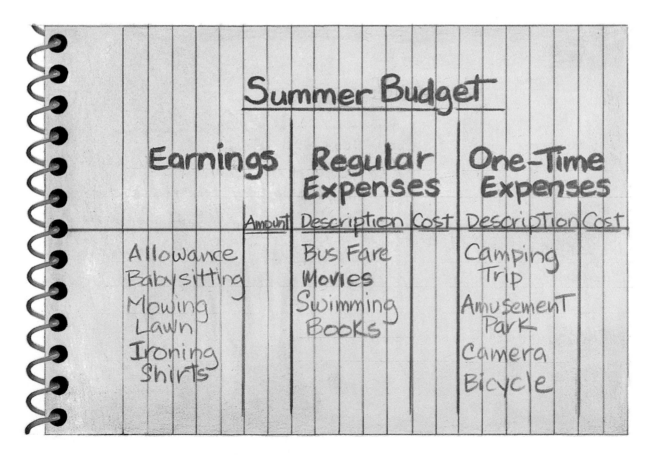

CHAPTER TEST

Multiply or divide. (page 196)

1. $77.28 \div 10$ **2.** $912.04 \div 100$ **3.** $0.105 \div 100$ **4.** $36.945 \div 1{,}000$

5. $602.046 \times 1{,}000$ **6.** $8.47 \times 1{,}000$ **7.** 35.04×100 **8.** 7.045×10

Divide. (pages 198 and 200)

9. $8\overline{)21.12}$ **10.** $17\overline{)162.52}$ **11.** $61\overline{)6.344}$ **12.** $19\overline{)14.44}$

13. $4\overline{)1.232}$ **14.** $6\overline{)0.018}$ **15.** $24\overline{)1.992}$ **16.** $67\overline{)404.01}$

17. $6\overline{)0.357}$ **18.** $95\overline{)3.8}$ **19.** $75\overline{)4.95}$ **20.** $16\overline{)24.8}$

21. $104.58 \div 45$ **22.** $116.5 \div 25$ **23.** $184.9 \div 43$

Draw a line of each length. (page 204)

24. 16 mm   **25.** 13 cm   **26.** 7.6 cm

Which unit would you use to measure? (pages 206, 210, and 212)
Write *millimeter, centimeter, meter,* or *kilometer.*

27. the length of a chalkboard   **28.** the height of a blade of grass

Write *milliliter* or *liter.*

29. the capacity of a barrel   **30.** the capacity of a thimble

Write *milligram, gram,* or *kilogram.*

31. the mass of a button   **32.** the mass of a tractor

Complete. (pages 206, 210, and 212)

33. $0.62 \text{ kg} = \blacksquare \text{ mg}$ **34.** $74 \text{ mL} = \blacksquare \text{ L}$

35. $6.2 \text{ m} = \blacksquare \text{ cm}$ **36.** $2{,}006 \text{ mL} = \blacksquare \text{ L}$

Solve. (pages 202–203, 208–209, and 214–215)

37. The forest service measured 136.75 cm of snow after a 5-day snowstorm on Razorback Mountain. During that storm, the average daily snowfall was 2.63 cm more than the previous storm's daily average. What was the average daily snowfall for the previous storm?

38. The water level at the Razorback Mountain reservoir increased by 4.76 cm after 7 days of warm temperatures and melting snow. Of that increase, 0.19 cm was due to a rainstorm. To the nearest hundredth of a centimeter, what was the average daily rise in the water level from snowmelt alone?

39. The heaviest snowstorm of the year on Razorback Mountain dropped 157.62 cm of snow in 6 hours. On the average, how much snow fell in 1 h during the first snowstorm of the year?

40. After a long drought, Razorback finally received fresh snow. The number of centimeters of snow that fell is a 2-digit number. Both digits are prime numbers. Their sum is 6. If you multiply the second digit by 4, the product has 0 in the ones place. How many centimeters of snow did Razorback Mountain receive?

BONUS

Choose the better price.

1. 5 onions for $1.95 or 3 for $1.47

2. 6 kiwi fruits for $2.10 or 7 for $2.24

3. 4 tires for $210.40 or 5 for $265.50

RETEACHING

A. Sometimes when you divide decimals, you have to write zeros in the quotient or in the dividend.

Find 15.35 ÷ 5.

Divide the whole number.

$$\begin{array}{r} 3 \\ 5\overline{)15.35} \\ \underline{15} \end{array}$$

Place the decimal point. Divide the tenths.

$$\begin{array}{r} 3.0 \\ 5\overline{)15.35} \\ \underline{15} \\ 3 \\ \underline{0} \\ 3 \end{array}$$ Write 0. Write 0.

Divide the hundredths.

$$\begin{array}{r} 3.07 \\ 5\overline{)15.35} \\ \underline{15} \\ 3 \\ \underline{0} \\ 35 \\ \underline{35} \end{array}$$

B. Find the quotient of 48.24 ÷ 5

Divide the whole number.

$$\begin{array}{r} 9 \\ 5\overline{)48.24} \\ \underline{45} \\ 3 \end{array}$$

Place the decimal point. Divide the tenths.

$$\begin{array}{r} 9.6 \\ 5\overline{)48.24} \\ \underline{45} \\ 3\,2 \\ \underline{3\,0} \\ 2 \end{array}$$

Divide the hundredths.

$$\begin{array}{r} 9.64 \\ 5\overline{)48.24} \\ \underline{45} \\ 3\,2 \\ \underline{3\,0} \\ 24 \\ \underline{20} \\ 4 \end{array}$$

Write a 0 in the dividend. Divide the thousandths.

$$\begin{array}{r} 9.648 \\ 5\overline{)48.240} \\ \underline{45} \\ 3\,2 \\ \underline{3\,0} \\ 24 \\ \underline{20} \\ 40 \\ \underline{40} \end{array}$$ Write 0.

Divide.

1. $8\overline{)0.74}$ **2.** $8\overline{)3.24}$ **3.** $7\overline{)42.14}$ **4.** $8\overline{)32.16}$ **5.** $4\overline{)44.36}$

6. $55\overline{)4.62}$ **7.** $40\overline{)283.6}$ **8.** $45\overline{)9.18}$ **9.** $42\overline{)3.15}$ **10.** $19\overline{)77.14}$

11. $5\overline{)47.33}$ **12.** $8\overline{)25.16}$ **13.** $4\overline{)83.14}$ **14.** $2\overline{)14.33}$ **15.** $5\overline{)17.2}$

16. 4.62 ÷ 55 **17.** 283.6 ÷ 40 **18.** 1.8 ÷ 12 **19.** 34.2 ÷ 90

20. 15.15 ÷ 5 **21.** 6.49 ÷ 2 **22.** 116.5 ÷ 25 **23.** 83.42 ÷ 4

ENRICHMENT

Order of Operations

When you solve a number sentence, you need to perform the operations in a certain order to get the correct answer.

From left to right, you multiply and divide, then add and subtract.

Find $10 - 2 \times 3$.
Here are two solutions.   Which is correct?

$$\underline{10 - 2} \times 3$$
$$\quad 8 \quad \times 3$$
$$\qquad 24$$

$$10 - \underline{2 \times 3}$$
$$10 - \quad 6$$
$$\qquad 4$$

Solved by subtracting and then multiplying

Solved by multiplying and then subtracting

The second solution is correct because it follows the rule: First multiply and divide; then add and subtract.

When parentheses are used in a number sentence, do the operations inside the parentheses first. Then do the operations outside, from left to right.

$$(5 + 7) \times 3 \qquad 8 \div (2 + 2)$$
$$12 \times 3 \qquad 8 \div 4$$
$$36 \qquad\qquad 2$$

Complete. Use the order of operations.

1. $7 \times 4 + 8$

2. $56 - 5 \times 8$

3. $14 + 8 \div 4$

4. $36 \div 6 - 4$

5. $22 + (8 \times 5)$

6. $8 - (4 + 2)$

7. $(46 - 22) \times 33$

8. $(45 + 9) \div 3$

9. $(32 + 48) \times 18$

10. $7 \times 8 + (3 + 2)$

11. $84 + (360 \div 15)$

12. $(6 + 3) \times (4 + 4)$

Work backwards from the answer and draw parentheses to show which operation was done first.

EXAMPLE: $4 \times 3 + 2 = 20 \longrightarrow 4 \times (3 + 2) = 20$, but $(4 \times 3) + 2 \neq 20$

13. $8 \times 6 - 4 = 16$

14. $36 + 9 \div 5 = 9$

15. $12 \div 2 \times 9 = 54$

16. $6 + 3 \times 7 = 63$

17. $6 + 3 \times 7 = 27$

18. $81 \div 9 + 9 = 18$

TECHNOLOGY

Here is a BASIC program that renames numbers of days as weeks.

```
10   LET D = 21
20   LET W = D / 7
30   PRINT D; " DAYS EQUAL"
40   PRINT W; " WEEKS"
```

1. What is printed when this program is RUN?

2. Write the line you would change to make the computer print this.

35 DAYS EQUAL
5 WEEKS

3. Write a program that stores 72 in a variable for hours. Have the computer compute the number of days and print this.

72 HOURS EQUAL
3 DAYS

Here is a short program that prints the sum of 7 and 9.

```
10   LET N1 = 7
20   LET N2 = 9
30   LET S = N1 + N2
40   PRINT S
```

When you RUN this program, it will print the number 16 on the screen. You might want to have the computer tell you which computation it is performing. To do this, add these extra lines to your program.

Instruction	The computer prints this.
40 PRINT "THE SUM OF"	THE SUM OF
50 PRINT N1	7
60 PRINT "AND"	AND
70 PRINT N2	9
80 PRINT "IS"	IS
90 PRINT S	16

Look closely at line 40 below. There are three pairs of quotation marks. The computer will print the letters between each set of quotation marks. Anything else must be a variable, so the computer prints the value of that variable. Here's the whole program.

```
10   LET N1 = 7
20   LET N2 = 9
30   LET S = N1 + N2
40   PRINT "THE SUM OF "; N1; " AND "; N2; " IS "; S
```

4. Write the line you would change to make the computer print this.
THE SUM OF 18 AND 9 IS 27

5. Write the line you would change to make the computer print this.
18 PLUS 9 EQUALS 27

6. Write a program that computes the quotient of 72 divided by 9 and that prints this.
72 DIVIDED BY 9 IS 8

You can use parentheses in a LET statement the same way you did in the PRINT statement. The computer will compute inside the parentheses first and then perform the rest of the calculations.

7. What is printed when this program is RUN?

```
10   LET N = 3 * (7 − 3)
20   PRINT "THE NUMBER IS "; N
```

You can have more than one set of parentheses in an expression.

```
10   LET N = (4 − 2) * (8 + 2)
20   PRINT "THE NUMBER IS "; N
```

The computer computes in the first set of parentheses and then in the second set of parentheses. At the very end, it multiplies 2 * 10, and stores the answer, 20, in N.

8. What is printed when you RUN this program?

```
10   LET F = (7 − 1) − (5 − 2)
20   PRINT "MY DOG HAS "; F; " FLEAS"
```

CUMULATIVE REVIEW

Write the letter of the correct answer.

1. $47\overline{)497}$

   a. 10   **b.** 10 R15
   c. 10 R27   **d.** not given

2. $6,744 \div 72$

   a. 94 R6   **b.** 98 R5
   c. 101 R1   **d.** not given

3. $9,943 \div 33$

   a. 298 R8   **b.** 301 R10
   c. 310   **d.** not given

4. $20\overline{)200}$

   a. 10   **b.** 20
   c. 100   **d.** not given

5. $\$76.80 \div 32$

   a. $2.40   **b.** $2.50
   c. $2.75   **d.** not given

6. $54\overline{)6,898}$

   a. 124 R2   **b.** 127 R40
   c. 127 R60   **d.** not given

7. 0.5×6.85

   a. 3.425   **b.** 3.445
   c. 4.755   **d.** not given

8. Estimate 37×522.

   a. 2,000   **b.** 3,000
   c. 20,000   **d.** 30,000

9. Write in standard form: 348 billion, 956 million, 729 thousand, 889.

   a. 34,895,672,989
   b. 348,956,729,889,000
   c. 348,956,729,889
   d. not given

10. Compare. Write $>$, $<$, or $=$ for ●.
0.26 ● 0.260

   a. $>$ **b.** $<$
   c. $=$ **d.** not given

11. 358×792

   a. 63,445   **b.** 238,436
   c. 283,426   **d.** not given

12. Michael's teacher is 3 times as old as Michael. Michael is 12 years old. Let n = the age of Michael's teacher. Choose the correct number sentence for solving the problem.

   a. $3 \times n = 12$ **b.** $3 + n = 12$
   c. $12 \times 3 = n$ **d.** not given

13. Dana's grandfather is 78 years old. He is 6 times as old as Dana. How old is Dana?

   a. 12   **b.** 13
   c. 14   **d.** not given

14. Forty students are going to a museum in vans. Each van can hold at most 11 students. How many vans are needed?

   a. 3 vans   **b.** $3\frac{7}{11}$ vans
   c. 4 vans   **d.** 7 vans

Could you describe a watermelon
to someone who has never seen
one? Try.

8 NUMBER THEORY, FRACTIONS

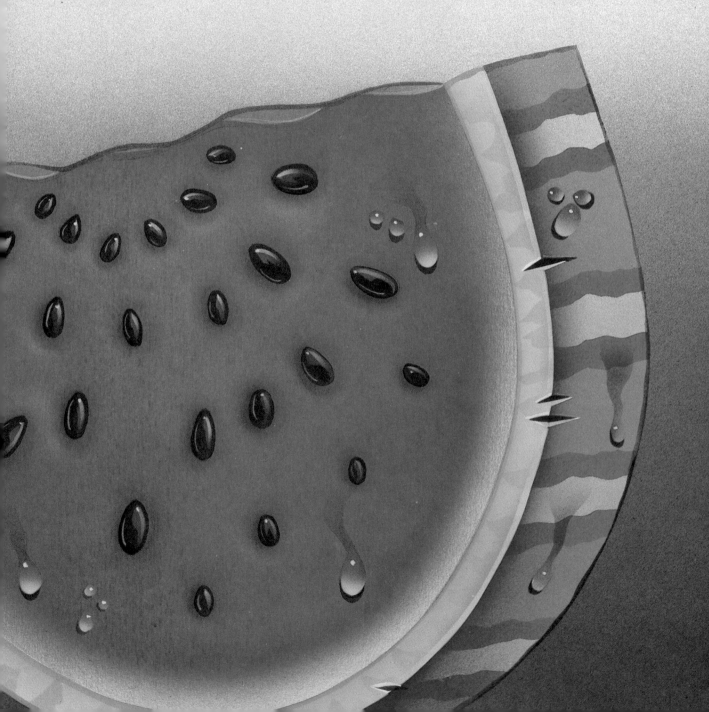

Least Common Multiples

A. Sometimes you may discuss with a friend what the two of you have in common. Numbers also may have characteristics that are common. You can use what you know about numbers to explore what they have in common.

Step 1: You and a partner each pick a different number between 2 and 9. Mentally multiply the number you chose by each of the numbers from 0 through 10. Record the products. These products are some of the **multiples** of the number that you have chosen.

Step 2: Compare the lists of multiples. What numbers do they have in common? Circle them. These are the **common multiples** of both numbers. What is the least number, other than 0, that has been circled? This is the **least common multiple** of the numbers.

Step 3: Choose other numbers and repeat what you have done. Try to find the least common multiple of three numbers.

Thinking as a Team

1. What number is a common multiple of any set of numbers?

2. What have you learned about how to find the least common multiple of a set of numbers? List your conclusions and discuss them with the class.

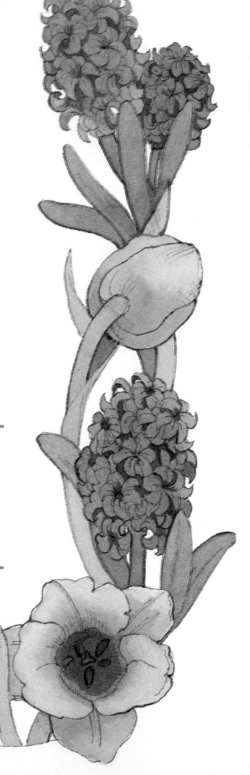

B. You can apply what you have discovered to the world around you.

Working as a Team

Your team is designing a display of potted plants for a local Spring Festival. Flower pots come in packs of 3. Tulip bulbs are sold in packs of 4 and hyacinth bulbs are sold in packs of 6.

Discuss with your team the design of your display.

You will need to think about these questions:

• What is the least number of packs of each that you must buy so that there will be one tulip and one hyacinth in each pot?

• How many tulips will you have? How many hyacinths? How many pots?

• What will the design be?

Discuss with the class how you solved this problem. Can you think of another way to solve the problem? How does this method compare with your original method?

Greatest Common Factor

A. You know that numbers can have common multiples. Work with a partner to explore other characteristics that numbers have in common.

Step 1: You and your partner should each write the numbers 0 through 9 on separate index cards. Shuffle the cards and place them in a pile on your desk. Pick two cards from the pile. Use them to form a 2-digit number. Then list all the numbers that have the number you formed as a multiple. These are the **factors** of the number you formed. Your partner should pick two cards to form a different number and list its factors.

Step 2: Compare the lists of factors. What numbers do they have in common? Circle them. These are the common factors of both numbers. What is the greatest number circled? This is the **greatest common factor** of the numbers.

Step 3: Form another number and repeat what you did in Steps 1 and 2. Try to find the greatest common factor of three numbers.

Thinking as a Team

1. How did you find the factors of each number that you formed? Discuss your method with the class. What other ways could you use to find the factors of a number?

2. What number is a common factor of any set of numbers?

3. Why is zero never a common factor?

4. What have you learned about finding the greatest common factor of a set of numbers? List your conclusions and discuss them with the class.

B. You can apply what you have discovered to the world around you.

Working as a Team

After completing the display of potted plants for the Spring Festival, your team helps make bouquets of flowers. You have

36 petunias	48 carnations
42 daffodils	24 marigolds

You want to use all of your petunias and carnations to make as many identical bouquets as possible. How many petunias and how many carnations will you put in each bouquet? How many bouquets will you make?

• How did you decide how many of each kind of flower to use?

• What difficulties did you have in solving this problem? Discuss them with the class.

• Compare your method to those of other teams. What other methods were used to solve the problem?

1. What is the greatest number of identical bouquets that you can make using any 2 kinds of flowers on the list? Which flowers will you use? How many of each kind will be in each bouquet?

2. What is the greatest number of identical bouquets that you can make using any 3 kinds of flowers. Which flowers will you use? How many flowers of each kind will you use in each bouquet?

3. What is the greatest number of identical bouquets that you can make using all of the flowers? How many flowers of each kind will you use in each bouquet?

Record your answers and discuss how you found them with the class.

Prime and Composite Numbers

A. A **prime number** has exactly two factors: itself and 1.

List all the factors of 19. $1 \times 19 = 19$

The factors of 19 are 1 and 19.
19 is a prime number.

Some other prime numbers are 2, 3, 5, 29, and 61.

B. A **composite number** has more than two factors.

List all the factors of 20. 1×20; 2×10; 4×5

The factors of 20 are 1, 2, 4, 5, 10, and 20.

20 is a composite number.

> Since it only has one factor, 1 is neither composite nor prime.

C. A composite number can be shown as the product of prime factors. This is called the **prime factorization** of the number. You can use a factor tree to help you write the prime factorization of 36.

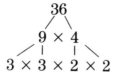

$$36$$
$$9 \times 4$$
$$3 \times 3 \times 2 \times 2$$

The prime factorization of 36 is $2 \times 2 \times 3 \times 3$.

Here are two more factor trees for 36.

$$36$$
$$6 \times 6$$
$$3 \times 2 \times 2 \times 3$$

$$36$$
$$3 \times 12$$
$$3 \times 4 \times 3$$
$$3 \times 2 \times 2 \times 3$$

Notice that the prime factors of 36 are always the same. The order of the factors is not important.

230

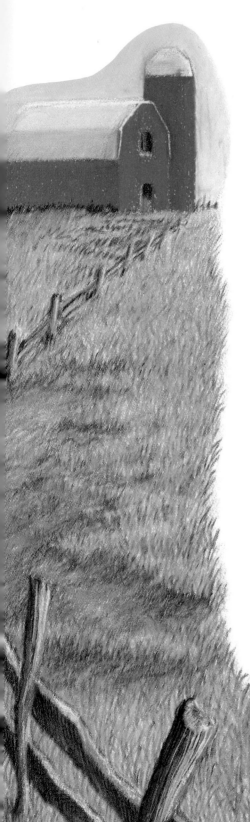

List all the factors of each number.

1. 8 **2.** 9 **3.** 14 **4.** 28 **5.** 32 **6.** 27

Write *prime* or *composite* to describe each number.

7. 5 **8.** 23 **9.** 21 **10.** 15 **11.** 81 **12.** 49

13. 93 **14.** 29 **15.** 53 **16.** 42 **17.** 97 **18.** 103

Copy and complete each factor tree.

19. 20
2 × 10
2 × ■ × ■

20. 24
6 × 4
2 × ■ × ■ × ■

21. 18
2 × ■
■ × ■ × ■

Draw a factor tree to write the prime factorization of each number.

22. 27 **23.** 32 **24.** 48 **25.** 45 **26.** 53

27. 81 **28.** 125 **29.** 132 **30.** 115 **31.** 113

CHALLENGE

Here is a way to find all the prime numbers between 1 and 50.

Copy the chart of the numbers 1 through 50.

Step 1: Cross out 1.
Step 2: Circle all the numbers that are multiples of

2 except 2.   3 except 3.   5 except 5.   7 except 7.

1. Are the circled numbers prime or composite?

2. Are the uncircled numbers prime or composite?

3. Write all the prime numbers between 1 and 50.

X	2	3	4	5	6	7	8	9	10
11	12	13	14	15	16	17	18	19	20
21	22	23	24	25	26	27	28	29	30
31	32	33	34	35	36	37	38	39	40
41	42	43	44	45	46	47	48	49	50

Fractions

A. Grain is stored in the 10 compartments of a cargo ship. If 4 compartments are filled with wheat, what fraction of the ship's compartments are filled?

You can write a fraction to show the part of the ship that has been filled.

numerator ⟶ $\underline{4}$ ⟵ number of parts filled
denominator ⟶ 10 ⟵ total number of parts

Read: four tenths.   Write: $\frac{4}{10}$, or 0.4.

Of the cargo compartments, $\frac{4}{10}$ are filled.

B. You can use a fraction to describe parts of a set. What fraction of the set is circles?

○ ○ ○ □ □ □ △ △ △

$\underline{3}$ ⟵ number of circles
9 ⟵ total number of shapes

Read: three ninths   **Write:** $\frac{3}{9}$.

C. You can use a number line to help you estimate the value of a fraction.

This number line shows $\frac{1}{8}$, $\frac{5}{8}$, and $\frac{7}{8}$.

Each fraction is between 0 and 1 on the number line.

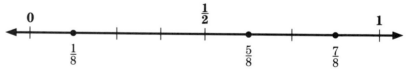

$\frac{1}{8}$ is close to 0. $\frac{5}{8}$ is close to $\frac{1}{2}$. $\frac{7}{8}$ is close to 1.

Checkpoint Write the letter of the correct answer.

What fraction of each drawing is shaded?

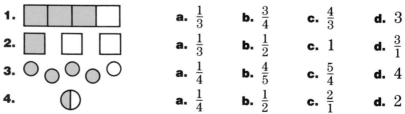

1.   **a.** $\frac{1}{3}$ **b.** $\frac{3}{4}$ **c.** $\frac{4}{3}$ **d.** 3

2.   **a.** $\frac{1}{3}$ **b.** $\frac{1}{2}$ **c.** 1   **d.** $\frac{3}{1}$

3.   **a.** $\frac{1}{4}$ **b.** $\frac{4}{5}$ **c.** $\frac{5}{4}$ **d.** 4

4.   **a.** $\frac{1}{4}$ **b.** $\frac{1}{2}$ **c.** $\frac{2}{1}$ **d.** 2

Write the fraction for the part that is shaded.

1.
2.
3.
4. ⬤ ○ ○
   ⬤ ○ ○
   ○ ○ ○
5. ⬤⬤⬤⬤⬤
   ⬤⬤⬤○○

Write the fraction.

6. one fourth

7. three fifths

8. seven twelfths

9. six sevenths

10. five ninths

11. two eighths

Write whether the fraction is close to *0*, close to *1*, or close to $\frac{1}{2}$.

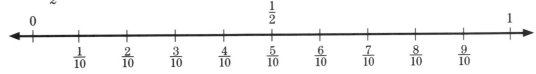

0     $\frac{1}{10}$ $\frac{2}{10}$ $\frac{3}{10}$ $\frac{4}{10}$ $\frac{5}{10}$ $\frac{6}{10}$ $\frac{7}{10}$ $\frac{8}{10}$ $\frac{9}{10}$ 1 $\frac{1}{2}$

12. $\frac{1}{10}$

13. $\frac{9}{10}$

14. $\frac{6}{10}$

15. $\frac{4}{10}$

16. $\frac{2}{10}$

17. $\frac{8}{10}$

Write the decimal.

18. $\frac{3}{10}$

19. $\frac{7}{10}$

20. $\frac{1}{10}$

21. $\frac{5}{10}$

22. $\frac{4}{10}$

23. $\frac{2}{10}$

24. $\frac{6}{10}$

25. $\frac{5}{10}$

26. $\frac{8}{10}$

27. $\frac{9}{10}$

★**28.** $\frac{10}{10}$

Solve.

29. Many years ago, farmers did not have machines to help them harvest their crops. They could only harvest 2 acres per day. If Mr. Pitts had a 12-acre field, what fraction of it could be harvested in one day?

★**30.** Jason had to plant two 40-acre fields. After one day, Jason had planted 11 acres of corn and 5 acres of squash. What fraction of his farm had Jason planted with corn and squash?

FOCUS: REASONING

Alan, Brad, and Clark are brothers. Alan and the oldest brother share a set of bunk beds. Brad is younger than Alan. Who shares the bunk beds with Alan?

PROBLEM SOLVING
Choosing the Operation

Remember that the wording of a problem and the
question it asks can give you hints about how to solve
the problem. You can use these hints to help you
choose the best operation to use.

Hints:

If you know	and you want to find	you can
• how many there are in two or more groups	how many there are in all	add.
• how many there are in one group • how many join it	the total number	add.
• how many there are in one group • the number taken away	how many are left	subtract.
• how many there are in each of two groups	how much larger one group is than the other	subtract to compare.
• how many there are in one group • how many there are in part of the group	how many there are in the remaining part of the group	subtract.
• the number in each group is the same • how many there are in each group • how many groups there are	how many there are in all	multiply.
• the number in each group is the same • how many there are in all • how many there are in each group	how many groups	divide.
• the number in each group is the same • how many there are in all • how many groups there are	how many in each group	divide.

Choose the best operation to solve each problem. Write the letter of the correct answer. Explain your choice.

1. The Dysons had 99 cattle in 1979. In 1984, they had 186 cattle. How many cattle did the Dysons acquire between 1979 and 1984?

   a. addition
   b. subtraction
   c. multiplication
   d. division

2. The Dysons' cattle eat 33,480 pounds of feed in 30 days. How much feed do they eat in 1 day?

   a. addition
   b. subtraction
   c. multiplication
   d. division

Solve.

3. The Dysons farm 75 acres of cornfields. If each acre yields 155.5 bushels of corn, how many bushels of corn do the Dysons harvest?

4. In 1977, Tom Dyson drove his tractor 7,181 miles. In 1978, he drove it 8,473 miles. He drove the tractor 7,811 miles in 1979, and in 1980, he drove 8,374 miles. Compare and order the mileages from the least to the greatest.

5. The Dyson's trailer carries 85 bales of hay. Each bale weighs 60.7 pounds. What is the total weight of the bales in the trailer?

6. The tractor cost the Dysons $45,000. The harvester cost $72,550. Estimate how much more was spent on the harvester than on the tractor.

7. When they first began to farm, the Dysons harvested 80 bushels of corn per day by hand. Using machines, they can harvest 3,500 bushels per day. By how much has their harvest production increased?

8. Last month, Tom drove the tractor for 27 days. After that, he repaired an axle, and noted that he had driven 3,294 miles that month. On the average, how many miles did Tom drive the tractor each day last month?

★9. In October, the Dysons sold 75 bushels of corn for $221.25. In November, they sold 75 bushels for $237.75. For how much less did the Dysons sell each bushel of corn in October?

★10. The Dysons have just sold some of their corn to a food company for $3.20 per bushel. If the price of corn falls to $2.80 per bushel next month, how much less will the Dysons receive for 10,000 bushels?

Equivalent Fractions

A. Ed divided his garden into 6 equal parts. He planted $\frac{1}{3}$ of the garden with string beans. How many sixths of the garden have string beans? You can draw a picture to find the answer.

$\frac{1}{6}$	$\frac{1}{6}$	$\frac{1}{6}$	$\frac{1}{6}$	$\frac{1}{6}$	$\frac{1}{6}$

$$\underbrace{\qquad}_{\frac{1}{3}} \quad \underbrace{\qquad}_{\frac{1}{3}} \quad \underbrace{\qquad}_{\frac{1}{3}}$$

Of the garden, $\frac{2}{6}$ is string beans.

$\frac{1}{3}$ and $\frac{2}{6}$ are **equivalent fractions.** They name the same part.

B. You can find equivalent fractions by multiplying both the numerator and the denominator of a fraction by the same number. That number cannot be zero.

$$\frac{1}{3} = \frac{1 \times 2}{3 \times 2} = \frac{2}{6} \qquad \frac{1 \times 3}{3 \times 3} = \frac{3}{9} \qquad \frac{1 \times 4}{3 \times 4} = \frac{4}{12}$$

So, $\frac{1}{3} = \frac{2}{6} = \frac{3}{9} = \frac{4}{12}$.

C. Complete.

$$\frac{2}{4} = \frac{\blacksquare}{8}$$

Think: $4 \times 2 = 8$.   So, $\frac{2 \times 2}{4 \times 2} = \frac{4}{8}$.

Checkpoint Write the letter of the correct answer.

Complete.

1. $\frac{3}{4} = \frac{\blacksquare}{8}$

a. 2
b. 3
c. 6
d. 7

2. $\frac{2}{3} = \frac{\blacksquare}{12}$

a. 2
b. 4
c. 6
d. 8

3. $\frac{3}{5} = \frac{6}{\blacksquare}$

a. 2
b. 5
c. 8
d. 10

Complete.

1. $\frac{1}{5} = \frac{1 \times 2}{5 \times 2} = \frac{\blacksquare}{\blacksquare}$

2. $\frac{1}{3} = \frac{1 \times 3}{3 \times 3} = \frac{\blacksquare}{\blacksquare}$

3. $\frac{1}{6} = \frac{1 \times 2}{6 \times 2} = \frac{\blacksquare}{\blacksquare}$

Write the next three equivalent fractions.

4. $\frac{3}{4}, \frac{6}{8}, \frac{9}{12}, \frac{\blacksquare}{\blacksquare}, \frac{\blacksquare}{\blacksquare}, \frac{\blacksquare}{\blacksquare}$

5. $\frac{1}{3}, \frac{2}{6}, \frac{3}{9}, \frac{\blacksquare}{\blacksquare}, \frac{\blacksquare}{\blacksquare}, \frac{\blacksquare}{\blacksquare}$

6. $\frac{1}{4}, \frac{2}{8}, \frac{3}{12}, \frac{\blacksquare}{\blacksquare}, \frac{\blacksquare}{\blacksquare}, \frac{\blacksquare}{\blacksquare}$

7. $\frac{2}{5}, \frac{4}{10}, \frac{6}{15}, \frac{\blacksquare}{\blacksquare}, \frac{\blacksquare}{\blacksquare}, \frac{\blacksquare}{\blacksquare}$

Complete.

8. $\frac{1}{10} = \frac{\blacksquare}{20}$

9. $\frac{1}{10} = \frac{\blacksquare}{30}$

10. $\frac{2}{4} = \frac{\blacksquare}{8}$

11. $\frac{1}{4} = \frac{\blacksquare}{12}$

12. $\frac{4}{8} = \frac{\blacksquare}{16}$

13. $\frac{4}{5} = \frac{\blacksquare}{10}$

14. $\frac{3}{6} = \frac{\blacksquare}{12}$

15. $\frac{3}{6} = \frac{\blacksquare}{18}$

16. $\frac{1}{5} = \frac{\blacksquare}{10}$

17. $\frac{2}{5} = \frac{\blacksquare}{10}$

18. $\frac{1}{5} = \frac{\blacksquare}{15}$

19. $\frac{5}{9} = \frac{10}{\blacksquare}$

20. $\frac{3}{4} = \frac{9}{\blacksquare}$

21. $\frac{6}{10} = \frac{12}{\blacksquare}$

★22. $\frac{2}{8} = \frac{1}{\blacksquare}$

For related activities see
Connecting Math Ideas, page 411.

23. Pat spent the weekend planting corn. She planted $\frac{1}{7}$ of it Saturday and $\frac{4}{28}$ of it Sunday. Did she plant the same amount of corn each day?

★24. Sally spent $\frac{1}{4}$ of a day planting tomatoes. Melanie spent 8 hours tending her garden. A day is 24 hours long. Who spent more time working in the garden?

CALCULATOR

You can use a calculator to find equivalent fractions.

$\frac{3}{25} = \frac{\blacksquare}{125}$

Divide the denominators:

Multiply the quotient by the numerator:

$\boxed{5} \ \boxed{\times} \ \boxed{3} \ \boxed{=} \ \boxed{15}$

So, $\frac{3}{25} = \frac{15}{125}$.

Use your calculator to find equivalent fractions.

1. $\frac{5}{9} = \frac{\blacksquare}{162}$

2. $\frac{4}{7} = \frac{\blacksquare}{105}$

3. $\frac{3}{18} = \frac{\blacksquare}{54}$

4. $\frac{5}{12} = \frac{\blacksquare}{144}$

Simplifying Fractions/Acting It Out

A. The Brennan family has a fruit farm. There are 12 orchards on their farm. Of these, 6 are apple orchards. This means that $\frac{6}{12}$ of the Brennan orchards are apple orchards.

Write $\frac{6}{12}$ in simplest form.

A fraction is in **simplest form** if the denominator and the numerator have no common factors greater than 1. You can find equivalent fractions by dividing the numerator and the denominator of a fraction by a common factor.

$$\frac{6}{12} = \frac{6 \div 2}{12 \div 2} = \frac{3}{6} \qquad \boxed{\frac{3}{6} \text{ is not in simplest form.}}$$

Continue dividing to find another fraction equivalent to $\frac{3}{6}$.

$$\frac{3}{6} = \frac{3 \div 3}{6 \div 3} = \frac{1}{2}$$

1 and 2 have no common factor greater than 1. So, $\frac{6}{12}$ in simplest form is $\frac{1}{2}$.

B. Another way to simplify a fraction is by dividing the numerator and the denominator by their greatest common factor.

Write $\frac{6}{12}$ in simplest form.

The greatest common factor of 6 and 12 is 6.
Divide both the numerator and the denominator by 6.

$$\frac{6}{12} = \frac{6 \div 6}{12 \div 6} = \frac{1}{2} \qquad \frac{6}{12} \text{ in simplest form is } \frac{1}{2}.$$

Checkpoint   Write the letter of the correct answer.

Find the equivalent fraction in simplest form.

1. $\frac{4}{12}$

   a. $\frac{1}{4}$
   b. $\frac{1}{3}$
   c. $\frac{2}{6}$
   d. $\frac{8}{24}$

2. $\frac{27}{30}$

   a. $\frac{1}{3}$
   b. $\frac{9}{10}$
   c. $\frac{3}{3}$
   d. 3

3. $\frac{75}{100}$

   a. $\frac{1}{25}$
   b. $\frac{15}{25}$
   c. $\frac{7}{10}$
   d. $\frac{3}{4}$

4. $\frac{12}{72}$

   a. $\frac{1}{12}$
   b. $\frac{3}{36}$
   c. $\frac{1}{6}$
   d. $\frac{2}{12}$

Divide to write the fraction in simplest form.

1. $\dfrac{4 \div 4}{8 \div 4} = $ ▩

2. $\dfrac{8 \div 4}{12 \div 4} = $ ▩

3. $\dfrac{8 \div 2}{10 \div 2} = $ ▩

4. $\dfrac{9 \div 9}{27 \div 9} = $ ▩

5. $\dfrac{10 \div 10}{30 \div 10} = $ ▩

6. $\dfrac{15 \div 5}{35 \div 5} = $ ▩

7. $\dfrac{45 \div 9}{54 \div 9} = $ ▩

8. $\dfrac{99 \div 11}{121 \div 11} = $ ▩

Complete.

9. $\dfrac{4}{8} = \dfrac{▩}{2}$

10. $\dfrac{2}{10} = \dfrac{▩}{5}$

11. $\dfrac{6}{27} = \dfrac{▩}{9}$

12. $\dfrac{8}{40} = \dfrac{▩}{5}$

13. $\dfrac{7}{56} = \dfrac{▩}{8}$

14. $\dfrac{6}{16} = \dfrac{▩}{8}$

15. $\dfrac{9}{24} = \dfrac{▩}{8}$

16. $\dfrac{13}{52} = \dfrac{▩}{4}$

17. $\dfrac{12}{62} = \dfrac{▩}{31}$

18. $\dfrac{63}{162} = \dfrac{▩}{18}$

Write the fraction in simplest form.

19. $\dfrac{4}{16}$

20. $\dfrac{6}{8}$

21. $\dfrac{8}{18}$

22. $\dfrac{10}{12}$

23. $\dfrac{12}{15}$

24. $\dfrac{18}{20}$

25. $\dfrac{60}{100}$

26. $\dfrac{7}{21}$

27. $\dfrac{15}{30}$

28. $\dfrac{14}{28}$

29. $\dfrac{20}{25}$

30. $\dfrac{4}{18}$

Solve. For Problem 32, use the Infobank.

31. Last year, the Makeys' wheat crop was 2.7 metric tons. Their silo is capable of storing 5 metric tons of wheat. How many more metric tons could it hold after last year's crop was stored?

32. Use the information about the leading wheat-growing states on page 418 to write and solve your own word problem.

FOCUS: REASONING

Solve. *Act it out* with a team if you need help.

1. One day, 4 friends were having a table tennis match. Every person played each of the others just one game. How many games were played?

2. Another day, 5 friends were having a table tennis match. Every person played each of the others just one game. How many games were played?

Compare and Order Fractions and Mixed Numbers

A. Compare $\frac{1}{3}$ and $\frac{2}{3}$.

Check to see that the denominators are the same.	Compare the numerators.
$\frac{1}{3}$ $\frac{2}{3}$	$1 < 2$

So, $\frac{1}{3} < \frac{2}{3}$.

B. Compare $\frac{1}{4}$ and $\frac{1}{3}$. The denominators are not the same.

Write the equivalent fractions for $\frac{1}{4}$ and $\frac{1}{3}$ that have a common denominator.

The least common multiple of 4 and 3 is 12.	Compare the numerators.
$\frac{1}{3} = \frac{4}{12}$ $\frac{1}{4} = \frac{3}{12}$	$\frac{4}{12} > \frac{3}{12}$

So, $\frac{1}{3} > \frac{1}{4}$.

C. Compare $3\frac{1}{3}$ and $3\frac{4}{9}$.

Compare the whole numbers.	Write an equivalent fraction with a common denominator.	Compare the fractions.
$3 = 3$	$\frac{1}{3} = \frac{3}{9}$	$\frac{3}{9} < \frac{4}{9}$

So, $3\frac{1}{3} < 3\frac{4}{9}$.

D. You can order $\frac{3}{4}$, $\frac{5}{8}$, and $\frac{2}{3}$ by comparing these fractions.

Write equivalent fractions that have a common denominator.	Compare to find the greatest fraction.	Continue comparing.
$\frac{3}{4} = \frac{18}{24}$	$\frac{18}{24}, \frac{15}{24}, \frac{16}{24}$	$\frac{16}{24} > \frac{15}{24}$
$\frac{5}{8} = \frac{15}{24}$	$\frac{18}{24} > \frac{16}{24}$	
$\frac{2}{3} = \frac{16}{24}$	$\frac{18}{24} > \frac{15}{24}$	

Once you have compared all of the fractions, you can write them in either order

from the least to the greatest: $\frac{5}{8}$, $\frac{2}{3}$, $\frac{3}{4}$; or,

from the greatest to the least: $\frac{3}{4}$, $\frac{2}{3}$, $\frac{5}{8}$.

Compare. Write >, <, or = for ●.

1. $\frac{1}{3}$ ● $\frac{2}{3}$ **2.** $\frac{3}{5}$ ● $\frac{4}{5}$ **3.** $\frac{5}{9}$ ● $\frac{2}{9}$ **4.** $\frac{2}{10}$ ● $\frac{7}{10}$ **5.** $\frac{3}{4}$ ● $\frac{1}{4}$

6. $\frac{4}{7}$ ● $\frac{3}{4}$ **7.** $\frac{6}{8}$ ● $\frac{3}{4}$ **8.** $\frac{1}{3}$ ● $\frac{2}{6}$ **9.** $\frac{1}{2}$ ● $\frac{5}{7}$ **10.** $\frac{2}{9}$ ● $\frac{1}{8}$

11. $3\frac{3}{9}$ ● $2\frac{1}{9}$ **12.** $5\frac{3}{8}$ ● $2\frac{7}{8}$ **13.** $4\frac{6}{8}$ ● $5\frac{4}{8}$ **14.** $7\frac{1}{7}$ ● $1\frac{6}{7}$ **15.** $2\frac{2}{3}$ ● $2\frac{3}{4}$

16. $\frac{2}{5}$ ● $\frac{4}{10}$ **17.** $\frac{5}{8}$ ● $\frac{3}{8}$ **18.** $2\frac{1}{2}$ ● $2\frac{3}{8}$ **19.** $\frac{5}{6}$ ● $\frac{4}{5}$ **20.** $1\frac{1}{3}$ ● $1\frac{1}{4}$

Write in order from the least to the greatest.

21. $\frac{3}{5}, \frac{2}{8}, \frac{1}{2}$ **22.** $\frac{1}{3}, \frac{2}{3}, \frac{1}{7}$ **23.** $\frac{2}{8}, \frac{2}{4}, \frac{2}{6}$ **24.** $\frac{4}{5}, \frac{2}{3}, \frac{3}{4}$

Write in order from the greatest to the least.

25. $\frac{3}{7}, \frac{1}{2}, \frac{2}{3}$ **26.** $\frac{3}{4}, \frac{1}{7}, \frac{2}{9}$ **27.** $\frac{1}{2}, \frac{4}{6}, \frac{2}{6}$ **28.** $\frac{3}{5}, \frac{3}{4}, \frac{3}{8}$

Solve.

29. During the first week of harvesting, one group of workers picked $\frac{2}{5}$ of the apple crop. A second group picked $\frac{3}{10}$ of the pear crop. Which group picked more of its crop?

30. Jesse makes his special juice. The recipe calls for $\frac{1}{2}$ gallon apple juice, $\frac{1}{6}$ gallon grape juice, and $\frac{1}{3}$ gallon pear juice. Order the ingredients from the least to the greatest.

MIDCHAPTER REVIEW

Find the least common multiple.

1. 2, 17   **2.** 5, 6   **3.** 9, 2   **4.** 7, 3

Find the greatest common factor.

5. 12, 18   **6.** 16, 24   **7.** 25, 24, 32, 48   **8.** 27, 45, 36

Complete.

9. $\frac{2}{3} = \frac{\blacksquare}{6}$ **10.** $\frac{3}{10} = \frac{\blacksquare}{20}$ **11.** $\frac{5}{9} = \frac{\blacksquare}{45}$ **12.** $\frac{2}{7} = \frac{\blacksquare}{21}$

Write the fraction in simplest form.

13. $\frac{8}{10}$ **14.** $\frac{9}{27}$ **15.** $\frac{17}{68}$ **16.** $\frac{15}{255}$

Write as a whole number or a mixed number.

17. $\frac{12}{4}$ **18.** $\frac{10}{9}$ **19.** $\frac{35}{6}$ **20.** $\frac{98}{7}$

PROBLEM SOLVING
Choosing a Strategy or Method

Write the strategy you choose. Then solve.

1. One farm contains 430 acres of land. Its owner plans to sell some of it at $4,000 per acre. How much money will the owner receive if he sells half his land?

2. The Lees and the Sands each owned 250-acre farms. They each bought another 75 acres. Today, the Lees have 354 acres. Who owns more land? How much more?

> Acting It Out
> Estimation
> Making a Model
> Using Outside Sources
> Choosing the Operation
> Writing a Number Sentence
> Checking for a Reasonable Answer
> Choosing/Writing a Sensible Question
> Checking That the Solution Answers
>   the Question
> Identifying Needed Information
> Solving Multistep Problems/Making a Plan

3. In 1989, there were 34 fewer farms in the state than in 1981. If there were 2,400 farms in 1989, how many farms were there in 1981?

4. The Parker farm has 3 times as many cattle as the Steinway farm. The Parkers have 90 cattle. How many cattle do the Steinways have?

5. An Alaskan chicken farmer sells 2,416 eggs in one month. The average hen on the farm lays about 16 eggs per month. About how many hens does the farmer have?

6. In 1988, a bushel of corn sold for $2.55. A bushel of wheat sold for $3.72. If a farmer sold 7,500 bushels of corn and 2 times as much wheat, was the farmer's income closer to $50,000 or to $75,000?

7. Jason Parker is loading bales of hay onto a mechanical arm. The arm moves the 50-pound bales up to the hayloft. Jason loads 1 bale every 5 seconds. How many bales will he load in 60 seconds?

8. Between 1970 and 1980, world production of eggs increased by 5,568,000 metric tons. In 1980, production was 26,700,000 metric tons. A metric ton equals 1,000 kilograms. How many metric tons of eggs were produced in 1970?

Write the strategy or method you choose. Then solve.

9. One farmer earned $12,600 from crop sales in 1988. Each year, she earns 0.04 times more than she did the previous year. How much will she earn in 1991?

10. Dan Parker wants to take 7 horses to Toni Steinway's farm. His trailer can hold only 2 horses. How many trips will Dan Parker have to make?

11. Between 1980 and 1983, the number of farms in Iowa decreased from 119,000 to 115,000. This decrease in farms continued at the same rate until 1989. About how many farms were there in 1989?

12. One acre of Toni Steinway's farmland is worth $2,000. When she bought it, she paid only $100 per acre. If Toni sold 80 acres of her land, how much profit would she make?

13. Last year, the Parkers earned $11,885 after expenses. The Steinways earned $2,100 more. The Jacksons earned as much from their large farm as the Parkers and the Steinways together. How much did the Jacksons earn?

14. The United States is the world's largest corn exporter. In one year, it exported 54,856,000 metric tons of corn. That same year, Argentina, exporting 9,112,000 metric tons, was second. Estimate how much larger the amount of corn the United States exported was than the amount exported by Argentina.

15. Nuts are an important agricultural product. In 1987, the United States produced 131,100 tons of pecans. In 1988, pecan production totaled 154,000 tons. With this information, what question can you answer?

16. One year, Canada produced 17,637,000 bushels of rye. The United States, producing 16,259,000 bushels, was close behind. In the United States, Nebraska produced 749,000 bushels, and Oklahoma produced 744,000 bushels. How many more bushels did Nebraska produce than Oklahoma?

17. A healthy apple tree can produce about 30 bushels of fruit. Recently, a fast-working farmer picked a record 270 bushels in 9 hours. If he completely picked one tree per hour, how many trees did he work on?

18. Look back at the problems you have solved. Talk about the ones that seemed difficult. What methods or processes did you use? Is there more than one way to think about these problems? Share ideas with your classmates.

Adding Like Fractions Using Models

A. Jean is raising a dairy cow named Bon Bon for her 4-H project. Jean makes cheese from the cow's milk. On Monday, Jean gives $\frac{3}{8}$ wheel of cheese to friends. On Thursday, she gives $\frac{4}{8}$ wheel to her 4-H club leader. How much cheese does Jean give away? You can use fraction pieces to make a model.

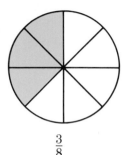
$$\frac{3}{8}$$

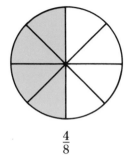
$$\frac{4}{8}$$

Count the shaded parts. There are $\frac{7}{8}$.

Add $\frac{3}{8} + \frac{4}{8}$.

To add fractions with like denominators, add the numerators. Write the sum over the denominator.

$$\frac{3}{8} + \frac{4}{8} = \frac{3+4}{8} = \frac{7}{8}$$

Jean gives away $\frac{7}{8}$ wheel of cheese.

B. Sometimes you need to rename the sum as a mixed number in simplest form.

$$\frac{3}{4} + \frac{3}{4} = \frac{3+3}{4} = \frac{6}{4} = 1\frac{2}{4}, \text{ or } 1\frac{1}{2}$$

Checkpoint Write the letter of the correct answer.

Add. The answer must be in simplest form.

1. $\frac{2}{4} + \frac{1}{4}$

   a. $\frac{3}{16}$

   b. $\frac{3}{8}$

   c. $\frac{3}{4}$

   d. $\frac{6}{5}$

2. $\frac{3}{5} + \frac{4}{5}$

   a. $\frac{7}{25}$

   b. $\frac{7}{10}$

   c. $\frac{7}{5}$

   d. $1\frac{2}{5}$

3. $\frac{5}{9} + \frac{7}{9}$

   a. $\frac{12}{81}$

   b. $1\frac{3}{9}$

   c. $\frac{4}{3}$

   d. $1\frac{1}{3}$

4. $\frac{9}{10} + \frac{2}{10}$

   a. $\frac{1}{10}$

   b. $\frac{7}{10}$

   c. $\frac{11}{10}$

   d. $1\frac{1}{10}$

Math Reasoning, page H202

Add. Write the sum in simplest form.

1. $\frac{3}{8} + \frac{2}{8}$

2. $\frac{2}{5} + \frac{1}{5}$

3. $\frac{4}{7} + \frac{2}{7}$

4. $\frac{7}{10} + \frac{2}{10}$

5. $\frac{2}{9} + \frac{5}{9}$

6. $\frac{1}{4} + \frac{1}{4}$

7. $\frac{3}{6} + \frac{1}{6}$

8. $\frac{3}{12} + \frac{5}{12}$

9. $\frac{2}{9} + \frac{1}{9}$

10. $\frac{5}{15} + \frac{5}{15}$

11. $\frac{6}{8} + \frac{5}{8}$

12. $\frac{2}{7} + \frac{5}{7}$

13. $\frac{5}{9} + \frac{8}{9}$

14. $\frac{2}{3} + \frac{1}{3}$

15. $\frac{3}{6} + \frac{4}{6}$

16. $\begin{array}{r} \frac{7}{12} \\ + \frac{9}{12} \\ \hline \end{array}$

17. $\begin{array}{r} \frac{7}{8} \\ + \frac{7}{8} \\ \hline \end{array}$

18. $\begin{array}{r} \frac{7}{10} \\ + \frac{5}{10} \\ \hline \end{array}$

19. $\begin{array}{r} \frac{4}{16} \\ + \frac{12}{16} \\ \hline \end{array}$

20. $\begin{array}{r} \frac{6}{12} \\ + \frac{5}{12} \\ \hline \end{array}$

21. $\begin{array}{r} \frac{2}{4} \\ + \frac{3}{4} \\ \hline \end{array}$

★22. $\frac{1}{4} + \frac{2}{4} + \frac{3}{4}$

★23. $\frac{2}{7} + \frac{3}{7} + \frac{1}{7}$

★24. $\frac{3}{6} + \frac{5}{6} + \frac{6}{6}$

★25. $\frac{7}{9} + \frac{5}{9} + \frac{6}{9}$

Solve. Draw pictures to help you.

26. Jean spends $\frac{2}{6}$ hour caring for Bon Bon on Monday. She spends $\frac{4}{6}$ hour with Bon Bon on Tuesday. How long does Jean spend with Bon Bon on Monday and Tuesday?

27. A special feed machine records how much each calf eats. Nell, a young calf, eats $\frac{2}{3}$ pound of feed in the morning and $\frac{2}{3}$ pound of feed in the afternoon. How much does Nell eat?

★28. Jean's family drinks the following amounts of milk in three days: $\frac{3}{4}$ gallon, $\frac{5}{4}$ gallon, $\frac{2}{4}$ gallon. How much milk does Jean's family drink in all?

ANOTHER LOOK

Complete.

1. 2 cm = ■ mm

2. 16 mm = ■ cm

3. 8.5 mm = ■ cm

4. 4 km = ■ m

5. 250 mm = ■ km

6. 8.75 km = ■ m

7. 375 mg = ■ g

8. 6 g = ■ mg

9. 1.3 g = ■ mg

10. 1.5 L = ■ mL

Adding and Subtracting Unlike Fractions

A. Jan bought $\frac{2}{3}$ pound of peanuts. Bob bought $\frac{1}{4}$ pound. Together, did they buy a whole pound of peanuts?

The fraction bars at the right can help you think about and compare fractions. They can also help you estimate their sums and differences.

You will need a sheet of paper, a pencil, and a ruler.
First, trace over $\frac{2}{3}$.
Now lay the end of your $\frac{2}{3}$ tracing next to the beginning of $\frac{1}{4}$ and trace it.
You now have a model of $\frac{2}{3} + \frac{1}{4}$.

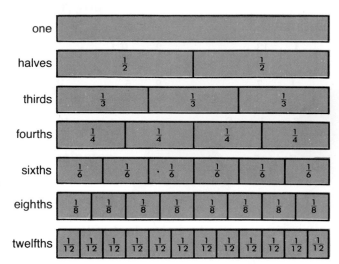

Working as a Team

1. Compare $\frac{2}{3} + \frac{1}{4}$ to the bar that shows one whole. Did Jan and Bob buy at least one whole pound of nuts?

2. Use the same method to estimate whether each sum is greater than one, equal to one, or less than one.

   a. $\frac{3}{4} + \frac{1}{3}$ **b.** $\frac{5}{8} + \frac{1}{4}$ **c.** $\frac{1}{2} + \frac{3}{4}$ **d.** $\frac{5}{6} + \frac{5}{12}$ **e.** $\frac{7}{12} + \frac{1}{6}$ **f.** $\frac{3}{4} + \frac{2}{8}$

3. Think of a way that you can use the fraction bars to find the exact sums. Compare your method to those of other teams.

B. Jan wanted to know how much more she has than Bob.

You can use the fraction bars to estimate the answer.

Trace over $\frac{2}{3}$ on your paper. Now trace $\frac{1}{4}$ *inside* your first tracing. The space between the end of the $\frac{1}{4}$ tracing and the end of the $\frac{2}{3}$ marking is the difference.

Does Jan have at least a half pound more of peanuts than Bob has?

Working as a Team

1. Use the same method to estimate whether each of these differences is greater than $\frac{1}{2}$, equal to $\frac{1}{2}$, or less than $\frac{1}{2}$.

   a. $\frac{7}{8} - \frac{1}{2}$ **b.** $\frac{3}{4} - \frac{1}{2}$ **c.** $\frac{1}{2} - \frac{1}{3}$ **d.** $\frac{11}{12} - \frac{1}{4}$ **e.** $\frac{6}{6} - \frac{2}{3}$ **f.** $\frac{9}{12} - \frac{1}{4}$

2. Think of a way that you can use the fraction bars to find the exact differences. Compare your method to those of other teams.

3. Name two fractions with unlike denominators whose sum is about 1.

4. Name two fractions with unlike denominators whose sum is about $\frac{1}{2}$.

5. Name three fractions with unlike denominators whose sum is about 1.

6. Name two fractions with unlike denominators whose difference is about $\frac{1}{2}$.

C. Jan and Bob decide to prepare nut mix for their friends. Jan has her own recipe. Bob finds one in a cookbook. Here are their recipes:

Jan's Recipe	**Bob's Recipe**
$\frac{2}{3}$ cup peanuts	$\frac{1}{4}$ cup peanuts
$\frac{1}{3}$ cup cashews	$\frac{1}{2}$ cup cashews
$\frac{1}{2}$ cup almonds	$\frac{1}{2}$ cup almonds
$\frac{3}{4}$ cup pistachios	$\frac{2}{3}$ cup pistachios

Thinking as a Team

1. Whose recipe serves more people?

2. How do you know?

3. One cup of nut mix serves 4 people. Which recipe would you use if you wanted to serve 8 people? Why?

4. Is the difference between the two recipes more or less than $\frac{1}{2}$ cup?

5. If Jan and Bob combined their recipes, would there be more or less than 4 cups of nuts?

More Adding and Subtracting Fractions

A. The chief grain crops grown in the United States are wheat, rice, corn, and barley. Barley is $\frac{1}{10}$ of grain production. Wheat is $\frac{2}{5}$ of grain production. Together, what part of the grain production are barley and wheat? How much more of the grain production is wheat than barley?

Sometimes you need to write fractions as equivalent fractions that have a common denominator before you can add or subtract.

$$\frac{1}{10} + \frac{2}{5} \quad\boxed{\frac{2 \times 2}{5 \times 2} = \frac{4}{10}}\quad \frac{2}{5} - \frac{1}{10}$$

$$\frac{1}{10} + \frac{4}{10} = \frac{4+1}{10} = \frac{5}{10} \qquad \frac{4}{10} - \frac{1}{10} = \frac{4-1}{10} = \frac{3}{10}$$

> To subtract fractions with like denominators, subtract the numerators. Write the difference over the denominator.

One half of the grain production is barley and wheat. Wheat is $\frac{3}{10}$ more of the production than barley.

B. Be sure to write the sum or the difference in simplest form.

$$\begin{array}{r} \frac{3}{4} = \frac{9}{12} \\ + \frac{3}{6} = \frac{6}{12} \\ \hline \frac{15}{12} = 1\frac{3}{12} = 1\frac{1}{4} \end{array} \qquad \begin{array}{r} \frac{5}{6} = \frac{20}{24} \\ - \frac{6}{8} = \frac{18}{24} \\ \hline \frac{2}{24} = \frac{1}{12} \end{array}$$

Checkpoint   Write the letter of the correct answer.

Add or subtract. Write the answer in simplest form.

1. $\frac{2}{3} + \frac{5}{6}$

    a. $\frac{10}{18}$

    b. $\frac{7}{9}$

    c. $\frac{9}{6}$

    d. $1\frac{1}{2}$

2. $\frac{1}{4} + \frac{5}{6}$

    a. $\frac{5}{24}$

    b. $\frac{6}{10}$

    c. $1\frac{1}{12}$

    d. $\frac{26}{24}$

3. $\frac{7}{10} - \frac{1}{10}$

    a. $\frac{6}{10}$

    b. $\frac{3}{5}$

    c. $\frac{4}{5}$

    d. $\frac{8}{10}$

4. $\frac{4}{5} - \frac{2}{4}$

    a. $\frac{3}{10}$

    b. $\frac{6}{20}$

    c. $\frac{6}{40}$

    d. $\frac{2}{1}$

Math Reasoning, page H202

Add. Write the sum in simplest form.

1. $\frac{2}{4} + \frac{1}{2}$ 2. $\frac{4}{9} + \frac{1}{3}$ 3. $\frac{5}{10} + \frac{2}{5}$ 4. $\frac{2}{7} + \frac{5}{14}$ 5. $\frac{3}{4} + \frac{5}{12}$

6. $\frac{2}{3} + \frac{5}{7}$ 7. $\frac{4}{11} + \frac{2}{3}$ 8. $\frac{3}{5} + \frac{4}{9}$ 9. $\frac{3}{7} + \frac{8}{9}$ 10. $\frac{1}{2} + \frac{2}{3}$

11. $\begin{array}{r} \frac{1}{9} \\ + \frac{2}{3} \\ \hline \end{array}$ 12. $\begin{array}{r} \frac{1}{5} \\ + \frac{4}{15} \\ \hline \end{array}$ 13. $\begin{array}{r} \frac{4}{7} \\ + \frac{12}{21} \\ \hline \end{array}$ 14. $\begin{array}{r} \frac{3}{7} \\ + \frac{5}{6} \\ \hline \end{array}$ 15. $\begin{array}{r} \frac{1}{12} \\ + \frac{5}{16} \\ \hline \end{array}$

Subtract. Write the difference in simplest form.

16. $\frac{5}{9} - \frac{2}{9}$ 17. $\frac{9}{12} - \frac{5}{12}$ 18. $\frac{5}{6} - \frac{1}{6}$ 19. $\frac{13}{16} - \frac{5}{16}$ 20. $\frac{9}{13} - \frac{6}{13}$

21. $\frac{9}{14} - \frac{2}{7}$ 22. $\frac{4}{9} - \frac{5}{27}$ 23. $\frac{3}{4} - \frac{3}{5}$ 24. $\frac{8}{9} - \frac{2}{3}$ 25. $\frac{9}{14} - \frac{3}{7}$

26. $\begin{array}{r} \frac{3}{5} \\ - \frac{3}{7} \\ \hline \end{array}$ 27. $\begin{array}{r} \frac{11}{12} \\ - \frac{1}{12} \\ \hline \end{array}$ 28. $\begin{array}{r} \frac{5}{6} \\ - \frac{1}{3} \\ \hline \end{array}$ 29. $\begin{array}{r} \frac{4}{9} \\ - \frac{3}{8} \\ \hline \end{array}$ 30. $\begin{array}{r} \frac{6}{7} \\ - \frac{1}{3} \\ \hline \end{array}$

Find n.

★31. $\frac{7}{10} + \frac{3}{5} + \frac{1}{4} = n$ ★32. $\frac{7}{10} - \frac{n}{10} = \frac{3}{10}$ ★33. $\frac{n}{8} + \frac{3}{8} = \frac{6}{8}$

Solve.

34. Workers harvest $\frac{2}{3}$ of the wheat crop in the morning. After lunch, the remaining $\frac{1}{3}$ of the crop is harvested. How much more was harvested in the morning?

35. Jody spends $\frac{1}{2}$ hour cleaning the tractor. Lon spends $\frac{1}{4}$ hour cleaning the wagon. How much time do both Jody and Lon spend cleaning?

36. Dan's crew harvested $\frac{9}{10}$ acre of wheat in one hour. Tom's crew harvested $\frac{1}{2}$ acre of wheat in one hour. How much more acreage did Dan's crew harvest than Tom's?

★37. Of the harvested wheat, $\frac{9}{10}$ will be sold. The rest will be used on the farm. What fraction of the wheat harvested will be used on the farm?

CHALLENGE   Patterns, Relations, and Functions

Find the pattern. Copy and complete.

1. $\frac{2}{5}, \frac{4}{5}, \frac{6}{5}, \frac{8}{5}, \frac{10}{5}, \blacksquare, \blacksquare, \blacksquare$

2. $\frac{1}{3}, \frac{1}{9}, \frac{1}{27}, \frac{1}{81}, \blacksquare, \blacksquare, \blacksquare$

Classwork/Homework, page H99   **More Practice, page H177**   **253**

Adding Mixed Numbers

A. Sandy lives in California. In the summer, she has a fruit-juice stand. On her first day, Sandy sells $2\frac{3}{8}$ gallons of apple juice. She also sells $3\frac{1}{8}$ gallons of orange juice. How many gallons of juice does Sandy sell?

Add $2\frac{3}{8} + 3\frac{1}{8}$.

Add the fractions.	Add the whole numbers.	Write the sum in simplest form.
$\begin{aligned} 2\frac{3}{8} \\ +\,3\frac{1}{8} \\ \hline \frac{4}{8} \end{aligned}$	$\begin{aligned} 2\frac{3}{8} \\ +\,3\frac{1}{8} \\ \hline 5\frac{4}{8} \end{aligned}$	$\begin{aligned} 2\frac{3}{8} \\ +\,3\frac{1}{8} \\ \hline 5\frac{4}{8} = 5\frac{1}{2} \end{aligned}$

Sandy sells $5\frac{1}{2}$ gallons of juice.

B. Add $5\frac{1}{2} + 3\frac{1}{4}$.

Find equivalent fractions with a common denominator.	Add the fractions.	Add the whole numbers.
$\begin{aligned} 5\frac{1}{2} = \quad 5\frac{2}{4} \\ +\,3\frac{1}{4} = \quad 3\frac{1}{4} \\ \hline \end{aligned}$	$\begin{aligned} 5\frac{1}{2} = 5\frac{2}{4} \\ +\,3\frac{1}{4} = 3\frac{1}{4} \\ \hline \frac{3}{4} \end{aligned}$	$\begin{aligned} 5\frac{1}{2} = 5\frac{2}{4} \\ +\,3\frac{1}{4} = 3\frac{1}{4} \\ \hline 8\frac{3}{4} \end{aligned}$

Checkpoint Write the letter of the correct answer.

Add. The answer must be in simplest form.

1. $2\frac{1}{3} + 3\frac{1}{3}$

a. $5\frac{1}{9}$
b. $5\frac{1}{6}$
c. $5\frac{2}{3}$
d. $23\frac{2}{3}$

2. $3\frac{3}{4} + 4$

a. $3\frac{7}{4}$
b. $7\frac{3}{4}$
c. $12\frac{3}{4}$
d. $34\frac{3}{4}$

3. $4\frac{1}{5} + 1\frac{4}{10}$

a. $4\frac{3}{5}$
b. $5\frac{1}{3}$
c. $5\frac{3}{5}$
d. $5\frac{6}{10}$

4. $7\frac{3}{4} + 6\frac{1}{5}$

a. $13\frac{3}{20}$
b. $13\frac{4}{9}$
c. $13\frac{19}{20}$
d. $13\frac{38}{40}$

Add. Write the sum in simplest form.

1. $3\frac{4}{7}$
$+ 5\frac{2}{7}$

2. $8\frac{9}{22}$
$+ 12\frac{11}{22}$

3. $17\frac{1}{4}$
$+ 4\frac{1}{4}$

4. $2\frac{1}{8}$
$+ 8\frac{5}{8}$

5. $9\frac{3}{10}$
$+ 4\frac{3}{10}$

6. $3\frac{1}{3}$
$+ 9\frac{1}{3}$

7. $2\frac{13}{23}$
$+ 1\frac{6}{23}$

8. $12\frac{2}{7}$
$+ 11\frac{7}{10}$

9. $5\frac{3}{5}$
$+ 5\frac{1}{5}$

10. $8\frac{7}{10}$
$+ 13\frac{1}{10}$

11. $4\frac{1}{2}$
$+ 4\frac{1}{4}$

12. $9\frac{2}{5}$
$+ 2\frac{7}{15}$

13. $13\frac{4}{9}$
$+ 15\frac{7}{18}$

14. $11\frac{1}{8}$
$+ 3\frac{13}{16}$

15. $5\frac{1}{6}$
$+ 1\frac{3}{4}$

16. $14\frac{1}{8} + 11\frac{1}{4}$

17. $7\frac{3}{14} + 2\frac{3}{7}$

18. $6\frac{1}{6} + 4\frac{8}{18}$

19. $14\frac{2}{3} + 1\frac{1}{3}$

20. $6\frac{2}{5} + 11\frac{2}{15}$

21. $3\frac{5}{6} + 8\frac{1}{6}$

22. $7\frac{7}{10} + 21\frac{5}{20}$

23. $11\frac{6}{7} + 9\frac{1}{21}$

24. $3\frac{4}{9} + 16\frac{1}{9}$

25. $4 + 1\frac{13}{14}$

26. $2\frac{11}{16} + 6\frac{3}{16}$

27. $15\frac{1}{2} + 7\frac{3}{17}$

★28. $12\frac{1}{3} + 1\frac{1}{2} + 2\frac{1}{6}$

★29. $4\frac{1}{8} + 7\frac{1}{24} + 11$

★30. $5\frac{1}{4} + 3\frac{1}{6} + 7\frac{3}{8}$

Solve.

31. Sandy plans to make fruit juice. She picks $1\frac{1}{3}$ bushels of grapes. She picks another $2\frac{1}{4}$ bushels of apricots. How many bushels of fruit does Sandy pick?

★32. Sandy mixed $1\frac{1}{4}$ quarts cranberry juice with $1\frac{1}{3}$ quarts apple juice. She added another $1\frac{1}{4}$ quarts strawberry juice. How much fruit punch did she make?

FOCUS: REASONING

Some farmers are taking their prize pigs to a county fair. On their way, they encounter a broad, deep river. Two boys are on the far bank with a small boat. The boat can only hold one farmer and one pig, or the two boys. How might the farmers get across?

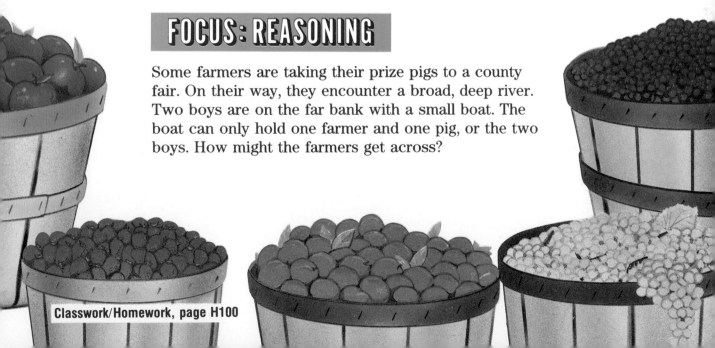

Adding Mixed Numbers with Renaming

A. Regina shops at the local market. She bought $5\frac{5}{16}$ pounds of ripe bananas and $4\frac{7}{8}$ pounds of green bananas. Did Regina buy more than 10 pounds of bananas?

You can estimate to answer this question.

Estimate $5\frac{5}{16} + 4\frac{7}{8}$.

Add the whole numbers.	**Estimate the sum of the fractions.**	**Add the sum of the whole numbers and the estimated sum of the fractions.**
$5\frac{5}{16} + 4\frac{7}{8}$	$5\frac{5}{16} + 4\frac{7}{8}$	$9 + 1\frac{1}{2} = 10\frac{1}{2}$
↓ ↓	↓ ↓	
$5 + 4 = 9$	$\frac{1}{2} + 1 = 1\frac{1}{2}$	So, $5\frac{5}{16} + 4\frac{7}{8} \approx 10\frac{1}{2}$.

Regina bought more than 10 pounds of bananas.

B. Regina's mother wanted to know how many pounds of bananas were bought.

Because an exact answer is needed, you need to add $5\frac{5}{16} + 4\frac{7}{8}$.

Find fractions with a common denominator.	**Add.**	**Write the sum in simplest form.**
$5\frac{5}{16} = 5\frac{5}{16}$	$5\frac{5}{16} = 5\frac{5}{16}$	$9\frac{19}{16} = 9 + 1\frac{3}{16}$
$+\, 4\frac{7}{8} = 4\frac{14}{16}$	$+\, 4\frac{7}{8} = 4\frac{14}{16}$	$= 10\frac{3}{16}$
	$9\frac{19}{16}$	

Regina bought $10\frac{3}{16}$ pounds of bananas.

Checkpoint Write the letter of the correct answer.

Add. The answer must be in simplest form.

1. $4\frac{6}{7} + 2\frac{1}{4}$

2. $3\frac{3}{9} + 5\frac{5}{6}$

3. $11\frac{11}{36} + 1\frac{2}{3}$

a. $6\frac{3}{28}$

b. $6\frac{31}{28}$

c. $7\frac{3}{28}$

d. $7\frac{31}{28}$

a. $8\frac{21}{18}$

b. $9\frac{1}{6}$

c. $9\frac{3}{18}$

d. $9\frac{21}{18}$

a. $11\frac{1}{36}$

b. $12\frac{1}{36}$

c. $12\frac{13}{36}$

d. $12\frac{35}{36}$

Write the letter of the best estimate.

1. $1\frac{2}{5} + 2\frac{3}{7}$

a. about 3
b. about 4
c. about 5

2. $9\frac{5}{8} + 3\frac{3}{4}$

a. about 12
b. about 14
c. about 15

3. $8\frac{1}{3} + 1\frac{7}{8} + \frac{4}{5}$

a. about 9
b. about 10
c. about 11

4. $2\frac{3}{5} + 1\frac{7}{8} + 3\frac{5}{6}$

a. about 6
b. about 9
c. about 10

Add. Write the answer in simplest form.

5. $\begin{array}{r} 7\frac{1}{2} \\ + 5\frac{3}{4} \\ \hline \end{array}$

6. $\begin{array}{r} 6\frac{5}{8} \\ + 1\frac{2}{3} \\ \hline \end{array}$

7. $\begin{array}{r} 9\frac{3}{4} \\ + 2\frac{15}{16} \\ \hline \end{array}$

8. $\begin{array}{r} 3\frac{4}{5} \\ + 4\frac{7}{10} \\ \hline \end{array}$

9. $\begin{array}{r} 1\frac{5}{8} \\ + 6\frac{1}{2} \\ \hline \end{array}$

10. $3\frac{4}{5} + 2\frac{2}{3}$ **11.** $5\frac{3}{7} + 8\frac{3}{4}$ **12.** $1\frac{3}{5} + 5\frac{5}{8}$ **13.** $4\frac{1}{2} + 11\frac{4}{7}$

14. $2\frac{6}{7} + 4\frac{1}{3}$ **15.** $5\frac{1}{2} + 3\frac{3}{5}$ **16.** $6\frac{1}{8} + 7\frac{15}{16}$ **17.** $9\frac{2}{3} + 3\frac{5}{8}$

18. $4\frac{3}{5} + 6\frac{4}{5}$ **★19.** $(9\frac{3}{5} + 6\frac{1}{20}) + 5\frac{1}{8}$ **★20.** $(2\frac{1}{8} + 3\frac{3}{4}) + 4\frac{1}{2}$ **★21.** $(7\frac{2}{3} + 5\frac{1}{5}) + 6\frac{3}{4}$

Solve.

22. Mr. Manti sells sausage. One morning, he sells $7\frac{1}{2}$ pounds of sausage to Regina and $5\frac{3}{4}$ pounds to Regina's cousin, Sophia. How many pounds of sausage does Mr. Manti sell to Regina and Sophia?

★23. Claudia brought 13 loaves of her delicious bread to sell at the market. She traded $1\frac{1}{2}$ loaves for some tomatoes. She sold $9\frac{1}{2}$ loaves. How many loaves did she have left?

CHALLENGE   Patterns, Relations, and Functions

Add to complete the fraction squares. Write each fraction in simplest form.

1.

2.
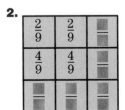

3.
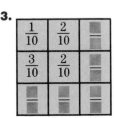

Subtracting Mixed Numbers

A. The Pickens family is having a barn raising. They need planks that are $4\frac{1}{4}$ feet long. Ned Class brings $5\frac{3}{4}$-foot planks. How much should Ned trim from the planks?

Find $5\frac{3}{4} - 4\frac{1}{4}$.

Subtract the fractions.	Subtract the whole numbers.	Write the difference in simplest form.
$\begin{aligned} 5\tfrac{3}{4} \\ -\,4\tfrac{1}{4} \\ \hline \tfrac{2}{4} \end{aligned}$	$\begin{aligned} 5\tfrac{3}{4} \\ -\,4\tfrac{1}{4} \\ \hline 1\tfrac{2}{4} \end{aligned}$	$\begin{aligned} 5\tfrac{3}{4} \\ -\,4\tfrac{1}{4} \\ \hline 1\tfrac{2}{4},\text{ or } 1\tfrac{1}{2}. \end{aligned}$

Ned should trim $1\frac{1}{2}$ feet from the planks.

B. Find $8\frac{1}{2} - 4\frac{1}{4}$.

Find equivalent fractions with a common denominator.	Subtract the fractions.	Subtract the whole numbers.
$\begin{aligned} 8\tfrac{1}{2} &= 8\tfrac{2}{4} \\ -\,4\tfrac{1}{4} &= 4\tfrac{1}{4} \\ \hline \end{aligned}$	$\begin{aligned} 8\tfrac{1}{2} &= 8\tfrac{2}{4} \\ -\,4\tfrac{1}{4} &= 4\tfrac{1}{4} \\ \hline &\quad\tfrac{1}{4} \end{aligned}$	$\begin{aligned} 8\tfrac{1}{2} &= 8\tfrac{2}{4} \\ -\,4\tfrac{1}{4} &= 4\tfrac{1}{4} \\ \hline &\ 4\tfrac{1}{4} \end{aligned}$

Other examples:

$$\begin{aligned} 5\tfrac{3}{5} \\ -\,2 \\ \hline 3\tfrac{3}{5} \end{aligned} \qquad\qquad \begin{aligned} 4\tfrac{2}{3} &= 4\tfrac{8}{12} \\ -\,1\tfrac{1}{4} &= 1\tfrac{3}{12} \\ \hline &\ 3\tfrac{5}{12} \end{aligned}$$

Checkpoint   Write the letter of the correct answer.

Subtract. The answer must be in simplest form.

1. $5\frac{3}{5} - 3$

a. $\frac{8}{5}$

b. 2

c. $2\frac{3}{5}$

d. $8\frac{3}{5}$

2. $6\frac{5}{8} - 4\frac{3}{8}$

a. $\frac{2}{8}$

b. $2\frac{1}{10}$

c. $2\frac{1}{4}$

d. $10\frac{1}{4}$

3. $7\frac{1}{2} - 2\frac{1}{8}$

a. $5\frac{1}{4}$

b. $5\frac{3}{8}$

c. $5\frac{5}{8}$

d. $9\frac{3}{8}$

Subtract. Write the difference in simplest form.

1. $2\frac{1}{2}$
-1

2. $6\frac{2}{3}$
-3

3. $3\frac{3}{4}$
$-2\frac{1}{4}$

4. $8\frac{5}{8}$
$-2\frac{1}{8}$

5. $9\frac{4}{7}$
$-8\frac{2}{7}$

6. $4\frac{1}{2}$
$-2\frac{1}{4}$

7. $9\frac{2}{3}$
$-3\frac{1}{6}$

8. $7\frac{1}{4}$
$-3\frac{1}{8}$

9. $9\frac{5}{8}$
$-2\frac{1}{2}$

10. $11\frac{1}{5}$
$-9\frac{1}{10}$

11. $5\frac{1}{3} - 5\frac{1}{4}$

12. $8\frac{3}{4} - 5\frac{1}{5}$

13. $9\frac{1}{4} - 6\frac{1}{6}$

14. $4\frac{2}{3} - 1\frac{2}{5}$

15. $12\frac{6}{7} - 3\frac{1}{4}$

16. $9\frac{1}{2} - 3\frac{1}{4}$

17. $3\frac{2}{3} - 1\frac{1}{4}$

18. $6\frac{1}{2} - 5$

19. $8\frac{5}{8} - 5\frac{1}{8}$

20. $8\frac{3}{5} - 2\frac{3}{10}$

21. $6\frac{1}{2} - 2\frac{1}{4}$

22. $7\frac{6}{7} - 1\frac{11}{14}$

23. $5\frac{2}{3} - 3\frac{4}{9}$

24. $4\frac{3}{4} - 1\frac{1}{12}$

25. $5\frac{7}{10} - 3\frac{1}{5}$

26. $7\frac{4}{5} - 5\frac{1}{2}$

Solve.

27. The Pickens family makes lunch for their barn-raising neighbors. They make $8\frac{1}{2}$ pounds of three-bean salad. Only $3\frac{1}{4}$ pounds are eaten. How much three-bean salad is left?

★28. Jamie Plunkett brings 25 pounds of flour for baking. Mr. Pickens uses $10\frac{1}{2}$ pounds of flour for rolls and $11\frac{1}{2}$ pounds for bread. How much flour does he have left?

NUMBER SENSE

You can estimate the differences between fractions by rounding each fraction to 0, $\frac{1}{2}$, or 1.

$\frac{11}{12}$ $-$ $\frac{5}{8}$
$\downarrow$ $\downarrow$

about 1 $-$ about $\frac{1}{2}$ $1 - \frac{1}{2} = \frac{1}{2}$

So, $\frac{11}{12} - \frac{5}{8} \approx \frac{1}{2}$.

Estimate the difference.

1. $\frac{13}{15} - \frac{3}{7}$

2. $\frac{11}{24} - \frac{1}{8}$

3. $\frac{7}{8} - \frac{1}{12}$

4. $\frac{8}{9} - \frac{21}{25}$

★5. $2\frac{4}{7} - 1\frac{1}{6}$

Subtracting Mixed Numbers with Renaming

A. Potter and Maggie opened a roadside vegetable stand for the summer. On opening day, they started with $4\frac{1}{4}$ bushels of corn. They sold $3\frac{3}{4}$ bushels. How much corn was left?

To find how much corn was left, you subtract.
Find $4\frac{1}{4} - 3\frac{3}{4}$.

Find fractions with a common denominator.

$$4\frac{1}{4}$$
$$-\,3\frac{3}{4}$$

Compare fractions. Rename if necessary.

$$\frac{1}{4} < \frac{3}{4}$$
$$4\frac{1}{4} = 3 + 1\frac{1}{4}$$
$$= 3\frac{5}{4}$$

Subtract.

$$4\frac{1}{4} = 3\frac{5}{4}$$
$$-\,3\frac{3}{4} = 3\frac{3}{4}$$
$$\frac{2}{4} = \frac{1}{2}$$

Of the corn, $\frac{1}{2}$ bushel was left.

B. Find $4\frac{1}{4} - 2\frac{1}{3}$.

Find fractions with a common denominator.

$$4\frac{1}{4} = 4\frac{3}{12}$$
$$-\,2\frac{1}{3} = 2\frac{4}{12}$$

Compare fractions. Rename if necessary.

$$\frac{3}{12} < \frac{4}{12}$$
$$4\frac{3}{12} = 3 + 1\frac{3}{12}$$
$$= 3\frac{15}{12}$$

Subtract.

$$4\frac{3}{12} = 3\frac{15}{12}$$
$$-\,2\frac{4}{12} = 2\frac{4}{12}$$
$$1\frac{11}{12}$$

Another example:

$$7 = 6\frac{2}{2}$$
$$-\,3\frac{1}{2} = 3\frac{1}{2}$$
$$3\frac{1}{2}$$

$$\boxed{7 = 6 + \frac{2}{2} = 6\frac{2}{2}}$$

Checkpoint Write the letter of the correct answer.

Subtract. The answer must be in simplest form.

1. $2\frac{1}{5} - 1\frac{4}{5}$ **a.** $\frac{2}{5}$ **b.** $1\frac{2}{5}$ **c.** $1\frac{5}{5}$ **d.** $3\frac{2}{5}$

2. $7\frac{2}{3} - 1\frac{3}{4}$ **a.** $5\frac{9}{12}$ **b.** $5\frac{11}{12}$ **c.** $6\frac{11}{12}$ **d.** $7\frac{11}{12}$

3. $5 - 3\frac{2}{3}$ **a.** $1\frac{1}{3}$ **b.** $1\frac{2}{3}$ **c.** $2\frac{1}{3}$ **d.** $8\frac{2}{3}$

Subtract. Write the difference in simplest form.

1. $5\frac{1}{4}$
   $-2\frac{3}{4}$

2. $3\frac{3}{10}$
   $-1\frac{7}{10}$

3. $7\frac{1}{6}$
   $-1\frac{1}{6}$

4. $4\frac{7}{16}$
   $-2\frac{13}{16}$

5. $8\frac{1}{4}$
   $-4\frac{1}{4}$

6. $6\frac{1}{5}$
   $-6\frac{1}{20}$

7. $18\frac{1}{3}$
   $-8\frac{5}{6}$

8. $3\frac{2}{5}$
   $-2\frac{13}{20}$

9. $12\frac{1}{6}$
   $-5\frac{5}{12}$

10. $14\frac{2}{3}$
    $-6\frac{11}{12}$

11. $7\frac{4}{9} - 5\frac{7}{9}$

12. $19\frac{7}{17} - 18\frac{11}{17}$

13. $11 - 2\frac{5}{7}$

14. $7 - 1\frac{9}{10}$

15. $13\frac{3}{6} - 3\frac{15}{18}$

16. $8\frac{3}{5} - 1\frac{4}{5}$

17. $14 - 6\frac{12}{21}$

18. $5\frac{1}{3} - 3\frac{2}{3}$

★19. $(4\frac{1}{4} - \frac{3}{4}) - \frac{1}{4}$

★20. $(1\frac{7}{11} - \frac{9}{11}) - \frac{3}{22}$

★21. $(19 - 7\frac{3}{7}) - \frac{3}{14}$

Solve.

22. Maggie received a delivery of 14 dozen eggs. Of these, $5\frac{5}{12}$ dozen were broken and had to be sent back. How many dozen did Maggie keep?

23. Maggie picked $5\frac{1}{2}$ pounds of plums in the morning. By the end of the day, Potter had sold $1\frac{2}{3}$ pounds of them. The rest were given to a hospital. How many pounds were given to the hospital?

★24. Potter and Maggie kept a chart of their first day's sales so that they would know what to stock the second day. Copy and complete the chart. Then decide what they should stock the second day.

VEGETABLES SOLD ON THE FIRST DAY

Vegetables	Stocked (pounds)	Sold (pounds)	Not sold
green peppers	8	$7\frac{3}{8}$	▨
mushrooms	5	$2\frac{3}{4}$	▨
peas	$7\frac{1}{2}$	3	▨
radishes	$8\frac{1}{4}$	$2\frac{3}{4}$	▨

PROBLEM SOLVING
Interpreting the Quotient and the Remainder

Some problems require division. Pay special attention
to the answer you get when you divide. You may need to

1. use both the quotient and the remainder,
2. drop the remainder,
3. round the answer to the next greater whole number, or
4. use only the remainder.

Alice is putting up a fence in her nursery. The section
of shrubbery she wants to fence measures 122 feet
around. She is building the fence with wood posts and
wire mesh which is sold in 16 foot rolls.

Divide

$$\begin{array}{r} 7 \text{ R}10 \\ 16\overline{)122} \\ \underline{112} \\ 10 \end{array}$$

Read each question. Think about how the answers
differ for each question.

Question	Action	Answer
1. How many rolls of wire mesh will actually be used?	Use both the quotient and the remainder.	$7\frac{5}{8}$ rolls will be used.
2. How many whole rolls of wire mesh will be used?	Drop the remainder.	7 whole rolls will be used.
3. How many rolls does she need to buy?	Round the quotient to the next greater whole number.	8 rolls are needed. (7 full rolls will be used. 1 roll will be cut.)
4. How many feet of the last roll will she use?	Use only the remainder.	10 feet will be used.

Write the letter of the correct answer.

1. Alice orders 250 bags of fertilizer to sell at her nursery. She sends a van to pick them up. The van holds 38 bags at a time. How many round trips will the van make?

$$250 \div 38 = 6 \text{ R}22$$

   a. 6 round trips
   b. 22 round trips
   c. 7 round trips

2. Alice is planting tulip bulbs. She can plant up to 16 bulbs per pot. She has 5,238 bulbs. How many pots will be completely filled with bulbs?

$$5,258 \div 16 = 328 \text{ R}10$$

   a. 328 pots
   b. 10 pots
   c. 329 pots

Solve.

3. Alice is planting saplings. Each sapling needs 5 square feet of space. How many saplings can she plant in 117 square feet of earth?

4. Alice's nursery has 210 decorative bushes. A landscaper buys 25 bushes in one month. How many bushes are left in the nursery?

5. A customer buys 150 flowerpots. The car he has holds 42 pots at a time. How many carloads will it take to transport the pots?

6. Alice is building a greenhouse for African violets. She has a 48-square-foot pane of glass. How many 5-square-foot windows can she cut?

7. Alice runs a sale on fragrant plants. Customers can buy a dozen for a reduced price. The dozen plants are packed into a box that has just enough room for them. If Alice sells 3,084 plants during the sale, how many boxes are used?

8. This year Alice sold 1,072 evergreens. She has to place her order for next year's stock. She expects to sell at least as many evergreens next year as she did this year. She has to order evergreens in shipments of 55. How many shipments should she order?

9. Alice is setting up her seed display. She can put 14 packs of seeds into each slot. How many slots will she need to display 1,138 packages of seeds?

★10. A greenhouse at Alice's nursery has 340 planters. Each planter holds 10 plants. Alice has 1,092 plants in the greenhouse. How many planters are completely empty?

CALCULATOR

Clear the calculator. Press these numbers and commands on your calculator. Watch the display. What does it show?

$$\boxed{0}\ \boxed{+}\ \boxed{1}\ \boxed{2}\ \boxed{=}\ \boxed{=}\ \boxed{=}$$

The display on most calculators will show 12, 24, 36.

Each time you press the $\boxed{=}$, the calculator adds 12 more to the total. This gives multiples of 12: 12 × 1, 12 × 2, 12 × 3, and so on. Find the first ten multiples of 12: 12, 24, 36, 48, 60, 72, 84, 96, 108, 120

You can use the calculator to help find the least common multiple of two different numbers. Find the first ten multiples of 15: Clear the calculator.

Press: $\boxed{0}\ \boxed{+}\ \boxed{1}\ \boxed{5}\ \boxed{=}\ \boxed{=}\ \boxed{=}\ \boxed{=}\ \boxed{=}\ \boxed{=}\ \boxed{=}\ \boxed{=}\ \boxed{=}\ \boxed{=}$

Display: 15, 30, 45, 60, 75, 90, 105, 120, 135, 150

You can see that 60 and 120 are in both sets of multiples. So, 60 is the LCM of 12 and 15.

Find the least common multiple of these sets of numbers on your calculator.

Numbers	Ten Multiples	Common Multiples	LCM
1. 28 7			
2. 50 60			
3. 22 33			
4. 3 5			
5. 14 6			

For a related activity, see *Connecting Math Ideas,* p. 411.

GROUP PROJECT

What Makes Your Garden Grow?

The problem: Jenny and Josh both had champion squash plants at the fair. "It was the right amount of sunlight," said Jenny. Josh believed it was the right amount of water. Can you find out the effect of sun and water on a plant's growth?

To see the effect of sunlight, follow these steps.
- Take two containers, and fill them with good soil.
- Plant several kidney, pinto, or lima beans in each pot.
- Mark one pot with a picture of the sun.
- Place both pots in a warm, light spot, and water them.
- After they sprout, give the pot with the picture of the sun 6 hours of sunlight every day. Then cover it with a cardboard box.
- Give the other pot only 3 hours of sun every day.
- At the end of 24 days, measure each plant. What is the difference?

Design your own experiment to show the difference between enough water and too little water on plant growth.

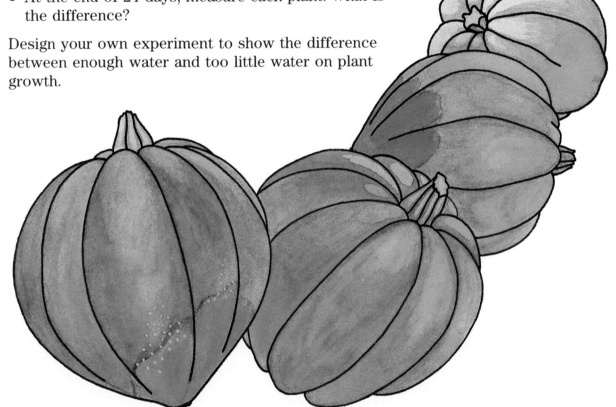

CHAPTER TEST

Find the least common multiple. (page 226)

Find the greatest common factor. (page 228)

1. 6, 8

2. 16, 24, 64

Write *prime* or *composite* to describe the number. (page 230)

Write the fraction for the part that is shaded. (page 232)

3. 21

4. 43

5.

6. △ △ △ ○ ○ ☐ ☐ ☐ ☐

Complete. (page 236)

Write in simplest form. (page 238)

7. $\frac{2}{5} = \frac{\blacksquare}{10}$

8. $\frac{5}{8} = \frac{10}{\blacksquare}$

9. $\frac{9}{27}$

10. $\frac{8}{40}$

Write as a whole number or as a mixed number. (page 240)

11. $\frac{9}{4}$

12. $\frac{16}{3}$

13. $\frac{49}{7}$

Write as a fraction. (page 240)

14. $4\frac{2}{3}$

15. $6\frac{3}{8}$

16. $4\frac{1}{2}$

Compare. Write >, <, or = for ●. (page 242)

17. $\frac{2}{5}$ ● $\frac{4}{9}$

18. $1\frac{3}{8}$ ● $1\frac{4}{12}$

Write in order from the least to the greatest. (page 242)

19. $\frac{1}{5}, \frac{1}{9}, \frac{1}{4}$

20. $\frac{1}{2}, \frac{5}{8}, \frac{2}{3}$

Estimate. (page 248)

21. $\frac{3}{8} + \frac{1}{16}$

22. $5\frac{1}{7} + 2\frac{3}{8}$

Add. Write the sum in simplest form. (pages 246, 250, 252, 254, and 256)

23. $\frac{3}{12} + \frac{11}{12}$

24. $\frac{2}{7} + \frac{3}{4}$

25. $\frac{5}{6} + \frac{3}{5}$

26. $\begin{array}{r} 6\frac{1}{3} \\ + 2\frac{1}{3} \\ \hline \end{array}$

27. $\begin{array}{r} 5\frac{7}{8} \\ + 3\frac{1}{8} \\ \hline \end{array}$

28. $\begin{array}{r} 4\frac{2}{3} \\ + 2\frac{3}{8} \\ \hline \end{array}$

29. $\begin{array}{r} 19\frac{7}{9} \\ + 8\frac{1}{6} \\ \hline \end{array}$

Subtract. Write the difference in simplest form.
(pages 252, 258, and 260)

30. $\frac{5}{6} - \frac{2}{6}$ **31.** $\frac{3}{4} - \frac{2}{9}$ **32.** $\frac{4}{5} - \frac{1}{6}$

33. 6 **34.** $3\frac{5}{8}$ **35.** $5\frac{1}{7}$ **36.** $4\frac{2}{3}$
    $-2\frac{1}{3}$ $-2\frac{7}{8}$ $-1\frac{3}{28}$ $-2\frac{3}{8}$

Solve. Write the letter of the operation you would use
to solve the problem. (pages 234–235)

37. Bob worked 38 hours on a dairy farm. Herb worked twice as many hours. How long did Herb work on the dairy farm?

   a. addition   **b.** subtraction
   c. multiplication   **d.** division

38. The 90 students in the agriculture course are placed in classes of no more than 20 students. How many classes are there?

   a. addition   **b.** subtraction
   c. multiplication   **d.** division

Write the letter of the correct answer. (pages 262–263)

39. Mr. Meyers harvested enough millet to fill all his grain bins, with 1,697 pounds left. He rented extra bins, each to hold 96 pounds of grain. How many bins did Mr. Meyers have to rent?

   a. 17   **b.** 18   **c.** 17 R64   **d.** $\frac{2}{3}$

40. Mr. Meyers's soybean crop totaled 10,214 pounds. He stored the crop in bins holding 92 pounds each. He sold all the soy except for that in the partly filled bin. How many pounds of soybeans did Mr. Meyers keep?

   a. 111   **b.** 111 R2   **c.** 2   **d.** $\frac{1}{46}$

BONUS

In each square below, choose the three fractions or
mixed numbers that, when added, give the greatest
sum. Then choose the three fractions or mixed
numbers that, when added, give the least sum.

1.

$\frac{4}{5}$	$\frac{6}{7}$	$\frac{2}{3}$	$\frac{7}{10}$
	$\frac{8}{12}$	$\frac{5}{8}$	$\frac{3}{5}$
$\frac{4}{16}$		$\frac{9}{11}$	$\frac{1}{8}$

2.

$2\frac{3}{8}$	$3\frac{3}{8}$	$2\frac{5}{6}$
$4\frac{3}{10}$	$2\frac{2}{3}$	$3\frac{7}{8}$
$3\frac{15}{20}$	$2\frac{3}{8}$	$4\frac{4}{5}$

RETEACHING

Before you can subtract mixed numbers, you may have to rename.

Find $7\frac{1}{5} - 4\frac{1}{3}$.

Find fractions that have like denominators.

$7\frac{1}{5} = 7\frac{3}{15}$
$-\ 4\frac{1}{3} = 4\frac{5}{15}$

Compare fractions. Rename if necessary.

$\frac{3}{15} < \frac{5}{15}$

$7\frac{3}{15} = 6 + 1 + \frac{3}{15}$

$\qquad = 6 + \frac{15}{15} + \frac{3}{15}$

$\qquad = 6\frac{18}{15}$

Subtract. Write the answer in simplest form.

$7\frac{3}{15} = 6\frac{18}{15}$
$-\ 4\frac{5}{15} = 4\frac{5}{15}$
$\qquad\quad\ \ 2\frac{13}{15}$

Another example:

$\quad 9\ = 8\frac{5}{5}$
$-\ 4\frac{1}{5} = 4\frac{1}{5}$
$\qquad\quad 4\frac{4}{5}$

$\boxed{9 = 8 + \frac{5}{5} = 8\frac{5}{5}}$

Subtract. Write the answer in simplest form.

1. $\quad 17\frac{1}{5}$
$\quad -\ 15\frac{2}{5}$

2. $\quad 9\frac{3}{10}$
$\quad -\ 7\frac{9}{10}$

3. $\quad 14$
$\quad -\ 12\frac{5}{6}$

4. $\quad 16\frac{2}{5}$
$\quad -\ 7\frac{4}{5}$

5. $\quad 14\frac{3}{11}$
$\quad -\ 2\frac{9}{11}$

6. $\quad 13\frac{1}{5}$
$\quad -\ 3\frac{3}{4}$

7. $\quad 21\frac{5}{6}$
$\quad -\ 9\frac{9}{10}$

8. $\quad 5\frac{3}{11}$
$\quad -\ 3\frac{1}{3}$

9. $\quad 18\frac{1}{9}$
$\quad -\ 8\frac{5}{6}$

10. $\quad 7$
$\quad -\ 4\frac{3}{5}$

11. $\quad 13\frac{2}{5}$
$\quad -\ 7\frac{4}{25}$

12. $\quad 3\frac{1}{5}$
$\quad -\ 1\frac{1}{3}$

13. $\quad 17\frac{5}{9}$
$\quad -\ 12\frac{1}{4}$

14. $\quad 4\frac{3}{7}$
$\quad -\ 2\frac{1}{4}$

15. $\quad 23\frac{5}{6}$
$\quad -\ 11\frac{2}{9}$

16. $9\frac{2}{5} - 4\frac{1}{2}$

17. $4 - 2\frac{1}{3}$

18. $2\frac{3}{8} - 1\frac{7}{8}$

19. $14\frac{2}{9} - 8\frac{2}{3}$

20. $12 - 3\frac{1}{5}$

21. $20\frac{2}{7} - 3\frac{1}{3}$

22. $8\frac{3}{10} - 5\frac{7}{10}$

23. $13\frac{2}{5} - 12\frac{3}{4}$

ENRICHMENT

Cross Products

To find the cross products of two fractions, multiply each numerator by the denominator in the other fraction. If the cross products are equal, the fractions are equivalent.

Are $\frac{4}{8}$ and $\frac{1}{2}$ equivalent fractions?

Cross multiply.

$$4 \times 2 \; \bullet \; 1 \times 8$$
$$8 \; = \; 8$$

The cross products are equal; so, the fractions are equivalent.

Write = or ≠. Use the cross products.

1. $\frac{3}{4} \; \bullet \; \frac{6}{8}$ 2. $\frac{5}{7} \; \bullet \; \frac{6}{9}$ 3. $\frac{4}{23} \; \bullet \; \frac{7}{29}$ 4. $\frac{2}{9} \; \bullet \; \frac{3}{8}$

5. $\frac{5}{15} \; \bullet \; \frac{3}{9}$ 6. $\frac{2}{3} \; \bullet \; \frac{9}{12}$ 7. $\frac{8}{18} \; \bullet \; \frac{4}{9}$ 8. $\frac{5}{6} \; \bullet \; \frac{7}{9}$

9. $\frac{4}{10} \; \bullet \; \frac{6}{15}$ 10. $\frac{5}{7} \; \bullet \; \frac{10}{14}$ 11. $\frac{3}{8} \; \bullet \; \frac{4}{9}$ 12. $\frac{3}{10} \; \bullet \; \frac{5}{15}$

13. $\frac{13}{19} \; \bullet \; \frac{7}{12}$ 14. $\frac{3}{5} \; \bullet \; \frac{9}{15}$ 15. $\frac{7}{8} \; \bullet \; \frac{9}{11}$ 16. $\frac{10}{25} \; \bullet \; \frac{2}{5}$

17. $\frac{12}{36} \; \bullet \; \frac{1}{3}$ 18. $\frac{9}{20} \; \bullet \; \frac{11}{25}$ 19. $\frac{8}{16} \; \bullet \; \frac{1}{2}$ 20. $\frac{5}{6} \; \bullet \; \frac{10}{12}$

Solve. Use cross products.

21. A mountaineering club makes two expeditions, one in May and one in July. In May, $\frac{4}{5}$ of the club goes on the expedition. In July, $\frac{2}{3}$ of the club goes on the expedition. Does the same fraction of the club go on each expedition?

22. Dan the milkman delivers $\frac{4}{10}$ of his weekly milk supply on Monday. On Tuesday, he delivers $\frac{2}{5}$ of his milk supply. Does Dan deliver the same fraction of his milk supply on each day?

CUMULATIVE REVIEW

Write the letter of the correct answer.

1. $742.7 \div 10$

   a. 7.427
   b. 74.27
   c. 7,427
   d. not given

2. A 10,000-meter run is how many kilometers long?

   a. 0.001 km
   b. 1 km
   c. 10 km
   d. not given

3. $96.15 \div 6$

   a. 16.02
   b. 16.025
   c. 16.25
   d. not given

4. Which unit would you use to measure the length of a pencil point?

   a. millimeters
   b. centimeters
   c. meters
   d. not given

5. $4.395 \div 15$

   a. 0.233
   b. 0.293
   c. 0.333
   d. not given

6. $6,372 + 3,498 + 65 + 412$

   a. 10,006
   b. 11,446
   c. 12,400
   d. not given

7. 0.7×0.25

   a. 0.175
   b. 0.555
   c. 0.715
   d. not given

8. Estimate $7,616,518 + 5,146,192$.

   a. 1,200,000
   b. 1,300,000
   c. 13,000,000
   d. 14,000,000

9. Order from the least to the greatest: 7.53, 7.503, 7.35, 5.

   a. 5, 7.53, 7.503, 7.35
   b. 7.35, 7.53, 5, 7.503
   c. 5, 7.35, 7.503, 7.53
   d. not given

10. Estimate $3,751 \div 5$.

    a. 7
    b. 70
    c. 700
    d. 7,000

11. $21,000 - 1,362$

    a. 19,638
    b. 19,748
    c. 20,362
    d. 20,638

12. Fred's car cost $8,799.00. Al's car cost $11,851.72. Herb's car cost $7,327.51 more than the combined cost of Fred's and Al's cars. What was the cost of Herb's car?

    a. $13,323.21
    b. $19,179.23
    c. $27,978.23
    d. not given

13. One year, Hank's Sporting Goods sold 327,523 baseballs, and Sal's Sporting Goods sold 299,858 baseballs. How many more baseballs did Hank's sell than Sal's?

    a. 27,665
    b. 38,775
    c. 627,387
    d. not given

Suppose your class is holding a carnival to raise money. What games would you organize? How much would you charge for each? How much money could you earn?

9 MULTIPLYING AND DIVIDING FRACTIONS
Customary Measurement

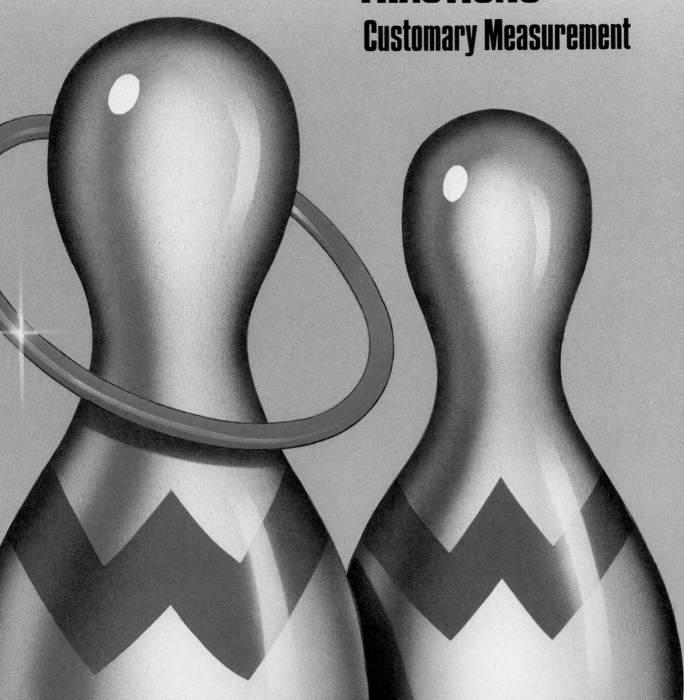

Multiplying Fractions Using Models

When the actors met for their first rehearsal, they discovered that boxes of props covered $\frac{1}{2}$ of the stage area. The stage crew quickly cleared $\frac{1}{3}$ of that area so that the rehearsal could begin. What part of the stage did the crew clear?

You can use a model to show $\frac{1}{3}$ of $\frac{1}{2}$.

Here is $\frac{1}{2}$ of the stage.

Here is $\frac{1}{3}$ of $\frac{1}{2}$.

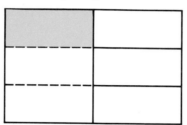

$\frac{1}{3}$ of $\frac{1}{2}$ is the same as $\frac{1}{6}$ of 1 whole.
The crew cleared $\frac{1}{6}$ of the stage.

You can use multiplication to find $\frac{1}{3}$ of $\frac{1}{2}$.
Multiply $\frac{1}{3} \times \frac{1}{2}$.

Multiply the numerators.
Multiply the denominators.

$$\frac{1}{3} \times \frac{1}{2} = \frac{1 \times 1}{3 \times 2} = \frac{1}{6}$$

If necessary, write the product in simplest form.

Multiply $\frac{2}{3} \times \frac{3}{4}$.

$$\frac{2}{3} \times \frac{3}{4} = \frac{2 \times 3}{3 \times 4} = \frac{6}{12} = \frac{1}{2}$$

Checkpoint   Write the letter of the correct answer.

Multiply. The answer should be in simplest form.

1. $\frac{1}{5} \times \frac{3}{5}$

a. $\frac{3}{25}$

b. $\frac{4}{25}$

c. $\frac{4}{10}$

d. $\frac{4}{5}$

2. $\frac{2}{3} \times \frac{3}{10}$

a. $\frac{1}{5}$

b. $\frac{5}{13}$

c. $\frac{5}{30}$

d. $\frac{6}{13}$

3. $\frac{5}{6} \times \frac{3}{4}$

a. $\frac{1}{3}$

b. $\frac{4}{5}$

c. $\frac{5}{8}$

d. $\frac{3}{2}$

Multiply. Write the answer in simplest form.

1. $\frac{1}{7} \times \frac{1}{5}$ **2.** $\frac{1}{3} \times \frac{1}{9}$ **3.** $\frac{1}{4} \times \frac{1}{2}$ **4.** $\frac{1}{7} \times \frac{1}{7}$ **5.** $\frac{1}{5} \times \frac{1}{8}$

6. $\frac{4}{9} \times \frac{2}{5}$ **7.** $\frac{7}{8} \times \frac{3}{4}$ **8.** $\frac{2}{3} \times \frac{5}{7}$ **9.** $\frac{4}{7} \times \frac{2}{9}$ **10.** $\frac{3}{8} \times \frac{3}{4}$

11. $\frac{2}{4} \times \frac{1}{2}$ **12.** $\frac{1}{8} \times \frac{4}{5}$ **13.** $\frac{1}{3} \times \frac{3}{4}$ **14.** $\frac{5}{9} \times \frac{1}{5}$ **15.** $\frac{1}{2} \times \frac{4}{5}$

16. $\frac{5}{6} \times \frac{2}{5}$ **17.** $\frac{3}{10} \times \frac{5}{6}$ **18.** $\frac{3}{4} \times \frac{2}{5}$ **19.** $\frac{3}{4} \times \frac{5}{6}$ **20.** $\frac{5}{8} \times \frac{2}{5}$

21. $\frac{4}{9} \times \frac{3}{4}$ ★**22.** $\frac{1}{2} \times \frac{1}{3} \times \frac{1}{4}$ ★**23.** $\frac{3}{7} \times \frac{1}{7} \times \frac{1}{3}$ ★**24.** $\frac{1}{4} \times \frac{3}{5} \times \frac{2}{3}$ ★**25.** $\frac{2}{5} \times \frac{2}{3} \times \frac{5}{8}$

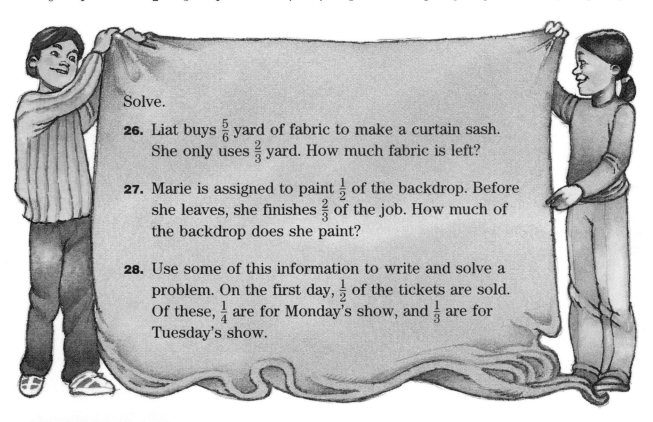

Solve.

26. Liat buys $\frac{5}{6}$ yard of fabric to make a curtain sash. She only uses $\frac{2}{3}$ yard. How much fabric is left?

27. Marie is assigned to paint $\frac{1}{2}$ of the backdrop. Before she leaves, she finishes $\frac{2}{3}$ of the job. How much of the backdrop does she paint?

28. Use some of this information to write and solve a problem. On the first day, $\frac{1}{2}$ of the tickets are sold. Of these, $\frac{1}{4}$ are for Monday's show, and $\frac{1}{3}$ are for Tuesday's show.

CHALLENGE

Take a shortcut when you multiply fractions. First divide by a common factor.

2 is a common factor of 2 and 4. Divide by 2; then multiply.

$$\frac{3}{\overset{}{\underset{2}{4}}} \times \frac{\overset{1}{2}}{7} = \frac{3 \times 1}{2 \times 7} = \frac{3}{14}$$

Use the shortcut to multiply.

1. $\frac{1}{3} \times \frac{6}{7}$ **2.** $\frac{1}{2} \times \frac{4}{9}$ **3.** $\frac{3}{5} \times \frac{5}{8}$ ★**4.** $\frac{2}{3} \times \frac{3}{10}$ ★**5.** $\frac{3}{4} \times \frac{8}{15}$

Multiplying Fractions and Whole Numbers

A. There are 12 students in the stage crew. Of these, $\frac{1}{3}$ are responsible for painting scenery. How many students paint scenery?

Find $\frac{1}{3}$ of 12. $\qquad$ **$\frac{1}{3} \times 12$**

Write the whole number as a fraction. $\qquad$ **$\frac{1}{3} \times \frac{12}{1}$**

Multiply the fractions. $\qquad$ **$\frac{1}{3} \times \frac{12}{1} = \frac{1 \times 12}{3 \times 1} = \frac{12}{3}$**

Write the product as a whole number. $\qquad \frac{12}{3} = 4$

4 students paint scenery.

B. Sometimes the answer is a fraction or a mixed number.

Find $\frac{1}{10} \times 5$. $\qquad$ **$\frac{1}{10} \times \frac{5}{1} = \frac{5}{10}$ or $\frac{1}{2}$**

Find $6 \times \frac{3}{4}$. $\qquad$ **$\frac{6}{1} \times \frac{3}{4} = \frac{18}{4} = 4\frac{2}{4}$ or $4\frac{1}{2}$**

Checkpoint Write the letter of the correct answer.

Multiply. The answer should be in simplest form.

1. $\frac{2}{5} \times 5$

a. $\frac{10}{25}$
b. $\frac{2}{25}$
c. 2
d. $1\frac{2}{5}$

2. $2 \times \frac{5}{12}$

a. $\frac{5}{6}$
b. $\frac{7}{12}$
c. $\frac{5}{24}$
d. $\frac{10}{24}$

3. $\frac{5}{6} \times 4$

a. $\frac{20}{24}$
b. $\frac{5}{24}$
c. $1\frac{1}{2}$
d. $3\frac{1}{3}$

Multiply. Write the answer in simplest form.

1. $\frac{1}{2} \times 8$ **2.** $4 \times \frac{3}{4}$ **3.** $10 \times \frac{2}{5}$ **4.** $\frac{3}{4} \times 8$ **5.** $6 \times \frac{2}{3}$

6. $2 \times \frac{1}{3}$ **7.** $\frac{2}{9} \times 4$ **8.** $\frac{3}{10} \times 3$ **9.** $5 \times \frac{1}{8}$ **10.** $\frac{2}{5} \times 2$

11. $3 \times \frac{2}{9}$ **12.** $\frac{5}{12} \times 2$ **13.** $2 \times \frac{3}{10}$ **14.** $\frac{3}{16} \times 4$ **15.** $2 \times \frac{3}{8}$

16. $\frac{5}{8} \times 10$ **17.** $6 \times \frac{3}{4}$ **18.** $\frac{5}{6} \times 8$ **19.** $12 \times \frac{7}{10}$ **20.** $14 \times \frac{3}{8}$

21. $\frac{5}{9} \times 6$ **22.** $6 \times \frac{3}{8}$ **23.** $64 \times \frac{1}{8}$ **24.** $6 \times \frac{7}{10}$ **25.** $\frac{1}{3} \times 25$

★26. $7 \times \frac{1}{8} \times \frac{1}{2}$ **★27.** $\frac{1}{4} \times 5 \times \frac{2}{5}$ **★28.** $\frac{2}{3} \times \frac{1}{6} \times 8$

Solve.

29. Margot draws a lamppost that is $\frac{2}{3}$ the height of the backdrop. If the backdrop is 9 feet high, how high is the lamppost?

30. Maya spends 2 hours gathering materials needed to create special effects. Then Ralph takes over for $\frac{1}{2}$ hour. How much time is spent on gathering the materials?

31. A gallon of paint usually costs $20. Students who shop at Myer's Paint Shop receive a discount equal to $\frac{1}{5}$ of the regular price. What is the amount of the discount?

32. Jeffrey has designed 40 posters to advertise the play. If he gives the publicity committee $\frac{3}{4}$ of them, how many posters does he have left?

CALCULATOR

Use your calculator to find the product of $\frac{7}{8} \times \frac{6}{7}$. You know that $\frac{7}{8}$ is the same as $8\overline{)7}$, or $7 \div 8$. So, $\frac{7}{8} \times \frac{6}{7}$ is the same as $(7 \div 8) \times (6 \div 7)$. You can use your calculator to find the product.

  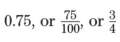 0.75, or $\frac{75}{100}$, or $\frac{3}{4}$

Use your calculator to solve.

1. $\frac{3}{4} \times \frac{2}{3}$ **2.** $\frac{3}{10} \times \frac{1}{3}$ **3.** $\frac{3}{8} \times \frac{4}{5}$ **4.** $\frac{3}{4} \times \frac{5}{6}$

5. $\frac{3}{8} \times \frac{2}{3}$ **6.** $\frac{9}{10} \times \frac{5}{12}$ **7.** $\frac{7}{8} \times \frac{64}{8}$ **8.** $\frac{9}{15} \times \frac{36}{27}$

Multiplying Fractions and Mixed Numbers

A. This year's musical is going to include a rainbow of colors and costumes. For the boys' shirts, $\frac{1}{2}$ bolt of red satin is needed. $5\frac{3}{4}$ times that is needed for the girls' skirts. How much red satin is needed for the skirts?

Find $5\frac{3}{4} \times \frac{1}{2}$.

Rename the mixed number.

$5\frac{3}{4} = \frac{23}{4}$

Multiply the fractions.

$\frac{23}{4} \times \frac{1}{2} = \frac{23}{8}$

Write the product as a mixed number.

$\frac{23}{8} = 2\frac{7}{8}$

For the girls' skirts, $2\frac{7}{8}$ bolts of satin are needed.

B. In some examples, you can write fractions for both factors before multiplying.

Find $6 \times 2\frac{1}{5}$. $\quad \frac{6}{1} \times \frac{11}{5} = \frac{66}{5} = 13\frac{1}{5}$

Find $3\frac{1}{9} \times 2\frac{1}{2}$. $\quad \frac{28}{9} \times \frac{5}{2} = \frac{140}{18} = 7\frac{7}{9}$

Checkpoint Write the letter of the correct answer.

Multiply. The answer should be in simplest form.

1. $\frac{2}{3} \times 1\frac{7}{8}$

2. $2 \times 4\frac{1}{8}$

3. $3\frac{1}{3} \times 5\frac{1}{4}$

a. $1\frac{7}{12}$

b. $1\frac{5}{12}$

c. $1\frac{1}{3}$

d. $1\frac{1}{4}$

a. $\frac{1}{16}$

b. $3\frac{1}{4}$

c. $8\frac{1}{4}$

d. $8\frac{1}{8}$

a. $\frac{210}{12}$

b. $15\frac{1}{2}$

c. $15\frac{3}{4}$

d. $17\frac{1}{2}$

Multiply. Write each product in simplest form.

1. $\frac{1}{2} \times 6\frac{2}{3}$ **2.** $\frac{2}{5} \times 5\frac{1}{2}$ **3.** $9\frac{1}{3} \times \frac{1}{6}$ **4.** $4\frac{1}{2} \times \frac{2}{3}$

5. $7 \times 3\frac{3}{4}$ **6.** $2\frac{2}{5} \times 5$ **7.** $4 \times 3\frac{1}{8}$ **8.** $2\frac{1}{2} \times 6$

9. $3\frac{2}{5} \times 4\frac{1}{4}$ **10.** $2\frac{1}{4} \times 1\frac{1}{6}$ **11.** $8\frac{2}{5} \times 3\frac{1}{8}$ **12.** $2\frac{1}{2} \times 3\frac{1}{3}$

13. $2\frac{1}{3} \times 1\frac{3}{5}$ **14.** $\frac{5}{6} \times 5\frac{1}{13}$ **15.** $\frac{2}{3} \times 8$ **16.** $3 \times 1\frac{5}{6}$

17. $1\frac{3}{5} \times 4\frac{3}{4}$ **18.** $\frac{1}{2} \times 3\frac{3}{5}$ **19.** $\frac{1}{3} \times 1\frac{1}{8}$ **20.** $2 \times 2\frac{1}{9}$

Solve.

21. The sparkling silver fabric used to create the nighttime sky weighs $10\frac{1}{2}$ pounds. The red velvet for the sunset weighs $\frac{2}{3}$ as much. How much does the red velvet weigh?

22. Use the advertisement to make up your own problem.

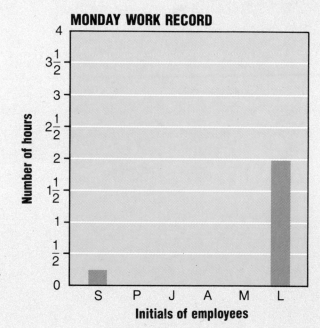

SALE
at Buttons and Bows
Get ¼ yard free for every
2½ yards of fabric you buy.

CHALLENGE

Each day the head of the costume department keeps track of how many hours each person works. Copy the graph, and use the data below to complete it. Who worked the most hours?

- Sue worked $\frac{1}{4}$ of an hour.
- Pete worked 2 times as much as Sue.
- José worked $1\frac{1}{2}$ times as much as Pete.
- Anne worked $4\frac{2}{3}$ times as much as José.
- Max worked $\frac{3}{7}$ of what Anne worked.
- Lily worked $1\frac{1}{3}$ times as much as Max.

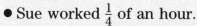

MONDAY WORK RECORD

Number of hours

Initials of employees

S P J A M L

PROBLEM SOLVING
Estimation

You can solve problems by using estimated amounts. Often when you estimate, you have to decide to what place you should round the numbers. You can estimate more closely by rounding numbers to different places.

The after-school film-club members rate the latest movies. The movies are rated as follows:

Points	Rating	
240 and under	*Tree House*	⌐
241–280	*Standing By*	★
281–320	*Greetings*	★ ★
321–360	*Broken Trail*	★ ★ ★
361–400	*Rain Go Away*	★ ★ ★ ★

Liza, a club member, is adding the points for 2 different films. She wants to quickly compare their ratings. She decides to estimate. Liza first rounds to the nearest ten and finds that the sums are the same. So, she rounds to the nearest whole number.

	A Winner Never Quits			*Forever*		
Acting	86.685---	90---	87	85.75---	90---	86
Cinematography	83.66-----	80---	84	84.75---	80---	85
Script	85.25-----	90---	85	89.50---	90---	90
Effects, costumes, etc.	71.25-----+ 70----+ 71			74.25----+ 70----+ 74		
		330	327		330	335

When you are comparing amounts that are close, you need a more exact estimate. If the more exact estimates are close, you can round to the nearest tenth or even hundredth. By rounding to the nearest whole number, Liza found that *Forever* received a slightly higher rating than *A Winner Never Quits*.

Estimate to solve.

1. The film club shows films every Wednesday from 3:30 to 5:30 P.M. The club members must leave no later than 5:45 P.M. This Wednesday they are showing these films.

   A Trail of Leaves—$22\frac{1}{2}$ min

   The Last Game —$36\frac{1}{2}$ min

   Clyde, the Pig —27 min

   Math Class —$15\frac{1}{4}$ min

   Will they be finished viewing by 5:30—5:35 P.M.?

2. One group of film-club members is videotaping a drama. So far they have spent these amounts.

   Videotape ————————————$9.39
   Duplicating the tape ————————$12.95
   Equipment rental ————————$49.98
   ($24.99/day)
   Props, Costumes ——————————$27.88

   They have a budget of $105.00. Do they have enough money to rent equipment for another day?

3. What rating should the following film receive? (Use the ratings on page 278.) *Greetings:* 84.575, 84.575, 78.66, 66.66.

4. The video club needs a camera and lights. A camera costs $279.85 to purchase. Lights cost $89.95 to buy. Rented equipment costs $24.99 a day for 12 days. Is it better over the year to buy or rent the equipment?

5. Ralph, the film-club president, counts 24 students who have paid the $0.90 admission to the showing. He also knows that last week the club earned $28.75. Has the club earned the $49.98 needed to pay for the rental of video equipment?

★6. Use the list below to make two film-club programs that take up at least 100 min but not more than 125 min each.

Scarlet Rose	$33\frac{1}{4}$ min
Tree House	$32\frac{1}{4}$ min
Standing By	$45\frac{1}{2}$ min
Parachute	$16\frac{2}{3}$ min
Broken Trail	$38\frac{1}{2}$ min
Rain Go Away	$75\frac{1}{2}$ min

★7. The group wants to purchase videos for their video library. The list on the right shows the videos they want and their prices. They have $164.41. Which videos could they purchase?

Together	$19.96
Raise the Flag	$21.75
Patty Malone	$29.00
Shiny Days	$18.75
Viola	$25.98
School Days	$36.98
Vegetable Soup	$29.99

Dividing Whole Numbers by Fractions

Daniela does the makeup for the actors in the play. She uses sticks of greasepaint. She needs $\frac{1}{2}$ stick to make up one actor. How many actors can she make up with 4 sticks of greasepaint?

You need to find how many $\frac{1}{2}$'s there are in 4 sticks.

To find how many, you divide.
You can use a picture to help you.

There are 8 halves in 4. $4 \div \frac{1}{2} = 8$

Check by multiplying. $8 \times \frac{1}{2} = 4$

Daniela can make up 8 actors.

Another example: $5 \div \frac{1}{3} =$ ■

There are 15 thirds in 5. $5 \div \frac{1}{3} = 15$

Check by multiplying. $15 \times \frac{1}{3} = 5$

Checkpoint Write the letter of the correct answer.

Divide.

1.

$3 \div \frac{1}{3} =$

a. 1

b. $3\frac{1}{3}$

c. 3

d. 9

2.

$6 \div \frac{1}{4} =$

a. $1\frac{1}{2}$

b. 6

c. 24

d. $6\frac{1}{4}$

3.

$3 \div \frac{1}{2} =$

a. $3\frac{1}{2}$

b. 5

c. 6

d. 7

Math Reasoning, page H203

Divide.

1. $3 \div \frac{1}{4}$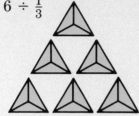

2. $5 \div \frac{1}{4}$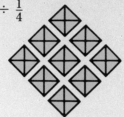

3. $4 \div \frac{1}{3}$

4. $6 \div \frac{1}{3}$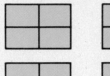

5. $9 \div \frac{1}{4}$

6. $4 \div \frac{1}{6}$

7. $4 \div \frac{1}{4}$

8. $7 \div \frac{1}{2}$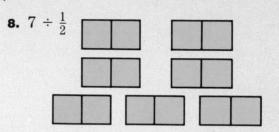

Solve. Draw a picture to help you.

9. The refreshment committee has 5 bottles of cider at the opening-night party. If $\frac{1}{4}$ bottle fills 1 cup, how many cups of cider are there?

10. The decoration committee has 15 yards of crepe paper to decorate the room. They use $\frac{1}{3}$ of it. How many yards do they use?

11. There are 6 cantaloupes to serve 48 people at the party. If each person eats $\frac{1}{4}$ melon, will there be enough melon for all? If not, how many more melons are needed?

12. Use this information to write and solve a problem of your own. Leonard has 6 boxes of napkins. Every table in the party room needs $\frac{1}{8}$ of a box of napkins.

MIDCHAPTER REVIEW

Multiply or divide. The answer should be in simplest form.

1. $\frac{7}{8} \times \frac{3}{4}$

2. $\frac{2}{3} \times \frac{3}{7}$

3. $5 \times \frac{1}{2}$

4. $\frac{9}{10} \times 11$

5. $2\frac{1}{4} \times 4\frac{4}{7}$

6. $2\frac{1}{3} \times 1\frac{3}{5}$

7. $6 \div \frac{1}{5}$

8. $12 \div \frac{1}{7}$

PROBLEM SOLVING
Making a Table To Find a Pattern

Sometimes you can make a table to find a pattern that will help you solve a problem.

> The River City High School is planning its yearly musical. In order to play certain music, the orchestra has to have a certain number of kinds of instruments. If there are 5 stringed instruments, there must be 3 woodwind instruments. If there are 10 strings, there must be 6 woodwinds. If there are 15 strings, there must be 9 woodwinds. How many woodwinds will be needed if 30 strings are used?

You can make a table to solve this problem by finding a pattern.

ORCHESTRA

Strings	5	10	15	
Woodwinds	3	6	9	

You can see that there is a pattern in the way the number of strings increases. The number increases by 5 each time. So, the next number in the table will be 20. The increase in woodwinds also shows a pattern. That number increases each time by 3. The next number in the table will be 12. Once you have figured out the pattern, you can use it to solve the problem by filling in the table until you reach 30 stringed instruments.

ORCHESTRA

Strings	5	10	15	20	25	30
Woodwinds	3	6	9	12	15	18

If 30 stringed instruments are used, the orchestra will need 18 woodwinds.

For additional activities, see *Connecting Math Ideas,* page 412.

Copy and complete the table to solve.

1. Day 1's rehearsal for the musical ran for 30 minutes. Day 2's rehearsal was 4 minutes longer. Day 3's rehearsal was 5 minutes longer than the previous day's. Rehearsal on Day 4 was 6 minutes longer than the one on Day 3. If the pattern continues, on which day would the rehearsal run for 60 minutes?

Day	1	2	3	▦	▦	▦	▦	▦	▦
Rehearsal time	▦	▦	▦	▦	▦	▦	▦	▦	▦

2. After how many days would the rehearsal last 90 minutes?

Solve. Make a table if needed.

3. The school auditorium has two levels: the main level and the balcony. When tickets for the musical went on sale, 4 balcony tickets were sold for every 3 main-level tickets. How many balcony tickets were sold if 45 tickets for the main level were sold?

4. If 33 tickets for the main level were sold, how many tickets for the balcony were sold?

5. One piece of scenery for the musical is attached to a pulley. When the stage manager uses a crank to turn the wheel of the pulley $1\frac{1}{2}$ times, the scenery is lowered 1 foot. How many times does the manager need to turn the pulley wheel in order to lower the scenery 12 feet?

6. How far is the scenery lowered after $13\frac{1}{2}$ turns?

7. During intermission, refreshments were sold. Jan sold rice cakes with cheese. For every 4 cakes she sold, she gave away 1. How many cakes did she give away if she sold 48?

Time

A. You can read time two ways.

| **9:45** |  |

Read 9:45 as 45 minutes after 9, or 15 minutes before 10.

A.M. is the time between 12:00 midnight and 12:00 noon.

P.M. is the time between 12:00 noon and 12:00 midnight.

B. Marcy is setting up a booth at her school fair. She began at 9:45 A.M. She finished at 1:00 P.M. How much time did Marcy need to set up her booth?

To find **elapsed time,** count the minutes and then the hours.

9:45 A.M. to 10:00 A.M. is 15 minutes.   10:00 A.M. to 1:00 P.M. is 3 hours.

Marcy needs 3 hours 15 minutes to set up her booth.

C. These units are used to measure time.

60 seconds (s) = 1 minute	7 days (d) = 1 week
60 minutes (min) = 1 hour	52 weeks (wk) = 1 year (y)
24 hours (h) = 1 day	12 months (mo) = 1 year
	365 days = 1 year

To rename larger units with smaller units, you can multiply.

4 wk = ■ d | 1 wk = 7 d |

4 × 7 = 28

4 wk = 28 d

To rename smaller units with larger units, you can divide.

48 h = ■ d | 24 h = 1 d |

48 ÷ 24 = 2

48 h = 2 d

Write *A.M.* or *P.M.*

1. The sun rises.   2. School begins.   3. Bedtime.

How much time has elapsed?

4. from to **11:00**
A.M.   A.M.

5. from **7:10** to **9:00**
A.M.   A.M.

6. from  to
P.M.   P.M.

7. from  to
A.M.   P.M.

Complete.

8. 4 d = ■ h   9. 6 min = ■ s   10. 4 wk = ■ d   11. 3 h = ■ min

12. 72 h = ■ d   13. 3 y = ■ d   14. $\frac{1}{2}$ h = ■ min   15. $\frac{1}{5}$ y = ■ d

Solve. In Exercises 18 and 19, *work backward* to find the answer to the question.

16. One class began to put up a used-toy booth at 8:45 A.M. They finished the booth at 10:15 A.M. How long did it take to build the booth?

17. Roberto began to work in the antique-clothing booth at 10:45 A.M. He worked steadily until 12:00 noon. For how long did Roberto work?

18. Marco finished working at 3:15 P.M. He had worked a total of 2 hours 10 minutes. At what time did he start working?

19. Kate finished working at 2:30 P.M. She had worked a total of 3 hours 45 minutes. At what time did she start working?

ANOTHER LOOK

Multiply.

1. 203
× 21

2. 304
× 34

3. 752
× 57

4. 197
× 68

5. 850
× 73

6. 48 × 700   7. 62 × 348   8. 86 × 427   9. 87 × 402   10. 58 × 329

Adding and Subtracting Time

A. Basketball practice lasted for 1 h 40 min on Monday, and 2 h 35 min on Tuesday. For how long did the team practice in the two days?

Add 1 h 40 min + 2 h 35 min.

Add the minutes.

$$1 \text{ h } 40 \text{ min}$$
$$+ 2 \text{ h } 35 \text{ min}$$
$$\overline{\hspace{1.5em} 75 \text{ min}}$$

Add the hours. Rename if necessary.

$$1 \text{ h } 40 \text{ min}$$
$$+ 2 \text{ h } 35 \text{ min}$$
$$\overline{3 \text{ h } 75 \text{ min}}$$

> **Think:**
> 3 h 75 min
> = 3 h + 1 h + 15 min
> = 4 h 15 min

The team practiced for 4 h 15 min in two days.

B. In two days, the team practiced for 4 h 15 min. John practiced for 2 h 55 min. For how much more time did the rest of the team practice?

Subtract 4 h 15 min − 2 h 55 min.

Subtract the minutes. Rename if necessary.

$$\overset{3}{\cancel{4}} \text{ h } \overset{75}{\cancel{15}} \text{ min}$$
$$- 2 \text{ h } 55 \text{ min}$$
$$\overline{\hspace{2em} 20 \text{ min}}$$

Subtract the hours.

$$\overset{3}{\cancel{4}} \text{ h } \overset{75}{\cancel{15}} \text{ min}$$
$$- 2 \text{ h } 55 \text{ min}$$
$$\overline{1 \text{ h } 20 \text{ min}}$$

The rest of the team practiced for 1 h 20 min more than John.

Checkpoint   Write the letter of the correct answer.

Add or subtract.

1.   5 h 35 min
     + 4 h 42 min

a. 10 h 27 min
b. 9 h 77 min
c. 10 h 7 min
d. 10 h 17 min

2.   4 min 26 s
     − 3 min 12 s

a. 0 min 14 s
b. 1 min 14 s
c. 1 min 38 s
d. 7 min 38 s

3.   3 h 48 min
     − 2 h 57 min

a. 1 min
b. 51 min
c. 1 h 51 min
d. 91 min

Add or subtract.

1.   4 h 16 min
    + 3 h 37 min

2.   2 h 28 min
    + 2 h 13 min

3.   7 min 19 s
    + 4 min 24 s

4.   5 min 32 s
    + 3 min 9 s

5.   1 min 25 s
    + 3 min 40 s

6.   4 h 18 min
    + 1 h 51 min

7.   7 min 52 s
    + 2 min 43 s

8.   2 h 27 min
    + 3 h 44 min

9.   7 h 52 min
    − 4 h 17 min

10.   8 min 42 s
    − 7 min 26 s

11.   6 h 35 min
    − 4 h 27 min

12.   9 min 36 s
    − 2 min 14 s

13.   5 min 13 s
    − 3 min 22 s

14.   7 h 28 min
    − 2 h 34 min

15.   11 h 13 min
    − 9 h 41 min

16.   3 min 2 s
    − 2 min 15 s

★17.   3 h 52 min 37 s
    + 2 h 21 min 43 s

★18.   7 h 19 min 22 s
    − 6 h 13 min 34 s

★19.   8 h 14 min 31 s
    − 5 h 25 min 37 s

Solve.

20. José learned his team's new play in only 1 h 20 min of practice on Tuesday and 1 h 45 min on Thursday. How long did it take José to learn the new play?

21. At 1:25 P.M. on the day of the big game, Steve realizes he forgot his sneakers. He has to be on the court by 3:15 P.M. How much time does he have to get his sneakers?

NUMBER SENSE

You can round to estimate numbers of hours.

54 h 47 min ≈ ■ h

54 h 47 min ≈ 55 h

Think: less than 30 minutes, round down.

more than 30 minutes, round up.

$$47 > 30$$
$$47 \approx 1 \text{ h}$$

Round to estimate the number of hours.

1. 3 h 22 min

2. 10 h 49 min

3. 6 h 31 min

4. 9 h 18 min

5. 1 h 11 min

6. 57 min

7. 8 h

8. 4 h 1 min

PROBLEM SOLVING
Using a Schedule

When you plan to take a bus, a train, or a plane from one place to another, you will find that a schedule is helpful. A bus schedule, for example, shows you where and when each bus stops along its route.

The regional softball play-off will take place at Allenwood School. Many students from neighboring towns will go to the game by bus.

Here is the information you should look for on a schedule.
- The heading tells you the endpoints of the bus route.
- The column headings show the towns and the streets where each bus stops.
- Some towns have two bus stops located at different streets.
- A dash (——) means that the bus does not stop.
- Since all the times shown are in the morning, A.M. appears under the headings for each column.

Use the schedule to answer this question. Gregory plans to take the bus that leaves from River Road in Newton at 7:50 A.M. At what time will he arrive in Allenwood?

Look at the schedule. Locate the entry that shows 7:50 A.M. under the Newton–River Road column. Follow the entry across to the Allenwood–Western Avenue column. The bus that leaves River Road at 7:50 A.M. will arrive in Allenwood at 8:48 A.M.

Here is the bus schedule they will use.

NEWTON TO ALLENWOOD							
Newton River Road	Newton Broad Street	Mayville Elm Street	Davis Gold Avenue	Hudson Pine Street	Gladstone Wyoming Avenue	Gladstone Main Street	Allenwood Western Avenue
A.M.	A.M.	A.M.	A.M.	A.M.	A.M.	A.M.	A.M.
5:50	6:05	6:11	6:17	6:24	6:29	6:33	6:43
——	——	6:21	6:27	6:34	6:39	6:43	6:53
6:05	6:20	6:26	——	6:37	——	6:44	6:54
7:00	7:16	7:23	7:30	7:37	7:42	7:47	7:57
7:10	7:26	7:33	7:40	7:47	7:52	7:57	8:07
7:25	——	——	——	7:52	——	——	8:12
——	——	7:53	8:00	8:07	8:12	8:17	8:27
7:40	7:56	8:03	8:10	8:17	8:22	8:27	8:37
7:50	8:07	8:14	8:20	8:27	8:33	8:38	8:48
——	——	8:24	8:30	8:37	8:43	8:48	8:58
8:10	8:27	8:34	8:40	8:47	8:53	8:58	9:08

Use the bus schedule to verify each statement. Write *true* or *false*.

1. The 7:50 A.M. bus from River Road arrives in Allenwood before the 8:14 A.M. bus from Mayville.

2. The 7:40 A.M. bus from River Road arrives in Allenwood 10 minutes earlier than the 7:50 A.M. bus.

3. It takes less time to ride from Davis to Hudson than from Mayville to Hudson.

4. The earliest bus to leave Mayville arrives in Gladstone before 6:30 A.M.

Use the bus schedule to solve each problem.

5. Jean and Mike want to arrive in Allenwood at 8:27 A.M. Jean lives in Hudson. Mike lives in Davis. They want to meet on the bus. At what time should each of them board the bus?

6. Maria lives near Broad Street in Newton. She wants to arrive in Allenwood shortly before 9:00 A.M. Which bus should she take?

7. Perry wants to go to Main Street in Gladstone. He boards the 7:33 A.M. bus in Mayville. If he rode for 19 minutes, would he be at his destination?

8. Stella boarded the 8:00 A.M. bus in Davis. She left the bus at Wyoming Avenue in Gladstone. Assuming the bus arrived on time, for how long did she ride?

9. The 6:20 A.M. bus from Broad Street in Newton is delayed 4 minutes. At what time will it arrive at Main Street in Gladstone?

10. How much longer does the trip from River Road in Newton to Allenwood take on the 7:50 A.M. bus than on the 5:50 A.M. bus? Why do you think so?

★11. Rick boards a bus at Broad Street in Newton at 7:26 A.M. Clara boards a bus in Hudson at 7:37 A.M. Who arrives in Allenwood first? How many minutes later does the second person arrive?

12. Paul lives in Davis. He wants to be in Allenwood 45 minutes before tickets for the big game go on sale. Tickets go on sale at 9:00 A.M. It will take about 5 minutes to walk from the Allenwood bus stop to the ticket booth. Which bus should Paul take?

Length: Inches

A. The members of the Carpenter's Club are building birdhouses. They need nails that are at least $1\frac{1}{2}$ inches long. Is this nail long enough?

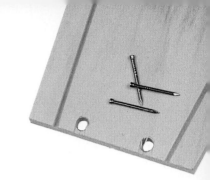

An **inch (in.)** is a customary unit of length. It can be used to measure the length of objects such as a paper clip or a picture frame.

The nail measures

2 inch to the nearest inch.

$1\frac{1}{2}$ in. to the nearest $\frac{1}{2}$ in.

$1\frac{2}{4}$ in. to the nearest $\frac{1}{4}$ in.

$1\frac{5}{8}$ in. to the nearest $\frac{1}{8}$ in.

$1\frac{9}{16}$ in. to the nearest $\frac{1}{16}$ in.

The nail measures $1\frac{9}{16}$ in. long. It is long enough.

B. You can find the distance around an object by measuring its sides and finding the sum of its measurements. Measure the distance around this shape.

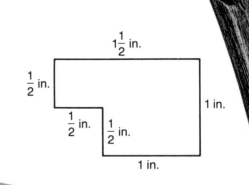

$1\frac{1}{2} + \frac{1}{2} + \frac{1}{2} + \frac{1}{2} + 1 + 1 = 5$

The distance is 5 inches.

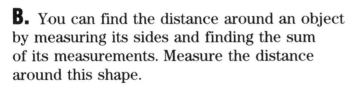

Measure this pencil to the nearest

1. inch. **2.** $\frac{1}{2}$ in. **3.** $\frac{1}{4}$ in. **4.** $\frac{1}{8}$ in. **5.** $\frac{1}{16}$ in.

Use a ruler to draw a line that is

6. $\frac{3}{4}$ in. **7.** $2\frac{3}{8}$ in. **8.** $3\frac{5}{16}$ in. **9.** $1\frac{7}{8}$ in.

Measure the distance around each.

10. **11.** **12.**

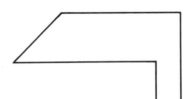

Solve.

13. Joe's birdhouse will be shaped like a triangle. A perch will go around all three sides. How many inches around will the perch be?

14. Ann uses two screwdrivers. One is $7\frac{3}{4}$ in. long. The other is $1\frac{1}{2}$ in. shorter. How long is the second screwdriver?

15. Ronnie is using nails of three different sizes. Each size is $\frac{1}{4}$ in. shorter than the next. The shortest nail is $1\frac{5}{8}$ in. What are the lengths of the other two nails?

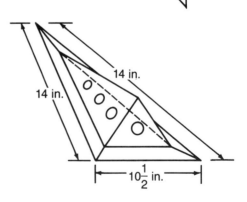

14 in.

14 in.

$10\frac{1}{2}$ in.

CHALLENGE

How long are these items? First estimate to the nearest $\frac{1}{2}$ in. Then measure. Copy and complete the table.

Object	this book	your thumb	your hand	your foot	a pencil
Estimate	■	■	■	■	■
Actual length	■	■	■	■	■

Feet, Yards, and Miles

If you have ever attended a track meet, you may have seen a 50-yard dash or a 6-mile run. Distances in track meets are often measured in yards and miles.

Here are several customary units of length that you should know.

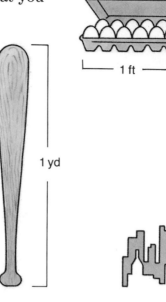

> 12 inches (in.) = 1 foot (ft)
> 3 ft = 1 yard (yd)
> 1,760 yd = 1 mile (mi)
> 5,280 ft = 1 mi

A **foot** can be used to measure objects. An egg carton is about a foot.

A **yard** can be used to measure objects. A baseball bat is about a yard.

A **mile** can be used to measure length. The distances between cities are measured in miles.

To rename larger units with smaller units, you can multiply.

4 ft = ■ in.   1 ft = 12 in.
4 × 12 = 48
4 ft = 48 in.

To rename smaller units with larger units, you can divide.

78 ft = ■ yd   3 ft = 1 yd
78 ÷ 3 = 26
78 ft = 26 yd

Other examples:

5 ft 7 in. = ■ in.   5 × 12 = 60
60 in. + 7 in. = 67 in.
5 ft 7 in. = 67 in.

2 mi = ■ yd   1,760 yd = 1 mi
2 × 1,760 = 3,520
2 mi = 3,520 yd

Checkpoint Write the letter of the correct answer.

Complete.

1. 3 ft = ■ in.
a. $\frac{1}{4}$
b. 24
c. 32
d. 36

2. 54 ft = ■ yd
a. $4\frac{1}{2}$
b. 18
c. 19
d. 648

3. 3 mi = ■ yd
a. 880
b. 1,760
c. 5,280
d. 5,290

Write *inches*, *feet*, or *yards*.

1. A desk may be 28 ▨ high.

2. An adult may be $5\frac{3}{4}$ ▨ tall.

3. A doorway may be 30 ▨ wide.

4. A person's arm may be 2 ▨ long.

Choose the appropriate unit of measure. Write *yd* or *mi*.

5. the distance a car travels in an hour

6. the distance you throw a ball

7. the length of a football field

8. the length of a piece of fabric

9. the distance to the sun

10. the length of shadows

11. the distance you can hit a golf ball

12. the distance you can walk in a day

Complete.

13. 5 ft = ▨ in.

14. 36 in. = ▨ ft

15. 120 in. = ▨ ft

16. 2 ft = ▨ in.

17. 5 ft 3 in. = ▨ in.

18. $1\frac{1}{2}$ ft = ▨ in.

19. 4 ft 7 in. = ▨ in.

20. 4 mi = ▨ yd

21. 5 yd = ▨ ft

22. 18 ft = ▨ yd

23. 1,760 yd = ▨ mi

24. 5,280 yd = ▨ mi

25. 440 yd = ▨ mi

26. $2\frac{1}{3}$ yd = ▨ in.

27. 2,640 ft = ▨ in.

Solve.

The results of Friday's track meet were posted on Monday morning. Copy and complete the chart to answer the questions.

28. Elva thought she ran the same distance as Frank. Was she correct?

29. Compare Bob's distance with Sam's and Lisa's. List them in order from who ran the greatest distance to who ran the least distance.

30. Sylvia ran this course around the school grounds. Find her total distance, and list it on the chart. Which runners ran farther than Sylvia? How many yards farther did they run?

TOTAL DISTANCE RUN

Runner	In feet	In yards	In miles
Elva	▨	1,320	▨
Sam	▨	880	▨
Frank	▨	▨	$\frac{3}{4}$
Lisa	▨	▨	$\frac{5}{8}$
Bob	▨	352	▨
Sylvia	▨	▨	▨

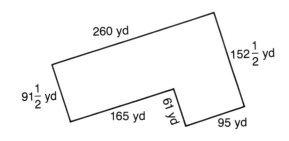

260 yd

$152\frac{1}{2}$ yd

$91\frac{1}{2}$ yd

165 yd

61 yd

95 yd

Cups, Pints, Quarts, and Gallons

Cups (c), **pints (pt)**, **quarts (qt)**, and **gallons (gal)** are customary units of capacity.

$$2 \text{ c} = 1 \text{ pt}$$
$$2 \text{ pt} = 1 \text{ qt}$$
$$4 \text{ qt} = 1 \text{ gal}$$

 1 cup (c)

 **1 pint (pt)**

1 quart (qt)

 **1 gallon (gal)**

To rename larger units with smaller units, you can multiply.

$$3 \text{ pt} = \blacksquare \text{ c}$$ | 1 pt = 2 c
$$2 \times 3 = 6$$
$$3 \text{ pt} = 6 \text{ c}$$

To rename smaller units with larger units, you can divide.

$$14 \text{ c} = \blacksquare \text{ pt}$$ | 2 c = 1 pt
$$14 \div 2 = 7$$
$$14 \text{ c} = 7 \text{ pt}$$

Write *cups*, *pints*, *quarts*, or *gallons*.

1. A full tank of gas may hold 15 ▨.

2. A juice glass may hold 2 ▨.

3. A barrel's capacity may be measured in ▨.

Complete.

4. $2 \text{ gal} = \blacksquare \text{ qt}$

5. $3 \text{ qt} = \blacksquare \text{ pt}$

6. $1 \text{ pt} = \blacksquare \text{ c}$

7. $3 \text{ gal} = \blacksquare \text{ qt}$

8. $4 \text{ c} = \blacksquare \text{ pt}$

9. $8 \text{ qt} = \blacksquare \text{ gal}$

10. $6 \text{ c} = \blacksquare \text{ pt}$

11. $4 \text{ pt} = \blacksquare \text{ qt}$

12. $2\frac{1}{4} \text{ gal} = \blacksquare \text{ qt}$

13. $3 \text{ c} = \blacksquare \text{ pt}$

★14. $3 \text{ gal } 2 \text{ qt} = \blacksquare \text{ qt}$

Solve.

15. Maria bakes 14 loaves of bread for the picnic. She needs 1 pt milk for each loaf. How many quarts of milk does she need?

16. Ralph needs $1\frac{1}{2}$ gal water to cook vegetables for the picnic. He has a 2-cup measuring cup. How many times must he fill the cup?

17. Use the recipe to write and solve a word problem.

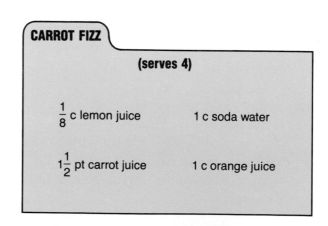

CARROT FIZZ

(serves 4)

$\frac{1}{8}$ c lemon juice   1 c soda water

$1\frac{1}{2}$ pt carrot juice   1 c orange juice

More Practice, page H180

Ounces, Pounds, and Tons

Ounces (oz), pounds (lb), and **tons (T)** are customary units of weight.

$$16 \text{ oz} = 1 \text{ lb}$$
$$2{,}000 \text{ lb} = 1 \text{ T}$$

1 ounce (oz)

1 pound (lb)

1 ton (T)

To rename larger units with smaller units, you can multiply.

$2 \text{ T} = $ ▦ lb
$\boxed{1 \text{ T} = 2{,}000 \text{ lb}}$
$2 \times 2{,}000 = 4{,}000$
$2 \text{ T} = 4{,}000 \text{ lb}$

To rename smaller units with larger units, you can divide.

$192 \text{ oz} = $ ▦ lb
$\boxed{16 \text{ oz} = 1 \text{ lb}}$
$192 \div 16 = 12$
$192 \text{ oz} = 12 \text{ lb}$

Write *ounces*, *pounds*, or *tons*.

1. An elephant may weigh 4 ▦.

2. A glass of milk may weigh 10 ▦.

3. A greeting card may weigh 1 ▦.

4. A full suitcase may weigh 25 ▦.

Complete.

5. 2 lb = ▦ oz

6. 4 lb = ▦ oz

7. 10 T = ▦ lb

8. 5 lb = ▦ oz

9. 112 oz = ▦ lb

10. 160 oz = ▦ lb

11. 10,000 lb = ▦ T

12. 500 lb = ▦ T

13. $1\frac{1}{4}$ lb = ▦ oz

14. $2\frac{3}{4}$ lb = ▦ oz

15. 224 oz = ▦ lb

16. 80 oz = ▦ lb

★17. 2 lb 6 oz = ▦ oz

★18. 5 lb 4 oz = ▦ oz

★19. 2 T 4 lb = ▦ lb

Solve.

20. The Green Thumb Club buys a 1-lb bag of seeds at Jack's Seed Store. The bag contains 8 packets. How many ounces does each packet weigh?

21. The club buys 35 oz of bluebell seeds for $8.10, and Jack adds a bonus of 10 oz. Including the bonus, how much did the club pay for each ounce of seed?

Fahrenheit Temperature

A. Temperature can be measured by using **degrees Fahrenheit (°F).** Look at the thermometer. The temperature is 30 degrees above zero, or 30°F. If the thermometer reads 30 degrees below zero, you write ⁻30°F.

B. If the temperature falls from 30°F to ⁻30°F, by how many degrees has the temperature changed?

Think: from 30 to 0 is 30.
from 0 to ⁻30 is 30.
30 + 30 = 60

The temperature falls 60°F.

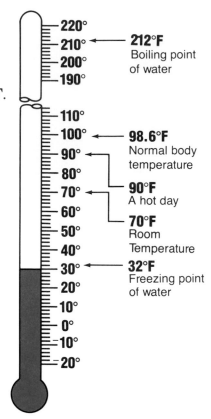

- 220°
- 210° ← **212°F** Boiling point of water
- 200°
- 190°
- 110°
- 100° ← **98.6°F** Normal body temperature
- 90°
- 80°
- 70° ← **90°F** A hot day
- 60°
- 50° ← **70°F** Room Temperature
- 40°
- 30° ← **32°F** Freezing point of water
- 20°
- 10°
- 0°
- 10°
- 20°

Write the temperature.

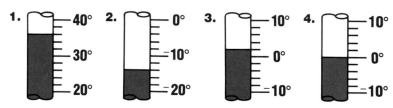

1. 40° 30° 20°   **2.** 0° 10° 20°   **3.** 10° 0° 10°   **4.** 10° 0° 10°

Copy and complete the chart.

	5.	6.	7.	8.
Starting temperature	0°F	⁻10°F	41°F	▩
Temperature change	rose 15°	▩	▩	rose 7°
Final temperature	▩	3°F	⁻11°F	⁻9°F

Choose the more suitable temperature for

9. a swim in a lake.   104°F or 45°F

10. a warm shower.   70°F or 115°F

Solve. For Problem 12, use the Infobank.

11. Mona records a temperature of 3°F at 8 A.M. in Springfield. Her noon recording is 18°F. By how many degrees has the temperature risen?

12. Use the information on page 419 to write and solve your own word problem.

Celsius Temperature

A. Temperature can also be measured by using **degrees Celsius (°C).** Look at the thermometer. It shows a normal room temperature of 20° above zero or 20°C. Below-zero Celsius temperatures can also be recorded. If the thermometer reads 20 degrees below zero, you write ‾20°C.

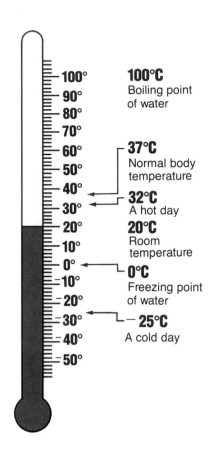

100°C	Boiling point of water
37°C	Normal body temperature
32°C	A hot day
20°C	Room temperature
0°C	Freezing point of water
‾25°C	A cold day

B. If the temperature rises from ‾20°C to 20°C, by how many degrees has the temperature changed?

Think: From ‾20 to 0 is 20.
From 0 to 20 is 20.
20 + 20 = 40

The temperature rises 40°C.

Write the temperature.

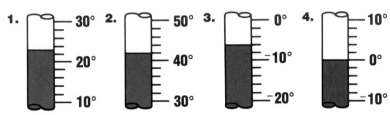

1. 30° 20° 10°
2. 50° 40° 30°
3. 0° ‾10° ‾20°
4. 10° 0° ‾10°

Copy and complete the chart.

	5.	6.	7.	8.
Starting temperature	12°C	‾2°C	51°C	▓
Temperature change	fell 12°	rose 10°	▓	fell 21°
Final temperature	▓	▓	39°C	‾5°C

Choose the more suitable temperature for

9. building a snowman. ‾2°C 35°C

10. a bowl of chicken soup. 49°C 77°C

Solve.

11. Dan uses an almanac to find world temperatures. The page is smudged, and he cannot tell whether the temperature at the North Pole is 40°C or ‾40°C. Which is the more likely temperature?

PROBLEM SOLVING
Using a Time-Zone Map

To find the difference in time between two places, you can use a time-zone map.

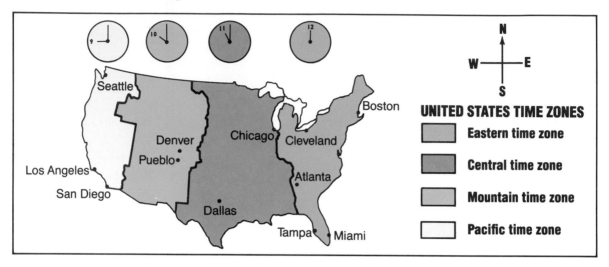

Chris lives in Cleveland. She wants to telephone her friend Pablo in San Diego at 10:00 A.M., Pacific time. At what time should she place the call?

Use the information on the time-zone map to help you solve this problem. This is how it is arranged.

- The headings tell you the names of the time zones.

- The colors and the heavy black lines show the areas of the time zones.

- The clocks show what time it is in each time zone when it is 12:00 noon in the Eastern time zone.

To find out when Chris should place her call:

- Locate the two places. Cleveland is in the Eastern time zone. San Diego is in the Pacific time zone.

- Look at the clocks. The time in San Diego is 3 hours earlier than it is in Cleveland. So, Eastern time is 3 hours later than Pacific time.

Chris should place her call at 1:00 P.M., Eastern time.

Write *true* or *false* for each statement.

1. Dallas and Tampa are in the same time zone.

2. It is 1 hour earlier in Boston than it is in Denver.

3. The Central time zone and the Pacific time zone are 2 hours apart.

Solve.

4. Debbie lives in Atlanta. Sue lives in Seattle. When Debbie wakes up at 7:30 A.M., what time is it where Sue lives?

5. Sue goes to bed in Seattle at 11:00 P.M. What time is it where Debbie lives?

6. At noon, Paul telephones his brother in Atlanta. Paul lives in Tampa. At what time does Paul's brother receive the call?

7. Gina drives from Cleveland to Chicago. Should she set her watch forward or backward? by how many hours?

8. Dan lives in Los Angeles. He left home at 10:00 A.M. He returned $11\frac{1}{2}$ hours later. At what time did he return home?

9. At 8:00 A.M., Dan's father left Denver to drive to Pueblo. He returned to Denver at 6:15 P.M. For how long had he been gone?

10. Kim lives on the West Coast, and Jan lives on the East Coast. Each begins dinner at 6:30 P.M. Both finish 1 hour later. At what time do both of them finish dinner?

11. It is 4:25 P.M. in Dallas. In another city, it is 1 hour later. In which time zone is that other city?

12. The National Guitar Company has offices in San Diego, Denver, Chicago, and Miami. All four offices are open daily from 8:30 A.M. to 5:00 P.M. At 3:30 P.M., Mountain time, which of the company's offices are open and which are closed?

★13. Suppose you fly from San Diego, California, to Boston, Massachusetts. Your plane takes off at 3:30 P.M., Pacific time. It lands at 11:40 P.M., Eastern time. How long did the flight take?

CALCULATOR

You can use a calculator to help you solve problems that involve many computations or computations with large numbers.

Units of Time
60 seconds = 1 minute
60 minutes = 1 hour
24 hours = 1 day
7 days = 1 week
12 months = 1 year
365 days = 1 year

Solve. Use the table if needed.

1. If your heart beats 75 times a minute, how many times does your heart beat in an hour?

2. How many times does your heart beat in a day?

3. How many times does your heart beat in a week?

4. How many times does your heart beat in a year?

5. Time your own heartbeat for 1 minute. Then answer problems 1–4 using that number.

6. If you could count one number each second for 24 hours each day, how long would it take you to count to 1 million? Write your answer as __ days, __ hours, __ minutes, __ seconds.

7. Could you count to 1 billion in your lifetime?

8. About how many years would it take?

9. Choose which will give the greatest amount.

   a. You are given 1 penny per second for 1 year.
   b. You are given $1 per minute for 3 weeks.
   c. You are given $2 a day for 20 years.

GROUP PROJECT

Having a Field Day

The problem: You are in charge of organizing the sports events for your school's field day. Decide how to schedule the events. Make a copy of the chart to help you.

Key Facts

- There are 100 students participating.
- You now have 8 adult volunteers to help organize and referee the events.
- You must have enough events to keep everyone involved for 4 hours.
- The athletic field is 100 yards long and 50 yards wide (the size of a football field).
- You want to award three ribbons for each event.

Key Questions

- What events should you include?
- Do you have enough space for more than one event per hour?
- How many people should participate in each event?
- How will students sign up for the events?
- Do you have enough adult help?
- Who will judge the events?
- Will you award ribbons after each event or at the end of the day?
- Will you invite parents to observe?

	Events	Players	Referee
First Hour			
Second Hour			
Third Hour			
Fourth Hour			

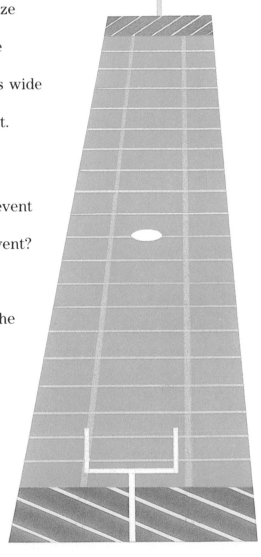

CHAPTER TEST

Multiply. Write the product in simplest form. (pages 272, 274, and 276)

1. $\frac{1}{9} \times \frac{1}{6}$

2. $\frac{2}{3} \times \frac{5}{8}$

3. $\frac{4}{9} \times \frac{7}{8}$

4. $5 \times \frac{2}{3}$

5. $\frac{9}{10} \times 5$

6. $13 \times \frac{4}{7}$

7. $6\frac{1}{8} \times 9\frac{7}{10}$

8. $12\frac{5}{6} \times \frac{7}{9}$

Divide. (page 280)

9. $9 \div \frac{1}{8}$

10. $12 \div \frac{1}{6}$

11. $2 \div \frac{1}{4}$

12. $6 \div \frac{1}{3}$

How much time has passed? (page 284)

Complete. (page 284)

13. from   to

A.M.   A.M.

14. $3 \text{ d} = \blacksquare \text{ h}$

15. $8 \text{ min} = \blacksquare \text{ s}$

Add or subtract. (page 286)

16. $\begin{array}{r} 5 \text{ h } 26 \text{ min} \\ + 3 \text{ h } 45 \text{ min} \\ \hline \end{array}$

17. $\begin{array}{r} 7 \text{ h } 11 \text{ min} \\ - 5 \text{ h } 25 \text{ min} \\ \hline \end{array}$

Measure the line to the nearest
(page 290) ———————————

18. inch

19. $\frac{1}{4}$ inch

20. $\frac{1}{8}$ inch

21. $\frac{1}{2}$ inch

Choose the appropriate unit. (page 292)
Write *in.*, *ft*, *yd*, or *mi*.

22. the length of a highway

23. the height of a volleyball net

24. the length of a key

Choose the appropriate unit. (pages 294 and 295)
Write *c*, *pt*, *qt*, or *gal*.

25. a bathtub

26. a milk bottle

27. a teapot

Write *ounces*, *pounds*, or *tons*.

28. an apple

29. a blue whale

30. a gorilla

Complete. (pages 292, 294, and 295)

31. $3 \text{ gal} = \blacksquare \text{ qt} = \blacksquare \text{ pt} = \blacksquare \text{ c}$

32. $64 \text{ oz} = \blacksquare \text{ lb}$

33. $2 \text{ mi} = \blacksquare \text{ yd} = \blacksquare \text{ ft} = \blacksquare \text{ in.}$

Copy and complete the chart. (pages 296 and 297)

	34.	35.	36.
Starting temperature	■	217°C	17°C
Temperature change	rose 13°	■	fell 25°
Final temperature	19°F	185°C	■

Solve. Make a table if needed. (pages 282 and 283)

37. The principal in Judy's school hands out a new-activities list to all the students in the school. There are only 4 copies for every 9 students. If there are 486 students in the school, how many copies does he hand out?

38. One day, all the students in Jack's school went to the auditorium for a presentation. There were 27 students for every 3 teachers in the auditorium. If there were 351 students in the auditorium, how many teachers were there?

Use the time zone map to solve the problems. (pages 298 and 299)

39. If it is 9:00 P.M. in New York, what time is it in San Francisco?

40. What time is it in Chicago if it is 7:00 A.M. in Denver?

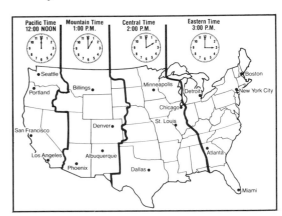

BONUS

Multiply the fractions in each row. Write the answers in simplest form.

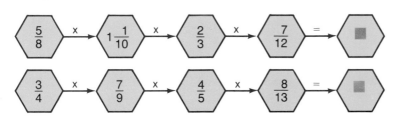

RETEACHING

A. Before you can multiply fractions and mixed numbers, you need to rename the mixed number as a fraction.

When renaming mixed numbers, remember these steps.

1. Multiply the whole numbers by the denominator.
$2\frac{3}{4} \rightarrow 4 \times 2 = 8$

2. Add the product to the numerator. $8 + 3 = 11$

3. Write the sum over the denominator. $2\frac{3}{4} \rightarrow \frac{11}{4}$

Find $3\frac{7}{9} \times \frac{1}{3}$.

Rename the mixed number.	Multiply the fractions.	Show the answer as a mixed number.
$3\frac{7}{9} = \frac{34}{9}$	$\frac{34}{9} \times \frac{1}{3} = \frac{34}{27}$	$\frac{34}{27} = 1\frac{7}{27}$

B. Sometimes you need to write fractions for both factors before multiplying.

Find $4 \times 6\frac{1}{9}$. $\frac{4}{1} \times \frac{55}{9} = \frac{220}{9} = 24\frac{4}{9}$

Another example:

Find $7\frac{5}{6} \times 3\frac{3}{4}$. $\frac{47}{6} \times \frac{15}{4} = \frac{705}{24} = 29\frac{3}{8}$

Multiply. Write the answer in simplest form.

1. $3\frac{1}{6} \times \frac{2}{3}$　　　　**2.** $10\frac{1}{2} \times \frac{1}{7}$　　　　**3.** $\frac{1}{2} \times 2\frac{8}{9}$　　　　**4.** $\frac{1}{10} \times 3\frac{3}{4}$

5. $\frac{6}{7} \times 7\frac{1}{6}$　　　　**6.** $5 \times 3\frac{2}{5}$　　　　**7.** $2\frac{4}{21} \times 9$　　　　**8.** $1\frac{5}{7} \times \frac{1}{2}$

9. $7\frac{7}{9} \times 2\frac{3}{5}$　　　　**10.** $2\frac{3}{4} \times 2\frac{5}{6}$　　　　**11.** $2\frac{7}{10} \times 8\frac{7}{9}$　　　　**12.** $6\frac{2}{5} \times 7\frac{3}{8}$

13. $8\frac{5}{12} \times \frac{3}{5}$　　　　**14.** $6\frac{4}{7} \times 1\frac{1}{4}$　　　　**15.** $4\frac{2}{3} \times 2\frac{3}{8}$　　　　**16.** $3 \times 2\frac{3}{4}$

17. $\frac{3}{5} \times 9\frac{5}{6}$　　　　**18.** $1\frac{9}{10} \times 7$　　　　**19.** $2\frac{1}{2} \times 10\frac{8}{9}$　　　　**20.** $2\frac{1}{3} \times \frac{4}{9}$

21. $4 \times \frac{6}{7}$　　　　**22.** $7\frac{1}{2} \times \frac{5}{6}$　　　　**23.** $5\frac{11}{15} \times 6\frac{2}{3}$　　　　**24.** $5\frac{1}{6} \times 5\frac{1}{7}$

ENRICHMENT

Reading a Road Map

A **road map** is like a satellite picture of the major streets and highways in an area. It shows the routes and distances between cities and towns. The *key* tells you what each symbol means.

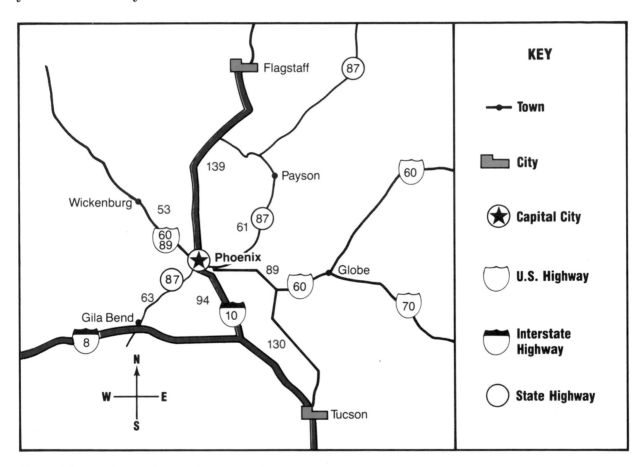

Note: The red numbers along the highways show the distances in miles between cities and towns.

Find the mileage from

1. Phoenix to Flagstaff.　　**2.** Phoenix to Globe.　　**3.** Gila Bend to Payson.

Find the shortest route between

4. Tucson and Phoenix.　　**5.** Phoenix and Gila Bend.　　**6.** Globe and Wickenburg.

7. Tucson and Payson.　　**8.** Gila Bend and Globe.　　**9.** Flagstaff and Tucson.

CUMULATIVE REVIEW

Write the letter of the correct answer.

1. A fraction for the part that is shaded.

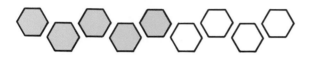

   a. $\frac{4}{9}$ **b.** $\frac{5}{9}$

   c. $\frac{4}{5}$ **d.** not given

2. Write in order from the greatest to the least: $\frac{19}{25}, \frac{5}{20}, \frac{7}{10}, \frac{4}{5}$.

   a. $\frac{7}{10}, \frac{4}{5}, \frac{5}{20}, \frac{19}{25}$ **b.** $\frac{4}{5}, \frac{5}{20}, \frac{7}{10}, \frac{19}{25}$

   c. $\frac{4}{5}, \frac{19}{25}, \frac{7}{10}, \frac{5}{20}$ **d.** not given

3. Write the answer in simplest form: $1\frac{5}{8} + 3\frac{3}{6}$.

   a. $4\frac{1}{8}$ **b.** $5\frac{1}{8}$

   c. $5\frac{3}{8}$ **d.** not given

4. Write the answer in simplest form: $\frac{2}{5} - \frac{3}{10}$.

   a. $\frac{1}{10}$ **b.** $\frac{2}{5}$

   c. $\frac{1}{2}$ **d.** not given

5. Write the answer in simplest form: $4 - 3\frac{2}{5}$.

   a. $\frac{3}{5}$ **b.** $1\frac{3}{5}$

   c. $2\frac{2}{5}$ **d.** not given

6. Write the answer in simplest form: $5\frac{1}{6} - 2\frac{3}{4}$.

   a. $2\frac{5}{12}$ **b.** $3\frac{5}{12}$

   c. $3\frac{11}{12}$ **d.** not given

7. $1.4 \text{ kg} = \blacksquare \text{ mg}$

   a. 0.0014 mg   **b.** 1,400 mg

   c. 140 mg   **d.** not given

8. $0.26 + 3.997 + 0.05$

   a. 4.2475   **b.** 4.317

   c. 3.275   **d.** not given

9. 3.67×0.9

   a. 0.313   **b.** 3.303

   c. 4.303   **d.** not given

10. $28,496 \div 9$

   a. 3,166 R2   **b.** 3,165

   c. 3,174 R4   **d.** not given

11. There are 1,375 people on the train to Tulsa. If each car on the train holds 65 people, how many cars are there?

   a. 21   **b.** 22

   c. 23   **d.** not given

12. The dining car on the train has 3 sittings for each meal. They serve 135 people at each breakfast sitting. A total of 150 more people are served at lunch. How many people are served at lunch?

   a. 345   **b.** 455

   c. 555   **d.** not given

Your class is planning a sight-seeing trip to the state capital. How will you travel there? How will you spend your time once you arrive? What will your costs be? Find a way to show the percent of the total cost that will be spent on each item.

10 RATIO AND PERCENT

Ratios

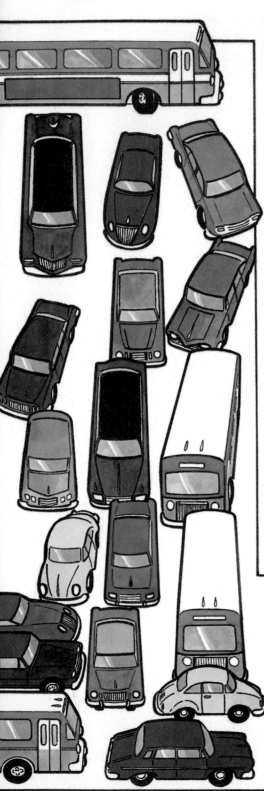

A. Every day at rush hour, there is a traffic jam at the Grove Street intersection in Rockville City. The city planners made a study of the area. In 1 hour, 15 cars and 4 buses stopped traffic. They compared the number of cars to the number of buses and decided to create a separate bus lane. What is the ratio of cars to buses?

We use **ratios** to compare two numbers.

The ratio of cars to buses is 15 to 4.

B. When you compare numbers in a ratio, be careful to write them in the correct order. You can write ratios in several ways.

Compare the number of buses to the number of cars.

$$4 \text{ to } 15 \qquad 4\!:\!15 \qquad \frac{4}{15}$$

Compare the number of buses to the total number of vehicles.

$$4 \text{ to } 19 \quad 4 \text{ out of } 19 \quad 4\!:\!19 \quad \frac{4}{19}$$

Compare the total number of vehicles to the number of cars.

$$19 \text{ to } 15 \qquad 19\!:\!15 \qquad \frac{19}{15}$$

Checkpoint
Write the letter of the correct answer.

Choose the ratio that matches.

1. 8:11

  a. 11:19

  b. 8 to 11

  c. $\frac{11}{8}$

  d. 8:3

2. 9 out of 10

  a. 1:9

  b. $\frac{10}{9}$

  c. 9:10

  d. 10:9

3. $\frac{22}{15}$

  a. 15 to 22

  b. 22:15

  c. 15 to 7

  d. 22:7

Math Reasoning, page H205

Write the ratio.

1. bicycles to tricycles

2. unicycles to bicycles

3. green cycles to yellow cycles

4. tricycles to unicycles

5. bicycles to all cycles

6. all cycles to green cycles

7. buses to cars

8. trucks to buses

9. red vehicles to blue vehicles

10. cars to buses

11. cars to all vehicles

12. all vehicles to red vehicles

Write each ratio as a fraction.

13. 1 out of 2

14. 7 to 8

15. 4:5

16. 100 to 350

17. 19 out of 20

18. 60:70

19. 21 out of 28

20. 3 to 4

Solve.

21. A study shows that, in one city, there are 5 bus riders to every 7 train riders. Write this ratio three ways.

22. City planners set aside 1 bicycle lane for every 6 automobile lanes. What is the ratio of bicycle lanes to automobile lanes?

CHALLENGE

Take a survey of how your classmates travel to school each morning. Copy the table, and record your results. Write a ratio for

1. the number of students who ride bicycles to the number who walk.

2. the number who ride the school bus to the number who travel by car.

MEANS OF TRANSPORTATION TO SCHOOL

Bus	
Car	
Walk	
Bicycle	

Equal Ratios

A. Mr. Chen wants to save fuel and to lessen traffic by starting a car pool at his company. He knows that he needs 1 car for every 5 people. How many cars will he need if 20 people join the car pool?

You can use **equal ratios** to find how many cars are needed. Two ratios are equal if they can be written as equivalent fractions.

Write the ratios comparing the number of cars to the number of people.

$$\frac{1}{5} \xleftarrow{\text{cars}} \xrightarrow{} \frac{n}{20} \quad \text{people}$$

Find equivalent fractions.

| **Think:** $5 \times 4 = 20.$ | $\frac{1}{5} = \frac{1 \times 4}{5 \times 4} = \frac{4}{20}$ |

Mr. Chen needs 4 cars for 20 people.

B. Mr. Chen makes a table to keep track of how many cars and people there are in the car pool. How many people can ride if he has 6 cars?

Complete.

Cars	1	2	3	4	5	6
People	5	10	15	20	25	■

$\frac{1}{5} = \frac{6}{n}$ | **Think:** $1 \times 6 = 6.$ | $\frac{1}{5} = \frac{1 \times 6}{5 \times 6} = \frac{6}{30}$

So, 30 people can ride in the car pool.

C. You can tell whether two ratios are equal by checking to see if they are equivalent fractions.

Are $\frac{3}{5}$ and $\frac{18}{35}$ equal ratios?

| **Think:** $3 \times 6 = 18.$ | $\frac{3}{5} = \frac{3 \times 6}{5 \times 6} = \frac{18}{30}$ |

$$\frac{18}{30} \neq \frac{18}{35}$$

So, $\frac{3}{5} \neq \frac{18}{35}$.

Find two equal ratios.

1. $\frac{1}{3} = \frac{2}{6} = \frac{\blacksquare}{\blacksquare} = \frac{\blacksquare}{\blacksquare}$

2. $\frac{2}{5} = \frac{4}{10} = \frac{\blacksquare}{\blacksquare} = \frac{\blacksquare}{\blacksquare}$

3. $\frac{3}{8} = \frac{6}{16} = \frac{\blacksquare}{\blacksquare} = \frac{\blacksquare}{\blacksquare}$

4. $\frac{2}{9} = \frac{4}{18} = \frac{\blacksquare}{\blacksquare} = \frac{\blacksquare}{\blacksquare}$

5. $\frac{3}{2} = \frac{9}{6} = \frac{\blacksquare}{\blacksquare} = \frac{\blacksquare}{\blacksquare}$

6. $\frac{5}{3} = \frac{10}{6} = \frac{\blacksquare}{\blacksquare} = \frac{\blacksquare}{\blacksquare}$

Find the missing number.

7. $\frac{3}{7} = \frac{15}{n}$

8. $\frac{6}{9} = \frac{48}{n}$

9. $\frac{5}{8} = \frac{n}{56}$

10. $\frac{11}{5} = \frac{n}{35}$

11. $\frac{3}{27} = \frac{n}{9}$

12. $\frac{12}{5} = \frac{60}{n}$

13. $\frac{10}{13} = \frac{n}{39}$

14. $\frac{8}{5} = \frac{n}{35}$

Copy and complete each ratio table.

15.

Number of cars	2	4	■	8
Number of headlights	4	■	12	■

16.

Number of cars	■	5	■	10	12	■
Number of doors	12	■	32	40	■	60

Write = or ≠ for ●.

17. $\frac{4}{50} ● \frac{20}{250}$

18. $\frac{3}{12} ● \frac{21}{86}$

19. $\frac{9}{15} ● \frac{56}{90}$

20. $\frac{18}{3} ● \frac{72}{12}$

21. $\frac{3}{11} ● \frac{18}{65}$

22. $\frac{8}{9} ● \frac{32}{36}$

23. $\frac{9}{13} ● \frac{36}{56}$

24. $\frac{5}{12} ● \frac{50}{122}$

Solve. For Problem 26, use the Infobank.

25. Mr. Chen is driving from New York to Chicago on business. He drives at a rate of 94 miles every 2 hours. How far does he drive in 4 hours?

26. Use the information on page 419 to solve. How far will the intercity bus travel in 2 hours?

Use the information on page 419 to solve.

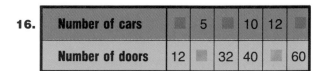

ANOTHER LOOK

Multiply.

1. $\begin{array}{r} 2,354 \\ \times 45 \\ \hline \end{array}$

2. $\begin{array}{r} 7,841 \\ \times 73 \\ \hline \end{array}$

3. $\begin{array}{r} 6,003 \\ \times 11 \\ \hline \end{array}$

4. $\begin{array}{r} 2,206 \\ \times 61 \\ \hline \end{array}$

5. $\begin{array}{r} 7,011 \\ \times 52 \\ \hline \end{array}$

6. $\begin{array}{r} 3,498 \\ \times 39 \\ \hline \end{array}$

PROBLEM SOLVING
Writing a Simpler Problem

Sometimes decimals, fractions, and large numbers make a problem seem difficult. It may be easier to use simpler numbers than those in the problem. Once you see how to get the answer, you can use the more difficult numbers to find the exact answer.

Rick owns the Go-to-School Bus Company. Each day, 4,368 students ride his buses to go to school. Each bus holds 42 students. How many busloads of students ride Rick's buses during a 5-day week?

Substitute simpler numbers for the numbers in the problem.

$$4,368 \longrightarrow 4,000$$
$$42 \longrightarrow 40$$

You multiply to find the total number of students who ride the bus in 5 days.

$$4,000 \times 5 = 20,000$$

Then you divide to find the number of busloads.

$$20,000 \div 40 = 500$$

Now you multiply and then divide, using the actual numbers in the problem.

$$4,368 \times 5 = 21,840 \qquad 21,840 \div 42 = 520$$

During a 5-day week, Rick's buses carry 520 busloads of students to school.

Write the letter of the better plan for simplifying each problem.

1. John has $52,000 that he wants to use to buy vans. Each van costs $12,942. Does he have enough money to buy 4 vans?

    a. Step 1: $12 × 4 = $48
        Step 2: $52 > $48

    b. Step 1: $52 − $12 = $40
        Step 2: $40 ÷ 4 = $10

2. A bus driver travels $13\frac{3}{10}$ miles from his garage to the first stop on his route. There are 24 stops along this route. The stops are $1\frac{1}{4}$ miles apart. How far does the bus travel from its garage to its last stop?

    a. Step 1: 24 × 1 = 24
        Step 2: 24 − 13 = 11

    b. Step 1: 24 × 1 = 24
        Step 2: 24 + 13 = 37

Solve. Use simpler numbers if needed.

3. A bridge is being built, which will shorten Lee's ride to school by $3\frac{7}{10}$ miles. She used to ride $4\frac{1}{4}$ miles to the old bridge and $5\frac{1}{2}$ miles from there to school. How long will Lee's ride be when she uses the new bridge?

4. Last year, John spent $48,789 to maintain his buses. He expects to spend twice as much this year. He has already spent $72,642. How much more money does he expect to pay for maintenance this year?

5. Many students ride bicycles to Hillsboro School. Seth rides $1\frac{3}{4}$ miles. Paul rides $1\frac{3}{10}$ miles farther than Seth. Myra rides $2\frac{1}{2}$ miles. How much farther does Paul ride than Myra?

6. John hired 12 new bus drivers. Each will earn $19,342 per year. The budget allows $240,000 to pay new drivers. Has he budgeted enough money to pay all the new drivers he has hired?

★7. On Monday, 1,302 students rode buses to school, and 504 students walked. Because it rained on Tuesday, $\frac{1}{2}$ of the students who walked on Monday rode buses. Each bus holds 42 students. How many busloads of students rode to school on Tuesday?

★8. Last year, 1,542 students went on school trips. It cost $7.89 per student. This year, there are 327 fewer students going on trips. But, it costs $9.45 per student. What is the difference in the total cost in the last two years?

Scale Drawings

A. A **scale drawing** is used as a model for an object. Designers draw "to scale" by reducing or enlarging all parts of the object.

Look at this scale drawing. The measurements of the Wright house have been drawn to the scale of 1 in.:10 ft. This means that 1 in. in the drawing is equivalent to 10 ft in the actual house.

How long is the back wall of the actual house?

You can use equal ratios to find the actual length of the wall.

Write a ratio for the scale.

1 in.:10 ft, or $\frac{1}{10}$.

Write a ratio for the length of the wall.

length in drawing $\longrightarrow$ 5 in.
actual length $\longrightarrow$ n ft

Use equal ratios to find the unknown length.

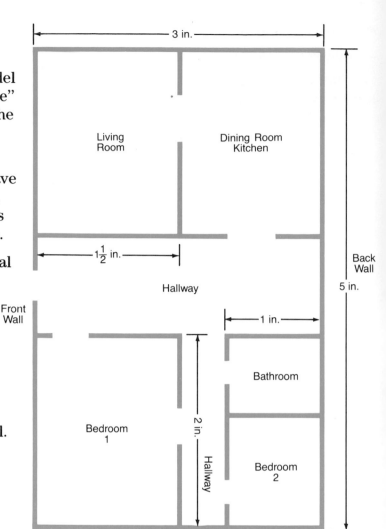

Scale: 1 in.: 10 feet

length in drawing (in.) $\longrightarrow$ $\dfrac{1}{10} = \dfrac{5}{n}$ | Think: $1 \times 5 = 5.$ | $\dfrac{1}{10} = \dfrac{1 \times 5}{10 \times 5} = \dfrac{5}{50}$
actual length (ft) $\longrightarrow$

The actual length of the back wall is 50 ft.

B. How long will a 20-foot-long bookcase appear to be in the scale drawing?

length in drawing (in.) $\longrightarrow$ $\dfrac{1}{10} = \dfrac{n}{20}$ | Think: $10 \times 2 = 20.$ | $\dfrac{1}{10} = \dfrac{1 \times 2}{10 \times 2} = \dfrac{2}{20}$
actual length (ft) $\longrightarrow$

The bookcase will appear to be 2 inches long in the drawing.

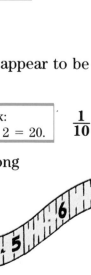

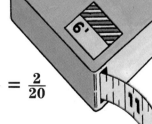

Use the scale drawing at the right to find the length and width of each room.

1. Living room
$l = \blacksquare; w = \blacksquare$

2. Dining room
$l = \blacksquare; w = \blacksquare$

3. Kitchen
$l = \blacksquare; w = \blacksquare$

4. Study
$l = \blacksquare; w = \blacksquare$

5. Pantry
$l = \blacksquare; w = \blacksquare$

6. Bathroom
$l = \blacksquare; w = \blacksquare$

Solve. Use Scale Drawing A.

7. What is the length of the wall that separates the dining room from the living room?

★**8.** Mrs. Wright is extending her living room and adding new furniture. The room will be 9 m long and 5 m wide. Use a scale of 1 cm : 0.5 m to draw the room. Then draw each piece of furniture from the chart in your scale drawing.

Scale Drawing A

Living Room   Dining Room

Pantry

Study   Kitchen

Bathroom

Scale: 1 cm: 3 m

Furniture	Actual length	Actual width
Sofa	2 m	1 m
Cabinets	3 m	0.5 m
Coffee table	1 m	0.5 m

MIDCHAPTER REVIEW

Write each ratio as a fraction.

1. 6 to 9   **2.** 17 out of 20   **3.** 14 to 30

4. 7 : 12

Write = or ≠ for ●.

5. $\frac{17}{34} \bullet \frac{35}{68}$ **6.** $\frac{4}{9} \bullet \frac{36}{81}$ **7.** $\frac{24}{64} \bullet \frac{3}{8}$

Use Scale Drawing B to find the length and the width of each room.

8. Kitchen
$l = \blacksquare; w = \blacksquare$

9. Bathroom
$l = \blacksquare; w = \blacksquare$

10. Living room
$l = \blacksquare; w = \blacksquare$

11. Bedroom
$l = \blacksquare; w = \blacksquare$

Scale Drawing B

Living Room   Kitchen

Bedroom   Bathroom

Scale: 1 in.: 12 ft

PROBLEM SOLVING
Using a Recipe

A recipe tells you the ingredients that are required, the steps to follow in preparing the dish, and the number of people it will serve. You may want to change the recipe to increase or decrease the number of servings.

MIGHTY MEAT LOAF

Makes 6 servings

3 eggs, beaten

4 pounds ground beef

$2\frac{1}{2}$ cups bread crumbs

$\frac{3}{4}$ cup minced onion

$\frac{1}{4}$ cup milk

$\frac{1}{4}$ cup ketchup

Blend eggs and meat. Add other ingredients. Mix well. Shape into an oval loaf. Bake in a shallow pan for about 1 hour at 350°F.

Bill wants to make Mighty Meat Loaf for a family dinner. He wants to make enough for 12 servings. How many eggs should he use?

You can write equal ratios to decide how many eggs Bill will need.

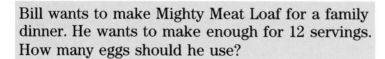

number of eggs
in recipe ⟶ $\dfrac{3}{6} = \dfrac{\blacksquare}{12}$ ⟵ number of eggs needed
number of servings → ⟵ number of servings
in recipe wanted

Find equivalent fractions.

$$6 \times 2 = 12 \qquad \frac{3}{6} = \frac{3 \times 2}{6 \times 2} = \frac{6}{12}$$

Bill will need 6 eggs for 12 servings.

Solve. Write the letter of the best answer.

1. Bill wants to make 18 servings of the meat loaf. If the recipe yields 9 servings and calls for $\frac{1}{4}$ cup of milk, how much milk will Bill use?

   a. $\frac{1}{3}$ cup   b. $\frac{1}{2}$ cup
   c. 3 cups   d. 4 cups

2. The meat-loaf recipe calls for $1\frac{1}{4}$ cup of bread crumbs. If this amount is used to make 6 servings, how many cups of bread crumbs will Bill need for 24 servings?

   a. $\frac{2}{24}$ cup   b. $8\frac{1}{4}$ cup
   c. 5 cups   d. 36 cups

Solve.

3. One soup recipe calls for 2 cups of broth. The recipe yields 5 servings. How much broth would you need for 15 servings?

4. A casserole recipe calls for $1\frac{1}{2}$ cups grated cheese. The casserole serves 8 people. How much cheese would you need for 24 servings?

5. To cook 3 cups of rice, you need 6 cups of water. What is the ratio of rice to water? How much water would you need for 6 cups of rice? for 9 cups of rice?

6. Larry is making date-nut bread. The recipe yields 1 loaf. Larry plans to bake 3 loaves. The recipe calls for $\frac{3}{4}$ cup chopped dates. How many cups of dates should Larry use?

★7. A chow-mein recipe calls for one 5–ounce can of water chestnuts. The recipe serves 6. Clara wants to serve 24 people. The store stocks only 10-ounce cans. How many 10-ounce cans should Clara buy?

★8. Sam's egg-salad recipe calls for 1 tablespoon of mustard. The recipe serves 9. Sam wants to serve 6. How much mustard should Sam use?
   (HINT: 3 teaspoons = 1 tablespoon)

Ratio and Percent

A. Sometimes you can *draw a picture* to help you explore ideas in mathematics. In this activity, you will use what you know about ratio to explore percent.

Step 1: Draw a 10 by 10 grid on graph paper.

- How many squares does the grid contain?

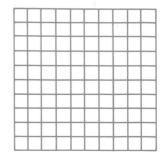

Step 2: Color 65 squares red.

- What is the ratio of red squares to the total number of squares in the grid? Write the ratio in three different ways.

- A **percent** (%) is the ratio of a number to 100. What percent of the grid is red?

Step 3: Color 30 squares green. Color the remaining squares in the grid yellow.

- What is the ratio of green squares to the total number of squares in the grid? What percent of the grid is green?

- What is the ratio of yellow squares to the total number of squares? What percent of the grid is yellow?

- What is the ratio of green and yellow squares to the total number of squares? What percent of the grid is green and yellow?

- What percent of the grid have you colored?

Working as a Team _____

1. Color different numbers of squares in another 10 by 10 grid. Exchange your grid with a teammate's. Write the ratio and the percent for the portion of the grid that is colored. Write the ratio and the percent for the portion that is not in color.

2. What can you say about the way in which ratio and percent are related? List your conclusions and discuss them with other teams.

Math Reasoning, page H205

B. Test scores are an example of how percent is used.

Suppose your teacher gave your class a math test that had 100 problems. At the right are the scores for six students in the class.

TEST SCORES

Billy	75%
Juan	88%
Reiko	93%
Amir	100%
Kathy	89%
Tamla	90%

Thinking as a Team

1. How many percentage points is each problem on the test worth?

2. What does the percent tell you about the number of problems that were answered correctly?

3. Can the percent tell you about the number of problems that were not answered correctly? How?

C. Your teacher gives a second math test. This time there are 50 problems on the test.

Thinking as a Team

1. How many percentage points is each problem on the test worth? How did you find the answer?

2. Here is a table that shows the number of questions that each of six students answered correctly. Write each test score in percent form.

Name	Number	Correct	Name	Number	Correct
Billy	48	■	Juan	44	■
Reiko	50	■	Amir	35	■
Kathy	46	■	Tamla	45	■

3. Does a score of 100% mean the same thing for a 100-problem test as it does for a 50-problem test? Why or why not?

4. Compare the percent score on the first test to the number correct on the second test of any one student. Why do you think your teacher uses percent to score tests?

For a related activity, see *Connecting Math Ideas*, page 412.

Percents and Decimals

A. You can make drawings to explore how percents and decimals are related.

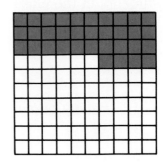

Step 1: Outline a 10 by 10 grid on graph paper. Shade enough small squares to show the decimal 0.34.

- What percent of the large square is shaded?

- Use the percent you found to complete this statement:

$$0.\,\blacksquare\ \blacksquare\ =\ \blacksquare\ \blacksquare\ \%$$

- Shade fewer than 10 squares on another grid. Write a decimal for the shaded part. Write a percent.

- Choose other decimals. Show them on graph paper. Then write them as percents.

Step 2: On a 10 by 10 grid, shade in enough squares to show the decimal 0.6.

- What percent of the squares are shaded?

- How can you rename a decimal written in tenths so that it will be easier to write as a percent?

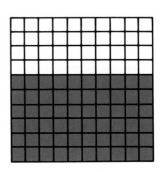

Step 3: Use a table like the one at the right to record two ways of writing the shaded parts of the grids. Repeat what you have done using other numbers.

Decimal	Percent
0.34	
0.6	

Thinking as a Team

1. How many places do you move the decimal point to rewrite a decimal as a percent?

2. How many places do you move the decimal point when you write a percent as a decimal?

3. When is it helpful to write a percent as a decimal?

4. How can you enter a percent into a calculator?

B. Write a decimal that is greater than 1, such as 1.25. Show it by using 10 by 10 grids on graph paper.

Thinking as a Team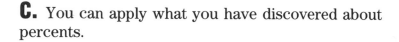

1. How many squares would you shade to show 1.25? How many would you shade to show 3.85 or 12.36?

2. How would you write 3.85 as a percent? How would you write 12.86 as a percent?

3. Write each decimal as a percent.
   1.25   2.01   2.5

C. You can apply what you have discovered about percents.

Thinking as a Team

1. You might have heard a sports star say, "I gave a 110% effort in the game." Is it possible to give a 110% effort? Why or why not?

2. Can you think of times when it is useful to use a percent greater than 100%?

3. Discuss the meaning of the following examples with your team.

   - You're going to feel 1,000% better!

   - The price of gold went up 150% in a month.

   - The number of deer in the forest has grown by 200%.

   - The manager of a factory made two different statements:

     "We produced 10% more this year than last year."
     "We produced 110% of what we did last year."

     Do the two statements mean the same thing? Why or why not?

Percents and Fractions

A. The students in fifth grade class at Lakeridge School got back their math tests. Amos and Judy told Mark about their test scores. Amos answered 4 out of 5 of the test questions correctly. Judy's score was 80%. Mark asked, "Which one of you has the higher score?" You can use what you know about ratio, fractions, and percent to answer this question.

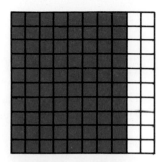

Step 1: Show 80% on a 10 by 10 grid.

- Name what you have shown as a decimal and as a fraction.

Step 2: On tracing paper, copy the outline of the 10 by 10 grid. Then draw lines separating it into 5 equal parts. Shade 4 of the parts red.

- Name the shaded part as a ratio and as a fraction.

Step 3: Place your tracing paper over the grid you made in Step 1.

- What do you notice? Write a number sentence to show what you have discovered.

- How many other ways can you write this?

- Who had the higher score, Amos or Judy?

Thinking as a Team

1. How does knowing that 75% is the ratio of 75 to 100 help you to write a fraction for 75%? What is that fraction in simplest form?

2. Write a fraction in simplest form for 50%. Write a fraction in simplest form for 5%.

B. Mark answered 17 out of the 20 questions on another test correctly. What percent will show his score?

Working as a Team

Think about this as you try to find Mark's score. If 4 out of 5 is equal to 80 out of 100, then 17 out of 20 is equal to _____ out of 100.

1. What is Mark's score? Describe how you found it.

2. Describe how you would find his score if $\frac{14}{20}$ of his answers had been correct.

C. Experiment with your calculator to discover how it can be used to find a percent equivalent to a fraction. You know that $\frac{3}{4}$ is equivalent to 75%.

Working as a Team

1. What mathematical operation does $\frac{3}{4}$ represent?

2. How do you write 75% as a decimal?

Try this with other fractions. Discuss with the class what you have discovered.

3. What will you do if your answer has decimal places beyond hundredths?

4. Suppose the decimal 6.5 appeared on your calculator display. Write this number as a mixed number. Write it as a percent.

5. When do you think you might want to write a percent as a fraction or a fraction as a percent? Discuss the reasons why you might want to do this.

Percent of a Number

In the United States, travel is one of the most popular vacation activities. Each year, millions of people travel to places throughout the United States and to other countries.

A travel agency arranges vacation trips for 1,500 people. Of these people, 65% travel by airplane. How many people travel by airplane?

Find 65% of 1,500.

Write 65% as a decimal.

$$65\% \longrightarrow \frac{65}{100} \longrightarrow 0.65$$

Multiply.

$$
\begin{array}{r}
1{,}5\,0\,0 \\
\times \quad 0.6\,5 \\
\hline
7\,5\,0\,0 \\
9\,0\,0\,0\,0 \\
\hline
9\,7\,5.0\,0
\end{array}
$$

Of the 1,500 people, 975 people travel by airplane.

Another example:

$$4\% \text{ of } 525 = n$$
$$0.04 \times 525 = n$$
$$21 = n$$
$$4\% \text{ of } 525 = 21$$

Checkpoint Write the letter of the correct answer.

Find the percent of each number.

1. 35% of 400

a. 32
b. 140
c. 140%
d. 14,000

2. 50% of 2,500

a. $\frac{1}{2}$
b. 1,250
c. 11,500
d. 125,000

3. 9% of 7,200

a. 638
b. 648
c. 800
d. 6,480

4. 81% of 100

a. 0.81
b. 8.1
c. 81
d. 100

Find the percent of each number.

1. 10% of 100
2. 75% of 20
3. 30% of 210
4. 90% of 30

5. 20% of 60
6. 80% of 640
7. 8% of 800
8. 60% of 590

9. 5% of 710
10. 90% of 660
11. 55% of 480
12. 25% of 212

13. 40% of 80
14. 70% of 450
15. 8% of 720
16. 30% of 350

17. 65% of 120
18. 50% of 44
19. 78% of 1,100
20. 4% of 200

21. 70% of 700
22. 25% of 4
★23. 125% of 16
★24. 225% of 100

Solve.

25. Ellen's class planned a bike trip during summer vacation. Only 40% of Ellen's class went on the trip. If there were 30 people in her class, how many people went biking?

26. Ellen's friends are planning a 9-day hike of 108 miles. How many miles should they hike each day if they want to hike the same number of miles each day?

27. Fritz has $300.00 to spend for his vacation. He budgets 60% of his money for transportation. How much money does he budget for transportation?

★28. The twenty-five members of the bicycle club want to fly to Italy in order to bike through the countryside. If a 400-seat plane is 90% full, how many seats are left?

NUMBER SENSE

Sometimes it is easier to find the percent of a number if you think of the percent as a fraction.

$$50\% = \frac{1}{2} \qquad 25\% = \frac{1}{4} \qquad 10\% = \frac{1}{10}$$

Use fractions to find the percent of the number.

$$50\% \text{ of } 120 \qquad\qquad 25\% \text{ of } 360 \qquad\qquad 10\% \text{ of } 780$$
$$= \frac{1}{2} \times 120 \qquad\qquad = \frac{1}{4} \times 360 \qquad\qquad = \frac{1}{10} \times 780$$
$$= \frac{120}{2} \qquad\qquad\quad = \frac{360}{4} \qquad\qquad\quad = \frac{780}{10}$$
$$= 60 \qquad\qquad\qquad = 90 \qquad\qquad\qquad = 78$$

So welcome to Fiji. Enjoy our shopping and our wonderful resorts. Enjoy the magic of a world untouched by the anger and violence that has affected so many destinations.

Find the percent of each number.

1. 10% of 200
2. 25% of 180
3. 50% of 66

4. 50% of 998
5. 10% of 510
6. 25% of 328

Finding Percents

A. The FunTime Toy Company owns 20 trucks. The owners plan to paint 5 of them red. What percent of the trucks will be painted red?

You need to find what percent of 20 is 5. Compare the part to the whole.

Write a fraction. | **Find an equivalent fraction with a denominator of 100.** | **Write the fraction as a percent.**

part $\longrightarrow$ $\frac{5}{20}$
whole $\longrightarrow$

$\frac{5 \times 5}{20 \times 5} = \frac{25}{100}$

25%

Of all FunTime's trucks, 25% will be painted red.

B. Sometimes you have to simplify to find an equivalent fraction with a denominator of 100.

8 is what percent of 40?

Write a fraction. | **Simplify.** | **Find an equivalent fraction that has a denominator of 100.** | **Write the fraction as a percent.**

part $\longrightarrow$ $\frac{8}{40}$
whole $\longrightarrow$

$\frac{8}{40} \div \frac{8}{8} = \frac{1}{5}$

$\frac{1 \times 20}{5 \times 20} = \frac{20}{100}$

20%

8 is 20% of 40.

Checkpoint Write the letter of the correct answer.

Solve.

1. What percent of 50 is 5?

a. 10
b. 20
c. 55
d. 250

2. What percent of 25 is 2?

a. 4
b. 8
c. $12\frac{1}{2}$
d. 50

3. 6 is what percent of 10?

a. 6
b. 10
c. 60
d. 600

Copy and complete the chart.

	1.	2.	3.	4.	5.	6.	7.	8.
Part	15	18	32	7	20	18	8	12
Whole	75	60	80	35	25	25	32	50
Percent	■	■	■	■	■	■	■	■

Compute.

9. What percent of 25 is 15?

10. 18 is what percent of 50?

11. What percent of 45 is 9?

12. 24 is what percent of 60?

13. 32 is what percent of 80?

14. What percent of 90 is 27?

15. 3 is what percent of 10?

16. What percent of 50 is 13?

Find the percent that each part is of the whole.

17. 9 calico cats
10 cats
■% are calico.

18. 1 goldfish
5 fish
■% are goldfish.

19. 19 black umbrellas
20 umbrellas
■% are black.

★20. 2 blue bicycles
8 yellow bicycles
10 white bicycles
■% are yellow.

★21. 9 pink flowers
6 red flowers
10 orange flowers
■% are pink.

★22. 12 brown dogs
36 spotted dogs
2 tan dogs
■% are tan.

Solve.

23. The FunTime Toy Company uses 12 out of their 20 trucks to deliver electronic games. What percent of the trucks deliver electronic games?

★24. On one day, 17 of FunTime's trucks were delivering. The other 3 trucks remained in the warehouse. What percent of the trucks remained in the warehouse?

ANOTHER LOOK

Multiply.

1. 0.07
× 0.8

2. 0.04
× 0.9

3. 0.05
× 0.3

4. 0.09
× 0.7

5. 0.03
× 0.4

6. 1.07
× 0.7

7. 7.04
× 5.3

8. 9.07
× 0.6

9. 7.02
× 9.2

10. 3.02
× 5.9

PROBLEM SOLVING
Using a Circle Graph

You can use a circle graph to show data given in percents and as fractional parts of a whole. The circle is divided into parts. A larger fraction or percent is shown by a larger part of the graph.

NUMBER OF CARS OWNED BY GREENTOWN FAMILIES

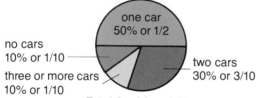

one car
50% or 1/2

no cars
10% or 1/10

three or more cars
10% or 1/10

two cars
30% or 3/10

Total families: 1,180

- The title tells you that this graph shows the number of cars owned by families in Greentown.
- Each part shows what percent or fraction of the families own a certain number of cars.

The percents must add up to 100%. The fractions must add up to 1.

- The size of each part shows the size of its percent or fractional part.

How many families own two cars?
First, find the part labeled *two cars*. What percent of the families own two cars? What fractional part of the families own two cars?

The graph tells you that 30%, or $\frac{3}{10}$, of the families in Greentown own two cars.

Then, find 30% of 1,180.
Write 30% as a decimal.
$30\% = 0.3$

$$\begin{array}{r} 1{,}180 \\ \times\ \ 0.3 \\ \hline 354 \end{array}$$

Of the Greentown families, 354 own two cars.

Write *true* or *false*.

1. The sum of the percents shown in a circle graph may be greater than 100%.

2. If a circle graph were divided into 4 equal parts, each part would be $\frac{1}{4}$ of the whole.

Use the circle graph to answer Exercises 3–6.

SUMMER ATTENDANCE AT TRANSPORTATION MUSEUM BY AGE GROUP

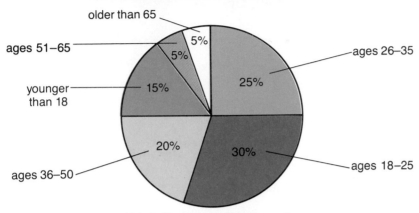

Total attendance: 9,900 people

3. What percent of the people who visited the museum were in the 26–35 age group?

4. The greatest percent of people who visited the museum were in which age group?

5. How many people were in the younger-than-18 age group?

6. How many people in the 26–35 age group attended the museum?

Circle graphs can be used to compare information. Use the three circle graphs below to solve each problem.

APPROXIMATE NUMBER OF MOTOR VEHICLES IN USE

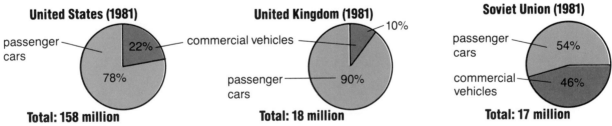

7. About how many passenger cars were in use in the United Kingdom in 1981?

8. Which of the countries had the greatest percent of passenger cars in use?

★9. Which country had the greatest number of passenger cars in use?

★10. To the nearest ten thousand, about how many more passenger cars than commercial vehicles were in use in the Soviet Union?

MATH COMMUNICATION

Scientists traveled from all over the world to see Dr. Magwich's plans for a new kind of flying machine made of superlight, superstrong clay. When they arrived, Dr. Magwich found that her list of supplies had been damaged by water and was unreadable. This is what Dr. Magwich had.

Dr. Magwich knew she needed clay, some nylon cloth for the wings, and some special liquid fuel. How much of each did she need?

Math has its own vocabulary. Such terms as *gallons*, *pounds*, and *yards* stand for units of measure. Dr. Magwich knew that *gallons* measure liquid, *pounds* measure solid weight, and *yards* measure length. Tell which item she put with each unit of measurement and write in the missing word. Choose from these terms.

pints	gallons	prime number
feet	inches	simplest form
pounds	miles	denominator
yards	numerator	mixed number

1. $31\frac{1}{2}$ is a kind of fraction called a _____.

2. If Dr. Magwich wrote $\frac{3}{6}$ as $\frac{1}{2}$, she would have written the fraction in its _____.

3. In $\frac{3}{4}$, 4 is the _____.

4. To measure enough fuel to fit in 2 cups, Dr. Magwich would use _____.

5. To show how far the flying machine would have to fly to reach the next city, Dr. Magwich would measure by _____.

6. A number that is divisible only by itself and 1 is called a _____.

GROUP PROJECT

Champ's Used Skateboards

The problem: Leroy is called "Champ" because he has been the skateboard champion in the neighborhood for so long. Everyone comes to him to find out about the latest safety equipment and for help fixing their boards. So Champ has decided to open a shop called Champ's Used Skateboards. What should he charge for his goods and services? Can you help? Discuss the Key Facts with your classmates; then make a price list.

Champ's Boards

new $120–$150 _____ now $60 ____

Professional Repair Shop

new $120–$150 _____ now $75 ____

Retired Reactor Gear

Helmet   new $32 ____ now _____

Gloves with fingers   new $15 ____ now _____

Gloves without fingers   new $14 ____ now _____

Knee Guards   new $26 ____ now _____

Elbow Guards   new $22 ____ now _____

Last Month's Magazines   new $1.50 ____ now _____

Key Facts

- Repairing skateboards can require a great deal of labor.
- Supplies needed are screws, paint, sandpaper, and glue.
- If the wheels need to be replaced, they cost $40 if they are new.
- Champ can take $5 to $10 off the price if an old skateboard is traded in when a newly repaired one is purchased.

CHAPTER TEST

Write each ratio as a fraction. (page 308)

1. 2:5   **2.** 5 out of 7   **3.** 10:3   **4.** 6 to 9

Write each fraction as a ratio. (page 308)

5. $\frac{3}{8}$ **6.** $\frac{12}{7}$ **7.** $\frac{8}{9}$ **8.** $\frac{14}{25}$

Find the missing number. (page 310)

9. $\frac{2}{3} = \frac{8}{n}$ **10.** $\frac{6}{11} = \frac{42}{n}$ **11.** $\frac{4}{5} = \frac{n}{25}$ **12.** $\frac{16}{7} = \frac{n}{28}$

Use the scale drawing at the right to find the length and width of each room. (page 314)

13. Living room   **14.** Study

15. Parlor   **16.** Balcony

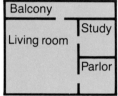

SCALE DRAWING

Balcony

Study

Living room

Parlor

Scale: 1 cm : 4m

Write the percent that describes the shaded part of the figure. (page 318)

17. red   **18.** blue

19. yellow   **20.** white

Write as a decimal. (page 320)

21. 18%   **22.** 52%   **23.** 9%   **24.** 27%

Write each percent as a fraction in simplest form. (page 322)

25. 11%   **26.** 32%   **27.** 49%   **28.** 83%

Find the percent of each number. (page 324)

29. 20% of 100   **30.** 40% of 600   **31.** 80% of 35   **32.** 6% of 950

Compute. (page 326)

33. What percent of 16 is 4?   **34.** 9 is what percent of 25?   **35.** What percent of 55 is 11?   **36.** 36 is what percent of 90?

Solve. Use simpler numbers if needed. (pages 312–313)

37. There are 25 students in Sam's class. Of that number, 40% ride the bus to school. In John's class, there are 35 students, and 60% of the students in his class ride the bus to school. How many students ride the bus to school in both John's and Sam's classes?

38. Jane's family drives 1,311 miles in 3 days to visit their grandmother. After the first day, they had driven $\frac{1}{3}$ of the way to their grandmother's. How many miles did they drive the first day?

Use the circle graph to solve. (pages 328–329)

1984 BUDGET FOR THE GREENVILLE HIGH FOOTBALL TEAM

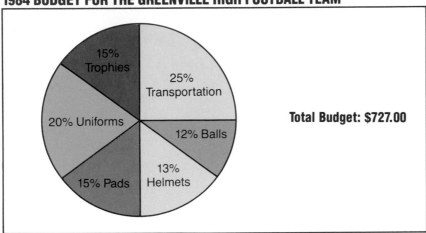

Total Budget: $727.00

39. How much did the team spend on transportation? on pads?

40. How much did the team spend on uniforms? on helmets?

BONUS

There are 200 coins in Hal's change jar.

1. If 20 coins are quarters, what percent are quarters?

2. If 30% are dimes, how many dimes does he have?

3. If $\frac{2}{5}$ of the coins are pennies, how many pennies does he have?

4. If 40 coins are nickels, what percent are nickels?

RETEACHING

A. To write a percent as a decimal or a fraction, think of a percent as the ratio of a number to 100.
So, 25% is 25 : 100, or $\frac{25}{100}$.

Write 73% as a decimal.
Think: 73% = $\frac{73}{100}$. Write 0.73.

Write 5% as a decimal.
Think: 5% = $\frac{5}{100}$. Write 0.05.

You can write a decimal as a percent.

Write 0.47 as a percent.
Think: 0.47 = $\frac{47}{100}$. Write 47%.

Write 0.06 as a percent.
Think: 0.06 = $\frac{6}{100}$. Write 6%.

B. You can also write a percent as a fraction or a fraction as a percent.

Write 65% as a fraction.

Percent   Fraction   Write in simplest form.
$65\% \longrightarrow \frac{65}{100} \longrightarrow \frac{13}{20}$

Write $\frac{11}{25}$ as a percent.

Find an equivalent fraction that has a denominator of 100.
$$\frac{11}{25} = \frac{11 \times 4}{25 \times 4} = \frac{44}{100}$$

Write the fraction as a percent.
$$\frac{44}{100} = 44\%$$

Write as a decimal.

1. 15%   **2.** 17%   **3.** 80%   **4.** 20%   **5.** 7%

Write as a percent.

6. 0.85   **7.** 0.54   **8.** 0.09   **9.** 0.08   **10.** 0.3

Write as a percent.

11. $\frac{15}{25}$ **12.** $\frac{48}{50}$ **13.** $\frac{4}{5}$ **14.** $\frac{1}{2}$ **15.** $\frac{20}{20}$

Write as a fraction in simplest form.

16. 85%   **17.** 30%   **18.** 9%   **19.** 42%   **20.** 116%

ENRICHMENT

Sales Tax and Discount

Some states and cities have **sales taxes.** The *sales tax* is a percentage of the cost of an item. It is added to that cost. When finding sales tax, round up. Pablo buys a book on the history of the railroad for $15.21. The sales tax is 6%. What is the total cost of the book?

Find 6% of $15.21.	Round up to the nearest cent.	Add to the cost of the book.
$15.21 $\times\ \ 0.06$ $\overline{\$0.9126}$	$0.9126 \rightarrow \$0.92$	$15.21 $+\ \ 0.92$ $\overline{\$16.13}$

The total cost of the book is $16.13.

Some stores give **discounts.** A *discount* is also a percentage of the cost of an item. It is subtracted from that cost. When finding discounts, round down. Harry buys a book on airplanes for $7.38. The store gives a discount of 5%. What is the cost of the book?

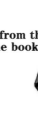

Find 5% of $7.38.	Round down to the nearest cent.	Subtract from the cost of the book.
$7.38 $\times\ \ 0.05$ $\overline{\$0.369}$	$0.369 \rightarrow \$0.36$	$7.38 $-\ \ 0.36$ $\overline{\$7.02}$

The cost of the book is $7.02.

Find the cost.

1. Price: $5.22
   Sales tax: 5%

2. Price: $6.22
   Sales tax: 6%

3. Price: $2.87
   Sales tax: 8%

4. Price: $9.47
   Sales tax: 4%

5. Price: $7.75
   Discount: 6%

6. Price: $5.33
   Discount: 7%

7. Price: $9.98
   Discount: 3%

8. Price: $1.28
   Discount: 5%

9. Price: $2.05
   Sales tax: 4%

10. Price: $8.12
    Discount: 9%

11. Price: $3.53
    Sales tax: 3%

12. Price: $4.07
    Discount: 10%

TECHNOLOGY

In BASIC, the computer will perform the operations inside the parentheses first.

1. Complete this program so that when you RUN it, it prints this.   4 PLUS 30 IS 34

```
10   LET A = (6 + ▧) / 4
20   LET B = (12 − 6) * (4 + ▧)
30   LET C = A + B
40   PRINT A; " PLUS "; B; " IS "; C
```

2. You can use parentheses in PRINT statements, too. What does the computer print when you give these instructions?

PRINT (6 * 4) / (2 + 2)
PRINT (10 / 2) − (5 − 2)

You can use a set of parentheses inside another set.

PRINT 10 − (5 * (3 − 1))

3. What will the computer print when you give these instructions?

PRINT (17 − (5 − 3)) / 5
PRINT 2 + ((2 * 3) − 4)

Notice that there are always the same number of left parentheses ⦅ as there are right parentheses ⦆.

Here is a four-line program that stores the number 1 in variable Z.

```
10   LET X = 1 + 2 + 3
20   LET Y = X * 4
30   LET Z = 25 − Y
40   PRINT Z
```

Here is a program that does the same computation on one line.

```
10   LET Z = 25 − ((1 + 2 + 3) * 4)
40   PRINT Z
```

4. Rewrite this program so that it does the computation on one line.

```
10   LET I = 5 + 4
20   LET J = I / 9
30   LET K = J − 1
40   PRINT K
```

Even without parentheses, the computer will do some parts of the computation before other parts. You already know that the computer will first calculate inside parentheses, if there are any. After those calculations are done, the computer will do all the multiplication and division from left to right. Then all the addition and subtraction is done from left to right. For instance, this PRINT statement will multiply 7 and 3 to find 21, and then add 3 and 21. It will print 24.

PRINT 3 + 7 * 3

Here is another example.

PRINT 9 − (8 / 2 + 5)

This instruction has a set of parentheses. The computer will start to do the computation inside the parentheses first. Inside the parentheses, there are two operations. The division is done first: $8 \div 2 = 4$. Then $4 + 5 = 9$. Now the rest of the equation is easy: $9 − 9 = 0$.

5. What will each instruction print?

PRINT 6 + 6 / 2

PRINT (6 + 6) / 2

PRINT 10 * 10 − 3

PRINT 10 * (10 − 3)

PRINT 8 * 10 − (5 * 6)

PRINT (6 − (8 − 5)) + 7

PRINT 10 * (15 − (2 * 5)) / 5

PRINT 8 / 2 + 10 − 5

CUMULATIVE REVIEW

Write the letter of the correct answer.

1. $\frac{4}{9} \times \frac{5}{6}$

   a. $\frac{9}{54}$ b. $\frac{10}{27}$

   c. $\frac{20}{15}$ d. not given

2. $\frac{1}{3}$ mile = ▦

   a. 1,760 ft b. 1,760 yd

   c. 5,280 ft d. not given

3. $15 \times \frac{1}{6}$

   a. $2\frac{1}{3}$ b. $2\frac{1}{2}$

   c. $3\frac{1}{2}$ d. not given

4. $\frac{1}{9} \times 81$

   a. $8\frac{1}{9}$ b. 9

   c. $9\frac{1}{9}$ d. not given

5. If the temperature falls from 55°F to
   ⁻55°F, by how many degrees has the
   temperature changed?

   a. 55° b. 100°

   c. 110° d. not given

6. 0.2×0.3

   a. 0.006 b. 0.6

   c. 6 d. not given

7. $\frac{5}{6} + \frac{7}{10}$

   a. $\frac{12}{16}$ b. $\frac{13}{15}$

   c. $1\frac{8}{15}$ d. not given

8. $6,736 \div 22$

   a. 36 R4 b. 306

   c. 306 R4 d. not given

9. $53 \times 5,697$

   a. 301,941 b. 305,750

   c. 315,351 d. not given

TRAIN SCHEDULE

Landstown to Cow Bluffs		
Landstown	**Poplar**	**Cow Bluffs**
12:10	12:24	12:55
1:30	1:44	2:15
4:55	5:09	5:40
Cow Bluffs to Landstown		
Cow Bluffs	**Poplar**	**Landstown**
6:14	6:19	6:53
6:38	6:44	7:12
6:54	6:59	7:34

Use the train schedule to answer the
questions.

10. How long does it take to ride from
    Landstown to Cow Bluffs?

    a. 15 min b. 35 min

    c. 45 min d. not given

11. When does the last train arrive in
    Landstown?

    a. 4:55 b. 6:53

    c. 7:34 d. not given

Use as many vocabulary words about geometry as is possible to describe our solar system. Or, if you prefer, draw a diagram of our solar system, and then label all the geometric shapes.

11 GEOMETRY

Basic Ideas of Geometry

You use geometry whenever you ask questions about the size, shape, volume, or position of anything. The word *geometry* comes from two Greek words that mean "earth" and "to measure."

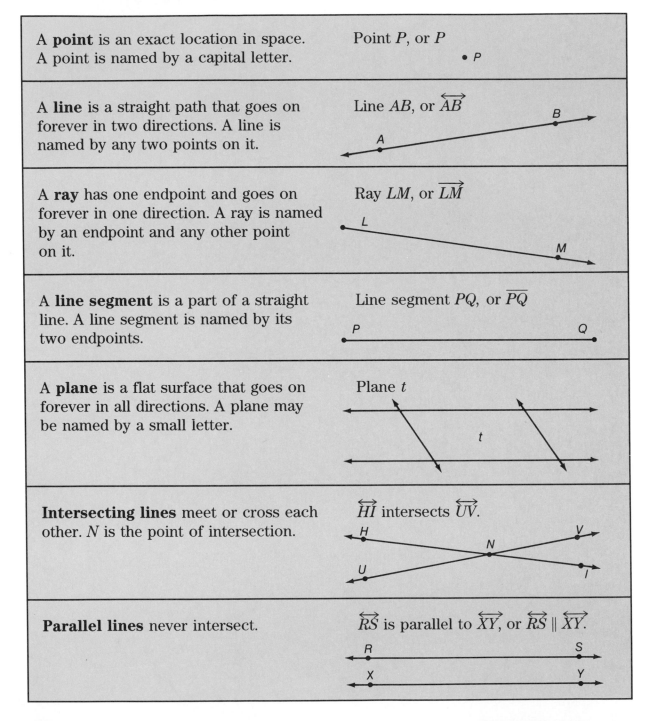

A **point** is an exact location in space. A point is named by a capital letter.	Point P, or P
A **line** is a straight path that goes on forever in two directions. A line is named by any two points on it.	Line AB, or $\overleftrightarrow{AB}$
A **ray** has one endpoint and goes on forever in one direction. A ray is named by an endpoint and any other point on it.	Ray LM, or $\overrightarrow{LM}$
A **line segment** is a part of a straight line. A line segment is named by its two endpoints.	Line segment PQ, or $\overline{PQ}$
A **plane** is a flat surface that goes on forever in all directions. A plane may be named by a small letter.	Plane t
Intersecting lines meet or cross each other. N is the point of intersection.	$\overleftrightarrow{HI}$ intersects $\overleftrightarrow{UV}$.
Parallel lines never intersect.	$\overleftrightarrow{RS}$ is parallel to $\overleftrightarrow{XY}$, or $\overleftrightarrow{RS} \parallel \overleftrightarrow{XY}$.

Identify and name each figure.

1.

2.

3.

4.

5.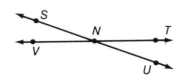

6.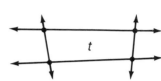

Name all the line segments.

7.

Copy the four points on a piece of paper, and then complete.

•D

8. Draw $\overline{BC}$.

9. Draw $\overleftrightarrow{AC}$.

10. Draw $\overrightarrow{AD}$.

11. Draw intersecting lines $\overleftrightarrow{AC}$ and $\overleftrightarrow{BD}$.

Draw the figure.

12. $\overleftrightarrow{AB} \parallel \overleftrightarrow{CD}$

13. $\overleftrightarrow{PQ}$ intersecting $\overleftrightarrow{RS}$ at point O

14. plane g

Complete. Use the diagram to answer.

15. Name the intersecting lines.

16. Name the parallel lines.

17. Name the points.

18. Name the line segments.

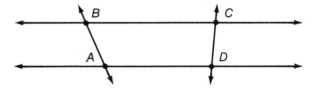

For a related activity, see **Connecting Math Ideas,** page 412.

NUMBER SENSE

Estimate what percent of the figure is shaded.

1.

2.

3.

4.

Angles

A. Angles are seen all around us. In this lesson, you will locate different kinds of angles and begin to explore some of their properties.

Tear off the corner of a piece of paper. The corner formed by two edges of the paper is called a **right** angle. It measures 90°.

- Use your right angle to find three other right angles around your desk or in this book.

- How many right angles are formed when a horizontal line and a vertical line intersect? These lines are called **perpendicular.** The point where these lines intersect is the **vertex** of the angles. Name 3 pairs of perpendicular lines that you see around you.

- If a right angle measures 90°, imagine what a 180° angle looks like. Describe it. It is called a **straight** angle.

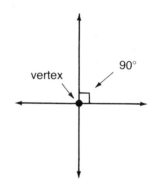

Look at the clock face that shows 9:00.

- What kind of angle do the hands of the clock form?

- Name 3 other times when the hands form the same angle.

- About how many times per hour do the hands of a clock form a right angle?

- What kind of angle do the hands of a clock form at 6:00?

- Name 3 other times when the hands form about the same angle.

B. Draw clocks showing these times: 1:45, 4:00, and 7:55. The angles shown by the hands of the clock at these times are called **obtuse** angles.

- How do obtuse angles compare to right angles?

- Name 3 other times when the hands of a clock form obtuse angles.

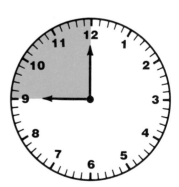

C. Draw clocks showing these times: 2:05, 4:30, and 10:45. The angles shown by these times are called **acute** angles.

- How do acute angles compare to right angles?
- Name 3 other times when the hands of a clock form acute angles.

Thinking as a Team _____

Imagine the following clock faces. Try to identify the kind of angle each pair of hands forms without drawing the time. Is it **acute, right, obtuse,** or **straight?**

8:55	3:00	6:30
10:25	5:01	7:45

Make up your own times. Challenge other students to identify the kind of angle formed.

D. As you have seen, angles are formed by two rays meeting at a common point. Use tracing paper to trace over angle A below. What kind of an angle is it? Place your tracing paper over each of the angles. Which angle is the same size as angle *A*?

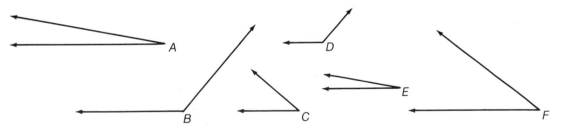

Thinking as a Team _____

Is the size of the angle affected by the length of the rays drawn to show it? *Hint:* Think about the hands of a small wristwatch compared to the hands of a large museum wall clock.

Measuring Angles

A. A **protractor** can be used to measure angles. Place the center of the protractor on the vertex of the angle.

∠*ABC* measures 40°.

Place the edge of the protractor so that one side of the angle crosses the zero mark on one of the scales.

∠*DEF* measures 120°.

Read the measure of the angle where the other side crosses the same scale.

B. To draw an angle of 55°, draw $\overrightarrow{BC}$. Place the center of the protractor on *B* so that the ray runs through 0. Find 55°, and mark point *A*. Draw $\overrightarrow{BA}$. ∠*ABC* measures 55°.

Use a protractor to measure each angle.

1.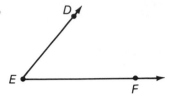

2.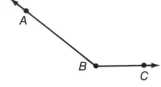

3.

4.

5.

6.

7.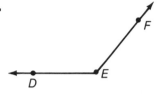

8.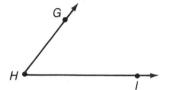

9.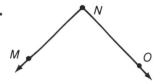

Draw each angle.

10. 135°	**11.** 60°	**12.** 30°	**13.** 45°	**14.** 127°
15. 37°	**16.** 100°	**17.** 145°	**18.** 166°	**19.** 9°
20. 15°	**21.** 78°	**22.** 132°	**23.** 59°	**24.** 5°
25. 170°	**26.** 40°	**27.** 120°	**28.** 50°	**29.** 149°

NUMBER SENSE

You can make a protractor and use it to sort angles.

To make a protractor:
1. Trace a circle.   **2.** Cut out the circle.
3. Fold it in half.   **4.** Label 0°, 90°, and 180°.

Copy and complete the chart.
Use your protractor to help sort these angles.

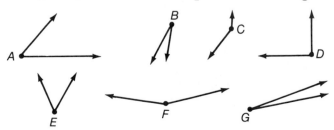

About 0°:	■
Less than 90°:	■
About 90°:	■
More than 90°:	■
About 180°:	■

Triangles

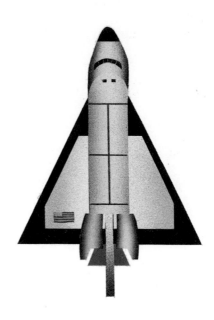

A. Rockets traveling through space do not need wings. When a space shuttle reenters Earth's atmosphere, it uses triangular wings to glide to a landing.

A **triangle** is any figure that has three sides and three angles.

Read: triangle *ABC*.
Write: △ *ABC*.

B. Some triangles have special names.

equilateral
All three sides
are of equal length.

isosceles
At least two sides are
of equal length.

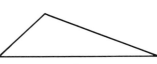
scalene
Each side is a
different length.

right
Has one
right angle.

acute
Has three
acute angles.

obtuse
Has one
obtuse angle.

C. The sum of the measures of the angles in any triangle is 180°.

Here is a way to show this.

Separate the angles
in △ *ABC*.

Place them along
a straight angle.

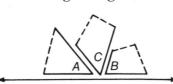

Since a straight angle measures 180°, the sum of the measures of the angles of △ *ABC* is 180°.

Name each triangle, and write if it is *equilateral, isosceles, scalene,* or *right.*

1.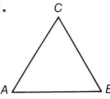

2.

3.

4.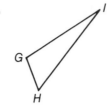

Name each triangle, and write if it is *right, obtuse,* or *acute.*

5.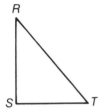

6.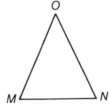

7.

8.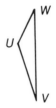

Find the measure of the missing angle.

9.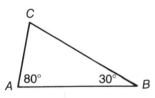

10.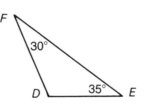

11.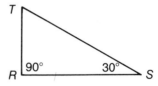

12.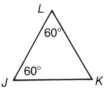

13.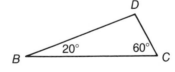

14.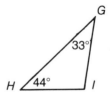

Solve.

15. This isosceles triangle has two angles of equal measure, and one angle of 90°. What is the measure of each of the other two angles?

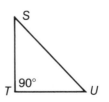

ANOTHER LOOK

Complete.

1. 20% of 50 = ▨

2. 80% of 25 = ▨

3. 60% of 30 = ▨

4. 40% of 75 = ▨

5. 90% of 60 = ▨

6. 90% of 90 = ▨

7. 70% of 70 = ▨

8. 80% of 50 = ▨

PROBLEM SOLVING
Making a Table To Find a Pattern

Many problems require that you find what comes next in a group of numbers, letters, or objects. To do this, you should study the information you are given to see whether there are any patterns that can be used as clues.

As a space probe descends to the surface of a planet, it begins to slow its speed to make a soft landing. It begins its descent at 1,024 miles from the surface of the planet, at a speed of 486 miles per hour. At 256 miles, the probe is moving at 162 miles per hour. At an altitude of 64 miles, it has slowed to 54 miles per hour, and at 16 miles, the probe is moving at 18 miles per hour. At what speed will the probe be moving when it is at an altitude of 1 mile?

You can make a table to show the pattern of changes in altitude and speed.

SPACE-PROBE DESCENT

Speed	486	162	54	18
Altitude	1,024	256	64	16

You can see that there is a pattern to the changes in speed and altitude. Each time, the speed is $\frac{1}{3}$ of the previous speed. The altitude is $\frac{1}{4}$ the previous altitude. By dividing the speed by 3, we know the next number in the pattern. By dividing the altitude by 4, the next number in that pattern can be found.

SPACE-PROBE DESCENT

Speed	486	162	54	18	6	2
Altitude	1,024	256	64	16	4	1

Copy and complete the table to solve.

1. In a simulator, astronauts practice docking spacecraft with other spacecraft. To succeed, they must reduce their speed to $\frac{1}{7}$ of their previous speed for every 10 km they come closer to the docking target. If they are traveling at 16,807 km/h at 50 km from the target, how fast will they be traveling at 20 km from the target?

DOCKING SIMULATION

Distance	60	50	40	30	20	10	0
Speed							

2. After docking, the astronauts increase their speed in the reverse of the docking pattern. What is their speed at 60 km?

Solve.

3. During a practice satellite launch from the simulator, the satellite is tracked by a computer. At 1 minute after release, the satellite is 100 yards from the launch vehicle. At 2 minutes, it is 180 yards away. At 3 minutes, the satellite is 324 yards from the launch vehicle, and at 4 minutes, 583.2 yards away. How far will the satellite have traveled at 6 minutes?

4. Space probes like the *Viking Lander* explore the surface of planets. One probe explores layers of soil. If it drills a hole that is 60 mm deep in 9 min, 50 mm deep in $7\frac{1}{2}$ min, and 40 mm deep at 6 min, how long has the probe been drilling when it reaches a depth of 20 mm?

★5. Astronauts need good reflexes to pilot spacecraft. The simulator flashes the pattern at the right on its screen. The astronaut has to find the next figure as fast as possible. What would the fourth figure in the pattern be?

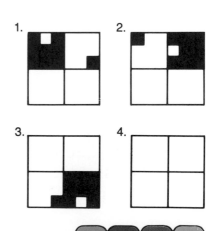

Polygons

A. Polygons are closed figures that consist of three or more line segments. They are closed figures because you can draw a line around their boundaries without ever coming to an end.

B. A **quadrilateral** is a polygon that has four sides.

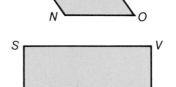

A quadrilateral whose opposite sides are the same length and are parallel to each other is a **parallelogram.** $\overline{DE} \parallel \overline{GF}$; $\overline{EF} \parallel \overline{DG}$.

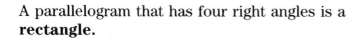

A parallelogram whose sides are all the same length is a **rhombus.**

A parallelogram that has four right angles is a **rectangle.**

A rectangle whose sides are all the same length is a **square.**

C. Other polygons are also named according to the number of sides they have.

| **pentagon** | **hexagon** | **octagon** | **decagon** |
| five sides | six sides | eight sides | ten sides |

A polygon whose sides and angles are all equal is a **regular polygon.**

D. A line segment that connects two vertices of a polygon and is not a side is a **diagonal.** $\overline{BD}$ is a diagonal of square *ABCD*.

Math Reasoning, page H207

Name the polygon.

1. 2. 3. 4.

5. 6. 7. 8.

9. 10. 11. 12.

Identify the polygon.

13. a quadrilateral whose opposite sides are parallel and are of equal length

14. a rectangle that has equal sides

15. a six-sided figure

16. a five-sided figure that has all sides and angles equal

17. a quadrilateral that has all sides equal but no right angles

Copy the figure. Draw its diagonals.

18. 19. 20.

Solve. Use the Infobank on page 420.

21. A constellation is a group of stars whose outline suggests a picture or a familiar shape. Name the shape of each highlighted constellation: Cetus, Orion, Pegasus, and Auriga.

Circles

A. The outline of a crater on the moon's surface suggests a circle. Scientists often use photographs to measure the size or the diameter of these circular craters.

Every point on a circle is the same distance from a point called the **center** of the circle.

A **chord** is a line segment that has its endpoints on the circle. $\overline{AD}$ and $\overline{BD}$ are chords.

A **diameter** is a chord that passes through the center of a circle. $\overline{BD}$ is a diameter. It is twice the length of the radius.

A **radius** is a line segment that has one endpoint on the circle and one endpoint on the center. $\overline{OC}$ is a radius.

B. You can use a compass to construct a circle that has a given radius.

Open the compass to the given radius.

Place the metal tip on a point, and turn the compass completely around the point.

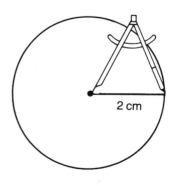

2 cm

Write *chord, radius,* or *diameter* for the given segment.

1.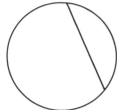
2.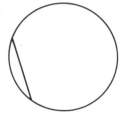
3.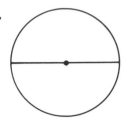
4.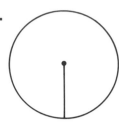

Copy and complete. Give the missing radius or diameter.

	5.	**6.**	**7.**	**8.**
Diameter	4 cm	▩	▩	26 cm
Radius	▩	5 cm	6 cm	▩

	9.	**10.**	**11.**	**12.**
Diameter	10 cm	▩	▩	44 cm
Radius	▩	18 cm	20 cm	▩

Use a compass to draw a circle that has the given radius.

13. 8 cm   **14.** 6 cm   **15.** 14 cm   **16.** 10 cm   **17.** 13 cm   **18.** 20 cm

Solve.

19. The Clavius Crater is one of the largest craters on the moon. The edge is about 130 km from the center of the crater. What is the diameter of the crater?

20. One crater has a diameter of 60 km. Another crater has a radius of 40 km. Which crater is wider?

MIDCHAPTER REVIEW

Use the figures at the right to answer.

1. Name all the line segments in Figure 1.

2. Name the parallel lines in Figure 1.

3. Use your protractor to find the measure of ∠B.

4. Find the measure of ∠C.

5. Is the triangle in Figure 2 right, equilateral, or isosceles?

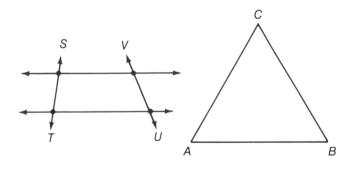

Fig. 1   Fig. 2

PROBLEM SOLVING
Choosing a Strategy or Method

Write the strategy or method you choose. Then solve.

1. An elevator takes people to the Moon Bus platform. A total of 25 people can fit in the elevator at one time. There are 279 people waiting for the elevator. Will the elevator make 11 trips or 12 trips to carry all the passengers to the platform?

Choosing the Operation
Making a Model
Writing a Number Sentence
Checking for a Reasonable Answer
Solving Multistep Problems/Making a Plan
Using a Schedule
Writing a Simpler Problem

Solve. All times given are Eastern Standard Time.

MOON BUS TRIPS TO LUNAR CITY San Francisco to Lunar City STARTING MAY 3830				
San Francisco	8:00 PM	11:00 PM	2:00 AM	5:00 AM
Dallas	9:35	———	———	6:30
Miami	10:50	1:55 AM	———	7:40
New York	11:40	2:45	5:30	8:30
Chicago	12:10 AM	3:15	6:00	———
Lunar City	8:15	11:00	2:05 PM	4:35 PM

2. You want to reach Lunar City by about 2:00 P.M. At what time would you have to leave New York?

3. Garth lives 25 minutes from the Miami bus stop. When must he leave home to catch the 7:40 A.M. bus?

4. You board the Moon Bus in San Francisco at 5:00 A.M. How many cities do you stop in before you arrive in Lunar City?

5. How long will it take you to go from Dallas to Lunar City if you take the bus that leaves San Francisco at 8:00 P.M.?

6. At what time would you leave San Francisco to make the quickest possible trip to Lunar City?

7. During a 4-week mission, an astronaut does exercises every other day. She works out with weights every 3 days. How many days a week will she do both?

Write the strategy or method you choose. Then solve.

8. The moon travels around Earth at a rate of 2,287 miles per hour. At that rate, how many miles does the moon travel between noon and 6:00 P.M.?

9. Mercury circles the sun at about 30 miles per second. Mars moves at about half that speed. In 1 hour, how many more miles has Mercury traveled than Mars?

10. The diameter of Venus is about 400 miles less than Earth's diameter. The diameter of Earth is about 7,900 miles. What is the diameter of Venus?

11. Jupiter is the largest planet. Its diameter is about 11.2 times that of Earth. If Earth's diameter is 7,900 miles, what is the diameter of Jupiter?

12. A day is much longer on the moon than it is on Earth. The ratio of moon days to Earth days is 3:42. Find the number of moon days that would equal 28 Earth days.

13. A rocket launch can burn 15 tons of fuel per second. At that rate, how many tons of fuel can it burn in 1 minute?

14. Gravity on the moon is only $\frac{1}{6}$ that of gravity on Earth. Someone who weighs 120 pounds on Earth would weigh only 20 pounds on the moon. How much would a person who weighs 32 pounds on the moon weigh on Earth?

15. The *Apollo 16 Rover* moon vehicle traveled 11.2 miles per second, a lunar record. At that rate, about how long would the vehicle take to travel a distance of 10 miles?

16. The moon is full of mountains and craters. Some lunar mountains rise to a height of 15,000 feet. That is about 75% of the height of North America's tallest peak, Mount McKinley. About how tall is Mount McKinley?

17. Look back at the problems you have solved. Talk about the ones that seemed difficult. What methods or processes did you use? Is there more than one way to think about these problems? Share ideas with your classmates.

Congruent Polygons

A. The solar panels of the space lab are **congruent** to each other. They are the same size and shape.

Line segments that have the same length are **congruent segments.**	A •————————————• B C •————————————• D Read: line segment *AB* is congruent to line segment *CD*. Write: $\overline{AB} \cong \overline{CD}$.
Angles that have the same measure are **congruent angles.**	H ∠ J ∠ Read: Angle *H* is congruent to angle *J*. Write: $\angle H \cong \angle J$.
Polygons that have the same size and shape are **congruent polygons.**	N △ L M T △ R S Read: Triangle *LMN* is congruent to triangle *RST*. Write: $\triangle LMN \cong \triangle RST$.

B. If two polygons are congruent, the matching or **corresponding** parts are congruent. *ABCD* ≅ *EFGH*

$\angle A \cong \angle E$ $\overline{AB} \cong \overline{EF}$
$\angle B \cong \angle F$ $\overline{BC} \cong \overline{FG}$
$\angle C \cong \angle G$ $\overline{CD} \cong \overline{GH}$
$\angle D \cong \angle H$ $\overline{DA} \cong \overline{HE}$

You can check whether two figures are congruent by tracing one and placing it over the other. If they match, the figures are congruent.

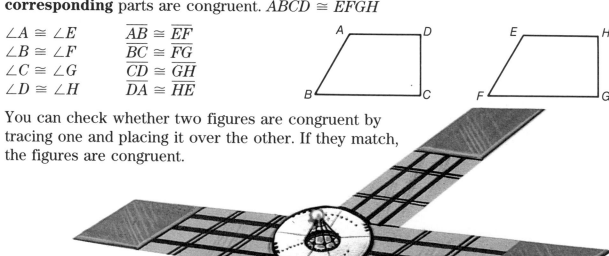

Is the line segment congruent to $\overline{AB}$? Write *yes* or *no*.
Use a ruler to measure. Trace to check.

1.

2.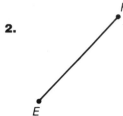

3. G   H

Is the angle congruent to $\angle J$? Write *yes* or *no*. Use a
protractor to measure. Trace to check.

4.

5.

6.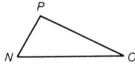

Is the figure congruent to $\triangle ABC$? Write *yes* or *no*. Use
a protractor and ruler to measure the angles and sides.
Trace to check.

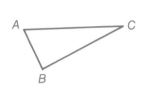

7.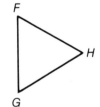

8.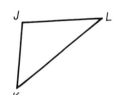

9.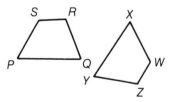

Figure $PQRS \cong$ Figure $WXYZ$
Use this information to answer Exercises 10 and 11.

10. Name the congruent sides.

11. Name the congruent angles.

FOCUS: REASONING

Long ago there was a great river. In the middle of the
river were two islands. The islands were connected to
the riverbanks and to each other by seven bridges.
Could a person cross all the bridges and never cross
the same bridge twice? If you think the answer is no,
copy the drawing with the least number of bridges
needed.

Symmetry/Acting It Out

If you could fold this picture of the *Saturn 5* rocket along the red line, one half would fit exactly on top of the other half. The red line is called a **line of symmetry.** The symmetrical shape of the *Saturn 5* helped it to fly to the edge of space.

Some figures have more than one line of symmetry.

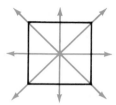 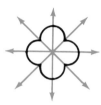 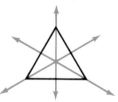

Some figures have no lines of symmetry.

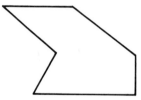 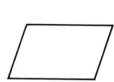 

Sometimes a picture that has two parts has a line of symmetry.

Is the blue line a line of symmetry? Write *yes* or *no*.

1.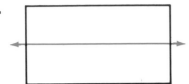

2.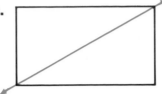

3.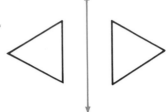

Copy each figure. Draw the line or lines of symmetry for each and count them.

4.

5.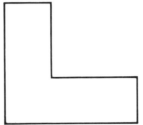

6.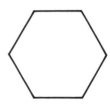

7.

8.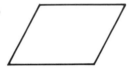

9.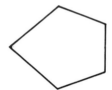

Copy and complete each figure so that the blue line is a line of symmetry.

10.

11.

12.

FOCUS: REASONING

Solve this puzzle. Use counters to *act out* the story, and show what the marchers did.

Ten marchers formed a triangle shape, as in Picture *A*. Then just three of the marchers moved, and the triangle shape in Picture *B* was formed. How was this done?

A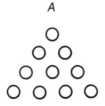

B

Similar Figures

A. An enlargement of a photograph allows small parts of the photo to be more clearly seen. The shapes of corresponding figures in the original and in the enlargement are the same.

Figures that have the same shape, but not necessarily the same size, are **similar.**

  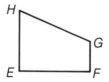

The two figures are similar.

Read: Quadrilateral *ABCD* is similar to quadrilateral *EFGH.*
Write: *ABCD* ~ *EFGH.*

B. In similar figures, the corresponding angles are congruent. △*STU* ~ △*KLM*

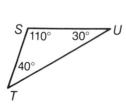 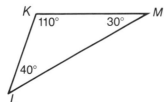

$\angle S \cong \angle K$
$\angle T \cong \angle L$
$\angle U \cong \angle M$

1. Name the figure that is similar to *ABCD*.

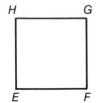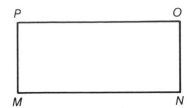

2. Name the triangle that is similar to △*ABC*.

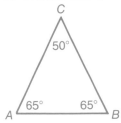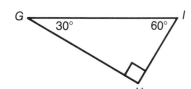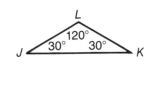

△*TUV* ~ △ *RPQ*. Use this information to answer Exercises 3 and 4.

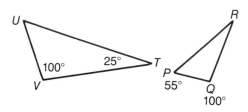

3. Find the measure of ∠*U*.

4. Find the measure of ∠*R*.

Write *true* or *false*. Draw pictures to help you.

5. All squares are similar.

6. All triangles are similar.

7. All parallelograms are similar.

8. All circles are similar.

9. Trace the triangle at the right. Then use your protractor to draw a triangle similar to the original one.

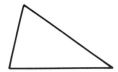

ANOTHER LOOK

Find the product. The answer must be in simplest form.

1. $\frac{1}{3} \times \frac{1}{3}$ **2.** $\frac{1}{3} \times \frac{1}{9}$ **3.** $\frac{4}{5} \times \frac{2}{3}$ **4.** $\frac{5}{8} \times \frac{1}{3}$ **5.** $\frac{1}{6} \times \frac{4}{7}$

6. $\frac{2}{7} \times \frac{1}{2}$ **7.** $\frac{4}{5} \times \frac{1}{6}$ **8.** $\frac{13}{14} \times \frac{2}{3}$ **9.** $\frac{8}{9} \times \frac{3}{4}$ **10.** $\frac{2}{5} \times \frac{3}{4}$

Points on a Grid

A. You can use a number pair, or **ordered pair,** to locate a point on a grid. The two numbers that you use are called **coordinates** of the point.

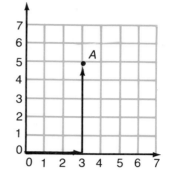

Find the location of point *A*.

Start at (0,0).
Move 3 spaces to the right.
Move 5 spaces up.
The ordered pair for point *A* is (3,5).

B. You can locate points on a grid and connect the points to form a geometric figure.

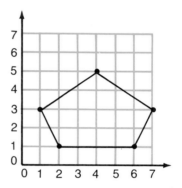

Locate (2,1), (1,3), (4,5), (7,3), and (6,1).

Connect the points in order to form a pentagon. Notice that the pentagon is a symmetrical figure.

Checkpoint Write the letter of the correct answer.

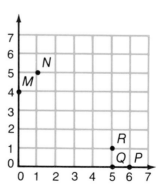

1. Name the ordered pair for *M*.

   a. 0   **b.** 4   **c.** (0,4)   **d.** (4,0)

2. Name the point for (5,1).

   a. *N*   **b.** *P*   **c.** *Q*   **d.** *R*

3. Name the point for (6,0).

   a. *N*   **b.** *P*   **c.** *M*   **d.** *Q*

4. Name the ordered pair for *Q*.

   a. (1,5)   **b.** (0,5)   **c.** (5,0)   **d.** (5,1)

Name the ordered pair for each point.

1. B 2. A 3. F 4. I

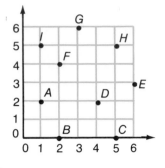

Name the point for each ordered pair.

5. (3,6) 6. (4,2) 7. (5,5) 8. (6,3)

Graph each set of points on a grid. Then connect the points in order to form a geometric figure. Is the figure symmetrical? Write *yes* or *no*.

9. (1,1), (1,3), (6,3), (6,1), (1,1)

10. (1,2), (3,9), (5,2), (1,2)

11. (1,6), (5,10), (9,6), (7,1), (3,1), (1,6)

12. (7,1), (9,3), (9,6), (3,6), (3,3), (5,1), (7,1)

13. (3,5), (2,7), (7,7), (6,5), (3,5)

14. (3,9), (6,9), (8,7), (6,2), (3,2), (1,4), (1,7), (3,9)

CHALLENGE

On many maps, points are located by the regions or sectors that they lie in, rather than by the grid lines. On the map of the moon's features, the crater Tycho is located in sector C1. Name the sector for each of the following features.

1. Mare Frigoris

2. Altai Mountains

3. Schichard Crater

4. Copernicus Crater

5. Mare Tranquillitas

6. Aristarchus Crater

Name the feature found in each of the following sectors.

7. A3

8. E5

9. C4

10. D1

11. C2

12. E4

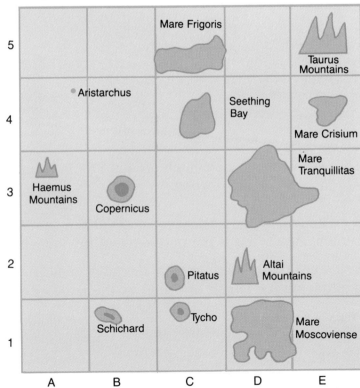

For a related activity, see *Connecting Math Ideas,* page 413.

Perimeter

A. When a rocket is launched into space, it gives off great amounts of heat and gas. To protect the scientists and workers, a fence is put up around the launch area. To find how much fence is needed, you need to know the perimeter of the launch area.

The **perimeter** of a figure is the distance around it. To find the perimeter, add the measures of its sides.

$$
\begin{array}{r}
75 \\
60 \\
75 \\
+\ 60 \\
\hline
270
\end{array}
$$

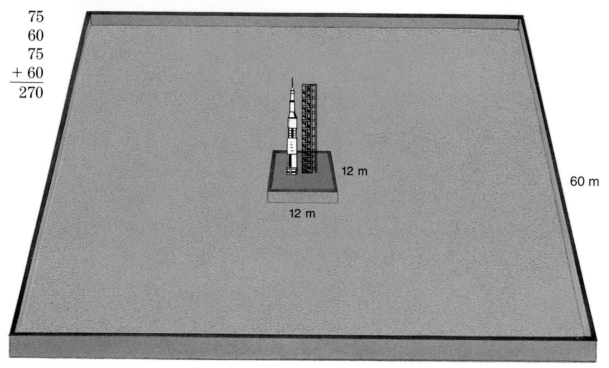

12 m

12 m

60 m

75 m

The perimeter of the launch area is 270 m. A total of 270 m of fence are needed.

B. The launchpad itself is a square at the center of the launch area. What is the perimeter of the launchpad?

You can find the perimeter of a regular polygon by multiplying the length of a side by the number of sides.

Find the measure of a side.	**Find the number of sides.**	**Multiply.**
12 m	**4**	$4 \times 12 = 48$

The perimeter of the launchpad is 48 m.

364

Find the perimeter of each figure.

1.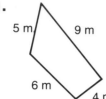
5 m   9 m   6 m   4 m

2.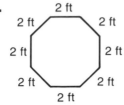
2 ft   2 ft   2 ft   2 ft   2 ft   2 ft   2 ft   2 ft

3.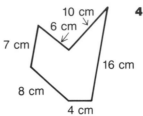
10 cm   6 cm   7 cm   16 cm   8 cm   4 cm

4.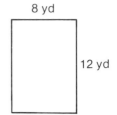
8 yd   12 yd

Use a centimeter ruler to find the perimeter of each figure.

5.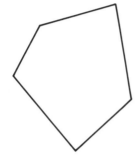

6.

7.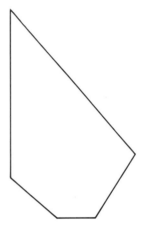

Solve.

8. A platform is constructed near the launchpad of a weather satellite. Everyone watching from the platform has a view of the launchpad. The platform has sides with lengths of 34 yd, 34 yd, 59 yd, and 59 yd. What is the perimeter of the platform?

For a related activity, see **Connecting Math Ideas,** page 413.

★9. Rusty constructs a model rocket that is an exact replica of the *Apollo 11* spaceship which landed on the moon. His launchpad is a regular hexagon that has one side 23 in. long. What is the perimeter of Rusty's launchpad?

CHALLENGE

You can find the perimeter of circular objects. First wrap a piece of string around the outside of the object. Then use a ruler to measure the string. This is the perimeter of the object. Try this at home using different-sized cans.

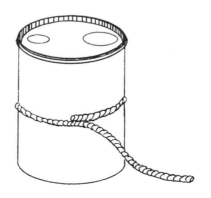

Area of Rectangles/Acting It Out

A. The *Viking Lander* was the first spacecraft to set down on the planet Mars. Many photographs of the surface of the planet were taken. Grids on the photographs allowed scientists to measure the precise areas that the photographs covered. What is the area of the grid on the photograph of Mars?

The **area** of a figure is the number of square units it contains. To find the area, you can count square units.

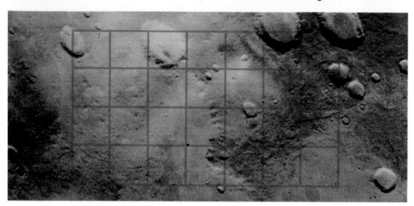

1 square centimeter (cm²)

There are 28 squares in the photograph.

Read: 28 square centimeters.
Write: 28 cm².

The units **km² (square kilometers), m² (square meters),** and **mm² (square millimeters)** are some other metric units of area.

B. You can also find the area of a rectangle by multiplying the length times the width.

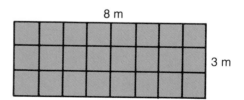

Area of rectangle = length × width
$A = l \times w$
$A = 8 \times 3$
$A = 24$
The area of the rectangle is 24 m².

C. You can find the area of a square the same way you would for a rectangle.

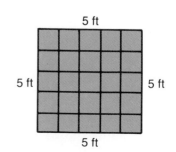

There are 5 rows of 5 squares.
So, $5 + 5 + 5 + 5 + 5 = 25$, or $5 \times 5 = 25$.
The area of the square is 25 ft².

Count to find the area.

1.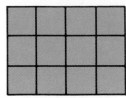

2.

3.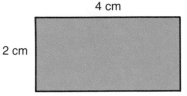

Multiply to find the area.

4.
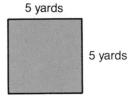
4 cm
2 cm

5.
5 yards
5 yards

6.
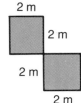
2 m
2 m
2 m
2 m

Multiply to find the area of the rectangle or square.

7. $l = 7$ m, $w = 4$ m

8. $l = 16$ ft, $w = 12$ ft

9. $l = 9$ mm, $w = 9$ mm

10. $l = 7$ km, $w = 6$ km

11. $l = 25$ miles, $w = 2$ miles

12. $l = 19$ in., $w = 5$ in.

13. $l = 15$ cm, $w = 15$ cm

14. $l = 42$ m, $w = 7$ m

15. $l = 28$ yd, $w = 28$ yd

16. $l = 9$ mm, $w = 5$ mm

17. $l = 50$ miles, $w = 8$ miles

18. $l = 30$ m, $w = 30$ m

19. a square: one side = 23 yards

★20. a square: perimeter = 36 cm

Solve.

21. Scientists plan to track the space shuttle with a laser beam fired from Earth and bounced off a target on the shuttle. The target is a rectangle 8 m wide and 10 m long. What is the area of the shuttle target?

22. Astronauts returning from the moon land their capsule in the ocean. This is called *splashdown*. If the section of ocean they are to land in is 12 miles long and 14 miles wide, what is the area of the splashdown site?

CHALLENGE

Seven lizards of equal length formed 2 squares, as shown. Then 1 lizard went away, and the other 6 lizards formed 5 squares. Show how this could be done. *Act it out*, using thin strips of paper as the lizards.

Area of Triangles

A. In this lesson, you will explore how to find the area of triangles. Drawings can be useful.

Step 1: On graph paper, draw two 10 by 14 rectangles and cut them out. Find the area of each rectangle.

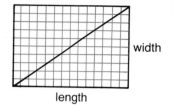

- How did you find the area? Show it as a formula.

- What units did you use to record the area?

Step 2: Cut diagonally across one rectangle as shown on the drawing at the right to make two triangles.

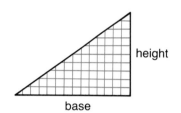

- What kind of triangles did you make?

- Place one triangle over the other. What do you notice?

Step 3: Compare the area of one triangle to the area of the rectangle.

- What do you notice about the area of the rectangle and the area of the right triangle?

- What is the area of the triangle?

- How would you check your answer?

- What do you notice about the base and the height of the triangle and the length and the width of the rectangle?

Step 4: Draw other pairs of rectangles on graph paper. Repeat Steps 1, 2, and 3 for each pair. Record your answers.

Thinking as a Team _____

1. Look at your answers. Use what you have discovered to write a formula for finding the area of a right triangle.

2. Test your formula by drawing other right triangles and finding their areas. How can you check your answers?

B. You can explore how to find the area of any triangle.

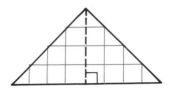

Step 1: On graph paper, draw triangles like those shown at the right. Then draw dotted lines perpendicular to the base of each triangle.

- What kind of angles are formed when you draw the dotted line? What kind of triangles?
- How does the height of each triangle formed by the dotted line relate to the height of the original triangle?
- How can this help you find the area of the original triangle?

Step 2: Find the areas of the original triangles.
- How did you find the areas?
- How can you check your answers?

Step 3: Work with a partner. Each of you is to draw another triangle. Repeat Steps 1 and 2 for each triangle drawn. Record your answers.

Thinking as a Team

1. Can you use the formula you discovered for finding the area of a right triangle to find the area of any triangle? Why or why not?

2. List what you have discovered about finding the area of a triangle. Compare your list to other teams.

C. You can apply what you have discovered.

Working as a Team

Walter, an aerospace engineer, is constructing a heat shield for the new spacecraft *Silosphere* out of 3 different kinds of metals. Each segment in the heat shield will be a certain shape. To make the heat shield Walter needs 80 triangles of metal A, 100 rectangles of metal B, and 50 triangles of metal C. Your team is responsible for ordering the metal.

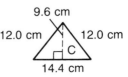

1. How much of metals A, B, and C will Walter need?

2. How much metal will Walter need in all?

For a related activity, see *Connecting Math Ideas,* page 414.

PROBLEM SOLVING
Drawing a Picture/Making a Model

If you have a problem you are not sure how to solve, it is often helpful to draw a picture or make a model of it. The picture or model can help you "see" the problem and decide how to solve it.

The fifth-grade class at Lakeview Elementary School is going on a field trip to the Space Museum. The first display they study is of the moon's surface. This square display is 12 ft by 12 ft. There is a rail around the display with posts that are 3 ft apart. How many posts are around the display of the moon's surface?

1. Draw and label a diagram of the display. Put as much information on the diagram as you can.

2. Reread the problem. Make sure your diagram fits the problem.

3. Solve the problem.

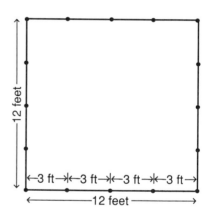

There are 16 posts around the display of the moon's surface.

Suppose you had grid paper and toothpicks. How could you make a model to solve the problem?

Write the letter of the picture you would use to solve the problem.

1. The Space Museum is 24 miles from Lakeview Elementary School. The bus driver picked up the fifth graders at school, drove 5 miles toward the museum, and remembered that he had forgotten the lunches. He drove back to the school for the lunches and then drove to the museum. How far did he drive in all?

a.
school 24 m museum

5m →
← 5m
24m →

b.
school 24 m museum

5m →
24m →

2. Ann, Beth, Carl, and Dennis were standing in line to buy tickets for the *Skylab* movie. Dennis was in front of Ann. Carl was between Ann and Dennis. Beth was at the end of the line. Who was first in line?

a.
Beth	Ann	Dennis	Carl
End			Front

b.
Beth	Ann	Carl	Dennis
End			Front

Draw a picture or make a model to solve each problem.

3. There is a rectangular poster of the planets on the wall of the museum. The poster is 36 inches by 24 inches. Around the edge of the poster, there is a tack every 12 inches to hold the poster on the wall. How many tacks are used to hold up the poster?

4. A large square bulletin board in the gift shop is covered with space posters. The bulletin board is 10 feet on a side. Each poster is a square that is 2 feet on a side. How many posters are on the bulletin board?

5. There is a display area showing a model *Skylab* station. The display area is 20 feet by 30 feet. There is a rail around the display area with posts every 5 feet. How many posts are around this display area?

6. Fran, Greg, Hans, and Ian were the first four students to get back on the bus. Greg got on before Fran but after Ian. Hans got on after Fran. Who was the first student on the bus?

7. A lunar vehicle stopped 50 feet from a boulder. The astronaut got out of the vehicle, walked 7 feet toward the boulder, and remembered that he had forgotten his camera. He walked back to the vehicle, got his camera, and then walked to the boulder. After taking a picture, he walked straight back to the lunar vehicle. How far did the astronaut walk in all?

★8. The museum staff is planning to paint the wall around a large mural that shows the history of space travel. The wall is 25 feet high and 100 feet wide. The mural is 10 feet high and 50 feet wide. How many square feet of wall space does the staff need to paint around the mural?

Solid Figures

A. The nose of the *Atlas Centaur* rocket has the shape of a cone. A *cone* is an example of a solid figure.

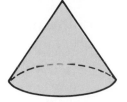

cone

B. Each flat surface of a prism is a **face.**
A prism has two congruent faces, called **bases.**
The rectangular prism in the figure has six faces.

Two faces intersect at an **edge.**
The rectangular prism has twelve edges.

The edges of a solid figure intersect at a **vertex.** The rectangular prism has eight vertices.

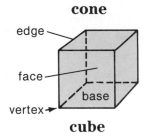

cube

A prism is often named by the shape of its base.

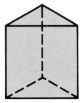

triangular prism

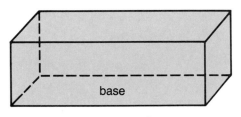

base

rectangular prism

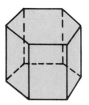

hexagonal prism

C. A **pyramid** has one base. The other faces are in the shape of triangles. A pyramid can be named by the shape of its base.

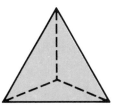

triangular pyramid

square pyramid

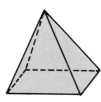

rectangular pyramid

hexagonal pyramid

Here are some other solid figures.

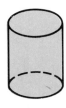

cylinder

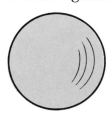

sphere

372

Name the solid figure that is shaped like the object.

1.

2.

3.

4.

5.

6.

7.

8.

Count the number of faces, edges, and vertices each figure has.

9.

■ faces
■ edges
■ vertices

10.

■ faces
■ edges
■ vertices

11.

■ faces
■ edges
■ vertices

Copy and complete the table.

Figure	Number of faces	Number of edges	Number of vertices
square pyramid	12. ■	13. ■	14. ■
hexagonal prism	15. ■	16. ■	17. ■
cone	★18. ■	★19. ■	★20. ■

CHALLENGE

The surface area of a figure is the sum of the areas of its faces.
Find the surface area of the rectangular prism shown at the right.

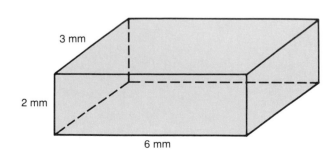

3 mm

2 mm

6 mm

Volume

A. The **volume** of a rectangular prism is the number of cubic units that are needed to fill it.

 1 cubic centimeter (cm^3)

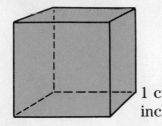 1 cubic inch (in.^{3})

To find the volume of a rectangular prism, you can count the number of cubic units.

Each layer has six cubic centimeters.
There are 2 layers.
6 + 6 = 12

The volume is 12 cubic centimeters.

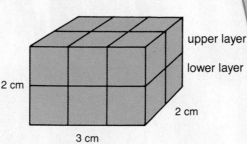

upper layer

lower layer

2 cm

2 cm

3 cm

You can also multiply to find the volume of a rectangular prism.

Volume of rectangular prism = length × width × height

$$V = l \times w \times h$$
$V = 3 \times 2 \times 2$
$V = 12$

B. Modular lockers on the space shuttle contain scientific equipment to be used for experiments. Each locker is 17 in. by 20 in. by 10 in. You can use the following formula to find the volume of the locker.

$$V = l \times w \times h$$
$V = 20 \times 17 \times 10$
$V = 3,400$

The volume of a modular locker is 3,400 in.^{3}

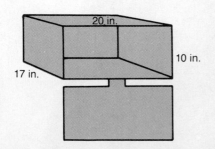

20 in.

10 in.

17 in.

Find the volume of each.

1.
3 cm
3 cm
1 cm

2.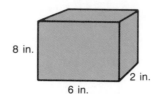
8 in.
2 in.
6 in.

3.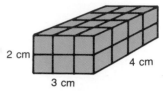
2 cm
4 cm
3 cm

4.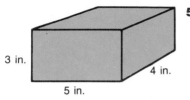
3 in.
4 in.
5 in.

5.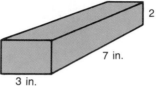
2 in.
7 in.
3 in.

6.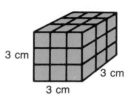
3 cm
3 cm
3 cm

Copy the table.
Use the formula $V = l \times w \times h$ to complete.

length (*l*)	width (*w*)	height (*h*)	Volume (*V*)
5 cm	3 cm	2 cm	**7.**
16 mm	12 mm	7 mm	**8.**
4 in.	1 in.	6 in.	**9.**
7 yd	5 yd	3 yd	**10.**
★**11.**	3 ft	5 ft	105 ft³

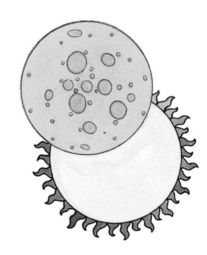

Solve.

12. An astronaut has a toolbox that is 24 in. long, 12 in. wide, and 8 in. high. What is the volume of the toolbox?

13. Find three boxes in your classroom. Estimate the volume of each. Then check the estimate by measuring and computing.

For a related activity, see ***Connecting Math Ideas,*** page 414.

FOCUS: REASONING

A rectangular box is about $1\frac{1}{2}$ ft long, $1\frac{3}{4}$ ft wide, and $2\frac{1}{4}$ ft high. A student wants to find the volume by filling the box with models of cubes that are 1 ft by 1 ft by 1 ft. Is this a reasonable way to find the volume? If not, what would you do? Explain.

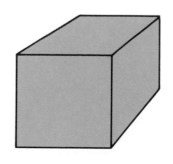

CALCULATOR

You can use a calculator to help you calculate perimeter and area. Convert any fractions to decimals.

Example: Find the perimeter of a square that measures $8\frac{1}{2}$ ft. per side. You can write $8\frac{1}{2}$ as 8.5.
To find the perimeter:

Press: [4] [×] [8] [.] [5] [=]

The display should show 34. The perimeter is 34 ft.

Copy and complete the table.

Room	Perimeter	Area
1. Living Room		
2. Kitchen		
3. Bedroom 1		
4. Bath		
5. House		

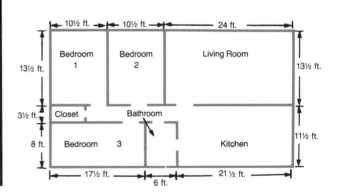

To the nearest 0.05 yd^2 how much carpet would it take to carpet these rooms?

What is the cost of each of the following if the carpet is $17 per square yard?

Room	Carpet Sq. Feet	Square Yards	Cost
Example: Living Room	324 ft^2	36 yd^2 (324 ÷ 9)	$ 612.00
6. Bedroom 2			
7. Bedroom 3			
8. Kitchen			
9. TOTAL			

376

GROUP PROJECT

Terrific Teaching Team

The problem: You and your friends are asked to help a group of younger children learn about solid figures and volume. Think about the Key Questions to help you decide what to do.

Key Questions

- What solid figures would you use in a first lesson with the children?
- Which would be more useful – *written material* about the figures, or *models* of the figures?
- In teaching about volume, what sorts of cubic unit models are available?
- Even if a small cube was not 1 centimeter on each side or 1 inch on each side, could it still be used to help explain volume to the younger children?

After discussing your ideas, demonstrate how you would:

Show models of different solid figures and describe the figures.

Construct models of two large rectangular prisms – one that is a cube, and one that is *not* a cube.

Describe each prism in different ways.

Measure the volume of an object using one type of cubic unit. Then measure it using a different type of unit. Discuss why the answers are different.

Make or find models that have a volume close to 1 cubic inch or 1 cubic centimeter.

CHAPTER TEST

Identify and name each figure. (page 340)

1.

S ————•———————•———— T

2.

G ————•————•———— H

3.

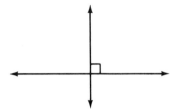

4.

L   M
•————————————•
A   B

Are the lines perpendicular? Write *yes* or *no*. (page 342)

5.

6.

Use your protractor to draw the following angles.
Identify them as acute, obtuse, right, or straight. (page 344)

7.   32°   **8.**   90°   **9.**   180°   **10.**   100°

11. Is the triangle equilateral or isoceles? (page 346)

12. Is the triangle acute or obtuse? (page 346)

Name the polygon or the part of a circle. (pages 350, 352)

13.   **14.**   **15.**   **16.**

17. Are the two figures congruent?
Write *yes* or *no*. (page 356)

18. Is the line a line of symmetry?
Write *yes* or *no*. (page 358)

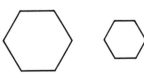

19. Find the measure of ∠R. (page 360)

20. Find the measure of ∠V. (page 360)

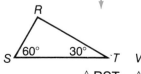

△RST ~ △UVW

378

Name the coordinates for each point. (page 362)

21. *A*

22. *D*

Name the point for each ordered pair. (page 362)

23. (2,3)

24. (5,1)

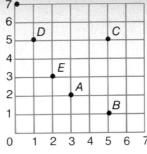

Find the perimeter. (page 364)

25. a square, one side = 9 in.

26. an equilateral triangle, one side = 6 ft

Find the area. (pages 366 and 368)

27. a triangle, $b = 6$ cm, $h = 9$ cm

28. a rectangle, $l = 7$ yd, $w = 6$ yd

Find the volume. (pages 372 and 374)

29. a rectangular prism, $l = 4$ ft, $w = 6$ ft, $h = 2$ ft

Solve. Make a table to find the pattern. (pages 348–349)

30. A *centrifuge* is used to test astronauts' ability to take high speeds. During one test, the centrifuge moved at 11 miles per hour in 0.5 seconds, 22 miles per hour in 1 second, 33 miles per hour after 1.5 seconds, and 44 miles per hour after 2 seconds. What was the machine's speed at 4, at 5.5, and at 8 seconds?

31. To test deceleration, the centrifuge was started at 264 miles per hour and slowed to 231 miles per hour after 4 seconds, 198 miles per hour after 8 seconds, and 165 miles per hour after 12 seconds. How fast was the machine moving after 20 seconds? How long did it take to stop?

Solve. (pages 370–371)

32. A mission specialist checks his plant experiments every 3 days, his fungus experiments every 4 days, and his crystal experiments every 6 days. During a 30-day mission, on which days does he check all 3 experiments?

33. The four astronauts boarded the shuttle. Karen entered before Ed but after Tom. Jerry entered after Karen but before Ed. In what order did they board?

RETEACHING

A. You can use a protractor to measure angles. Place the center of the protractor on the vertex of the angle.

Place the edge of the protractor so that one side of the angle crosses the zero mark on one of the scales.

Read the measure of the angle where the other side crosses the same scale.

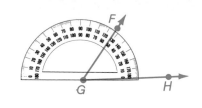

B. To draw an angle of 165°, draw $\overrightarrow{MN}$. Place the center of the protractor on M so that the rays run through 0°. Find the obtuse mark for 165°, and mark point L. Draw $\overrightarrow{ML}$.

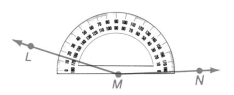

Use a protractor to measure each angle.

1.   **2.**   **3.**

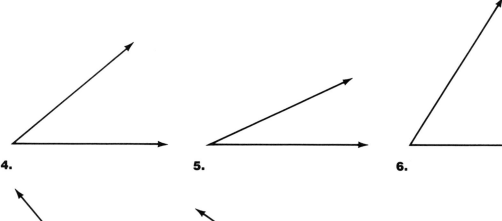

4.   **5.**   **6.**

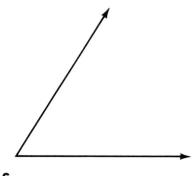

Use a protractor to draw each angle.

7. 32°	**8.** 80°	**9.** 35°	**10.** 12°
11. 90°	**12.** 125°	**13.** 165°	**14.** 147°
15. 40°	**16.** 85°	**17.** 135°	**18.** 63°
19. 114°	**20.** 155°	**21.** 16°	**22.** 59°

ENRICHMENT

Slides, Flips, and Turns

If you *slide* a figure along a line, you obtain a
translation.

If you *flip* a figure about a line of symmetry, you obtain
a **reflection.**

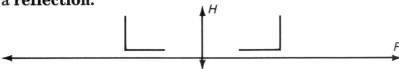

If you *turn* a figure on a curved path around a point,
you obtain a **rotation.**

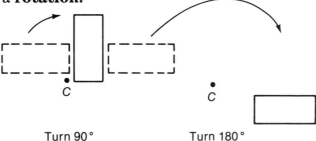

Turn 90°   Turn 180°

In Exercises 1, 2, and 3, begin by drawing figure *B*.
Then draw the required figure.

1. a translation of figure *B*

2. a reflection of figure *B*

3. a rotation of figure *B*

4. Draw a different figure, and show a
   translation, a reflection, and a
   rotation of it.

CUMULATIVE REVIEW

Write the letter of the correct answer.

1. Compute $\frac{7}{8} = \frac{21}{\blacksquare}$.

   a. 16   **b.** 20
   c. 24   **d.** not given

2. Write as a percent: $\frac{92}{100}$.

   a. 9.2%   **b.** 92%
   c. 920%   **d.** not given

3. Write 75% as a fraction.

   a. $\frac{2}{3}$ **b.** $\frac{3}{4}$
   c. $\frac{4}{5}$ **d.** not given

4. Write 58% as a decimal.

   a. 0.058   **b.** 0.508
   c. 0.58   **d.** not given

5. 37% of 1,500

   a. 540   **b.** 550
   c. 555   **d.** not given

6. What percent of 25 is 5?

   a. 20%   **b.** 125%
   c. 500%   **d.** not given

7. $9 \div \frac{1}{5}$

   a. $\frac{1}{45}$ **b.** 45
   c. 90   **d.** not given

8. Which unit would you use to measure the mass of a pen?

   a. milligrams   **b.** grams
   c. kilograms   **d.** not given

9. $4,056 \div 45$

   a. 9 R6   **b.** 90
   c. 90 R6   **d.** not given

10. $18\overline{)\$36.90}$

   a. $2.05   **b.** $2.0527
   c. $20.52   **d.** not given

11. 121×483

   a. 57,443   **b.** 65,975
   c. 72,323   **d.** not given

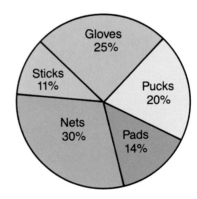

Total Costs: $2,500

12. How much was spent on pucks?

   a. $500.00   **b.** $1,000.00
   c. $1,500.00   **d.** not given

13. How much was spent on nets?

   a. $75.00   **b.** $750.00
   c. $1,250.00   **d.** not given

Some communities in the United States were planned more carefully than others. Have you looked at a map of your town or city? Are the streets arranged in any kind of pattern? Is the layout of the oldest part of the city different from the layout of the modern part? Draw a map of your town. Label areas of historic interest.

12 STATISTICS AND PROBABILITY

Making a Bar Graph

The population of the thirteen original colonies changed from 1660 to 1780. You can make a **bar graph** to show and compare population growth.

To make a bar graph:

1. Round the numbers in the data table to a convenient place.

2. Draw and label the vertical and horizontal axes. Choose intervals between the numbers that best display the data. Title the graph.

3. Draw the bars on the graph.

You can see from the graph how the population grew from 1660 to 1780.

You can also draw the graph using a computer graphing program.

POPULATION OF AMERICAN COLONIES: 1660–1780

Year	Actual population	Rounded to hundreds of thousands
1660	75,058	100,000
1690	210,372	200,000
1720	466,185	500,000
1750	1,170,760	1,200,000
1780	2,780,369	2,800,000

POPULATION OF AMERICAN COLONIES: 1660–1780

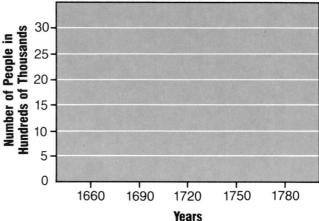

POPULATION OF AMERICAN COLONIES: 1660–1780

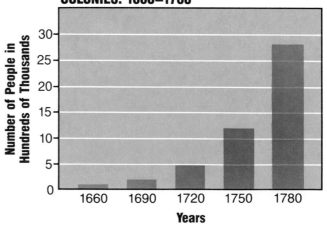

Solve.

1. The table lists the populations of California and of four other states in 1850. Copy and complete the bar graph. Use the data in the table. Round each population to the nearest tenth of a million.
3,097,394 ⟶ 3.1 million

POPULATIONS OF SELECTED STATES: 1850

State	Actual population	Rounded amounts
New York (N.Y.)	3,097,394	
California (Calif.)	92,597	
Michigan (Mich.)	397,654	
Virginia (Va.)	1,119,348	
Tennessee (Tenn.)	1,002,717	

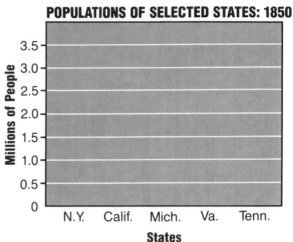

2. Which states have about double the population of Michigan?

3. The table lists some results of the 1980 census. Use the table to write and solve your own problem.

PEOPLE PER SQUARE MILE: 1980

State	People per square mile
New York (N.Y.)	371
Florida (Fla.)	180
California (Calif.)	151
Texas (Tex.)	54

4. Make a bar graph that shows the number of students in each grade at your school. Use it to estimate the size of next year's classes.

ANOTHER LOOK

Solve.

1. 6325 g = ▓ kg
2. 300 m = ▓ km
3. 15 kg = ▓ g
4. 932 km = ▓ m

5. 388 m = ▓ mm
6. 8,043 mL = ▓ L
7. 93 km = ▓ cm
8. 13 L = ▓ mL

Making a Pictograph

Pictographs use symbols to represent large numbers. You can draw a pictograph to show the growth of United States cotton production from 1790 to 1810.

To make a pictograph:

1. Round the numbers in the data table to a convenient place.

U.S. COTTON PRODUCTION: 1790–1810

Year	Bales of cotton	Bales in five thousands
1790	3,000	5,000
1795	17,000	15,000
1800	73,000	75,000
1805	148,000	150,000
1810	178,000	180,000

2. List the years vertically as shown in the chart. Title the graph.

U.S. COTTON PRODUCTION: 1790–1810

Year	Bales of cotton
1790	
1795	
1800	
1805	
1810	

3. Choose a symbol to represent an approximate amount of cotton.

Let □ = 10,000 bales
Let ▷ = 5,000 bales

List the symbols. Replace the numbers with symbols. Complete the pictograph.

U.S. COTTON PRODUCTION: 1790–1810

Year	Bales of cotton
1790	▷
1795	□▷
1800	□□□□□□□▷
1805	□□□□□□□□□□□□□□□
1810	□□□□□□□□□□□□□□□□□□

□ = 10,000 bales   ▷ = 5,000 bales

You can see from the pictograph how cotton production increased from 1790 to 1810. Draw the pictograph again with a computer graphing program.

Solve.

1. Copy and complete the pictograph. Use the data in the table.

U.S. CORN PRODUCTION: 1940–1980

Year	Bushels of corn
1940	2,500,000,000
1950	3,000,000,000
1960	4,500,000,000
1970	4,000,000,000
1980	6,500,000,000

U.S. CORN PRODUCTION: 1940–1980

Year	Bushels of corn
1940	
1950	
1960	
1970	
1980	

◯ = 1 billion bushels

2. Use the information from the pictograph to tell whether corn production should rise or fall by 1990.

3. The table lists the average number of bushels harvested per acre for certain crops grown in the United States. Round the numbers to the nearest ten thousand. Let △ = 10,000 bushels. Then make a pictograph that uses all of this information.

HARVESTS OF SOME U.S. CROPS

Farm crop	Bushels per acre	Rounded amounts
Corn	91,000	
Sorghum	46,300	
Wheat	33,400	
Rye	24,400	

4. Native Americans taught the Pilgrims how to grow corn, one of America's favorite vegetables. Make a pictograph that gives your classmates' favorite vegetables.

ANOTHER LOOK

Find the area of

1. a triangle.

base = 4 in.
height = 19 in.
area = ▨

2. a square.

sides = 9 mm
area = ▨

3. a rectangle.

length = 17 km
width = 4 km
area = ▨

4. a triangle.

base = 12 yd
height = 13 yd
area = ▨

Making a Broken-Line Graph

Broken-line graphs are used to show a continuing trend during a period of time. You can make a broken-line graph to show the growth of railroads in the United States from 1840 to 1870.

To make a broken-line graph:

1. Round the numbers in the data table to a convenient place.

GROWTH OF U.S. RAILROADS: 1840–1870

Year	Miles of track	Miles in thousands
1840	2,818	3,000
1845	4,633	5,000
1850	9,021	9,000
1855	18,374	18,000
1860	30,626	31,000
1865	35,085	35,000
1870	52,933	53,000

2. Draw and label the vertical and horizontal axes. Choose intervals between the numbers that best display the data. Title the graph.

3. Place the points on the graph. Then connect all the points with line segments.

You can see from the graph how the railroads grew from 1840 to 1870. You can also make a graph using a computer graphing program.

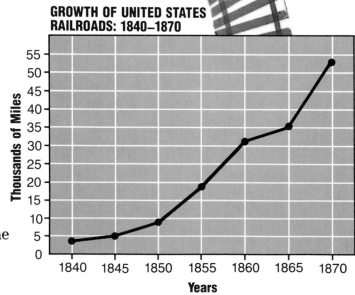

GROWTH OF UNITED STATES RAILROADS: 1840–1870

388

Solve.

1. About 122 million cars use the roads in the United States. Copy and complete the broken-line graph to show car sales in the United States.

U.S. CAR SALES: 1982–1987

Year	Number of cars	Rounded amounts (in millions)
1982	7,982,000	8
1983	9,182,000	9
1984	10,390,000	10
1985	11,042,000	11
1986	11,460,000	11
1987	10,278,000	10

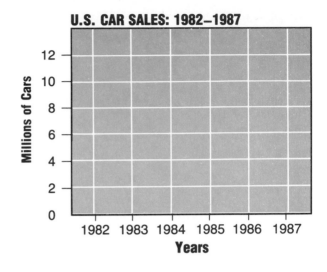

U.S. CAR SALES: 1982–1987

2. According to your broken-line graph, did car sales go up or down between 1982 and 1984? Do you think car sales went up or down between 1987 and 1990?

3. Use the data in the table to make a broken-line graph to show car sales in the United States from 1946 to 1950.

U.S. CAR SALES: 1946–1950

Year	Number of cars
1946	2,100,000
1947	3,500,000
1948	3,900,000
1949	5,100,000
1950	6,600,000

4. What is different about the trend shown in the broken-line graph from 1982 to 1987 and the trend shown in the graph from 1946 to 1950?

MIDCHAPTER REVIEW

Choose a set of data from the Infobank starting on page 415. Display this data using a bar graph, a pictograph, or broken-line graph. Explain why you used the type of graph you displayed.

PROBLEM SOLVING
Interpreting a Graph

Graphs are a good way to show and compare data. But you must be careful when comparing graphs. Sometimes they can be misleading.

> Use the two line graphs to answer the question. Which area had more miles of railroad track in 1880, the United States or Europe?

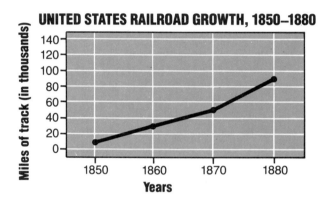

UNITED STATES RAILROAD GROWTH, 1850–1880

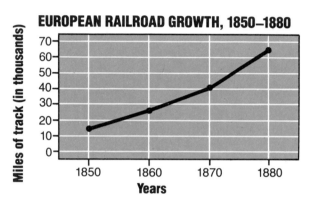

EUROPEAN RAILROAD GROWTH, 1850–1880

- The title and the labels at the bottom tell you that both graphs show railroad growth between 1850 and 1880. The graph at the left shows railroad growth in the United States. The graph at the right shows railroad growth in Europe.

- The labels at the left side of each graph mark the number of miles of railroad track in each area. The spaces are marked in 20,000-mile units on the first graph. The second graph is marked in 10,000-mile units.

- You have to read carefully to compare the information in these graphs. The broken line appears to be about the same, but the information is not presented in the same way in both graphs.

  By using the scale at the left of each graph, you can see that Europe had 65,000 miles of track in 1880. The United States had 90,000 miles of track in 1880. In 1880, the United States had more miles of railroad track.

Math Reasoning, page H209

Use the information in the graphs to solve each
problem.

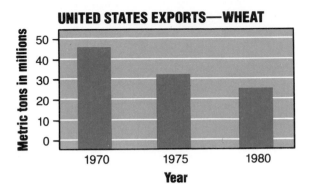

UNITED STATES EXPORTS—WHEAT

Metric tons in millions

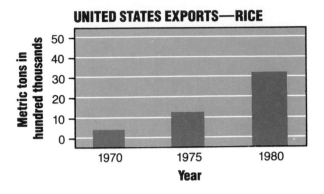

UNITED STATES EXPORTS—RICE

Metric tons in hundred thousands

1. Did the United States export more wheat or more rice in 1975?

2. Did the United States export more wheat or more rice in 1980?

3. Which export shows the greatest change between 1970 and 1980?

4. About how many more metric tons of rice were exported in 1980 than in 1970?

5. Which export had the greatest decrease?

6. How many more metric tons of wheat were exported in 1970 than in 1975?

7. Did rice exports in 1980 equal wheat exports in 1975?

8. In which years shown did the United States export more than 1,000,000 metric tons of wheat?

9. In which years shown did the United States export more than 1,000,000 metric tons of rice?

10. In which years shown did the United States export more rice than wheat?

Mean, Median, Mode, and Range

A. In this activity, you will explore other ways of comparing data. To do this you will use counters to make *models* of numbers.

Working as a Team

Step 1: Have each member of your team pick a number between 1 and 9 until you form a set of 5 numbers. The same number can be picked more than once. When a number is picked, make a stack of that many counters. Record the set of numbers on a chart like the one shown.

Set of Numbers	
Range	
Median	
Mode	
Mean	

Step 2: Compare the tallest and the shortest stacks. How many more counters are in the tallest stack? This is the **range** of your set. Record it on the chart.

- Write a number sentence to show how you found the range.

Order the stacks from tallest to shortest. The number of counters in the stack in the middle is the **median.** Record the median. Do any of the stacks have the same number of counters? The number that appears most often is the **mode.** Record the mode, if any.

Step 3: Place the stacks on top of each other to form one large stack. Can you separate this stack into 5 groups of equal size? If so, how many counters are in each group? This is the average or **mean** of your set. If you cannot form groups of equal size, how can you describe the mean? Record the mean on the chart.

- Is there a way to calculate the mean?

Step 4: Repeat what you have done with other sets of numbers. Try sets that have more than 5 numbers in them.

Compare your teams' methods and results with those of other teams.

B. You can apply what you have learned to other numerical data.

Working as a Team

Step 1: Choose a question to ask other students in your class. Here are some possibilities:

- What is your age?
- What is your height?
- How long have you been attending our school?

Ask the question of at least 10 students.

Step 2: Discuss each of the following before you find the range, the median, the mode, and the mean for the data:

- How will you record the answers?
- Discuss which is the easiest way to compute the range and the mean: mentally, using pencil and paper, or on a calculator.

Step 3: On your own, find the range, the mode, the median, and the mean for your team's data. Then discuss your results with the other members of your team.

- How are your results different?
- How are they the same?
- What do the results tell you about the data?

Share your results with the class. Discuss how they found their results.

Choose a topic to research. Here are some possibilities:

- How old each of the Presidents of the United States was when he took office.
- How long each President served.
- How long each President lived.

Gather the numerical data and find the range, the mode, the median, and the mean. Share your results with the class and discuss what you learned about the data you found.

PROBLEM SOLVING
Making a Diagram

Making a diagram can help you solve some problems. One kind of diagram that is often helpful is a tree diagram. A tree diagram is so named because it resembles the branches of a tree.

> The United States has honored leaders such as George Washington, Thomas Jefferson, and Abraham Lincoln. National holidays and monuments have been dedicated to them, and pictures of each appear on money and stamps. How can you list the number of honors all three Presidents could have received?

You can use a tree diagram to solve this problem easily. First, list the possibilities. Then, count them.

Person	Honor	Possibility
G. Washington	Holiday	Washington–Holiday
	Monument	Washington–Monument
	Money	Washington–Money
	Stamp	Washington–Stamp
T. Jefferson	Holiday	Jefferson–Holiday
	Monument	Jefferson–Monument
	Money	Jefferson–Money
	Stamp	Jefferson–Stamp
A. Lincoln	Holiday	Lincoln–Holiday
	Monument	Lincoln–Monument
	Money	Lincoln–Money
	Stamp	Lincoln–Stamp

There are 12 possibilities. Another way to find the number of possibilities is to multiply the number of people by the number of honors.

$$\begin{array}{ccccc} \text{people} & & \text{honors} & & \text{possibilities} \\ 3 & \times & 4 & = & 12 \end{array}$$

Math Reasoning, page H210

Copy and complete each diagram.

1. Bruce, James, or Karen is going to give a report on a famous person from United States history. That person can choose Thomas Paine, John Adams, or James Madison. How many possibilities are there?

Student	**Report**	**Possibility**
	Paine	Bruce—Paine
Bruce	Adams	Bruce—Adams

2. The students of Hill School are going to put up a lobby display as part of their study of United States history. They can display a copy of the Declaration of Independence, the Constitution, or the Bill of Rights. The document can be displayed in a wall case, a glass cabinet, or a pedestal case. How many possibilities are there?

Document	**Display**	**Possibility**
	wall	Declaration—wall
Declaration	cabinet	Declaration—cabinet

For each problem, predict the number of possibilities. Then draw a tree diagram to verify your prediction. In the last column of the tree diagram, list all the possibilities.

3. Chris, Sandy, Kim, or Rita is going to portray a famous woman from the Revolutionary War period. She can be Abigail Adams, Dolley Madison, Betsy Ross, or Martha Washington. How many possibilities are there?

4. One of 6 fifth-grade classes in Abbey School is going to do a presentation about a famous person in our country's history. The possible subjects are John Adams, Ben Franklin, Alexander Hamilton, or George Washington. How many possibilities are there?

Probability

A. George Washington is said to have thrown a silver dollar across the Potomac River. What is the probability that it landed heads?

It is **equally likely** that the coin will land either heads or tails.

Probability can be shown as a fraction.

$$\frac{\text{Number of favorable outcomes (heads)}}{\text{Number of possible outcomes (heads + tails)}} = \frac{1}{2}$$

There is 1 chance out of 2 of heads. So, the probability of the coin landing heads is $\frac{1}{2}$.

B. Is it equally likely that the spinner will stop on red or on yellow?

Find the probability of each event.

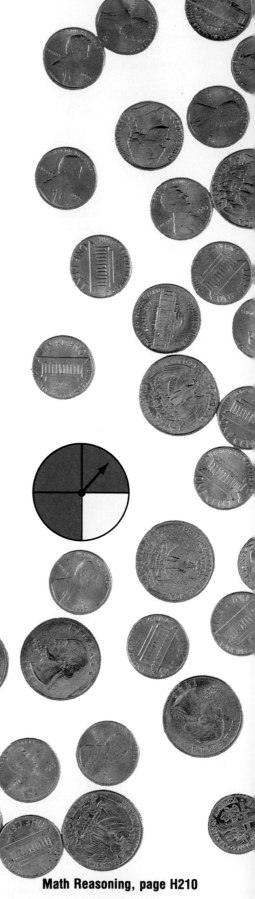

Stopping on red
Favorable outcomes: 3
Possible outcomes: 4
Probability: $\frac{3}{4}$

Stopping on yellow
Favorable outcomes: 1
Possible outcomes: 4
Probability: $\frac{1}{4}$

$$\frac{3}{4} > \frac{1}{4}$$

It is more probable that the spinner will stop on red. The two events are **not equally likely.**

Suppose you pick one marble from the jar with your eyes closed. Then you return it to the jar. Write a fraction for the probability of picking

1. a red marble.
2. a green marble.
3. a yellow marble.
4. a blue marble.
★5. a green or a blue marble.
★6. a blue or a yellow marble.

Suppose the cards are turned face down and rearranged. You pick one card. Then you return it. Write a fraction for the probability of picking

7. the letter *W*.
8. the letter *T*.
9. the letter *N*.
10. a vowel.
11. a consonant.

WASHINGTON

Solve.

Jamie is going to write a report about a President on this chart. Suppose he places all the names in a hat and picks one. What is the probability that

12. he will pick George Washington?

13. he will pick a President whose first name is John?

14. he will pick a President whose last name begins with *M*?

15. he will pick a President who was born in South Carolina?

16. he will pick a President who was born in New York or in Massachusetts?

★17. he will pick a President who was *not* born in Massachusetts?

President	Birthplace
George Washington	Virginia
John Adams	Massachusetts
Thomas Jefferson	Virginia
James Madison	Virginia
James Monroe	Virginia
John Quincy Adams	Massachusetts
Andrew Jackson	South Carolina
Martin Van Buren	New York

More Probability

A. What is the probability that the spinner will stop on a color of the United States flag?

$$\frac{\text{Favorable outcome (red + white + blue)}}{\text{Possible outcomes (red + white + blue)}} = \frac{3}{3}, \text{ or } 1$$

It is **certain** that the spinner will stop on a color of the flag.

So, the probability of a certain event is 1.

What is the probability that the spinner will stop on green?

$$\frac{\text{Favorable outcomes (green)}}{\text{Possible outcomes (red + white + blue)}} = \frac{0}{3}, \text{ or } 0$$

It is **impossible** that the spinner will stop on green.

So, the probability of an impossible event is 0.

B. Andy plans to spin the spinner 30 times. He can predict about how many times the spinner will stop on red, on white, or on blue.

To make a prediction, multiply the probability of each separate event by the total number of spins.

Event	Total spins	Predicted outcome
$\frac{1}{3}$ (probability of red)	× 30	About 10 spins will stop on red.
$\frac{1}{3}$ (probability of white)	× 30	About 10 spins will stop on white.
$\frac{1}{3}$ (probability of blue)	× 30	About 10 spins will stop on blue.

Andy spins the spinner 30 times. He keeps a tally of his results. A **tally** is a way to record results.

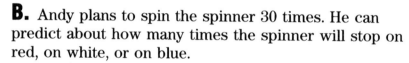

Outcome	Prediction	Tally
Red	10	ⵄ卌 ⵏⵏⵏ
White	10	卌 ⵏⵏⵏ
Blue	10	卌 卌 ⵏⵏⵏ

ǀ = 1 spin

卌 = 5 spins

Andy's results are close to his predicted outcome.

Suppose you pick a marble from the bag. Predict the probability of each event below. Write *certain* or *impossible* for each event. What is the probability of picking

1. a yellow marble?
2. a red or a green marble?
3. a white marble?
4. a green or a red marble?

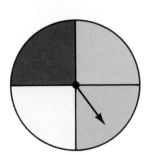

Use the spinner for Exercises 5–7.

5. Suppose you spin the spinner. List all the possible outcomes.
6. Is the spinner as likely to stop on green as on red?
7. What is the probability that the spinner will stop on either red or green?

8. List all the possible outcomes for tossing a coin. Next, as an experiment, predict how many times a coin will land heads in 50 tosses. Then toss a coin 50 times and record the results. Was your prediction accurate?

9. Suppose a coin is tossed 200 times. Predict how many times it will land heads in 200 tosses. Then combine your results from Exercise 8 with the results of three classmates. Was your prediction accurate? Now predict how many times a coin will land heads in 500 tosses.

CHALLENGE

When there is an even number of numbers, the median is the average of the two middle numbers. Find the median: 12, 15, 17, 25, 33, 36

middle numbers

$(17 + 25) \div 2 = 21$ The median is 21.

Find the median.

1. 11, 13, 23, 27, 28, 30
2. 3, 7, 9, 16
3. 8, 11, 13, 21, 26, 29
4. 23, 24, 27, 31, 36, 37
5. 4, 5, 7, 9, 15, 28, 29, 39
6. 18, 36, 41, 47, 49, 53, 55, 56

PROBLEM SOLVING
Choosing a Strategy or Method

Write the strategy or method you choose. Then solve.

1. Some early settlers traveled across the United States. After 3 days, they had gone 48 miles. After 6 days, they had gone 96 miles. After 9 days, they had gone 144 miles. At that rate, how long did it take them to go 432 miles?

> Acting It Out
> Guessing and Checking
> Making a Model
> Working Backward
> Making an Organized List
> Making a Table
> Making a Diagram
> Drawing a Picture

2. A bookshop is having a sale on books about United States history. The owner decorates the store for the sale with red, white, and blue ribbons. If he uses 2 colors at a time, how many possible color combinations can he make?

3. At the "Americana Sale," you can choose 3 books for $25: 1 about agriculture, industry, or transportation; 1 about explorers, inventors, or Presidents; and 1 about literature or science. From how many combinations of subjects can you choose?

4. Grizzly bears were a danger faced by pioneers. Grizzly bears are very large. The weight of one particular grizzly is a 3-digit number. The sum of its digits is 14. The last digit is 0. If you drop that 0, the new number is not evenly divisible by 2, 5, or 7. What is the number?

5. Many pioneers died young, but Daniel Boone was an exception. The two digits of his age when he died have a product of 48. The 2-digit number is not evenly divisible by 17. What was Daniel Boone's age when he died?

6. Two mapmakers were canoeing down a river. After 15 minutes, they had gone 0.7 mile down the river. After 30 minutes, they had gone 1.4 miles, and after 45 minutes, 2.1 miles. Their destination was 11.2 miles away. For how long did they travel?

7. Daniel has two groups of crayons. The first group has a green crayon and a yellow crayon. The second group has a blue, a red, and a purple crayon. Daniel picks a crayon from each group. List all the possible pairs of colors that are outcomes for the two picks.

Write the strategy or method you choose. Then solve.

8. United States workers spend about 40 hours a week on the job. In the last century, the figure was different. It is also a 2-digit number. The difference between the digits is 6, and the sum of the digits is less than 10. If you multiply this number by 5, the product has a 0 in the ones and the tens places. How many hours did workers spend on the job each week in the last century?

9. The bookshop has another "Americana Sale." Customers can buy 1 hardcover or softcover book on discoveries, battles, or amazing feats; 1 hardcover or softcover book about art, music, or films; and 1 hardcover or softcover book on famous United States citizens. From how many combinations can the customers choose?

10. Books are displayed on 6 racks. Each rack holds books about a different subject. The subjects are history, science, literature, biography, politics, and art. If the racks are set up in pairs around the store, how many combinations of the 6 subjects are possible?

11. When explorers reached the new land, they hiked through the woods for $2\frac{1}{2}$ hours and stopped. Then they hiked 3 hours and made camp. On the next day, they hiked for a total of $6\frac{1}{2}$ hours, and on the third day, they hiked for $7\frac{1}{2}$ hours. At that rate, for how many hours altogether had they hiked after the fifth day?

12. Jack bought some books at the "Americana Sale." He donated $\frac{1}{2}$ of them to the library. He gave each of 3 friends the same number of books. He kept twice the number of books he gave to any of his friends. If he kept 4 books, how many books did he buy?

13. Traders traded beads and shells for Native American artifacts. One trader put 6 beads and 4 shells into a bag. He picked out 5 things at random to trade. How many combinations of beads and shells could he have picked out?

14. The town of Farmdale began with 200 people. After one year, there were 300 people. After the second year, the population had grown to 400, and in one more year, it had grown to 500 people. At that rate, what was the population in 7 years?

15. From this lesson, choose one problem that you've already solved. Show how it can be solved by using a method that is different from the one you used originally.

LOGICAL REASONING

A. A statement that is true or false is a logical statement.
STATEMENT: It will snow on Thursday.

If it snows on Thursday, then the statement is *true*.
If it does not snow, then the statement is *false*.

Two statements that have exactly the same meaning
are called **equivalent** statements. Whenever one statement
is true, then the other statement is also true.

a. I am taller than my brother.
b. My brother is shorter than I. } Equivalent statements

a. The stoplight is green. } Not equivalent statements
b. The stoplight is not red. If the stoplight is yellow, then only *b* is true.

Polygon *ABCD* is a rectangle.
Write whether the statement is *true*
or *false*.

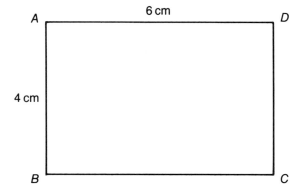

1. *ABCD* is a square.
2. *ABCD* is a parallelogram.
3. The perimeter of *ABCD* is 10 cm.
4. *ABCD* is a triangle.
5. *ABCD* is a quadrilateral.

Write whether statements *a* and *b* are *equivalent*
or *not equivalent*.

6. a. Yesterday was Tuesday.
  b. Tomorrow is Thursday.

7. a. Next month is January.
  b. Next month is not May.

8. a. Every day in May was rainy.
  b. May 15th was a sunny day.

9. a. Some of my friends are boys.
  b. None of my friends are girls.

10. a. Every visitor was unfriendly.
   b. None of the visitors were
   friendly.

11. a. My favorite number is less
   than 8.
   b. My favorite number is not
   greater than 8.

GROUP PROJECT

Numbers, Numbers, Numbers!

The problem: In a certain game, there are three green cards and four red cards. You use the cards to form numbers.

Key Facts

- The cards are mixed and laid, facedown, in two piles. You pick a card, without looking, from each pile.
- You are as likely to pick one card as another.
- The green card gives the tens digit of the number.
- The red card gives the ones digit of the number.

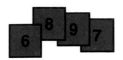

1. Predict the number of two-digit numbers that can be formed.

2. Suppose you pick a green card and a red card 24 times. Predict how many times a two-digit number less than 30 will be formed.

3. Suppose you pick a green card and a red card 120 times. Predict how many times a two-digit number less than 30 will be formed.

4. Make *models* of the cards. Test the predictions you made for Problems 2 and 3.

5. Discuss how you can show all the possible two-digit numbers that can be formed. Show them in an organized way.

6. What is the probability that a number less than 30 will be formed?

CHAPTER TEST

Solve. Copy and complete each graph using the information in the table to its left. (pages 384, 386, and 388)

1. Round each population to the nearest million.

U.S. FARM POPULATION

Year	Actual population	Rounded amounts
1900	29,875,000	
1925	31,190,000	
1950	23,048,000	
1975	8,253,000	

2. In which year was farm population about double the 1975 figure?

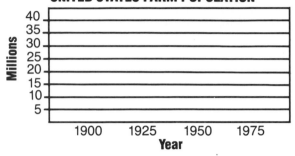

3. Round each number to the nearest half million.

NUMBER OF FARMS IN U.S.

Year	Actual number of farms	Rounded amounts
1900	5,737,000	
1925	6,471,000	
1950	5,648,000	
1975	2,314,000	

4. Were there more farms in 1900 or 1950?

NUMBER OF FARMS IN THE UNITED STATES

Year	Number of farms
1900	
1925	
1950	
1975	

○ = 1,000,000   ◖ = 500,000

5. Round each number to the nearest ten million.

TOTAL ACRES OF FARMLAND

Year	Actual number of acres	Rounded amounts
1900	839,000,000	
1925	924,000,000	
1950	1,202,000,000	
1975	905,600,000	

6. Has the number of acres of farmland increased steadily since 1900?

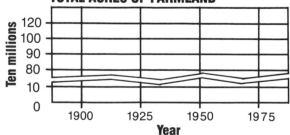

Find the mean, median, mode, and range. (page 392)

7. 109, 90, 91, 90

8. 83, 27, 83, 39, 42, 83, 42

A bowl has 14 beads. 3 are red, 2 are yellow, 4 are blue, and 5 are green. (page 396)

Write a fraction for the probability of picking a

9. red bead.   **10.** blue bead.   **11.** yellow bead.   **12.** green bead.

A bag has 4 beads. 3 are brown, and 1 is orange.
Predict the probability of each event by writing *certain* or *impossible*. (page 398)

What is the probability of picking a

13. red bead? **14.** brown or orange bead? **15.** orange or brown bead? **16.** blue bead?

Solve. Use the graphs below. (pages 390–391)

POPULATION PER SQUARE KILOMETER OF THE CONTINENTS

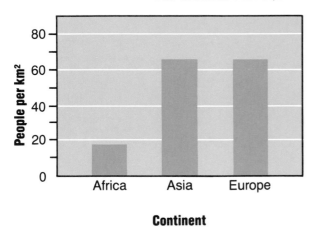

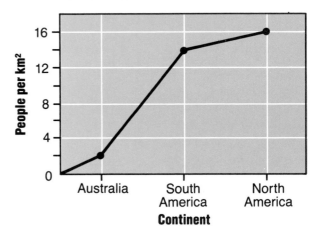

17. Does North America or Europe have more people per square kilometer?

18. Does Asia or South America have more people per square kilometer?

Solve. Use a tree diagram. (pages 394–395)

19. Ron, Liz, or Clara is going to do a report on philanthropists in New York history. That person will choose one of the Coopers, Houstons, Astors, or Rockefellers for the report. How many possibilities are there?

20. A report on one of six signers of the Declaration of Independence will be made by either Sarah or Kyle. How many possibilities are there?

RETEACHING

A. Look at the spinner at the right. What is the probability that the spinner will stop on blue?

It is **equally likely** that the spinner will stop either on blue or on yellow.

Probability can be shown as a fraction.

$$\frac{\textbf{number of favorable outcomes (blue)}}{\textbf{number of possible outcomes (blue and yellow)}} = \frac{1}{2}$$

There is 1 chance in 2 that the spinner will stop on blue. So, the probability of blue is $\frac{1}{2}$.

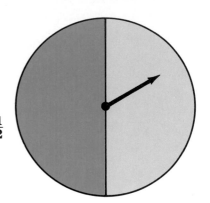

B. Find the probability of each event.

Stopping on _A_	**Stopping on _B_**
Favorable outcomes: 1	Favorable outcomes: 2
Possible outcomes: 3	Possible outcomes: 3
Probability: $\frac{1}{3}$	Probability: $\frac{2}{3}$

$$\frac{1}{3} < \frac{2}{3}$$

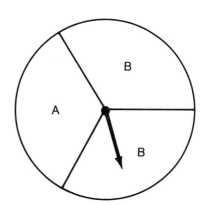

It is more probable that the spinner will stop on _B_. The two events are **not equally likely**.

Write the probability as a fraction.
What is the probability that the first marble to be picked from the box will be

1. red?　　　**3.** white?

2. yellow?　　**4.** blue?

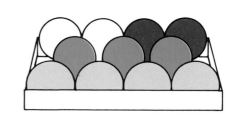

You have 26 cards each with a different letter of the alphabet written on it: 5 vowels and 21 consonants. What is the probability that you will pick

1. a **_G_** card?　　　**2.** an **_S_** card?

3. a **vowel** card?　　**4.** a **consonant** card?

ENRICHMENT

Double-Bar Graphs

Double-bar graphs are used to compare similar kinds of information. The bar graph below shows the population growth in the pioneer towns of Sage and Indian Bend between 1800 and 1860.

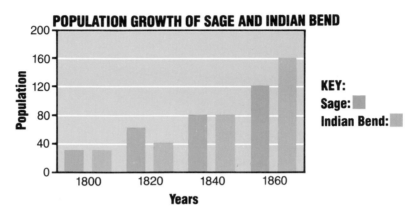

The key explains how to read the bars on the graph. The axis represents a different set of information. The titles of the axes identify this information.

Use the graph to answer the questions.

1. Between which two years did the population of Indian Bend double?

2. In which year was the population of Indian Bend greater than that of Sage? How many people lived in Sage that year?

Copy and complete the bar graph. Use the data in the chart.

NUMBER OF FARMS IN SAGE AND INDIAN BEND

Year	Sage	Indian Bend
1800	4	3
1820	6	7
1840	5	9
1860	8	15

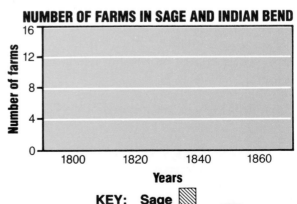

TECHNOLOGY

You can write BASIC programs to solve problems. Suppose you need to solve a problem such as this.

There are 340 children in a school. Of them, 25% are involved in sports. How many children are involved in sports?

You could write a computer program to give you the answer. Here's one way to do it.

```
10   LET NC = 340
20   LET P = .25
30   LET SP = NC * P
40   PRINT SP; " CHILDREN ARE INVOLVED IN SPORTS"
```

This program stores the total number of children in a variable NC. It stores the percent in P. Remember that percents can be written as decimals. The answer is in SP. When you RUN this program, it will print this.

85 CHILDREN ARE INVOLVED IN SPORTS

1. Rewrite two lines of the program above so that you find the answer to this problem.

There are 270 children in another school. Of them, 20% are involved in sports. How many children are involved in sports?

2. What will the program print when it is RUN?

You can use parentheses to help solve multistep problems.

The fifth-grade class has a bake sale that lasts for three hours. They sell 60 baked goods in all. They sell 13 baked goods in the first hour and 30 in the second hour. How many baked goods do they sell in the third hour?

Here is one way to solve this problem.

```
10   LET SP = 60 − (13 + 30)
20   PRINT "THEY SOLD "; SP; " BAKED GOODS IN
THE THIRD HOUR."
```

3. Write a program to solve this problem.

The music teacher teaches four classes per day. She has 27 students in her first class, 14 students in her second class, and 20 students in her fourth class. She has 79 students in all. How many students does she have in her third class?

4. Write a program that has 20 print statements. The program should print the numbers 1 through 20. Each print statement should compute with the numbers 2, 3, and 4 only. You can add, subtract, multiply, or divide these three numbers. Here's a start.

```
10   PRINT 4 − 3
20   PRINT 4 / 2
30   PRINT 3 * (4 ÷ 4)
40   PRINT (4 / 2) * 2
```

When you use a comma in a PRINT statement, it acts like the tab key on your typewriter. It moves the cursor to the next printing area, or **print zone.**

Statement:	The computer will print this.
PRINT 1,2	1 2

Statement:	The computer will print this.
PRINT "HI","THERE"	HI THERE

5. Finish writing this program. It should print the number of students in each of three classes.

```
10   LET C1 = 15
20   LET C2 = 20
30   LET C3 = 23
40   LET T = C1 + C2 + C3
50   PRINT "CLASS 1",C1
```

When you RUN the program, it should print this.

```
CLASS 1   15
CLASS 2   20
CLASS 3   23
TOTAL     58
```

CUMULATIVE REVIEW

Write the letter of the correct answer.

1. Classify the angle.

a. acute   b. obtuse
c. right   d. not given

2. Find the area of a triangle with base = 5 m; height = 8 m.

a. 13   b. 20
c. 40   d. not given

3. Find the area of a rectangle with length = 7 m; width = 4 m.

a. 11 m   b. 11 m^2
c. 14 m   d. not given

4. Find the volume of a cube with an edge of 9 in.

a. 729 in.^{3} b. 729 in.^{2}
c. 81 in.^{3} d. not given

5. Find the perimeter of a regular pentagon with a side 14 cm long.

a. 70 cm^2 b. 70 cm
c. 196 cm   d. not given

6. Give the name for *AB*.

a. radius   b. diameter
c. chord   d. not given

7. Choose the best unit for measuring the weight of a bowling ball.

a. milligrams   b. grams
c. kilograms   d. not given

8. 70% of 250

a. 150   b. 175
c. 200   d. not given

9. Write the answer in simplest form: $14\frac{5}{6} - 12\frac{7}{8}$.

a. $1\frac{23}{24}$ b. $2\frac{1}{24}$
c. $2\frac{23}{24}$ d. not given

10. Find the mean. 4, 7, 6, 10, 8

a. 4   b. 6
c. 7   d. not given

11. The Exotic Fruit Company delivers 6,783 coconuts in one week. The coconuts are packed 21 to a crate. How many crates do they deliver?

a. 323   b. 325
c. 142,443   d. not given

12. An office-supply company orders 3,575 pens. The pens are delivered in boxes, with no more than 43 to a box. How many boxes are delivered?

a. 83   b. 84
c. 85   d. not given

Connecting Math Ideas

Page 237   Exploring Patterns in Fractions

Use 10 red and 10 black checkers or slips of paper as objects.

1. Make a group of 5 objects so that $\frac{1}{5}$ of the group is red. How can you change the group so that $\frac{2}{5}$ of the new group is red?

2. Continue changing the group so that $\frac{3}{5}$ is red and $\frac{4}{5}$ is red. What pattern do you see? Do the fractions that represent red checkers get larger or smaller?

For Exercises 3–4, start with a new group of objects.

3. Make a group of objects so that $\frac{1}{6}$ of the group is black. How can you change the group so that $\frac{1}{7}$ of the new group is black?

4. Change the group again so that $\frac{1}{8}$ is black and $\frac{1}{9}$ is black. What pattern do you see? Do the fractions that represent black checkers get larger or smaller?

 Use a calculator for Exercises 5–6.

5. Start with any fraction. Choose a counting number and keep adding it to the numerator. Record your fractions. What pattern do you see?

6. Start with any fraction. Choose a counting number and keep adding it to the denominator. Record your fractions. What pattern do you see?

Page 264   Using Guessing and Checking

Guess what the answer is. Then *check* to see whether the guess is correct. If not, guess again.

1. The least common multiple (LCM) of two numbers is 12. One number is 2 more than the other. What are the two numbers?

2. The LCM of two numbers is 30. One number is 4 less than the other. What are the two numbers?

3. The product of two prime numbers is 187. What are the two numbers?

4. The product of two prime numbers is 161. What are the two numbers?

Page 282 Using a Computer to Find Ordered Pairs

Here is a BASIC program that explores ordered pairs.

```
10  INPUT S
20  PRINT "IF THERE ARE"; S; "STRINGS"
30  LET W = S / 5 * 3
40  PRINT "THEN THERE ARE"; W; "WOODWINDS"
50  PRINT " (S,W) = "; "("; S; ","; W; ")"
60  END
```

Use the program to answer questions such as "How many woodwinds are there in an orchestra with 60 strings?" (36) "with 695 strings?" (417) Develop similar programs for Exercises 3–7 on page 283.

Page 319 Drawing a Picture to Explore Ratio and Percent

Solve. *Draw a picture* for Exercise 1.

1. On a 10-problem math test, a student got 9 problems correct. Draw a 10 by 10 grid. Shade enough squares so that the ratio of the shaded part to the total number of squares is $\frac{9}{10}$.

2. How many points is each problem on the test worth? What percent is the student's score on the test?

Page 341 Using a Simpler Problem

Solve.

Keith says: "I drew a plane. In it, I drew 12 horizontal lines and 16 vertical lines. How many points of intersection are there?" Before you try to answer his question, solve one or two *simpler problems* like this one:

2 horizontal lines
5 vertical lines
■ points of intersection

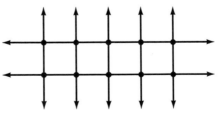

Now use the results from the simpler problem to answer Keith's question.

Page 363 Working Backward to Locate Points on a Grid

Solve by *working backward*. Making a graph or a drawing can help you.

1. An ant was placed on a grid. It crawled 4 spaces to the right. Then it was at (6, 0). At what point did the ant start?

2. A fly was placed on a grid. It crawled 3 spaces to the right and 1 space up. Then it was at (4, 3). At what point did the fly start?

Page 365 Exploring Circumference

1. The perimeter of a circle is called its **circumference.** Find three circular objects that are different sizes. Measure the diameter (d) and circumference (C) of each circle. Use string to help you measure. Record the data (d and C) for each object.

2. For each circle you measured in Exercise 1, divide the circumference by the diameter. Use a calculator to find the quotient. Is the answer a little more than 3 in each case?

3. For any circle, $C \div d$, or $\frac{C}{d}$, is always the same. The Greek letter π (*pi*) is the symbol used for $\frac{C}{d}$. $\pi \approx 3.14$. If a circle has a circumference of 6.28 inches, about how many inches long is the diameter?

4. Since $\frac{C}{d} = \pi$, a formula for the circumference of a circle is often given as $C = \pi \times d$. Using 3.14 for π, find the circumference of a circle if its diameter is 4 inches; if its diameter is 10 inches.

5. Suppose you know the length of a radius. Is the first equation or the second equation a formula for the circumference of a circle?

$$C = \pi \times \tfrac{1}{2} \times r \qquad C = \pi \times 2 \times r$$

6. Estimate the circumference of a circle if its radius is 3 inches; if its radius is 10 inches.

BANDS OF THE ATMOSPHERE: LOWER BOUNDARIES

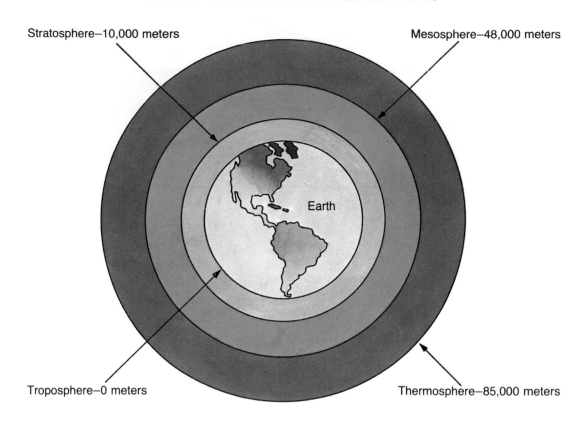

Stratosphere—10,000 meters

Mesosphere—48,000 meters

Earth

Troposphere—0 meters

Thermosphere—85,000 meters

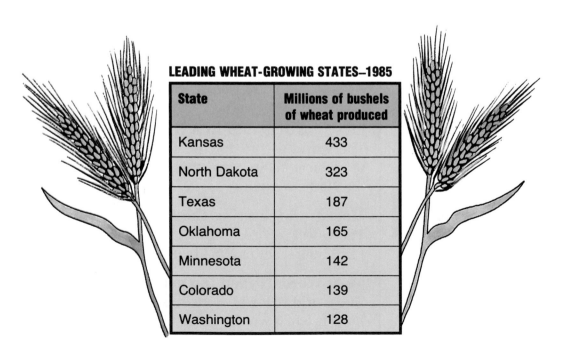

LEADING WHEAT-GROWING STATES—1985

State	Millions of bushels of wheat produced
Kansas	433
North Dakota	323
Texas	187
Oklahoma	165
Minnesota	142
Colorado	139
Washington	128

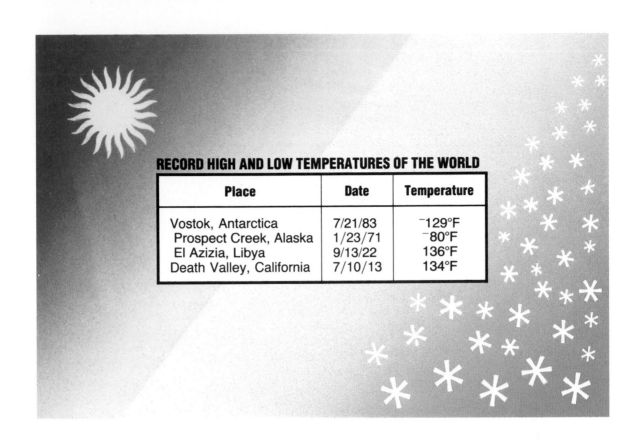

RECORD HIGH AND LOW TEMPERATURES OF THE WORLD

Place	Date	Temperature
Vostok, Antarctica	7/21/83	⁻129°F
Prospect Creek, Alaska	1/23/71	⁻80°F
El Azizia, Libya	9/13/22	136°F
Death Valley, California	7/10/13	134°F

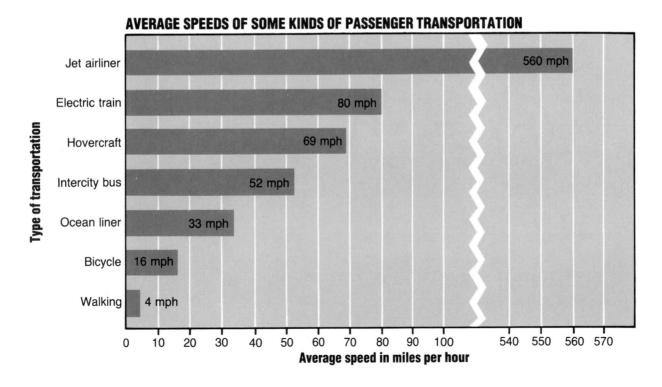

AVERAGE SPEEDS OF SOME KINDS OF PASSENGER TRANSPORTATION

Type of transportation

- Jet airliner — 560 mph
- Electric train — 80 mph
- Hovercraft — 69 mph
- Intercity bus — 52 mph
- Ocean liner — 33 mph
- Bicycle — 16 mph
- Walking — 4 mph

Average speed in miles per hour

SHAPES IN THE CONSTELLATIONS

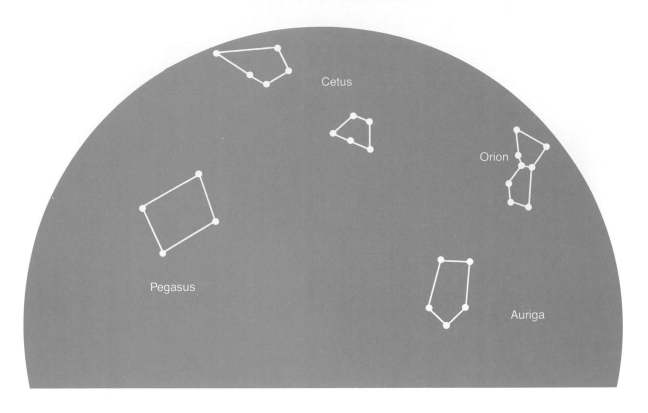

PRESIDENTIAL HEIGHT AND WEIGHT CHART

Name	Height	Weight in pounds
Herbert Hoover	5 ft 11 in.	200
Franklin Roosevelt	6 ft 2 in.	200
Harry Truman	5 ft 9 in.	165
Dwight Eisenhower	5 ft 10½ in.	180
John Kennedy	6 ft	175
Lyndon Johnson	6 ft 3 in.	210
Richard Nixon	5 ft 11½ in.	175
Gerald Ford	6 ft	200
Jimmy Carter	5 ft 9½ in.	175
Ronald Reagan	6 ft 1 in.	185
George Bush	6 ft 2 in.	195

STUDENT HANDBOOK

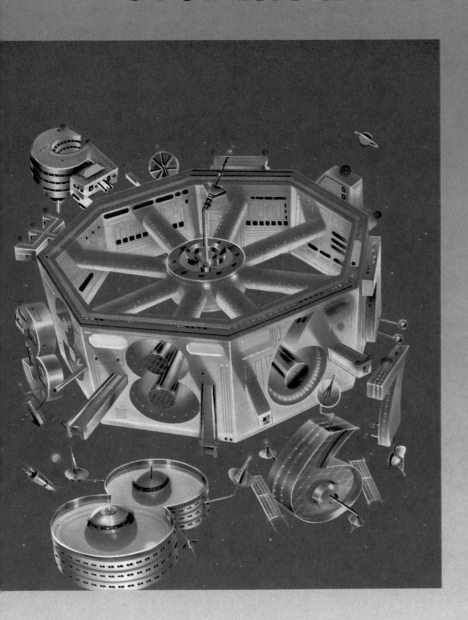

Write the value of the underlined digit.

1. 7̲19

2. 6,90̲4

3. 81̲,319

4. 5̲9,002

5. 13̲7,646

6. 17,4̲01

Write in standard form.

7. 80,000 + 300 + 2

8. 900,000 + 20,000 + 7,000 + 800 + 40 + 3

9. 10,000 + 8,000 + 700 + 30 + 4

10. 30,000 + 1,000 + 600 + 70 + 6

11. 600,000 + 50,000 + 4,000 + 300 + 20 + 2

12. 20,000 + 3,000 + 900 + 90 + 9

Write in expanded form.

13. 8,954

14. 71,683

15. 444,296

16. 9,851

17. 123,478

18. 54,911

19. 19,672

20. 263,548

Solve.

21. Pablo Picasso created 13,500 paintings and designs in his lifetime. What is the value of the digit 3 in 13,500?

Write the value of the underlined digit.

1. 2,314,<u>6</u>09

2. 1<u>3</u>,491,732

3. 4,5<u>8</u>6,916,300

4. <u>1</u>6,000,932,134

5. 14,09<u>6</u>,475

6. 412,000,000,6<u>1</u>9

Write in standard form.

7. 732 million, 37 thousand

8. 154 billion, 82 million, 15 thousand, 6 hundred 11

9. 99 million, 2 thousand, 7 hundred

10. 225 billion, 137 million, 985 thousand, 8 hundred 44

Write the word name for each.

11. 679,020,111

12. 802,313,602,033

Write the numbers shown in the chart in standard form.

	Billions	Millions	Thousands	Ones
13.	0	5	10	225
14.	3	26	309	76
15.	0	78	910	562
16.	1	112	680	269

Compare. Use >, <, or = .

1. 3,743 ◯ 3,842

2. 930 ◯ 903

3. 345,011 ◯ 345,101

4. 98,701 ◯ 98,701

5. 8,808 ◯ 18,808

6. 71,814 ◯ 17,757

7. 65,000 ◯ 56,000

8. 2,112 ◯ 11,121

9. 123,456 ◯ 231,456

10. 77,777 ◯ 757,770

11. 898,989 ◯ 898,989

12. 24,422 ◯ 24,420

13. 716,671 ◯ 716,671

14. 6,001 ◯ 6,010

15. 678,876 ◯ 778,876

Order from the least to the greatest.

16. 158, 157, 149, 152

17. 241, 313, 165, 156

18. 756, 509, 821, 312

19. 2,496; 1,231; 996; 2,946

Order from the greatest to the least.

20. 7,560; 8,903; 7,712; 8,900

21. 5,022; 5,018; 5,015; 5,005

22. 612; 9,612; 11,342; 10,342

Use the four-step plan to solve each problem. Find the information you need in the chart.

- State the problem in your own words.
- Tell which tools you will use.
- Solve the problem.
- Check your solution.

CARROLLTON SUMMER SOFTBALL LEAGUE

Team	Wins	Losses	Ties	Team	Wins	Losses	Ties
Tigers	16	3	0	Prostars	9	11	0
Oldtimers	15	3	2	Thunderers	7	11	2
Generals	11	8	1	Anglers	6	13	1
Phantoms	10	10	0	Sunshiners	5	15	0

1. Which team won two more games than the Anglers lost?

2. How many more games did the Tigers win than the Prostars?

3. Which team lost three times as many games as it won?

4. Which team won three times as many games as the Oldtimers lost?

5. How many more losses did the Sunshiners have than the Generals?

6. Which two teams together won as many games as the Generals won?

7. How many games did the Tigers and the Generals win altogether?

8. Which team could have tied its record with the Prostars if it had won two of the games it tied?

Add.

1. $\begin{array}{r}7\\+7\\\hline\end{array}$	2. $\begin{array}{r}8\\+4\\\hline\end{array}$	3. $\begin{array}{r}6\\+1\\\hline\end{array}$	4. $\begin{array}{r}3\\+3\\\hline\end{array}$	5. $\begin{array}{r}2\\+9\\\hline\end{array}$	6. $\begin{array}{r}7\\+5\\\hline\end{array}$
7. $\begin{array}{r}4\\+9\\\hline\end{array}$	8. $\begin{array}{r}3\\+7\\\hline\end{array}$	9. $\begin{array}{r}9\\+8\\\hline\end{array}$	10. $\begin{array}{r}1\\+0\\\hline\end{array}$	11. $\begin{array}{r}5\\+7\\\hline\end{array}$	12. $\begin{array}{r}3\\+6\\\hline\end{array}$

Write the missing number.

13. $6 + 3 = 3 + \underline{\quad?\quad}$

14. $5 + \underline{\quad?\quad} = 5$

15. $2 + 0 = \underline{\quad?\quad} + 2$

16. $1 + 2 = \underline{\quad?\quad} + 1$

17. $\underline{\quad?\quad} + 9 = 17$

18. $3 + \underline{\quad?\quad} = 9$

19. $(4 + \underline{\quad?\quad}) + 5 = 16$

20. $(1 + 3) + \underline{\quad?\quad} = 13$

21. $6 + (\underline{\quad?\quad} + 8) = 18$

22. $1 + (\underline{\quad?\quad} + 9) = 13$

23. $(8 + \underline{\quad?\quad}) + 6 = 18$

24. $354 + \underline{\quad?\quad} = 512$

25. $6 + \underline{\quad?\quad} = 12$

26. $9 + \underline{\quad?\quad} = 10$

27. $\underline{\quad?\quad} + 5 = 9$

28. $\underline{\quad?\quad} + 3 = 7$

29. $3 + \underline{\quad?\quad} = 11$

30. $2 + \underline{\quad?\quad} = 5$

Copy and solve. Then match the letters and numbers to answer the riddle. If you put a mother duck and six ducklings in a box, what would you have?

A $\underline{\quad?\quad} + 4 = 10$

U $\underline{\quad?\quad} + 8 = 12$

S $\underline{\quad?\quad} + 7 = 14$

R $6 + 5 = \underline{\quad?\quad}$

E $8 + \underline{\quad?\quad} = 13$

C $\underline{\quad?\quad} + 8 = 11$

F $9 + 7 = \underline{\quad?\quad}$

B $8 + \underline{\quad?\quad} = 9$

X $\underline{\quad?\quad} + 6 = 8$

K $\underline{\quad?\quad} + 8 = 17$

O $7 + \underline{\quad?\quad} = 15$

A $\underline{\quad?\quad} + 7 = 13$

Q $3 + 9 = \underline{\quad?\quad}$

O $6 + \underline{\quad?\quad} = 14$

$$\underline{\overset{?}{6}\ \overset{?}{1}\ \overset{?}{8}\ \overset{?}{2}}\ \ \underline{\overset{?}{8}\ \overset{?}{16}}\ \ \underline{\overset{?}{12}\ \overset{?}{4}\ \overset{?}{6}\ \overset{?}{3}\ \overset{?}{9}\ \overset{?}{5}\ \overset{?}{11}\ \overset{?}{7}}$$

Add or subtract.

1. $\begin{array}{r} 15 \\ -\ 7 \\ \hline \end{array}$	2. $\begin{array}{r} 5 \\ +\ 6 \\ \hline \end{array}$	3. $\begin{array}{r} 10 \\ -\ 8 \\ \hline \end{array}$	4. $\begin{array}{r} 9 \\ -\ 5 \\ \hline \end{array}$	5. $\begin{array}{r} 8 \\ +\ 1 \\ \hline \end{array}$	6. $\begin{array}{r} 12 \\ -\ 7 \\ \hline \end{array}$
7. $\begin{array}{r} 14 \\ -\ 5 \\ \hline \end{array}$	8. $\begin{array}{r} 7 \\ +\ 9 \\ \hline \end{array}$	9. $\begin{array}{r} 12 \\ -\ 6 \\ \hline \end{array}$	10. $\begin{array}{r} 15 \\ -\ 6 \\ \hline \end{array}$	11. $\begin{array}{r} 8 \\ +\ 9 \\ \hline \end{array}$	12. $\begin{array}{r} 8 \\ -\ 3 \\ \hline \end{array}$
13. $\begin{array}{r} 16 \\ -\ 8 \\ \hline \end{array}$	14. $\begin{array}{r} 7 \\ -\ 1 \\ \hline \end{array}$	15. $\begin{array}{r} 3 \\ +\ 9 \\ \hline \end{array}$	16. $\begin{array}{r} 10 \\ -\ 2 \\ \hline \end{array}$	17. $\begin{array}{r} 12 \\ -\ 4 \\ \hline \end{array}$	18. $\begin{array}{r} 7 \\ +\ 8 \\ \hline \end{array}$
19. $\begin{array}{r} 6 \\ +\ 9 \\ \hline \end{array}$	20. $\begin{array}{r} 11 \\ -\ 9 \\ \hline \end{array}$	21. $\begin{array}{r} 14 \\ -\ 7 \\ \hline \end{array}$	22. $\begin{array}{r} 6 \\ -\ 1 \\ \hline \end{array}$	23. $\begin{array}{r} 5 \\ +\ 4 \\ \hline \end{array}$	24. $\begin{array}{r} 17 \\ -\ 8 \\ \hline \end{array}$

25. $7 - 3$

26. $14 - 9$

27. $4 + 1$

28. $9 + 9$

29. $8 - 6$

30. $7 + 6$

Copy and complete.

31. $6 + 4 = 10$

 $10 - \underline{\ ?\ } = 4$

32. $7 + 5 = 12$

 $12 - \underline{\ ?\ } = 7$

33. $4 + 9 = 13$

 $13 - \underline{\ ?\ } = 9$

34. $3 + 8 = 11$

 $11 - \underline{\ ?\ } = 8$

35. $8 + 4 = 12$

 $12 - \underline{\ ?\ } = 4$

36. $7 + 7 = 14$

 $14 - \underline{\ ?\ } = 7$

Write a family of facts for each group of numbers.

37. 3, 6, 9

 ▮ + ▮ = ▮

 ▮ + ▮ = ▮

 ▮ − ▮ = ▮

 ▮ − ▮ = ▮

38. 15, 8, 7

 ▮ + ▮ = ▮

 ▮ + ▮ = ▮

 ▮ − ▮ = ▮

 ▮ − ▮ = ▮

39. 11, 6, 5

 ▮ + ▮ = ▮

 ▮ + ▮ = ▮

 ▮ − ▮ = ▮

 ▮ − ▮ = ▮

Use with pages 12–13.

Write the two numbers whose sum is about

1. 100.

62
41   20
95

2. 1,000.

876
316   532
125

3. 100.

35
89 72
48

4. 100.

25
16   58
47

5. 1,000.

271
912   469
752

6. 1,000.

191
621   573
789

Estimate. Write > or <.

7. 27 + 89 ◯ 100

8. 96 + 86 ◯ 200

9. 37 + 76 ◯ 100

10. 296 + 167 ◯ 400

11. 293 + 324 ◯ 600

12. 397 + 389 ◯ 800

13. 331 + 378 + 351 ◯ 1,000

14. 735 + 422 + 819 ◯ 2,000

15. 5,375 + 6,906 ◯ 10,000

16. 7,961 + 203 + 89 ◯ 10,000

Estimate. First write your rough estimate. Then write your adjusted estimate.

17.
391
85
414
+ 120

18.
735
252
176
+ 349

19.
$8.61
7.08
1.95
+ 3.50

20.
4,681
5,267
3,408
+ 2,835

21. Volunteers at the summer fest want to sell 500 balloons. They have inflated 227 red, 86 orange, 192 blue, and 15 green balloons. Estimate how many balloons are inflated. Have they inflated more or less than 500 balloons?

22. The lemonade vendor needs to begin the day with $20.00 in change. There are $8.75 in quarters, $3.85 in nickels, $4.30 in dimes, and $0.97 in pennies in the money box. Estimate the amount of money in the box. Does the vendor have $20.00 in change?

Round each number to the nearest hundred and to the nearest thousand.

1. 7,468   **2.** 3,456   **3.** 4,663   **4.** 2,598

5. 1,553   **6.** 3,221   **7.** 5,532   **8.** 7,298

9. 985   **10.** 723   **11.** 12,339   **12.** 10,675

Estimate. Write > or <.

13. 4,679 + 4,598 ◯ 9,000   **14.** 8,486 + 11,783 ◯ 21,000

15. 7,395 + 2,931 ◯ 10,000   **16.** 4,211 + 5,724 + 2,916 ◯ 13,000

17. 8,716 + 9,831 ◯ 18,000   **18.** 6,327 + 2,469 + 3,782 ◯ 12,000

Estimate the total population in

19. the two largest cities.

20. the two smallest cities.

21. Beeville and Honeydale.

City	Population
Clovertown	7,862
Honeydale	5,041
Springmill	46,215
Beeville	8,961
Fairview	39,560
Clearland	2,319

Solve.

22. Farmer Barber harvested 27,216 bushels of wheat and 15,536 bushels of soybeans last year. He had contracted a harvest of 45,000 bushels of grain with the local market. Estimate his total grain harvest. Did he produce as much grain as he thought he would?

23. Many airlines give a free trip to people who fly 100,000 miles or more within one year. The following table shows Carla's travel this year. Estimate the total number of miles flown. Will Carla win a free trip?

Jan.–Mar.	33,261 miles
Apr.–June	35,892 miles
July–Sept.	28,723 miles
Oct.–Dec.	17,219 miles

Estimate to solve.

1. The Clinton Block Association is renovating an old school for a community center. The block association needs 700 feet of lumber for some new walls. A lumber company donates 234 feet of lumber and the block association buys 352 feet and finds 210 feet of lumber in the basement of the old school. Do they have enough lumber?

2. The old school auditorium is being converted into a town-meeting hall. The first section of the meeting hall will have 65 seats. The second section will have 47 seats. The third and fourth sections will have 82 seats each. Estimate the minimum number of seats available in the new meeting hall.

3. Local residents have donated 900 books for a library at the community center. They use bookshelves from the old school to hold the books. One bookshelf holds 235 books. Another holds 315 books, and the last one they find holds 304 books. Do they have enough bookshelf space for the books?

4. A building-supply store donates 500 shingles to repair the old school roof, which leaks in 3 places. In one spot, 230 of the old shingles need to be replaced. In the last 2 places, 110 shingles need to be replaced in each place. Are there enough new shingles for the job?

5. It is going to cost $750 to build a game room in the new community center. Local children earn $110 washing cars. A bake sale raises $230, and a neighborhood street fair raises $516. Is there enough money to build the game room?

6. When the community center opens, residents hold a 3-day fair to celebrate and raise money for an operating fund. They make $125 the first day, $234 the second day, and $220 the last day. What is the minimum amount of money in the fund?

Add.

1. 178
    + 15

2. $3.67
    + 5.03

3. 402
    + 336

4. 516
    + 191

5. $2.25
    + 7.37

6. 870
    + 169

7. 441
    + 386

8. 101
    + 889

9. 743
    + 302

10. 29
    + 17

11. 648
    + 296

12. 194
    + 372

13. 64
    + 17

14. 479
    + 813

15. 765
    + 479

16. 810
    + 843

17. 218
    + 93

18. 599
    + 848

19. $6.69
    + 6.69

20. 711
    + 954

21. $5.42
    + 2.24

22. 702
    + 199

23. 654
    + 456

24. 37
    + 64

25. 735
    + 211

26. 804
    + 687

27. $6.22
    + 9.54

28. 605
    + 599

29. 14
    + 57

30. 111
    + 111

31. 12 + 35

32. 43 + 19

33. $5.45 + $3.32

34. 13 + 88

35. 73 + 58

36. 391 + 142

37. 108 + 63

38. $44 + $92

39. 77 + 99

Solve.

40. On Thursday, the Olympia Theater sold 173 mezzanine tickets and 258 balcony tickets. How many tickets were sold in all?

Find the sum.

1. $913.09
 + 113.44

2. 11,692
 + 84,241

3. 60,155
 + 79,849

4. 33,003
 + 10,225

5. 7,652
 + 1,826

6. 10,697
 + 39,401

7. 9,594
 + 2,454

8. 1,809
 + 6,869

9. $78.08
 + 16.03

10. 40,081
 + 23,916

11. $66.22
 + 61.80

12. 10,750
 + 64,325

13. 89,705
 + 65,721

14. 706,656
 + 197,038

15. 3,768
 + 2,118

16. 1,001 + 3,016

17. 19,333 + 41,666

18. 11,991 + 18,492

19. 5,080 + 2,777

20. $61.33 + $49.67

21. 14,603 + 13,199

22. 7,444 + 1,611

23. $111.60 + $198.22

24. $171.44 + $186.52

25. 6,097 + 8,211

Solve.

26. 7,612
 + 1,830

27. 2,091
 + 2,900

28. 6,421
 + 1,738

29. 4,681
 + 4,001

30. 149,036
 + 20,045

31. 17,868
 + 16,455

32. 13,411
 + 22,894

33. 5,827
 + 2,718

34. 9,047
 + 2,963

Add. Check by adding up.

1. 304 915 + 126	**2.** 1,349 9,002 + 542	**3.** 42 24 + 41	**4.** 63 36 + 60	**5.** 3,455 600 + 4,253
6. $1.89 2.12 + 5.08	**7.** 301 54 + 607	**8.** 1,000 280 + 2,151	**9.** 5,622 3,325 + 1,699	**10.** 456 302 + 111
11. 200 300 + 100	**12.** $65.54 46.34 + 72.04	**13.** 812 769 + 1,110	**14.** 1,575 844 + 3,709	**15.** $71.19 45.95 + 53.54
16. 15 17 + 23	**17.** 18 16 + 81	**18.** $95.44 61.87 + 52.09	**19.** 8,673 1,303 + 280	**20.** 1,357 2,468 + 3,051
21. 624 1,879 + 313	**22.** $95.78 7.46 + 56.23	**23.** 502 815 + 27	**24.** $0.34 6.91 + 4.57	**25.** 8,141 1,767 + 340
26. 250 6,510 + 132	**27.** 498 62 + 818	**28.** 1,582 4,743 + 1,956	**29.** $150.15 150.15 + 150.15	**30.** 3,537 2,225 + 2,568

31. 250 + 60 + 84

32. 59 + 102 + 88 + 33

33. $9.99 + $18.50 + $31.57

34. 95 + 37 + 10

Solve.

35. Bobby collected 125 space figures. Joann collected 423 space figures. Jordan collected 57 space figures. How many space figures did they collect in all?

Solve each problem. Use the Infobank on pages 415–420 if you need additional facts.

1. Kansas produced 433 million bushels of wheat in 1985. Minnesota produced 142 million bushels of wheat in the same year. How many bushels did the two states produce in all?

2. Texas produced 187 million bushels of wheat in 1985. North Dakota produced even more. How many bushels of wheat were produced by both states in 1985?

3. In 1982, Oklahoma produced 228 million bushels of wheat. How much did Oklahoma produce in 1985? Write the difference between what Oklahoma produced in 1982 and what it produced in 1985.

4. Minnesota, Colorado, and Washington produced similar amounts of wheat. Which state produced the most? How much did the three states produce in all?

5. Glen and Bryant Ferris are planning a camping trip. Glen decides to buy his supplies from Explorer's Outfitters, Inc. Glen needs to buy a sleeping bag, knapsack, and flashlight. How much money will he spend?

6. Bryant Ferris plans to buy a compass, a canteen, and hiking boots from Explorer's Outfitters, Inc. He has $72.50. Does he have enough to buy these supplies? If he has money left over, write the amount.

7. Tillie is doing research on the winners of the women's 100-meter dash in the 1988 Olympics. She reads that Florence Griffith-Joyner won the gold medal. Evelyn Ashford won the silver medal. How much time separated the two winners?

8. The sum of the times of the three fastest runners in the women's 100-meter dash in the 1960 Olympics is 34.75 seconds. Is this sum greater than or less than the sum of the times of the 1988 winners? Write the difference between the two sums.

9. Whitney read that 4,514 people participated in a game of musical chairs in 1982. In 1988, how many more people participated in a game of musical chairs?

10. In 1982, David Scott set the world record for the most hours playing the piano. To the nearest hundred, how many hours did he play?

Subtract.

1.	229 − 196	2.	271 − 162	3.	359 − 43	4.	57 − 46	5.	$6.25 − 4.37
6.	61 − 26	7.	881 − 25	8.	95 − 49	9.	717 − 454	10.	$9.38 − 6.73
11.	439 − 112	12.	46 − 25	13.	84 − 27	14.	538 − 77	15.	$9.51 − 8.66

16. 162 − 51   17. 776 − 549   18. 49 − 31

19. 697 − 639   20. 79 − 36   21. 27 − 11

Use the following information to answer the questions.
Six students at Arrow School have stamp collections. Rita has
103 stamps, Frank has 62, Barry has 115, Julio has 77, Irene
has 54, and Sue has 93.

22. How many more stamps does Rita have than Irene?

23. How many more stamps does Sue have than Julio?

24. How many more stamps do Frank and Sue have together than
Barry?

Find the difference.

1. 8,462 − 6,311	**2.** $891.26 − 55.77	**3.** 177,640 − 172,999	**4.** 568,981 − 398,765	**5.** 876,064 − 391,009
6. 7,983 − 3,194	**7.** 171,725 − 49,836	**8.** 4,506 − 1,134	**9.** 842,172 − 531,185	**10.** $9,712.91 − 144.54
11. 9,763 − 985	**12.** 634,449 − 463,490	**13.** 79,442 − 1,693	**14.** 99,241 − 8,743	**15.** 666,666 − 135,782
16. 988,816 − 87,153	**17.** 9,931 − 3,778	**18.** 325,421 − 213,789	**19.** 125,575 − 100,989	**20.** 243,542 − 198,988
21. 679,222 − 51,325	**22.** 1,775 − 318	**23.** 43,725 − 5,839	**24.** $324.58 − 83.69	**25.** 457,274 − 381,989

26. 2,714 − 986

27. $6.43 − $3.78

28. 922 − 157

29. 6,270 − 3,150

30. $2.37 − $1.49

31. 478 − 289

Solve.

32. Mr. Sal Delmonico, a radio and TV salesperson, has sold items to about 35,390 people. He believes he has talked to 116,896 people in his career. How many more people has he talked to than he has sold to?

Find the difference.

1. 900,001 − 100,009	**2.** $100.50 − 29.58	**3.** 9,030 − 6,001	**4.** 4,001 − 3,002	**5.** 980,052 − 242,578

1. 900,001 − 100,009 **2.** $100.50 − 29.58 **3.** 9,030 − 6,001 **4.** 4,001 − 3,002 **5.** 980,052 − 242,578

6. 80,400 − 78,925 **7.** 1,102 − 594 **8.** 507,900 − 407,700 **9.** $410.06 − 329.24 **10.** 70,004 − 22,228

11. $40.03 − 19.01 **12.** $330.00 − 317.67 **13.** 103 − 77 **14.** 300,700 − 199,999 **15.** 601,010 − 573,467

16. 700,072 − 625,849 **17.** 107,008 − 99,889 **18.** $10.09 − 10.08 **19.** 806,502 − 512,321 **20.** 700,090 − 59,102

21. $90.08 − 16.94 **22.** 7,006 − 3,943 **23.** 702,003 − 225,679 **24.** 412,000 − 367,451 **25.** 1,090 − 564

26. 400 − 136 **27.** 600,543 − 317,624 **28.** $100.06 − 96.69 **29.** 58,001 − 42,828 **30.** 100,005 − 99,436

31. 954,000 − 621,311 **32.** 2,100 − 1,414

33. 200 − 108 **34.** 407 − 122

35. 26,034 − 14,785 **36.** 3,703 − 988

Solve.

37. Mrs. Johnson went to buy new school clothes for her daughter Sarah. She began with $125.00. When she finished her shopping, she had $18.51 left. How much had she spent shopping?

Write the letter of the operation that would solve the problem.

1. A herd of 31 antelope joined another herd of 27 antelope and formed a new herd. How large was this new herd?
   a. addition   b. subtraction

2. On the tundra, a herd of 48 caribou met another herd. They formed a new herd of 144. How many caribou were in the other herd?
   a. addition   b. subtraction

Choose the operation. Then solve.

3. A flock of 247 monarch butterflies migrated to the south. Of the 247, 133 headed toward Florida, and the rest headed toward Mexico. How many headed toward Mexico?

4. There was a school of 28 dolphins. One year, 8 dolphins were born. If none of the herd dies, how many dolphins will be in the school at the end of the year?

5. Of a school of 751 goldfish, 323 were captured and sold as pets. How many were left?

6. While traveling south, a flock of 23 snow geese stopped near a pond. While there, 4 of the geese stood guard while the others ate. How many geese ate?

7. Prairie dogs are rodents that live in large "cities" beneath the plains. One prairie-dog city had 4,000 prairie dogs. If 435 of them were above ground at one time, how many were below ground?

8. Each year, herds of wild horses swim from Chincoteague Island in Virginia to the mainland. If 504 horses of 2,800 made the swim one year, how many were left behind?

9. A pair of penguins took turns sitting on an egg. The male sat for a total of 396 hours. If the female sat for the same number of hours, how long did it take for the egg to hatch?

10. Another pair of penguins sat on an egg for 864 hours. For how many hours more than the other pair did this pair sit on their egg?

Write each as a decimal.

1.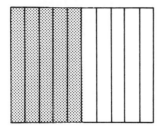

2.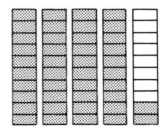

3.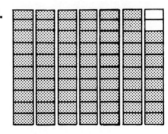

4. two and seven tenths

5. seven and two tenths

6. nine and four tenths

7. nine tenths

8. nineteen and nine tenths

9. ninety-nine and one tenth

Copy and complete this place-value chart. Write each decimal on the place-value chart.

10. 2.4   **11.** 0.3   **12.** 93.3

	Tens	Ones	Tenths
10.			
11.			
12.			

Write the word name for each decimal.

13. 0.5

14. 3.6

15. 10.4

16. 15.2

17. 8.7

18. 13.3

Solve.

19. The sailfish is a fast animal. In Florida, a sailfish was clocked at sixty-eight and one tenth mph. Write that number as a decimal.

20. The giant tortoise can only travel five yards in forty-three and five tenths seconds. Write that number as a decimal.

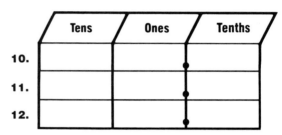

Write each as a decimal.

1.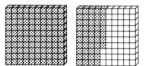

2.

3.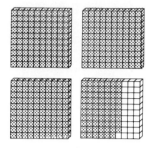

4. one and twenty-five hundredths

5. one hundred forty and eleven hundredths

6. sixty-one and eight hundredths

7. sixty-one hundredths

8. twelve and five hundredths

Write the word name for each number.

9. 6.83

10. 0.91

11. 405.64

12. 39.01

Use the figure at the right.

13. Write the decimal for the number of squares shaded in Figure X.

14. Write the decimal for the number of squares shaded in Figure Y.

15. Write the decimal for the number of squares shaded in Figure Y and Figure Z together.

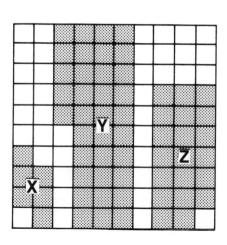

Write each as a decimal.

1. ten and three hundred five thousandths

2. ten and thirty-five thousandths

3. one and three hundred fifty-one thousandths

4. twelve thousandths

Write the word name for each decimal.

5. 76.016

6. 0.009

7. 5.803

8. 58.003

Write the value of the underlined digit.

9. 0.4<u>2</u>7

10. 6,214.<u>7</u>98

11. 16.09<u>1</u>

12. <u>3</u>.101

13. 5.6<u>7</u>1

14. 8,<u>6</u>90.352

15. 7.59<u>8</u>

16. 4,367.<u>0</u>51

Write the decimal. Complete the chart.

	Thousands	Hundreds	Tens	Ones	Tenths	Hundredths	Thousandths
17.	1	2	3	4	0	0	0
18.	0	0	2	2	3	1	0
19.	4	0	1	0	6	0	0
20.	0	0	0	0	4	1	5
21.	5	7	0	4	3	9	7
22.	0	3	9	1	9	7	8

Can you use the bar graph to answer these questions?

1. Which activity uses the most calories?

2. Which activity is the most popular?

Solve.

3. Are more calories burned while running or walking?

4. Lance ate 3 strawberries. They equaled 12.0 calories. Which activity could burn that number of calories in one minute?

5. About 10 string beans equal 7 calories. How many of these activities could burn that number of calories in less than one minute?

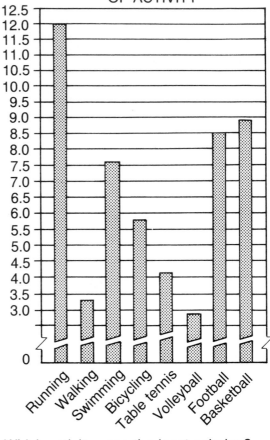

CALORIES USED PER MINUTE OF ACTIVITY

6. Which activity requires more calories, football or basketball?

7. Which activity uses the least calories?

8. How many calories does a game of table tennis burn per minute?

9. Which uses more calories, bicycling or swimming?

Compare. Write >, <, or = .

1. 0.259 ◯ 0.333

2. 0.33 ◯ 0.025

3. 0.16 ◯ 0.052

4. 0.6 ◯ 0.60

5. 0.093 ◯ 0.090

6. 2.013 ◯ 2.103

7. 6.07 ◯ 6.070

8. 1.56 ◯ 1.506

9. 2.1 ◯ 2.110

Write in order from the least to the greatest.

10. 0, 0.675, 0.009

11. 0.09, 0, 0.25

12. 0.057, 0.01, 0.052

13. 1.01, 2.41, 0.241

Write in order from the greatest to the least.

14. 0.055, 0.005, 0.55

15. 2.015, 2.51, 2.105

16. 6.14, 0.16, 0.64

17. 8.07, 8.083, 8.7

18. In order to find the honey, the bee must find its way to the smallest decimal in the honeycomb. Find the trail from the greatest to the least. Write the numbers of the honeycomb cells through which the bee must travel. Be sure to write the numbers in the correct order.

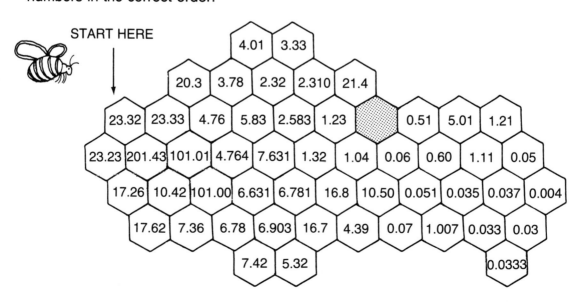

START HERE

Round to the nearest whole number.

1. 1.3

2. 13.725

3. 3.7

4. 21.82

5. 6.54

6. 72.271

7. 12.15

8. 3.4

9. 14.15

10. 5.13

11. 40.45

12. 18.447

13. 7.105

14. 7.501

15. 8.86

Round to the nearest tenth.

16. 40.101

17. 0.146

18. 2.044

19. 6.40

20. 6.405

21. 7.09

22. 0.251

23. 0.215

24. 2.457

25. 2.15

26. 26.39

27. 5.707

28. 23.029

29. 7.054

30. 8.349

Round to the nearest hundredth.

31. 2.222

32. 2.224

33. 0.205

34. 3.141

35. 3.145

36. 0.007

37. 0.526

38. 0.948

39. 0.692

40. 11.445

41. 8.234

42. 71.111

43. 29.009

44. 7.001

45. 0.003

Solve.

46. Keisha rode her bicycle 4.36 kilometers.
Round this number to the nearest tenth.

Estimate. Write =, >, or <.

1. 7.68 + 2.39 ◯ 9

2. 39.63 + 19.92 ◯ 60

3. 8.962 + 0.729 ◯ 10

4. 0.898 + 0.201 ◯ 1

5. 3.371 + 1.596 ◯ 6

6. 0.51 + 0.47 ◯ 1

7. 2.73 + 0.801 ◯ 3

8. 5.36 + 0.089 ◯ 6

9. 3.97 + 6.68 ◯ 10

10. 4.87 + 4.75 + 3.45 ◯ 15

11. 46.71 + 31.375 + 27.62 ◯ 100

12. 24.92 + 59.06 + 11.17 ◯ 90

Write the letter of the best estimate.

13. 4.68 + 5.83 + 6.77   **a.** 1,800   **b.** 15   **c.** 18

14. 2.98 + 2.65 + 0.89   **a.** 7   **b.** 70   **c.** 700

15. 9.76 + 7.65 + 6.96   **a.** 22   **b.** 30   **c.** 25

16. 7.67 + 3.89 + 2.08   **a.** 12   **b.** 14   **c.** 16

Estimate. Write =, >, or <.

17. 36.71 − 27.85 ◯ 10

18. 78.91 − 69.34 ◯ 9

19. 47.87 − 19.9 ◯ 30

20. 51.77 − 29.6 ◯ 20

21. 8.87 − 0.968 ◯ 7

22. 11.45 − 10.55 ◯ 1

23. 73.081 − 27.6 ◯ 50

24. 97.6 − 63.911 ◯ 30

25. 27.61 − 18.09 ◯ 10

Round to numbers that you can compute mentally.
Write the letter of the best mental estimate.

26. 51.7 − 27.92   **a.** 10   **b.** 20   **c.** 15

27. 76.63 − 35.089   **a.** 30   **b.** 40   **c.** 50

28. 69.71 − 57.8   **a.** 10   **b.** 20   **c.** 25

29. 47.89 − 12.98   **a.** 20   **b.** 30   **c.** 40

30. 81.59 − 27.62   **a.** 50   **b.** 60   **c.** 70

Solve. Explain why you would *overestimate* or *underestimate*.

1. Don needs to perform at least 24 hours of community service to earn his citizenship merit badge. Here is his record so far.
   Week 1: 3.2 hours   **Week 5:** 3.4 hours
   Week 2: 2.5 hours   **Week 6:** 5.6 hours
   Week 3: 5.2 hours   **Week 7:** 2.8 hours
   Week 4: 2.9 hours   **Week 8:** 2.1 hours
   Has Don earned his merit badge?

2. Jill is on the phone ordering the following items: scout manuals for $67.80; mess kits for $49.50; and day packs for $88.88. The troop has exactly $208. Do they have enough money to pay for Jill's order?

3. The troop is going to camp out at Rottinwood Camp. The camp has room for 120 scouts. If 22 scouts go from Company *A*, 44 scouts go from Company *B*, and 36 scouts go from Company *C*, will there be enough room at the camp?

4. Each scout must spend 90 hours in the wilderness to earn a camping merit badge. Here are some times for the first 3 outings.
   Tim: 11.2; 10.5; 30.9   Janie: 36.2; 20.7; 11.9
   Carol: 20.5; 31.6; 48.1   Biff: 31.8; 23.2; 40.4
   Scott: 24.9; 44.2; 51.3   Juanita: 30.5; 47.6; 30.8
   Which scouts have earned their merit badges?

5. Biff is making plaster casts of animal footprints. He has only enough equipment to make one cast at a time. It takes 3.2 hours for the plaster to dry in a bear print, 2.3 hours for it to dry in a raccoon print, and 1.2 hours for it to dry in a deer print. Will 9 hours be enough time to make all 3 casts?

Add. You may need to write equivalent decimals before adding.

1. 3.95
     + 0.350

2. 9.1
     + 4.90

3. 66.09
     + 5.099

4. 0.990
     + 7.119

5. 3.142
     + 27.008

6. 2.97
     + 0.97

7. $75.07
     + 9.99

8. $437.78
     + 6.45

9. 0.6
       0.7
     + 0.3

10. 1.5
        4.60
      + 3.63

11. 5.47
        0.08
      + 11.59

12. 9.463
        11.354
      + 15.789

13. 0.49
      + 0.56

14. $5.75
        2.47
      + 6.93

15. $45.36
        36.45
      + 17.71

16. 0.49
      + 0.38

17. 0.54
      + 7.38

18. $5.75
        3.82
      + 6.93

19. 6.42
        4.62
      + 2.46

20. $75.37
        11.55
      + 10.81

21. 4.27 + 0.55

22. 33.81 + 6.493

23. 1.08 + 4.35 + 3.87

24. 2.03 + 5.16 + 7.21

Add. Find the first digit of each sum below. Copy the riddle onto a separate sheet of paper. Write the letter above the digit to solve the riddle.

25. 3.62
      + 4.185
             = H

26. 763.2
      + 49.8
             = N

27. 0.887
      + 9.023
             = A

28. 54.128
      + 3.2
             = T

29. 32.661
      + 33.101
             = G

30. 29.26
      + 16.98
             = I

31. 22.436
      + 187.3
             = O

32. 99.999
      + 1.001
             = W

What state name sounds like a lot of laundry?

?	?	S	H	?	?	?	?	?	?
1	9		7	4	8	6	5	2	8

Use with pages 60–61.

Subtract. You may need to write an equivalent decimal before subtracting.

1. 0.2
− 0.19

2. 81.08
− 78.17

3. 91.17
− 4.29

4. 9.16
− 8.25

5. $7.45
− 5.65

6. 53.56
− 47.90

7. 76.70
− 67.80

8. 34.02
− 5.89

9. $65.71
− 4.65

10. 13.00
− 9.36

11. $76.57
− 39.24

12. 8.69
− 5.24

13. 34.7
− 16.83

14. 101.06
− 100.98

15. 135.86
− 32.45

16. 0.57
− 0.06

17. 0.71
− 0.66

18. 1.09
− 0.38

19. $2.00
− 1.23

20. 43.80
− 4.99

21. $13.03
− 4.67

22. $64.00
− 15.07

23. 79.00
− 0.43

24. $53.99
− 30.79

25. $67.89
− 0.24

26. 6.02 − 6.00

27. 120.78 − 94.96

28. 18.17 − 9.29

29. 0.5 − 0.28

30. 0.93 − 0.07

31. 3.14 − 1.99

32. 16.61 − 11.91

33. 7.05 − 4.01

Solve.

34. A bird's flying speed was measured at 106.25 mph in the U.S.S.R. Another bird in India was recorded at a speed of 171.8 mph. Which country had the faster bird and by how much?

35. The fastest racehorse was recorded at a speed of 43.26 mph. Round this speed to the nearest tenth, and then to the nearest whole number.

Write the letter of the correct answer.

1. A roll of 24-exposure color print film costs $2.60. A 36-exposure roll costs $1.80 more. How much does the 36-exposure roll cost?
   a. $n = \$1.80 + \$2.60$
   b. $n = \$2.60 - \$1.80$

2. Wallet-size reprints cost $0.30 each, and large prints cost $3.75 each. Sally orders one of each. How much does she spend?
   a. $n = \$3.75 - \$0.30$
   b. $n = \$3.75 + \$0.30$

Write an equation. Then solve.

3. Pepe bought a roll of 36-exposure color print film for $3.68. The film costs $7.75 to develop. How much did Pepe spend in all?

4. Film for 36 color slides costs $5.69. Developing the film costs $4.75. If Lulu has $11.00, will she have enough to buy the film and have it developed?

5. A 20-exposure roll of color print film costs $4.75 to develop. The same size roll of color slides costs $1.80 less to develop. How much does it cost to develop a 20-exposure roll of slides?

6. Edna found an old photo of her grandparents. She had it enlarged and framed at a cost of $14.70. She also had 2 wallet-size reprints made at a cost of $0.75 each. How much did Edna spend?

7. Jody is sending away the 2 rolls of film she shot on her vacation to be developed. Each roll costs $3.25 to be developed. For what amount should Jody make out her check?

8. Zoe took some photographs of the Greek Festival for *The Journal*. The newspaper paid her $60.00 for them. Zoe's expenses came to $26.30. What was Zoe's profit?

9. Arnold took a picture of each of his classmates and one of the teacher. He found a lab that charged $12.75 for developing and printing his roll of film. The shipping charge was $1.25. How much money will Arnold need?

10. Al had a photo of his puppy enlarged at a cost of $11.95. The tax came to $0.94. He paid with a 20-dollar bill. How much change did Al get?

Use the Associative Property to find the products.

1. $2 \times (50 \times 8)$

2. $(7 \times 25) \times 4$

3. $2 \times (500 \times 6)$

4. $(6 \times 25) \times 4$

5. $2 \times (40 \times 8)$

6. $(8 \times 20) \times 5$

7. $(6 \times 30) \times 3$

8. $10 \times (60 \times 7)$

9. $(4 \times 8) \times 25$

Complete.

10. $5 \times 4 = \underline{\ ?\ } \times 5$

11. $(2 \times 3) \times \underline{\ ?\ } = 2 \times (3 \times 6)$

12. $7 \times \underline{\ ?\ } = 7$

13. $6 \times (5 + 8) = (6 \times \underline{\ ?\ }) + (6 \times 8)$

14. $3 \times 7 \times 5 = \underline{\ ?\ } \times 5 \times 7$

15. $9 \times 5 = 5 \times \underline{\ ?\ }$

16. $8 \times \underline{\ ?\ } = 0$

17. $2 \times (7 + 6) = (\underline{\ ?\ } \times 7) + (2 \times 6)$

18. $4 \times 3 \times 2 = \underline{\ ?\ }$

19. $9 \times 0 = \underline{\ ?\ }$

20. $1 \times 6 = \underline{\ ?\ }$

21. $(4 \times 2) \times 5 = \underline{\ ?\ }$

22. $5 \times (5 \times 4) = \underline{\ ?\ }$

23. $3 \times (5 \times 2) = \underline{\ ?\ }$

Complete. Write the name of the property.

24. $6 \times (4 + 7) = (6 \times 4) + (\underline{\ ?\ } \times \underline{\ ?\ })$

25. $5 \times (3 + 4) = 15 + \underline{\ ?\ }$

26. $(2 \times 4) \times 2 = 2 \times (\underline{\ ?\ } \times 2)$

27. $3 \times 4 \times 7 = 3 \times \underline{\ ?\ } \times 4$

28. $(1 \times 9) \times 6 = 1 \times (9 \times \underline{\ ?\ })$

Solve.

29. Stephanie has a pen pal in India and another in Italy. If she receives 3 letters per year from each pen pal, how many letters will she receive in 3 years?

30. Stephanie's Italian pen pal telephones her every year on her birthday. If they talk for 8 minutes per call, how many minutes will they talk over 5 years?

Multiply.

1. 10 × 6	**2.** 30 × 4	**3.** 1,000 × 10	**4.** 200 × 2	**5.** 60 × 7
6. 2,000 × 30	**7.** 10 × 8	**8.** 100 × 9	**9.** 5,000 × 40	**10.** 70 × 5
11. 10 × 7	**12.** 8,000 × 30	**13.** 6,000 × 20	**14.** 800 × 800	**15.** 40 × 7
16. 9,000 × 40	**17.** 60 × 6	**18.** 4,000 × 70	**19.** 5,000 × 90	**20.** 3,000 × 20

21. 70 × 3,000

22. 500 × 500

23. 8 × 60

24. 4 × 4,000

25. 9 × 80

26. 2 × 1,000

Multiply. Copy the riddle on a separate sheet of paper. Then match the letters to solve.

27. 1,000 × 9 = M	**28.** 7,000 × 50 = T	**29.** 30,000 × 20 = N	**30.** 800 × 5 = P	**31.** 4,000 × 6 = Y
32. 60 × 9 = A	**33.** 9,000 × 9 = K	**34.** 4,000 × 70 = I	**35.** 1,000 × 10 = S	**36.** 10 × 80 = E

What do you say when you order turtle soup?

$\dfrac{?}{9,000}$ $\dfrac{?}{540}$ $\dfrac{?}{81,000}$ $\dfrac{?}{800}$ $\quad$ $\dfrac{?}{280,000}$ $\dfrac{?}{350,000}$ $\qquad$ $\dfrac{?}{10,000}$ $\dfrac{?}{600,000}$ $\dfrac{?}{540}$ $\dfrac{?}{4,000}$ $\dfrac{?}{4,000}$ $\dfrac{?}{24,000}$

Without finding the exact answer, write the letter of the answer that is reasonable.

1. Allie plays guitar in a group called the Squealers. The group also includes a drummer, a bass player, a pianist, a singer, and one other guitarist. How many members are there in the band?
   a. 2   b. 6   c. 20

2. Each member of the Squealers received $20 for playing at the county fair. How much did the entire band earn at the county fair?
   a. $20   b. $120   c. $1,200

3. Allie bought 10 blank tapes to record the band's music. If each tape cost $2.00, how much did she spend?
   a. $20.00   b. $2.00   c. $200.00

4. The Squealers went on a nationwide tour. They went to 30 cities. They played an average of 3 shows in each city. About how many shows did they play in all?
   a. 9   b. 90   c. 600

5. On their tour, the group spent 3 days in each of 30 cities. How many days did their tour last?
   a. 30 days
   b. 90 days
   c. 365 days

6. The Squealers earned a total of $20,750 on their tour. They spent $3,246 on expenses. How much money did they make in profit?
   a. $17,504
   b. $1,750.40
   c. $24,000

7. The group played in a school auditorium. There were 60 rows of seats and 100 seats in each row. Every seat was taken. How many people came to the concert?
   a. 60   b. 6,000   c. 600

8. One day the Squealers gave a free concert in the park. Each of the 6 members of the group put up 100 posters advertising the concert. How many posters did they put up all together?
   a. 60   b. 6,000   c. 600

9. The Squealers recorded an album on tape. It had 10 songs that lasted 3 minutes each. How long was the tape?
   a. 30 minutes
   b. 90 minutes
   c. 300 minutes

10. The group wanted 10 copies of the tape to send to 10 local radio stations. How many copies did they need?
    a. 10
    b. 60
    c. 100

Estimate.

1. 301
    × 19

2. 37
    × 29

3. $7.17
    × 9

4. 532
    × 73

5. 41
    × 21

6. 54
    × 13

7. $9.06
    × 9

8. 48
    × 11

9. 212
    × 82

10. 33
     × 14

11. 62
     × 13

12. $5.88
     × 8

13. 481
     × 39

14. 86
     × 49

15. 952
     × 81

16. $8.15
     × 2

17. 417
     × 72

18. 594
     × 38

19. 63
     × 29

20. 74
     × 18

21. $7.05
     × 7

22. 366
     × 89

23. 67
     × 12

24. 875
     × 75

25. 99
     × 41

26. 28
     × 36

27. 603
     × 25

28. $1.15
     × 6

29. 851
     × 36

30. $4.44
     × 3

31. 39 × 89

32. 22 × $9.16

33. 95 × 266

34. 13 × 184

35. 58 × 364

36. 47 × 333

Estimate.

37. Every day, Jeremy crosses the Silver Gate Bridge 4 times. He crosses once to go to school, once to go home for lunch, once to go back to school, and once to return home. If Jeremy goes to school 186 days in a year, about how many times does he cross the bridge?

38. When Jeremy arrives at school, he and his friend Carlos exercise before class begins. If together they do a total of 30 jumping jacks, about how many exercises do they do each year? HINT: There are 186 school days.

Solve. Find an estimate or an exact answer as needed.

1. Marvin needs to raise $500 to repair the wall to the racoon display at his game farm. The admission fee to the farm is $1.75. If 295 people visit the farm during the week, will Marvin earn enough money to repair the wall?

2. The local zoo covers 1,043 acres. The state park nearby is almost 4 times as large as the zoo. About how large is the state park?

3. The members of the Zoo Club want to buy three books about some of the animals they saw during their last trip to the zoo. They have exactly $17.50 in their budget to spend on books.

   The cost of each book is:

   Bats by Night $5.23
   Hungry Hippos $3.79
   Lions Live $9.58

   Do they have enough money?

4. The Zoo Club also has $185 to spend on new t-shirts. There are 25 members in the club. The t-shirts cost $6.95 each. Does the club have enough money to buy each member a new t-shirt?

Multiply.

1.	31	2.	151	3.	563	4.	$0.34	5.	307
	× 9		× 4		× 4		× 8		× 5

6.	$3.46	7.	789	8.	50	9.	93	10.	36
	× 2		× 3		× 6		× 5		× 6

11.	819	12.	53	13.	117	14.	648	15.	$5.40
	× 4		× 6		× 3		× 9		× 3

16.	68	17.	$7.10	18.	353	19.	44	20.	254
	× 9		× 2		× 4		× 5		× 3

21. 6 × 32

22. 4 × 601

23. 5 × $2.50

24. 2 × $10.20

25. 7 × 17

26. 3 × 48

27. 8 × 64

28. 9 × $1.83

29. 7 × 211

Multiply.

Help Juanita find her dog. Find your answers on the map.
Then make a list of the places the dog visited.

30.	81	31.	43	32.	191	33.	388	34.	817	35.	749
	× 7		× 9		× 5		× 6		× 4		× 8

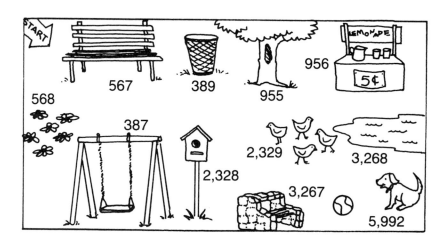

Multiply. Estimate to check your answer.

1. 2,340
    × 3

2. $62.51
    × 4

3. 5,928
    × 7

4. 1,598
    × 2

5. 12,067
    × 5

6. 4,789
    × 8

7. 7,234
    × 8

8. 9,560
    × 3

9. $85.21
    × 4

10. 5,344
    × 6

11. $26.98
    × 9

12. 15,300
    × 2

13. 1,351
    × 9

14. 6,205
    × 3

15. 3,482
    × 5

16. 24,059
    × 3

17. 7,846
    × 7

18. $52.83
    × 6

19. 4,763
    × 4

20. 9,368
    × 2

21. 5 × 8,650

22. 3 × 22,121

23. 4 × $97.14

24. 2 × 13,053

25. 7 × 5,822

26. 6 × $46.79

Solve.

27. Captain Juarez has been the skipper of the ferryboat *Isabelle* for 6 years. If he averages 3,550 trips a year across Wellington Sound, how many trips has he made during his 6 years as skipper?

28. During that period, the *Isabelle* carried about 15,820 people and about 11,915 cars per year. How many people did the ship carry during Captain Juarez's time as skipper? How many cars?

Estimation	Writing a Number Sentence
Choosing the Operation	Checking for a Reasonable Answer

Write the strategy or method you choose. Then solve.

1. Jill is making a box kite and two delta kites. She needs 8 sticks for each box kite and 2 sticks for each delta kite. How many sticks does she need in all?

2. Jeff has a piece of string 42 inches long. He uses 36 inches to make a kite tail. How many inches of string does he have left?

3. Jill has 4 feet of red paper, 5 feet of blue paper, and 8 feet of yellow paper for making kites. How many feet of paper does she have in all?

4. Jeff wants to buy a box kite that costs $4.29, a ball of string that costs $1.50, and a delta kite that costs $2.95. About how much will Jeff spend?

5. Jill bought 2 box kites for $2.69 each and a flat kite for $3.25. How much did she spend for the kites?

6. A kite store has 6 boxes of string. Each box has 25 balls of string in it. How many balls of string are there in all?

7. Jeff is making 3 kites. One is 42 inches long, another is 36 inches long, and the third is 38 inches long. About how many inches long would all three kites be if Jeff measured them from end to end?

8. Alfie bought a kite for each of his 4 nephews. The kites were $3.80 each. How much did Alfie spend on the kites?

Use with page 90.

| Estimation | Acting It Out | Writing a Number Sentence |
| Choosing the Operation | Making a Model | Checking for a Reasonable Answer |

Write the strategy or method you choose. Then solve.

1. Jill buys paper and string for $6.75 to make kites. She pays with a $10 bill. How much change does she get?

2. Tom and Nicky go to the hobby shop and buy paper for $1.50, string for $0.75, and glue for $0.80. How much change do they receive from $5.00?

3. Louise buys 5 ribbons for her kite tail. Each ribbon costs $0.22. About how much money does she spend on the ribbon?

4. Jennifer went to the store and bought kites for her 6 cousins. Each kite cost $2.70. How much money did she spend?

5. Mark tangled his kite in a tree and spent $1.40 for glue and $2.60 for tape to fix the kite. He paid for the items with $5.00. What was his change?

6. Elspeth made a Japanese dragon kite. She spent $7.30 on paper, $5.10 on silk ribbons, $0.75 on glue, and $2.41 on glitter and sequins. About how much did she spend?

7. Christina decided to make a delta kite. The kite was 3 feet long, and the tail was 8 feet long. What was the total length of the kite and tail?

8. Judy bought a kite for $4.50 and string for $1.25. She paid with a $10 bill and received $3.25 as change. Judy went back to the cashier to explain the mistake. What was the mistake?

9. Richard bought a box kite for $6.15 and a flat kite for $4.45. Was his total bill closer to $10 or to $15?

10. Tom is making 4 kites. He needs 3 sheets of paper for each kite. How many sheets of paper does he need in all?

Multiply.

1. $\begin{array}{r} 61 \\ \times\ 10 \\ \hline \end{array}$

2. $\begin{array}{r} 137 \\ \times\ 35 \\ \hline \end{array}$

3. $\begin{array}{r} \$27.46 \\ \times\ \ \ \ 14 \\ \hline \end{array}$

4. $\begin{array}{r} 289 \\ \times\ 27 \\ \hline \end{array}$

5. $\begin{array}{r} 8,100 \\ \times\ \ \ \ 30 \\ \hline \end{array}$

6. $\begin{array}{r} \$35.28 \\ \times\ \ \ \ 46 \\ \hline \end{array}$

7. $\begin{array}{r} 47 \\ \times\ 80 \\ \hline \end{array}$

8. $\begin{array}{r} 511 \\ \times\ 33 \\ \hline \end{array}$

9. $\begin{array}{r} 749 \\ \times\ 25 \\ \hline \end{array}$

10. $\begin{array}{r} 1,678 \\ \times\ \ \ \ 69 \\ \hline \end{array}$

11. $\begin{array}{r} 2,022 \\ \times\ \ \ \ 50 \\ \hline \end{array}$

12. $\begin{array}{r} 94 \\ \times\ 11 \\ \hline \end{array}$

13. $\begin{array}{r} 310 \\ \times\ 20 \\ \hline \end{array}$

14. $\begin{array}{r} \$85.16 \\ \times\ \ \ \ 47 \\ \hline \end{array}$

15. $\begin{array}{r} 509 \\ \times\ 73 \\ \hline \end{array}$

16. $\begin{array}{r} 87 \\ \times\ 19 \\ \hline \end{array}$

17. $\begin{array}{r} 923 \\ \times\ 40 \\ \hline \end{array}$

18. $\begin{array}{r} 3,187 \\ \times\ \ \ \ 36 \\ \hline \end{array}$

19. $\begin{array}{r} \$56.41 \\ \times\ \ \ \ 50 \\ \hline \end{array}$

20. $\begin{array}{r} \$67.99 \\ \times\ \ \ \ 43 \\ \hline \end{array}$

21. $25 \times 7,654$

22. $90 \times \$87.33$

23. $17 \times 9,113$

24. $81 \times 4,555$

25. $96 \times 1,036$

26. 70×306

27. $13 \times 5,939$

28. $43 \times 7,026$

Multiply.

29. $\begin{array}{r} 1,241 \\ \times\ \ \ \ 37 \\ \hline \end{array}$

30. $\begin{array}{r} 304 \\ \times\ 99 \\ \hline \end{array}$

31. $\begin{array}{r} 5,028 \\ \times\ \ \ \ 74 \\ \hline \end{array}$

32. $\begin{array}{r} 4,512 \\ \times\ \ \ \ 17 \\ \hline \end{array}$

33. $\begin{array}{r} 1,476 \\ \times\ \ \ \ 34 \\ \hline \end{array}$

34. $\begin{array}{r} 82 \\ \times\ 19 \\ \hline \end{array}$

35. $\begin{array}{r} 3,594 \\ \times\ \ \ \ 27 \\ \hline \end{array}$

36. $\begin{array}{r} 932 \\ \times\ 64 \\ \hline \end{array}$

37. $\begin{array}{r} 946 \\ \times\ 73 \\ \hline \end{array}$

38. $\begin{array}{r} 2,086 \\ \times\ \ \ \ 45 \\ \hline \end{array}$

Multiply.

1. 562
   × 349

2. 197
   × 200

3. 843
   × 656

4. $9.72
   × 498

5. 235
   × 176

6. $8.64
   × 973

7. 621
   × 517

8. 743
   × 459

9. 253
   × 186

10. 346
    × 300

11. 472
    × 931

12. 869
    × 500

13. $7.42
    × 610

14. 596
    × 372

15. 260
    × 418

16. 563
    × 927

17. $7.99
    × 683

18. 348
    × 297

19. 900
    × 193

20. 426
    × 317

21. 718 × 569

22. 201 × 462

23. 537 × $6.28

24. 343 × $1.58

25. 985 × 611

26. 257 × 316

27. 306 × 719

28. 634 × 811

Solve.

29. The novelist who has written the most books is Kathleen Lindsey. Each of her books is about 278 pages long and has about 117 words per page. About how many words does each book contain?

30. About how many total pages were there in her 904 novels?

Complete the plan by writing the missing step.

1. The Sioux Indians lived on the Great Plains. One day, a Sioux tribe sent out 7 parties to gather food. If each party contained four smaller groups of five Indians each, then how many Indians went on the expedition?
Step 1: Find out how many Indians were in each party.

Step 2:

2. One Sioux village had 17 tipis. Ten of them were small tipis that housed 2 people in each. The others were large tipis that housed three people in each. How many people lived in the village?
Step 1:

Step 2: Find the sum of the people living in small and large tipis.

Make a plan. Then solve.

3. Tipis were made of buffalo hide. Each small tipi was made of 4 buffalo hides. Each large tipi was made of 8 hides. In Small Foot Village, there were 14 large tipis and one small tipi. How many buffalo hides were used to make all the tipis in the village?

4. Araho Village had 20 tipis, each of which housed 2 villagers. If each villager owned two ponchos, then how many ponchos were there in the village?

5. Winter was coming soon, and so the villagers started to make winter coats. There were 12 adults and 6 children who needed coats. One buffalo hide was used to make 3 children's coats or 2 adults' coats. How many hides were needed?

6. Ten villagers traveled to their winter campsite. They brought 14 horses along. Each villager rode his or her own horse, and the remaining horses were used to carry supplies. If each horse carried 172 pounds, how many pounds of supplies did the villagers bring?

7. Presley goes to the American Indian College of Art in New Mexico. In his first year, Presley did 3 paintings on buffalo hide, 6 on canvas, and the rest on paper. If he did 18 pieces of work, how many did he paint on paper?

8. Presley went to visit his 3 younger brothers on the reservation. He brought each of them 5 packs of baseball cards as a present. If each pack cost $0.25, how much money did Presley spend?

Use with pages 96–97.

Estimate. Write > or <.

1. 3.7 × 42.1 ◯ 120

2. 9.13 × $1.62 ◯ $14

3. 5.6 × 3.2 ◯ 20

4. 3.69 × 1.35 ◯ 6

5. 4.3 × $8.75 ◯ $40

6. 2.4 × 8.9 ◯ 16

7. 7.6 × $24.50 ◯ $200

8. 1.3 × 3.2 ◯ 3

9. 6.11 × 8.42 ◯ 48

10. 2.7 × 43.62 ◯ 100

11. 6.8 × $5.24 ◯ $40

12. 3.8 × 7.7 ◯ 32

Estimate.

13. 34.72
    × 6.3

14. $6.65
    × 4.1

15. 7.5
    × 3.6

16. 46.7
    × 1.15

17. 2.6
    × 5.3

18. 10.31
    × 2.2

19. 5.94
    × 7.9

20. $32.89
    × 7.3

21. 23.9
    × 11.1

22. 52.35
    × 4.8

23. 7.3
    × 4.5

24. $6.13
    × 5.78

Estimate.

25. Cal Cool usually uses 83.8 kilowatt-hours of electricity each month. After he bought an air conditioner, he estimated his use would be 1.4 times as great. Did he expect to use more or less than 168 killowatt-hours per month?

26. Hal Heater's average monthly electric bill during the summer is $38.95. He uses 1.8 times as much electricity during the winter. Is his average monthly bill in winter more or less than $70?

Work backward to solve the problems. Make a flowchart if you need to. Work forward to check your answers.

1. In a summer reading program, Cathy Stuart read 14 more short stories than her sister Denise, and Denise read 8 fewer than her brother Ron. Ron read 53 short stories. How many short stories did Cathy read?

2. Rachel, Tim, Ralph, and Elena went on a fishing trip. Rachel caught 4 more fish than Ralph, but 6 less than Tim. Elena caught 11 more fish than Tim. Ralph caught 10 fish. How many fish did Elena catch?

3. Nina and her friends spent a Saturday picking up aluminum cans for recycling. Nina picked up 9 fewer cans than Todd. Todd picked up 4 more than Gonzalo. If Gonzalo picked up 46 cans, how many cans did Nina pick up?

4. On the first day of school, Ms. Garner told her class to write an essay about their summer vacations. Kris's essay was 3 paragraphs longer than Bob's. Lauren's essay was 8 paragraphs shorter than Kris's. If Bob's essay was 15 paragraphs long, how long was Lauren's essay?

5. Phil, Eric, and Jilda picked the oranges from the trees in Phil's back yard. Phil picked 32 oranges. Eric picked twice as many as Jilda. Jilda picked 17 fewer oranges than Phil. How many oranges did Eric pick?

6. The Pembrook County Fair had a 15-minute walnut-shelling contest. Patty shelled 22 more walnuts than Jerry. Steve shelled 19 less than Patty. Jerry shelled 38 walnuts. How many walnuts did Steve shell?

7. Three farmers planted wheat in their fields. Mr. Whitney planted 5 acres fewer than Mr. Inez. Mrs. Reilly planted 12 more acres than Mr. Whitney. Mr. Inez planted 44 acres of wheat. How many acres of wheat did Mrs. Reilly plant?

8. Roger baked a batch of peanut butter cookies. He ate 4 of them while they were still warm from the oven. His little sister and brother together ate 12 more while the cookies were cooling. That night, the family ate 15 peanut butter cookies, but there were still 6 left. How many cookies did Roger bake?

Multiply.

1. 7.4 × 4

2. 3.8 × 2

3. 0.01 × 26

4. 43 × 3.4

5. 758 × 0.79

6. $0.06 × 117

7. $6.70 × 49

8. 0.333 × 9

9. 114 × 0.005

10.
$$\begin{array}{r} 5.12 \\ \times\ \ \ 33 \\ \hline \end{array}$$

11.
$$\begin{array}{r} 0.04 \\ \times\ \ \ 16 \\ \hline \end{array}$$

12.
$$\begin{array}{r} 0.12 \\ \times\ \ \ 88 \\ \hline \end{array}$$

13.
$$\begin{array}{r} 0.19 \\ \times\ \ 459 \\ \hline \end{array}$$

14.
$$\begin{array}{r} 39 \\ \times\ 0.01 \\ \hline \end{array}$$

15.
$$\begin{array}{r} 26 \\ \times\ 0.05 \\ \hline \end{array}$$

16.
$$\begin{array}{r} \$6.74 \\ \times\ \ \ 13 \\ \hline \end{array}$$

17.
$$\begin{array}{r} 831 \\ \times\ 0.041 \\ \hline \end{array}$$

18.
$$\begin{array}{r} 3.91 \\ \times\ \ \ 47 \\ \hline \end{array}$$

19.
$$\begin{array}{r} 0.006 \\ \times\ \ \ \ 89 \\ \hline \end{array}$$

20.
$$\begin{array}{r} 0.109 \\ \times\ \ \ \ 99 \\ \hline \end{array}$$

21.
$$\begin{array}{r} 5.656 \\ \times\ \ \ \ 31 \\ \hline \end{array}$$

Multiply. Then copy the letter for each product on a separate sheet of paper.

22.
$$\begin{array}{r} 57.333 \\ \times\ \ \ \ 24 \\ \hline \end{array}$$
O

23.
$$\begin{array}{r} 722.999 \\ \times\ \ \ \ \ 48 \\ \hline \end{array}$$
O

24.
$$\begin{array}{r} \$42.98 \\ \times\ \ \ \ 611 \\ \hline \end{array}$$
W

25.
$$\begin{array}{r} 563.253 \\ \times\ \ \ \ \ 20 \\ \hline \end{array}$$
D

26.
$$\begin{array}{r} \$24.07 \\ \times\ \ \ \ 561 \\ \hline \end{array}$$
R

27.
$$\begin{array}{r} \$949.24 \\ \times\ \ \ \ \ 66 \\ \hline \end{array}$$
O

28.
$$\begin{array}{r} 796.678 \\ \times\ \ \ \ \ 32 \\ \hline \end{array}$$
G

29.
$$\begin{array}{r} \$1,000.64 \\ \times\ \ \ \ \ \ 23 \\ \hline \end{array}$$
K

$$\frac{\ \ \ ?\ \ \ }{25{,}493.696}$$

$$\frac{\ \ \ ?\ \ \ }{1{,}375.992}$$

$$\frac{\ \ \ ?\ \ \ }{34{,}703.952}$$

$$\frac{\ \ \ ?\ \ \ }{11{,}265.06}$$

$$\frac{\ \ \ ?\ \ \ }{\$26{,}260.78}$$

$$\frac{\ \ \ ?\ \ \ }{\$62{,}649.84}$$

$$\frac{\ \ \ ?\ \ \ }{\$13{,}503.27}$$

$$\frac{\ \ \ ?\ \ \ }{\$23{,}014.72}$$!!

Make an organized list. Solve.

1. Al, Bob, Carlos, and Doug enter the boy's junior division of the tennis tournament. Each boy will be matched against each other boy only once. How many matches will there be?

2. Fay, Graciela, Helen, Roy, Sam, and Ted buy box seats for the tournament. There are 3 rows of 2 seats each in the box. Each girl sits next to a boy. How many possible boy-girl pairs are there?

3. At the end of the tournament, trophies are given out for the first-place, second-place and third-place winners in each division. There are 8 divisions in all. How many trophies are awarded?

4. On the third day of the tournament, four matches are played. Joe has enough money to purchase tickets to 3 of the matches. From how many possible combinations of matches can Joe choose?

5. In the semifinals of the Girls' Junior Division, Lea plays Mindy and Nan plays Olga. The winners of those matches will play each other in the finals. How many possible combinations of players could there be for the finals?

6. As soon as one player wins 3 sets in the final match of the tennis tournament, that player is declared the winner. There can be 5 sets at most in the final match. How many different ways can the tournament final be won?

Make an organized list. Solve.

7. There are 4 juice stands on the tournament grounds. Karl, Leroy, Melanie, Norma, and Paula take turns selling juice. How many possible combinations of juice sellers are there? On the last day of the tournament, Karl stays home. How many possible combinations of sellers are there on that day?

8. There are 3 souvenir stands on the tournament grounds. Kim, Stanley, Monica, Judy, Cindy, and Bill work at the stands in pairs. How many possible pairs are there? The souvenir stands are such a success that two stands are added. One person works in each stand. How many possible combinations of workers are there then?

9. Four trophies will be awarded after the tournament. There are 6 semifinalists. How many possible combinations of winners can there be? How many if there are only 4 semifinalists?

10. Ann, Bill, Cindy, Dan, Ed, and Fay are in the elimination round. There can be only two winners, one girl and one boy. How many possible pairs of winners can there be? How many possible pairs would there be if Fay were eliminated?

Multiply.

1. 4.3
  × 0.7

2. 0.84
  × 0.6

3. 1.9
  × 0.52

4. 32.95
  ×   0.8

5. 11.7
  × 2.2

6. 0.56
  × 0.4

7. 0.99
  × 0.9

8. 0.5
  × 0.37

9. 24.13
  ×   0.7

10. 8.1
  × 0.65

11. 0.77
  × 2.3

12. 0.8
  × 0.09

13. 21.12
  ×   0.3

14. 0.53
  × 8.2

15. 4.65
  × 0.5

16. 0.4×0.97

17. 0.39×5.2

18. 0.28×14.4

Multiply. Round the product to the nearest cent.

19. $0.47
  ×   0.9

20. $35.79
  ×   0.3

21. $6.82
  ×   0.5

22. $51.98
  ×   0.6

23. $7.23
  ×   0.4

Solve.

24. The Holts use an average of 287.9 kilowatt-hours of electricity each month during the winter. During the summer, they use 1.5 times as much electricity each month. What is their summer monthly average number of kilowatt-hours?

25. The Fongs used 184.7 kilowatt-hours of electricity in April. If they pay $0.66 per kilowatt-hour, how much was their April bill to the nearest cent?

Multiply.

1. 5.7 × 0.63

2. 8 × $0.01

3. $0.05 × 0.6

4. 0.6 × 0.6

5. 0.09 × 35.5

6. 0.93 × 0.05

7. $0.71 × 4

8. 7.5 × 0.09

9. 20 × 0.63

10. $8.50 × 32

11.
$$\begin{array}{r} 0.08 \\ \times\ 9.8 \\ \hline \end{array}$$

12.
$$\begin{array}{r} \$2.64 \\ \times\ \ \ 12 \\ \hline \end{array}$$

13.
$$\begin{array}{r} 0.69 \\ \times\ 3.2 \\ \hline \end{array}$$

14.
$$\begin{array}{r} 0.97 \\ \times\ 0.6 \\ \hline \end{array}$$

15.
$$\begin{array}{r} 0.15 \\ \times\ 0.3 \\ \hline \end{array}$$

16.
$$\begin{array}{r} 0.9 \\ \times\ 0 \\ \hline \end{array}$$

17.
$$\begin{array}{r} 0.721 \\ \times\ \ \ 89 \\ \hline \end{array}$$

18.
$$\begin{array}{r} 0.863 \\ \times\ \ \ 13 \\ \hline \end{array}$$

19.
$$\begin{array}{r} 0.004 \\ \times\ \ 100 \\ \hline \end{array}$$

20.
$$\begin{array}{r} 0.115 \\ \times\ 1,000 \\ \hline \end{array}$$

21.
$$\begin{array}{r} 0.678 \\ \times\ \ 800 \\ \hline \end{array}$$

22.
$$\begin{array}{r} 0.234 \\ \times\ \ 144 \\ \hline \end{array}$$

23.
$$\begin{array}{r} 0.78 \\ \times\ 0.7 \\ \hline \end{array}$$

24.
$$\begin{array}{r} 1.52 \\ \times\ 0.3 \\ \hline \end{array}$$

25.
$$\begin{array}{r} 0.219 \\ \times\ \ \ 2 \\ \hline \end{array}$$

26.
$$\begin{array}{r} 1.46 \\ \times\ 0.2 \\ \hline \end{array}$$

Solve.

27. Carol can ride her bike 7.5 miles in 1 hour. At that rate, how many miles can she travel in 3.25 hours?

28. Gary's car can travel 24.7 miles on a gallon of gas. How many miles can the car travel on 5.4 gallons?

29. Emil's famous chef's salad recipe calls for 2.5 cups of shredded cheese. If Emil triples the recipe, how many cups of shredded cheese would he need?

30. One inch equals about 2.54 centimeters. How many centimeters are in 7.25 inches?

Choose the information you would need to be able to solve each problem. Write the letter of the correct answer.

1. While playing tennis for one hour, a person burns up 438 calories. How many more calories would a person burn while running for an hour?
   a. distance a person runs
   b. calorie intake
   c. calories burned while running

2. While doing strenuous work such as digging, a person breathes 5 times as often per minute as he or she does while resting. How many more breaths per minute is that?
   a. breaths per minute while resting
   b. breaths per minute while digging
   c. both a and b

Solve. If there is not enough information, write what information you would need.

3. In 1982, Americans ate about 265 eggs per person. In the same year, the price of an egg in the state of Hawaii was $0.10. How much did the average person living in that state spend on eggs in 1982?

4. A pound of ground beef cost $1.49 in Hawaii in 1983. In that year, Americans bought 106.5 pounds of ground beef per person. How much did the average Hawaiian spend on ground beef?

5. In 1980, Americans consumed about 28.9 pounds of citrus fruits and 17.9 pounds of apples per person. Was that more than or less than all other fruits consumed per person in 1980?

6. In 1983, a pound of dry beans cost $0.46. Ricardo's chili recipe calls for 2.5 pounds of beans. How much did he have to spend on beans each time he prepared chili in 1983?

7. In 1982, the price of tuna in Honolulu was $1.17 for a 6.5 ounce can. In 1983, the price was $0.95. How much more expensive was tuna in 1982?

8. In 1982, a half-gallon of milk cost $0.43 more in Honolulu than it did on the mainland. Was that difference greater or smaller than in 1983?

9. American teenage boys eat 5.3 pounds of food per person each day. This equals a total of 1,935 pounds of food a year. What is the cost per year for feeding 2 teenage boys?

10. In 1984, Americans ate 250 million pounds of popcorn. One pound of popcorn costs about $0.58. About how much did the average American spend on popcorn that year?

Divide.

1. $3\overline{)9}$ 2. $5\overline{)20}$ 3. $2\overline{)4}$ 4. $7\overline{)14}$ 5. $6\overline{)24}$

6. $4\overline{)12}$ 7. $2\overline{)12}$ 8. $5\overline{)30}$ 9. $4\overline{)32}$ 10. $8\overline{)16}$

11. $3\overline{)21}$ 12. $6\overline{)42}$ 13. $7\overline{)63}$ 14. $2\overline{)18}$ 15. $5\overline{)45}$

16. $9\overline{)36}$ 17. $6\overline{)54}$ 18. $7\overline{)35}$ 19. $8\overline{)56}$ 20. $9\overline{)81}$

21. $24 \div 3$ 22. $32 \div 8$ 23. $28 \div 7$

24. $45 \div 5$ 25. $48 \div 6$ 26. $63 \div 9$

Solve.

27. The school has 21 cheerleaders. On the field, they stand in 3 equal rows. How many cheerleaders are there in each row?

28. There were 45 cars in the parking lot during the game. If there were 9 cars in each row, how many rows of cars were there?

Solve to complete each family of facts.

1. 2×3

   3×2

   $6 \div 3$

   $6 \div 2$

2. 5×6

    6×5

   $30 \div 5$

   $30 \div 6$

3. 4×7

    7×4

  $28 \div 4$

  $28 \div 7$

Write the family of facts for each set of numbers.

4.

42	6	7

☐ × ☐ = ☐

☐ × ☐ = ☐

☐ ÷ ☐ = ☐

☐ ÷ ☐ = ☐

5.

9	4	36

☐ × ☐ = ☐

☐ × ☐ = ☐

☐ ÷ ☐ = ☐

☐ ÷ ☐ = ☐

6.

8	5	40

☐ × ☐ = ☐

☐ × ☐ = ☐

☐ ÷ ☐ = ☐

☐ ÷ ☐ = ☐

Divide.

7. $6\overline{)18}$ **8.** $8\overline{)0}$ **9.** $1\overline{)5}$ **10.** $5\overline{)45}$ **11.** $9\overline{)54}$ **12.** $2\overline{)10}$

13. $5\overline{)30}$ **14.** $4\overline{)36}$ **15.** $7\overline{)42}$ **16.** $8\overline{)64}$ **17.** $3\overline{)0}$ **18.** $9\overline{)45}$

19. $0 \div 4$ **20.** $20 \div 5$ **21.** $9 \div 1$

Solve.

22. 5×5 **23.** 8×6 **24.** 7×9

25. 6×4 **26.** 9×3 **27.** 4×8

Divide.

1. 7 ÷ 2

2. 23 ÷ 4

3. 13 ÷ 3

4. 44 ÷ 5

5. 38 ÷ 6

6. 17 ÷ 4

7. 23 ÷ 3

8. 33 ÷ 9

9. 35 ÷ 8

10. 29 ÷ 4

11. 39 ÷ 7

12. 14 ÷ 4

13. 52 ÷ 8

14. 11 ÷ 3

15. 20 ÷ 7

16. 39 ÷ 5

17. 19 ÷ 2

18. 33 ÷ 5

19. 17 ÷ 3

20. 23 ÷ 6

21. 9 ÷ 2

22. 28 ÷ 5

23. 43 ÷ 9

24. 29 ÷ 6

25. 13 ÷ 8

26. 47 ÷ 7

27. 15 ÷ 2

28. 30 ÷ 4

29. 59 ÷ 9

30. 30 ÷ 8

Copy and complete the Input/Output table.

INPUT	OUTPUT
10 ÷ 3 =	
27 ÷ 4 =	
44 ÷ 9 =	
37 ÷ 5 =	
34 ÷ 6 =	
17 ÷ 2 =	
74 ÷ 8 =	

Write the letter of the operation that would solve the problem.

1. The Incan Empire existed long ago. The Inca had no written language. Instead, they tied knots in strings and sent the strings as messages. Topa was carrying 10 strings. Each string had 9 knots tied in it. How many knots were there in the strings Topa carried?
   a. multiplication   **b.** division

2. One message contained 126 knots. Each knot was part of a code that helped the runner remember the message. If there were 9 knots in each string, how many pieces of string were needed for the message?
   a. multiplication   **b.** division

Choose the operation and solve.

3. The Inca never discovered the wheel. Instead, they transported things on the backs of animals called llamas. Suppose the Incan emperor had 117 gold bricks, and each llama could carry 9 bricks. How many llamas would the emperor need to carry his load?

4. A team of 56 llamas was traveling across the Incan Empire. They came to a river, which they had to cross on a boat. The boat could hold only 7 llamas at a time. How many trips did the boat have to make in order to take all the llamas across the river?

5. The Inca built some of their temples of pure gold. If one temple had eight walls, each made of 256 gold bricks, how many bricks would it have taken to build the temple?

6. Manco earned 20 gold coins a year for 50 years. Each year, he spent 9 gold coins. If the emperor took 7 gold coins in taxes each year and Manco saved the rest, how many coins could Manco have saved in 50 years?

7. Suppose a farm cost 147 gold coins. Manco and six of his friends wanted to buy a farm to work together. Each of them had 13 gold coins. Were they able to purchase a farm?

8. Becky and Carmelita read about the Inca in their math book. They decided to make a secret knot-code in string. They each had $3. A store sold 25 feet of heavy string for $3. How many feet of string could Becky and Carmelita buy?

Use with pages 136–137.

Is the number evenly divisible by 2? Write *yes* or *no.*

1. 28   **2.** 67   **3.** 106   **4.** 849

5. 390   **6.** 1,121   **7.** 2,643   **8.** 764

9. 25,312   **10.** 17,736   **11.** 32,451   **12.** 51,750

Is the number evenly divisible by 5? Write *yes* or *no.*

13. 35   **14.** 90   **15.** 506   **16.** 285

17. 428   **18.** 1,005   **19.** 18,330   **20.** 21,559

21. 27,475   **22.** 31,860   **23.** 19,305   **24.** 40,651

Is the number evenly divisible by 10? Write *yes* or *no.*

25. 80   **26.** 645   **27.** 750   **28.** 1,100

29. 486   **30.** 3,240   **31.** 12,590   **32.** 20,005

33. 38,370   **34.** 55,550   **35.** 16,321   **36.** 42,794

Is the first number evenly divisible by the second? Write *yes* or *no.*

37. 72, 9   **38.** 58, 7   **39.** 45, 5

40. 90, 10   **41.** 32, 5   **42.** 27, 3

Solve. Write *true* or *false.*

43. If a number is divisible by 5, then it is always divisible by 10.

44. If a number is divisible by 10, then it is always divisible by 5.

Write how many digits each quotient will contain.

1. $7\overline{)1,443}$ 2. $5\overline{)139}$ 3. $8\overline{)4,793}$ 4. $3\overline{)736}$

5. $6\overline{)485}$ 6. $2\overline{)157}$ 7. $9\overline{)273}$ 8. $8\overline{)911}$

Write the best estimate.

9. $4\overline{)185}$	4	40	400	10. $5\overline{)6,750}$	10	100	1,000
11. $6\overline{)1,985}$	3	30	300	12. $7\overline{)2,915}$	40	400	4,000
13. $9\overline{)826}$	9	90	900	14. $8\overline{)2,316}$	20	200	2,000
15. $4\overline{)219}$	5	50	500	16. $7\overline{)3,592}$	50	500	5,000
17. $9\overline{)28,312}$	30	300	3,000	18. $6\overline{)17,392}$	30	300	3,000
19. $3\overline{)89,312}$	300	3,000	30,000	20. $8\overline{)41,493}$	50	500	5,000

Estimate.

21. $6\overline{)3,145}$ 22. $9\overline{)7,316}$ 23. $7\overline{)4,892}$

24. $5\overline{)2,475}$ 25. $4\overline{)4,019}$ 26. $6\overline{)3,715}$

Estimate.

27. Tour guides at the park need to separate 293 students into 8 groups. Will there be more or less than 40 students per group?

28. The class was collecting fallen leaves to put into a scrapbook. They collected 119 leaves and can put 4 leaves on 1 page. Estimate to see whether 30 pages will be enough to mount 119 leaves.

29. Each seat on the bus can hold 3 people. There are 131 students who must go on the last bus home. Will the bus need more or less than 40 seats to hold 131 students?

Read the problem. Write the letter of the number sentence
that solves the problem.

1. Elmer decided to build and sell bird
   cages. The material for each bird cage
   cost $1.57. If he built 35 bird cages, how
   much was Elmer's total cost?
   a. $1.57 \times n = 35$
   b. $1.57 \times 35 = n$
   c. $1.57 + 35 = n$

2. Julianna liked to paint. She decided to
   sell her paintings for $1.50 each. The
   material for each painting cost $0.37.
   How much money can she earn from
   each painting?
   a. $1.50 - 0.37 = n$
   b. $1.50 \times n = 0.37$
   c. $0.37 = n \times 1.50$

Write a number sentence. Solve.

3. Armand's father taught him how to make
   wooden bookends. Armand made 44
   bookends and sold them. He charged
   $3.50 for each bookend. How much
   money did Armand earn?

4. Chandra and Bobby sewed 54 shirts.
   They sold them for $5.95 each. If they
   sold nine shirts, how much money did
   they earn?

5. Lisa makes puppets. She sells them for
   $3.00 each. Last month, she made
   $21.00. How many puppets did Lisa sell?

6. Jeff trades baseball and football cards.
   Last year, he ended up with 620
   baseball cards and 516 football cards.
   How many more baseball cards did he
   have?

7. John learned how to build boxes in metal
   shop. He sold the boxes to his friends.
   He made 6 boxes and sold them for a
   total of $27.00. How much did John
   charge for each box?

8. Bill helped Mr. Johnson paint his house.
   Mr. Johnson paid Bill $2.00 per hour.
   Bill made a total of $33.00 on the job.
   How many hours did he work?

9. Annette set up a lemonade stand outside
   her house. She charges $0.50 per glass.
   How much money will Annette earn if she
   sells 25 glasses?

10. Sue baked cookies for the bake sale.
    She made 5 dozen cookies and
    charged $0.15 per cookie. How much
    money did Sue earn?

Divide.

1. $\frac{22}{2}$ 2. $\frac{45}{3}$ 3. $\frac{60}{5}$ 4. $\frac{40}{4}$

5. $\frac{32}{2}$ 6. $\frac{39}{3}$ 7. $95 \div 5$ 8. $120 \div 3$

9. $68 \div 2$ 10. $66 \div 1$ 11. $17 \div 4$ 12. $180 \div 6$

13. $180 \div 9$ 14. $50 \div 3$ 15. $81 \div 5$ 16. $75 \div 4$

17. $5\overline{)145}$ 18. $9\overline{)300}$ 19. $4\overline{)128}$ 20. $6\overline{)179}$ 21. $7\overline{)345}$

22. $9\overline{)486}$ 23. $3\overline{)183}$ 24. $8\overline{)602}$ 25. $9\overline{)855}$ 26. $6\overline{)456}$

27. $8\overline{)742}$ 28. $7\overline{)619}$ 29. $5\overline{)325}$ 30. $4\overline{)237}$ 31. $9\overline{)659}$

Solve.

32. The hiking club has 171 packages of trail mix. If the packages are divided equally into 3 cartons, how many packages are there in each carton?

33. The hiking club has 8 members. They must carry 112 pounds of equipment with them. If each member carries the same amount, how many pounds is that?

Divide.

1. 250 ÷ 2   **2.** 404 ÷ 4   **3.** 333 ÷ 3   **4.** 342 ÷ 2

5. 590 ÷ 5   **6.** 800 ÷ 4   **7.** 477 ÷ 3   **8.** 482 ÷ 2

9. 4)786   **10.** 3)603   **11.** 7)859   **12.** 7)2,845

13. 4)699   **14.** 5)4,090   **15.** 8)7,444   **16.** 2)1,001

17. 6)5,892   **18.** 7)6,252   **19.** 4)2,674   **20.** 6)1,089

21. 4)1,868   **22.** 6)4,536   **23.** 7)1,841   **24.** 8)2,760

Solve.

25. Roane's Services paid a total of $2,934 for 3 identical office desks. How much did each desk cost?

26. Foresters counted 1,845 trees on a 5-acre piece of land. If all the acres are equally wooded, about how many trees are on each acre?

27. A scout leader is handing out boxes of cookies for the scouts to sell. There are 1,080 boxes of cookies and 9 scouts. If the cookies are divided evenly, how many boxes should each scout receive?

28. A tour group of 1,168 people wants to visit historic sites in Europe. If only 8 tour guides are available, how many tourists must each tour guide take?

Divide. Multiply to check your answer.

1. 6)7,536   **2.** 3)8,538   **3.** 2)3,046   **4.** 8)9,978

5. 4)8,712   **6.** 7)9,425   **7.** 5)9,790   **8.** 9)9,999

9. 2)10,946   **10.** 7)16,709   **11.** 9)21,486   **12.** 8)33,736

13. 5)17,935   **14.** 4)10,749   **15.** 3)17,547   **16.** 6)34,122

17. 2)13,795   **18.** 7)53,123   **19.** 9)84,789   **20.** 2)84,336

21. 4)92,704   **22.** 6)75,526   **23.** 8)99,776   **24.** 5)74,365

The Las Cruces Camp Scouts decide to organize a camping trip. Read each statement. Then, write questions that the scouts should answer before making a decision.

1. The camp scouts have to decide how far they can travel for their camping trip.

2. They need to set a date for the camping trip.

3. The scouts need to figure out how long the camping trip should be.

4. They need to decide how much food to bring.

5. They must plan how to have water for cooking, drinking, and washing.

6. They need to decide how they are going to get to the campsite.

Divide.

1. 3)90

2. 6)60

3. 7)285

4. 2)100

5. 4)820

6. 5)703

7. 6)642

8. 7)911

9. 4)3,212

10. 5)4,800

11. 3)1,824

12. 6)4,744

13. 9)9,612

14. 2)8,604

15. 5)20,390

16. 4)10,438

17. 980 ÷ 7

18. 616 ÷ 2

19. 1,821 ÷ 3

20. 3,650 ÷ 5

Solve.

21. The Swallow Kite Company puts 5 streamers on each kite. How many kites can the company make with 1,024 streamers? How many streamers are left?

Use with pages 152–153.

Divide.

1. $2.52 ÷ 6

2. $37.45 ÷ 5

3. $835.84 ÷ 8

4. 3)$2.16

5. 8)$1.68

6. 7)$4.83

7. 4)$8.40

8. 6)$6.54

9. 2)$8.96

10. 9)$9.45

11. 8)$25.60

12. 6)$43.50

13. 9)$84.33

14. 7)$42.63

15. 6)$244.50

16. 5)$345.75

17. 4)$847.24

18. 3)$421.53

19. 5)$394.75

20. 8)$491.36

21. 3)$141.69

22. 7)$629.93

23. 9)$4.32

Solve.

24. John buys an 8-ounce jar of peanuts for $1.12. How much do the peanuts cost per ounce?

25. The bill for 8 desk lamps is $891.84. How much does each lamp cost?

26. A group of 7 students went to see a movie. The tickets for all 7 students cost $33.25. What was the cost of each ticket?

27. A box of 6 pencils sells for $0.42. What is the price per pencil?

Solve.

1. Brenda and John are going fishing in Maine. They will have 28 lures to share between them. How many lures will each have? How many will be left?

2. John went digging for worms with his 3 friends. He found 32 worms and divided them equally among the group. How many worms did each person have?

3. John and Brenda brought enough hush puppies to the camp fish fry so that each of the 31 campers could have one. John packed the hush puppies 5 per box. He only brought full boxes. How many boxes did he bring?

4. Brenda's group caught 75 trout. They kept the trout on stringers that would hold 9 trout each. How many full stringers did they have?

5. Brenda and John spent a rainy weekend tying 37 flies. They kept them in a special fly box that had a separate little box for each fly. If the boxes were in rows of 4, how many rows of boxes contained flies? How many flies were in the last row?

6. John needed 52 new fishhooks. He bought as many as he could in boxes of 8. The rest he bought separately. How many boxes did he buy? How many hooks did he buy separately?

7. John and his dad brought 27 pieces of bait. They caught 8 smallmouth bass. If it took them 3 pieces of bait to catch each fish, how many pieces did they have left? Would there be enough bait left to catch another fish?

Divide.

1. $30\overline{)270}$ 2. $40\overline{)240}$ 3. $70\overline{)630}$ 4. $10\overline{)80}$ 5. $40\overline{)400}$

6. $80\overline{)720}$ 7. $20\overline{)180}$ 8. $50\overline{)400}$ 9. $70\overline{)630}$ 10. $10\overline{)50}$

11. $40\overline{)360}$ 12. $90\overline{)810}$ 13. $50\overline{)250}$ 14. $90\overline{)450}$ 15. $70\overline{)350}$

16. $80\overline{)400}$ 17. $70\overline{)490}$ 18. $60\overline{)480}$ 19. $90\overline{)720}$ 20. $60\overline{)180}$

21. $10\overline{)20}$ 22. $20\overline{)100}$ 23. $60\overline{)420}$ 24. $10\overline{)30}$ 25. $30\overline{)270}$

26. $250 \div 50$ 27. $450 \div 90$

28. $\frac{80}{40}$ 29. $\frac{120}{60}$ 30. $\frac{720}{80}$

Write how many digits each quotient will contain.

1. $12\overline{)2,295}$ **2.** $23\overline{)4,578}$ **3.** $31\overline{)6,892}$ **4.** $11\overline{)3,216}$ **5.** $26\overline{)1,175}$

6. $42\overline{)5,827}$ **7.** $53\overline{)4,895}$ **8.** $26\overline{)5,236}$ **9.** $33\overline{)15,607}$ **10.** $49\overline{)51,416}$

Write the best estimate.

11. $15\overline{)1,837}$ 10   100   1,000   **12.** $24\overline{)3,698}$ 10   100   1,000

13. $32\overline{)9,156}$ 20   200   2,000   **14.** $86\overline{)1,129}$ 10   100   1,000

15. $19\overline{)214,234}$ 1,000 10,000 100,000   **16.** $26\overline{)181,562}$ 6,000 60,000 600,000

17. $74\overline{)795}$ **18.** $21\overline{)839}$ **19.** $23\overline{)675}$ **20.** $62\overline{)3,235}$

21. $14\overline{)1,569}$ **22.** $26\overline{)5,531}$ **23.** $32\overline{)9,864}$ **24.** $43\overline{)2,988}$

25. $16\overline{)3,351}$ **26.** $31\overline{)1,567}$ **27.** $42\overline{)4,456}$ **28.** $52\overline{)1,645}$

Estimate.

29. A bicycle touring company put $6,350.00 into its profit-sharing fund. Twelve workers are to receive equal shares of the profits. One worker wants to buy a new TV with his share. The TV costs $679.00. Will he have enough money from his share to buy the TV? Estimate to answer this question.

30. An employee of the company receives $148.00 as a bonus. She decides to use her bonus to buy a book bag for each of the 27 children in the community. Each book bag costs $5.00. Will she have enough money from her bonus? Estimate to answer this question.

Checking for a Reasonable Answer	Choosing the Operation	Solving Two-Step Problems/
Estimation	Writing a Number	Making a Plan
Acting It Out	Sentence	Identifying Needed Information

Write the strategy or method you choose. Then solve.

1. The Tlingit Indians live in Alaska. In the past, they traveled in large canoes. If 3 canoes were traveling from one village to another, and each canoe could hold 18 people, how many people could go?

2. The Tlingit held parties called *potlatches.* At each potlatch, the host would give most of his possessions to his guests. If a host gave away 78 baskets, how many did each guest receive?

3. The Tlingit could meet their needs by working about 30 hours a week. Estimate how many hours the Tlingits worked in a year. (HINT: 52 weeks = 1 year)

4. One host of a potlatch gave away 35 robes of mink, 50 robes of deerskin, and 7 robes of bearskin. How many robes were given away?

5. A potlatch would last 3 days. If 3 trays of smoked salmon were eaten each day, and the host had 13 trays to start with, how many trays of salmon were left to give as gifts?

6. At one potlatch, there were 51 baskets of dried salmon. At the feast, 19 baskets of salmon were eaten. The remaining baskets were divided equally among 8 honored guests. How many baskets did each receive?

7. The most prized gifts were blankets made of mountain-goat wool and cedar. To make 5 of these blankets took 10 months. How long did it take to make each blanket?

8. The Tlingit fished for salmon. If 7 people caught 63 fish and divided them equally, what was each person's share of the fish?

Checking for a Reasonable Answer	Choosing the Operation	Solving Two-Step Problems/ Making a Plan
Estimation	Writing a Number Sentence	Identifying Needed Information
Acting It Out	Guessing and Checking	

Write the strategy or method you choose. Then solve.

1. The Tlingit Indians in Alaska have power fishing boats. Each day, the catch per boat is about 2,000 salmon. If 4 boats go out together, how many salmon can they bring in?

2. Joe See lives in the Tlingit community of Sitka. He wants to visit his sister in Juneau. His boat can travel at a speed of 14 miles per hour. How long will the trip take?

3. Joe wants to buy his sister a dress that she saw in the window of a dress shop. How much money should he bring with him?

4. A family of 5 brought sandwiches for lunch with them. If they brought 15 sandwiches and divided them equally, how many did each family member get?

5. Joe See decided to take his family on a trip to Wrangell. The ferry left Sitka at 1:00 and arrived in Wrangell at 5:00 that same afternoon. The ferry traveled at a speed of 25 miles per hour. How many miles was the trip to Wrangell?

6. The people who live along the coastline of Alaska often travel by ferryboat. The *Tustumena* sails overnight from Anchorage to Kodiak Island. Sleeping cabins are available. Each sleeps 2. How many cabins would a family of 5 need?

7. Once in Wrangell, Joe See's children bought some T-shirts for a total of $8.60. Then the family went out to dinner. The dinner cost $23.50. Joe brought $70.00 with him to spend. How much money did he have left?

8. Going home, Joe and his family got a ride on a fishing boat. They left Wrangell at 10:00 A.M. They stopped in Petersburg for 2 hours and 15 minutes. They arrived home at 5:00 P.M. How long was the trip home without the stop?

Use with pages 170–171.

Divide.

1. $14\overline{)77}$ 2. $18\overline{)169}$ 3. $12\overline{)84}$ 4. $25\overline{)190}$ 5. $16\overline{)83}$

6. $24\overline{)150}$ 7. $36\overline{)115}$ 8. $47\overline{)290}$ 9. $26\overline{)60}$ 10. $56\overline{)254}$

11. $26\overline{)78}$ 12. $21\overline{)47}$ 13. $31\overline{)220}$ 14. $39\overline{)352}$ 15. $17\overline{)140}$

16. $100 \div 23$ 17. $85 \div 42$ 18. $100 \div 14$

19. $135 \div 27$ 20. $334 \div 36$ 21. $360 \div 58$

22. $111 \div 35$ 23. $95 \div 15$ 24. $517 \div 64$

25. $108 \div 33$ 26. $243 \div 58$ 27. $100 \div 47$

Copy the problems and complete. Use the quotient of each problem to find the divisor of the following problem. Then combine the quotients to find out how many chairs were used in the largest game of musical chairs.

 $68\overline{)272}$ $\boxed{?}1\overline{)205}$ $\boxed{?}9\overline{)59}$ $9\boxed{?}\overline{)364}$

$\underline{?},\ \underline{?}\ \ \underline{?}\ \ \underline{?}$

Divide.

1. $22\overline{)379}$

2. $29\overline{)673}$

3. $11\overline{)283}$

4. $47\overline{)3,160}$

5. $25\overline{)357}$

6. $28\overline{)572}$

7. $62\overline{)982}$

8. $24\overline{)728}$

9. $92\overline{)1,666}$

10. $31\overline{)1,962}$

11. $26\overline{)293}$

12. $43\overline{)2,677}$

13. $53\overline{)925}$

14. $84\overline{)2,218}$

15. $51\overline{)1,080}$

16. $32\overline{)2,026}$

17. $43\overline{)3,497}$

18. $71\overline{)3,852}$

19. $82\overline{)\$51.66}$

20. $47\overline{)1,557}$

21. $\$4.48 \div 32$

22. $578 \div 94$

23. $738 \div 21$

Read each problem. Estimate an answer.

1. If you jumped rope without stopping for 5 minutes, about how many times would you jump?

2. About how long would it take you to write the title of this book 15 times?

3. Estimate how many shelves would be needed in your classroom to hold 60 math books if each shelf is 2 feet long.

4. If a class studied about 10 pages a week in their math textbook, about how long would it take to study all the chapters?

5. If you could place small boxes of crayons flat in an empty half-gallon milk carton, about how many boxes would it take to reach the top of the carton?

6. If you drink an 8-ounce glass of milk 3 times a day, about how many glasses would you drink in 3 months?

7. Imagine that you are walking from one end of your classroom to the other. How many steps would you have to take?

8. If 26 fifth-grade students stood in a straight line one arm's distance apart, about how many feet long would the line be?

9. About how long a table would be needed to seat a class of 30 students if nobody sat at the ends?

10. Philadelphia's City Hall Tower is 548 feet high. How many shoe boxes would you have to stack on end to equal the height of that building?

Divide.

1. 75)4,367 **2.** 48)397 **3.** 34)2,834 **4.** 86)5,492

5. 96)4,292 **6.** 65)3,643 **7.** 54)$41.58 **8.** 36)4,785

9. 68)4,635 **10.** 46)1,674 **11.** 27)$7.83 **12.** 28)1,597

13. 93)3,674 **14.** 83)6,425 **15.** 35)2,279 **16.** 58)2,971

17. 7,413 ÷ 96 **18.** 811 ÷ 66

19. 5,552 ÷ 75 **20.** 1,926 ÷ 37

21. $\frac{1,015}{24}$ **22.** $\frac{340}{26}$ **23.** $\frac{1,539}{95}$

Use with pages 178–179.

Divide.

1. $16\overline{)1,646}$

2. $17\overline{)8,381}$

3. $41\overline{)14,975}$

4. $26\overline{)7,046}$

5. $23\overline{)8,114}$

6. $11\overline{)\$35.64}$

7. $18\overline{)3,100}$

8. $12\overline{)4,428}$

9. $42\overline{)5,292}$

10. $33\overline{)7,129}$

11. $59\overline{)9,314}$

12. $29\overline{)\$94.25}$

Divide. Then copy and complete the cross-number puzzle.

Across

a. $882 \div 14$

c. $9,637 \div 23$

f. $10,366 \div 71$

h. $\frac{14,508}{39}$

Down

a. $1,273 \div 19$

b. $1,769 \div 61$

d. $9,114 \div 49$

e. $10,087 \div 11$

g. $5,250 \div 125$

Divide.

1. $4,800 \div 8$

2. $2,092 \div 4$

3. $4,558 \div 9$

4. $306 \div 3$

5. $3,045 \div 5$

6. $6,409 \div 8$

7. $5\overline{)4,545}$

8. $27\overline{)13,669}$

9. $4\overline{)1,207}$

10. $8\overline{)\$56.32}$

11. $6\overline{)607}$

12. $22\overline{)8,910}$

13. $28\overline{)\$67.20}$

14. $33\overline{)11,221}$

15. $14\overline{)7,089}$

16. $56\overline{)19,048}$

17. $13\overline{)3,978}$

18. $17\overline{)\$34.17}$

19. $20\overline{)4,037}$

20. $27\overline{)9,722}$

21. $30\overline{)9,067}$

22. $18\overline{)7,238}$

Write the letter of the correct answer.

1. Pluto is the most distant planet from the sun. It takes Pluto about 248 Earth-years to complete one orbit around the sun. Americans live about 74 years. About how many American lifetimes does it take for Pluto to complete one orbit?
   a. 3.35 lifetimes
   b. 3.35 years
   c. 174 years

2. For about 20 Earth-years of each orbit, Pluto crosses the orbit of Neptune. During this time, Neptune is the most distant planet from the sun. For how many Earth-years does Pluto remain the most distant planet from the sun?
   a. 20 years
   b. 228 years
   c. 12.4 times

Solve.

3. Mercury is the closest planet to the sun. Mercury's year lasts about 88 Earth-days. About how many Earth-weeks are in each Mercury-year?

4. One year on Jupiter is equal to 12 years on Earth. How old would a 72-year-old American be in Jupiter-years?

5. In Earth-years, Zorn is 12 years old. In Jupiter-years, his mother is 2 years older than he is. How old is she in Earth-years?

6. A year is 365 days. This is the length of time it takes Earth to orbit the sun. It takes the moon about 30 days to orbit Earth. About how many times does the moon orbit Earth in 1 year?

7. One Mercury-day equals about 24 weeks and 2 days on Earth. About how many Earth-days is one Mercury-day?

8. One year on Jupiter is equal to 156 Earth-weeks. About how many Earth-days are in one Jupiter-year?

9. Jill has a telescope on her roof. It magnifies heavenly bodies up to 125 times larger than she could see them without the telescope. How many times larger would the heavenly bodies appear if the telescope were twice as powerful?

10. Jill is looking at the rings of Saturn through her telescope. They appear 50 times larger than she could see them without the telescope. Jill switches to a lens that is 4 times as powerful. How many times larger are the rings now?

Multiply or divide.

1. 5.7 ÷ 10

2. 40 ÷ 100

3. 10 × 0.08

4. 100 × 3.971

5. 6 ÷ 10

6. 0.041 ÷ 10

7. 71.2 × 1,000

8. 0.028 × 100

9. 103.17 ÷ 1,000

10. 3.4 × 100

11. 4.7 ÷ 100

12. 0.032 × 1,000

Copy and complete the charts.

x	10	100	1,000
13. 0.5			
14. 0.013			
15. 6.317			
16. 79.8			

÷	10	100	1,000
17. 16.35			
18. 24			
19. 418			
20. 0.7			

Use the information below to answer the questions.

Child	Daily piggy-bank deposits
Ari	$0.59
Ted	$1.26
Mara	$0.31

21. How much will each child have after 100 days?

Ari   Ted

          Mara

22. Each child then withdraws the whole amount in 10 equal withdrawals. How much is each withdrawal?

Ari   Ted

          Mara

Divide.

1. $37\overline{)9.176}$

2. $9\overline{)14.67}$

3. $29\overline{)3.625}$

4. $5\overline{)8.35}$

5. $13\overline{)49.66}$

6. $7\overline{)2.961}$

7. $3\overline{)0.1671}$

8. $31\overline{)12.772}$

9. $8\overline{)36.8}$

10. $57\overline{)407.55}$

11. $89\overline{)59.986}$

12. $11\overline{)89.452}$

13. $42\overline{)219.66}$

14. $17\overline{)2.091}$

15. $62\overline{)26.536}$

16. $39\overline{)121.68}$

17. $12\overline{)64.92}$

18. $91\overline{)240.24}$

19. $18\overline{)115.56}$

20. $80\overline{)14.880}$

21. $0.9 \div 3$

22. $36.4 \div 26$

23. $1.2 \div 4$

24. $4.8 \div 8$

25. $15.68 \div 7$

26. $22.23 \div 19$

27. $15.54 \div 7$

28. $3.72 \div 3$

29. $37.14 \div 6$

Divide.

1. 2.7 ÷ 4

2. 1.8 ÷ 12

3. 28.21 ÷ 13

4. 3.036 ÷ 6

5. 4.035 ÷ 5

6. 83.64 ÷ 41

7. 9)0.0954

8. 81)2.268

9. 34)2.72

10. 44)2.552

11. 29)3.422

12. 43)45.15

13. 62)1.3888

14. 55)22.275

15. 8)0.384

16. 49)0.392

17. 87)8.787

18. 26)52.208

19. 51)229.601

20. 83)24.9581

21. 68)4.012

Use the guess-and-check method to solve for each blank.

1. In 1956, Lorraine Crapp was the first woman to break 5 minutes for the 400-meter freestyle swim, a record that stood for _____?_____ years.

This 2-digit number is divisible by 2, 4, and 8. The difference between its digits is 5. The number is less than 50. What is the number?

2. The Three Day Event is an equestrian competition designed to test the all-around ability of horse and rider. It includes cross-country obstacles _____?_____ inches high.

This is a 2-digit number. The sum of its digits is 11. The difference between its digits is 3. The product when doubled is a 2-digit number. What is the number?

3. In the 44 years from 1921 to 1965, which are known as the Yankee dynasty, the New York Yankees won 29 pennants and _____?_____ world championships.

This 2-digit number is divisible by 5 and 4 but *not* by 3 or 7. The number is less than 2 dozen. What is the number?

4. In basketball, the net, made of white cord, is suspended from an orange-painted iron ring _____?_____ cm in diameter.

This 2-digit number is divisible by 9 and 3. If you reverse its digits, it is divisible by 9, 6, and 3. The sum of its digits is 9, and the difference between them is 1. What is the number?

5. Tse-tung Chuang, a three-time Chinese table-tennis champion, began his training in the Children's Palace, Chingshan, Peking, at the age of _____?_____ years.

This 2-digit number is divisible by 2. The sum of its digits is less than half a dozen. When multiplied by 3, the product has a 2 in the ones place. What is the number?

6. In 1956, Betty Cuthbert, an Australian sprinter, won three Olympic gold medals at the age of _____?_____ .

This is a 2-digit number less than 50. The sum of its digits is divisible by 9. The difference between its digits is divisible by 7. What is the number?

7. The track bicycle, used for sprinting, is fitted with silk-covered tubular tires weighing as little as _____?_____ grams.

This is a 3-digit number with 1 in the tens place. The sum of the other 2 digits is divisible by 2 and 4 but *not* by 6 or 8. The number is less than 300. What is the number?

8. In 1888, the Yale football team beat all its 13 opponents with a total score of _____?_____ points to 0.

This is a 3-digit number. It is divisible by 2. The sum of its first 2 digits is 15. The sum of its last 2 digits is 17. What is the number?

Use the guess-and-check method to solve for each blank.

9. One of the dragonflylike species of insects is comparatively large. It has a wingspread of _____?_____ inches.

   This 2-digit number is divisible by 2 and 3. The sum of its digits is 3. The number is greater than one dozen. What is the number?

10. If all the offspring of a pamace fly were to survive long enough to reproduce, there would be _____?_____ generations by the end of a year.

    This is an odd 2-digit number divisible by 5. The sum of its digits is 7, and the difference between them is 3. What is the number?

11. If all its members survived, the 25th generation of flies would be so large that all the individuals packed tightly together would form a ball of flies _____?_____ million miles in diameter.

    This even 2-digit number is divisible by 3, as is the difference between its digits. The sum of its digits is divisible by 5. What is the number?

12. An ant can lift _____?_____ times its own weight.

    This 3-digit number is less than 500 and is divisible by 9, 5, 3, and 2. The sum of its digits is 9. The difference between its first 2 digits is one. It has a 0 in the ones place. What is the number?

13. Insects have a size range nearly _____?_____ times greater than mammals. An Atlas moth can be almost 3,000 times as large as the smallest fly.

    This 2-digit number is divisible by 2 and 3 but *not* by 4 or 9. The difference between its digits is equal to their sum. What is the number?

14. If you added _____?_____ to the number of times a cricket chirped in 15 seconds, you would get the temperature in degrees Fahrenheit.

    This 2-digit number is divisible by 3, as are the sum of and the difference between its digits. When multiplied by 2, the product is a 2-digit number with 8 in the ones place. What is the number?

15. Flies include some of the fastest flying insects. The horsefly has been clocked at more than _____?_____ miles per hour.

    This is a 2-digit number. The sum of its digits is 4. The difference between its digits is 2. The number is greater than 25. What is the number?

16. When the temperature in a beehive drops below _____?_____ degrees F, the bees form a dense ball that moves slowly about the hive, feeding on stored food.

    This 2-digit number is divisible by 3 but *not* by 2. The difference between its digits is 2. If the digits were reversed, it would be divisible by 5. What is the number?

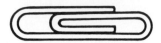

Measure the length of the paper clip to the nearest

1. cm

2. mm

Measure the length of the pencil to the nearest

3. cm

4. mm

Draw a line that measures

5. 43 mm

6. 7 cm

7. 5.5 cm

8. 28 mm

Write the distance around each shape.

9.

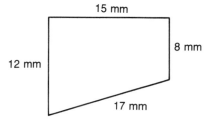

35 mm   25 mm
32 mm

10.

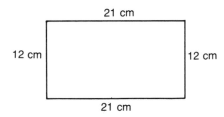

21 cm
12 cm   12 cm
21 cm

11.

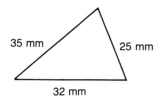

15 mm
8 mm
12 mm
17 mm

12.

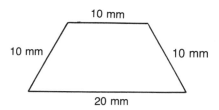

10 mm
10 mm   10 mm
20 mm

Which unit would you use to measure the length?
Write *mm, cm, m,* or *km.*

1. distance from Texas to Iowa

2. height of a room

3. length of a teacher's desk

4. distance a plane travels

5. width of a ring

6. length of a ladybug

7. length of a car

8. length of a shoestring

Choose the appropriate unit.
Write *mm, cm, m,* or *km.*

9. A grasshopper is 30 ____?____ long.

10. A comb is 10 ____?____ long.

11. The distance from California to Pennsylvania is 3,000 ____?____ .

12. A baseball bat is 1 ____?____ long.

13. A scarf is 160 ____?____ long.

14. Sabina's hand is 15 ____?____ long.

Complete.

15. 0.03 m = ____?____ cm

16. 3,500 m = ____?____ km

17. 60 mm = ____?____ cm

18. 7 km = ____?____ m

19. 78 cm = ____?____ m

20. 95 m = ____?____ km

21. 6,411 m = ____?____ km

22. 9.5 cm = ____?____ mm

23. 64.8 m = ____?____ cm

24. 150 cm = ____?____ m

25. 11,230 m = ____?____ km

26. 0.02 km = ____?____ m

Use with pages 206–207.

Write the letter for the information that is not needed.

1. The Washington Market Block Association is having a block party to raise $1,000 to fix up their park. They sold 124 tickets at $4.00 each. How much money did they make selling tickets?

   a. They sold 124 tickets.

   b. They need $1,000 in all.

   c. Tickets sold for $4.00 each.

2. At the block party, Kim Lee won the beanbag toss. He scored 27.6 points in all. He threw the beanbag 3 times. About how many points did he score each time he threw the beanbag?

   a. Kim Lee won the beanbag toss.

   b. He threw the beanbag 3 times.

   c. He scored a total of 27.6 points.

Write the extra information. Then solve.

3. Benches for the park cost $85.00 each. A group of 16 businessmen and 12 businesswomen donated $1,360. How many benches can they buy?

4. There were 20 old benches in the park, but $\frac{3}{4}$ of them had to be replaced. The remaining 5 were repaired at a cost of $61.15. What was the cost of repairs per bench?

5. Jack Peatmoss, a volunteer, worked a total of 200 hours planting 860 plants. There were 126 shrubs and the rest were flower bulbs. How many flowers did Jack plant?

6. Jack planted borders along the park walkways for 4 days. He averaged 71.5 feet of border each day. This was 3.2 feet more than his previous average. How many feet of walkway did Jack border?

7. Nancy volunteered to paint the new benches. It took her 12 hours to paint 10 benches. It took her 3 days to do the job. How long did it take her to paint one bench?

8. Nancy can run 10 times around the park in 50 minutes. It takes Mary 3 minutes more to run the same distance. How long does it take Nancy to run around the park 1 time?

Which unit would you use to measure the capacity?
Write *mL* or *L*.

1. a soup ladle

2. an eyedropper

3. a large pitcher

4. a watering can

5. a small oil can

6. a teaspoon

7. a gasoline tank

8. a small glass

9. a rain barrel

10. a bathtub

11. a kitchen sink

12. a tablespoon

Complete.

13. 0.7 L = _____?_____ mL

14. 3,500 mL = _____?_____ L

15. 1.248 L = _____?_____ mL

16. 624 mL = _____?_____ L

17. 11 L = _____?_____ mL

18. 0.09 L = _____?_____ mL

19. 14.6 L = _____?_____ mL

20. 8,000 mL = _____?_____ L

21. 2 L = _____?_____ mL

22. 0.53 L = _____?_____ mL

23. 78 mL = _____?_____ L

24. 8,779 mL = _____?_____ L

25. 16 L = _____?_____ mL

26. 651 mL = _____?_____ L

27. 14,300 mL = _____?_____ L

28. 5,000 mL = _____?_____ L

29. 0.032 L = _____?_____ mL

30. 1.06 L = _____?_____ mL

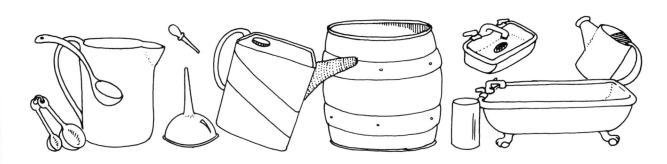

Use with pages 210–211.

Kilograms, Grams, and Milligrams

Which unit would you use to measure the mass?
Write *mg*, *g*, or *kg*.

1. a spider

2. a dump truck

3. a crate of oranges

4. a grain of sand

5. a bag of cement

6. an apple

Copy and complete.

7. $0.07 \text{ g} = \underline{\quad ? \quad}_{A} \text{ mg}$

8. $860 \text{ g} = \underline{\quad ? \quad}_{B} \text{ kg}$

9. $1.4 \text{ kg} = \underline{\quad ? \quad}_{C} \text{ g}$

10. $63 \text{ mg} = \underline{\quad ? \quad}_{D} \text{ g}$

11. $1 \text{ kg} = \underline{\quad ? \quad}_{E} \text{ mg}$

12. $9 \text{ kg} = \underline{\quad ? \quad}_{G} \text{ mg}$

13. $0.402 \text{ g} = \underline{\quad ? \quad}_{H} \text{ mg}$

14. $139 \text{ mg} = \underline{\quad ? \quad}_{K} \text{ g}$

15. $0.7 \text{ g} = \underline{\quad ? \quad}_{L} \text{ mg}$

16. $969 \text{ g} = \underline{\quad ? \quad}_{N} \text{ kg}$

17. $0.4 \text{ g} = \underline{\quad ? \quad}_{O} \text{ mg}$

18. $45.9 \text{ g} = \underline{\quad ? \quad}_{P} \text{ mg}$

19. $755 \text{ mg} = \underline{\quad ? \quad}_{R} \text{ kg}$

20. $8.4 \text{ g} = \underline{\quad ? \quad}_{T} \text{ mg}$

21. $0.08 \text{ kg} = \underline{\quad ? \quad}_{U} \text{ g}$

Copy the rhyme. Write the letters that match your answers to
complete the rhyme.

There once was a man from $\underline{\quad ? \quad}$ $\underline{\quad ? \quad}$ $\underline{\quad ? \quad}$ $\underline{\quad ? \quad}$
45,900   1,000,000   0.000755   80

Who did tricks his dog

Spot $\underline{\quad ? \quad}$ $\underline{\quad ? \quad}$ $\underline{\quad ? \quad}$ $\underline{\quad ? \quad}$ $\underline{\quad ? \quad}$ $\underline{\quad ? \quad}$, $\underline{\quad ? \quad}$ $\underline{\quad ? \quad}$ $\underline{\quad ? \quad}$
1,400   400   80   700   0.063   0.969   8,400   0.063   400

When he sat up to $\underline{\quad ? \quad}$ $\underline{\quad ? \quad}$ $\underline{\quad ? \quad}$,
0.86   1,000,000   9,000,000

He tripped over his $\underline{\quad ? \quad}$ $\underline{\quad ? \quad}$ $\underline{\quad ? \quad}$,
700   1,000,000   9,000,000

And he $\underline{\quad ? \quad}$ $\underline{\quad ? \quad}$ $\underline{\quad ? \quad}$ $\underline{\quad ? \quad}$ $\underline{\quad ? \quad}$ $\underline{\quad ? \quad}$ while old
0.86   70   0.000755   0.139   1,000,000   0.063

Spot cried $\underline{\quad ? \quad}$ $\underline{\quad ? \quad}$ $\underline{\quad ? \quad}$ $-$ $\underline{\quad ? \quad}$ $\underline{\quad ? \quad}$ $\underline{\quad ? \quad}$.
0.86   400   400   402   400   400

Complete the plan by writing the missing step.

1. Julio exercises 5 days a week. Each day he works on a rebounder for 10 minutes to warm up. Then, he rows for 15 minutes and lifts weights for half an hour. How much time does Julio spend exercising in one week?
   Step 1: Find Julio's total exercising time for one day.

   Step 2:

2. Jennifer Krall exercises 45 minutes 3 times a week. How many hours does she exercise in 6 weeks? (HINT: 60 minutes = 1 hour)

   Step 1: Find the number of minutes Jennifer exercises in 1 week.
   Step 2: Find the number of minutes Jennifer exercises in 6 weeks.

   Step 3:

Make a plan for each problem. Solve.

3. During the football season, Carlos gained 255 yards in 75 carries, and Aaron gained 304 yards in 95 carries. Who gained more yards per carry?

4. During baseball season, Marty practiced 3 days a week, 2 hours each day. Tim practiced 5 days a week, 1 hour each day. Who spent more hours practicing?

5. During the basketball season, Karen got 165 rebounds in 15 games. Maria got 224 rebounds in 20 games. Which girl got more rebounds per game?

6. During one 15-game soccer season, 120 liters of orange juice were drunk by the 16 members of the team. About how much juice did each member drink during one game?

7. Janice could run a kilometer twice as fast as Burt could. Burt could run a kilometer 7 seconds faster than Eliot. If Eliot could run a kilometer in 12 minutes 7 seconds, how fast could Janice run?

8. Roland could run half a kilometer in 4 minutes. At that rate, how would his time compare with Janice's?

9. Suzuki could run 2 kilometers in 10 minutes. She wanted to know whose time was better, hers or Janice's. Who had the better time?

10. One afternoon, 15 children formed teams for a 4-person relay race. One team had only 3 runners, and so one person had to run twice as far as everyone else. If the course was 300 meters long, how far did that person have to run?

Write the first six multiples of each number.

1. 3

2. 30

3. 1

4. 11

5. 16

6. 7

Write the first three common multiples.

7. 1, 7

8. 4, 5

9. 2, 6

10. 3, 5

11. 6, 8

12. 15, 30

Write the least common multiple.

13. 2, 3

14. 2, 5

15. 12, 18

16. 4, 6

17. 10, 25

18. 5, 6

19. 8, 12

20. 7, 10

21. 4, 9

22. 10, 15

23. 8, 10

24. 3, 5

25. 5, 15

26. 9, 12

27. 3, 4

28. 7, 28

29. 3, 7

30. 12, 30

31. 8, 14

32. 9, 15

Write the least common multiple. Then match the answer and the letter below to break the code.

33. 5, 9

34. 7, 8

35. 4, 15

36. 9, 36

$$\frac{?}{T} \qquad \frac{?}{O} \qquad \frac{?}{P} \qquad \frac{?}{A}$$

What has eyes but cannot see?

$$\frac{?}{36} \quad \frac{?}{60} \quad \frac{?}{56} \quad \frac{?}{45} \quad \frac{?}{36} \quad \frac{?}{45} \quad \frac{?}{56}$$

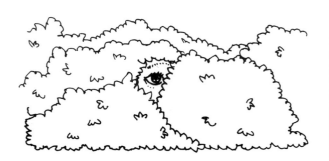

List the factors of each number.

1. 15   **2.** 20   **3.** 14

4. 35   **5.** 21   **6.** 25

7. 16   **8.** 32   **9.** 45

List the common factors.

10. 2, 6   **11.** 16, 24   **12.** 9, 14

13. 30, 75   **14.** 25, 55   **15.** 40, 64

16. 40, 50   **17.** 6, 30   **18.** 36, 75

Write the greatest common factor.

19. 5, 15   **20.** 18, 24   **21.** 7, 21   **22.** 4, 16

23. 3, 9   **24.** 12, 44   **25.** 14, 35   **26.** 16, 18

27. 9, 27   **28.** 5, 6   **29.** 12, 18   **30.** 10, 24

31. 3, 24   **32.** 11, 33   **33.** 12, 15   **34.** 14, 49

35. 15, 33   **36.** 24, 32   **37.** 15, 35   **38.** 28, 42

39. 2, 10   **40.** 12, 20   **41.** 22, 33   **42.** 6, 7

43. 4, 12   **44.** 18, 45   **45.** 16, 40   **46.** 5, 20

47. 8, 20   **48.** 15, 25   **49.** 16, 32   **50.** 16, 20

51. 6, 15   **52.** 18, 36   **53.** 7, 14   **54.** 8, 12

Write *prime* or *composite* to describe each number.

1. 40   2. 17   3. 31

4. 27   5. 45   6. 19

7. 42   8. 39   9. 56

10. 29   11. 70   12. 37

13. 44   14. 60   15. 84

Copy and complete each factor tree.

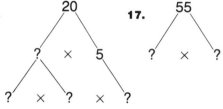

16.

17.

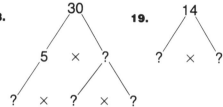

18.

19.

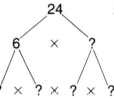

20.

21.

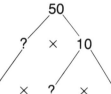

22.

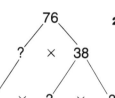

23.

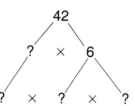

Use a factor tree to write the prime factorization of each number. Other factor trees are possible.

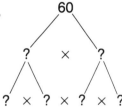

24.

25.

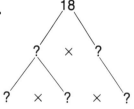

26.

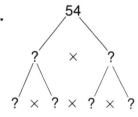

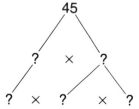

27.

28.

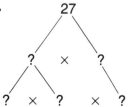

29.

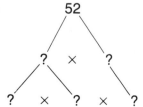

Write the fraction for the part that is shaded.

1.

2.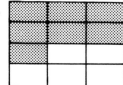

3.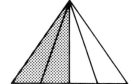

4.

5.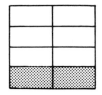

6.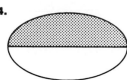

7.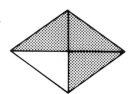

8.

9.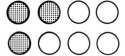

10.

11.

12.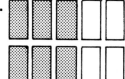

Write the fraction.

13. two ninths

14. one twelfth

15. five sevenths

16. seven tenths

17. three eighths

18. four sixths

Write the decimal.

19. $\frac{8}{10}$

20. $\frac{6}{10}$

21. $\frac{9}{10}$

22. $\frac{1}{10}$

23. $\frac{2}{10}$

24. $\frac{7}{10}$

Choose the operation that you could use to solve the problem.

1. Burke and his brother caught 11 Pacific salmon at Bristol Bay, Alaska. The next week they caught 29 more. How many fish have they caught so far?

   a. multiplication   b. subtraction

   c. division   d. addition

2. In 7 days, Burke caught 21 rainbow trout in a stream near Ketchikan. On average, how many trout did he catch each day?

   a. subtraction   b. division

   c. multiplication   d. addition

Solve.

3. To catch graling, Burke used 3 fishing lines, each 45 feet long. How long were all 3 lines together?

4. Burke paid $4.50 for 6 containers of live bait. How much did each container cost?

5. Burke caught 4 trout that weighed an average of 2.3 pounds each. What was the weight of all 4 trout?

6. Burke went fishing with 19 pieces of bait. The fish got 7 pieces before Burke decided to try another spot. How many pieces of bait did Burke have left?

7. A coho salmon swam 2.5 km upstream one day and 2.2 km the next. How many kilometers did it swim in all?

8. Burke paddled his canoe 4.66 km one day and 5.25 km the next. How far did he paddle in all?

Complete.

1. $\frac{1}{2} = \frac{1 \times 2}{2 \times 2} =$ _____ ?

2. $\frac{4}{5} = \frac{4 \times 4}{5 \times 4} =$ _____ ?

3. $\frac{1}{4} = \frac{1 \times 5}{4 \times 5} =$ _____ ?

4. $\frac{1}{5} = \frac{1 \times 3}{5 \times 3} =$ _____ ?

5. $\frac{2}{5} = \frac{2 \times 6}{5 \times 6} =$ _____ ?

6. $\frac{5}{6} = \frac{5 \times 2}{6 \times 2} =$ _____ ?

7. $\frac{3}{4} = \frac{3 \times 6}{4 \times 6} =$ _____ ?

8. $\frac{1}{3} = \frac{1 \times 4}{3 \times 4} =$ _____ ?

9. $\frac{2}{3} = \frac{2 \times 9}{3 \times 9} =$ _____ ?

10. $\frac{7}{10} = \frac{?}{40}$

11. $\frac{8}{12} = \frac{32}{?}$

12. $\frac{10}{11} = \frac{?}{66}$

13. $\frac{8}{16} = \frac{?}{64}$

14. $\frac{9}{15} = \frac{45}{?}$

15. $\frac{5}{8} = \frac{?}{32}$

16. $\frac{3}{5} = \frac{6}{?}$

17. $\frac{6}{10} = \frac{24}{?}$

18. $\frac{2}{4} = \frac{?}{36}$

Write the next three equivalent fractions.

19. $\frac{3}{5}, \frac{6}{10}, \frac{9}{15}$

20. $\frac{1}{6}, \frac{2}{12}, \frac{3}{18}$

21. $\frac{2}{3}, \frac{4}{6}, \frac{6}{9}$

22. $\frac{5}{7}, \frac{10}{14}, \frac{15}{21}$

Solve.

23. There are 28 students in Ivan's class. On a museum trip, $\frac{3}{4}$ of the students liked the space-exploration exhibit better than the computer exhibit. Write $\frac{3}{4}$ as an equivalent fraction that has a denominator of 28.

Complete.

1. $\dfrac{8 \div 2}{10 \div 2} = \underline{\quad ? \quad}$

2. $\dfrac{14 \div 14}{28 \div 14} = \underline{\quad ? \quad}$

3. $\dfrac{7 \div 7}{35 \div 7} = \underline{\quad ? \quad}$

4. $\dfrac{60 \div 12}{96 \div 12} = \underline{\quad ? \quad}$

5. $\dfrac{54 \div 9}{63 \div 9} = \underline{\quad ? \quad}$

6. $\dfrac{10 \div 10}{40 \div 10} = \underline{\quad ? \quad}$

7. $\dfrac{6 \div 6}{12 \div 6} = \underline{\quad ? \quad}$

8. $\dfrac{30 \div 15}{45 \div 15} = \underline{\quad ? \quad}$

9. $\dfrac{16 \div 2}{18 \div 2} = \underline{\quad ? \quad}$

Is the fraction in simplest form? Write *yes* or *no*. If not, write the fraction in simplest form.

10. $\dfrac{1}{3}$

11. $\dfrac{2}{4}$

12. $\dfrac{2}{3}$

13. $\dfrac{1}{4}$

14. $\dfrac{6}{8}$

15. $\dfrac{16}{18}$

16. $\dfrac{6}{7}$

17. $\dfrac{10}{20}$

18. $\dfrac{11}{12}$

19. $\dfrac{5}{6}$

20. $\dfrac{12}{21}$

21. $\dfrac{40}{50}$

22. $\dfrac{3}{8}$

23. $\dfrac{7}{14}$

24. $\dfrac{15}{18}$

25. $\dfrac{20}{25}$

26. $\dfrac{7}{8}$

27. $\dfrac{24}{40}$

28. $\dfrac{17}{20}$

29. $\dfrac{21}{28}$

Write each fraction in simplest form. Write the letter above the fraction in simplest form to solve the riddle. What did Debra buy at the Alphabet Clothes Store?

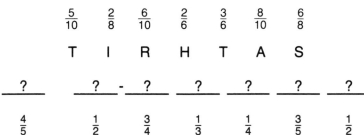

$\dfrac{5}{10}$	$\dfrac{2}{8}$	$\dfrac{6}{10}$	$\dfrac{2}{6}$	$\dfrac{3}{6}$	$\dfrac{8}{10}$	$\dfrac{6}{8}$
T	I	R	H	T	A	S

$\underline{\quad ? \quad} \quad \underline{\quad ? \quad} - \underline{\quad ? \quad} \quad \underline{\quad ? \quad} \quad \underline{\quad ? \quad} \quad \underline{\quad ? \quad} \quad \underline{\quad ? \quad}$

$\dfrac{4}{5} \qquad \dfrac{1}{2} \qquad \dfrac{3}{4} \qquad \dfrac{1}{3} \qquad \dfrac{1}{4} \qquad \dfrac{3}{5} \qquad \dfrac{1}{2}$

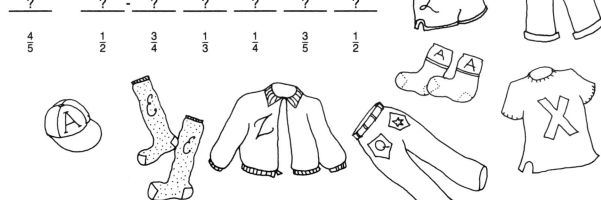

Write a mixed number and a fraction for the part that is shaded.

1.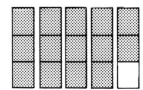

2.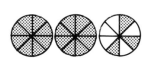

3.

4.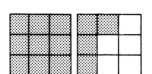

5.

6.

Write as a whole number or as a mixed number.

7. $\frac{19}{6}$ **8.** $\frac{29}{3}$ **9.** $\frac{16}{5}$ **10.** $\frac{31}{6}$

11. $\frac{11}{4}$ **12.** $\frac{41}{5}$ **13.** $\frac{37}{8}$ **14.** $\frac{63}{9}$

15. $\frac{25}{5}$ **16.** $\frac{27}{20}$ **17.** $\frac{38}{9}$ **18.** $\frac{50}{13}$

Write as a fraction.

19. $2\frac{3}{7}$ **20.** 7 **21.** $1\frac{3}{5}$ **22.** $7\frac{5}{9}$

23. $2\frac{1}{6}$ **24.** $9\frac{1}{3}$ **25.** $3\frac{3}{7}$ **26.** 25

27. $4\frac{1}{6}$ **28.** $8\frac{2}{5}$ **29.** $5\frac{1}{2}$ **30.** $16\frac{4}{5}$

Compare. Write $>$, $<$, or $=$.

1. $\frac{10}{12}$ ◯ $\frac{4}{6}$

2. $\frac{1}{5}$ ◯ $\frac{2}{5}$

3. $\frac{1}{2}$ ◯ $\frac{6}{12}$

4. $7\frac{1}{4}$ ◯ $7\frac{3}{4}$

5. $\frac{3}{5}$ ◯ $\frac{5}{6}$

6. $3\frac{8}{9}$ ◯ $6\frac{5}{9}$

7. $5\frac{1}{7}$ ◯ $5\frac{3}{21}$

8. $\frac{7}{8}$ ◯ $\frac{1}{4}$

9. $\frac{2}{3}$ ◯ $\frac{10}{11}$

10. $\frac{8}{10}$ ◯ $\frac{9}{10}$

11. $\frac{5}{15}$ ◯ $\frac{3}{5}$

12. $1\frac{2}{6}$ ◯ $1\frac{1}{5}$

13. $\frac{7}{8}$ ◯ $\frac{2}{3}$

14. $\frac{1}{2}$ ◯ $\frac{5}{10}$

15. $\frac{3}{7}$ ◯ $\frac{1}{4}$

16. $\frac{5}{11}$ ◯ $\frac{6}{11}$

17. $3\frac{2}{3}$ ◯ $2\frac{2}{4}$

18. $\frac{7}{8}$ ◯ $\frac{5}{8}$

19. $2\frac{1}{2}$ ◯ $4\frac{1}{9}$

20. $5\frac{4}{10}$ ◯ $4\frac{2}{5}$

Write in order from the least to the greatest.

21. $\frac{1}{2}$, $\frac{1}{4}$, $\frac{6}{8}$

22. $\frac{10}{12}$, $\frac{4}{6}$, $\frac{3}{4}$

23. $\frac{3}{5}$, $\frac{4}{7}$, $\frac{4}{5}$

24. $\frac{7}{10}$, $\frac{2}{3}$, $\frac{5}{6}$

25. $\frac{2}{3}$, $\frac{4}{9}$, $\frac{7}{9}$

26. $\frac{1}{3}$, $\frac{1}{2}$, $\frac{3}{7}$

Write in order from the greatest to the least.

27. $\frac{2}{5}$, $\frac{1}{3}$, $\frac{4}{15}$

28. $\frac{1}{2}$, $\frac{3}{4}$, $\frac{5}{12}$

29. $\frac{1}{2}$, $\frac{3}{5}$, $\frac{5}{8}$

30. $\frac{2}{3}$, $\frac{2}{6}$, $\frac{5}{6}$

31. $\frac{4}{12}$, $\frac{7}{8}$, $\frac{6}{12}$

32. $\frac{5}{7}$, $\frac{3}{4}$, $\frac{6}{7}$

Use only the fractions that are greater than $\frac{1}{2}$. Write the corresponding letters in order to answer the riddle.

What are fractions when they are arranged from the greatest to the least?

$\frac{3}{11}$ $\frac{9}{10}$ $\frac{1}{6}$ $\frac{8}{9}$ $\frac{3}{8}$ $\frac{6}{7}$ $\frac{1}{3}$ $\frac{1}{4}$ $\frac{10}{12}$ $\frac{3}{4}$ $\frac{2}{6}$ $\frac{5}{7}$ $\frac{4}{10}$ $\frac{7}{10}$ $\frac{5}{11}$ $\frac{3}{12}$ $\frac{6}{9}$ $\frac{2}{7}$ $\frac{7}{12}$ $\frac{3}{9}$ $\frac{4}{8}$

F A P L J L T Q I N B O K R A S D R E X R

Acting It Out	Writing a Number Sentence	Checking That the Solution
Estimation	Checking for a Reasonable	Answers the Question
Using Outside Sources	Answer	Identifying Needed Information
Choosing the Operation	Choosing/Writing a	Solving Multistep Problems/
	Sensible Question	Making a Plan

Write the strategy or method you choose. Then solve.

1. Mount Aconcagua is the tallest mountain in the Western Hemisphere. It is about 22,840 feet high. Some climbers took 4 days to climb the mountain and half as long to descend. How many feet did the climbers descend per day?

2. Mount Saint Helens is a volcano in the Cascade Mountains. During the 1980 eruptions, about 300 meters of its peak were blasted away. After these eruptions, the volcano's elevation was 2,549 meters. What was its height before the eruptions?

3. The highest peaks in the Middle Rocky Mountains are Kings Peak, 13,528 feet high, and Gannett Peak, 13,804 feet high. What is the total height of these two peaks?

4. New York City is approximately 60 feet above sea level. Mount Everest is about 29,000 feet above sea level. About how many times higher is Mount Everest than New York City?

5. The Amazon River in South America is about 4,000 miles long. A boat travels about 19 miles a day. With this information, what question can you answer?

6. The Zambezi River in Africa is 1,600 miles long. The Zambezi is twice as long as the Saint Lawrence River. How long is the Saint Lawrence River?

7. Mount Fuji in Japan is about 12,000 feet high. A group climbed to the top of Mount Fuji. About how many feet did the group climb each day?

8. Dale and Roy give trail rides in the Sierra Nevadas. Each customer pays $6.00 per mile for a ride that lasts about 3 hours. The horses travel at about 3 miles per hour. About how much per customer does the trail ride cost?

Acting It Out	Writing a Number Sentence	Checking That the Solution
Estimation	Checking for a Reasonable	Answers the Question
Using Outside Sources	Answer	Identifying Needed Information
Choosing the Operation	Choosing/Writing a	Solving Multistep Problems/
	Sensible Question	Making a Plan

Write the strategy or method you choose. Then solve.

1. Mount Rainier is 14,410 feet high. Mount Washington is 6,288 feet high. The sum of these two mountain peaks is just 378 feet more than the height of Mount McKinley. What is the height of Mount McKinley?

2. When a cougar is born, it weighs about 1.1 pounds. An average adult cougar weighs about 176 pounds. It takes a cougar $2\frac{1}{2}$ years to reach adult weight. How much weight does a cougar gain a month if it gains the same amount each month? (HINT: 12 months = 1 year)

3. Bob Simmons wants to take a group of 25 schoolchildren and 8 adult chaperons on a picnic across the river. Bob's boat can carry a total of 5 people, including Bob. How many trips will Bob have to make?

4. Bay Shore Sporting Goods is having a big sale. Leather mountain-climbing boots are on sale for $89.95 a pair. Alberta Parker bought a pair for everyone in her family. The total cost was $539.70. How many pairs of boots did Alberta buy?

5. Alberta saved about $90 by buying the boots on sale. About how much did she save on each pair of boots?

6. Alberta also bought 2 pairs of polythermal socks for everyone in her family. The socks were on sale at 3 pairs for $14.99. With this information, what question can you answer?

7. The total price of the 12 pairs of polythermal socks before the sale was $84.00. What was the price of one pair of socks?

8. The total price of the mountain-climbing boots on sale was $539.70, and the total price of the polythermal socks on sale was $59.96. If Alberta gave the cashier $600.00, how much change did she get back?

Add. Write the sum in simplest form. You may wish to use models to help you.

1. $\frac{3}{4} + \frac{3}{4}$

2. $\frac{1}{7} + \frac{2}{7}$

3. $\frac{4}{9} + \frac{4}{9}$

4. $\frac{5}{7} + \frac{4}{7}$

5. $\frac{2}{3} + \frac{2}{3}$

6. $\frac{1}{6} + \frac{2}{6}$

7. $\frac{3}{8} + \frac{1}{8}$

8. $\frac{5}{9} + \frac{2}{9}$

9. $\frac{4}{5} + \frac{3}{5}$

10. $\begin{array}{r} \frac{3}{7} \\ + \frac{5}{7} \\ \hline \end{array}$

11. $\begin{array}{r} \frac{5}{9} \\ + \frac{5}{9} \\ \hline \end{array}$

12. $\begin{array}{r} \frac{7}{10} \\ + \frac{2}{10} \\ \hline \end{array}$

13. $\begin{array}{r} \frac{5}{12} \\ + \frac{5}{12} \\ \hline \end{array}$

14. $\begin{array}{r} \frac{4}{5} \\ + \frac{1}{5} \\ \hline \end{array}$

15. $\begin{array}{r} \frac{6}{7} \\ + \frac{5}{7} \\ \hline \end{array}$

16. $\begin{array}{r} \frac{1}{3} \\ + \frac{1}{3} \\ \hline \end{array}$

17. $\begin{array}{r} \frac{3}{15} \\ + \frac{4}{15} \\ \hline \end{array}$

18. $\begin{array}{r} \frac{5}{9} \\ + \frac{8}{9} \\ \hline \end{array}$

19. $\begin{array}{r} \frac{11}{15} \\ + \frac{12}{15} \\ \hline \end{array}$

20. $\begin{array}{r} \frac{6}{7} \\ + \frac{6}{7} \\ \hline \end{array}$

21. $\begin{array}{r} \frac{7}{13} \\ + \frac{5}{13} \\ \hline \end{array}$

22. $\begin{array}{r} \frac{7}{20} \\ + \frac{4}{20} \\ \hline \end{array}$

23. $\begin{array}{r} \frac{7}{10} \\ + \frac{3}{10} \\ \hline \end{array}$

24. $\begin{array}{r} \frac{6}{11} \\ + \frac{7}{11} \\ \hline \end{array}$

25. $\begin{array}{r} \frac{9}{14} \\ + \frac{2}{14} \\ \hline \end{array}$

Write 0, $\frac{1}{2}$, or 1 to complete.

1. $\frac{9}{10}$ is close to ____?____.

2. $\frac{6}{13}$ is close to ____?____.

3. $\frac{2}{8}$ is close to ____?____.

4. $\frac{5}{30}$ is close to ____?____.

5. $\frac{3}{19}$ is close to ____?____.

6. $\frac{11}{20}$ is close to ____?____.

7. $\frac{7}{15}$ is close to ____?____.

8. $\frac{1}{30}$ is close to ____?____.

9. $\frac{4}{5}$ is close to ____?____.

10. $\frac{12}{15}$ is close to ____?____.

11. $\frac{11}{12}$ is close to ____?____.

12. $\frac{4}{9}$ is close to ____?____.

Estimate.

13. $\frac{4}{5} + \frac{4}{9}$

14. $\frac{1}{2} + \frac{7}{12}$

15. $\frac{14}{15} + \frac{7}{8}$

16. $\frac{1}{5} + \frac{1}{16}$

17. $\frac{9}{12} + \frac{1}{4}$

18. $\frac{8}{9} + \frac{9}{10}$

19. $\frac{1}{7} + \frac{1}{4}$

20. $\frac{5}{8} + \frac{1}{4}$

21. $\frac{7}{8} + \frac{1}{3}$

22. $\frac{3}{7} + \frac{2}{5}$

23. $\frac{1}{5} + \frac{1}{6}$

24. $\frac{3}{4} + \frac{1}{2}$

25. $\frac{1}{4} + \frac{1}{9}$

26. $\frac{1}{8} + \frac{3}{16}$

27. $\frac{1}{2} + \frac{1}{2}$

28. $\frac{11}{12} + \frac{2}{9}$

29. $\frac{10}{11} + \frac{2}{9}$

30. $\frac{4}{10} + \frac{1}{7}$

31. $\frac{3}{15} + \frac{9}{12} + \frac{2}{11}$

32. $\frac{1}{5} + \frac{6}{7} + \frac{8}{10}$

33. $\frac{13}{14} + \frac{1}{4} + \frac{9}{20}$

34. $\frac{6}{8} + \frac{7}{9} + \frac{5}{6}$

35. $\frac{10}{13} + \frac{7}{16} + \frac{8}{18}$

36. $\frac{17}{20} + \frac{2}{3} + \frac{4}{9}$

Solve.

37. Emily pours apple juice for her brother, her sister, and herself. She pours $\frac{4}{9}$ cup for her brother, $\frac{1}{3}$ cup for her sister, and $\frac{9}{10}$ cup for herself. Estimate how many cups Emily pours.

Add. Write the sum in simplest form.

1. $\dfrac{3}{4}$
   $+\dfrac{3}{8}$

2. $\dfrac{3}{5}$
   $+\dfrac{1}{3}$

3. $\dfrac{1}{6}$
   $+\dfrac{2}{3}$

4. $\dfrac{3}{10}$
   $+\dfrac{1}{4}$

5. $\dfrac{2}{5}$
   $+\dfrac{9}{10}$

6. $\dfrac{5}{7}$
   $+\dfrac{1}{14}$

7. $\dfrac{1}{3}$
   $+\dfrac{8}{9}$

8. $\dfrac{7}{8}$
   $+\dfrac{1}{2}$

9. $\dfrac{5}{6}$
   $+\dfrac{2}{9}$

10. $\dfrac{5}{12}$
    $+\dfrac{9}{10}$

11. $\dfrac{2}{9}$
    $+\dfrac{2}{3}$

12. $\dfrac{7}{10}$
    $+\dfrac{1}{8}$

13. $\dfrac{1}{5}$
    $+\dfrac{3}{10}$

14. $\dfrac{7}{12}$
    $+\dfrac{7}{15}$

15. $\dfrac{3}{4}$
    $+\dfrac{7}{8}$

16. $\dfrac{1}{6}$
    $+\dfrac{1}{8}$

17. $\dfrac{1}{2}$
    $+\dfrac{3}{16}$

18. $\dfrac{2}{3}$
    $+\dfrac{4}{9}$

19. $\dfrac{1}{6} + \dfrac{2}{3}$

20. $\dfrac{1}{6} + \dfrac{5}{9}$

21. $\dfrac{7}{10} + \dfrac{2}{5}$

22. $\dfrac{1}{7} + \dfrac{3}{8}$

23. $\dfrac{2}{3} + \dfrac{7}{9}$

24. $\dfrac{1}{10} + \dfrac{3}{5}$

25. $\dfrac{2}{5} + \dfrac{7}{15}$

26. $\dfrac{1}{2} + \dfrac{1}{4}$

27. $\dfrac{2}{3} + \dfrac{5}{6}$

28. $\dfrac{3}{10} + \dfrac{1}{2}$

29. $\dfrac{1}{4} + \dfrac{5}{8}$

30. $\dfrac{5}{6} + \dfrac{7}{10}$

Solve.

31. Luis and Carolyn have 3 hours to paint a room. During that time, Luis paints $\dfrac{3}{10}$ of the room and Carolyn paints $\dfrac{3}{5}$. How much of the room is painted?

32. Carolyn used $\dfrac{5}{6}$ gallon of paint. Luis used $\dfrac{1}{12}$ gallon of paint. How much paint did they use in all?

Subtract. Write the difference in simplest form.

1. $\frac{6}{9}$ $-\frac{4}{9}$

2. $\frac{2}{5}$ $-\frac{1}{6}$

3. $\frac{4}{6}$ $-\frac{7}{12}$

4. $\frac{7}{8}$ $-\frac{1}{4}$

5. $\frac{11}{15}$ $-\frac{2}{15}$

6. $\frac{3}{5}$ $-\frac{1}{2}$

7. $\frac{5}{6}$ $-\frac{1}{3}$

8. $\frac{17}{20}$ $-\frac{13}{20}$

9. $\frac{11}{12}$ $-\frac{1}{2}$

10. $\frac{5}{9}$ $-\frac{1}{3}$

11. $\frac{1}{6}$ $-\frac{1}{9}$

12. $\frac{10}{11}$ $-\frac{2}{11}$

13. $\frac{2}{9}$ $-\frac{1}{81}$

14. $\frac{3}{10}$ $-\frac{3}{25}$

15. $\frac{7}{8}$ $-\frac{1}{2}$

16. $\frac{11}{12}$ $-\frac{5}{12}$

17. $\frac{6}{10}$ $-\frac{2}{5}$

18. $\frac{16}{19}$ $-\frac{13}{19}$

19. $\frac{5}{7}$ $-\frac{1}{7}$

20. $\frac{4}{5}$ $-\frac{2}{15}$

21. $\frac{5}{6}$ $-\frac{2}{3}$

22. $\frac{11}{14}$ $-\frac{5}{14}$

23. $\frac{23}{24}$ $-\frac{14}{24}$

24. $\frac{2}{3}$ $-\frac{1}{3}$

25. $\frac{14}{15}$ $-\frac{1}{15}$

26. $\frac{15}{26}$ $-\frac{2}{13}$

27. $\frac{5}{8}$ $-\frac{3}{8}$

28. $\frac{9}{11}$ $-\frac{8}{11}$

29. $\frac{10}{27}$ $-\frac{7}{27}$

30. $\frac{3}{10}$ $-\frac{2}{15}$

31. $\frac{9}{10} - \frac{3}{10}$

32. $\frac{13}{15} - \frac{4}{15}$

33. $\frac{1}{2} - \frac{3}{7}$

34. $\frac{2}{3} - \frac{1}{6}$

35. $\frac{7}{12} - \frac{5}{12}$

36. $\frac{8}{9} - \frac{4}{9}$

37. $\frac{9}{11} - \frac{3}{11}$

38. $\frac{1}{3} - \frac{1}{4}$

39. $\frac{3}{8} - \frac{9}{24}$

Use with pages 252–253.

Add. Write the sum in simplest form.

1. $15\frac{1}{6}$
   $+\ 9\frac{1}{4}$

2. $21\frac{1}{5}$
   $+\ 6\frac{2}{3}$

3. $3\frac{2}{9}$
   $+\ 5\frac{2}{9}$

4. $9\frac{6}{7}$
   $+\ 12$

5. $8\frac{1}{6}$
   $+\ 11\frac{3}{9}$

6. $17\frac{1}{6}$
   $+\ 1\frac{7}{12}$

7. $25\frac{1}{3}$
   $+\ 2\frac{2}{4}$

8. $4\frac{1}{6}$
   $+\ \frac{1}{2}$

9. $1\frac{2}{3} + 1$

10. $1\frac{1}{2} + 20\frac{1}{6}$

11. $2\frac{7}{9} + 3\frac{1}{9}$

12. $14\frac{1}{4} + 1\frac{1}{4}$

13. $5\frac{1}{3} + 15\frac{1}{8}$

14. $6\frac{2}{9} + 11\frac{1}{18}$

15. $10\frac{5}{6} + 6$

16. $19 + 7\frac{1}{2}$

17. $3\frac{3}{7} + 4\frac{1}{3}$

18. $5 + 2\frac{1}{5}$

19. $9\frac{1}{4} + 3\frac{1}{2}$

20. $1\frac{1}{2} + 3\frac{1}{4}$

21. $4 + 4\frac{3}{8}$

22. $5\frac{1}{3} + 1\frac{1}{2}$

23. $7\frac{2}{5} + 4\frac{3}{10}$

24. $6\frac{5}{8} + 8\frac{1}{8}$

25. $3\frac{1}{3} + 4\frac{1}{6}$

26. $2\frac{1}{2} + 4\frac{3}{8}$

27. $1\frac{5}{8} + 2\frac{1}{4}$

28. $12\frac{1}{2} + 11\frac{2}{3}$

29. $5\frac{2}{5} + 2\frac{3}{4}$

Use with pages 254–255.

Write the letter of the best estimate.

1. $5\frac{1}{10} + 3\frac{7}{8}$

   a. about 8

   b. about 9

   c. about 10

2. $8\frac{1}{4} + 4\frac{1}{9}$

   a. about 12

   b. about 13

   c. about 16

3. $9\frac{1}{8} + 2\frac{2}{7}$

   a. about 9

   b. about 10

   c. about 11

4. $3\frac{7}{12} + \frac{1}{5}$

   a. about 2

   b. about 3

   c. about 4

Add. Write the sum in simplest form.

5. $7\frac{3}{4} + 4\frac{1}{4}$

6. $8\frac{4}{5} + 1\frac{4}{5}$

7. $12\frac{11}{12} + 3\frac{1}{4}$

8. $6\frac{3}{10} + 8\frac{9}{10}$

9. $5\frac{9}{10} + 2\frac{1}{6}$

10. $7\frac{5}{18} + 10\frac{5}{6}$

11. $12\frac{3}{7} + 3\frac{5}{7}$

12. $4\frac{5}{6} + 2\frac{1}{3}$

13. $5\frac{1}{3} + 6\frac{2}{3}$

14. $9\frac{11}{16} + 9\frac{1}{2}$

15. $8\frac{1}{2} + 10\frac{2}{3}$

16. $6\frac{3}{4} + 7\frac{1}{3}$

17. $1\frac{7}{15} + 1\frac{3}{5}$

18. $6\frac{2}{3} + 4\frac{7}{9}$

19. $5\frac{7}{10} + 5\frac{7}{20}$

20. $11\frac{7}{8} + 3\frac{3}{12}$

21. $3\frac{1}{2} + 1\frac{3}{4}$

22. $2\frac{2}{3} + 2\frac{2}{3}$

23. $5\frac{9}{10} + 6\frac{2}{5}$

24. $7\frac{5}{6} + 7\frac{5}{6}$

25. $3\frac{5}{9} + 8\frac{13}{18}$

26. $4\frac{7}{8} + 3\frac{1}{6}$

Subtract. Write the difference in simplest form.

1. $12\frac{7}{9}$
   $- \ 9\frac{2}{6}$

2. $11\frac{5}{7}$
   $- \ 8\frac{1}{2}$

3. $20\frac{1}{3}$
   $- \ 8\frac{2}{15}$

4. $16\frac{10}{11}$
   $- \ 9$

5. $13\frac{9}{13}$
   $- \ 3\frac{6}{13}$

6. $5\frac{18}{21}$
   $- \ 3\frac{2}{3}$

7. $9\frac{1}{3}$
   $- \ 1\frac{3}{10}$

8. $14\frac{7}{8}$
   $- \ 7\frac{2}{3}$

9. $10\frac{2}{3}$
   $- \ 3\frac{1}{6}$

10. $12\frac{3}{4}$
    $- \ 5$

11. $8\frac{11}{14}$
    $- \ 3\frac{5}{7}$

12. $9\frac{1}{2}$
    $- \ 6\frac{1}{2}$

13. $5\frac{3}{4}$
    $- \ 2\frac{1}{2}$

14. $14\frac{3}{4}$
    $- \ 9$

15. $6\frac{2}{3}$
    $- \ 1$

16. $7\frac{6}{9}$
    $- \ 5\frac{1}{3}$

17. $6\frac{5}{7}$
    $- \ 1\frac{2}{7}$

18. $9\frac{5}{6}$
    $- \ 8\frac{1}{2}$

19. $4\frac{4}{5}$
    $- \ 2\frac{1}{10}$

20. $5\frac{2}{3}$
    $- \ 3\frac{4}{9}$

21. $4\frac{3}{4} - 2\frac{1}{4}$

22. $6\frac{3}{8} - 5\frac{1}{8}$

23. $10\frac{6}{7} - 8\frac{3}{14}$

24. $8\frac{5}{8} - 1$

25. $7\frac{8}{9} - 3\frac{4}{9}$

26. $8\frac{3}{4} - 2\frac{1}{2}$

Solve.

27. Felipe wants to be on the track team. On his first day of training, he runs $6\frac{1}{4}$ times around the track. The second day, he runs $8\frac{1}{2}$ times around the track. How many more times did he run around the track on the second day?

Subtracting Mixed Numbers with Renaming

Subtract. Write the answer in simplest form.

1. $8 - 3\frac{1}{3}$

2. $5\frac{1}{4} - 2\frac{3}{4}$

3. $7\frac{1}{4} - 2\frac{1}{3}$

4. $9\frac{5}{8} - 2\frac{6}{8}$

5. $10\frac{1}{5} - 5\frac{7}{10}$

6. $6 - 2\frac{1}{7}$

7. $3\frac{1}{4} - 1\frac{7}{8}$

8. $8\frac{1}{2} - 7\frac{11}{12}$

9. $11\frac{2}{20} - 3\frac{7}{10}$

10. $4 - 3\frac{1}{2}$

11. $4\frac{1}{4} - 2\frac{3}{4}$

12. $10\frac{1}{3} - 6\frac{1}{2}$

13. $7\frac{2}{5} - 2\frac{4}{5}$

14. $9 - 7\frac{1}{3}$

15. $8\frac{1}{5} - 3\frac{1}{4}$

Subtract.

16. $\begin{array}{r} 3\frac{2}{3} \\ -1\frac{6}{7} \\ \hline \end{array}$

17. $\begin{array}{r} 6 \\ -2\frac{5}{12} \\ \hline \end{array}$

18. $\begin{array}{r} 7\frac{1}{5} \\ -3\frac{5}{6} \\ \hline \end{array}$

19. $\begin{array}{r} 8\frac{3}{4} \\ -2\frac{4}{5} \\ \hline \end{array}$

20. $\begin{array}{r} 8\frac{5}{24} \\ -1\frac{11}{12} \\ \hline \end{array}$

21. $\begin{array}{r} 7\frac{1}{11} \\ -5\frac{1}{2} \\ \hline \end{array}$

22. $\begin{array}{r} 4\frac{1}{6} \\ -2\frac{2}{3} \\ \hline \end{array}$

23. $\begin{array}{r} 7\frac{4}{7} \\ -3\frac{11}{14} \\ \hline \end{array}$

24. $\begin{array}{r} 12\frac{5}{9} \\ -7\frac{2}{3} \\ \hline \end{array}$

25. $\begin{array}{r} 5\frac{1}{4} \\ -3\frac{5}{6} \\ \hline \end{array}$

26. $\begin{array}{r} 7\frac{1}{5} \\ -4\frac{9}{10} \\ \hline \end{array}$

27. $\begin{array}{r} 6\frac{1}{2} \\ -3\frac{3}{4} \\ \hline \end{array}$

Write the letter of the correct answer.

1. A group of 27 senior citizens are going on a hike along the Peconic River. They plan to drive to the river. If each car can hold 5 people, how many cars will they need?

   a. 5   **b.** $5\frac{1}{2}$ **c.** 6

2. The group walked 3 miles in 4 hours before stopping for lunch. How far did they walk in one hour?

   a. $\frac{3}{4}$ of a mile
   b. $1\frac{1}{3}$ miles
   c. 1 mile

Solve.

3. Sally is in charge of food for the senior citizens' river hike. Sally can put 10 sandwiches into each pack. If 38 sandwiches are needed, how many packs will Sally put together?

4. At the Bay Shore Senior Citizens Center, 39 members have signed up for a two-day hike in the Catskill Mountains. Each tent has room for 7 adults. How many tents will be needed?

5. While on a 5-hour hike, a group of 5th graders walked 12 miles. How far did they walk in 1 hour?

6. How far could twice as many 5th graders walk in 5 hours?

7. On a river-rafting trip, each raft carried a total of 9 people. If 53 people took the trip, how many rafts were used?

8. There is 1 guide for every 8 people who go on the river-rafting trip. If 55 people decide to go rafting, how many guides will be needed?

9. On a canoe trip, each canoe holds only 3 people. If 14 people want to go on the trip, how many canoes will they need?

10. If 21 sandwiches were divided equally among the 14 people, how many would each person get?

11. There are 45 people who have signed up for a canoe trip. The guide will bring 4 packs of food for each person. If 21 packs of food fit into each waterproof container, how many waterproof containers will the guide bring?

12. If the waterproof containers are divided among 15 boats, how many boats would carry containers?

Multiply. Write the answer in simplest form. You may use models to help you.

1. $\frac{1}{2} \times \frac{1}{4}$

2. $\frac{3}{4} \times \frac{8}{9}$

3. $\frac{1}{4} \times \frac{1}{6}$

4. $\frac{1}{5} \times \frac{1}{3}$

5. $\frac{1}{10} \times \frac{1}{3}$

6. $\frac{6}{7} \times \frac{1}{2}$

7. $\frac{3}{4} \times \frac{5}{6}$

8. $\frac{1}{3} \times \frac{1}{7}$

9. $\frac{2}{5} \times \frac{1}{5}$

10. $\frac{1}{5} \times \frac{1}{8}$

11. $\frac{1}{4} \times \frac{6}{7}$

12. $\frac{3}{8} \times \frac{2}{3}$

13. $\frac{1}{2} \times \frac{1}{9}$

14. $\frac{2}{3} \times \frac{1}{8}$

15. $\frac{7}{8} \times \frac{5}{7}$

16. $\frac{1}{9} \times \frac{1}{4}$

17. $\frac{1}{6} \times \frac{1}{7}$

18. $\frac{1}{5} \times \frac{1}{2}$

19. $\frac{1}{4} \times \frac{1}{3}$

20. $\frac{3}{10} \times \frac{1}{3}$

21. $\frac{3}{5} \times \frac{2}{3}$

22. $\frac{4}{9} \times \frac{1}{2}$

23. $\frac{1}{4} \times \frac{1}{8}$

24. $\frac{1}{8} \times \frac{4}{5}$

Multiply. Then copy the riddle. Match the letters to answer the riddle.

25. $\frac{4}{5} \times \frac{3}{8}$ B

26. $\frac{1}{9} \times \frac{1}{8}$ R

27. $\frac{1}{2} \times \frac{6}{7}$ C

28. $\frac{1}{5} \times \frac{1}{10}$ K

29. $\frac{7}{8} \times \frac{2}{3}$ E

30. $\frac{4}{7} \times \frac{9}{10}$ A

31. $\frac{3}{7} \times \frac{1}{3}$ T

32. $\frac{1}{7} \times \frac{1}{9}$ G

33. $\frac{5}{6} \times \frac{3}{5}$ U

34. $\frac{1}{5} \times \frac{5}{6}$ A

35. $\frac{4}{5} \times \frac{5}{7}$ R

36. $\frac{3}{4} \times \frac{4}{5}$ G

What has four wheels and flies?

| $\frac{?}{\frac{1}{63}}$ | $\frac{?}{\frac{18}{35}}$ | $\frac{?}{\frac{1}{72}}$ | $\frac{?}{\frac{3}{10}}$ | $\frac{?}{\frac{1}{6}}$ | $\frac{?}{\frac{3}{5}}$ | $\frac{?}{\frac{7}{12}}$ |

| $\frac{?}{\frac{1}{7}}$ | $\frac{?}{\frac{4}{7}}$ | $\frac{?}{\frac{1}{2}}$ | $\frac{?}{\frac{3}{7}}$ | $\frac{?}{\frac{1}{50}}$ |

Multiplying Fractions and Whole Numbers

Multiply. Write the answer in simplest form.

1. $\frac{1}{2} \times 6$

2. $2 \times \frac{1}{2}$

3. $8 \times \frac{5}{6}$

4. $\frac{1}{4} \times 24$

5. $\frac{1}{4} \times 30$

6. $10 \times \frac{1}{2}$

7. $\frac{1}{7} \times 14$

8. $\frac{1}{4} \times 32$

9. $25 \times \frac{3}{5}$

10. $\frac{1}{9} \times 60$

11. $33 \times \frac{2}{3}$

12. $\frac{1}{4} \times 100$

13. $\frac{4}{7} \times 21$

14. $64 \times \frac{1}{4}$

15. $\frac{2}{9} \times 48$

16. $\frac{5}{6} \times 60$

17. $\frac{4}{5} \times 15$

18. $\frac{4}{7} \times 21$

19. $40 \times \frac{7}{8}$

20. $96 \times \frac{1}{5}$

21. $100 \times \frac{7}{10}$

22. $20 \times \frac{4}{5}$

23. $49 \times \frac{2}{7}$

24. $\frac{1}{3} \times 3$

Write $\frac{1}{3}$ of each number.

25. 21

26. 28

27. 39

28. 45

29. 65

30. 24

31. 52

32. 10

Write $\frac{1}{4}$ of each number.

33. 43

34. 14

35. 1,000

36. 80

37. 28

38. 100

39. 17

40. 21

Write $\frac{3}{4}$ of each number.

41. 12

42. 1,000

43. 28

44. 16

45. 50

46. 100

47. 25

48. 20

Use with pages 274–275.

Multiply. Write each product in simplest form.

1. $\frac{3}{4} \times 1\frac{1}{3}$

2. $6 \times 10\frac{1}{2}$

3. $2\frac{1}{6} \times \frac{1}{2}$

4. $1\frac{3}{4} \times \frac{2}{5}$

5. $2\frac{2}{3} \times 1\frac{1}{4}$

6. $\frac{5}{6} \times 1\frac{2}{3}$

7. $\frac{5}{6} \times 1\frac{1}{2}$

8. $2\frac{1}{6} \times \frac{2}{5}$

9. $3\frac{1}{3} \times \frac{1}{3}$

10. $\frac{4}{5} \times 4\frac{1}{2}$

11. $\frac{2}{3} \times 6\frac{1}{4}$

12. $\frac{3}{4} \times 2\frac{1}{6}$

13. $6 \times \frac{2}{3}$

14. $3\frac{3}{5} \times 1\frac{1}{2}$

15. $\frac{2}{7} \times 9\frac{1}{2}$

16. $\frac{1}{4} \times 2\frac{5}{6}$

17. $8 \times \frac{7}{8}$

18. $\frac{3}{8} \times 1\frac{1}{7}$

19. $3\frac{3}{4} \times 1\frac{1}{2}$

20. $9 \times \frac{3}{8}$

21. $\frac{5}{6} \times 6$

22. $9\frac{1}{2} \times \frac{2}{3}$

23. $5\frac{1}{5} \times \frac{1}{4}$

24. $3\frac{1}{3} \times \frac{1}{9}$

25. $4\frac{1}{4} \times 2\frac{1}{2}$

26. $\frac{3}{7} \times 1\frac{1}{3}$

27. $\frac{1}{10} \times 4\frac{1}{6}$

28. $\frac{1}{9} \times 8\frac{1}{2}$

29. $5\frac{1}{2} \times \frac{2}{7}$

30. $\frac{2}{3} \times 5\frac{2}{5}$

Copy and complete the fraction rings. Multiply the fraction in the center by the outside number. Write the answer in the outermost ring.

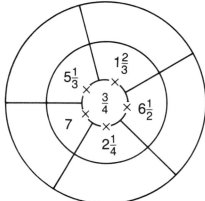

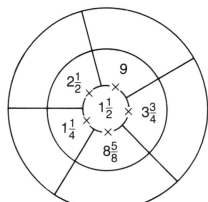

Estimate to solve.

1. The Jambon Drama Club is putting on the play *Knights of the Round Table*. The club may use the auditorium from 4:30 P.M. to 6:30 P.M. They must leave no later than 6:45 P.M. Here is their rehearsal schedule:

Act 1: $15\frac{1}{4}$ minutes Act 3: $27\frac{1}{2}$ minutes

Act 2: 36 minutes Act 4: $22\frac{1}{2}$ minutes

Will the club be finished rehearsing by 6:45 P.M.?

2. The club has a budget of $225 for the play. So far, they have spent the following amounts of money.

$42.75: costumes $12.50: special effects

$61.50: props $44.62: equipment rental

$30.47: scenery   ($22.31 per day)

              $32.50: lights

Do they have enough money to rent equipment for 2 more days?

3. The club needs a switchboard to control the lights and sound effects. A new switchboard costs $356.75 plus $57.50 for installation. Renting one costs $33.10 per day. They would need to rent a switchboard for 14 days. Would it be more economical to purchase or to rent the equipment?

4. Sal Laloco is in charge of box office sales. Before the show opens, he sells 112 tickets at $1.95 per ticket. The club has $98 in the treasury. Does the club have enough money to buy a spotlight for $305?

5. Jennifer and Patti will play the leads in *Sisters of Lucy*. Each girl will be on stage for different lengths of time.

	Jennifer	Patti
Act 1	27.8 min	22.5 min
Act 2	18.4 min	23.2 min
Act 3	26.2 min	17.4 min

Which girl will be on stage longer?

Divide.

1.

$4 \div \frac{1}{4}$

2.

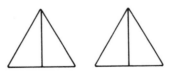

$2 \div \frac{1}{2}$

3.

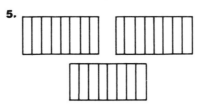

$8 \div \frac{1}{2}$

4.

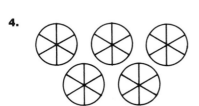

$5 \div \frac{1}{6}$

5.

$3 \div \frac{1}{8}$

6.

$4 \div \frac{1}{5}$

7. $1 \div \frac{1}{2}$

8. $2 \div \frac{1}{5}$

9. $2 \div \frac{1}{7}$

10. $7 \div \frac{1}{8}$

11. $4 \div \frac{1}{6}$

12. $12 \div \frac{1}{3}$

13. $2 \div \frac{1}{9}$

14. $5 \div \frac{1}{5}$

15. $14 \div \frac{1}{2}$

16. $8 \div \frac{1}{5}$

17. $5 \div \frac{1}{9}$

18. $6 \div \frac{1}{3}$

19. $6 \div \frac{1}{4}$

20. $7 \div \frac{1}{6}$

21. $10 \div \frac{1}{2}$

22. $20 \div \frac{1}{5}$

23. $40 \div \frac{1}{2}$

24. $50 \div \frac{1}{2}$

25. $16 \div \frac{1}{5}$

26. $30 \div \frac{1}{5}$

27. $15 \div \frac{1}{3}$

28. $6 \div \frac{1}{5}$

29. $11 \div \frac{1}{4}$

30. $31 \div \frac{1}{2}$

Copy and complete each table. Solve.

1. The local ball park can seat 1,200 people and has standing room for 300. Before a game is played, 75 people enter the stadium every minute. If everybody who enters tries to get a seat, how long would it take for 600 seats to be filled?

Number of minutes								
Number of people								

2. At that rate, in how much time would the standing room be filled?

3. If 300 people attend the game, there must be 2 hot dog vendors. If 600 people attend, there must be 4 hot dog vendors. How many people are at a game when there are 8 hot dog vendors?

Number of vendors				
Number of people				

4. How many vendors should there be for 750 people?

5. When 450 people attend the game, 3 souvenir stands are open. When there are 900 people, 6 stands are open. How many people will 9 souvenir stands serve?

Number of stands			
Number of people			

Use with pages 282–283.

Copy and complete the tables to solve the problems.

1. Fritz was teaching little Sal to catch a ball. When they stood 5 feet apart, Sal caught 6 of 8 balls. At 6 feet, Sal caught 5 of 8 balls. At 7 feet, he caught every other ball. If the trend continued, how many balls would Sal have caught at a distance of 10 feet?

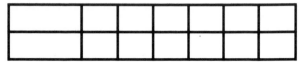

2. Anne wants to find out whether she can shoot better fast or slowly. When she shoots fast, she makes 3 shots in 15 seconds, 6 shots after 30 seconds, and 9 shots after 45 seconds. When she shoots slowly, she makes 1 shot in 15 seconds, 5 shots after 30 seconds, and 9 shots after 45 seconds. If this trend continues, how many baskets will she have made after shooting fast for 90 seconds? How many shooting slowly?

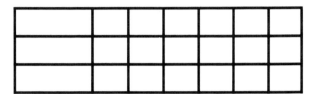

3. Thad is throwing basketballs through a hoop to improve his accuracy. When he is 1 yard away from the hoop, he throws 9 of 10 balls through the hoop. When he is 4 yards away, he throws 7 of 10 balls through the hoop. He throws 5 of 10 balls through the hoop when he is 7 yards away. At this rate and from 16 yards away, how many of 10 throws will be good?

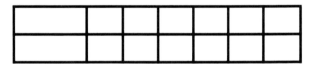

Write *A.M.* or *P.M.*

1. Breakfast is served.

2. The bus brings you to school.

3. School ends.

4. The sun sets.

How much time has passed?

5.

from	to
12:00	**4:00**
Noon	P.M.

_____?_____ h _____?_____ min

6.

from	to
6:10	**7:45**
A.M.	A.M.

_____?_____ h _____?_____ min

7.

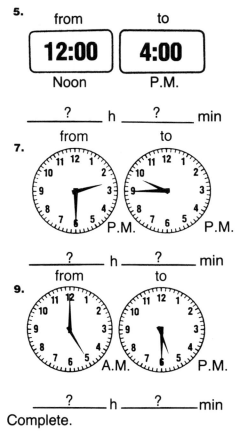

from   to

_____?_____ h _____?_____ min

8.

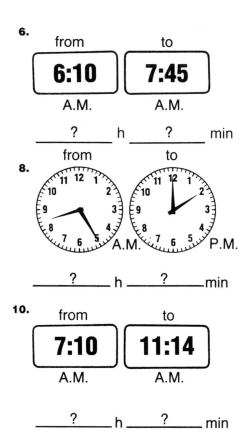

from   to

_____?_____ h _____?_____ min

9.

from   to

_____?_____ h _____?_____ min

10.

from	to
7:10	**11:14**
A.M.	A.M.

_____?_____ h _____?_____ min

Complete.

11. $3 \text{ y} = $ _____?_____ mo

12. $4 \text{ min} = $ _____?_____ s

13. $120 \text{ s} = $ _____?_____ min

14. $\frac{5}{6} \text{ h} = $ _____?_____ min

15. $\frac{2}{7} \text{ wk} = $ _____?_____ d

16. $730 \text{ d} = $ _____?_____ y

Use with pages 284–285.

Add.

1. 3 h 10 min
   + 1 h 14 min

2. 3 h 40 min
   + 8 h 25 min

3. 6 min 32 s
   + 9 min 20 s

4. 8 h 44 min
   + 1 h 6 min

5. 12 h 12 min
   + 3 h 15 min

6. 5 h 24 min
   + 2 h 19 min

7. 7 h 22 min
   + 3 h 41 min

8. 4 min 50 s
   + 9 min 7 s

9. 22 min 16 s
   + 34 min 18 s

10. 5 min 39 s
    + 5 min 29 s

11. 9 h 14 min
    + 5 h 32 min

12. 9 h 36 min
    + 4 h 11 min

Subtract.

13. 7 h 45 min
    − 3 h 29 min

14. 18 h 59 min
    − 12 h 23 min

15. 8 min 32 s
    − 6 min 13 s

16. 18 h 39 min
    − 14 h 50 min

17. 5 h 22 min
    − 1 h 50 min

18. 28 min 18 s
    − 16 min 28 s

19. 16 min 45 s
    − 6 min 40 s

20. 10 min 10 s
    − 3 min 35 s

21. 7 min 30 s
    − 4 min 20 s

22. 2 h 51 min
    − 1 h 52 min

23. 3 h 18 min
    − 2 h 10 min

24. 48 min 25 s
    − 46 min 35 s

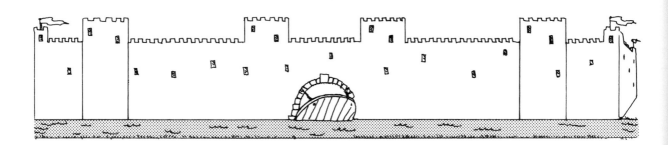

Solve.

25. Janna spent 3 h 26 min putting together a model castle on Saturday. On Monday, she spent 1 h 15 min working on it. How long did she spend in all?

26. It took Janna 15 h 18 min to complete a model bridge. The model castle took 17 h 9 min. How much longer did it take to put the castle together?

Use the schedule to solve.

Canoe tours	Departs	Arrives	Distance	Remarks
Riverview to Stacey	9:00 A.M.	1:00 P.M.	10 miles	Calm water
Riverview to Deep Eddy	9:00 A.M.	3:00 P.M.	14 miles	White water
Stacey to Deep Eddy	10:00 A.M.	12:30 P.M.	4 miles	White water
Stacey to Mark's Landing	2:00 P.M.	7:00 P.M.	10 miles	Sunset tour small islands
Deep Eddy to Mark's Landing	11:00 A.M.	3:30 P.M.	6 miles	Calm water small islands
Riverview to Mark's Landing	11:30 A.M.	3:30 P.M. Next day	20 miles	Calm water white water small islands overnight camp at Stacey
All trips require advance reservations. Reserve 1 week in advance for day trips, 2 weeks for overnight camping trips.				

1. Gina and Nicky are taking two trips, from Riverview to Stacey, and from Stacey to Mark's Landing. How long will they have between trips?

2. Paul and Jan want to meet at Deep Eddy. If Paul leaves from Riverview, and Jan leaves from Stacey, when is the earliest they could meet?

3. Gloria takes the overnight tour. The tour leaves Stacey at 11:30 A.M. At about what time did the tour reach Stacey the previous day?

4. Jim is taking the bus to Stacey to go on the Stacey/Deep Eddy trip. The bus ride takes 45 minutes. When must the bus leave to reach Stacey in time?

5. On March 1, Susan and Tina decided to take the overnight trip to Mark's Landing. What is the earliest day they could take the trip?

6. Ralph decides to take two trips, one from Riverview to Deep Eddy, and the other from Deep Eddy to Mark's Landing. Can he take both trips the same day?

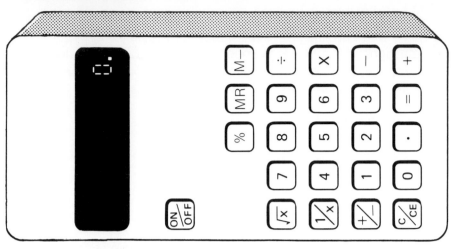

Measure this calculator to the nearest

1. inch

2. $\frac{1}{2}$ in.

3. $\frac{1}{4}$ in.

4. $\frac{1}{8}$ in.

5. $\frac{1}{16}$ in.

Use a ruler to draw a line that is

6. $1\frac{1}{2}$ in.

7. $3\frac{1}{4}$ in.

8. $2\frac{7}{16}$ in.

9. $4\frac{3}{8}$ in.

Solve.

Paco is making a kite. He is using two wooden sticks and a sheet of plastic to make the kite.

10. What is the total length of the pieces of wood?

11. What is the distance around the kite?

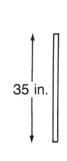

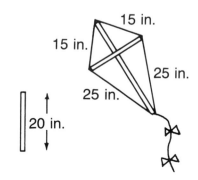

15 in.

15 in.

25 in.

25 in.

35 in.

20 in.

Write *inches*, *feet*, or *yards*.

1. A chair may be 3 _____?_____ high.

2. A spoon may be 6 _____?_____ long.

3. A television screen may be 21 _____?_____ wide.

4. The distance around a jogging track may be 440 _____?_____ .

Choose the appropriate unit of measure. Write *yd* or *mi*.

5. the length of the Colorado River

6. the length of a carpet

7. the distance from Illinois to Mexico

8. the length of an Olympic swimming pool

9. the length of a football field

10. the height of a window

Complete.

11. 15 ft = _____?_____ yd

12. 1 mi = _____?_____ ft

13. 1 yd = _____?_____ in.

14. 2 yd = _____?_____ ft

15. 5,280 ft = _____?_____ yd

16. 2 mi = _____?_____ yd

Solve.

17. The *Give-Me-A-Tip* newspaper carriers all have routes which cover less than 1 mile. Copy and complete the chart to find out the distance of each carrier's route.

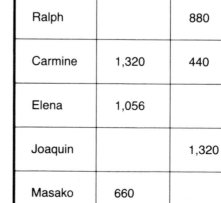

LENGTH OF ROUTE

	Feet	Yards	Miles
Ralph		880	$\frac{1}{2}$
Carmine	1,320	440	
Elena	1,056		$\frac{1}{5}$
Joaquin		1,320	
Masako	660		

Write *ounces*, *pounds*, or *tons*.

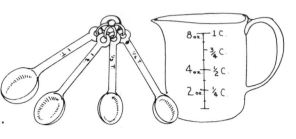

1. A bag of oranges may weigh 4 _____?_____ .

2. A tomato may weigh 5 _____?_____ .

3. A truckload of topsoil may weigh $\frac{1}{2}$ _____?_____ .

4. A handful of cherries may weigh 10 _____?_____ .

Complete.

5. 3 lb = _____?_____ oz

6. 2,000 lb = _____?_____ T

7. 32 oz = _____?_____ lb

8. 20 lb = _____?_____ oz

9. 20,000 lb = _____?_____ T

10. 20 oz = _____?_____ lb

11. 15 T _____?_____ lb

12. $2\frac{1}{2}$ lb = _____?_____ ozs

13. 2 T = _____?_____ lb

14. 400 oz = _____?_____ lb

15. 1,000 lb = _____?_____ T

16. 64 oz = _____?_____ lb

17. 8 lb = _____?_____ oz

18. $1\frac{1}{2}$ T = _____?_____ lb

19. 1,500 lb = _____?_____ T

Write *cups*, *pints*, *quarts*, or *gallons*.

20. A thermos may hold 3 _____?_____ of milk.

21. A fish tank may hold 8 _____?_____ of water.

22. A pitcher may hold 2 _____?_____ of juice.

23. A small carton may hold 1 _____?_____ of cream.

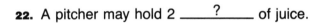

Complete.

24. 2 c = _____?_____ pt

25. 20 qt = _____?_____ gal

26. 10 pt = _____?_____ qt

27. 6 qt = _____?_____ pt

28. 3 gal = _____?_____ qt

29. 4 pt = _____?_____ c

30. 16 qt = _____?_____ gal

31. 6 c = _____?_____ pt

32. 6 pt = _____?_____ qt

Write the Fahrenheit temperature.

1.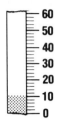

2.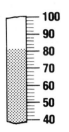

3.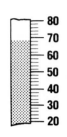

4.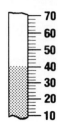

Copy and complete the chart.

	Starting temperature	Temperature change	Final temperature
5.	40°F	fell 15°	
6.	21°F	rose 12°	

Write the Celsius temperature.

7.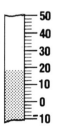

8.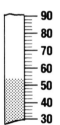

9.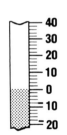

10.

Copy and complete the chart.

	Starting temperature	Temperature change	Final temperature
11.	37°C	fell	20°C
12.		rose 6°	16°C

Use with pages 296–297.

TIME ZONES OF THE CONTIGUOUS UNITED STATES

Pacific time

Eastern time

Mountain time

Central time

Seattle

Oakland

Chicago

Boston

New York

Dallas

Houston

Tampa

New Orleans

Solve.

1. Sandy gets home from school in New York at 3:45 P.M. If his cousin in Houston also gets home at 3:45, how long does Sandy have to wait before calling her?

2. A flight from Tampa, Florida, to Oakland, California, takes 6 hours. If you leave Tampa at 11:00 A.M., to what time will you have to set your watch when you arrive?

3. The Chicago ball team will play a game in Seattle at 6:05 P.M., Pacific time. What time will the game begin on television in Chicago?

4. If the team played in Boston at 6:00 P.M., Eastern time, what time would the game begin on television in Chicago?

5. The Tra-la-la Music Company has offices in Seattle, Houston, Boston, and Chicago. If all the offices open at 9:00 A.M., what is the earliest time the manager in Boston can call all the other offices?

6. All the offices of the Tra-la-la Music Company close at 5:00 P.M. nationwide. If it is 4:45 in Houston and the Houston office wants to call the Chicago office, will it still be open?

Copy and complete the table to show each ratio three ways.

1.		5 to 6	$\frac{5}{6}$
2.	1:2		$\frac{1}{2}$
3.	15:10	15 to 10	
4.		4 to 4	$\frac{4}{4}$
5.	42:42		$\frac{42}{42}$
6.	300:500	300 to 500	

Write the ratio.

7. apples to pears

8. bananas to lemons

9. apples to lemons

10. pears to apples

11. bananas to pieces of fruit

12. pieces of fruit to pears

Write each ratio as a fraction.

13. 8 of 9

14. 2 of 5

15. 1 of 7

16. 5 of 8

17. 3 of 10

18. 9 of 25

19. 11 of 64

20. 13 of 36

21. 6 of 13

22. 4 of 11

23. 3 of 14

24. 18 of 27

What ratio am I?

25. I am the ratio of the greatest common factor of 8 and 12 to the least common multiple of 8 and 12.

26. I am the ratio of the greatest prime factor of 10 to the greatest prime factor of 28.

Equal Ratios

Write two equal ratios.

1. $\frac{4}{5} = \frac{8}{10}$

2. $\frac{3}{7} = \frac{6}{14}$

3. $\frac{8}{9} = \frac{16}{18}$

4. $\frac{7}{10} = \frac{14}{20}$

5. $\frac{1}{2} = \frac{2}{4}$

6. $\frac{3}{4} = \frac{6}{8}$

Write the missing term of the equal ratio.

7. $\frac{1}{2} = \frac{?}{14}$

8. $\frac{3}{8} = \frac{24}{?}$

9. $\frac{5}{2} = \frac{?}{10}$

10. $\frac{9}{10} = \frac{?}{30}$

11. $\frac{5}{12} = \frac{?}{24}$

12. $\frac{4}{6} = \frac{?}{18}$

13. $\frac{7}{3} = \frac{?}{21}$

14. $\frac{5}{6} = \frac{35}{?}$

15. $\frac{6}{7} = \frac{?}{42}$

16. $\frac{2}{9} = \frac{18}{?}$

17. $\frac{1}{4} = \frac{4}{?}$

18. $\frac{3}{4} = \frac{?}{20}$

19. $\frac{9}{5} = \frac{?}{25}$

20. $\frac{9}{4} = \frac{36}{?}$

21. $\frac{5}{7} = \frac{?}{63}$

22. $\frac{6}{9} = \frac{48}{?}$

23. $\frac{7}{4} = \frac{?}{24}$

24. $\frac{3}{2} = \frac{?}{16}$

25. $\frac{8}{7} = \frac{?}{35}$

26. $\frac{5}{9} = \frac{40}{?}$

Write = or ≠.

27. $\frac{2}{3} \bigcirc \frac{18}{24}$

28. $\frac{1}{5} \bigcirc \frac{6}{30}$

29. $\frac{7}{4} \bigcirc \frac{28}{16}$

30. $\frac{5}{8} \bigcirc \frac{40}{72}$

31. $\frac{1}{4} \bigcirc \frac{4}{16}$

32. $\frac{9}{4} \bigcirc \frac{45}{16}$

33. $\frac{1}{6} \bigcirc \frac{5}{36}$

34. $\frac{7}{21} \bigcirc \frac{1}{3}$

Write the letter of the ratio that is equal to the given ratio.

Given ratio	A	B	C	
$\frac{1}{4}$	$\frac{3}{12}$	$\frac{4}{1}$	$\frac{5}{12}$	**35.**
$\frac{3}{2}$	$\frac{4}{6}$	$\frac{6}{4}$	$\frac{4}{8}$	**37.**
$\frac{4}{7}$	$\frac{16}{28}$	$\frac{5}{8}$	$\frac{16}{21}$	**39.**
$\frac{8}{9}$	$\frac{18}{16}$	$\frac{13}{14}$	$\frac{72}{81}$	**41.**

Given ratio	A	B	C	
$\frac{2}{3}$	$\frac{14}{15}$	$\frac{8}{12}$	$\frac{3}{2}$	**36.**
$\frac{5}{9}$	$\frac{10}{27}$	$\frac{10}{18}$	$\frac{15}{24}$	**38.**
$\frac{6}{7}$	$\frac{7}{6}$	$\frac{12}{13}$	$\frac{18}{21}$	**40.**
$\frac{8}{5}$	$\frac{24}{15}$	$\frac{15}{10}$	$\frac{30}{25}$	**42.**

Solve. Write a simpler problem if you need to.

1. Irma is a postal carrier. She drives $1\frac{3}{4}$ miles to work. Her delivery route begins $\frac{1}{2}$ mile from the post office and is $2\frac{2}{3}$ miles long. How many miles has Irma traveled when she reaches the end of her route?

2. One day, Ely's checking account shows a balance of $57.04. He writes a check for $21.50 to pay the telephone bill and a check for $15.35 to pay the electric bill. The next day, Ely deposits $243.97 in his checking account. What is his balance that day?

3. Chopin's "Waltz in C-Sharp Minor" is 3 minutes 45 seconds long. His "Waltz in E-flat" is 5 minutes 22 seconds long. His "Heroic Polonaise" is 7 minutes 3 seconds long. His "Ballade in G Minor" is 9 minutes 13 seconds long. If the 4 pieces were taped on a 30-minute cassette, how much blank time would there be left?

4. Wayne types about 50 words per minute. A typical double-spaced page contains 500 words. How long does it take Wayne to type $9\frac{1}{2}$ pages?

5. Inez earns $3.00 per hour sorting empty cans for recycling. She is saving money to buy a gift for her mother. The gift she has chosen costs $22.98. She will spend $0.85 for a card and $1.25 for wrapping paper. So far, Inez has saved $6.50. How many more hours must she work in order to reach her goal?

6. Enzio bought a hunk of cheese weighing 3 pounds at the store. He saved half of it for the macaroni and cheese dish he will cook for dinner. He made sandwiches for himself and 5 friends with the rest. How much cheese did he use for each sandwich?

7. Ilana cut the pattern for a skirt she is sewing. The length of a panel is $28\frac{1}{2}$ inches. Of that, $\frac{5}{8}$ inch will be used for the waistband seam, $\frac{1}{4}$ inch for finishing the lower rough edge and $2\frac{1}{2}$ inches for the hem. What is the final length of the skirt?

Juan makes a scale drawing of Main Street.
Scale: 1 cm : 4 m

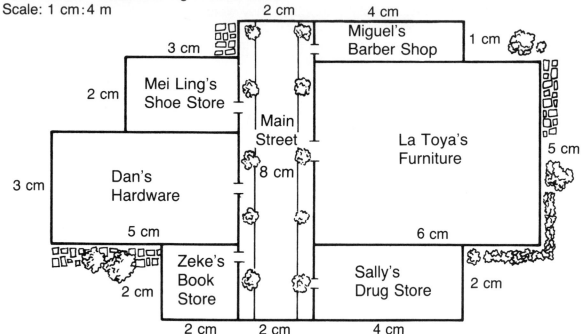

Use the scale drawing above to find the length and width of each store.

1. Mei Ling's Shoe Store

$l =$ ____?____ ; $w =$ ____?____

2. Miguel's Barber Shop

$l =$ ____?____ ; $w =$ ____?____

3. La Toya's Furniture

$l =$ ____?____ ; $w =$ ____?____

4. Sally's Drug Store

$l =$ ____?____ ; $w =$ ____?____

5. Zeke's Book Store

$l =$ ____?____ ; $w =$ ____?____

6. Dan's Hardware

$l =$ ____?____ ; $w =$ ____?____

Solve.
Use the scale drawing above.

7. What is the length of the wall between Mei Ling's Shoe Store and Dan's Hardware?

8. The door to La Toya's Furniture is 2 m wide. How wide would it be on the scale drawing?

Alaskan sourdoughs were prospectors who traveled alone through the Alaskan wilderness searching for gold. They were called sourdoughs because they carried sourdough starter pots strapped to their packs. They used these pots whenever they wanted to make a batch of sourdough bread.

Alaskan Sourdough Bread

$\frac{2}{3}$ cup sourdough starter

1 pack active dry yeast

$1\frac{1}{3}$ cup warm water

$3\frac{3}{4}$ cup unsifted all-purpose flour

$2\frac{1}{8}$ teaspoon salt

$\frac{1}{2}$ teaspoon baking soda

---

1. Jenny wants to make two batches of sourdough bread. How many cups of sourdough starter will she need?

2. Jenny makes two batches of the bread. How many teaspoons of salt will she need?

3. Jenny has $10\frac{1}{2}$ cups of flour. Can she make 3 batches of the sourdough bread? How much more flour would she need?

4. Rick and Dave plan to make sourdough bread for their family-reunion picnic. They make $4\frac{1}{2}$ batches of the bread. How much flour do they need?

5. Rick has a 10-lb bag of flour that equals about $18\frac{1}{2}$ cups. Will he have enough flour to make $4\frac{1}{2}$ batches of sourdough bread?

A   B   C   D

Use Figures A–D. Copy and complete the table.

	Figure	Ratio of shaded part to whole	Write as "per 100"	Write using %
1.	A	26 to 100		
2.	B		7 per 100	
3.	C			58%
4.	D	83 to 100		

Write the percent.

5. $\frac{51}{100}$

6. $\frac{46}{100}$

7. $\frac{4}{100}$

8. $\frac{19}{100}$

9. 12 of 100

10. 2 to 100

11. 84:100

12. 59:100

13. 65:100

14. 87 to 100

15. 61 per 100

16. 74 of 100

17. 3 of 100

18. 38:100

19. 94:100

20. 8 of 100

21. 17 to 100

22. 5:100

23. 37 of 100

24. 98 per 100

25. a ratio of 35 to 100

Write as a percent.

1. 0.42	**2.** 0.76	**3.** 0.30	**4.** 0.80
5. 0.05	**6.** 0.09	**7.** 0.1	**8.** 0.6
9. 0.62	**10.** 0.43	**11.** 0.86	**12.** 0.94
13. 0.60	**14.** 0.70	**15.** 0.5	**16.** 0.3
17. 0.04	**18.** 0.02	**19.** 0.4	**20.** 0.03
21. 0.36	**22.** 0.79	**23.** 0.07	**24.** 0.83
25. 0.73	**26.** 0.87	**27.** 0.32	**28.** 0.88
29. 0.95	**30.** 0.45	**31.** 0.18	**32.** 0.06
33. 0.8	**34.** 0.19	**35.** 0.01	**36.** 0.65

Write as a decimal.

37. 35%	**38.** 76%	**39.** 42%	**40.** 93%
41. 32%	**42.** 5%	**43.** 7%	**44.** 10%
45. 30%	**46.** 52%	**47.** 67%	**48.** 37%
49. 2%	**50.** 8%	**51.** 31%	**52.** 20%
53. 90%	**54.** 14%	**55.** 48%	**56.** 64%
57. 86%	**58.** 99%	**59.** 17%	**60.** 24%
61. 43%	**62.** 53%	**63.** 84%	**64.** 33%

Copy and complete the table. Write each fraction in simplest form.

	Fraction	Decimal	Percent
1.	$\frac{1}{2}$		
2.		0.25	
3.			30%
4.		0.75	
5.	$\frac{4}{5}$		
6.			60%

Write each percent as a fraction in simplest form.

7. 50% **8.** 25% **9.** 14% **10.** 60%

11. 30% **12.** 11% **13.** 15% **14.** 20%

Write each fraction as a percent.

15. $\frac{42}{100}$ **16.** $\frac{58}{100}$ **17.** $\frac{1}{4}$ **18.** $\frac{2}{5}$

19. $\frac{41}{50}$ **20.** $\frac{8}{25}$ **21.** $\frac{9}{20}$ **22.** $\frac{1}{2}$

23. $\frac{7}{10}$ **24.** $\frac{19}{50}$ **25.** $\frac{10}{25}$ **26.** $\frac{3}{4}$

27. $\frac{16}{100}$ **28.** $\frac{2}{25}$ **29.** $\frac{3}{10}$ **30.** $\frac{4}{5}$

Find the percent of each number.

1. 20% of 70
2. 50% of 30
3. 70% of 240

4. 40% of 100
5. 9% of 1,400
6. 4% of 200

7. 3% of 3,600
8. 10% of 250
9. 28% of 300

10. 90% of 130
11. 76% of 500
12. 1% of 1,200

13. 34% of 400
14. 70% of 20
15. 43% of 200

16. 30% of 120
17. 5% of 100
18. 8% of 300

19. 2% of 1,600
20. 52% of 400
21. 65% of 20

22. 12% of 450
23. 40% of 160
24. 6% of 150

25. 60% of 180
26. 74% of 200
27. 95% of 60

28. 300% of 100
29. 50% of 12
30. 20% of 50

Copy and complete each equation. Write the letter that has the same number as the equation answer to solve the riddle.

C   30% of 120
E   60% of 90

A   10% of 70
T   70% of 140

E   40% of 200
H   99% of 200

H   75% of 200
A   20% of 60

Which animal wouldn't you trust?

$$\frac{?}{7} \quad \frac{?}{36} \; \frac{?}{198} \; \frac{?}{80} \; \frac{?}{54} \; \frac{?}{98} \; \frac{?}{12} \; \frac{?}{150}$$

Find the percent that each part is of the whole.

1. 3 dimes
10 coins

_____?_____ % are dimes.

2. 4 red cars
16 cars

_____?_____ % are red.

3. 5 mysteries
25 books

_____?_____ % are mysteries.

4. 6 oak trees
12 trees

_____?_____ % are oak.

5. 2 roses
20 flowers

_____?_____ % are roses.

6. 4 horses
100 animals

_____?_____ % are horses.

Compute.

7. What percent of 25 is 10?

8. 14 is what percent of 28?

9. What percent of 30 is 6?

10. 36 is what percent of 48?

11. 27 is what percent of 45?

12. What percent of 70 is 21?

13. 44 is what percent of 55?

14. 23 is what percent of 50?

15. What percent of 80 is 24?

16. 75 is what percent of 300?

17. What percent of 40 is 2?

18. 10 is what percent of 1,000?

What percent is the first number of the second?

19. 12, 30

20. 16, 25

21. 19, 50

22. 32, 40

23. 16, 64

24. 3, 60

25. 45, 90

26. 14, 35

Solve.

27. The flag of Mathmania has 60 stars. Of these, 36 are blue. What percent of the stars are blue?

28. The flag has 20 stripes. There are 6 red stripes. What percent of the stripes are not red?

Answer *true* or *false*.

1. The part of a circle graph that represents $\frac{1}{3}$ is smaller than the part that represents 50%.

2. If a circle graph were divided into 5 unequal parts, each part would be 20% of the whole.

Use the circle graph to solve.

TELEPHONES IN USE WORLDWIDE

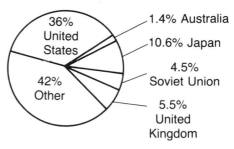

3. What proportion of the world's telephones shown in the graph are used in specific countries?

4. In which country are the greatest number of telephones in use?

5. To the nearest million, how many more telephones are in use in the United Kingdom than in the Soviet Union?

6. Of the countries shown, which has the smallest percentage of telephones in use?

Use both circle graphs to solve.

MONEY SPENT BY UNITED STATES TOURISTS IN EUROPE

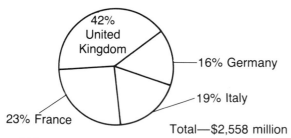

MONEY SPENT BY EUROPEAN TOURISTS IN THE UNITED STATES

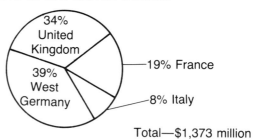

7. Was more money spent by American tourists visiting Europe or by Europeans visiting the United States?

8. Who spent more money, American tourists visiting France or German tourists visiting the United States?

9. In which 2 countries combined did American tourists spend about as much as they did in the United Kingdom?

10. How much more money was spent by Americans visiting Europe than by Europeans visiting the United States?

Identify and name each figure.

1.

_____

2.

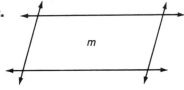

m

_____

3.

_____

4.

_____

5.

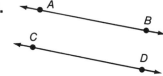

_____

6.

_____

7. Name all the rays.

Construct a figure that includes everything listed in questions 8–11.

8. Draw $\overline{PR}$.

9. Draw $\overrightarrow{PQ}$.

10. Draw $\overleftrightarrow{PS}$ intersecting $\overrightarrow{QS}$.

11. Draw $\overline{QR}$.

•R
Q•   S
             •

•
P

Complete. Use the diagram to answer.

12. Name all the lines.

13. Name three points on $\overleftrightarrow{JL}$.

14. Name the point where $\overleftrightarrow{JN}$ intersects $\overleftrightarrow{LM}$.

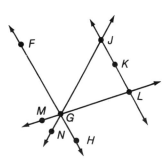

15. Name two parallel lines.

16. Name two rays with endpoint *K*.

Are the lines perpendicular? Write *yes* or *no*.

1.

2.

3.

4.

Give three different names for each angle.

5.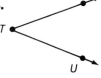

6.

7.

Name the vertex, the sides, and the angle.

8.

9.

Write whether the angle is *right, acute, obtuse,* or *straight.*

10.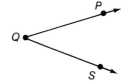

11.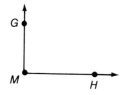

12.

13.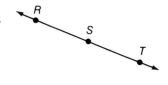

14.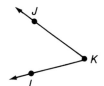

15.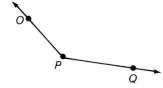

Use a protractor to measure the angle.

1.

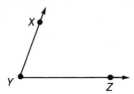

2.

3.

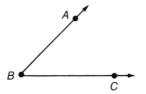

4.

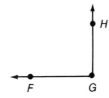

5.

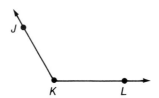

6.

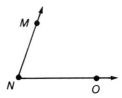

7.

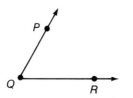

8.

Draw each angle.

9. 35°

10. 125°

Name each triangle, and write if it is *equilateral*, *isosceles*, or *scalene*.

1.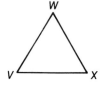

2.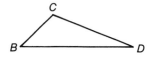

3.

Name each triangle, and write if it is *right*, *obtuse*, or *acute*.

4.

5.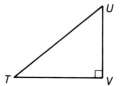

6.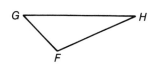

Write the measure of the missing angle.

7.

8.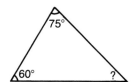

9.

Construct triangles with the angles given. Label each triangle *equilateral*, *isosceles*, or *scalene*.

10. 18°, 22°, 140°

11. 40°, 40°, 100°

12. 45°, 90°, 45°

13. 60°, 60°, 60°

14. 45°, 110°, 25°

15. 30°, 75°, 75°

Complete the tables to solve the problems.

1. Dennis and Larry went on a trip to Mexico. Dennis kept track of the time that the sun set each night they spent in Acapulco. It set at 7:00 P.M., 7:03 P.M., 7:06 P.M., and 7:09 P.M. On which night did the sun set at 7:18 P.M.?

Night	1	2	3	4				
Time	7:00	7:03	7:06	7:09				

2. During the trip, Larry used a tape recorder to practice his Spanish every day for 9 days. His schedule for the first 3 days was 15, 20, and 25 minutes. If he followed the same pattern for all 9 days, how long did he practice his Spanish on the ninth day?

Day	1	2	3						
Minutes	15	20	25						

3. Larry and Dennis were sitting at their window watching the excursion boats leave from the harbor. A boat left at 8:15 A.M., 8:22 A.M., 8:30 A.M., 8:39 A.M., and 8:49 A.M. At what time did the next four boats leave from the harbor?

Boat	1	2	3	4	5	6	7	8	9
Time	8:15	8:22	8:30	8:39	8:49				

4. Larry and Dennis were in no hurry to go home after their vacation. On the first day of the trip home, they traveled 200 miles. On the second day, they only traveled 185 miles. On the third day, they traveled 170 miles, and so on. If they followed this pattern, and if the trip took 6 days, how many miles did they travel on the trip home?

Day	1	2	3	4	5	6
Miles	200	185	170			

Make a table to answer each question.

1. Dennis and Larry found a diagram of an ancient Aztec ritual. The arrows show how many squares a warrior danced forward and how many squares he danced back before going forward again. Make a table to show the dance pattern. How many steps, in which direction, did the warrior take next?

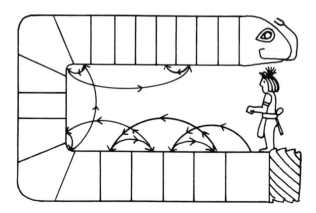

2. In one ancient storehouse, Dennis found some wall markings showing counts for sacks of grain and cocoa. The first marks indicate 2 sacks of grain and 1 of cocoa. Make a table to show the ratio of grain to cocoa. If there were 16 sacks of grain, how many sacks of cocoa would there be?

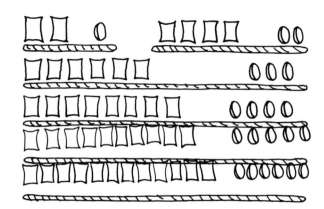

3. Larry saw an ancient tally. Part of the tally had been destroyed. A friend explained that the slash marks were used to record the amount of corn harvested in a year. The circles showed how much corn was used that year. Make a table to show the pattern.
a. If the pattern continued, what would the missing tallies have been?

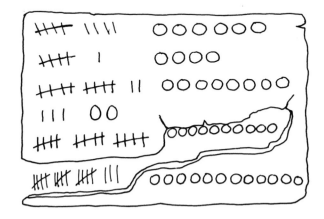

b. What fraction of the corn was used each year?

Name the polygon.

1.  **2.**  **3.**   **4.**

5.  **6.**   **7.**  **8.**

Identify the polygon.

9. a ten-sided figure

10. a six-sided figure that has all sides and angles equal

11. a quadrilateral that has four right angles and four equal sides

12. a three-sided figure

Copy the figures. Draw all the diagonals from point C.

13. 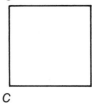 **14.**   **15.**

Copy the figures. Draw all the diagonals from each vertex.

16.  **17.**

Write *chord*, *radius*, or *diameter* for the given segment.

1.

2.

3.

4.

5.

6.

7.

8.

Write the diameter of a circle with the given radius.

9. 1 cm   **10.** 3 cm   **11.** 5 cm   **12.** 10 cm   **13.** 28 cm

Write the radius of a circle with the given diameter.

14. 6 cm   **15.** 12 cm   **16.** 20 cm   **17.** 28 cm   **18.** 60 cm

Use a ruler and a compass to draw a circle that has a

19. radius of 3 cm.   **20.** diameter of 4 cm.

Choosing the Operation	Checking for a Reasonable Answer	Using a Schedule
Writing a Number Sentence	Solving Multistep Problems/	Writing a Simpler Problem
	Making a Plan	

Write the strategy or method you choose. Then solve.

1. Mary is spending 2 days in Billings, Montana. She can spend $82 for food and entertainment. If she spends $20 a day for food, how much money will she have left for entertainment?

2. If a flight from New York to Los Angeles stops in St. Louis for 45 minutes, what is the total travel time?

SKYHAPPY AIRLINE FLIGHTS FROM NEW YORK		
Leave New York	**Arrive**	**New York Time**
8:30 A.M.	St. Louis	12:00 noon
8:30 A.M.	New Orleans	1:00 P.M.
8:45 A.M.	Atlanta	12:30 P.M.
9:00 A.M.	Miami	3:30 P.M.
10:00 A.M.	Dallas	3:00 P.M.
1:00 P.M.	Phoenix	6:00 P.M.
1:00 P.M.	Denver	5:00 P.M.
1:00 P.M.	Billings	5:15 P.M.
1:15 P.M.	Los Angeles	8:15 P.M.
2:00 P.M.	Seattle	9:00 P.M.

3. How much longer does it take to fly from New York to New Orleans than it takes to fly from New York to St. Louis?

4. How much more time does the trip from New York to Miami take than the trip from New York to Dallas?

5. James flew Skyhappy Airlines to Borneo. His round-trip ticket cost $680. Instead of flying back home from Borneo, James cashed in half of his ticket and flew to Buenos Aires. If his ticket to Buenos Aires cost $200, how much money did the airline refund to James?

6. When James arrived home, he had 6 rolls of film to be developed and printed. The cost was $7.25 a roll for prints. Later, he found a store that would develop and print film for $6.30 a roll. How much money would James have saved if he had taken his film to the less expensive place?

Choosing the Operation	Checking for a Reasonable Answer	Using A Schedule
Writing a Number Sentence	Solving Multistep Problems/ Making a Plan	Writing a Simpler Problem

Write the strategy or method you choose. Then solve.

1. Ralph has a recipe for Hungarian goulash. It calls for 1 pound of beef and 3 carrots. The recipe feeds 3 people. If Ralph wants to feed 5 people, how many more carrots should he add? How much more beef does he need?

2. Dino had a recipe for spaghetti sauce. It calls for 2 cans of tomato sauce and $\frac{1}{4}$ cup of chopped onion. The recipe feeds 5 people. If Dino wants to feed 15 people, how many cans of sauce does he need? How much onion does he need?

3. Skyhappy Airlines flies 20% of its flights to Europe, 35% to California, and 35% to New York. The airline plans to discontinue its flights to Europe and divert these planes to California and New York. If the flights to Europe are divided equally, what percent of all Skyhappy flights will go to New York? What percent will go to California?

4. The rest of Skyhappy Airlines flights go to Texas. What percent of the flights go to Texas?

TRAIN SCHEDULE

City	Departs
Haverhill	8:05 A.M.
Bradford	8:10 A.M.
Lawrence	8:18 A.M.
Andover	8:27 A.M.
Ballardvale	8:37 A.M.
Reading	8:42 A.M.
Melrose	8:50 A.M.
Malden	8:56 A.M.
Boston	9:11 A.M.

5. How long is the train ride from Haverhill to Reading?

6. How long does the train take to run its entire route from Haverhill to Boston?

Is the line segment congruent to $\overline{RS}$?
Write *yes* or *no*. Use a ruler to measure. Trace to check.

1.

2.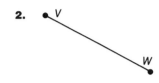

3.

Is the angle congruent to $\angle M$? Write *yes* or *no*.
Use a protractor to measure. Trace to check.

4.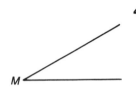

5.

6.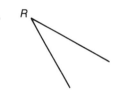

Is the figure congruent to Figure *JKLM*? Write *yes* or *no*.
Use a protractor and ruler to measure the angles and sides.
Trace to check.

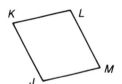

7.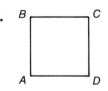

8.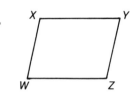

9.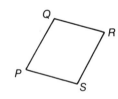

$\triangle ABC$ is congruent to $\triangle FGH$. Write the corresponding angle
or side.

10. $\overline{AB}$

11. $\overline{BC}$

12. $\angle B$

13. $\overline{FH}$

14. $\angle H$

15. $\angle A$

 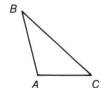 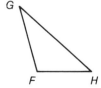

Is the dotted line a line of symmetry? Write *yes* or *no*.

1.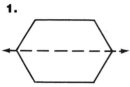

2.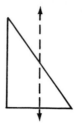

3.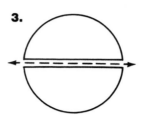

4.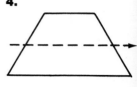

Copy the figures. Draw all lines of symmetry for each figure.
Then count the lines.

5.

6.

7.

8.

9.

10.

Copy and complete each figure so that the dotted line is a
line of symmetry.

11.

12.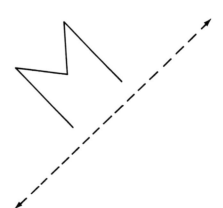

1. Name the figure that is similar to *GHIJK*.

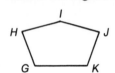   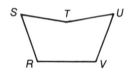

2. Name the triangle that is similar to △*QRS*.

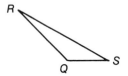 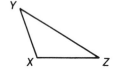 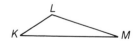 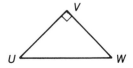

Figure *LMNO* is similar to figure *CDEF*.
Use this information to answer Questions 3–5.

3. Find the measure of ∠*M*.

4. Find the measure of ∠*E*.

5. Find the measure of ∠*C*.

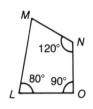 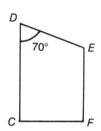

Write *true* or *false*.

6. All equilateral triangles are similar.

7. All rectangles are similar.

8. All regular pentagons are similar.

Ari wants to carpet the den, which is the same shape as the
garage, but half the size. Draw a floor plan of the den.
Scale: 1 mm : 1 ft

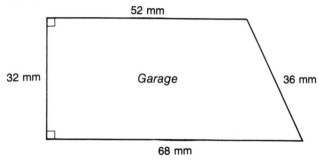

Name the ordered pair for each point.

1. G

2. N

3. L

4. H

5. S

6. O

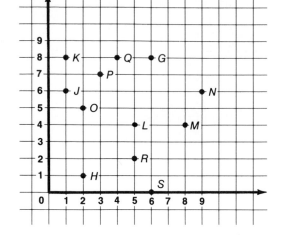

Name the point for each ordered pair.

7. (8,4)

8. (3,7)

9. (1,6)

10. (5,2)

11. (4,8)

12. (1,8)

Graph the points for each figure on a grid.
Then connect the points in
order for each figure.

Figure *ABCD*:
A(1,9); B(3,13); C(5,9); D(3,5)

Figure *EFGH*:
E(8,1); F(7,3); G(8,5); H(9,3)

13. Are figures *ABCD* and
EFGH similar?

Figure *JKLM*:
J(7,10); K(8,13); L(12,13);
M(11,10)

Figure *NPQR*:
N(11,7); P(13,9); Q(18,9)
R(16,7)

14. Are figures *JKLM* and
NPQR similar?

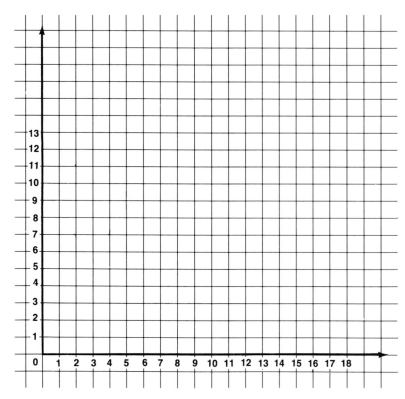

Use with pages 362–363.

Find the perimeter of each figure.

1.

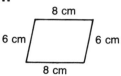

8 cm
6 cm — 6 cm
8 cm

2.

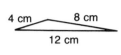

9 cm
9 cm — 9 cm
9 cm

3.

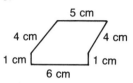

4 cm — 8 cm
12 cm

4.

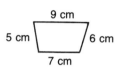

9 cm
5 cm — 6 cm
7 cm

5.

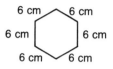

6 cm — 6 cm
6 cm — 6 cm
6 cm — 6 cm

6.

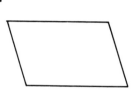

5 cm
4 cm — 4 cm
1 cm — 1 cm
6 cm

Use a centimeter ruler to find the perimeter of each figure.

7.

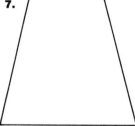

Perimeter:

8.

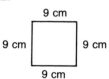

Perimeter:

9.

Perimeter:

Find the perimeter.

10. a rectangle whose sides measure 8 cm, 3 cm, 8 cm, and 3 cm

11. a pentagon with each side 7 cm

12. a polygon whose sides measure 6 cm, 4 cm, 8 cm, 2 cm, and 5 cm

13. a triangle whose sides measure 16 cm, 18 cm, and 20 cm

Count to find the area.

1.

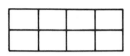

_____?_____ square units

2.

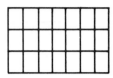

_____?_____ square units

3.

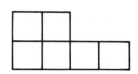

_____?_____ square units

Multiply to find the area.

4.

4 cm

8 cm

_____?_____ cm²

5.

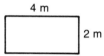

4 m

2 m

_____?_____ m²

6.

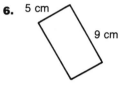

5 cm

9 cm

_____?_____ cm²

7.

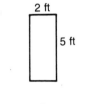

2 ft

5 ft

_____?_____ ft²

8.

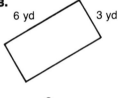

6 yd   3 yd

_____?_____ yd²

9.

9 in.

7 in.

_____?_____ in.²

Multiply to find the area of the rectangle or square.

10. l = 8 cm, w = 3 cm

11. l = 9 cm, w = 2 cm

12. l = 10 in., w = 10 in.

13. l = 4 ft, w = 2 ft

14. l = 12 in., w = 9 in.

15. l = 10 m, w = 4 m

Count to find the area.

1.

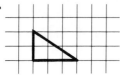

_____?_____ square units

2.

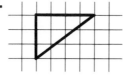

_____?_____ square units

3.

_____?_____ square units

Multiply to find the area.

4.

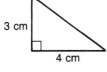

3 cm, 4 cm

_____?_____ cm²

5.

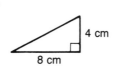

4 cm, 8 cm

_____?_____ cm²

6.

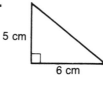

5 cm, 6 cm

_____?_____ cm²

7.

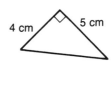

4 cm, 5 cm

_____?_____ cm²

8.

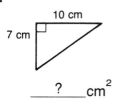

7 cm, 10 cm

_____?_____ cm²

9.

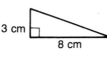

3 cm, 8 cm

_____?_____ cm²

10.

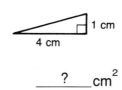

4 cm, 1 cm

_____?_____ cm²

11.

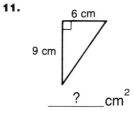

6 cm, 9 cm

_____?_____ cm²

Copy and complete the chart.

A TRIANGLE

	Base	Height	Area
12.	5 ft	4 ft	_____?_____ ft²
13.	3 cm	10 cm	_____?_____ cm²
14.	7 mi	2 mi	_____?_____ mi²
15.	3 m	12 m	_____?_____ m²
16.	2 cm	5 cm	_____?_____ cm²
17.	11 in.	4 in.	_____?_____ in.²
18.	6 ft	6 ft	_____?_____ ft²

Draw a picture or make a model to solve each problem.

1. A museum is planning an exhibit about fossils. The exhibit area is a square with sides that measure 8 feet. The curator plans to put lights around the exhibit. There will be a light every 2 feet around the exhibit. How many lights will be used?

2. Janice is doing an experiment with a rubber ball. She holds the ball 5 feet above the floor and releases it. The ball falls to the floor and bounces back to a height of 4 feet. It falls again and bounces back to a height of 3 feet. This happens 5 times before the ball comes to rest. How far does the ball travel during the experiment?

3. Gary is making a mosaic. The mosaic will be 30 inches by 12 inches. He is using tiles that measure 3 inches by 3 inches. How many tiles will Gary use in his mosaic?

4. Dale is planning to put lights around his pool. The pool is a rectangle that measures 30 feet by 60 feet. A light should be placed every 5 feet around the pool. How many lights will Dale need for the pool?

5. Cynthia is setting up a hall for a concert. The space for the audience measures 40 feet by 20 feet. Each row of chairs is 20 feet wide. Cynthia plans to allow 2 feet between rows. How many rows of chairs can she set up in the space?

6. John is planting a garden. Its size measures 24 feet by 15 feet. Each row is 15 feet long. He plans to allow $1\frac{1}{2}$ feet between rows. How many rows can he plant in the garden?

Name the solid figure that is shaped like the object.

1.

2.

3.

4.

5.

6.

7.

8.

Count the number of faces, edges, and vertices each figure has.

9.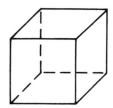

_____?_____ faces

_____?_____ edges

_____?_____ vertices

10.

_____?_____ faces

_____?_____ edges

_____?_____ vertices

11.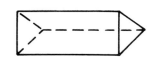

_____?_____ faces

_____?_____ edges

_____?_____ vertices

Copy and complete the table.

	Number of faces	Number of edges	Number of vertices
Triangular pyramid	**12.** ___?___	**13.** ___?___	**14.** ___?___
Rectangular prism	**15.** ___?___	**16.** ___?___	**17.** ___?___
Pentagonal prism	**18.** ___?___	**19.** ___?___	**20.** ___?___

Find the volume of each.

1.

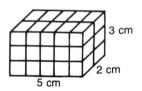

3 cm

2 cm

5 cm

2.

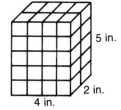

4 m

3 m

4 m

3.

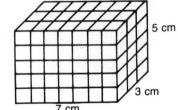

5 cm

3 cm

7 cm

4.

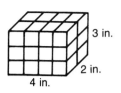

3 in.

2 in.

4 in.

5.

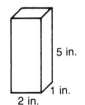

5 in.

2 in.

4 in.

6.

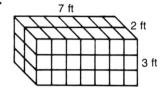

7 ft

2 ft

3 ft

7.

3 cm

1 cm

6 cm

8.

5 in.

1 in.

2 in.

9.

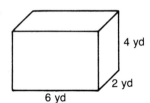

4 yd

2 yd

6 yd

Use the formula $V = l \times w \times h$. Copy and complete the table.

RECTANGULAR PRISMS

Length (*l*)	Width (*w*)	Height (*h*)	Volume (*V*)
7 in.	2 in.	1 in.	**10.** ____?____
10 yd	4 yd	5 yd	**11.** ____?____
6 mi	4 mi	7 mi	**12.** ____?____
11 m	2 m	6 m	**13.** ____?____

Use with pages 374–375.

Solve.

1. Each year thousands of people immigrate to the United States. This table gives the number of immigrants to the United States from 1983 to 1987. Copy and complete the bar graph. Use the data in the table and round the number of immigrants to the nearest ten thousand.

IMMIGRATION

Year	Number of immigrants	Rounded numbers
1983	605,000	
1984	615,000	
1985	650,000	
1986	662,000	
1987	599,000	

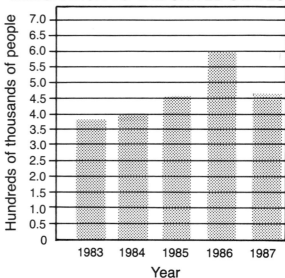

IMMIGRATION TO THE UNITED STATES

2. In 1980, the U.S. Bureau of the Census calculated the most populous cities. The table shows the four largest cities. Copy and complete the bar graph to show the data. Round the populations to the nearest tenth of a million.

CITY POPULATIONS

City	Population	Rounded numbers
New York City	17,412,652	
Los Angeles	11,497,568	
Chicago	7,937,326	
Philadelphia	5,680,000	

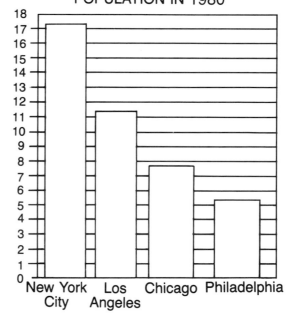

POPULATION IN 1980

Solve.

1. This table shows how many miles four people run in one week. Copy and complete the pictograph to show the number of miles each person runs in one week. Let 🚶 = 6 miles. Let 🚶 = 3 miles.

Person	Miles run in one week
Larry	30 miles
Kirk	18 miles
Lisa	36 miles
Debbie	45 miles

MILES RUN IN ONE WEEK

🚶 = 6 miles	🚶 = 3 miles
Person	Number of miles
Larry	
Kirk	
Lisa	
Debbie	

2. The Running Deer Shoe Company is designing a new line of sneakers. The Jaguar is made for basketball players, the Olympian for runners, and the Buddy Smith for tennis players. The company is also producing a sneaker called the Walking Deer for older people, and one called the Little Deer for children. Let 👟 = 100,000 sneakers produced and 👟 = 50,000. Copy and complete the pictograph to show the number of sneakers produced in one year.

SNEAKERS PRODUCED IN ONE YEAR

Jaguar	350,000
Olympian	300,000
Buddy Smith	250,000
Walking Deer	500,000
Little Deer	150,000

SNEAKERS PRODUCED IN ONE YEAR

👟 = 100,000 produced	👟 = 50,000 produced
Jaguar	
Olympian	
Buddy Smith	
Walking Deer	
Little Deer	

Use with pages 386–387.

1. Each year many thousands of dollars are spent to buy dogs. Copy and complete the broken-line graph to show dog sales in the United States.

UNITED STATES SALES OF DOGS

1980	$200,000
1981	$600,000
1982	$300,000
1983	$200,000
1984	$500,000
1985	$400,000
1986	$300,000

2. Use the data in the table to make a broken-line graph to show sales at the Puppy Town Pet Store.

SALES AT PUPPY TOWN PET STORE

1980	$15,000
1981	$20,000
1982	$25,000
1983	$30,000
1984	$40,000
1985	$35,000

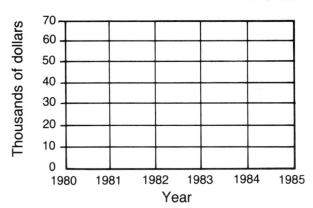

Use the graphs below to answer the questions.

BICYCLES SOLD BY THE CYCLORAMA CO.   BICYCLES SOLD BY THE BIKELAND CO.

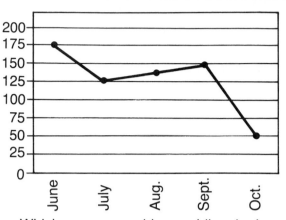 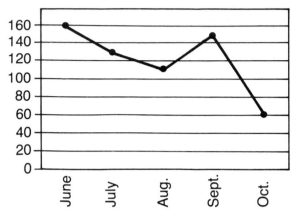

1. Which company sold more bikes in June, Cyclorama or Bikeland?

2. Which company sold more bikes in August? About how many more?

3. Did Bikeland sell more bikes in August or September? About how many more?

4. Are the summer months good or bad for bicycle sales?

5. In which months did Cyclorama and Bikeland have nearly the same number of sales?

6. Which company had a sharper drop in sales in October?

7. Which company had the sharpest increase in sales in a single month? Which month was it? How many more bikes did they sell than the month before?

First write the mean. Then write the median.

1. 7, 6, 5

2. 6, 17, 26, 3, 8

3. 23, 11, 17, 4, 20

4. 70, 32, 68, 15, 25

5. 3, 7, 1, 5, 9

6. 9, 3, 12

7. 44, 16, 22, 8, 10

8. 5, 2, 22, 7, 19

First write the mode. Then write the range.

9. 14, 3, 27, 62, 3, 42

10. 79, 24, 18, 24, 5, 10

11. 91, 86, 17, 17, 23, 59

12. 33, 66, 77, 22, 33

13. 203, 118, 154, 3, 203

14. 5, 25, 5, 35, 5, 75

15. 62, 26, 62, 216, 21, 61

16. 1, 11, 1, 11, 1, 1

Solve.

17. Each week, the Armstrong family reads quite a few books from the local library. This year, they read 40 books in January, 33 books in February, 42 books in March, 67 books in April, and 33 books in May. For those 5 months, what is the mean number of books they read in 1 month?

18. Mrs. Armstrong works at the local library. It is her job to record the number of books borrowed each day. On Monday, 27 people each checked out a book. On both Tuesday and Wednesday, 30 people each borrowed a book. On Thursday, 46 people each borrowed a book, and on Friday, 37 people each borrowed a book. What is the mean number of books borrowed? What is the mode?

Solve. Use a tree diagram if needed.

1. The members of the Science Club decide to create a club banner. The cloth for the banner could be blue, brown, yellow, green, gold, or white. The letters for the banner could be white, black, or blue. How many combinations of cloth and letters are possible?

2. For Science Day the club wants to create an exhibit on three of the original Mercury astronauts: Scott Carpenter, John Glenn, and Gus Grissom. The exhibit will show scenes from the lives of these astronauts using a VCR, a slide projector, or a movie projector. The club decides to use a different piece of equipment for each astronaut. How many combinations are possible?

3. In addition to the exhibit, 5 members of the club want to give reports on famous American scientists and inventors. They have information on Benjamin Franklin, Thomas Jefferson, George Washington Carver, Thomas Edison, Rachel Carson, and An Wang. How many possibilities are there?

4. For the club outing, the members must decide to go to the Space Museum or to the Museum of Natural History. In either place, they can attend a lecture, see a film, or see a special exhibit. What are their choices?

Make a tree diagram to solve each problem.

1. The Hyatt family is planning a wilderness vacation. They are thinking about going to one of three places: Yellowstone National Park, Grand Canyon National Park, or Grand Teton National Park. Once they have decided where they will go, the Hyatts must decide what they would most like to do there. They can go camping, backpacking, or white-water rafting. What are all the choices they have?

2. The Hyatts decide to go rafting. They can take a 2-day trip, a 5-day trip, or a 1-week trip down the Yellowstone River, the Lewis River, the Snake River, or the Gibbon River. What are their choices?

3. One morning, the Hyatts decide to have lunch at the Snake River Lodge. They can order one item from each group for lunch.

Group A	Group B	Group C
baked ham	green beans	fruit cup
veal chops	tossed salad	tapioca
chicken saute		melon medley

What combinations of food can they order from the menu?

Celia bought some beads at the Make-It-Yourself Jewelry Store. In a bag, she brought home 2 orange beads, 1 yellow bead, 3 red beads, and 2 blue beads. Suppose Celia picks a bead from the bag without looking.

1. How many equally likely outcomes are there?

2. What is the probability of picking a yellow bead?

3. What is the probability of picking a blue bead?

4. What is the probability of picking a red bead?

Suppose you are playing a game. Imagine the cards are all placed in a hat. You pick one card. Then you return it.

Jump up and down three times.	Get each player a glass of juice.
Get each player a glass of juice.	Each player gets you a glass of juice.
Do a household chore for the player on your right.	The player on your left does a household chore for you.
The player on your left does a household chore for you.	Jump up and down three times.
Pick the next game.	The player on your left does a household chore for you.

Find the probability for each event. Write a fraction for each probability.

What is the probability of

5. doing a household chore?

6. picking the next game?

7. jumping up and down three times?

8. having someone do a household chore for you?

9. having another player do something for you?

10. getting each player a glass of juice?

Predict the probability of each event below.
Write *certain* or *impossible* for each event.
There are 12 beads in a can: 6 beads are
white and 6 beads are green.
What is the probability of picking

1. a blue bead?

2. a white or green bead?

3. a green or white bead?

4. a yellow bead?

The 6 sides of this cube each have a
different letter: *A*, *B*, *C*, *D*, *E*, or *F*. Suppose
you toss the cube and note which letter
comes out on top.

5. What is the probability that the letter on
top is *C*?

6. What is the probability that the letter
on top is a vowel?

Suppose you toss the cube 60 times. Predict the number of
times the letter on top will be

7. *C*

8. *X*

9. a vowel

10. *E*

11. before *G* in the alphabet

Solve.

12. Hector builds a maze for his guinea pig.
The maze has 3 ways to escape and 10
ways to get lost. What is the probability
of Hector's guinea pig finding its way
through the maze?

13. While Hector cleaned the cage, his
guinea pig got lost in the house. There
are 2 doors leading outside, 2 doors
leading upstairs, and 1 door to the
cellar. Is the guinea pig as likely to go
upstairs as to go outside?

Acting It Out	Making an Organized List	Making a Table
Guessing and Checking	Solving Multistep Problems/	Making a Diagram
Making a Model	Making a Plan	Drawing a Picture

Write the strategy or method you choose. Then solve.

1. Dr. Thinkhard is working on a formula for a chemical that will produce seedless raspberries. He knows the formula is a combination of agents *W, X, Y,* and *Z,* but he does not know the correct order of the agents. How many possible orders are there?

2. Next weekend, Dr. Thinkhard plans to have a garage sale. He sets up a display of his old test tubes, beakers, and Bunsen burners and makes a sign — "Any 2 for $1.00." What are all of the possible pairs of objects that people could buy for $1.00? (HINT: Remember that people could buy two of the same item.)

3. To test his formula for seedless raspberries, Dr. Thinkhard made a few batches of the chemical. He discovered that he could make a batch of the chemical in 0.8 hour. How long would it take him to make 3 batches? How many batches could he make in 4.8 hours?

4. One batch of the chemical for raspberries weighs a certain number of grams. The number has 2 digits and is divisible by 3. The sum of the digits is 9. If you subtract the tens digit from the ones digit, you get the tens digit. How much does the batch weigh?

Acting It Out	Making an Organized List	Making a Table
Guessing and Checking	Solving Multistep Problems/	Making a Diagram
Making a Model	Making a Plan	Drawing a Picture

Write the strategy or method you choose. Then solve.

1. Dr. Thinkhard has tested a formula to produce seedless raspberries. Not every batch of his seedless-raspberry formula was successful. Of the first 8 batches, 6 produced seedless raspberries. Of 16 batches, 12 produced seedless berries. If this pattern continues, how many batches can Dr. Thinkhard expect to be successful out of 48 batches?

2. When Dr. Thinkhard went to the patent office to register his formula, he had trouble finding the right room. He went to a floor that had 10 rooms on one side. The rooms were labeled 1 through 10. A woman in the first room told him to go 4 rooms up the hall. A man in that room told him to go back 2 rooms. Finally, a janitor told him to go 6 rooms up, and then Dr. Thinkhard was at the right room. Which room was it?

3. Dr. Thinkhard made a list of 6 chemicals that he uses in many formulas. Each formula uses 2 different chemicals. Using the numbers 1 through 6 to stand for the 6 chemicals, find how many different formulas are possible.

4. Dr. Thinkhard refined his formula and had a high success rate. This rate was given as a percent. The success rate is a two-digit number that is greater than 75. The sum of the digits is 14, and the product of the digits is 48. What was Dr. Thinkhard's success rate?

5. Dr. Thinkhard worked 12 hours yesterday on his project. He worked twice as long in the afternoon than in the morning. How many hours did he work in the morning? How many hours did he work in the afternoon?

6. Dr. Thinkhard's total budget for lab equipment is $350.00. He would like to buy a lab table for $82.00, 12 beakers at $4.98 each, and 10 racks of test tubes at $14.67 each. How much money will be left in his budget?

MORE PRACTICE

Chapter 1, page 7 _____

Compare. Write >, <, or = for ●.

1. 639 ● 693
2. 536 ● 5,360
3. 3,777 ● 3,770
4. 821 ● 1,218

5. 579,038 ● 578,900
6. 11,010 ● 101
7. 357 ● 357
8. 770 ● 707

Order from the greatest to the least.

9. 3,275; 3,725; 375; 7,253
10. 3,297; 32,097; 2,397; 79
11. 923; 293; 329

12. 27,357; 27,573; 27,753; 27,735
13. 238; 328; 832
14. 6,750; 7,560; 6,570

Order from the least to the greatest.

15. 39,008; 39,080; 30,980; 39,800
16. 6,235; 6,523; 65,023; 65,325

17. 72,555; 75,525; 57,575; 75,557
18. 4,659; 46,000; 4,600; 460

Chapter 1, page 18 _____

Estimate.

1.   189
     − 52

2.   236
     − 45

3.   568
    − 327

4. $1.74
    − 0.37

5.   483
    − 269

6.   641
    − 230

7. $3.68 − $1.54
8. 502 − 79
9. 876 − 637

10. 276 − 139
11. 710 − 335
12. 787 − 436

13. 875 − 693
14. 407 − 259
15. $6.72 − $3.59

Chapter 1, page 23 _____

Add.

1.   356,081
     +   7,974

2.   597,269
     +   4,813

3.   918,597
     + 24,987

4. $323.89
     + 527.35

5.   87,405
     + 62,567

6.   14,822
     + 3,502

7. $63.52
     + 35.98

8.   128,507
     + 43,089

9. $65.73 + $32.98
10. 238,996 + 55,071
11. 329,554 + 817,111

12. $829.10 + $523.75
13. 134,431 + 58,111
14. 699,935 + 2,708

Chapter 1, page 25

Add.

1. 33,204
  3,224
+ 9

2. 42,549
  35,240
  1,289
+ 97

3. $15.29
  3.59
+ 7.23

4. 87,853
  9,725
  14
+ 12

5. 36,133
  3,411
+ 3

6. $12.23 + $13.11

7. 47 + 3,116 + 542

8. 74,141 + 81,094 + 778

9. $37.89 + $19.98 + $3.23

10. 36,415 + 52,554 + 3,516 + 45

11. 27,055 + 38 + 2,913 + 516

Chapter 1, page 31

Subtract.

1. 237,155
− 12,791

2. $11.98
− 9.53

3. 84,695
− 499

4. 26,215
− 6,013

5. 114,458
− 73,817

6. $32.15
− 27.43

7. 26,337
− 633

8. 174,296
− 6,092

9. $95.18
− 59.37

10. 788,213
− 1,381

11. 385,883 − 56,867

12. 354,867 − 190,662

13. 54,923 − 4,712

14. 45,824 − 23,555

15. $46.44 − $38.56

16. 3,856 − 255

Chapter 1, page 33

Subtract.

1. $5.05
− 1.53

2. 708
− 72

3. 5,608
− 4,225

4. 90,009
− 5,270

5. 94,600
− 82,345

6. 9,005
− 254

7. 5,000
− 1,051

8. $4.03
− 3.29

9. 600,059
− 77,544

10. 230,009
− 127,122

11. 95,800 − 1,436

12. 865,005 − 552,244

13. 597,008 − 34,634

14. $6.08 − $5.05

15. $3,020.50 − $2,531.54

16. 3,670 − 647

Chapter 2, page 47

Write as a decimal.

1. twenty-two hundredths

2. nine and eleven hundredths

3. five hundredths

4. one hundred and seventy-nine hundredths

Write the word name for each decimal.

5. 6.47   **6.** 49.08   **7.** 2.76   **8.** 9.99   **9.** 0.82

10. 18.77   **11.** 44.89   **12.** 33.64   **13.** 80.05   **14.** 0.01

Chapter 2, page 49

Write as a decimal.

1. five and twenty-one thousandths

2. sixty-one thousandths

3. two hundred ninety-eight thousandths

4. six and four thousandths

Write the word name for each decimal.

5. 7.123   **6.** 8.365   **7.** 0.001   **8.** 0.021   **9.** 1.605

Write the value of the blue digit.

10. 713.307   **11.** 4.099   **12.** 0.263

13. 593.004   **14.** 427.446   **15.** 978.219

Chapter 2, page 53

Compare. Write >, <, or = for ●.

1. 6.23 ● 6.32   **2.** 5.678 ● 5.6   **3.** 0.2 ● 0.20

4. 5.21 ● 5.021   **5.** 0.033 ● 0.33   **6.** 7.005 ● 5.707

Write in order from the least to the greatest.

7. 3.62, 36.2, 3.602   **8.** 0.018, 0.008, 0.801   **9.** 5.29, 5.2, 5.9

10. 6.098, 6.908, 6.089   **11.** 0.123, 1.013, 1.01   **12.** 32.9, 32.09, 3.29

Write in order from the greatest to the least.

13. 63.3, 6.33, 6.503   **14.** 0.012, 0.001, 0.011   **15.** 4.12, 0.412, 4.012

16. 0.81, 0.811, 0.085   **17.** 5.5, 5.55, 5.555   **18.** 28.13, 2.813, 28.3

Chapter 2, page 55

Round to the nearest whole number.

1. 3.52
2. 7.88
3. 2.39
4. 18.72
5. 135.26

6. 14.99
7. 12.05
8. 0.876
9. 5.23
10. 11.71

Round to the nearest tenth.

11. 14.29
12. 11.31
13. 15.65
14. 0.15
15. 2.54

16. 18.327
17. 72.275
18. 4.332
19. 4.37
20. 7.89

Round to the nearest hundredth.

21. 0.429
22. 0.215
23. 2.321
24. 8.588
25. 7.327

26. 0.813
27. 0.587
28. 25.631
29. 27.328
30. 52.551

Chapter 2, page 61

Add.

1. 2.27 + 5.8
2. 3.653 + 27.94
3. 7.2 + 5.364
4. 8.53 + 9.78
5. 6.038 + 3.25

6. 4.037 2.653 + 8.215
7. 8.503 5.675 + 2.137
8. 6 52.83 + 0.2
9. 0.3 0.5 + 6.3
10. 7.87 2.21 + 0.54

11. 5.23 + 11.25
12. 16.32 + 25.238 + 2.1
13. 823.7 + 0.69

Chapter 2, page 63

Subtract.

1. 28.3 − 0.28
2. $873.29 − 565.38
3. 87.11 − 60.42
4. $72.25 − 61.15
5. 67.14 − 28.09

6. 6.58 − 5.39
7. 61.4 − 0.04
8. 27.52 − 16.45
9. 7.56 − 4.87
10. 22.11 − 19.67

11. 5 − 0.07
12. 28.3 − 0.28
13. 8.06 − 5.57
14. 32.3 − 29.5

Multiply.

1. 5
    $\times 0$

2. 9
    $\times 8$

3. 7
    $\times 6$

4. 4
    $\times 5$

5. 6
    $\times 3$

6. 3×8

7. $(4 \times 2) \times 5$

8. $(6 \times 0) \times 5$

9. $7 \times (1 \times 3)$

10. 8×0

11. 7×7

12. 9×9

13. 5×7

Copy and complete. Write the name of the property.

14. $6 \times (7 + 4) = (6 \times 7) + (\blacksquare \times \blacksquare)$

15. $72 \times (63 \times 87) = (72 \times \blacksquare) \times 87$

16. $5 \times (3 + 4) = (5 \times 3) + (5 \times \blacksquare)$

17. $9 \times \blacksquare = 3 \times 9$

18. $8 \times \blacksquare = 0$

19. $5 \times \blacksquare = 5$

Multiply.

1. 80
    $\times 4$

2. 600
    $\times 5$

3. $5{,}000$
    $\times 20$

4. $8{,}000$
    $\times 7$

5. $6{,}000$
    $\times 400$

6. 70
    $\times 10$

7. 400
    $\times 40$

8. $7{,}000$
    $\times 40$

9. $7{,}000$
    $\times 300$

10. $9{,}000$
    $\times 5$

11. 70×900

12. $400 \times 6{,}000$

13. 10×20

14. 30×300

15. 70×800

16. $800 \times 4{,}000$

17. $60 \times 5{,}000$

18. $90 \times 3{,}000$

Multiply.

1. 635
    $\times 7$

2. 72
    $\times 5$

3. $\$8.62$
    $\times 6$

4. 23
    $\times 4$

5. 906
    $\times 7$

6. $4 \times \$3.28$

7. 9×17

8. $3 \times \$6.50$

9. 4×433

10. 6×133

11. 2×325

12. 5×115

13. 9×100

14. 5×141

15. 7×63

16. 8×35

17. 2×48

Chapter 3, page 89

Multiply.

1. 1,110
× 7

2. 5,731
× 5

3. $12.35
× 6

4. 6,742
× 9

5. 21,051
× 8

6. 42,323
× 2

7. 9,881
× 7

8. 1,441
× 2

9. 62,058
× 4

10. $29.88
× 8

11. 8 × 31,223
12. 5 × 1,422
13. 5 × $52.18
14. 4 × 41,526

15. 9 × $75.30
16. 7 × 12,481
17. 5 × 11,010
18. 3 × 2,313

19. 6 × 1,000
20. 8 × 82,116
21. 2 × $81.54
22. 6 × 3,647

Chapter 3, page 93

Multiply.

1. $6.25
× 91

2. 711
× 75

3. 4,078
× 57

4. 23
× 42

5. $52.19
× 83

6. 556
× 20

7. $7.23
× 78

8. 12
× 11

9. 72
× 53

10. 2,456
× 74

11. 77 × $3.52
12. 64 × $82.99
13. 28 × 4,329
14. 33 × 8,269

15. 53 × 78
16. 23 × 827
17. 67 × 235
18. 14 × 12

Chapter 3, page 95

Multiply.

1. 477
× 177

2. 753
× 480

3. $3.96
× 279

4. 105
× 566

5. 704
× 639

6. $3.28
× 215

7. 450
× 347

8. 442
× 208

9. 603
× 578

10. $9.79
× 281

11. 647 × 745
12. 323 × $9.99
13. 409 × 653
14. 231 × 828

Chapter 4, page 107

Estimate. Write > or < for ●.

1. 4.4×7.6 ● 25   **2.** 4.2×7.5 ● 27   **3.** 2.6×4.9 ● 10

4. 6.3×25.2 ● 150   **5.** $\$6.62 \times 3.29$ ● $25   **6.** 2.68×25.45 ● 55

Estimate.

7.
$$8.7 \\ \times\, 3.1$$

8.
$$16.6 \\ \times\, 7.32$$

9.
$$\$8.27 \\ \times\,\,\, 5.6$$

10.
$$\$21.17 \\ \times\,\,\,\,\,\, 2.1$$

Chapter 4, page 115

Multiply.

1.
$$4.8 \\ \times\, 0.68$$

2.
$$49.5 \\ \times\,\,\, 0.09$$

3.
$$0.76 \\ \times\,\,\, 0.8$$

4.
$$0.93 \\ \times\,\,\, 0.7$$

5.
$$6.28 \\ \times\,\,\, 0.3$$

6. 0.21×3.35 **7.** 0.3×31.23 **8.** 0.61×43.33 **9.** 0.2×27.27

Multiply. Round the product to the nearest cent.

10.
$$\$36.78 \\ \times\,\,\,\,\,\, 0.13$$

11.
$$\$7.28 \\ \times\,\,\,\, 0.6$$

12.
$$\$33.59 \\ \times\,\,\,\,\, 0.39$$

13.
$$\$2.15 \\ \times\,\,\,\, 0.3$$

14.
$$\$6.23 \\ \times\,\,\,\, 0.5$$

Chapter 4, page 117

Multiply.

1.
$$0.42 \\ \times\,\, 0.2$$

2.
$$0.4 \\ \times 0.1$$

3.
$$3.6 \\ \times 0.02$$

4.
$$2.2 \\ \times 0.03$$

5.
$$0.17 \\ \times 0.3$$

6. 2.2×0.04 **7.** 0.3×0.31 **8.** 1.1×0.07 **9.** 4.1×0.02

Multiply. Round the product to the nearest cent.

10.
$$\$2.02 \\ \times\,\,\,\, 0.2$$

11.
$$\$0.07 \\ \times\,\,\,\, 0.4$$

12.
$$\$0.03 \\ \times\,\,\,\, 1.3$$

13.
$$\$0.78 \\ \times\,\,\,\, 0.1$$

14.
$$\$0.31 \\ \times\,\,\,\, 0.3$$

Chapter 5, page 135

Divide.

1. $5\overline{)38}$ **2.** $7\overline{)44}$ **3.** $3\overline{)25}$ **4.** $8\overline{)49}$ **5.** $9\overline{)53}$

6. $6\overline{)46}$ **7.** $5\overline{)19}$ **8.** $9\overline{)32}$ **9.** $7\overline{)61}$ **10.** $3\overline{)27}$

11. $35 \div 6$ **12.** $59 \div 8$ **13.** $13 \div 2$ **14.** $87 \div 9$ **15.** $15 \div 7$

16. $43 \div 7$ **17.** $11 \div 3$ **18.** $71 \div 8$ **19.** $21 \div 4$ **20.** $64 \div 9$

21. $\frac{68}{8}$ **22.** $\frac{39}{7}$ **23.** $\frac{26}{4}$ **24.** $\frac{80}{9}$ **25.** $\frac{77}{8}$

Chapter 5, page 145

Divide.

1. $3\overline{)111}$ **2.** $3\overline{)87}$ **3.** $2\overline{)106}$ **4.** $6\overline{)76}$ **5.** $4\overline{)221}$

6. $5\overline{)391}$ **7.** $4\overline{)55}$ **8.** $9\overline{)198}$ **9.** $6\overline{)72}$ **10.** $6\overline{)386}$

11. $87 \div 6$ **12.** $740 \div 9$ **13.** $105 \div 5$ **14.** $145 \div 5$ **15.** $429 \div 7$

16. $225 \div 9$ **17.** $433 \div 5$ **18.** $69 \div 3$ **19.** $887 \div 9$ **20.** $232 \div 9$

21. $\frac{488}{8}$ **22.** $\frac{556}{9}$ **23.** $\frac{644}{7}$ **24.** $\frac{333}{8}$ **25.** $\frac{265}{5}$

Chapter 5, page 147

Divide.

1. $3\overline{)1,782}$ **2.** $6\overline{)5,046}$ **3.** $9\overline{)991}$ **4.** $7\overline{)917}$ **5.** $2\overline{)858}$

6. $6\overline{)5,988}$ **7.** $3\overline{)2,739}$ **8.** $4\overline{)867}$ **9.** $2\overline{)421}$ **10.** $9\overline{)1,227}$

11. $874 \div 5$ **12.** $884 \div 2$ **13.** $968 \div 8$ **14.** $495 \div 2$ **15.** $818 \div 7$

16. $798 \div 7$ **17.** $847 \div 7$ **18.** $865 \div 4$ **19.** $6,235 \div 5$ **20.** $484 \div 4$

21. $\frac{1,870}{5}$ **22.** $\frac{826}{2}$ **23.** $\frac{963}{3}$ **24.** $\frac{4,137}{7}$ **25.** $\frac{757}{4}$

Chapter 5, page 149 _____

Divide.

1. $8\overline{)16{,}888}$
2. $7\overline{)32{,}121}$
3. $4\overline{)5{,}353}$
4. $3\overline{)64{,}008}$

5. $5\overline{)69{,}564}$
6. $4\overline{)18{,}517}$
7. $2\overline{)8{,}438}$
8. $8\overline{)61{,}728}$

9. $20{,}686 \div 3$
10. $24{,}755 \div 6$
11. $37{,}180 \div 9$
12. $84{,}242 \div 9$

13. $67{,}255 \div 5$
14. $6{,}779 \div 2$
15. $48{,}793 \div 3$
16. $5{,}139 \div 4$

Chapter 5, page 153 _____

Divide.

1. $2\overline{)6{,}818}$
2. $5\overline{)5{,}009}$
3. $2\overline{)7{,}018}$
4. $2\overline{)66{,}094}$
5. $3\overline{)4{,}515}$

6. $8\overline{)6{,}437}$
7. $8\overline{)1{,}659}$
8. $7\overline{)761}$
9. $6\overline{)67{,}625}$
10. $9\overline{)63{,}099}$

11. $6{,}358 \div 9$
12. $82{,}527 \div 3$
13. $19{,}511 \div 3$
14. $94{,}441 \div 2$

15. $6{,}808 \div 2$
16. $1{,}807 \div 2$
17. $1{,}859 \div 9$
18. $1{,}221 \div 4$

19. $758 \div 7$
20. $7{,}269 \div 9$
21. $79{,}266 \div 6$
22. $2{,}835 \div 4$

Chapter 5, page 155 _____

Divide.

1. $3\overline{)\$641.91}$
2. $8\overline{)\$52.00}$
3. $2\overline{)\$124.64}$
4. $2\overline{)\$73.08}$

5. $3\overline{)\$299.22}$
6. $2\overline{)\$3.60}$
7. $6\overline{)\$58.80}$
8. $6\overline{)\$190.74}$

9. $\$506.87 \div 7$
10. $\$12.00 \div 3$
11. $\$15.00 \div 5$
12. $\$88.98 \div 2$

13. $\$396.48 \div 4$
14. $\$89.82 \div 6$
15. $\$259.04 \div 8$
16. $\$66.36 \div 4$

17. $\$106.35 \div 3$
18. $\$0.63 \div 7$
19. $\$8.10 \div 3$
20. $\$36.27 \div 3$

Divide.

1. $30\overline{)180}$ 2. $40\overline{)320}$ 3. $20\overline{)160}$ 4. $10\overline{)60}$ 5. $70\overline{)210}$

6. $80\overline{)640}$ 7. $20\overline{)40}$ 8. $50\overline{)200}$ 9. $40\overline{)120}$ 10. $60\overline{)360}$

11. $490 \div 70$ 12. $540 \div 90$ 13. $480 \div 80$ 14. $180 \div 90$ 15. $250 \div 50$

16. $\frac{720}{80}$ 17. $\frac{320}{40}$ 18. $\frac{90}{30}$ 19. $\frac{550}{50}$ 20. $\frac{240}{60}$

Estimate.

1. $22\overline{)364}$ 2. $36\overline{)576}$ 3. $32\overline{)838}$ 4. $86\overline{)2,759}$ 5. $42\overline{)964}$

6. $72\overline{)4,598}$ 7. $22\overline{)6,922}$ 8. $73\overline{)8,351}$ 9. $23\overline{)8,842}$ 10. $93\overline{)2,857}$

11. $457 \div 11$ 12. $2,614 \div 84$ 13. $3,234 \div 77$ 14. $7,174 \div 58$

15. $\frac{8,495}{55}$ 16. $\frac{1,917}{21}$ 17. $\frac{2,983}{58}$ 18. $\frac{3,553}{71}$ 19. $\frac{4,264}{44}$

Divide.

1. $23\overline{)767}$ 2. $11\overline{)793}$ 3. $71\overline{)4,028}$ 4. $65\overline{)813}$ 5. $22\overline{)1,369}$

6. $33\overline{)431}$ 7. $21\overline{)869}$ 8. $83\overline{)6,343}$ 9. $72\overline{)6,565}$ 10. $31\overline{)2,932}$

11. $\$55.44 \div 88$ 12. $5,952 \div 27$ 13. $2,491 \div 53$ 14. $6,298 \div 77$ 15. $5,337 \div 62$

16. $794 \div 44$ 17. $\$80.51 \div 97$ 18. $2,983 \div 58$ 19. $7,115 \div 85$ 20. $1,752 \div 22$

Chapter 6, page 179

Divide.

1. $13\overline{)793}$
2. $12\overline{)\$7.32}$
3. $63\overline{)1,384}$
4. $55\overline{)3,740}$
5. $78\overline{)3,539}$

6. $83\overline{)4,112}$
7. $42\overline{)817}$
8. $73\overline{)\$37.23}$
9. $83\overline{)2,655}$
10. $47\overline{)2,867}$

11. $829 \div 23$
12. $1,517 \div 46$
13. $\$16.10 \div 46$
14. $864 \div 12$
15. $979 \div 12$

16. $\frac{4,896}{68}$
17. $\frac{769}{55}$
18. $\frac{1,383}{22}$
19. $\frac{1,659}{46}$
20. $\frac{1,459}{21}$

Chapter 6, page 181

Divide.

1. $79\overline{)9,218}$
2. $33\overline{)16,938}$
3. $35\overline{)4,480}$
4. $81\overline{)57,964}$
5. $11\overline{)6,751}$

6. $79\overline{)9,717}$
7. $11\overline{)6,754}$
8. $65\overline{)16,575}$
9. $32\overline{)9,896}$
10. $73\overline{)67,087}$

11. $19,078 \div 84$
12. $27,653 \div 72$
13. $8,567 \div 31$
14. $9,362 \div 77$

15. $5,088 \div 24$
16. $19,674 \div 31$
17. $15,868 \div 41$
18. $15,228 \div 42$

19. $\frac{8,625}{69}$
20. $\frac{22,911}{81}$
21. $\frac{26,157}{78}$
22. $\frac{27,837}{42}$
23. $\frac{7,819}{55}$

Chapter 6, page 183

Divide.

1. $93\overline{)28,090}$
2. $81\overline{)32,564}$
3. $22\overline{)\$13.20}$
4. $54\overline{)21,999}$
5. $91\overline{)36,541}$

6. $42\overline{)8,509}$
7. $91\overline{)9,454}$
8. $76\overline{)8,134}$
9. $58\overline{)40,865}$
10. $52\overline{)26,439}$

11. $14,738 \div 71$
12. $7,589 \div 36$
13. $\$6.66 \div 74$
14. $23,334 \div 33$

15. $6,615 \div 11$
16. $5,762 \div 32$
17. $11,548 \div 57$
18. $14,849 \div 21$

19. $\frac{60,756}{86}$
20. $\frac{20,012}{33}$
21. $\frac{6,888}{34}$
22. $\frac{29,766}{42}$
23. $\frac{6,720}{32}$

Divide.

1. $9\overline{)67.32}$ **2.** $32\overline{)11.84}$ **3.** $23\overline{)57.73}$ **4.** $97\overline{)22.31}$ **5.** $13\overline{)70.98}$

6. $21\overline{)6.51}$ **7.** $8\overline{)50.4}$ **8.** $33\overline{)36.63}$ **9.** $23\overline{)55.43}$ **10.** $14\overline{)11.746}$

11. $51\overline{)4.539}$ **12.** $42\overline{)38.22}$ **13.** $52\overline{)449.28}$ **14.** $70\overline{)8.40}$ **15.** $25\overline{)11.25}$

16. $2.282 \div 7$ **17.** $69.72 \div 83$ **18.** $9.152 \div 2$ **19.** $118.56 \div 76$

Divide.

1. $25\overline{)1.25}$ **2.** $2\overline{)1.27}$ **3.** $32\overline{)64.64}$ **4.** $48\overline{)28.848}$ **5.** $16\overline{)6.8}$

6. $32\overline{)6.496}$ **7.** $79\overline{)3.397}$ **8.** $25\overline{)12.3}$ **9.** $22\overline{)9.13}$ **10.** $41\overline{)8.241}$

11. $11.67 \div 15$ **12.** $45.32 \div 44$ **13.** $1.44 \div 36$ **14.** $1.92 \div 96$

15. $0.32 \div 16$ **16.** $46.09 \div 55$ **17.** $8.505 \div 21$ **18.** $7.84 \div 35$

Measure the length of the piece of string to the nearest

1. ▨ cm   **2.** ▨ mm   **3.** ▨ cm ▨ mm

Draw a line that measures

4. 4 cm   **5.** 9.7 cm   **6.** 15 cm   **7.** 2.3 cm   **8.** 12 cm

Measure to find the distance around each shape.

9.   **10.**

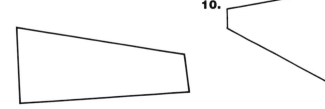

Which unit would you use to measure?
Write *millimeter, centimeter, meter,* or *kilometer.*

1. the length of a football field

2. the length of a pencil

3. the distance to the moon

4. the height of a flagpole

5. the diameter of a thumbtack

6. an airplane flight

Complete.

7. 23 km = ■ m

8. 7 mm = ■ cm

9. 0.03 m = ■ cm

10. 0.427 cm = ■ mm

11. 0.76 m = ■ cm

12. 8,050 m = ■ km

Which unit would you use to measure the capacity?
Write *milliter* or *liter.*

1. a bathtub

2. a swimming pool

3. a bottle cap

4. a pond

5. a straw

6. a cooler

Complete.

7. 4.5 L = ■ mL

8. 0.57 L = ■ mL

9. 352 mL = ■ L

10. 3,232 L = ■ mL

11. 0.565 L = ■ mL

12. 3,252 mL = ■ L

Which unit would you use to measure the mass?
Write *milligram, gram,* or *kilogram.*

1. a piece of paper

2. a dinosaur

3. a frog

4. an ocean liner

5. a feather

6. a paperweight

Complete.

7. 21,000 kg = ■ mg

8. 63 g = ■ mg

9. 56.4 g = ■ kg

10. 320 mg = ■ kg

11. 323 g = ■ mg

12. 72.5 kg = ■ g

Find the least common multiple.

1. 7, 6
2. 2, 5, 4
3. 3, 9
4. 7, 8
5. 3, 4, 8

6. 6, 30
7. 4, 7
8. 5, 9, 3
9. 2, 11
10. 3, 13

11. 4, 6, 8
12. 2, 5, 8
13. 3, 4
14. 8, 9
15. 7, 14, 21

16. 3, 8
17. 4, 9
18. 6, 12, 8
19. 2, 7, 5
20. 2, 9

21. 4, 6, 9
22. 3, 6, 10
23. 4, 7
24. 2, 6
25. 2, 17

Find the greatest common factor.

1. 16, 28
2. 8, 18
3. 8, 26
4. 14, 44
5. 56, 64

6. 72, 96
7. 24, 38
8. 6, 42
9. 22, 58
10. 21, 49

11. 33, 51
12. 9, 54
13. 24, 26
14. 5, 20
15. 34, 64

16. 30, 55
17. 9, 12
18. 26, 48
19. 27, 63
20. 77, 84

21. 56, 90
22. 60, 90
23. 45, 81
24. 14, 38
25. 21, 48

26. 28, 58
27. 40, 50
28. 12, 18, 24
29. 18, 36, 45
30. 16, 24, 32

Complete.

1. $\frac{6}{8} = \frac{3}{\blacksquare}$
2. $\frac{3}{9} = \frac{\blacksquare}{3}$
3. $\frac{20}{25} = \frac{\blacksquare}{5}$
4. $\frac{27}{54} = \frac{1}{\blacksquare}$
5. $\frac{4}{6} = \frac{2}{\blacksquare}$

6. $\frac{18}{24} = \frac{3}{\blacksquare}$
7. $\frac{4}{34} = \frac{2}{\blacksquare}$
8. $\frac{20}{45} = \frac{\blacksquare}{9}$
9. $\frac{10}{16} = \frac{\blacksquare}{8}$
10. $\frac{6}{9} = \frac{2}{\blacksquare}$

11. $\frac{9}{27} = \frac{\blacksquare}{3}$
12. $\frac{16}{64} = \frac{1}{\blacksquare}$
13. $\frac{36}{90} = \frac{2}{\blacksquare}$
14. $\frac{72}{84} = \frac{\blacksquare}{7}$
15. $\frac{88}{99} = \frac{8}{\blacksquare}$

Write the fraction in simplest form.

16. $\frac{2}{38}$
17. $\frac{3}{6}$
18. $\frac{6}{72}$
19. $\frac{25}{125}$
20. $\frac{9}{12}$

21. $\frac{2}{8}$
22. $\frac{36}{144}$
23. $\frac{20}{50}$
24. $\frac{26}{39}$
25. $\frac{2}{4}$

Estimate.

1. $\frac{1}{5} + \frac{7}{8}$ 2. $\frac{2}{7} + \frac{6}{9}$ 3. $\frac{5}{11} + \frac{3}{10}$ 4. $\frac{4}{9} + \frac{6}{7}$ 5. $\frac{7}{8} + \frac{7}{8} + \frac{3}{7}$

6. $\frac{1}{8} + \frac{2}{3}$ 7. $\frac{4}{7} + \frac{2}{5}$ 8. $\frac{7}{9} + \frac{7}{13}$ 9. $\frac{4}{5} + \frac{3}{8}$ 10. $\frac{5}{6} + \frac{1}{9} + \frac{2}{5}$

11. $\frac{6}{15} + \frac{3}{8}$ 12. $\frac{7}{8} + \frac{17}{20}$ 13. $\frac{5}{8} + \frac{4}{5}$ 14. $\frac{2}{5} + \frac{6}{7}$ 15. $\frac{7}{14} + \frac{2}{9} + \frac{8}{9}$

16. $\frac{5}{9} + \frac{7}{12}$ 17. $\frac{9}{10} + \frac{3}{7}$ 18. $\frac{6}{7} + \frac{11}{15}$ 19. $\frac{1}{2} + \frac{8}{9}$ 20. $\frac{1}{7} + \frac{16}{17} + \frac{4}{9}$

Add. Write the answer in simplest form.

1. $\frac{3}{5} + \frac{1}{10}$ 2. $\frac{3}{4} + \frac{1}{8}$ 3. $\frac{4}{9} + \frac{3}{5}$ 4. $\frac{1}{6} + \frac{2}{3}$ 5. $\frac{1}{2} + \frac{6}{7}$

6. $\frac{7}{9} + \frac{3}{4}$ 7. $\frac{3}{4} + \frac{5}{8}$ 8. $\frac{5}{6} + \frac{1}{2}$ 9. $\frac{2}{5} + \frac{7}{8}$ 10. $\frac{2}{3} + \frac{8}{9}$

11. $\frac{1}{2} + \frac{3}{4}$ 12. $\frac{9}{10} + \frac{4}{5}$ 13. $\frac{2}{3} + \frac{4}{9}$ 14. $\frac{5}{8} + \frac{1}{2}$ 15. $\frac{1}{12} + \frac{5}{8}$

16. $\begin{array}{r} \frac{5}{9} \\ + \frac{5}{18} \\ \hline \end{array}$ 17. $\begin{array}{r} \frac{4}{5} \\ + \frac{6}{9} \\ \hline \end{array}$ 18. $\begin{array}{r} \frac{8}{15} \\ + \frac{7}{10} \\ \hline \end{array}$ 19. $\begin{array}{r} \frac{5}{6} \\ + \frac{6}{7} \\ \hline \end{array}$ 20. $\begin{array}{r} \frac{4}{9} \\ + \frac{8}{12} \\ \hline \end{array}$

Subtract. Write the answer in simplest form.

1. $\frac{8}{9} - \frac{1}{9}$ 2. $\frac{5}{7} - \frac{2}{3}$ 3. $\frac{4}{6} - \frac{1}{6}$ 4. $\frac{5}{6} - \frac{3}{4}$ 5. $\frac{7}{8} - \frac{2}{5}$

6. $\frac{5}{7} - \frac{3}{7}$ 7. $\frac{2}{4} - \frac{1}{4}$ 8. $\frac{6}{10} - \frac{2}{7}$ 9. $\frac{5}{9} - \frac{1}{2}$ 10. $\frac{2}{3} - \frac{1}{3}$

11. $\frac{2}{3} - \frac{5}{9}$ 12. $\frac{3}{5} - \frac{3}{10}$ 13. $\frac{1}{2} - \frac{1}{4}$ 14. $\frac{5}{9} - \frac{1}{3}$ 15. $\frac{7}{10} - \frac{1}{5}$

16. $\begin{array}{r} \frac{3}{4} \\ - \frac{3}{10} \\ \hline \end{array}$ 17. $\begin{array}{r} \frac{2}{5} \\ - \frac{1}{4} \\ \hline \end{array}$ 18. $\begin{array}{r} \frac{8}{9} \\ - \frac{3}{4} \\ \hline \end{array}$ 19. $\begin{array}{r} \frac{1}{2} \\ - \frac{1}{7} \\ \hline \end{array}$ 20. $\begin{array}{r} \frac{2}{3} \\ - \frac{1}{5} \\ \hline \end{array}$

Estimate.

1. $1\frac{3}{5} + 4\frac{4}{9}$ **2.** $10\frac{1}{8} + 1\frac{4}{7}$ **3.** $5\frac{1}{8} + 7\frac{5}{6}$ **4.** $9\frac{3}{5} + 2\frac{5}{6}$ **5.** $8\frac{3}{10} + 5\frac{5}{6}$

Add. Write the answer in simplest form.

6. $7\frac{3}{4} + 3\frac{4}{5}$ **7.** $8\frac{5}{6} + 2\frac{2}{9}$ **8.** $5\frac{9}{10} + 1\frac{3}{4}$ **9.** $6\frac{1}{6} + 6\frac{9}{10}$ **10.** $3\frac{1}{2} + 5\frac{4}{7}$

11. $5\frac{1}{4} + 7\frac{5}{6}$ **12.** $6\frac{1}{2} + 10\frac{7}{9}$ **13.** $1\frac{2}{5} + 1\frac{2}{3}$ **14.** $4\frac{1}{3} + 1\frac{3}{4}$ **15.** $6\frac{5}{6} + 9\frac{1}{4}$

16. $\begin{array}{r} 8\frac{2}{5} \\ + 10\frac{3}{4} \\ \hline \end{array}$ **17.** $\begin{array}{r} 10\frac{3}{5} \\ + 2\frac{3}{4} \\ \hline \end{array}$ **18.** $\begin{array}{r} 6\frac{4}{7} \\ + 4\frac{1}{2} \\ \hline \end{array}$ **19.** $\begin{array}{r} 4\frac{3}{4} \\ + 5\frac{7}{10} \\ \hline \end{array}$ **20.** $\begin{array}{r} 1\frac{1}{2} \\ + 5\frac{5}{9} \\ \hline \end{array}$

Subtract. Write the answer in simplest form.

1. $8\frac{3}{8} - 2\frac{1}{8}$ **2.** $5\frac{6}{7} - 1\frac{3}{4}$ **3.** $3\frac{2}{5} - 1\frac{1}{5}$ **4.** $13\frac{7}{9} - 6$ **5.** $5\frac{5}{7} - 3\frac{2}{6}$

6. $12\frac{2}{3} - 5$ **7.** $8\frac{5}{9} - 3$ **8.** $7\frac{3}{4} - 4\frac{3}{8}$ **9.** $12\frac{2}{3} - 3\frac{1}{6}$ **10.** $14\frac{5}{6} - 12\frac{1}{2}$

11. $17\frac{2}{3} - 8\frac{1}{9}$ **12.** $15\frac{1}{2} - 14$ **13.** $16\frac{7}{10} - 10\frac{1}{2}$ **14.** $13\frac{7}{8} - 1\frac{3}{4}$ **15.** $3\frac{1}{3} - 1\frac{1}{6}$

16. $\begin{array}{r} 10\frac{7}{9} \\ - 9\frac{1}{3} \\ \hline \end{array}$ **17.** $\begin{array}{r} 11\frac{3}{4} \\ - 8\frac{1}{2} \\ \hline \end{array}$ **18.** $\begin{array}{r} 18\frac{7}{8} \\ - 1\frac{3}{4} \\ \hline \end{array}$ **19.** $\begin{array}{r} 14\frac{1}{2} \\ - 7 \\ \hline \end{array}$ **20.** $\begin{array}{r} 16\frac{2}{3} \\ - 3 \\ \hline \end{array}$

Subtract. Write the answer in simplest form.

1. $6\frac{1}{6} - 1\frac{3}{4}$ **2.** $4\frac{1}{4} - 1\frac{2}{5}$ **3.** $2\frac{1}{10} - 1\frac{1}{6}$ **4.** $20\frac{3}{5} - 4\frac{2}{3}$ **5.** $15\frac{2}{3} - 3\frac{3}{4}$

6. $8\frac{2}{9} - 2\frac{1}{2}$ **7.** $20 - 9\frac{1}{4}$ **8.** $10\frac{1}{3} - 1\frac{2}{3}$ **9.** $8\frac{3}{10} - 2\frac{7}{10}$ **10.** $16\frac{3}{10} - 13\frac{5}{6}$

11. $19\frac{1}{2} - 8\frac{2}{3}$ **12.** $13\frac{1}{3} - 6\frac{1}{2}$ **13.** $11\frac{3}{7} - 4\frac{5}{7}$ **14.** $18\frac{1}{2} - 15\frac{2}{3}$ **15.** $15\frac{1}{6} - 11\frac{7}{10}$

16. $\begin{array}{r} 8\frac{2}{10} \\ - 2\frac{3}{4} \\ \hline \end{array}$ **17.** $\begin{array}{r} 9 \\ - 8\frac{1}{2} \\ \hline \end{array}$ **18.** $\begin{array}{r} 19\frac{1}{9} \\ - 2\frac{1}{6} \\ \hline \end{array}$ **19.** $\begin{array}{r} 17\frac{3}{6} \\ - 13\frac{5}{6} \\ \hline \end{array}$ **20.** $\begin{array}{r} 9\frac{2}{5} \\ - 8\frac{1}{2} \\ \hline \end{array}$

Chapter 9, page 273

Multiply. Write the product in simplest form.

1. $\frac{2}{3} \times \frac{1}{10}$
2. $\frac{1}{6} \times \frac{2}{3}$
3. $\frac{3}{7} \times \frac{1}{4}$
4. $\frac{1}{4} \times \frac{2}{5}$
5. $\frac{5}{6} \times \frac{1}{4}$

6. $\frac{1}{2} \times \frac{3}{4}$
7. $\frac{1}{8} \times \frac{1}{10}$
8. $\frac{2}{5} \times \frac{3}{4}$
9. $\frac{2}{3} \times \frac{3}{5}$
10. $\frac{1}{2} \times \frac{2}{9}$

11. $\frac{3}{4} \times \frac{4}{5}$
12. $\frac{4}{7} \times \frac{2}{5}$
13. $\frac{1}{3} \times \frac{5}{6}$
14. $\frac{2}{7} \times \frac{1}{3}$
15. $\frac{3}{4} \times \frac{5}{7}$

16. $\frac{1}{2} \times \frac{2}{3}$
17. $\frac{4}{7} \times \frac{3}{8}$
18. $\frac{1}{6} \times \frac{3}{5}$
19. $\frac{5}{8} \times \frac{2}{3}$
20. $\frac{1}{2} \times \frac{3}{5}$

21. $\frac{4}{5} \times \frac{7}{8}$
22. $\frac{2}{7} \times \frac{5}{9}$
23. $\frac{1}{3} \times \frac{1}{5}$
24. $\frac{4}{9} \times \frac{1}{6}$
25. $\frac{7}{9} \times \frac{1}{2}$

Chapter 9, page 277

Multiply. Write the product in simplest form.

1. $\frac{3}{8} \times 4\frac{2}{3}$
2. $2\frac{5}{6} \times 8$
3. $\frac{4}{9} \times 1\frac{1}{8}$
4. $3\frac{1}{2} \times 2\frac{2}{3}$
5. $\frac{4}{7} \times 2\frac{2}{8}$

6. $8\frac{1}{4} \times \frac{5}{6}$
7. $7 \times 4\frac{2}{9}$
8. $6 \times 3\frac{4}{9}$
9. $8\frac{2}{5} \times \frac{1}{2}$
10. $\frac{2}{3} \times 4\frac{1}{8}$

11. $4\frac{4}{5} \times 3\frac{2}{3}$
12. $3\frac{1}{3} \times \frac{7}{8}$
13. $3\frac{2}{5} \times \frac{5}{6}$
14. $2\frac{4}{7} \times 4\frac{3}{4}$
15. $1\frac{1}{6} \times 4\frac{3}{4}$

16. $5\frac{2}{9} \times 7\frac{1}{2}$
17. $2\frac{1}{4} \times \frac{1}{6}$
18. $10\frac{2}{3} \times \frac{3}{8}$
19. $5 \times 3\frac{1}{5}$
20. $\frac{1}{2} \times 9\frac{1}{3}$

21. $2\frac{7}{10} \times \frac{2}{9}$
22. $\frac{3}{7} \times 2\frac{1}{4}$
23. $2\frac{1}{4} \times 3\frac{2}{3}$
24. $3\frac{3}{4} \times \frac{7}{10}$
25. $\frac{3}{7} \times 2\frac{1}{3}$

Chapter 9, page 281

Divide.

1. $9 \div \frac{1}{7}$
2. $13 \div \frac{1}{2}$
3. $36 \div \frac{1}{6}$
4. $85 \div \frac{1}{2}$
5. $30 \div \frac{1}{5}$

6. $45 \div \frac{1}{9}$
7. $25 \div \frac{1}{10}$
8. $66 \div \frac{1}{3}$
9. $24 \div \frac{1}{8}$
10. $30 \div \frac{1}{8}$

11. $18 \div \frac{1}{9}$
12. $75 \div \frac{1}{10}$
13. $80 \div \frac{1}{6}$
14. $75 \div \frac{1}{5}$
15. $7 \div \frac{1}{7}$

16. $8 \div \frac{1}{8}$
17. $26 \div \frac{1}{4}$
18. $52 \div \frac{1}{3}$
19. $44 \div \frac{1}{4}$
20. $6 \div \frac{1}{8}$

21. $48 \div \frac{1}{3}$
22. $90 \div \frac{1}{4}$
23. $35 \div \frac{1}{10}$
24. $21 \div \frac{1}{7}$
25. $16 \div \frac{1}{6}$

Add or subtract.

1. 3 h 14 min
    + 1 h 39 min

2. 12 min 15 s
    − 4 min 35 s

3. 6 h 5 min
    − 1 h 14 min

4. 2 h 35 min
    + 7 h 47 min

5. 2 min 4 s
    + 9 min 29 s

6. 45 h 12 min
    − 18 h 25 min

7. 8 h 30 min
    + 12 h 45 min

8. 24 h 6 min
    − 8 h 16 min

9. 16 h 21 min
    − 3 h 34 min

10. 47 min 12 s
    + 9 min 25 s

11. 12 h 39 min
    − 10 h 45 min

12. 55 min 12 s
    + 18 min 6 s

13. 4 min 55 s
    + 5 min 32 s

14. 8 h 45 min
    − 5 h 20 min

15. 29 min 7 s
    − 10 min 15 s

16. 6 h 25 min
    + 5 h 55 min

Write *inches*, *feet*, or *yards*.

1. A car may be 10 ▦ long.

2. A book may be 10 ▦ wide.

3. A house may be 20 ▦ high.

4. A chalkboard may be 3 ▦ wide.

Complete.

5. 6 yd = ▦ in.

6. 7 ft = ▦ in.

7. 10,560 yd = ▦ mi

8. 48 in. = ▦ ft

9. $5\frac{1}{2}$ ft = ▦ in.

10. 12 yd = ▦ ft

11. 1 mi = ▦ ft

12. 54 in. = ▦ yd

13. 10 ft = ▦ in.

14. 24 ft = ▦ yd

15. 96 in. = ▦ ft

16. 6 mi = ▦ yd

Write *cups*, *pints*, *quarts*, or *gallons*.

1. A coffee mug may hold 2 ▦.

2. A water tank may hold 200 ▦.

3. A bathtub may hold 25 ▦.

4. An oilcan may contain 1 ▦.

Complete.

5. $5\frac{1}{4}$ gal = ▦ qt

6. 2 pt = ▦ gal

7. 12 c = ▦ pt

8. 8 qt = ▦ gal

9. 48 c = ▦ gal

10. 2 gal = ▦ pt

11. 4 qt = ▦ c

12. 3 pt = ▦ c

13. 5 gal = ▦ c

14. 7 qt = ▦ c

15. 16 pt = ▦ gal

16. 7 c = ▦ pt

Find the next two equal ratios.

1. $\frac{1}{4} = \frac{2}{8} = \frac{\blacksquare}{\blacksquare} = \frac{\blacksquare}{\blacksquare}$

2. $\frac{2}{3} = \frac{6}{9} = \frac{\blacksquare}{\blacksquare} = \frac{\blacksquare}{\blacksquare}$

3. $\frac{4}{5} = \frac{8}{10} = \frac{\blacksquare}{\blacksquare} = \frac{\blacksquare}{\blacksquare}$

Find the missing number.

4. $\frac{84}{18} = \frac{14}{n}$

5. $\frac{n}{16} = \frac{15}{48}$

6. $\frac{16}{n} = \frac{96}{36}$

7. $\frac{99}{54} = \frac{n}{6}$

8. $\frac{n}{10} = \frac{33}{30}$

9. $\frac{18}{90} = \frac{1}{n}$

10. $\frac{50}{n} = \frac{100}{86}$

11. $\frac{n}{37} = \frac{12}{74}$

Write = or ≠ for ●.

12. $\frac{15}{8}$ ● $\frac{90}{48}$

13. $\frac{14}{18}$ ● $\frac{8}{2}$

14. $\frac{1}{13}$ ● $\frac{2}{19}$

15. $\frac{18}{16}$ ● $\frac{108}{96}$

16. $\frac{12}{21}$ ● $\frac{5}{3}$

17. $\frac{2}{4}$ ● $\frac{12}{24}$

18. $\frac{16}{13}$ ● $\frac{17}{6}$

19. $\frac{4}{21}$ ● $\frac{11}{14}$

Chapter 10, page 319

Write as a percent.

1. $\frac{94}{100}$

2. $\frac{13}{100}$

3. $\frac{85}{100}$

4. $\frac{64}{100}$

5. $\frac{7}{100}$

6. $\frac{76}{100}$

7. $\frac{3}{100}$

8. $\frac{91}{100}$

9. $\frac{1}{100}$

10. $\frac{42}{100}$

11. $\frac{11}{100}$

12. $\frac{57}{100}$

13. $\frac{37}{100}$

14. $\frac{99}{100}$

15. $\frac{12}{100}$

16. 4:100

17. 18 out of 100

18. 29:100

19. 48 per 100

20. 95:100

21. 42 to 100

22. 6:100

23. 17 per 100

24. 32 per 100

25. 48 out of 100

26. 11:100

27. 55 to 100

Chapter 10, page 321

Write as a percent.

1. 0.62

2. 0.83

3. 0.32

4. 0.92

5. 0.66

6. 0.79

7. 0.78

8. 0.23

9. 0.07

10. 0.48

11. 0.19

12. 0.05

13. 0.09

14. 0.34

15. 0.17

Write as a decimal.

16. 72%

17. 15%

18. 4%

19. 86%

20. 49%

21. 97%

22. 6%

23. 51%

24. 63%

25. 8%

26. 13%

27. 25%

28. 7%

29. 35%

30. 14%

Chapter 10, page 323

Write each percent as a fraction in simplest form.

1. 90%   **2.** 76%   **3.** 68%   **4.** 31%   **5.** 48%

6. 60%   **7.** 26%   **8.** 74%   **9.** 35%   **10.** 2%

Write each fraction as a percent.

11. $\frac{9}{100}$ **12.** $\frac{3}{4}$ **13.** $\frac{2}{5}$ **14.** $\frac{3}{10}$ **15.** $\frac{6}{25}$

16. $\frac{1}{20}$ **17.** $\frac{7}{28}$ **18.** $\frac{7}{10}$ **19.** $\frac{3}{25}$ **20.** $\frac{6}{20}$

Chapter 10, page 325

Find the percent of each number.

1. 20% of 100   **2.** 6% of 250   **3.** 74% of 2,000   **4.** 6% of 350

5. 70% of 30   **6.** 60% of 470   **7.** 10% of 7   **8.** 80% of 65

9. 55% of 500   **10.** 35% of 700   **11.** 40% of 600   **12.** 15% of 900

13. 2% of 650   **14.** 4% of 950   **15.** 75% of 500   **16.** 5% of 240

17. 8% of 850   **18.** 50% of 660   **19.** 25% of 1,000   **20.** 44% of 500

Chapter 10, page 327

Compute.

1. What percent of 15 is 12?   **2.** 91 is what percent of 910?   **3.** What percent of 500 is 90?   **4.** 7 is what percent of 35?

5. What percent of 20 is 6?   **6.** What percent of 700 is 63?   **7.** 3 is what percent of 15?   **8.** 9 is what percent of 300?

Find the percent that each part is of the whole.

9. 2 blue cars
10 cars
■% are blue.

10. 7 white houses
14 houses
■% are white.

11. 2 black mice
5 mice
■% are black.

Identify and name each figure.

1.

2.

3.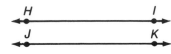

Draw each figure.

4. line segment $\overline{XY}$

5. plane t

6. intersecting lines $\overleftrightarrow{TU}$ and $\overleftrightarrow{VW}$ at point Z

Is the figure congruent to $\triangle ABC$? Write *yes* or *no*.

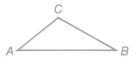

1.

2.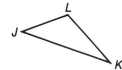

3.

Is the figure congruent to $\triangle STUV$? Write *yes* or *no*.

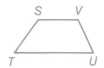

4.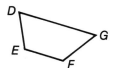

5.

6.

Is the figure congruent to $\square VWXY$? Write *yes* or *no*.

7.

8.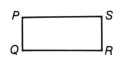

9.

Find the perimeter of each figure.

1.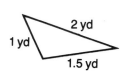

2.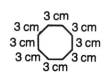

3.

4.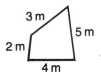

5. a pentagon
each side = 2 ft

6. a square
each side = 3 cm

7. a rectangle
2 sides = 6 yd
2 sides = 2 yd

Find the area.

1.

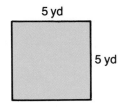

5 yd

5 yd

2.

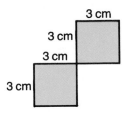

3 cm

3 cm

3 cm

3 cm

3.

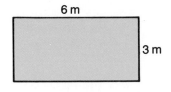

6 m

3 m

4. $l = 9$ cm $w = 4$ cm

5. $l = 12$ ft $w = 6$ ft

6. $l = 19$ in. $w = 7$ in.

7. $l = 4$ m $w = 4$ m

8. $l = 17$ km $w = 10$ km

9. $l = 8$ mi $w = 5$ mi

10. $l = 20$ yd $w = 7$ yd

11. $l = 9$ mm $w = 8$ mm

12. $l = 16$ ft $w = 11$ ft

Find the area.

1.

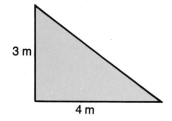

3 m

4 m

2.

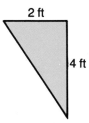

2 ft

4 ft

3.

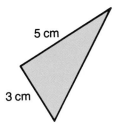

5 cm

3 cm

4. $b = 9$ m $h = 10$ m

5. $b = 6$ yd $h = 14$ yd

6. $b = 7$ in. $h = 7$ in.

7. $b = 11$ ft $h = 13$ ft

8. $b = 4$ mm $h = 7$ mm

9. $b = 10$ cm $h = 13$ cm

10. $b = 7$ km $h = 12$ km

11. $b = 5$ ft $h = 8$ ft

12. $b = 8$ mi $h = 9$ mi

Find the volume.

1.

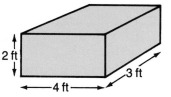

2 ft

3 ft

4 ft

2.

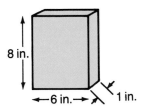

8 in.

6 in.

1 in.

3.

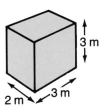

3 m

2 m

3 m

4. $l = 9$ in. $w = 3$ in. $h = 4$ in.

5. $l = 10$ mm $w = 6$ mm $h = 6$ mm

6. $l = 8$ km $w = 8$ km $h = 8$ km

7. $l = 32$ yd $w = 1$ yd $h = 2$ yd

8. $l = 16$ ft $w = 5$ ft $h = 9$ ft

9. $l = 20$ m $w = 7$ m $h = 7$ m

Copy and complete the bar graph. Use the data in the table. Round each number to the nearest tenth of a million. Then answer each question.

AREA OF THE UNITED STATES—1790–1970

Year	Area in square miles	Rounded
1790	888,811	
1820	1,788,006	
1850	2,992,747	
1880	3,022,387	
1970	3,618,467	

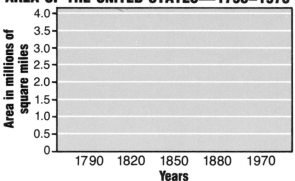

AREA OF THE UNITED STATES—1790–1970

1. During which period did the area of the United States double in size?

2. About how much did the area of the United States increase between 1880 and 1970?

Copy and complete the broken-line graph. Use the data in the table. Round each number to the nearest tenth of a billion. Then answer each question.

POSTAL INCOME IN FIVE CITIES—1980

City	Income	Rounded
Boston	$224,428,760	
Chicago	$528,233,991	
Los Angeles	$271,136,828	
New York	$666,377,778	
St. Louis	$127,427,555	

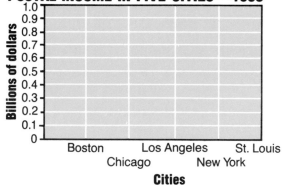

POSTAL INCOME IN FIVE CITIES—1980

1. Which city had the most postal income? Which city had the least postal income?

2. Which two cities had almost the same postal income?

Chapter 12, page 393

Find the mean and the median.

1. 5, 4, 3
2. 25, 20, 15, 10, 18
3. 12, 8, 6, 2, 4
4. 9, 10, 11, 14, 19
5. 32, 18, 24, 42, 14
6. 7, 5, 9, 1, 4

Find the mode and the range.

7. 68, 52, 44, 68
8. 102, 34, 76, 34
9. 3, 9, 21, 9, 18
10. 29, 17, 51, 47, 17
11. 54, 26, 32, 54
12. 4, 1, 5, 11, 5

Chapter 12, page 397

Write a fraction for the probability of picking

1. a blue marble.
2. a red marble.
3. a green marble.
4. a yellow marble.
5. a pink marble.
6. a black marble.

Write a fraction for the probability of picking

7. a *1* card.
8. a *2* card.
9. a *3* card.
10. a *4* card.
11. a *5* card.
12. a *7* card.

Chapter 12, page 399

Predict the probability of each event.
Write *certain* or *impossible* for each event.

What is the probability of picking

1. a green marble?
2. a yellow or black marble?
3. a black or yellow marble?
4. a red marble?

What is the probability of landing on

5. blue?
6. red or white?
7. green?
8. green or yellow?

MATH REASONING

Chapter 1

Logical Reasoning, pages 2–3

Use subtraction to change the blue digit to a zero.

1. 843,652   **2.** 215,814   **3.** 657,195   **4.** 973,854

Logical Reasoning, pages 12–13

John forgot his school locker number. He remembers that the number has three digits. He knows that the sum of the digits is 9 and that the digits are odd numbers. He also knows that there are 120 lockers in all.

Use the information to find John's locker number.

Challenge, pages 16–17

Solve.

1. What is the least 2-digit number that can be rounded to 100?

2. What is the greatest 3-digit number that can be rounded to 100?

Chapter 1

Visual Thinking, pages 22–23

 Use your calculator to change the numbers to words.

Enter each number into your calculator. Add 1,000 to the number. Write the answer. Then turn your calculator upside down and write the word shown on the display.

1. six thousand, seven hundred thirty-eight
2. four hundred sixty thousand, three hundred seventy-five
3. five hundred seventy-six thousand, three hundred forty-five
4. fifty-six thousand, three hundred thirty-four

Challenge, pages 24–25

 Use a calculator to find the missing digits.

1.
```
   9 8 5
   4 5 3
 + 2 3 8
 ───────
 1,■■ 6
```

2.
```
       8
      7 9
    4 2 4
    5 8 9
  + 6 3 5
  ───────
  1,■■■
```

3.
```
   2 7 2
   1 6 4
   2 7 8
 +   9 6
 ───────
 ■■ 0
```

4.
```
      4 7 6
    5, 7 2 7
   6 5, 3 3 2
    1, 5 9 8
 + 5 3, 8 6 3
 ───────────
 ■■■,9 9 6
```

5.
```
          9
    3, 0 7 8
        4 4
      8 5 6
 + 2 3, 7 1 0
 ───────────
 ■■, 6 ■■
```

Logical Reasoning, pages 30–31

Subtraction can be used to find missing digits. Use number facts as clues to find the missing digits.

Example:

```
                    4  13  15  13
   5, 4 6 3         5,  4   6   3     Think:   13 − ■ = 9     So,   5,463
 −■,■ 8■          −■,  ■   8   ■             15 − 8 = 7          −2,784
 ───────          ──────────────            13 − ■ = 6          ──────
 2, 6 7 9           2,  6   7   9             4 − ■ = 2           2,679
```

1.
```
   9, 7 2 6
 −■, 4■■
 ─────────
 3, 2 8 8
```

2.
```
   6 7, 5 2 1
 −3■, 4 6■
 ───────────
 ■9, 0■8
```

3.
```
 ■4, 9 0 5
 −1 8, 0■5
 ──────────
 6,■ 9 0
```

4.
```
 ■6, 0 8 7
 −   9,■■8
 ──────────
 7, 0 3 9
```

Chapter 2

Logical Reasoning, pages 44–45

1. Use the digits 0, 2, 4, 6, 8 and a decimal point to write the greatest number possible and the least number possible.

2. Use the digits 1, 3, 7, 3, 9 and a decimal point to write the greatest number possible and the least number possible.

Challenge, pages 48–49

Use the three digits and a decimal point to write eighteen different numbers. Remember that a number like .346 is not a three-digit number. Because it is less than 1, it is written as 0.346 and is a four-digit number.

1. 364   2. 751   3. 468

Logical Reasoning, pages 52–53

What is the missing number in the pattern?

1. 2.1, 0.21, 0.021, ■   2. 0.241, ■, 24.1, 241

3. 0.58, 0.59, 0.6, ■   4. 1.98, 1.99, ■, 2.1

Math Reasoning

Chapter 2

Challenge, pages 54–55

If a decimal is rounded to a whole number, the zeros to the right of the decimal point may be omitted.

Example: Round 3,472.378 to the nearest whole number.

$$3,472.378 \rightarrow 3,472.000 \text{ or } 3,472$$

1. Write a sentence to explain why this is true.

2. Round 5,682.432 to the nearest hundred, the nearest ten, and the nearest one.

Logical Reasoning, pages 56–57

Heather and Jenny were shopping. Their purchases included items that cost $5.12, $6.78, and $8.09. The girls each estimated the total cost in a different way.

Example:

Heather's method:			Jenny's method:		
$5.12	$5.12		$5.12	$\rightarrow$	$5.00
6.78	6.78 } about $1		6.78	$\rightarrow$	7.00
+8.09	+8.09		+8.09	$\rightarrow$	+8.00
$19	So, $19 + $1 = $20.				$20.00

1. Describe the method Heather used to estimate the total cost.

2. Describe the method Jenny used to estimate the total cost.

3. Which method would you choose? Why?

Challenge, pages 62–63

Copy each subtraction sentence. Insert decimal points to make a true number sentence.

1. $347 - 15 = 3.32$ **2.** $347 - 15 = 1.97$ **3.** $347 - 15 = 19.7$

4. $347 - 15 = 33.2$ **5.** $347 - 15 = 346.85$ **6.** $347 - 15 = 345.5$

Math Reasoning

Chapter 3

Logical Reasoning, pages 78–79

When a certain 1-digit number is multiplied by 100, the product is 720 more than the product of the number and 10. What is the number?

Challenge, pages 82–83

You can use front-end estimation in multiplication. Estimate the product of two numbers by multiplying their lead digits and then writing zeros in the product.

Example:

Find the lead digit. Multiply.	Count the places after the lead digit.		Write zeros in the product.
$\begin{array}{r} 21{,}873 \\ \times\ \ \ \ 7 \\ \hline 14 \end{array}$	$\begin{array}{r} 21{,}873 \\ \times\ \ \ \ 7 \\ \hline 14 \end{array}$	Four places mean four zeros.	$\begin{array}{r} 21{,}873 \\ \times\ \ \ \ 7 \\ \hline 140{,}000 \end{array}$

Estimate each product.

1. $54{,}250 \times 2$

2. $13{,}211 \times 4$

3. $6{,}844 \times 6$

4. $830{,}040 \times 3$

Visual Thinking, pages 86–87

You can often discover patterns when you see an arrangement of numbers. Look at the multiples of 9 on the chart. They are organized in rows and columns.

09	18	27	36	45	54	63	72	81	90
99	108	117	126	135	144	153	162	171	180	189
198	207	216	225	234	243	252	261	270	279	288
297	306	315	324	333	342	351	360	369	378	387

1. Look at the first row. What pattern can you find in the ones place? in the tens place?

2. Look down each column. What pattern can you find in the ones place? in the tens place? in the hundreds place?

3. What other patterns can you find in this arrangement of numbers?

4. Use the data from the patterns to write a fifth row.

Math Reasoning

Chapter 3

Challenge, pages 92–93

"Keep moving" was the most important rule on a wagon train. The pioneers who left Independence, Missouri, in the spring had only five months to cross the western mountains. If they did not make it, they could be trapped by the winter snowstorms. Because of this, the leader of the wagon train had to calculate the group's progress carefully.

The wagon train was moving at a speed of 17 miles a day.

1. If a wheel broke and it took 3 days to repair, how many miles would the wagons travel in a week?
2. How far would the wagons travel in 4 weeks and 2 days?
3. About how far would the wagons travel in 5 months?

Logical Reasoning, pages 94–95

Find the missing digits.

1.
```
      8 0 ■
  ×   ■ ■ 3
  ─────────
    2 4 0 6
  1 ■ 0 4 0
+ 8 0 ■ 0 0
  ─────────
  9 8, ■ 4 6
```

2.
```
      7 ■ 3
  ×   ■ 4 ■
  ─────────
    2 1 3 9
  2 8 ■ 2 0
+ 1 4 ■ 6 0 0
  ───────────
  1 7 ■, 2 5 9
```

Challenge, pages 96–97

In a race on Fun Day, each person wore swim fins and balanced an apple on his or her head. The first runner to finish scored 100 points, the second 90 points, and the third 80 points. From that, 10 points were subtracted for each time the runner dropped the apple during the race. Use the score card to calculate the number of points for each runner. Who scored the most points?

	Missy	Chris	Julie
Place at finish	Third	First	Second
Times apple dropped	4	9	3

Math Reasoning

Chapter 4

Challenge, pages 106–107

Estimate the products. List the number sentences in order from the least to the greatest according to the estimated products.

$$85.3 \times 0.8$$
$$18.31 \times 18$$
$$129.8 \times 10.2$$
$$43.9 \times 0.7$$
$$82.63 \times 2.5$$
$$287.3 \times 2.6$$
$$57.1 \times 31.25$$

Challenge, pages 110–111

A magic square always has the same sum for each row, column, and diagonal. Multiply each number in the first magic square by 0.6 to create a new square. Three boxes of the new square have been filled in for you.

16	2	3	13
5	11	10	8
9	7	6	12
4	14	15	1

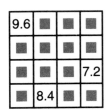

1. What is the sum for each row and column of the first square?

2. Is the new square a magic square? If so, what is the sum for each row and column?

Logical Reasoning, pages 112–113

   10¢ = $0.10

1¢ = $0.01

 $1 = $1.00

$10 = $10.00

 TEN

$100 = $100.00

 100

$1,000 = $1,000.00

Use the least number of coins and bills possible to show a picture of each decimal.

1. $423.56   **2.** $1,372.30   **3.** $2,030.06   **4.** $3,405.18

Chapter 4

Logical Reasoning, pages 114–115

Which is the better buy?

1. a bag of 6 boxes of raisins for $1.09, or 8 boxes of raisins for $1.20

2. 6 cans of fruit juice for a total of $2.79, or 12 cans of fruit juice for $5.19

3. a bag of 10 apples for $3.90, or 10 apples for $0.39 each

Logical Reasoning, pages 116–117

Choose two decimals between 0 and 1. Find the product.

1. Is the product greater than or less than the two factors?
2. Try other examples. Do you get the same results?
3. Is the product always greater than or always less than the two factors?
4. Is the product greater than or less than 1?

Choose two decimal numbers greater than 1.
Find the product.

5. Is the product greater than or less than the two factors?
6. Try other examples. Do you get the same results?
7. Is the product always greater than or always less than the two factors?

Challenge, pages 118–119

A waterfall is an excellent source of energy. This energy used to be measured in horsepower. To find how much horsepower a waterfall can produce, first multiply the speed of the water times the distance that the water falls. Then multiply that product by 0.1.

Identify the needed information.

1. If the speed of a waterfall is 500 cubic feet per second, what is the horsepower produced?

2. If you know the distance the water falls is 60 feet, do you have enough information to solve? If so, solve.

Math Reasoning

Chapter 5

Challenge, pages 130–131

Here is a quick way to find the sum of all the numbers in a series. First, complete the series in the first row. Then, write the series backwards under these numbers. Add each set of numbers. You see that all these sums are the same.

1.2,	1.4,	1.6,	1.8,	2.0,	2.■,	2.■,	2.■,	2.8
2.8,	2.■,	2.■,	2.■,	2.0,	1.8,	1.6,	1.4,	1.2
4.0	■	■	■	4.0	■	■	■	4.0

To find the sum of all the numbers in the series, multiply 4 by the number of items in the series. $4 \times 9 = 36$

Then divide by 2. $36 \div 2 = 18$
So, $1.2 + 1.4 + 1.6 + 1.8 + 2.0 + 2.2 + 2.4 + 2.6 + 2.8 = 18$.

Complete the series and find the sum of the numbers.

3.4, 3.8, 4.2, 4.6, ■, ■, ■, ■, ■

Logical Reasoning, pages 134–135

1. When you divide by 3, the remainder can be 0, 1, or 2. The remainder cannot be 3. Why?

2. List the remainders you can get when you divide by each number.

   a. 2   **b.** 4   **c.** 5   **d.** 6   **e.** 7   **f.** 8   **g.** 9

Logical Reasoning, pages 138–139

Here is a way to decide whether a number is divisible by 4.

1. Is 600 divisible by 4? Explain.

2. Is 128 divisible by 4? Explain. (*Hint:* $128 = 100 + 28$)
   Think: $4 \times 25 = 100$ and $4 \times 7 = 28$.

3. How can you check whether 128 is divisible by 4?

4. Is 236 divisible by 4? Explain. (*Hint:* $236 = 200 + 36$)

5. What do you notice about the last two digits of numbers that are divisible by four?

6. Write a rule for divisibility by 4.

Math Reasoning

Chapter 5

Visual Thinking, pages 142–143

1. Use each graph to write five true statements. Use this information to write questions.

2. Choose a statement to write a subtraction number sentence. Solve.

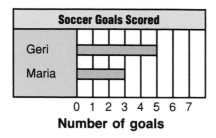 

Challenge, pages 144–145

Find the missing digits.

1.
```
      2 ■
   ■)■ 7
     ■
    1 ■
    ■ 6
      ■
```

2.
```
      1 ■
   ■)■ 8
     ■
    3 ■
    3 ■
      ■
```

Challenge, pages 146–147

In the following division problems, each letter represents a digit. The letter O represents zero.

Solve to break the code and find the digit that stands for each letter.

1.
```
   S)L8TP
     LR
     14
     PL
     L1
     LP
      0
```

2.
```
   B )2DCC
      AO
      3C
      DA
      DC
      DA
       D
```

Chapter 6

Challenge, pages 166–167

Divide. Match the remainder in each problem to the code to find the message.

2	3	4	5	6	7	8	9
X	U	T	N	A	E	P	R

1. $80\overline{)326}$

2. $90\overline{)815}$

3. $50\overline{)257}$

4. $30\overline{)242}$

5. $60\overline{)128}$

6. $40\overline{)127}$

7. $20\overline{)149}$

8. $70\overline{)144}$

Challenge, pages 168–169

Estimate the quotient with paper and pencil or mental math. Use a calculator to find the exact answer. Compare the exact answer with the estimate. Is the answer reasonable?

Example: $3{,}122 \div 14$

Think: $14\overline{)31}$. The quotient begins in the hundreds place. It will have three digits. The estimated answer is 200. The exact answer is 223.

Problem	Estimated Answer	Exact Answer
1. $216 \div 18$	■	■
2. $943 \div 23$	■	■
3. $2{,}800 \div 25$	■	■
4. $6{,}560 \div 32$	■	■

Challenge, pages 172–173

Fill in each box with the missing digit.

1.
```
        7 R ■7
   ■3)■ 7 ■
     1 6 1
     ■ 7
```

2.
```
         7 R ■9
  3 ■)2 5 ■
      2 3 8
      ■ 9
```

Math Reasoning

Student Handbook   **H197**

Chapter 6

Challenge, pages 174–175

If you know the answer and the divisor to a division problem, can you find the dividend?
You can use a calculator to help you.

Example: 49 R3 = ■ ÷ 24

[4] [9] [×] [2] [4] [+] [3] [=] [1179.] ← dividend

Use a calculator to find the dividend.

1. 52 R4 = ■ ÷ 23

2. 36 R2 = ■ ÷ 29

3. 705 R8 = ■ ÷ 16

4. 39 R70 = ■ ÷ 81

Challenge, pages 176–177

Mary estimates she sleeps about 196,560 minutes a year. About how many hours a week does she sleep? About how many hours a day does she sleep?

Challenge, pages 178–179

Solve.

1. I am greater than the remainder in 54)401. I am less than the remainder in 35)307. I am an odd number.

What number am I? ■

2. I am greater than the remainder in 94)728. I am less than the remainder in 84)494. I am an even number.

What number am I? ■

3. I am greater than the remainder in 23)324. I am less than the remainder in 42)467. I am an odd number.

What number am I? ■

4. I am greater than the remainder in 27)695. I am less than the remainder in 36)779. I am an even number.

What number am I? ■

Math Reasoning

Chapter 7

Challenge, pages 196–197

 Use a calculator to answer Exercises 1–3.

1. 3.428 ÷ 10 **2.** 342.8 ÷ 10 **3.** 34.28 ÷ 10

4. Write a statement about dividing by 10 and the location of the decimal point.

Use a calculator to answer Exercises 5–7.

5. 3.428 ÷ 100 **6.** 342.8 ÷ 100 **7.** 34.28 ÷ 100

8. Write a statement about dividing by 100 and the location of the decimal point.

Challenge, pages 198–199

Write the missing digits.

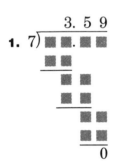
1.

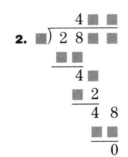
2.

Visual Thinking, pages 204–205

Meteorologists, scientists who study weather, measure rainfall very precisely. Look at the measuring tapes pictured. One tape is marked only in centimeters and the other in both millimeters and centimeters.

Use a centimeter ruler to measure the rain in the barrel. Record your measurements in centimeters and millimeters. Tell which is more precise.

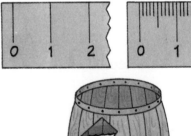

Math Reasoning

Chapter 7

Logical Reasoning, pages 206–207

Make a drawing that illustrates the problem.

A train is passing through a tunnel.
The tunnel is 1 kilometer long.
The train is 1 kilometer long.
The train is traveling at a rate
of 1 kilometer per minute.

How long will it take the train to pass through the tunnel?

Challenge, pages 210–211

Imagine that you are visiting a desert
planet where water is used as money.
You have 25 liters of water as you look
in the store window.

1. How much water will it cost to buy
one of each item in the window?

2. How much water will you have left over?

Logical Reasoning, pages 212–213

The words used in the metric system come from two ancient
languages, Greek and Latin.

- The origins of the word *meter* can be found in both languages.
  The Greek word *metron* and the Latin word *metrum* both
  mean "measure."

- The word *kilo* comes from the Greek *chilioi*, meaning
  "thousand." Use *kilo* to indicate 1,000 of a measure.

- The word *deci* comes from the Latin *decimus*, meaning "tenth."
  Use *deci* to indicate 0.1 of a measure.

You can use these words to understand many units of measure,
such as a gram, which is a unit of mass, and a meter, which is a
unit of length.

1. How many grams are in 1
kilogram less 8 decigrams?

2. How many meters are
in 2 kilometers less 5
decimeters?

Chapter 8

Challenge, pages 228–229

The product of three whole numbers is 2,280.
The three numbers have no common factors except 1.

What are the numbers?

Challenge, pages 230–231

Twin primes are prime numbers that differ by 2. Here are the first two pairs of twin primes.

3 and 5   5 and 7

1. Find the next five pairs of twin primes.

2. How many pairs of twin primes less than 100 are there?

Visual Thinking, pages 232–233

Look at these fractions: $\frac{1}{1}, \frac{1}{2}, \frac{1}{3}, \frac{1}{4}.$

$\frac{1}{1}$ [ ]

$\frac{1}{2}$ [|]

$\frac{1}{3}$ [| |]

$\frac{1}{4}$ [| | |]

1. If the denominator increases and the numerator stays the same, what happens to the values of the fractions?

Look at these fractions: $\frac{2}{2}, \frac{3}{2}, \frac{4}{2}, \frac{5}{2}.$

2. Draw fraction bars to show what happens to the values of the fractions if the denominator stays the same and the numerator increases.

Chapter 8

Challenge, pages 238–239

You can use factor trees to see whether a fraction is in simplest form. To see whether $\frac{6}{25}$ is in simplest form, use factor trees. Make one factor tree for the numerator and another for the denominator.

Remember that the foundation of a factor tree is made up of prime factors. The prime factors in the factor tree for 6 are different from the prime factors in the factor tree for 25. When this happens, a fraction is in simplest form. So, $\frac{6}{25}$ is in simplest form.

Use factor trees to decide whether each fraction is in simplest form. Write *yes* or *no*.

1. $\frac{36}{49}$ 　　　　　 **2.** $\frac{15}{22}$ 　　　　　 **3.** $\frac{27}{42}$

Challenge, pages 246–247

Copy the exercises. Write + or − in each ● to make a true number sentence.

1. $\frac{9}{10}$ ● $\frac{4}{10}$ ● $\frac{8}{10} = \frac{1}{2}$ 　　　　　 **2.** $\frac{9}{12}$ ● $\frac{1}{12}$ ● $\frac{6}{12} = \frac{1}{3}$

3. $\frac{6}{9}$ ● $\frac{5}{9}$ ● $\frac{2}{9} = \frac{1}{3}$ 　　　　　 **4.** $\frac{2}{6}$ ● $\frac{3}{6}$ ● $\frac{1}{6} = \frac{2}{3}$

5. $\frac{7}{16}$ ● $\frac{4}{16}$ ● $\frac{5}{16} = \frac{1}{2}$ 　　　　　 **6.** $\frac{9}{15}$ ● $\frac{4}{15}$ ● $\frac{5}{15} = \frac{2}{3}$

Challenge, pages 252–253

Find the missing denominator.

1. $\frac{5}{6} - \frac{5}{\blacksquare} = \frac{5}{18}$ 　　　　　 **2.** $\frac{3}{8} - \frac{1}{\blacksquare} = \frac{5}{24}$

3. $\frac{1}{\blacksquare} - \frac{1}{5} = \frac{2}{15}$ 　　　　　 **4.** $\frac{1}{\blacksquare} - \frac{3}{10} = \frac{1}{5}$

Math Reasoning

Chapter 9

Challenge, pages 272–273

Multiply. Write the answer in simplest form. Match the letter to the answer below to solve the riddle.

1. $\frac{3}{5} \times \frac{5}{7} = \blacksquare$ G

2. $\frac{2}{3} \times \frac{4}{5} = \blacksquare$ H

3. $\frac{1}{3} \times \frac{2}{5} = \blacksquare$ D

4. $\frac{5}{7} \times \frac{7}{8} = \blacksquare$ N

5. $\frac{2}{3} \times \frac{3}{8} = \blacksquare$ O

6. $\frac{4}{9} \times \frac{3}{4} = \blacksquare$ T

7. $\frac{9}{10} \times \frac{5}{9} = \blacksquare$ U

8. $\frac{1}{8} \times \frac{3}{5} = \blacksquare$ A

Riddle: What kind of nut doesn't have a shell?

Answer: $\dfrac{?}{\frac{3}{40}}$ $\dfrac{?}{\frac{2}{15}}$ $\dfrac{?}{\frac{1}{4}}$ $\dfrac{?}{\frac{1}{2}}$ $\dfrac{?}{\frac{3}{7}}$ $\dfrac{?}{\frac{8}{15}}$ $\dfrac{?}{\frac{5}{8}}$ $\dfrac{?}{\frac{1}{2}}$ $\dfrac{?}{\frac{1}{3}}$

Challenge, pages 276–277

Find the missing whole number in each problem.

1. $3\frac{1}{2} \times \blacksquare = 7$

2. $4\frac{1}{3} \times \blacksquare = 13$

3. $10\frac{1}{4} \times \blacksquare = 41$

4. $5\frac{1}{6} \times \blacksquare = 31$

5. $7\frac{1}{8} \times \blacksquare = 57$

6. $12\frac{1}{10} \times \blacksquare = 121$

Logical Reasoning, pages 280–281

Solve.

1. Divide 20 by $\frac{1}{2}$ and add 10. What is the answer?

2. Divide 10 by $\frac{1}{5}$ and add 5. What is the answer?

3. Divide 30 by $\frac{1}{10}$ and add 10. What is the answer?

Math Reasoning

Chapter 9

Logical Reasoning, pages 286–287

Counting backward on a clock is a method you can use to help you be on time. Suppose you have a piano lesson on Saturday at 11:00 A.M. and you want to do some errands and visit a friend along the way.

Stop	Time it Will Take
Friend's house	25 minutes
Bakery	10 minutes
Library	10 minutes
Lesson	10 minutes

1. Count backward to find what time you will have to leave home.

2. What other method can you use to find the same answer?

Challenge, pages 290–291

At the time of King Henry I of England, a yard was the distance from the tip of the king's nose to the end of his thumb. How far is it from the tip of your nose to the end of your thumb? Work with three classmates, and record your measurements in a table. Then answer the questions. You may have to round to the nearest inch to rename in yards.

DISTANCE FROM NOSE TO THUMB

Name	In inches	In yards
Jennifer	$19\frac{1}{2}$	$\frac{20}{36}$

1. Whose measurement is the longest? the shortest?

2. What is the difference between the longest and the shortest?

3. What is the average in inches of all the measurements? Compare your table with those of other groups.

4. Find out the average distance for the whole class in inches, and then rename it in yards.

Challenge, pages 292–293

Customary units of measurement are based upon the human body, as are the words we use to name these units of measurement. One *foot* describes the length of a human foot. One *hand* describes the width of a hand (4 inches). The word *inch* comes from the Latin word *uncia*, which described the width of the thumb. One *inch* can be thought of as one *thumb*.

1. How wide is your desk in feet and thumbs?
2. How wide is your desk in hands and thumbs?

Math Reasoning

Chapter 10

Logical Reasoning, pages 308–309

Mrs. Olivia drives to work and back each day on a toll road. She stops 5 times each way to deposit the tolls. Each toll is either $0.25 or $0.50. The ratio of the number of $0.25 tolls to the number of $0.50 tolls is 1:4 each way.

Do you have enough information to find out how much Mrs. Olivia spends each day on tolls? If so, how much does she spend?

Challenge, pages 318–319

A **sequence** of numbers is a set of ordered numbers that form a pattern. When you discover the rule for the pattern, you can extend the pattern.

   0.5, 0.9, 1.3, 1.7, ■, ■, ■

You add 0.4 to each number to find the next number. So, the next three numbers in the sequence are 2.1, 2.5, and 2.9.

Find the missing numbers in each sequence.

1. $\frac{8}{2}, \frac{7}{3}, \frac{6}{4}, \frac{■}{■}, \frac{■}{■}, \frac{■}{■}$

2. 18%, 27%, 36%, 45%, ■, ■, ■

3. 80%, 78.5%, 77%, 75.5%, ■, ■, ■

4. $\frac{7}{2}, \frac{6}{4}, \frac{5}{6}, \frac{■}{■}, \frac{■}{■}, \frac{■}{■}$

Challenge, pages 322–323

 You can use a calculator to write a fraction as a percent.

Example: Write a percent for $\frac{2}{5}$.

First, divide the numerator by the denominator.
Then, multiply the decimal answer by 100.

So, $\frac{2}{5} = 40\%$.

Use a calculator to find a percent for each fraction.

1. $\frac{3}{5}$ **2.** $\frac{3}{10}$ **3.** $\frac{9}{50}$ **4.** $\frac{17}{25}$ **5.** $\frac{13}{20}$ **6.** $\frac{7}{8}$

Chapter 10

Logical Reasoning, pages 324–325

The whole is represented by 100%.

Nicole finds that 40% of her pictures were taken indoors and 80% were taken out of town. This adds up to 120%. How can this be true?

Visual Thinking, pages 326–327

Look at the drawing of a parking lot. Notice the total number of spaces, the number of spaces filled, and the kinds of vehicles that are parked. The first space in each of the four rows is reserved for handicapped persons.

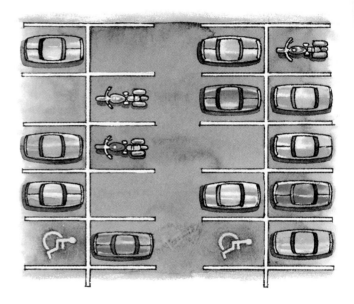

1. What percent of spaces are vacant?
2. What percent of spaces in each row are filled?
3. What percent of spaces for handicapped persons are filled?
4. Write a fraction for the number of motorcycles parked in the lot compared to the total number of spaces.

Challenge, pages 328–329

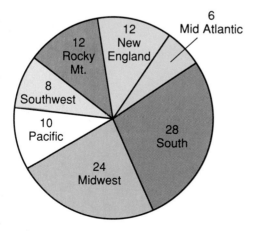

United States senators represent the interests of the people in their regions. The circle graph shows the different regions of the country and the number of senators from each region.

1. Which region is represented by the most senators?

2. Which regions are represented by the same number of senators?

3. How many men and women serve in the Senate altogether?

Math Reasoning

Chapter 11

Challenge, pages 340–341

Start with these four line segments.
Draw five more segments to make the word
TEN.

Visual Thinking, pages 342–343

Look around your classroom. Find two acute angles, two right
angles, and two obtuse angles. Then close your eyes and picture
one room in your house. Identify one acute angle, one right angle,
and one obtuse angle. Copy and complete the chart with brief
descriptions of these angles.

Acute angles	Right angles	Obtuse angles

Challenge, pages 350–351

In a **regular polygon,** all the sides are the same length, and all
the angles measure the same number of degrees.

1. Is the hexagon shown a regular polygon?
   Explain.

2. Can you draw another hexagon on dot paper
   that is a regular polygon? Explain.

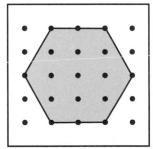

Chapter 11

Visual Thinking, pages 358–359

The answer in this calculator display shows two lines of symmetry.

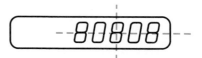

 Use a calculator to solve each problem. Then tell how many lines of symmetry the answer has.

1. $3,434 \div 34$ **2.** $676,767 \div 67$ **3.** 99×89 **4.** 27×37

Logical Reasoning, pages 362–363

Sara and Jack are playing the Treasure Hunt Game. When Jack asks a coordinate location, Sara must respond with north or south and east or west to indicate which direction he must travel to find the treasure. Use the grid and these clues to discover where Sara hid the treasure from Jack.

Jack asks whether the treasure is at (4, 3). Sara replies no, go east and north.

Jack asks whether the treasure is at (11, 6). Sara replies no, go east and south.

Jack asks whether the treasure is at (13, 5). Sara replies no, go west one space and south one space.

Where did Sara hide the treasure?

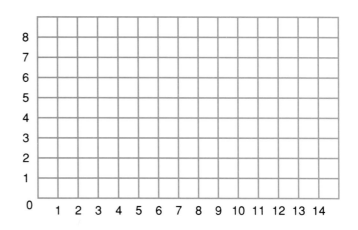

Logical Reasoning, pages 364–365

To write a mathematical rule, you must use logical reasoning based on examples you have already seen.

Write a rule for finding the perimeter of each figure.

1.

rhombus

2.

equilateral triangle

3.

parallelogram

Chapter 12

Visual Thinking, pages 386–387

The symbols used on a pictograph sometimes indicate what the graph displays.

1. If the symbol 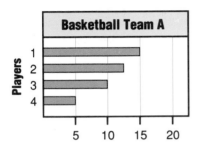 is on a pictograph, what information might the graph contain?

2. If the symbol ♪ is on a pictograph, what information might the graph contain?

Visual Thinking, pages 390–391

Use the information in the graphs to answer the questions.

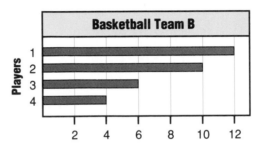

1. Who scored more points—Player 1 from Team A, or Player 1 from team B?

2. About how many points did each team score?

Logical Reasoning, pages 392–393

Look at the table. It lists a range of amounts of certain vitamins that are needed daily by children and adults. Use the table to answer the questions.

1. Why do you think there are ranges of amounts and not precise amounts?

2. Which two vitamins do children and adults need the least of?

3. Which vitamins do men and women need in about the same amounts as children?

VITAMIN REQUIREMENTS

	Men	**Women**	**Children (ages 1–14)**
Vitamin B₁	1.2–1.4 mg	1.0–1.1 mg	0.7–1.4 mg
Niacin	16–19 mg	13–14 mg	9–18 mg
Vitamin C	60 mg	60 mg	45–50 mg
Vitamin E	10 mg	8 mg	5–8 mg

4. How many grams of Vitamin C does an adult need every day?

5. Estimate how many grams of vitamin B₁ a 14-year-old might need in a whole year.

Math Reasoning

Chapter 12

Visual Thinking, pages 394–395

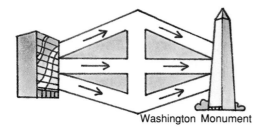

Washington Monument

The Reed family stayed in Washington, D.C. for a week. Each day they took a different road to tour the city. All the roads shown are one-way. How many different routes could the Reed family have taken from their hotel to the Washington Monument?

Logical Reasoning, pages 396–397

1. Make 4 cards, one each of red, yellow, blue, and green. Put them into a bag. The probability that you will draw a red card without looking is 1 out of 4. Complete the table.

PREDICTIONS

Draws	4	8	12	16	20
Red card	1	■	■	■	■

2. Now draw a card from the bag several times. Return the card to the bag after each draw. Complete the table. Compare the results with your predictions.

RESULTS

Draws	4	8	12	16	20
Red card	■	■	■	■	■

Challenge, pages 398–399

One of the most famous names in mathematics is that of Blaise Pascal (blehz pas KAL). Blaise Pascal was a French mathematician and philosopher of the 17th century who taught himself geometry at the age of 12 and wrote his first book on mathematics at the age of 16. Among his contributions were the theory of probability (with Pierre de Fermat), Pascal's Law in physics, and Pascal's Triangle, pictured here.

1. Can you discover how each row in Pascal's Triangle is formed?

2. Complete the next row.

3. What patterns or sequences can you find?

Pascal's Triangle

```
          1
        1   1   ◀— row 1
      1   2   1   ◀— row 2
    1   3   3   1   ◀— row 3
  1   4   6   4   1
1   5  10  10   5   1
```

Math Reasoning

TABLE OF MEASURES

TIME

1 minute (min) = 60 seconds (s)   1 year (y) = 12 months
1 hour (h) = 60 minutes   1 year = 52 weeks
1 day (d) = 24 hours   1 year = 365 days
1 week (wk) = 7 days

METRIC UNITS

LENGTH
1 centimeter (cm) = 10 millimeters (mm)
1 meter (m) = 100 centimeters (cm)
1 kilometer (km) = 1,000 meters

CAPACITY
1 liter (L) = 1,000 milliliters (mL)

MASS
1 gram (g) = 1,000 milligrams (mg)
1 kilogram (kg) = 1,000 grams

TEMPERATURE
0° Celsius (°C) . . . . Water freezes
100° Celsius (°C) . . . . Water boils

CUSTOMARY UNITS

LENGTH
1 foot (ft) = 12 inches (in.)
1 yard (yd) = 3 feet
1 mile (mi) = 5,280 feet
1 mile = 1,760 yards

WEIGHT
1 pound (lb) = 16 ounces (oz)
1 ton (T) = 2,000 pounds

CAPACITY
1 pint (pt) = 2 cups (c)
1 quart (qt) = 2 pints
1 gallon (gal) = 4 quarts

TEMPERATURE
32° Fahrenheit (°F) . . . . Water freezes
212° Fahrenheit (°F) . . . . Water boils

FORMULAS

AREA   Rectangle $A = l \times w$

Triangle $A = \frac{1}{2}(b \times h)$

VOLUME   Rectangular Prism $V = l \times w \times h$

SYMBOLS

$<$ is less than

$>$ is greater than

$\neq$ is not equal to

$\approx$ is approximately equal to

$4 \div 2$ 4 divided by 2

% percent

$3:5$ the ratio 3 to 5

° degree

• A point A

$\overleftrightarrow{AB}$ line AB

$\overrightarrow{AB}$ ray AB

$\overline{AB}$ line segment AB

$\angle ABC$ angle ABC

$\triangle ABC$ triangle ABC

$\parallel$ is parallel to

$\cong$ is congruent to

$\sim$ is similar to

(5,3) the ordered pair 5,3

GLOSSARY

Acute Angle An angle that measures less than 90°.

Acute triangle A triangle that has three acute angles.

Addends Numbers that are added.
Example:

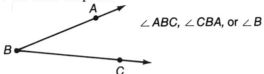

Angle A figure formed by two different rays that have the same endpoint.

∠ABC, ∠CBA, or ∠B

Area The number of square units needed to cover a surface.

Associative Property of Addition If the grouping of addends is changed, the sum remains the same.
Example: $(2 + 3) + 6 = 2 + (3 + 6)$

Associative Property of Multiplication If the grouping of factors is changed, the product remains the same.
Example: $(2 \times 2) \times 4 = 2 \times (2 \times 4)$

Average The average, or mean, of a set of numbers is the sum of the numbers divided by the number of addends.

BASIC *BASIC* stands for "Beginner's All-purpose Symbolic Instructional Code," a computer language.

Chord A line segment that has endpoints on a circle.

Circle A circle consists of all points in one plane that are the same distance from one point, called the *center*.

Circumference The distance around a circle.

Commutative Property of Addition If the order of two addends is changed, the sum remains the same.
Example: $6 + 3 = 3 + 6$

Commutative Property of Multiplication If the order of the factors is changed, the product remains the same.
Example: $7 \times 4 = 4 \times 7$

Composite number A number that has more than two factors.
Example: 24 is a composite number because it has 8 factors: 1, 2, 3, 4, 6, 8, 12, and 24.

Cone A solid figure that has a circular base and one vertex.

Congruent Figures that are exactly the same shape and size are congruent.

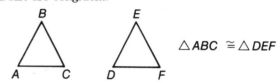

△ABC ≅ △DEF

Cube A solid figure that has six square faces.

Cylinder A solid figure that has two congruent circular bases.

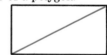

Debug To fix the problems in a computer program so that it will do what you want it to do.

Decimal A number that uses place value and a decimal point to show tenths, hundredths, thousandths, etc.
Examples: 0.09, 37.1486

Degree A unit of measure for circles, angles, and temperature.

Denominator In $\frac{5}{8}$, 8 is the denominator. It tells the total number of parts or groups.

Diagonal A line segment that is not a side and that joins two vertices of a polygon.

Diameter A chord that passes through the center of a circle.

A⎯•⎯B

Digit Any of the individual numerals 0, 1, 2, 3, 4, 5, 6, 7, 8, or 9 that are used to build the base-ten name for a number.

Distributive Property To find the product of a number times the sum of two addends, you can multiply each addend by the number and then add the products.
Example: $4 \times (3 + 8) = (4 \times 3) + (4 \times 8)$

Dividend The number that is divided.
Example: $10 \div 2 = 5$

$$2\overline{)10}$$

dividend ———

Divisible A number is divisible by another if it can be divided by that number with no remainder.
Example: 9 is divisible by 3, but not by 4.

Divisor The number that divides the dividend.
Example: $16 \div 8 = 2$

$$8\overline{)16}$$

divisor

Edge Two faces of a solid intersect at an edge.

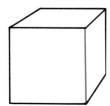

Equation A mathematical sentence that has an equals sign.

Equilateral triangle A triangle that has three sides of equal length.

Equivalent fractions Two or more fractions that name the same number.
Example: $\frac{6}{8} = \frac{3}{4}$

Even number A number that has the digit 0, 2, 4, 6, or 8 in the ones place. It is divisible by 2.

Expanded numeral A numeral expanded to show the value of each digit.
Example: $57,305 = 50,000 + 7,000 + 300 + 5$

Face The flat surfaces of a prism.

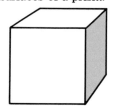

Factors Numbers that are multiplied.
Example: $3 \times 5 = 15$

Factors

Flowchart A diagram that shows the steps to do something.

FOR/STEP/NEXT A three-part command that makes a computer repeat a step a given number of times.
```
10   FOR N = 2 TO 10 STEP 2
20   PRINT N
30   NEXT N
```
makes a computer print the numbers 2, 4, 6, 8, and 10.

Fraction A fraction is used to name parts of a whole, or parts of a group.

Gram A unit of mass in the metric system.

Greatest Common Factor The greatest common factor of two or more numbers is the greatest number that is a factor of each number.
Example: 9 is the greatest common factor of 18 and 27.

Hexagon A six-sided polygon.

IF/THEN A command that tells a computer to make a decision.
Example: If $N < 10$ THEN 40 tells a computer to go to line 40 if the number in the storage place N is less than 10.

Inequality A number sentence that contains $<$, $>$, or $\neq$.

Intersecting lines Lines that meet or cross at one point.

Isosceles triangle A triangle that has at least two congruent sides.

Least common denominator The least common multiple of the denominators of two or more fractions.
Example: For $\frac{1}{5}$ and $\frac{2}{3}$, 15 is the least common denominator.

Least common multiple The least common multiple of two or more numbers is the smallest number other than 0 that is a common multiple.
Example: For 4 and 7, 28 is the least common multiple.

Line A line is a straight path that goes on forever in two directions.

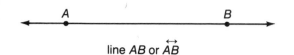

line *AB* or $\overleftrightarrow{AB}$

Line of symmetry The line along which a symmetrical figure can be folded so that the two halves match exactly.

Line segment A line segment is a part of a straight line. It is named by its endpoints.

line segment *AB* or $\overline{AB}$

LIST A command that tells a computer to show the program lines that are stored in its memory.

Liter A unit of liquid capacity in the metric system.

Mean The mean, or average, of a set of numbers is the sum of the numbers divided by the number of addends in the set.

Median The median is the middle number in an ordered set of numbers.

Meter A unit of length in the metric system.

Mixed Number A mixed number has a whole number part and a fraction part, such as $4\frac{2}{3}$.

Mode The mode is the number that occurs most often in a set of numbers.

Multiple A multiple of a number is the product of that number and any other whole number. Example: 10, 25, and 40 are multiples of 5.

Number line A line used to show numbers in order.

Number sentence An equation or inequality.
Examples: $13 - 5 = 8$ $n \times 4 = 32$
           $3 \times 4 < 16$ $8 + 6 > 11$

Numeral A name for a number.

Numerator In $\frac{6}{7}$, 6 is the numerator. It tells how many parts you are talking about.

Obtuse Angle An angle that measures more than 90° but less than 180°.

Obtuse triangle A triangle that has an obtuse angle.

Odd number A number that has 1, 3, 5, 7, or 9 in the ones place. It is not divisible by 2.

Ordered pair A pair of numbers, used to locate a point on a grid.

Parallel lines Lines in a plane that never intersect.

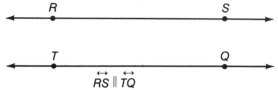

$\overleftrightarrow{RS} \parallel \overleftrightarrow{TQ}$

Parallelogram A quadrilateral whose opposite sides are the same length and are parallel.

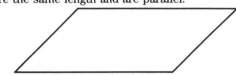

Pentagon A five-sided polygon.

Perimeter The distance around a polygon—the sum of the lengths of its sides.

Period A group of three digits in a numeral set off by commas.

Perpendicular lines Lines that intersect and form right angles.

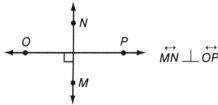

$\overleftrightarrow{MN} \perp \overleftrightarrow{OP}$

Plane A flat surface that goes on forever in all directions.

Point A point is an exact location in space.

Polygon A closed figure formed by line segments.

Prime factorization A composite number can be shown to be the product of its prime factors. Example: The prime factorization of 18 is
      $2 \times 3 \times 3$.

Prime number A prime number has exactly two factors, itself and 1.

PRINT A command that tells a computer to output information on a screen or on paper.

Prism A polyhedron that has two congruent bases in parallel planes and whose other faces are parallelograms.

Probability A comparison of the number of favorable outcomes to the total number of possible outcomes.

Property of One for Multiplication If one factor is 1, then the product is always the other factor.

Property of Zero for Addition If one of the addends is zero, the sum is equal to the other addend.
Example: $7 + 0 = 7, 0 + 9 = 9$

Property of Zero for Multiplication If one factor is 0, the product is always 0.
Example: $8 \times 0 = 0, 9{,}672 \times 0 = 0$

Protractor An instrument used to measure angles.

Pyramid A solid that has three or more faces that are triangles that have a common vertex and one face that is a polygon.

Quadrilateral A polygon with four sides.

Quotient The result of a division.
Example: $36 \div 4 = 9 \leftarrow$ quotient $\rightarrow \dfrac{7}{6\overline{)42}}$

Radius A line segment that has one endpoint on the circle and one endpoint on the center.

Range The difference between the greatest and the least number in a set of numbers.

Ratio A comparison between two numbers.

Ray A part of a line that begins at an endpoint and goes on forever in one direction.

ray AB or $\overrightarrow{AB}$

Rectangle A parallelogram that has four right angles.

Rectangular prism A three-dimensional figure that has six faces and eight corners. Its bases are rectangular.

Rhombus A parallelogram whose sides are all the same length.

Right angle An angle that measures 90°.

Right triangle A triangle that has one right angle.

RND(1) In a computer program, RND(1) makes a computer pick a random 9-place decimal between 0 and 1.

Scalene triangle A triangle with no congruent sides.

Similar figures Figures that have the same shape but not necessarily the same size.

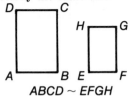
$ABCD \sim EFGH$

Simplest form A fraction is in simplest form if its numerator and denominator have no common factors other than 1.

Sphere A solid figure that has a surface that has all points the same distance from its center.

Square A rectangle whose sides are all the same length.

Standard numeral The usual way to name a number.
Example: The standard numeral for thirty-four is 34.

Symmetry A figure is symmetrical when there is a line about which the figure can be folded. The resulting figure matches the original.

Triangle A three-sided polygon.

Vertex The common endpoint of the sides of an angle or two sides of a polygon.

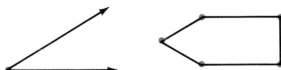

Volume The number of cubic units needed to fill a solid figure.

Whole numbers Any of these numbers:
0, 1, 2, 3, . . .

Index

Learning Resources

The Learning Resources can be traced, colored, and cut out.
These resources can be used as tools to help you understand
math concepts and solve problems.

Number Lines

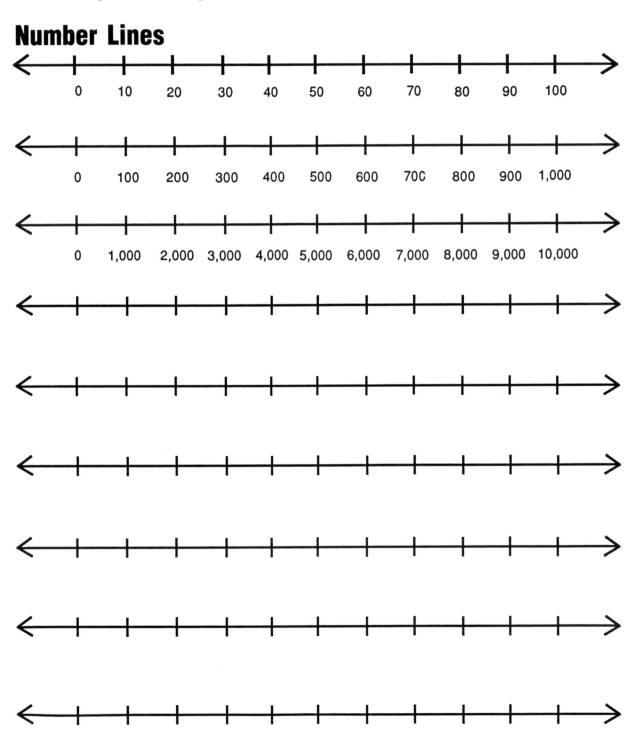

Fraction Circles

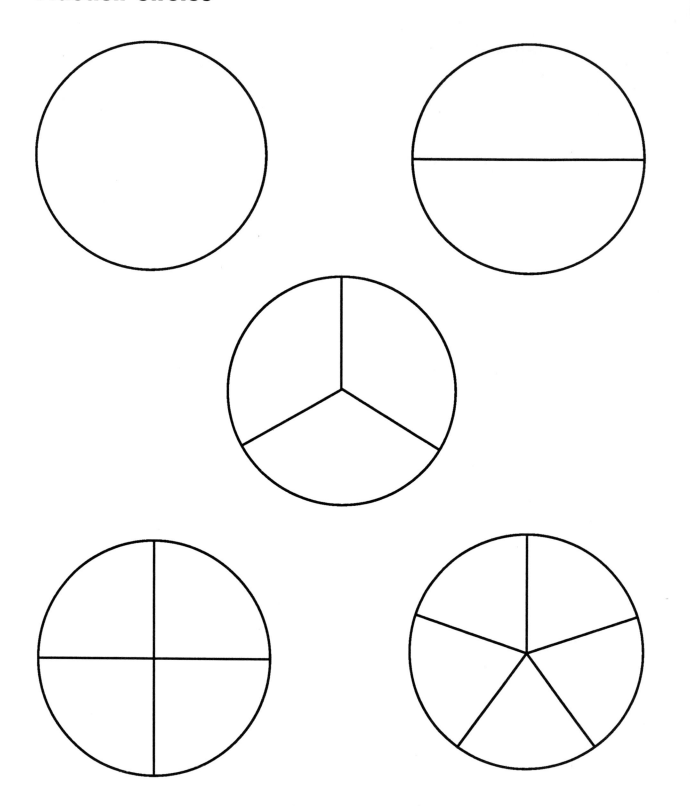

Fraction Circles

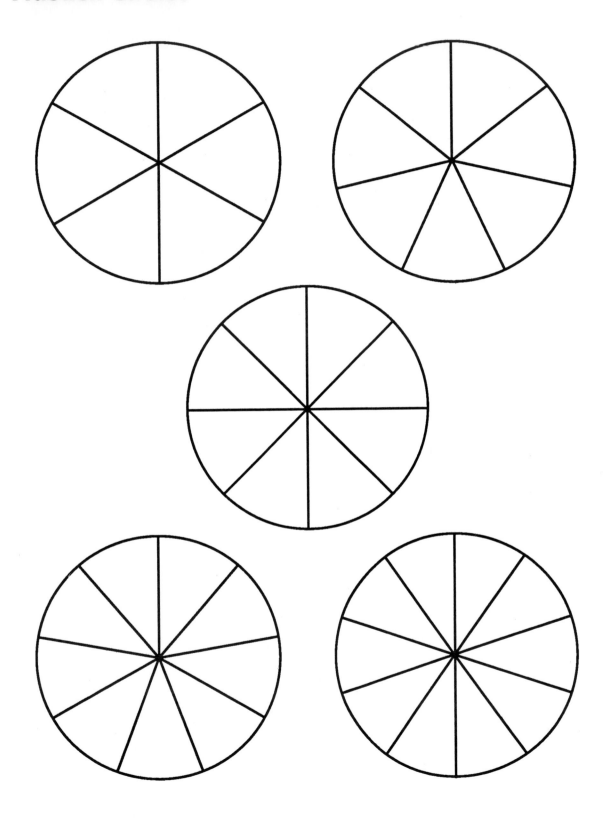

Fraction Bars

| $\frac{1}{10}$ | | | | | | | | | |

| $\frac{1}{9}$ | | | | | | | | |

| $\frac{1}{8}$ | | | | | | | |

| $\frac{1}{7}$ | | | | | | |

| $\frac{1}{6}$ | | | | | |

| $\frac{1}{5}$ | | | | |

| $\frac{1}{4}$ | | | |

| $\frac{1}{3}$ | | |

| $\frac{1}{2}$ | |

| 1 |

Plane Geometric Shapes

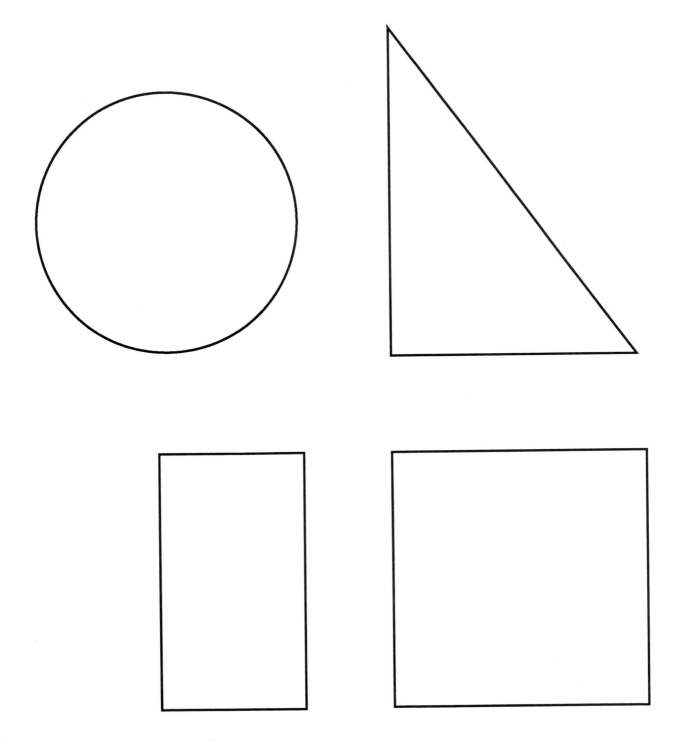

Plane Geometric Shapes

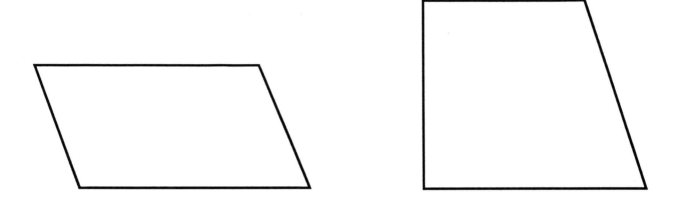

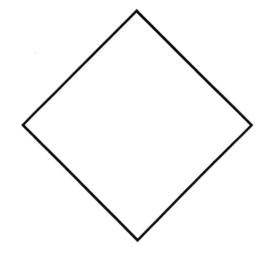

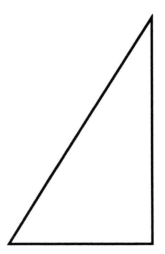

Plane Geometric Shapes

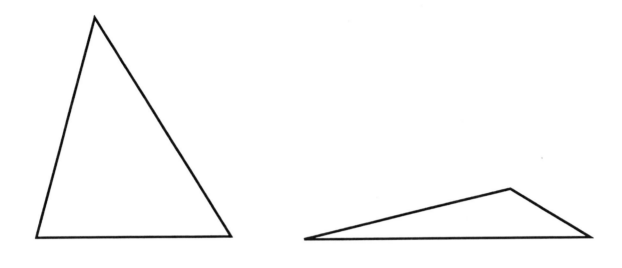

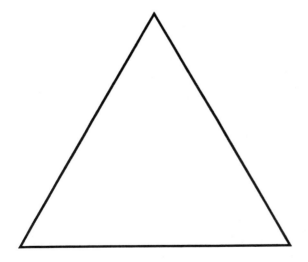

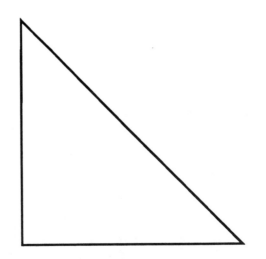

Plane Geometric Shapes

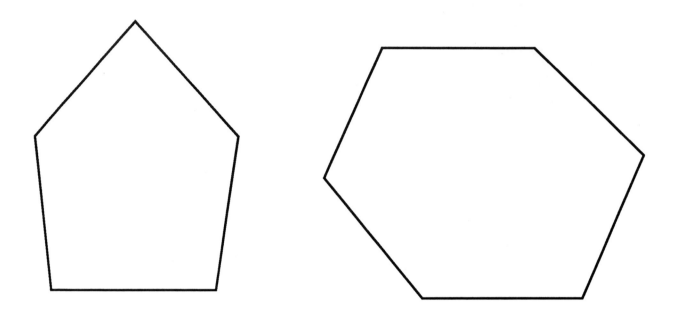

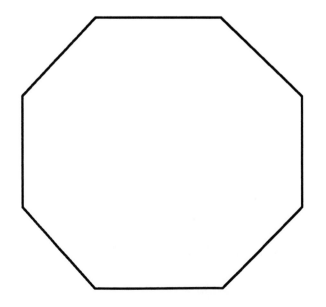

Tangram

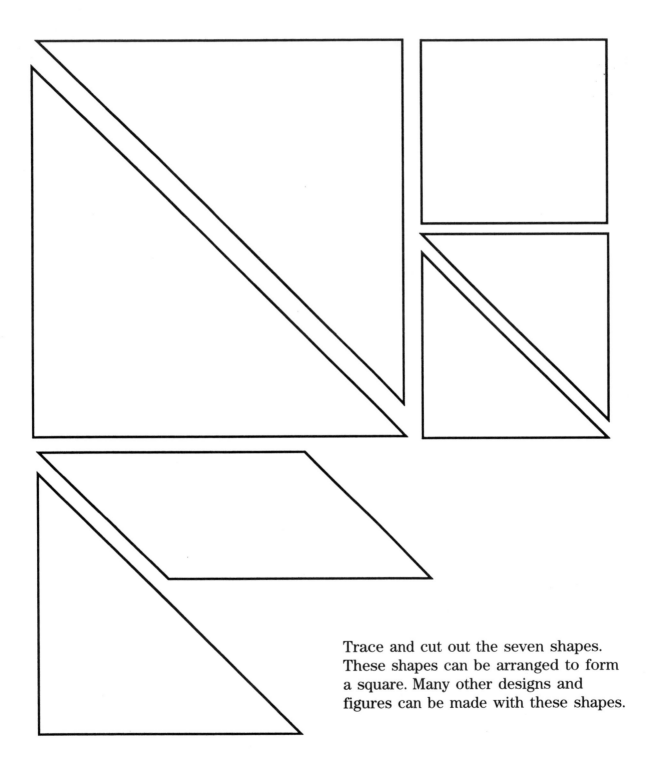

Trace and cut out the seven shapes. These shapes can be arranged to form a square. Many other designs and figures can be made with these shapes.

Solid Geometric Shapes

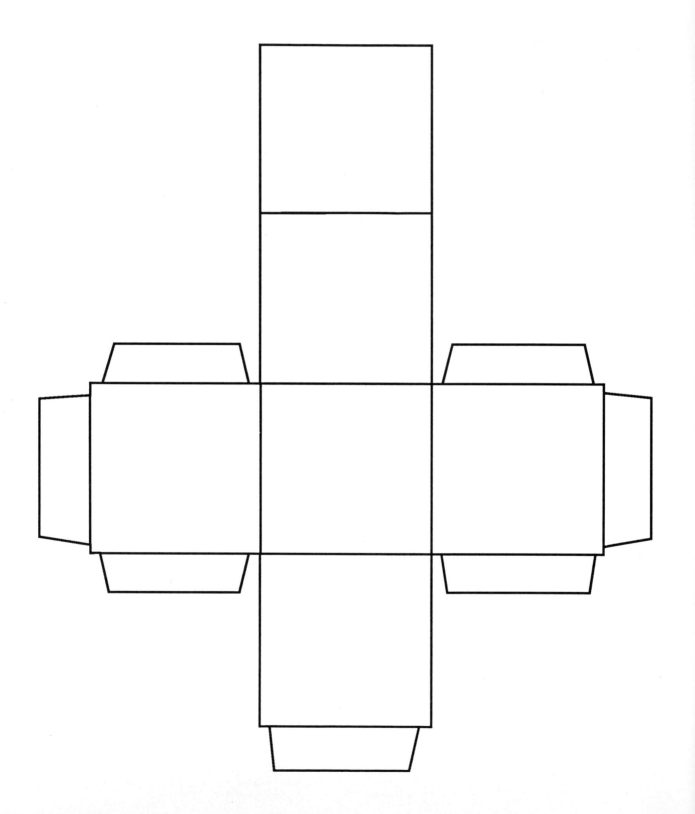

Solid Geometric Shapes

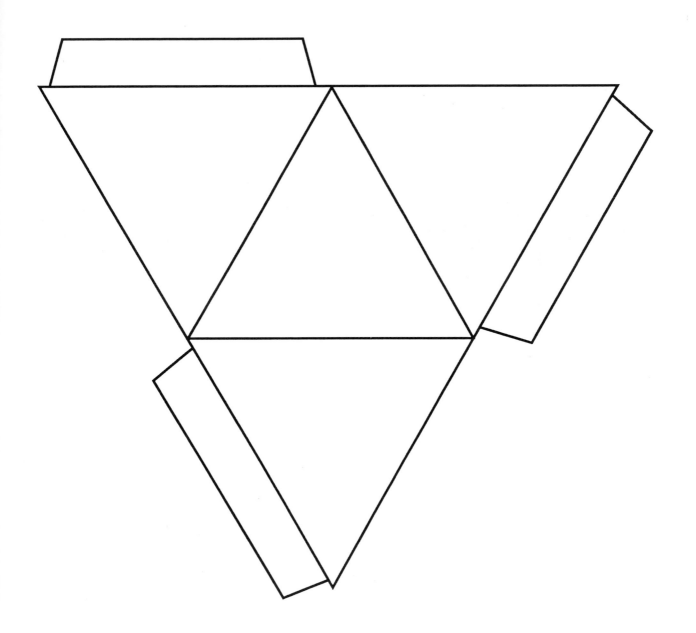

Solid Geometric Shapes

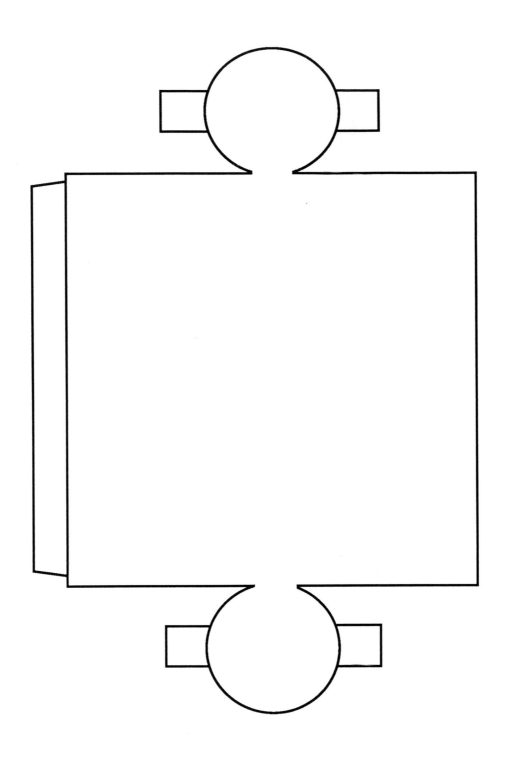

Solid Geometric Shapes

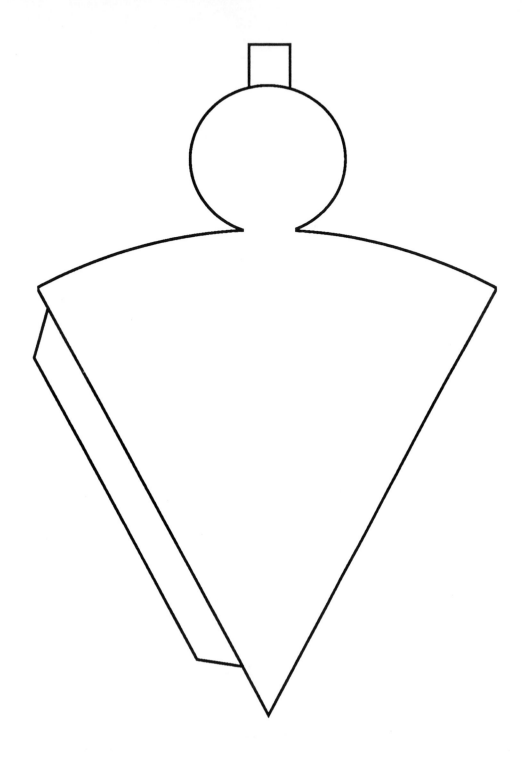

Solid Geometric Shapes

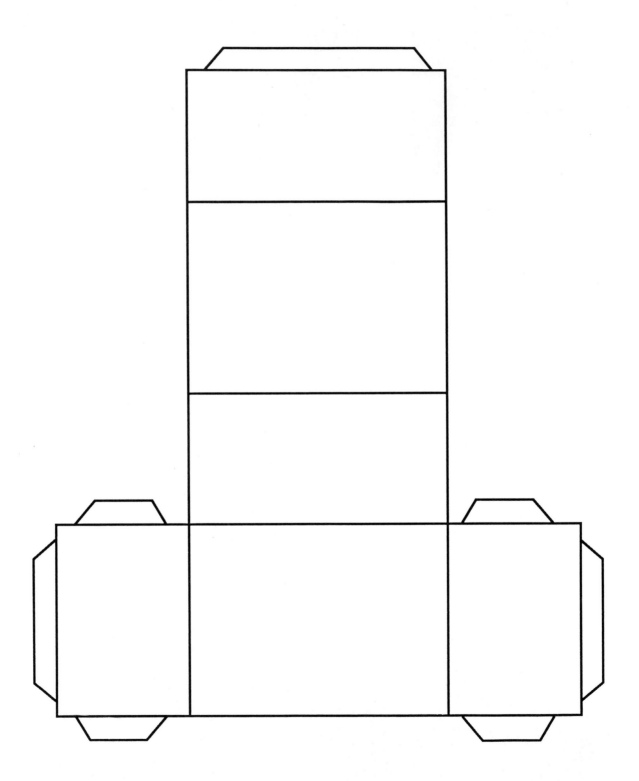